MACROECONOMICS

PRINCIPLES AND POLICY

NINTH EDITION 2004 UPDATE

Macroeconomics: Principles and Policy, 9e 2004 Update

William J. Baumol and Alan S. Blinder

Vice President / Editorial Director:
Jack W. Calhoun

Vice President / Editor-in-Chief:
Dave Shaut

Publisher of Economics
Michael B. Mercier

Acquisitions Editor:
Michael W. Worls

Developmental Editor:
Sarah K. Dorger

Sr. Marketing Manager:
Brian Joyner

Sr. Marketing Coordinator:
Jenny Garamy

Production Editor:
Daniel C. Plofchan

Manufacturing Coordinator:
Sandee Milewski

Manager of Technology, Editorial:
Vicky True

Sr. Technology Project Manager:
Peggy Buskey

Sr. Media Editor:
Pam Wallace

Compositor:
Pre-Press Company, Inc.
East Bridgewater, MA

Sr. Design Project Manager:
Michelle Kunkler

Cover and Internal Designer:
Elm Street Publishing
Services, Inc.

Photography Manager:
Deanna Ettinger

Photography Research:
Elm Street Publishing
Services, Inc.

Printer:
QuebecorWorld
Versailles, KY

Library of Congress Control
Number: 2004104031

Package ISBN: 0-324-20165-6

Book ISBN: 0-324-28232-X

CD-ROM ISBN: 0-324-28990-1

For permission to use material from
this text or product, submit a request
online at
http://www.thomsonrights.com.

Any additional questions about per-
missions can be submitted by email
to thomsonrights@thomson.com

MACROECONOMICS

PRINCIPLES AND POLICY

NINTH EDITION 2004 UPDATE

William J. Baumol

New York University and Princeton University

Alan S. Blinder

Princeton University

THOMSON

SOUTH-WESTERN

Australia · Canada · Mexico · Singapore · Spain · United Kingdom · United States

Dear Instructors:

Thank you for your interest in and support of **Macroeconomics: Principles and Policy.** We are proud of the fact that over the past 25 years our book has introduced millions of students to the world of economics in a way that engages their interest and opens their eyes to aspects of real economic life that they did not understand before.

The economy changes all the time, but some economic principles endure. These principles are the same as those that have guided us now through nine editions. Ever since the First Edition, **Macroeconomics: Principles and Policy** was predicated on the view that practical issues and developments in the economy should influence the content of an introductory economics course. Issues should drive students to the principles rather than the other way around. This educational philosophy is most evident in our chapter-opening real-world problems, used as launching pads for subsequent analyses.

Over the many editions, the **Ideas for Beyond the Final Exam** have been a favorite element of students and instructors alike. We believe that certain economic ideas are so important that students should remember them for a long time. To help students identify the most crucial concepts, we have selected nine from among the many presented in this book. Each of the Ideas for Beyond the Final Exam is highlighted with an icon in the margin and discussed in depth as it occurs throughout the course of the book.

As we move into the Ninth Edition and its 2004 Update, we have refined our text and its ancillary components in numerous ways—all designed to provide today's students with the best possible ways to learn economics at the introductory level. But our philosophy remains unchanged: we seek to equip students with the tools they need to understand the world they live in. So, for example, after 10 years without a recession (1991–2001), and with little worry about inflation, it is no wonder that we found instructors asking us for more material on long-run growth. We have provided this—and even given it "first billing" in Chapters 5 and 6. But we have not succumbed to the temptation to downplay the importance of recessions and the monetary and fiscal responses to them—aspects of reality which returned in 2001.

We are grateful to our reviewers, who helped us produce this edition. Some of the changes to the Ninth Edition consist of, but are not limited to:

- The introductory chapters, 1–3, have been condensed considerably. (They ran to 5 chapters in the Eighth Edition; some of this now appears in appendixes.)
- Chapter 5 includes substantial changes on the coverage of economic growth.
- An all-new Chapter 6 adds material on economic growth that did not appear in previous editions.
- To make room for this new material, the early chapters on aggregate demand have been condensed, saving one chapter.
- Chapter 14 reflects extensive changes to bring the discussion of deficits *and* surpluses (and their relation to monetary policy) up to date.

Beyond the textbook itself, the Ninth Edition offers new and improved technology supplements. **Xtra!** is a student tutorial that is packaged with every new text. This interactive multimedia CD-ROM, provided at no additional cost, offers self-testing, graphing workshops, and CNN video lectures and applications. The Web site for the ninth edition is much improved, with added resources for both instructors and students. WebTutor is now available with the new edition of **Principles and Policy**. This online course management program allows the instructor to organize classroom support materials and communications with students easily and effectively. WebTutor also provides added tutorials to review critical text material chapter by chapter. Concepts are reinforced through extensive exercises, problems, cases, flashcards, self-tests, and other tools.

We thank the loyal adopters of our text for your continuing support and believe that you will enjoy this new edition. For those instructors who have not used our text, but are considering doing so, we believe that we have provided you with extremely valuable tools to launch your students into the world of economics and give them the opportunity to advance further in this exciting discipline.

We hope you enjoy teaching from the book as much as we have enjoyed writing it.

Sincerely,
William J. Baumol
Alan S. Blinder

ABOUT THE AUTHORS

WILLIAM J. BAUMOL

William J. Baumol was born February 26, 1922, in an area of New York City that has since come to be known as Fort Apache. He received his BSS at the College of the City of New York in 1942 and his Ph.D. at the University of London in 1949.

He is Professor of Economics at New York University and Senior Research Economist and Professor Emeritus at Princeton University. He is a frequent consultant to the management of major firms in a wide variety of industries in the United States and other countries, as well as to a number of governmental agencies. In several fields, including the telecommunications and electric utility industries, current regulatory policy is based on his explicit recommendations. Among his many contributions to economics are research on the theory of the firm, the contestability of markets, productivity convergence among nations, and the economics of the arts and other services—indeed, the "cost disease of the personal services" is often referred to as "Baumol's disease." In addition to economics, he taught a course in wood sculpture at Princeton for about 20 years.

He has been president of the American Economic Association, and three other professional societies. He is an elected member of the National Academy of Sciences, created by the U.S. Congress, and of the American Philosophical Society, founded by Benjamin Franklin. He is also on the board of trustees of the National Council on Economic Education, and of the Theater Development Fund. He is the recipient of ten honorary degrees and many other awards and honors.

Baumol is the author of 36 books and hundreds of journal and newspaper articles, and his writings have been translated into more than a dozen languages.

ALAN S. BLINDER

Alan S. Blinder was born in New York City and attended Princeton University, where one of his teachers was William Baumol. After earning a master's degree at the London School of Economics and a Ph.D. at MIT, Blinder returned to Princeton, where he has taught since 1971. He is currently the Gordon S. Rentschler Memorial Professor of Economics and co-director of Princeton's Center for Economic Policy Studies, which he founded.

In January 1993, Blinder went to Washington as part of President Clinton's first Council of Economic Advisers. Then, from June 1994 through January 1996, he served as vice chairman of the Federal Reserve Board. He thus played a role in formulating both the fiscal and monetary policies of the 1990s, topics discussed extensively in this book. Blinder has been involved with several financial businesses as a consultant, has served on the board of the American Stock Exchange, and is now a partner in the Promontory Financial Group.

For more than 10 years, Blinder wrote newspaper and magazine columns on economic policy, and his op-ed pieces still appear regularly in various newspapers. He also appears frequently on CNN and CNBC, and is a regular commentator on PBS's "Nightly Business Report."

Blinder has been vice president of the American Economic Association and is a member of both the American Philosophical Society and the American Academy of Arts and Sciences. He has two grown sons, two grandsons, and lives in Princeton with his wife, where he plays tennis as often as he can.

BRIEF CONTENTS

TABLE OF CONTENTS

PART IV THE UNITED STATES IN THE WORLD ECONOMY 299

CHAPTER 16 INTERNATIONAL TRADE AND COMPARATIVE ADVANTAGE 301

CHAPTER 17 THE INTERNATIONAL MONETARY SYSTEM: ORDER OR DISORDER? 323

PREFACE

As this 9th Edition Update was being prepared, the U.S. economy appeared finally to be shaking off the after-effects of the 2001 recession and entering a period of sustained growth. Many other countries were showing signs of growth as well. That makes it entirely appropriate that the 9th Edition places far greater emphasis on growth than previous editions did. After all, despite occasional serious business downturns, it is still growth that matters most for standards of living in the long run. Indeed, surveys of users and potential users have indicated a desire for a more detailed treatment of economic growth, and we have been delighted to comply.

Accordingly, the Ninth Edition adds an entirely new chapter on the macroeconomics of growth (Chapter 6), plus additional material on growth in several other chapters (especially Chapters 5 and 13). To make room for these additions, we have shortened some of the macroeconomic discussion that appeared in the Eighth Edition—for example, by collapsing three chapters into two.

This Update reflects many of the significant changes that have taken place in the U.S. and world economies since the 9th Edition was originally published. For example, the state of the U.S. and other economies looks much better, but the federal budget looks much worse.

It has been said that economics is no laughing matter, and that an economist is a person who, having observed something that works in reality, wonders whether it works in theory! This book contains its share of theoretical material. But the theory is not merely an exercise in making students miserable; it is driven by issues that are real and current. And every discussion of theory is related to applications, so as to offer students a continuing sense of the relevance of the material to reality. As used by physicists, biologists, and economists—indeed in all the fields of research in colleges and universities—the word *theory* simply means a thorough and rigorous explanation. For example, economists believe that foreign trade can harm some workers but makes most members of the community better off. We need theory to explain why. Or another example: Average incomes of people who live in market economies have grown far faster than those of others in countries where the economy is directed by government planners. Again, theory can explain why.

To maintain prosperity, to offer a better future to those who are now less educated, and to deal with the enormous economic problems of the poorer nations of the world, we need to understand the effects of international trade and of improvements in technology. Do they make most of us better off by making products cheaper, so that our incomes go further? Or do they threaten our incomes by making us more vulnerable to foreign competition and labor-saving technology? Such crucial issues are addressed throughout this book.

In addition to its entirely new material, many parts of the book have been extensively rewritten and reorganized for easier comprehension. Quite a few of these changes were suggested by users of the book and by others whose opinions we solicited in an extensive survey. For example, we have abbreviated the introductory materials in Part I from the previous five chapters down to three. In each of these chapters, we were careful to retain the features that readers reported as being helpful in earlier editions.

NOTE TO THE STUDENT

May we offer a suggestion for success in your economics course? Unlike some of the other subjects you may be studying, economics is cumulative: Each week's lesson builds upon what you have learned before. You will save yourself a lot of frustration— and a lot of work—by keeping up on a week-to-week basis. To assist you in doing so, we provide a chapter summary, a list of important terms and concepts, and a selection of questions to help you review the contents of each chapter. Making use of these learning aids will help you to master the material in your economics course. For additional assistance, we have prepared student supplements to help reinforce the concepts in this book and provide opportunities for practice and feedback. The following list indicates the ancillaries that provide the learning tools designed specifically to be helpful to students.

THE SUPPORT PACKAGE

As economic education incorporates new technologies, we have expanded and improved our extensive learning package to accommodate instructor and student needs.

For the Instructor

Instructor's Manual   David O'Hara of Metropolitan State University has extensively revised the *Instructor's Manual*. Every chapter includes detailed chapter outlines, teaching tips and suggestions, answers to end-of-chapter questions in the main text, and questions for classroom discussion. Included in this edition's *Instructor's Manual* is an Activities Manual, which provides instructors with classroom games, activities, and demonstrations designed to illustrate and enliven important economic concepts. These activities have been tremendously popular with instructors and are very useful for classroom learning. (ISBN 0-03-035502-8)

Macroeconomics Test Bank   The updated and revised *Macroeconomics Test Bank* by Edward F. Stuart of Northeastern Illinois University consists of more than 200 questions per chapter covering Chapters 1–3 and 21–35 in the text. Every question has been checked to ensure the accuracy and clarity of the answers and painstakingly revised to address the main text revisions. The *Test Bank* includes true/false, multiple-choice, and short-answer questions that assess students' critical thinking skills. Easy, medium, and difficult questions outline the process that students must use to arrive at their answers: recall, application, and integration. Questions are organized by text section to help instructors pick and choose their selections with ease. (ISBN 0-03-035562-1)

Computerized Test Banks   ExamView—Computerized Testing Software contains all of the questions in the printed *Test Bank*. ExamView is an easy-to-use test creation software compatible with both Microsoft Windows and Macintosh. Instructors can add or edit questions, instructions, and answers and select questions by previewing them on the screen, selecting them randomly, or selecting them by number. Instructors can also create and administer quizzes online, whether over the Internet, a local-area network (LAN), or a wide-area network (WAN). (ISBN 0-03-035472-2)

Instructor's Resource CD-ROM   Get quick access to all instructor ancillaries from your desktop. This easy-to-use CD-ROM lets you review, edit, and copy exactly what you need in the format you want. The IRCD contains electronic versions of the *Instructor's Manual*, both *Test Banks*, both the lecture and resource PowerPoint presentations, ExamView Files, and Transparency Masters. (ISBN 0-03-035494-3)

Principles of Economics Video *Principles of Economics* is a 40-minute videotape that offers students an insightful overview of ten common economic principles: Tradeoffs, Opportunity Cost, Marginal Thinking, Incentives, Trade, Markets, Government's Role, Productivity, Inflation, and the Phillips Curve.

Principles of Economics shows viewers how to apply economic principles to their daily lives. This video is filled with interviews from some of the country's leading economists and includes profiles of real students facing economic choices, as well as showing the economy's impact on U.S. and foreign companies.

This video can be used at the beginning of a term to give students a general overview of economics, or used one section at a time prior to teaching one of these principles in your course. (ISBN 0-03-032626-5)

Turner Learning/CNN Economics Video with Integration Guide Professors can bring the real world into the classroom by using the Turner Learning/CNN Economics Video. This video provides current stories of economic interest. The accompanying integration guide provides a summary and discussion questions for each clip. The video is produced in cooperation with Turner Learning Inc. (ISBN 0-324-14778-3)

PowerPoint Lecture and Resource Slides Available only on the Web site and the IRCD are two versions of the PowerPoint presentation. The first is a comprehensive and user-friendly lecture presentation (ISBN 0-03-035532-X) for use in the classroom. This presentation consists of speaking points and chapter outlines that are accompanied by graphs and tables, many of which are animated, from the main text. The art and graphic resource slides (ISBN 0-324-17384-9) provide the instructor with all of the tables and figures from the main text.

Transparency Acetates Full-color transparency acetates for all important figures and tables in the ninth edition are available for use on an overhead projector. They are available to adopters upon request. (ISBN 0-324-17385-7)

Web Site Valuable resources for instructors can be found on the Internet at http://baumol.swlearning.com. For instructors, the PowerPoint presentations, *Instructor's Manual*, and a sample chapter of the printed *Test Bank* are available at the Instructor Resources section of the site.

Web Tutor/Web Tutor Advantage Online learning is growing at a rapid pace. Whether instructors are planning to offer courses at a distance, or to offer a Web-enhanced classroom, South-Western/Thomson Learning offers them a solution with WebTutor. WebTutor provides instructors with text-specific content that interacts in the two leading Course Management Systems available in Higher Education—WebCT and Blackboard. WebTutor is a turnkey solution for instructors who want to begin using technology like Blackboard or WebCT but do not have Web-ready content available or do not want to be burdened with developing their own content. South-Western offers two levels of WebTutor—WebTutor and WebTutor Advantage.

WebTutor—An interactive study guide, WebTutor uses the Internet to turn everyone in your class into a front-row student. WebTutor offers quizzing, concept review, flashcards, discussion forums, and more. Instructor tools are also provided to assist communication between students and faculty.

WebTutor Advantage—More than just an interactive study guide, WebTutor Advantage delivers innovative learning aids that actively engage students. Benefits include automatic and immediate feedback from quizzes; interactive, multimedia-rich explanation of concepts, such as flash-animated graphing tutorials and graphing exercises that utilize an online graph-drawing tool; streaming video applications; online exercises; flashcards; and greater interaction and involvement through online discussion forums. Powerful instructor tools are also provided to assist communication and collaboration between students and faculty.

For more information about the WebTutor products, please contact your local sales representative.

Favorite Ways to Learn Economics Instructor's Edition   David Anderson of Centre College and Jim Chasey of Homewood Flossmoor High School have created an instructor's edition to accompany *Favorite Ways to Learn Economics*. Using experiments to bring economic education to life is a growing trend and for good reason. It works! Students are far more likely to retain new knowledge when it is reinforced with hands-on experiments. *Favorite Ways to Learn Economics* is a lab manual for the classroom and for individual study. This manual of experiments and problem sets reinforces the key principles of microeconomics and macroeconomics covered in most college and AP courses. Students will enjoy this active approach to learning and instructors will see improvement in their students' comprehension. Like a finely tuned lecture, these experiments and problem sets bring economics to life. (ISBN 0-03-032771-7)

For the Student

Study Guide   Craig Swan of the University of Minnesota has revised the student *Study Guide* to make it an even more valuable tool for understanding the text's main concepts. The *Study Guide*, which is available in comprehensive (ISBN 0-03-035539-7) and macro (ISBN 0-03-035547-8) split versions, includes:

- Learning objectives
- Lists of important terms and concepts for every chapter
- Quizzes that help students test their understanding and comprehension of concepts
- Multiple-choice tests for self-understanding
- Lists of supplementary readings and study questions for every chapter
- "Economics in Action" sections that use current news articles to illustrate economic concepts
- "Economics Online" exercises that outline useful Internet and Web sources for economic data and information. Periodic updates of these sources will be provided at http://baumol.swcollege.com within the Interactive Study Center.

The Wall Street Journal Edition   *The Wall Street Journal* is synonymous with the latest word on business, economics, and public policy. *Economics: Principles and Policy* makes it easy for students to apply economic concepts to this authoritative publication, and for you to bring the most up-to-date, real-world events into your classroom. For a nominal additional cost, *Economics: Principles and Policy* can be packaged with a card entitling students to a 15-week subscription to both the print and interactive versions of *The Wall Street Journal*. Instructors who have at least ten students activate their subscriptions will automatically receive their own free subscription. Contact your South-Western/Thomson Learning sales representative for package pricing and ordering information.

InfoTrac College Edition   If you bought a new copy of the InfoTrac College Edition of this text, don't forget to take advantage of your subscription. With InfoTrac College Edition, you can receive anytime, anywhere, online access to a database of full-text articles from hundreds of scholarly and popular periodicals. You can use its fast and easy search tools to find what you're looking for among the tens of thousands of articles—updated daily and dating back as far as four years—all in this single Web site. It's a great way to locate resources for papers and projects without having to travel to the library. **To log on and get started, visit http://www.infotrac-college.com**

Xtra! CD-ROM   Baumol Xtra! CD-ROM, packaged with every new text, provides students with complimentary access to the robust set of additional online learning tools found at **http://baumolXtra.swlearning.com**. Here is a tour through some of the study support features you will find there:

The Graphing Workshop

For most students, graphing is one of the most difficult aspects of the Principles course. The Graphing Workshop is your one-stop learning resource for help in mastering the language of graphs. You'll explore important economic concepts through a unique learning system made up of tutorials, interactive tools, and exercises that teach you how to interpret, reproduce, and explain graphs:

- **SEE IT!** Animated graphing tutorials provide step-by-step graphical presentations and audio explanations.
- **TRY IT!** Interactive graphing exercises have you practice manipulating and interpreting graphs with GraphIt—a hands-on Java graphing tool. You can check your work online.
- **APPLY IT!** Interactive graphing assignments challenge you to apply what you have learned by creating your own graph from scratch to analyze a specific scenario. You can print out and/or e-mail answers to your instructor for grading.

Video Lecture and Applications

Via streaming video, difficult concepts from each chapter are explained and illustrated by an economics instructor. These "Ask the Instructor" video clips can be extremely helpful review and clarification tools if you had trouble understanding an in-class lecture or if you are more of a visual learner who sometimes has difficulty grasping concepts as they are presented in the text. In addition, CNN video segments bring the "real world" right to your desktop. The accompanying CNN video exercises help to illustrate how economics is an important part of your daily life.

Additional Self-Testing Opportunities

In addition to the open-access chapter-by-chapter quizzes found at the Baumol Product Support Web site (http://baumol.swlearning.com), Baumol Xtra! offers you an opportunity to practice for midterms and finals by taking online quizzes that span multiple chapters.

econ@pps: (Economic Applications)

These economic applications are also available through the Baumol Xtra! CD. EconDebate Online, EconNews Online, EconData Online, and EconLinks Online, all deepen your understanding of theoretical concepts through hands-on exploration and analysis of the latest economic news stories, policy debates, data and Web sites. These applications are updated on a regular basis.

Web Site   Valuable resources for students can be found on the Internet at the Baumol textbook support site: http://baumol.swlearning.com. The Interactive Study Center provides students with links to economics-related Internet sites, automatically graded practice quizzes, and PowerPoint slides for their review. Also at the Web site are a sample chapter from the study guide, access to Baumol Xtra! and other resources.

South-Western Economics Resource Center   A unique, rich, and robust online resource for economics instructors and students, **http://economics.swlearning.com** provides customer service and product information, teaching and learning tips and tools, information about careers in economics, access to all of our text-supporting Web sites, and other cutting-edge educational resources.

Economics Alive! CD-ROMs   These interactive multimedia study aids for economics are the high-tech, high-fun way to study economics. Through a combination of animated presentations, interactive graphing exercises, and simulations, the core principles of economics come to life and are driven home in an upbeat and entertaining way. Macroeconomics Alive! CD-ROM (ISBN 0-538-86850-3)

For more details, visit the Economics Alive! Web site at http://econalive. swlearning.com.

Favorite Ways to Learn Economics   Authors David Anderson of Centre College and Jim Chasey of Homewood Flossmoor High School use experiments to bring economic education to life—a growing trend, for good reason. It works! Students are far more likely to retain new knowledge when it is reinforced with hands-on experiments. *Favorite Ways to Learn Economics* is a lab manual for the classroom and for individual study that contains experiments and problem sets that reinforce the key principles of microeconomics and macroeconomics covered in most college and AP courses. Students will enjoy this active approach to learning, and instructors will see improvement in their students' comprehension. Like a finely tuned lecture, these experiments and problem sets bring economics to life. (ISBN 0-03-032741-5)

Economics: Hits on the Web   This resource booklet supports students' research efforts on the World Wide Web. This manual covers materials such as: an introduction to the World Wide Web, browsing the Web, finding information on the World Wide Web, email, email discussion groups and newsgroups, and documenting Internet sources for research. It also provides a list of the hottest economic sites on the Web. (ISBN 0-759-30740-7)

The Tobacco Wars   *The Tobacco Wars*, by Walter Adams of Michigan State University and James W. Brock of Miami University of Ohio, presents the economic theory surrounding the tobacco litigation as a creative dialogue between many key players in the debate—including tobacco industry executives, consumers, attorneys, economists, health care professionals, historians, and political activists. Their fictional conversations illustrate the real-life issues, controversies, and points of view currently at play, giving readers a balanced and provocative framework to reach their own conclusions. The text provides a unique way to illustrate microeconomic principles, such as:

- consumer behavior
- industrial organization and public policy
- antitrust policy
- externalities, social costs, and market imperfections

(ISBN 0-324-01296-9)

NOTE TO THE INSTRUCTOR

In trying to improve the book from one edition to the next, we rely heavily on our experiences as teachers. But our experience using the book is minuscule compared with that of the hundreds of instructors who use it nationwide. If you encounter problems or have suggestions for improving the book, we urge you to let us know by writing to us in care of South-Western / Thomson Learning, 5191 Natorp Blvd., Mason, OH 45040. Such letters are invaluable, and we are glad to receive both praise and suggestions for improvement. Many such suggestions that were accumulated since publication of the Eighth Edition have found their way into this new book. Suggested course outlines for both one-semester and one-quarter courses appear in the *Instructor's Manual*.

IN GRATITUDE

Finally, we are pleased to acknowledge our mounting indebtedness to the many who have generously helped us in our efforts through the more than quarter century of existence of this book. We have often needed help in dealing with some of the many subjects that an introductory textbook must cover. Our friends and colleagues Albert Ando, Charles Berry, Rebecca Blank, William Branson, the late Lester Chandler, Gregory Chow, Avinash Dixit, the late Robert Eisner, Susan Feiner, the late Stephen Goldfeld, Claudia Goldin, Ronald Grieson, Daniel Hamermesh, Yuzo Honda, Peter Kenen, Melvin Krauss, Herbert Levine, the late Arthur Lewis, Burton Malkiel, Edwin Mills, Janusz Ordover, Uwe Reinhardt, Harvey Rosen, Laura Tyson, and Martin Weitzman have all given generously of their knowledge in particular areas over the course of nine editions. We have learned much from them, and have shamelessly relied on their help.

Economists and students at colleges and universities other than ours offered numerous useful suggestions for improvements, many of which we have incorporated into this ninth edition. We must single out Professor David Lucking-Reiley of the *University of Arizona*, whose sharp eye led to many useful suggestions. We also wish to thank Mohsen Bahmani, *University of Wisconsin–Milwaukee*; Justino De La Cruz, *University of Texas at San Antonio*; Catalina Amuedo-Dorantes, *San Diego State University*; Michael Dowd, *University of Toledo*; James Frew, *Willamette University*; Brad Kamp, *University of South Florida*; Evelyn Lehrer, *University of Illinois at Chicago*; Norman Obst, *Michigan State University*; Anthony O'Brien, *Lehigh University*; David O'Hara, *Metropolitan State University*; Robert Rosenman, *Washington State University*; Dan Rubenson, *Southern Oregon University*; Jeffrey T. Stewart, *Miami University*; Brian Trinque, *University of Texas at Austin*; Vivian Charles Walsh, *Muhlenberg College*; and Mark Witte, *Northwestern University* for their insightful reviews.

We also wish to thank the many economists who responded to our survey; their responses were invaluable in planning this revision: Bahram Adranoh, *University of Portland*; Christie Agioutanti, *City University of New York, Bernard M. Baruch College*; Terence Alexander, *Iowa State University*; Bobur Alimov, *University of Connecticut*; Polly Allen, *University of Connecticut*; W. David Allen, *University of Alabama–Huntsville*; Eric Allmeroth, *Lake Tahoe Community College*; John E. Anderson, *University of Nebraska*; Ourania Antonopoulos, *New York University*; Rozhyer Q. Aware, *South Dakota State University*; Mohsen Bahmani, *University of Wisconsin–Milwaukee*; Benjamin Balak, *University of North Carolina–Chapel Hill*; Erol Balkan, *Hamilton College*; Jennifer A. Ball, *California State University–Long Beach*; Sudeshna C. Bandyopadhyay, *West Virginia University*; Alexander Barbara, *University of Minnesota*; Debra Barbezot, *Colby College*; Gustavo Barboza, *Wabash College*; Donald N. Baum, *University of Nebraska–Omaha*; Anoop Bhargova, *Mount St. Mary's College–Weekend College*; Todd M. Bihaw, *University of New Hampshire–Manchester*; Cihan Bilginsoy, *University of Utah*; David Black, *University of Toledo*; Ben Blair, *Mississippi State University*; Howard Bodenhorn,

Lafayette College; Giacomo Bonanno, *University of California–Davis*; David J. Bonko, *Northwestern Electronic Institute*; Lawrence W. Boyd, *University of Hawaii*; Morgan K. Bridge, *Mesa State College*; Bonnie-Anne Briggs, *Gates Chili High School*; Jozell Brister, *Abilene Christian University*; Robert Buchele, *Smith College*; Joyce Burnette, *Wabash College*; Tim Burson, *Queens College*; Tony Cafarelli, *Ursuline College*; Gerard A. Cahill, *Florida Institute of Technology*; Sara J. Cameron, *Forest Lake High School*; Carl Campbell, *Northern Illinois University*; Rob Carey, *Tri-County Technical College*; Amber Casolari, *Glendale College*; Gene N. Chang, *University of Toledo*; Yongsung Chang, *University of Pennsylvania*; Parama Chavdhory, *New York University*; Stephen J. Conroy, *University of West Florida*; Sean Corcoran, *University of Maryland–College Park*; Michael D. Corley, *Kennesaw State University*; Rhonda R. Cormon, *University of Northern Colorado*; Kevin M. Coughlin, *Iona College*; Eleanor D. Craig, *University of Delaware*; Mark Crain, *George Mason University*; Brendon M. Cunningham, *Hartwick College*; Joseph Dahms, *Hood College*; Norm Dalsted, *Colorado State University*; Richard Depolt, *Wake Forest University*; Diane Dewar, *State University of New York–Albany*; Joseph E. Dragonette, *Saint Joseph's University*; Marie Duggan, *Keene State College*; Joseph G. Eisenhauer, *Canisius College*; Mona El Shazly, *Columbia College*; Morris Eskenazl, *Delaware Technical and Community College*; Eleanor Fapohunda, *State University of New York–Farmingdale*; Michael Farrell, *California State University–Long Beach*; Farzad Farsio, *Montana State University–Billings*; Shokoofeh Fazel, *College of Business*; Louis Felicetta, *Fairleigh Dickinson University*; Tawni Hunt Ferrarini, *Northern Michigan University*; Janis Barry Figuerson, *Fordham College of Lincoln Center*; Nelson Henrique Barbosa Filho, *Saint Francis College*; Gina B. Finn, *Canterbury School*; William C. Freund, *Pace University*; Frank Gamrat, *Duquesne University*; Frank Garland, *Tri-County Technical College*; George Gayle, *University of Pittsburgh*; Dusmann A. Gbane, Jr., *Oakland University*; Charles Geiss, *University of Missouri–Columbia*; G. Reza Ghorashi, *Stockton*; Kenneth P. Gilliam, *Kennesaw State University*; Annie Goldman, *San Francisco State University*; Jon Goldstein, *Bowdoin College*; Lyndon E. Goodridge, *College of Life Science and Agriculture*; Crauford Goodwin, *Duke University*; Randall B. Goodwin, *Kennesaw State University*; Jerry Gray, *Williamette University*; Ernest H. Greene, *New York University*; Paul W. Grimes, *Mississippi State University*; Elias O. Grivoyannis, *Yeshivd University*; Jang-Ting Guo, *University of California–Riverside*; Brian Gurney, *Montana State University–Billings*; A.R. Gutowsky, *California State University–Sacramento*; Charles W. Haase, *San Francisco State University*; Simon Hakim, *Temple University*; John M. Halstead, *University of New Hampshire*; Karen Klassen Harder, *Bethel College*; Richard R. Hawkins, *University of West Florida*; Sally Hays, *California State University–Fresno*; David Hemenway, *Harvard School of Public Health*; Gerald Hendrickson, *University of New Mexico*; Bruce Herrick, *Washington and Lee University*; Aref A. Hervani; *Miami University*, Paul Hettler, *Duquesne University*; Andrew T. Hill, *University of Delaware*; Nathtali Hoffman, *Elmira College*; Don Holley, *Boise State University*; Sandra F. Holsonback, *Muhlenberg College*; Seungmo Jeff Hong, *Fordham University*; Linda M. Hooks, *Washington and Lee University*; Farrokh Hormezi, *Pace University Graduate Center*; James Hornsten, *Bowdoin College*; Harold A. Horowitz, *Yeshiva College*; Joshua Hoyt, *Madison Area Technical College*; Chia-Hsin Hu, *George Washington University*; Julio Huato, *Saint Francis College*; Kelly C. Hughes, *South Dakota State University*; Samira Hussein, *Johnson County Community College*; Iliona Ilieva, *Fordham University*; Robin Imgrund, *Alleghany College of Maryland*; Petros Isannatos, *Kettering University*; Eric Isenberg, *Washington University–St. Louis*; Oded Izaaeli, *Oakland University*; Alexei Izyumov, *University of Louisville*; Aaron Jackson, *University of Oregon*; Don C. Jackson, *Abilene Christian University*; Eric D. Jacobson, *University of Delaware*; David G. Jaques, *California State Polytechnic University*; Jon Jonakin, *Tennessee Technological University*; Derek C. Jones, *Hamilton College*; Robert K. Jordan, *University of Southern Maine*; James Karakos, *Washtenaw Community College*; Roger Kaufman, *Smith College*; Rosa Keanini, *Sacramento City College*; Kristen Keith, *University of Toledo*; Feisal Khan, *Hobart and William Smith College*; Mariam Khawar, *Elmora College*; Benjamin Kim, *University of Nebraska*; Han J. Kim, *South*

Dakota State University; Janice Kinghorn, *Anitoch College*; Kivanc Kirgiz, *Duke University*; Fred Klunk, *Shippensburg University*; Mary Knasinski, *University of Wisconsin–Milwaukee*; Sinan Koont, *Dickinson College*; Janet Koscianski, *Shippensburg University*; George Kosicki, *College of The Holy Cross*; Bob Kruse, *Northwest College*; Timur Kuran, *University of Southern California*; Jorge L. Laboy, *University of Connecticut*; Tom Larson, *California State University–Los Angeles*; Pareena Lawrence, *University of Minnesota*; Daviel Lee, *Shippenburg University*; Dulee Maria Leon, *Santa Monica College*; Tony Leong, Jr., *University of Berkeley*; Cathleen Leue, *University of Oregon*; Allan Lisse, *Abington College, Penn State University*; Melody Lo, *Purdue University*; Charlotte Lott, *Chatham College*; Terry Lucas, *Kennesaw State University*; Leonel R. Lucero, *Fordham University*; Pirudas Lwamugira, *Fitchburg State College*; Daniel McGowan, *Hobart and William Smith*; Mike McIlhon, *Metro State University*; Donald M. McLeod, *University of Wyoming*; Stanley McMillen, *University of Connecticut*; Sunil Maheshwan, *Clark University*; Alberto B. Manalo, *University of New Hampshire*; H.G. Mannur, *Smith College*; David M. Massey, *West Chester University*; Peter Matthews, *Middlebury College*; Shah M. Mehrabi, *Montgomery College*; Gretchen Mester, *University of Oregon*; Carrie A. Meyer, *George Mason University*; Jeffrey A. Michael, *Towson University*; Genna Miller, *Duke University*; Phillip A. Miller, *University of Missouri*; Gregory L. Miller, *Wallace Community College–Selma*; Michael S. Miller, *DePaul University*; Nader N. Mobini, *California State University–Sacramento*; C.A. Moerneman, *Delta College*; Edward Montgomery, *University of Maryland*; Roger V. Moore, *College of New Jersey*; Myra Moore, *University of Georgia*; W.D. Morgan, *University of California–Santa Barbara*; Panos Mourdoukoutas, *Long Island University*; Stephanie Murphy, *Culinary Institute of America*; M. Nagano, *Scottsdale Community College*; P.C. Nair, *Montgomery College*; John A. Naylor, *Wabash College*; Neil Niman, *University of New Hampshire*; Mohamad Hisham B. Mohd. Noh, *Glendale Community College*; Lee Norma, *Idaho State University*; Ingmar Nyman, *Hunter College*; S.C. Nzeako, *City of New York, Borough of Manhattan Community College*; William Oakland, *Tulane University*; Patrick O'Halloran, *University of Wisconsin–Waukesha*; David O'Hara, *Metropolitan State University*; Olligbenga Onafowora, *Susquehanna University*; Anthony M. Opyrchal, *University of Detroit–Mercy*; Joseph Ottoy, *Central Michigan University*; Harvey Pacil, *Towson University*; Kerry Pannell, *Bowdoin College*; Ravi Papamoswaran, *Oakland University*; Walter G. Park, *American University*; Perry L. Patterson, *Wake Forest University*; Sam Pavel, *Kalamazoo College*; William F. Payne, *Murray State University*; Paul Pecorino, *University of Alabama*; Mark Pernecky, *St. Olaf College*; Phillip E. Petitt, *University of Massachusetts*; David R. Poma, *St. Francis College*; Jennie Popp, *University of Arkansas*; Jonathan Powers, *Knox College*; Rahim M. Quazi, *University of Georgia*; Kolleen J. Rask, *College of The Holy Cross*; Cadwell Ray, *University of Tulsa*; J. Martin Redfern, *University of Arkansas*; Cordelia Reimers, *Hunter College*; Louis-Phillippe Reston, *Kalamazoo College*; W. Gregory Rhodus, *Bentley College*; Jack Richards, *Portland State University*; Paul Ridgeun, *Gwynedd-Mercy College*; David Ring, *State University of New York–Oneonta*; Meenakshi Rishi, *Ohio Northern University*; Bruce Roberts, *University of Southern Maine*; Robert Rosenman, *Washington State University*; Robert A. Rosenthal, *Stonehill College*; Howard N. Ross, *Baruch College, City University of New York*; Raj Roy, *University of Toledo*; Kim J. Ruhl, *University of Minnesota*; Steven L. Rundle, *Biola University*; Renee Sanders, *East Mississippi Community College*; John Schnell, *University of Alabama–Huntsville*; Daniel A. Seiver, *Miami University*; Tayyeb Shabbir, *University of Pennsylvania*; Edward Shepard, *Le Moyne College*; Anna Shostya, *Hunter College*; Arleatha M. Simms, *Saint Paul's College*; Lynnette Smyth, *Gordon College*; John A. Sondey, *South Dakota State University*; Jeffrey T. Stewart, *Miami University*; Sara Solnick, *University of Vermont*; Camille Soltau, *Washington State University*; Abdol S. Soofi, *University of Wisconsin–Milwaukee*; Denise Stanley, *California State University–Fullerton*; Jeff Stensland, *Metropolitan State*; Della L. Sue, *Marist College*; Gilbert Suzawa, *University of Rhode Island*; William J. Swift, *Hofstra University*; Jennifer E. Tessendorf, *Hobart and William Smith College*; Booi Themeli, *Fordham University*; James A. Thorson, *Southern Connecticut State University*; Jerry Thursby, *Purdue*

University; Joanne Tokle, *Idaho State University*; Robert Tokle, *Idaho State University*; Henry Townsend, *George Washington University*; Evvidiki Tsounta, *University of Minnesota*; Fred Tyler, *Fordham University*; Joshua Utt, *Washington State University*; Evert Van Der Heide, *Calvin College*; Richard Vogel, *State University of New York–Farmingdale*; Marc Von Der Ruhr, *St. Norbers College*; Karen Vorst, *University of Missouri–Kansas City*; Lawrence Waldman, *University of New Mexico*; Neal T. Wallace, *Portland State University*; Richard Watson, *University of California–Santa Barbara*; Jim Weaver, *Longview Community College*; David Weber, *U.S. Coast Guard Academy*; Robert J. Wechman, *Lehman College–City University of New York*; Ross D. Weiner, *City College of New York*; Mark Weinstock, *Hunter College*; Barbara A. Weins-Tuers, *Penn State–Altoona*; Thomas Weiss, *University of Kansas*; Toni Weiss, *Tulane University*; Mark Witte, *Northwestern University*; Katherine Wolfe, *University of Pittsburgh*; Richard Su Xiong, *University of Wisconsin–Milwaukee*; Donald E. Yett, *University of Southern California*; James Dale Yohe, *University of West Florida*; Ben Young, *University of Missouri–Kansas City*; Ali Zadeh, *Susquehanna University*; Peter Zaleski, *Villanova University*; Sourushe Zandvakili, *University of Cincinnati*; Jason Zimmerman, *South Dakota State University*; Duo Zhang, *West Virginia University*.

Obviously, the book you hold in your hands was not produced by us alone. An essential role was played by the staff at the former Harcourt College Publishers, including Thomas Gay, Executive Editor for Economics and Laurie Runion, Developmental Editor. We also wish to thank the staff at South-Western/Thomson Learning, including: Mike Roche, Vice President and Team Director; Mike Mercier, Publisher of Economics; Mike Worls, Acquisitions Editor; the late Jeff Gilbreath, Senior Developmental Editor; Sarah K. Dorger, Developmental Manager; Janet Hennies and Lisa Lysne, Executive Marketing Managers; Brian Joyner, Senior Marketing Manager; Michelle Kunkler, Design Manager; and Dan Plofchan, Production Editor, as well as the staff at Elm Street Publishing Services, Inc., Pre-Press Company, Inc., and OffCenter Concepts, Inc. It was a pleasure to deal with them, and we appreciate their understanding of our approaches, our goals, and our idiosyncrasies.

We also thank our intelligent and delightful secretaries and research coworkers at Princeton University and New York University, Kathleen Hurley and Janeece Roderick Lewis, who struggled successfully with the myriad tasks involved in completing the manuscript. Above all, Professor Baumol owes an un-repayable debt to his friend and longstanding partner, Sue Anne Batey Blackman, who updated much of the materials and contributed draft paragraphs, illustrative items, and far more with her usual insight and diligence. By now, Sue Anne undoubtedly knows more about the book than the authors do.

And, finally, we must not omit our continuing debt to our wives, Hilda Baumol and Madeline Blinder. They have now suffered through nine editions and the inescapable neglect and distraction the preparation of each new edition imposes. Their tolerance and understanding has been no minor contribution to the project.

William J. Baumol
Alan S. Blinder

To my four children, Ellen, Daniel, and now Sabrina and Jim.

W.J.B.

To Malcolm and Levi, the new generation.

A.S.B.

GETTING ACQUAINTED WITH ECONOMICS

Welcome to economics! Some of your fellow students may have warned you that "Econ is boring." Don't believe them—or at least, don't believe them too much. It is true that studying economics may not be as much fun as, say, studying literature or film. But a first course in economics can be an eye-opening experience. There is a vast and important world out there—the economic world—and this book is designed to help you understand it better.

Have you ever wondered whether jobs will be plentiful or scarce when you graduate? Or why a college education becomes more and more expensive? Was the government right to sue Microsoft? Why can't pollution be eliminated? How did the U.S. economy manage to grow so rapidly in the 1990s while Japan's economy stagnated? If any of these questions have piqued your curiosity, read on. You may find economics to be more interesting than you had thought!

The three chapters of Part I introduce you to both the subject matter of economics and to some of the methods that economists use to study their subject.

1

What Is Economics?

Why does public discussion of economic policy so often show the abysmal ignorance of the participants? Why do I so often want to cry at what public figures, the press, and television commentators say about economic affairs?

ROBERT M. SOLOW

Economics is a broad-ranging discipline, both in the questions it asks and the methods it uses to seek answers. Many of the world's most pressing problems are economic in nature. The first part of this chapter is intended to give you some idea of the sorts of issues that economic analysis helps to clarify and the kinds of solutions that economic principles suggest. The second part briefly introduces the tools that economists use—tools you are likely to find useful in your career, personal life, and role as an informed citizen, long after this course is over.

CONTENTS

IDEAS FOR BEYOND THE FINAL EXAM

Elephants may never forget, but people do. We realize that most students inevitably forget much of what they learn in a course—perhaps with a sense of relief—soon after the final exam.

Nevertheless, we hope that you *will* remember some of the most important economic ideas and, even more important, the ways of thinking about economic issues that are taught in this course. To help you identify some of the most crucial concepts, we have selected nine from the many in this book. Some offer key insights into the workings of the economy. Several bear on important policy issues that appear in newspapers. Others point out common misunderstandings that occur among even the most thoughtful lay observers. Most of them indicate that it takes more than just common sense to analyze economic issues effectively. As the opening quote of this chapter suggests, many learned judges, politicians, and university administrators who failed to understand basic economic principles could have made wiser decisions than they did.

Try this one on for size. Imagine you own a widget manufacturing company that rents a warehouse. Your landlord raises your rent by $10,000 per year. Should you raise the price of your widgets to try to recoup some of your higher costs? Or should you do the opposite—lower your price to try to sell more and spread the so-called overhead over more products? In fact, as we shall see in Chapter 7, both answers are probably wrong!

Each of the nine *Ideas for Beyond the Final Exam*, many of which are counterintuitive, will be sketched briefly here. More important, each will be discussed in depth when it occurs in the course of the book, where it will be called to your attention by a special icon in the margin. So don't expect to master these ideas fully now. But do notice how some of the ideas arise again and again as we deal with different topics. By the end of the course you will have a better sense of when common sense works and when it fails. And you will be able to recognize common fallacies that are all too often offered as pearls of wisdom by public figures, the press, and television commentators.

IDEAS FOR BEYOND THE FINAL EXAM

Idea 1: How Much Does It Really Cost?

Because no one has infinite riches, people are constantly forced to make choices. If you purchase a new computer, you may have to give up that trip you had planned. If a business decides to retool its factories, it may have to postpone its plans for new executive offices. If a government expands its defense program, it may be forced to reduce its outlays on school buildings.

Economists say that the true costs of such decisions are not the number of dollars spent on the computer, the new equipment, or the military, but rather *the value of what must be given up in order to acquire the item*—the vacation trip, the new executive offices, and the new schools. These are called **opportunity costs** because they represent the *opportunities* the individual, firm, or government must forgo to make the desired expenditure. Economists maintain that rational decision making must be based on opportunity costs, not just dollar costs (see Chapter 2).

The cost of a college education provides a vivid example. How much do you think it *costs* to go to college? Most people are likely to answer by adding together your expenditures on tuition, room and board, books, and the like, and then deducting any scholarship funds you may receive. Suppose that amount comes to $15,000.

Economists keep score differently. They first want to know how much you would be earning if you were not attending college. Suppose that salary is $16,000 per year. This may seem irrelevant, but because you *give up* these earnings by attending college, they must be added to your tuition bill. You have that much less income because of your education. On the other side of the ledger, economists would not count *all* of

The **opportunity cost** of some decision is the value of the next best alternative that must be given up because of that decision (for example, working instead of going to school).

the university's bill for room and board as part of the costs of your education. They would want to know how much *more* it costs you to live at school rather than at home. Economists would count only this *extra* cost as an educational expense. On balance, college is probably costing you much more than you think.

Idea 2: Attempts to Repeal the Laws of Supply and Demand—The Market Strikes Back

When a commodity is in short supply, its price naturally tends to rise. Sometimes disgruntled consumers badger politicians into "solving" this problem by making the high prices illegal—by imposing a ceiling on the price. Similarly, when supplies are abundant—say, when fine weather produces extraordinarily abundant crops—prices tend to fall. Falling prices naturally dismay producers, who often succeed in getting legislators to impose price floors.

But such attempts to repeal the laws of supply and demand usually backfire and sometimes produce results virtually the opposite of those intended. Where rent controls are adopted to protect tenants, housing grows scarce because the law makes it unprofitable to build and maintain apartments. When price floors are placed under agricultural products, surpluses pile up because people buy less.

As we will see in Chapter 3 and elsewhere in this book, such consequences of interference with the price mechanism are no accident. They follow inevitably from the way in which free markets work.

Idea 3: The Surprising Principle of Comparative Advantage

Japan produces many products that Americans buy in huge quantities—including cars, cameras, and electronic equipment. American manufacturers often complain about Japanese competition and demand protection from the flood of imports that, in their view, threatens American standards of living. Is this view justified?

Economists think not. They maintain that both sides normally gain from international trade. But what if the Japanese were able to produce *everything* more cheaply than we can? Wouldn't Americans be thrown out of work and our nation be impoverished?

A remarkable result, called the law of *comparative advantage*, shows that, even in this extreme case, the two nations can still benefit by trading and that each can gain as a result! We will explain this principle first in Chapter 2 and then more fully in Chapter 16. But for now a simple parable will make the reason clear.

Suppose Sally grows up on a farm and is a whiz at plowing. But she is also a successful country singer who earns $4,000 per performance. Should Sally turn down singing engagements to leave time to work the fields? Of course not. Instead she should hire Alfie, a much less efficient farmer, to do the plowing for her. Sally may be better at plowing, but she earns so much more by singing that it makes sense for her to specialize in that and leave the farming to Alfie. Although Alfie is a less skilled farmer than Sally, he is an even worse singer.

So Alfie earns his living in the job at which he at least has a *comparative* advantage (his farming is not as inferior as his singing), and both Alfie and Sally gain. The same is true of two countries. Even if one of them is more efficient at everything, both countries can gain by producing the things they do best *comparatively*.

Idea 4: Trade Is a Win-Win Situation

One of the most fundamental ideas of economics is that *both* parties must expect to gain something in a *voluntary* exchange. Otherwise, why would they both agree to trade? This principle seems self-evident. Yet it is amazing how often it is ignored in practice.

For example, it was widely believed for centuries that in international trade one country's gain from an exchange must be the other country's loss (Chapter 16). Analogously, some people feel instinctively that if Ms. A profits handsomely from a deal with Mr. B, then Mr. B must have been exploited. Laws sometimes prohibit mutually beneficial exchanges between buyers and sellers—as when a loan transaction is banned because the interest rate is "too high" (Chapter 5), or when a willing worker is condemned to remain unemployed because the wage she is offered is "too low," or when the resale of tickets to sporting events ("ticket scalping") is outlawed even though the buyer is happy to get the ticket that he could not obtain at a lower price (Chapter 3).

In every one of these cases, and many more, well-intentioned but misguided reasoning blocks the mutual gains that arise from voluntary exchange—and thereby interferes with one of the most basic functions of an economic system (see Chapter 2).

Idea 5: The Importance of Thinking at the Margin

We will devote many pages of this book to explaining and extolling a type of decision-making process called *marginal analysis*, which we can best illustrate through an example.

Suppose an airline is told by its accountants that the full cost of transporting one passenger from Los Angeles to New York is $300. Can the airline profit by offering a reduced fare of $200 to students who fly on a standby basis? The surprising answer is probably yes. The reason is that most of the costs of the flight must be paid whether the plane carries 20 passengers or 120 passengers.

Costs such as maintenance, landing rights, and ground crews are irrelevant to the decision of whether to carry additional standby passengers at reduced rates. The only costs that *are* relevant are the *extra* costs of writing and processing additional tickets, the food and beverages consumed by these passengers, the additional fuel required, and so on. These so-called *marginal costs* are probably quite small in this example. Any passenger who pays the airline more than its marginal cost adds something to the company's profit. So it probably is more profitable to let students ride at low fares than to leave the seats empty.

In many real cases, a failure to understand marginal analysis leads decision makers to reject advantageous possibilities like the reduced fare in our example. These people are misled by using *average* rather than *marginal* cost figures in their calculations—an error that can be quite costly.

Idea 6: Externalities: A Shortcoming of the Market Cured by Market Methods

Markets are very adept at producing the goods that consumers want and in just the quantities they desire. They do so by rewarding those who respond to what consumers want and who produce these products economically. This all works out well as long as each exchange involves only the buyer and the seller—and no one else. But some transactions affect third parties who were not involved in the decision. Examples abound. Electric utilities that generate power for Midwestern states also produce pollution that kills freshwater fish in upstate New York. A farmer sprays crops with toxic pesticides, but the poison seeps into the groundwater and affects the health of neighboring communities.

Such social costs are called *externalities* because they affect parties *external* to the economic transactions that cause them. Externalities escape the control of the market mechanism because no financial incentive motivates polluters to minimize the damage they do. So business firms make their products as cheaply as possible, disregarding any environmental harm they may cause.

Yet we can point out a way for the government to use the market mechanism to control undesirable externalities. If the electric utility and the farmer are charged for the clean air and water they use up, just as they are charged for any coal and fertilizer they consume, then they will have a financial incentive to reduce the amount of pollution they generate. Thus, in this case, economists believe that market methods are often the best way to cure one of the market's most important shortcomings.

▌Idea 7: The Trade-Off Between Efficiency and Equality

Wages and income have grown more unequal in the United States since the late 1970s. Highly skilled workers have pulled away from low-skilled workers. The rich have grown richer while the poor have become (relatively) poorer. Yet U.S. unemployment has been much lower than that in Europe for many years. And in many European countries inequality has not grown more extreme.

Many economists see these phenomena as two sides of the same coin. Europe and the United States have made different choices regarding how best to balance the conflicting claims of greater economic efficiency (more output and jobs) versus greater equality.

Roughly speaking, the American solution is to let markets work to promote efficiency—something they are very good at doing—with only minimal government interferences to reduce economic inequalities. But much of continental Europe takes a different view. They find it scandalous that many Americans work for less than $6 per hour, with virtually no fringe benefits and no job security. European laws mandate not only relatively high minimum wages but also substantial fringe benefits and employment protections. Of course, European taxes must be much higher to pay for these programs.

As economists see it, each system's virtue is also its vice. There is an agonizing *trade-off* between the *size* of a nation's output and the degree of *equality* with which that output is distributed. European-style policies designed to divide the proverbial economic pie more equally inadvertently can cause the size of the pie to shrink. American-style arrangements that promote maximal efficiency and output may permit or even breed huge inequalities. Which system is better? There is no clear answer.

▌Idea 8: The Short-Run Trade-Off Between Inflation and Unemployment

The U.S. economy was lucky in the second half of the 1990s. A set of fortuitous events—falling energy prices, tumbling computer prices, a rising dollar, and so on—pushed inflation down even while unemployment fell to its lowest level in almost 30 years. During the 1970s and early 1980s, the United States was not so fortunate. Skyrocketing prices for food and, especially, energy sent both inflation and unemployment up to extraordinary heights. In both episodes, then, inflation and unemployment moved in the same direction.

But economists maintain that neither of these two episodes was "normal." When we are experiencing neither unusually good luck (as in the 1990s) nor exceptionally bad luck (as in the 1970s), there is a *trade-off between inflation and unemployment*—meaning that low unemployment normally makes inflation rise and high unemployment normally makes inflation fall. We will study the mechanisms underlying this trade-off in Parts II and III, especially Chapter 15. It poses one of the fundamental dilemmas of national economic policy.

▌Idea 9: Productivity Growth Is (Almost) Everything in the Long Run

In Geneva, Switzerland, today, a worker in a watch factory turns out more than 100 times as many mechanical watches per year as her ancestors did three centuries earlier. The *productivity* of labor (output per hour of work) in cotton production has probably gone up more than 1,000-fold in 200 years. It is estimated that rising labor productivity has increased the standard of living of a typical American worker more than sevenfold in the past century. (See Chapter 5.)

Other economic issues such as unemployment, monopoly, and inequality are also important to us all and will receive much attention in this book. But in the long run, nothing has as great an effect on our material well-being and the amounts society can afford to spend on hospitals, schools, and social amenities as the rate of growth of productivity—the amount that an average worker can produce in an hour. Chapter 5 points out that what appears to be a small increase in productivity growth can have a huge effect on a country's standard of living over a long period of time because productivity compounds like the interest on savings in a bank. Similarly, a slowdown in productivity growth that persists for a substantial number of years can have a devastating effect on living standards.

Epilogue

These ideas are some of the more fundamental concepts you will find in this book—ideas that we hope you will retain beyond the final exam. There is no need to master them right now, for you will hear much more about each as you progress through the book. By the end of the course, you may be amazed to see how natural, or even obvious, they will seem.

INSIDE THE ECONOMIST'S TOOL KIT

We turn now from the kinds of *issues* economists deal with to some of the tools they use to grapple with them.

Economics as a Discipline

Although economics is clearly the most rigorous of the social sciences, it nevertheless looks decidedly more "social" than "scientific" when compared with, say, physics. An economist must be a jack of several trades, borrowing modes of analysis from numerous fields. Mathematical reasoning is often used in economics, but so is historical study. And neither looks quite the same as when practiced by a mathematician or a historian. Statistical inference plays a major role in modern economic inquiry, although economists had to modify standard statistical procedures to fit their kinds of data.

The Need for Abstraction

Some students find economics unduly abstract and "unrealistic." The stylized world envisioned by economic theory seems only a distant cousin to the world they know. There is an old joke about three people—a chemist, a physicist, and an economist—stranded on an island with an ample supply of canned food but no tools to open the cans. The chemist thinks that lighting a fire under the cans would burst the cans. The physicist advocates building a catapult with which to smash the cans against some boulders. The economist's suggestion? "Let's assume we have a can opener."

Economic theory *does* make some unrealistic assumptions; you will encounter several of them in this book. But some abstraction from reality is necessary because of the incredible complexity of the economic world, not because economists like to sound absurd.

Compare the chemist's simple task of explaining the interactions of compounds in a chemical reaction with the economist's complex task of explaining the interactions of people in an economy. Are molecules motivated by greed or altruism, by envy or ambition? Do they ever emulate other molecules? Do forecasts about them influence their behavior? People, of course, do all these things and many, many more. It is therefore vastly more difficult to predict human behavior than to predict chemical reactions. If economists tried to keep track of every feature of human behavior, they would never get anywhere. Thus:

Abstraction from unimportant details is necessary to understand the functioning of anything as complex as the economy.

"Yes, John, we'd all like to make economics less dismal. . . "

SOURCE: From *The Wall Street Journal*. Permission, Cartoon Features Syndicate.

Note: The 19th Century British writer, Thomas Carlyle, described economics as the "dismal science," a label that stuck.

Map © by RMC, R.L.04-S-14. http://www.randmcnally.com.

■ MAP 1

Detailed Road Map of Los Angeles

Abstraction means ignoring many details so as to focus on the most important elements of a problem.

■ MAP 2

Major Los Angeles Arteries and Freeways

An analogy will make clear why economists **abstract** from details. Suppose you have just arrived for the first time in Los Angeles. You are now at the Los Angeles Civic Center—the point marked *A* in Maps 1 and 2, which are alternative maps of part of Los Angeles. You want to drive to the Los Angeles County Museum of Art, point *B* on each map. Which map would be more useful?

Map 1 has complete details of the Los Angeles road system. This makes it hard to read and hard to use as a way to find the art museum. For this purpose, Map 1 is far too detailed, although for some other purposes (for example, locating some small street in Hollywood) it may be far better than Map 2.

In contrast, Map 2 omits many minor roads—you might say they are *assumed away*—so that the freeways and major arteries stand out more clearly. As a result of this simplification, several routes from the Civic Center to the Los Angeles County Museum of Art emerge. For example, we can take the Hollywood Freeway west to Alvarado Boulevard, go south to Wilshire Boulevard, and then head west again. Although we *might* find a shorter route by poring over the details in Map 1, most strangers to the city would be better off with Map 2. Similarly, economists try to *abstract* from a lot of confusing details while retaining the essentials.

Map 3, however, illustrates that simplification can go too

Map © by RMC, R.L.04-S-14. http://www.randmcnally.com.

MAP 3

Greater Los Angeles Freeways

SOURCE: California Department of Transportation.

far. It shows little more than the major interstate routes that pass through the greater Los Angeles area, and therefore will not help a visitor find the art museum. Of course, this map was never intended to be used as a detailed tourist guide, which brings us to an important point:

There is no such thing as one "right" degree of abstraction for all analytic purposes. The proper degree of abstraction depends on the objective of the analysis. A model that is a gross oversimplification for one purpose may be needlessly complicated for another.

Economists are constantly seeking analogies to Map 2 rather than Map 3, treading the thin line between useful generalizations about complex issues and gross distortions of the pertinent facts. For example, suppose you want to learn why some people are fabulously rich while others are abjectly poor. People differ in many ways, too many to enumerate, much less to study. The economist must ignore most of these details to focus on the important ones. The color of a person's hair or eyes is probably not important for the problem, but, due to racial discrimination, the color of his or her skin probably is. Height and weight may not matter, but education probably does. Proceeding in this way, we can pare Map 1 down to the manageable dimensions of Map 2. But there is a danger of going too far, stripping away some of the crucial factors, so that we wind up with Map 3.

The Role of Economic Theory

Some students find economics "too theoretical." Let's consider what we mean by a **theory.**

A **theory** is a deliberate simplification of relationships used to explain how those relationships work.

To an economist or natural scientist, the word *theory* means something different from what it means in common parlance. In science, a theory is *not* an untested assertion of alleged fact. The statement that aspirin provides protection against heart attacks is not a theory; it is a *hypothesis,* which will prove to be true or false once the right sorts of experiments have been completed. Instead, a theory is a deliberate simplification (abstraction) of reality that attempts to explain how some relationships work. It is an *explanation* of the mechanism behind observed phenomena. Thus, gravity forms the basis of theories that describe and explain the paths of the planets. Similarly, Keynesian theory (discussed in Parts II and III) seeks to describe and explain how government policies affect unemployment and prices in the national economy.

People who have never studied economics often draw a false distinction between *theory* and *practical policy.* Politicians and businesspeople, in particular, often reject abstract economic theory as something that is best ignored by "practical" people. The irony of these statements is that:

It is precisely the concern for policy that makes economic theory so necessary and important.

To analyze policy options, economists are forced to deal with *possibilities that have not actually occurred.* For example, to learn how to shorten periods of high unemployment, they must investigate whether a proposed new policy that has never been tried can help. Or to determine which environmental programs will be most effective, they must understand how and why a market economy produces pollution and what might happen if the government taxed industrial waste discharges and automobile emissions. Such questions require some *theorizing*, not just examination of the facts, because we need to consider possibilities that have never occurred.

The facts, moreover, can sometimes be highly misleading. Data often indicate that two variables move up and down together. But this statistical **correlation** does not prove that either variable *causes* the other. For example, when it rains, people drive their cars more slowly and there are also more traffic accidents. But no one thinks that slower driving causes more accidents. Rather, we understand that both phenomena are caused by a common underlying factor—more rain. How do we know this? Not just by looking at the correlation between data on accidents and driving speeds. Data alone tell us little about cause and effect. We must use some simple *theory* as part of our analysis.

> Two variables are said to be **correlated** if they tend to go up or down together. Correlation need not imply causation.

Similarly, we must use theoretical analysis, and not just data alone, to understand *how*, if at all, different government policies will lead to lower unemployment or *how* a tax on emissions will reduce pollution.

Statistical correlation need not imply causation. Some theory is usually needed to interpret data.

What Is an Economic Model?

An **economic model** is a representation of a theory or a part of a theory, often used to gain insight into cause and effect. The notion of a "model" is familiar enough to children; and economists—like other scientists—use the term in much the same way that children do.

> An **economic model** is a simplified, small-scale version of some aspect of the economy. Economic models are often expressed in equations, by graphs, or in words.

A child's model airplane looks and operates much like the real thing, but it is much smaller and simpler, so it is easier to manipulate and understand. Engineers for Boeing also build models of planes. Although their models are far larger and much more elaborate than a child's toy, they use them for much the same purposes: to observe the workings of these aircraft "up close" and to experiment with them to see how the models behave under different circumstances. ("What happens if I do this?") From these experiments, they make educated guesses as to how the real-life version will perform.

Economists use models for similar purposes. The late A. W. Phillips, the famous engineer-turned-economist who discovered the "Phillips curve" (discussed in Chapter 15), was talented enough to construct a working model of the determination of national income in a simple economy by using colored water flowing through pipes. For years this contraption has graced the basement of the London School of Economics. While we will explain the models with words and diagrams, Phillips's engineering background enabled him to depict the theory with tubes, valves, and pumps.

Because many of the models used in this book are depicted in diagrams, for those of you who need review, we explain the construction and use of various types of graphs in the appendix to this chapter. Don't be put off by seemingly abstract models. Think of them as useful road maps. And remember how hard it would be to find your way around Los Angeles without one.

SOURCE: Science and Society Picture Library

A.W. Phillips built this model in the early 1950s to illustrate Keynesian theory.

Reasons for Disagreements: Imperfect Information and Value Judgments

"If all the earth's economists were laid end to end, they could not reach an agreement," the saying goes. Politicians and reporters are fond of pointing out that economists can be found on both sides of many public policy issues. If economics is a science, why do economists so often disagree? After all, astronomers do not debate whether the earth revolves around the sun or vice versa.

This question reflects a misunderstanding of the nature of science. Disputes are normal at the frontier of any science. For example, astronomers once did argue vociferously over whether the earth revolves around the sun. Nowadays, they argue about gamma-ray bursts, young red supergiants, and other esoterica. These arguments go mostly unnoticed by the public because few of us understand what they are talking about. But economics is a *social* science, so its disputes are aired in public and all sorts of people feel competent to join economic debates.

Furthermore, economists actually agree on much more than is commonly supposed. Virtually all economists, regardless of their politics, agree that taxing polluters is one of the best ways to protect the environment, that rent controls can ruin a city (Chapter 3), and that free trade among nations is usually preferable to the erection of barriers through tariffs and quotas (see Chapter 16). The list could go on and on. It is probably true that the issues about which economists agree *far* exceed the subjects on which they disagree.

Finally, many disputes among economists are not scientific disputes at all. Sometimes the pertinent facts are simply unknown. For example, the appropriate financial penalty to levy on a polluter depends on quantitative estimates of the harm done by the pollutant. But good estimates of this damage may not be available. Similarly, while there is reasonable scientific agreement that the earth is slowly warming, there are huge disagreements over how costly global warming may be. Such disputes make it difficult to agree on a concrete policy proposal.

Another important source of disagreements is that economists, like other people, come in all political stripes: conservative, middle-of-the-road, liberal, radical. Each may have different values, and so each may hold a different view of the "right" solution to a public policy problem—even if they agree on the underlying analysis. Here are two examples:

1. We suggested early in this chapter that policies that lower inflation are likely to raise unemployment. Many economists believe they can measure the amount of unemployment that must be endured to reduce inflation by a given amount. But they disagree about whether it is worth having, say, 3 million more people out of work for a year to cut the inflation rate by 1 percent.
2. In designing an income tax, society must decide how much of the burden to put on upper-income taxpayers. Some people believe the rich should pay a disproportionate share of the taxes. Others disagree, believing it is fairer to levy the same income tax rate on everyone.

Economists cannot answer questions like these any more than nuclear physicists could have determined whether dropping the atomic bomb on Hiroshima was a good idea. The decisions rest on moral judgments that can be made only by the citizenry through its elected officials.

Although economic science can contribute theoretical and factual knowledge on a particular issue, the final decision on policy questions often rests either on information that is not currently available or on social values and ethical opinions about which people differ, or on both.

SUMMARY

1. To help you get the most out of your first course in economics, we have devised a list of nine important ideas that you will want to retain *Beyond the Final Exam*. Briefly, they are the following:

   a. **Opportunity cost** is the correct measure of cost.

   b. Attempts to fight market forces often backfire.

   c. Nations can gain from trade by exploiting their *comparative advantages*.

d. Both parties gain in a voluntary exchange.

e. Good decisions typically require *marginal analysis* that weighs incremental costs against incremental benefits.

f. Externalities may cause the market mechanism to malfunction, but this defect can be repaired by market methods.

g. There is a trade-off between efficiency and equality. Many policies that promote one damage the other.

h. In the short run, policymakers face a trade-off between inflation and unemployment. Policies that reduce one normally increase the other.

i. In the long run, *productivity* is almost the only thing that matters for a society's material well-being.

2. Common sense is not always a reliable guide in explaining economic issues or to making economic decisions.

3. Because of the great complexity of human behavior, economists are forced to *abstract* from many details, to make generalizations that they know are not quite true, and to organize what knowledge they have in terms of some theoretical structure called a "model."

4. Correlation need not imply causation.

5. Economists use simplified models to understand the real world and predict its behavior, much as a child uses a model railroad to learn how trains work.

6. Although these models, if skillfully constructed, can illuminate important economic problems, they rarely can answer the questions that confront policymakers. Value judgments are needed for this purpose, and the economist is no better equipped than anyone else to make them.

KEY TERMS

Opportunity cost 4   Theory 10   Economic Model 11

Abstraction 9   Correlation 11

QUESTIONS FOR REVIEW

1. Think about how you would construct a model of how your college is governed. Which officers and administrators would you include and exclude from your model if the objective were one of the following:

a. To explain how decisions on financial aid are made

b. To explain the quality of the faculty

Relate this to the map example in the chapter.

2. Relate the process of abstraction to the way you take notes in a lecture. Why do you not try to transcribe every word uttered by the lecturer? Why don't you write down just the title of the lecture and stop there? How do you decide, roughly speaking, on the correct amount of detail?

3. Explain why a government policymaker cannot afford to ignore economic theory.

APPENDIX   Using Graphs: A Review[1]

As noted in the chapter, economists often explain and analyze models with the help of graphs. Indeed, this book is full of them. But that is not the only reason for studying how graphs work. Most people will deal with graphs in the future, perhaps frequently. You will see them in newspapers. If you become a doctor, you will use graphs to keep track of your patients' progress. If you join a business firm, you will use them to check profit or performance at a glance. This appendix introduces some of the techniques of graphic analysis—tools you will use throughout the book and, more importantly, very likely throughout your working career.

GRAPHS USED IN ECONOMIC ANALYSIS

Economic graphs are invaluable because they can display a large quantity of data quickly and because they facilitate data interpretation and analysis. They enable the eye to take in at a glance important statistical relationships that would be far less apparent from written descriptions or long lists of numbers.

TWO-VARIABLE DIAGRAMS

Much of the economic analysis found in this and other books requires that we keep track of two **variables** simultaneously.

[1]Students who have a nodding acquaintance with geometry and feel quite comfortable with graphs can safely skip this appendix.

A variable is something measured by a number; it is used to analyze what happens to other things when the size of that number changes (varies).

For example, in studying how markets operate, we will want to keep one eye on the *price* of a commodity and the other on the *quantity* of that commodity that is bought and sold.

For this reason, economists frequently find it useful to display real or imaginary figures in a two-variable diagram, which simultaneously represents the behavior of two economic variables. The numerical value of one variable is measured along the horizontal line at the bottom of the graph (called the *horizontal axis*), starting from the **origin** (the point labeled "0"), and the numerical value of the other variable is measured up the vertical line on the left side of the graph (called the *vertical axis*), also starting from the origin.

The "0" point in the lower-left corner of a graph where the axes meet is called the origin. Both variables are equal to zero at the origin.

Figures 1-1(a) and 1-1(b) are typical graphs of economic analysis. They depict an imaginary *demand curve*, represented by the red dots in Figure 1-1(a) and the heavy red line in Figure 1-1(b). The graphs show the price of natural gas on their vertical axes and the quantity of gas people want to buy at each price on the horizontal axes. The dots in Figure 1-1(a) are connected by the continuous red curve labeled *DD* in Figure 1-1(b).

Economic diagrams are generally read just as one would read latitudes and longitudes on a map. On the demand curve in Figure 1-1, the point marked *a* represents a hypothetical combination of price and quantity of natural gas demanded by customers in St. Louis. By drawing a horizontal line leftward from that point to the vertical axis, we learn that at this point the average price for gas in St. Louis is $3 per thousand cubic feet. By dropping a line straight down to the horizontal axis, we find

TABLE 1-1	Quantities of Natural Gas Demanded at Various Prices				
Price (per thousand cubic feet)	$2	$3	$4	$5	$6
Quantity demanded (billions of cubic feet per year)	120	80	56	38	20

that consumers want 80 billion cubic feet per year at this price, just as the statistics in Table 1-1 show. The other points on the graph give similar information. For example, point *b* indicates that if natural gas in St. Louis costs only $2 per thousand cubic feet, quantity demanded would be higher—it would reach 120 billion cubic feet per year.

Notice that information about price and quantity is *all* we can learn from the diagram. The demand curve will not tell us what kinds of people live in St. Louis, the sizes of their homes, or the condition of their furnaces. It tells us about the quantity demanded at each possible price—no more, no less.

A diagram abstracts from many details, some of which may be quite interesting, so as to focus on the two variables of primary interest—in this case, the price of natural gas and the amount of gas that is demanded at each price. All of the diagrams used in this book share this basic feature. They cannot tell the reader the "whole story," any more than a map's latitude and longitude figures for a particular city can make someone an authority on that city.

THE DEFINITION AND MEASUREMENT OF SLOPE

One of the most important features of economic diagrams is the rate at which the line or curve being sketched runs uphill or downhill as we move to the right. The demand curve in Figure 1-1 clearly slopes downhill (the price falls) as we follow it to the right (that is, as consumers demand more gas). In such instances, we say that *the curve has a negative slope, or is negatively sloped, because one variable falls as the other one rises.*

The slope of a straight line is the ratio of the vertical change to the corresponding horizontal change as we move to the right along the line or, as it is often said, the ratio of the "rise" over the "run."

The four panels of Figure 1-2 show all of the possible slopes for a straight-line relationship between two unnamed variables called *Y* (measured along the vertical axis) and *X*

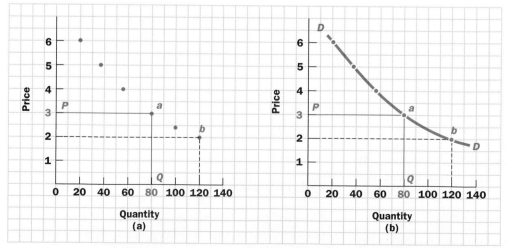

■ FIGURE 1-1   A Hypothetical Demand Curve for Natural Gas in St. Louis

NOTE: Price is in dollars per thousand cubic feet; quantity is in billions of cubic feet per year.

■ FIGURE 1-2   Different Types of Slope of a Straight-Line Graph

(measured along the horizontal axis). Figure 1-2(a) shows a *negative slope*, much like our demand curve in the previous graph. Figure 1-2(b) shows a *positive slope*, because variable Y rises (we go uphill) as variable X rises (as we move to the right). Figure 1-2(c) shows a *zero slope*, where the value of Y is the same irrespective of the value of X. Figure 1-2(d) shows an *infinite slope*, meaning that the value of X is the same irrespective of the value of Y.

Slope is a numerical concept, not just a qualitative one. The two panels of Figure 1-3 show two positively sloped straight lines with different slopes. The line in Figure 1-3(b) is clearly steeper. But by how much? The labels should help you compute the answer. In Figure 1-3(a) a horizontal movement, AB, of 10 units ($13 - 3$) corresponds to a vertical movement, BC, of 1 unit ($9 - 8$). So the slope is $BC/AB = 1/10$. In Figure 1-3(b), the same horizontal movement of 10 units corresponds to a vertical movement of 3 units ($11 - 8$). So the slope is $3/10$, which is larger—the rise divided by the run is greater in Figure 1-3 (b).

By definition, the slope of any particular straight line remains the same, no matter where on that line we choose to measure it. That is why we can pick any horizontal distance, AB, and the corresponding slope triangle, ABC, to measure slope. But this is not true for curved lines.

Curved lines also have slopes, but the numerical value of the slope differs at every point along the curve as we move from left to right.

The four panels of Figure 1-4 provide some examples of *slopes of curved lines*. The curve in Figure 1-4(a) has a negative slope everywhere, and the

■ FIGURE 1-3   How to Measure Slope

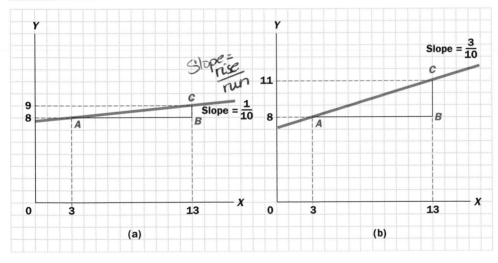

■ FIGURE 1-4   Behavior of Slopes in Curved Graphs

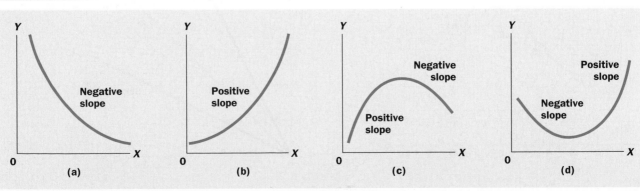

curve in Figure 1-4(b) has a positive slope everywhere. But these are not the only possibilities. In Figure 1-4(c) we encounter a curve that has a positive slope at first but a negative slope later on. Figure 1-4(d) shows the opposite case: a negative slope followed by a positive slope.

We can measure the slope of a smooth curved line numerically *at any particular point* by drawing a *straight* line that *touches*, but does not *cut*, the curve at the point in question. Such a line is called a **tangent** to the curve.

> **The slope of a curved line at a particular point is defined as the slope of the straight line that is tangent to the curve at that point.**

Figure 1-5 shows tangents to the red curve at two points. Line *tt* is tangent at point *T*, and line *rr* is tangent at point *R*. We can measure the slope of the curve at these two points by applying the definition. The calculation for point *T*, then, is the following:

$$\text{Slope at point } T = \text{Slope of line } tt = \frac{\text{Distance } BC}{\text{Distance } BA}$$

$$= \frac{(1-5)}{(3-1)} = \frac{-4}{2} = -2$$

A similar calculation yields the slope of the curve at point *R*, which, as we can see from Figure 1-5, must be smaller numerically. That is, the tangent line *rr* is less steep than line *tt*:

$$\text{Slope at point } R = \text{Slope of line } rr$$

$$= \frac{(5-7)}{(8-6)} = \frac{-2}{2} = -1$$

EXERCISE   Show that the slope of the curve at point *G* is about 1.

What would happen if we tried to apply this graphical technique to the high point in Figure 1-4(c) or to the low point in Figure 1-4(d)? Take a ruler and try it. The tangents that you construct should be horizontal, meaning that they should have a slope exactly equal to zero. It is always true that where the slope of a smooth curve changes from positive to negative, or vice versa, there will be at least one point whose slope is zero.

> **Curves shaped like hills, such as Figure 1-4(c), have a zero slope at their *highest* point. Curves shaped like valleys, such as Figure 1-4(d), have a zero slope at their *lowest* point.**

RAYS THROUGH THE ORIGIN AND 45° LINES

The point at which a straight line cuts the vertical (*Y*) axis is called the **Y-intercept.**

> **The Y-intercept of a line or a curve is the point at which it touches the vertical axis (the Y-axis). The X-intercept is defined similarly.**

For example, the *Y*-intercept of the line in Figure 1-3(a) is a bit less than 8.

> **Lines whose Y-intercept is zero have so many special uses in economics and other disciplines that they have been given a special name: a ray through the origin, or a ray.**

Figure 1-6 shows three rays through the origin, and the slope of each is indicated in the diagram. The ray in the center (whose slope is 1) is particularly useful in many economic applications because it marks points where *X* and *Y* are equal (as long as *X* and *Y* are measured in the same units). For example, at point *A* we have *X* = 3 and *Y* = 3; at point *B*, *X* = 4 and *Y* = 4. A similar relation holds at any other point on that ray.

■ FIGURE 1-5   How to Measure Slope at a Point on a Curved Graph

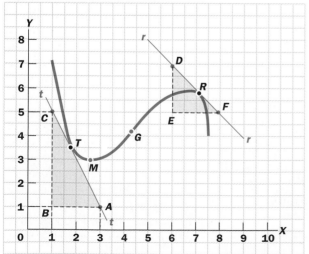

■ FIGURE 1-6   Rays Through the Origin

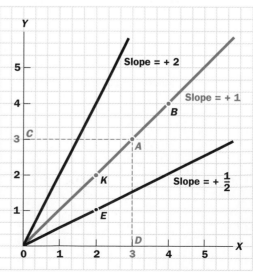

How do we know that this is always true for a ray whose slope is 1? If we start from the origin (where both X and Y are zero) and the slope of the ray is 1, we know from the definition of slope that

$$\text{Slope} = \frac{\text{Vertical change}}{\text{Horizontal change}} = 1$$

This implies that the vertical change and the horizontal change are always equal, so the two variables must always remain equal. Any point along that ray (for example, point A) is exactly equal in distance from the horizontal and vertical axes (length DA = length CA)—the number on the X-axis (the abscissa) will be the same as the number on the Y-axis (the ordinate).

Rays through the origin with a slope of 1 are called **45° lines** because they form an angle of 45° with the horizontal axis. A 45° line marks off points where the variables measured on each axis have equal values.[2]

If a point representing some data is above the 45° line, we know that the value of Y exceeds the value of X. Conversely, whenever we find a point below the 45° line, we know that X is larger than Y.

SQUEEZING THREE DIMENSIONS INTO TWO: CONTOUR MAPS

Sometimes problems involve more than two variables, so two dimensions just are not enough. This is unfortunate, because the surface of a sheet of paper is only two-dimensional. When we study a business firm's decision-

[2]The definition assumes that both variables are measured in the same units.

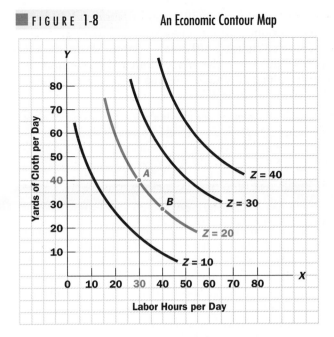

FIGURE 1-8 An Economic Contour Map

FIGURE 1-7 A Geographic Contour Map

SOURCE: Mount Everest. Alpenvereinskarte. Vienna: Kartographische Anstalt Freytag-Berndt und Artaria, 1957, 1988.

making process, for example, we may want to keep track simultaneously of three variables: how much labor it employs, how much raw material it imports from foreign countries, and how much output it creates.

Luckily, economists can use a well-known device for collapsing three dimensions into two—a *contour map*. Figure 1-7 is a contour map of the summit of Mt. Everest on the border of Nepal and Tibet. On some of the irregularly shaped "rings" on this map, we find numbers (like 8500) indicating the height (in meters) above sea level at that particular spot on the mountain. Thus, unlike the more usual sort of map, which gives only latitudes and longitudes, this contour map (also called a topographical map) exhibits *three* pieces of information about each point: latitude, longitude, and altitude.

Figure 1-8 looks more like the contour maps encountered in economics. It shows how some third variable, called Z (think of it as a firm's output, for example), varies as we change either variable X (think of it as a firm's employment of labor) or variable Y (think of it as the use of imported raw material). Just like the map of Mt. Everest, any point on the diagram conveys three pieces of data. At point A, we can read off the values of X and Y in the conventional way (X is 30 and Y is 40), and we can also note the value of Z by checking the contour line on which point A falls. (It is on the $Z = 20$ contour.) So point

A is able to tell us that 30 hours of labor and 40 yards of cloth produce 20 units of output per day. The contour line that indicates 20 units of output shows the various combinations of labor and cloth a manufacturer can use to produce 20 units of output. Economists call such maps **production indifference maps.**

A production indifference map is a graph whose axes show the quantities of two inputs that are used to produce some output. A curve in the graph corresponds to some given quantity of that output, and the different points on that curve show the different quantities of the two inputs that are enough to produce the given output.

Although most of the analyses presented in this book rely on the simpler two-variable diagrams, contour maps will find their applications.

SUMMARY

1. Because graphs are used so often to portray economic models, it is important for students to acquire some understanding of their construction and use. Fortunately, the graphics used in economics are usually not very complex.

2. Most economic models are depicted in two-**variable** diagrams. We read data from these diagrams just as we read the latitude and longitude on a map: each point represents the values of two variables at the same time.

3. In some instances, three variables must be shown at once. In these cases, economists use contour maps, which, as the name suggests, show "latitude," "longitude," and "altitude" all at the same time.

4. Often, the most important property of a line or curve drawn on a diagram will be its **slope**, which is defined as the ratio of the "rise" over the "run," or the vertical change divided by the horizontal change. Curves that go uphill as we move to the right have positive slopes; curves that go downhill have negative slopes.

5. By definition, a straight line has the same slope wherever we choose to measure it. The slope of a curved line changes, but the slope at any point on the curve can be calculated by measuring the slope of a straight line tangent to the curve at that point.

KEY TERMS

Variable 13

Origin (of a graph) 14

Slope of a straight (or curved) line 14

Tangent to a curve 16

Y-intercept 16

Ray through the origin, or ray 16

45° line 17

Production indifference map 18

QUESTIONS FOR REVIEW

1. Portray the following hypothetical data on a two-variable diagram:

Academic Year	Total Enrollment	Enrollment in Economics Courses
1994–1995	3,000	300
1995–1996	3,100	325
1996–1997	3,200	350
1997–1998	3,300	375
1998–1999	3,400	400

Measure the slope of the resulting line, and explain what this number means.

2. From Figure 1-5, calculate the slope of the curve at point *M*.

3. Colin believes that the number of job offers he will get depends on the number of courses in which his grade is B+ or better. He concludes from observation that the following figures are typical:

Number of grades of B+ or better	0	1	2	3	4
Number of job offers	1	3	4	5	6

Put these numbers into a graph like Figure 1-1(a). Measure and interpret the slopes between adjacent dots.

4. In Figure 1-6, determine the values of *X* and *Y* at point *K* and at point *E*. What do you conclude?

5. In Figure 1-8, interpret the economic meaning of points *A* and *B*. What do the two points have in common? What is the difference in their economic interpretation?

2

Scarcity and Choice: *The* Economic Problem

Our necessities are few but our wants are endless.

FORTUNE COOKIE INSCRIPTION

Understanding what the market system does well and what it does badly is this book's central task. But to address this complex question, we must first answer a simpler one: What do economists expect the market to accomplish?

The most common answer is that the market resolves what is often called *the* fundamental economic problem: All decisions are constrained by the scarcity of available resources. A dreamer may envision a world free of want, in which everyone, even in Africa and Central America, drives a BMW and eats caviar, but the earth lacks the resources needed to make that dream come true.

Because resources are scarce, all economic decisions involve *trade-offs*. Should you use that $5 bill to buy a hoagie or some new diskettes for your computer files? Should General Motors invest more money in assembly lines or in research? A well-functioning market system facilitates and guides such decisions, assigning each hour of labor and each kilowatt-hour of electricity to the task where, it is hoped, the input will best serve the public.

This chapter shows how economists analyze choices like these. The same basic principles, based on the concept of *opportunity cost,* apply to the decisions made by business firms, governments, and society as a whole. Many of the most basic ideas of economics, such as *efficiency, division of labor, comparative advantage, exchange,* and *the role of markets* appear here for the first time.

CONTENTS

Issue: What to Do about the Budget Deficit?

For roughly 15 years, from the early 1980s until the late 1990s, how to reduce the federal budget deficit was the top economic issue of the day. Presidents Ronald Reagan, George H.W. Bush, and Bill Clinton all battled with Congress over tax and spending *priorities*. Which programs should be cut? What taxes should be raised?

Then, thanks to a combination of strong economic growth and deficit-reducing policies, the budget deficit melted away like springtime snow and actually turned into a budget *surplus* for a few fiscal years (1998 through 2001). For a while, the need to make agonizing *choices* seemed to disappear—or so it seemed. But it was an illusion. Even during the brief era of budget surpluses, hard choices still had to be made. The U.S. government could not afford *everything*. Then, as the stock market collapsed, the economy slowed, and President George W. Bush pushed a series of tax cuts through Congress, the budget surpluses quickly turned back into deficits again—the largest deficits in our history.

SOURCE: © 2002 PhotoDisc

As the 2004 Presidential campaign geared up, the fiscal questions were the familiar ones of the 1980s and 1990s. Which spending programs should be cut and which ones should be increased? Which, if any, of the Bush tax cuts should be repealed—or replaced by other tax cuts? Even a government with an annual budget of over $2 *trillion* was forced to set priorities and make hard choices.

Even when resources are quite generous, they are never unlimited. So everyone must still make tough choices. An *optimal* decision is one that chooses the most desirable alternative *among the possibilities permitted by the available resources*, which are always scarce in this sense.

SCARCITY, CHOICE, AND OPPORTUNITY COST

Resources are the instruments provided by nature or by people that are used to create goods and services. Natural resources include minerals, soil, water, and air. Labor is a scarce resource, partly because of time limitations (the day has only 24 hours) and partly because the number of skilled workers is limited. Factories and machines are resources made by people. These three types of resources are often referred to as *land, labor,* and *capital.* They are also called *inputs* or *factors of production.*

One of the basic themes of economics is scarcity: the fact that **resources** are always limited. Even Philip II, of Spanish Armada fame and ruler of one of the greatest empires in history, had to cope with frequent rebellions in his armies when he could not meet their payrolls or even provide basic provisions. In more recent years, the U.S. government has been agonizing over difficult budget decisions even though it spends about 2 trillion dollars—that's $2,000,000,000,000—annually.

But the scarcity of *physical resources* is more fundamental than the scarcity of funds. Fuel supplies, for example, are not limitless, and some environmentalists claim that we should now be making some hard choices—such as keeping our homes cooler in winter and warmer in summer and living closer to our jobs. Although energy may be the most widely discussed scarcity, the general principle applies to all of the earth's resources—iron, copper, uranium, and so on. Even goods produced by human effort are in limited supply because they require fuel, labor, and other scarce resources as inputs. We can manufacture more cars, but the increased use of labor, steel, and fuel in auto production will mean that we must cut back on something else, perhaps the production of refrigerators. This all adds up to the following fundamental principle of economics, which we will encounter again and again in this text:

**Virtually all resources are *scarce,* meaning that humans have less of them than we would like. There-
fore, choices must be made among a *limited* set of possibilities, in full recognition of the inescapable
fact that a decision to have more of one thing means that we will have less of something else.**

In fact, one popular definition of economics is the study of how best to use *limited*
means to pursue *unlimited* ends. Although this definition, like any short statement,
cannot possibly cover the sweep of the entire discipline, it does convey the flavor of
the economist's stock in trade.

To illustrate the true cost of an item, consider the decision to produce additional
cars, and therefore to produce fewer refrigerators. Although the production of a car
may cost $15,000 per vehicle, or some other money amount, *its real cost to society is the
refrigerators that society must forgo to get an additional car.* If the labor, steel, and energy
needed to manufacture a car are sufficient to make 30 refrigerators, the **opportunity
cost** of a car is 30 refrigerators. The principle of opportunity cost is so important that
we will spend most of this chapter elaborating on it in various ways.

> The **opportunity cost** of any decision is the value of the next best alternative that the decision forces the decision maker to forgo.

**IDEAS FOR
BEYOND THE
FINAL EXAM**

HOW MUCH DOES IT REALLY COST? *The Principle of Opportunity Cost*   Economics examines the
options available to households, businesses, governments, and entire societies, given the limited resources at their command. It studies the logic of how people can make rational decisions from among
competing alternatives. One overriding principle governs this logic—a principle we introduced in
Chapter 1 as one of the *Ideas for Beyond the Final Exam:* With limited resources, a decision to have
more of one thing is simultaneously a decision to have *less* of something else. Hence, the relevant
cost of any decision is its *opportunity cost*—the value of the next best alternative that is given up. **Rational decision** making must be based on opportunity-cost calculations.

Opportunity Cost and Money Cost

Because we live in a market economy where (almost) everything has its price, students
often wonder about the connection or difference between an item's *opportunity cost* and
its *market price.* What we just said seems to divorce the two concepts: The true opportunity cost of a car is not its market price but the value of the other things (like refrigerators) that could have been made or purchased instead.

> A **rational decision** is one that best serves the objec-tives of the decision maker, whatever those objectives may be. Such objectives may include a firm's desire to max-imize its profits, a govern-ment's desire to maximize the welfare of its citizens, or an-other government's desire to maximize its military might. The term *rational* connotes neither approval nor disap-proval of the objective itself.

But isn't the opportunity cost of a car related to its money cost? The normal answer is yes. The two costs are usually closely tied because of the way in which a market economy sets prices. Steel, for example, is used to manufacture both automobiles
and refrigerators. If consumers value items that can be made with
steel (such as refrigerators) highly, then economists would say that
the *opportunity cost* of making a car is high. But, under these circumstances, a well-functioning price system will assign a high price to
steel, which will therefore make the *money cost* of manufacturing a car
high as well. In summary:

**If the market functions well, goods that have high opportunity costs will also
have high money costs. In turn, goods that have low opportunity costs will also
have low money costs.**

Yet it would be a mistake to treat opportunity costs and explicit
monetary costs as identical. For one thing, sometimes the market
does not function well, and hence assigns prices that do not accurately reflect opportunity costs.

Moreover, some valuable items may not bear explicit price tags at all. We encountered one such example in Chapter 1, where we noted that the opportunity cost of a
college education may differ sharply from its explicit money cost. Why? Because one
important item is typically omitted from the money-cost calculation: the *market value
of your time,* that is, the wages you could earn by working instead of attending college.
Because you give up these potential wages, which can amount to $15,000 per year or
more, so as to acquire an education, they must be counted as a major part of the opportunity cost of going to college.

"O.K., who can put a price on love? Jim?"

Other common examples where money costs and opportunity costs diverge are goods and services that are given away "free." For example, some early settlers of the American West destroyed natural amenities such as forests and buffalo herds, which had no market price, leaving later generations to pay the opportunity costs in terms of lost resources. Similarly, you incur no explicit monetary cost to acquire an item that is given away for free. But if you must wait in line to get the "free" commodity, you incur an opportunity cost equal to the value of the next best use of your time.

SCARCITY AND CHOICE FOR A SINGLE FIRM

The **outputs** of a firm or an economy are the goods and services it produces.

The **inputs** used by a firm or an economy are the labor, raw materials, electricity and other resources it uses to produce its outputs.

The nature of opportunity cost is perhaps clearest in the case of a single business firm that produces two **outputs** from a fixed supply of **inputs**. Given current technology and the limited resources at its disposal, the more of one good the firm produces, the less of the other it will be able to make. Unless managers explicitly weigh the desirability of each product against the other, they are unlikely to make rational production decisions.

Consider the example of Farmer Jones, whose available supplies of land, machinery, labor, and fertilizer are capable of producing the various combinations of soybeans and wheat listed in Table 2-1. Obviously, devoting more resources to soybean production means that Farmer Jones will produce less wheat.

Table 2-1 indicates, for example, that if Jones grows only soybeans, the harvest will be 40,000 bushels. But if he reduces his soybean production to 30,000 bushels, he can also grow 38,000 bushels of wheat. Thus, *the opportunity cost of obtaining 38,000 bushels of wheat is 10,000 fewer bushels of soybeans.* Put another way, the opportunity cost of 10,000 more bushels of soybeans is 38,000 bushels of wheat. The other numbers in Table 2-1 have similar interpretations.

The Production Possibilities Frontier

Figure 2-1 presents this same information graphically. Point *A* indicates that one of the options available to the farmer is to produce 40,000 bushels of soybeans and zero wheat. Thus, point *A* corresponds to the first line of Table 2-1, point *B* to the second line, and so on. Curves similar to *AE* appear frequently in this book; they are called **production possibilities frontiers.** Any point *on or inside* the production possibilities frontier is attainable. Points *outside* the frontier cannot be achieved with the available resources and technology.

TABLE 2-1   Production Possibilities Open to a Farmer

Bushels of Soybeans	Bushels of Wheat	Label in Figure 2-1
40,000	0	A
30,000	38,000	B
20,000	52,000	C
10,000	60,000	D
0	65,000	E

A **production possibilities frontier** shows the different combinations of various goods that a producer can turn out, given the available resources and existing technology.

Because resources are limited, the production possibilities frontier always slopes downward to the right. The farmer can *increase* wheat production (move to the right in Figure 2-1) only by devoting more land and labor to growing wheat. But this choice simultaneously *reduces* soybean production (the curve moves downward) because less land and labor remain available for growing soybeans.

Notice that, in addition to having a negative slope, our production possibilities frontier *AE* has another characteristic; it is "bowed outward." What does this curvature mean? In short, as larger and larger quantities of resources are transferred from the production of one output to the production of another, the additions to the second product decline.

Suppose Farmer Jones initially produces only soybeans, using even land that is comparatively most productive in wheat cultivation (point *A*). Now he decides to switch some land from soybean production into wheat production. Which part of the land will he switch? If Jones is sensible, he will use the part relatively most productive in growing wheat. As he shifts to point *B*, soybean production falls from 40,000 bushels to 30,000 bushels as wheat production rises from zero to 38,000 bushels. A sacrifice of only 10,000 bushels of soybeans "buys" 38,000 bushels of wheat.

Imagine now that the farmer wants to produce still more wheat. Figure 2-1 tells us that the sacrifice of an additional 10,000 bushels of soybeans (from 30,000 bushels to 20,000 bushels) will yield only 14,000 more bushels of wheat (see point *C*). Why? The main reason is that *inputs tend to be specialized.* As we noted at point *A*, the farmer was using resources for soybean production that were relatively more productive in growing wheat. Consequently, their relative productivity in soybean production was low. When these resources are switched to wheat production, the yield is high.

But this trend cannot continue forever, of course. As more wheat is produced, the farmer must utilize land and machinery with an even greater productivity advantage in growing soybeans and a smaller productivity advantage in growing wheat. This is why the first 10,000 bushels of soybeans forgone "buys" the farmer 38,000 bushels of wheat, whereas the second 10,000 bushels of soybeans "buys" only 14,000 bushels of wheat. Figure 2-1 and Table 2-1 show that these returns continue to decline as wheat production expands: The next 10,000-bushel reduction in soybean production yields only 8,000 bushels of additional wheat, and so on.

As we can see, the *slope* of the production possibilities frontier graphically represents the concept of *opportunity cost*. Between points *C* and *B*, for example, the opportunity cost of acquiring 10,000 additional bushels of soybeans is 14,000 bushels of forgone wheat; between points *B* and *A*, the opportunity cost of 10,000 bushels of soybeans is 38,000 bushels of forgone wheat. In general, as we move upward to the left along the production possibilities frontier (toward more soybeans and less wheat), the opportunity cost of soybeans in terms of wheat increases. Looking at the same thing the other way, as we move downward to the right, the opportunity cost of acquiring wheat by giving up soybeans increases.

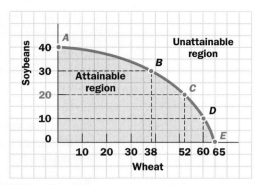

NOTE: Quantities are in thousands of bushels per year.

■ FIGURE 2-1
Production Possibilities Frontier for Production by a Single Firm

■ The Principle of Increasing Costs

We have just described a very general phenomenon with applications well beyond farming. The **principle of increasing costs** states that as the production of one good expands, the opportunity cost of producing another unit of this good generally increases.

This principle is not a universal fact—exceptions do arise. But it does seem to be a technological regularity that applies to a wide range of economic activities. As our farming example suggests, the principle of increasing costs is based on the fact that resources tend to be at least somewhat specialized. So we lose some of their productivity when those resources are transferred from doing what they are relatively *good* at to what they are relatively *bad* at. In terms of diagrams such as Figure 2-1, the principle simply asserts that the production possibilities frontier is bowed outward.

Perhaps the best way to understand this idea is to contrast it with a case in which no resources are specialized so costs do not increase as output proportion changes. Figure 2-2 depicts a production possibilities frontier for producing black shoes and brown shoes. Because the labor and machinery used to produce black shoes are just as good at producing brown shoes, the frontier is a straight line. If the firm cuts back its production of black shoes by 10,000 pairs, it can get 10,000 additional pairs of brown shoes. It loses no productivity in the switch because resources are not specialized.

More typically, however, as a firm concentrates more of its productive capacity on one commodity, it is forced to employ inputs that are better suited to making another commodity. The firm is forced to vary the proportions in which it uses inputs because of the limited quantities of some of those inputs. This fact also explains the typical curvature of the firm's production possibilities frontier.

The **principle of increasing costs** states that as the production of a good expands, the opportunity cost of producing another unit generally increases.

■ FIGURE 2-2
Production Possibilities Frontier with No Specialized Resources

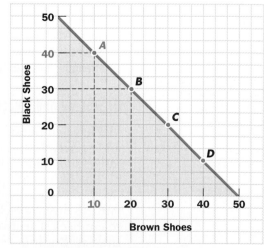

NOTE: Quantities are in thousands of pairs per week.

SCARCITY AND CHOICE FOR THE ENTIRE SOCIETY

Like an individual firm, the entire economy is also constrained by its limited resources and technology. If the public wants more aircraft and tanks, it will have to give up some boats and automobiles. If it wants to build more factories and stores, it will have to build fewer homes and sports arenas. In general:

The position and shape of the production possibilities frontier that constrains society's choices are determined by the economy's physical resources, its skills and technology, its willingness to work, and how much it has devoted in the past to the construction of factories, research, and innovation.

Because so many nations have debated whether to reduce or augment military strength for so long, let us illustrate the nature of society's choices by the example of choosing between military might (represented by missiles) and civilian consumption (represented by automobiles). Just like a single firm, the economy as a whole faces a production possibilities frontier for missiles and autos, determined by its technology and the available resources of land, labor, capital, and raw materials. This production possibilities frontier may look like curve *BC* in Figure 2-3. If most workers are employed in auto plants, car production will be large, but the output of missiles will be small. If the economy transfers resources out of auto manufacturing when consumer demand declines, it can, by congressional action, alter the output mix toward more missiles (the move from *D* to *E*). However, something is likely to be lost in the process because physical resources are specialized. The fabric used to make car seats will not help much in missile production. The principle of increasing costs strongly suggests that the production possibilities frontier curves downward toward the axes.

We may even reach a point where the only resources left are not very useful outside of auto manufacturing. In that case, even a large sacrifice of automobiles will get the economy few additional missiles. That is the meaning of the steep segment, *FC*, on the frontier. At point *C* there is little additional output of missiles as compared to point *F*, even though at *C* automobile production has been given up entirely.

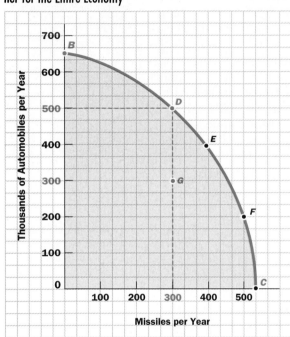

FIGURE 2-3

Production Possibilities Frontier for the Entire Economy

The downward slope of society's production possibilities frontier implies that hard choices must be made. Civilian consumption (automobiles) can be increased only by decreasing military expenditure, not by rhetoric or wishing. The curvature of the production possibilities frontier implies that, as defense spending increases, it becomes progressively more expensive to "buy" additional military strength ("missiles") by sacrificing civilian consumption.

Scarcity and Choice Elsewhere in the Economy

We have emphasized that limited resources force hard choices on business managers and society as a whole. But the same type of choices arises elsewhere—in households, universities, and other nonprofit organizations, as well as the government.

The nature of opportunity cost is perhaps most obvious for a household that must decide how to divide its income among the goods and services that compete for the family's attention. If the Simpson family buys an expensive new car, it may be forced to cut back sharply on some other purchases. This fact does not make it unwise to buy the car. But it does make it unwise to buy the car until the family considers the full

The Military-Civilian Output Trade-Off in Reality

T he arms race may have ground to a halt, but space-age technology that helped keep the peace for 50 years is now being channeled in new directions. Literally hundreds of companies have had to face the new reality: Find other applications for current products, or perish.

The innovations have been spectacular. A rocket parts plant in Colorado developed a racing bike frame made from thermoplastic and reinforced carbon fiber. Composite materials, including boron filaments, graphites, and carbon fibers, have long been principal components in jet aircraft. Today, they are as likely to be found in golf club shafts, tennis rackets, ski poles, and even hockey sticks. Race car companies are trying to take advantage of strong, lightweight materials in car designs.

Spillover benefits haven't been limited to the sports industry. E-Systems, which still does big defense business, demonstrated an innovative touch by adapting spy satellite technology to improve tumor-detection capabilities in mammograms. New uses have even been found for shuttered military bases. San Francisco's Treasure Island Naval Station, for example, is now being used as a movie studio.

SOURCE: © SuperStock

SOURCES: Tim Smart, "Beating Swords into Golf Clubs?" *Business Week*, April 18, 1994, p. 85; "Uncle Sam's Fire Sales," *U.S. News & World Report*, January 9, 1995; "Aerospace and Defense," *Forbes*, January 3, 1994, p. 106.

implications for its overall budget. If the Simpsons are to utilize their limited resources most effectively, they must explicitly acknowledge that the opportunity costs of the car are the things they will forgo as a result—perhaps a vacation and an expensive new TV set.

 ### Issue Revisited: Coping with the Budget Deficit

Even a rich and powerful nation like the United States must cope with the limitations implied by scarce resources. The necessity for choice imposed on governments by the limited amount they feel they can afford to spend is similar in character to the problems faced by business firms and households. For the goods and services that it buys from others, a government must prepare a budget similar to that of a very large household. For the items it produces itself—education, police protection, libraries, and so on—it faces a production possibilities frontier much like a business firm does. Even though the U.S. government will spend over $2\frac{1}{4}$ trillion in 2004, some of the most acrimonious debates between President Bush and his critics arise from disagreements about how the government's limited resources should be allocated among competing uses. Even if unstated, the concept of opportunity cost is central to these debates.

THE CONCEPT OF EFFICIENCY

So far, our discussion of scarcity and choice has assumed that either the firm or the economy always operates on its production possibilities frontier rather than *below* it. In other words, we have tacitly assumed that, whatever the firm or economy decides to do, it does so *efficiently*.

A set of outputs is said to be produced **efficiently** if, given current technological knowledge, there is no way one can produce larger amounts of any output without using larger input amounts or giving up some quantity of another output.

Economists define efficiency as the absence of waste. An efficient economy utilizes all of its available resources and produces the maximum amount of output that its technology permits.

To see why any point on the economy's production possibilities frontier in Figure 2-3 represents an efficient decision, suppose for a moment that society has decided to produce 300 missiles. The production possibilities frontier tells us that if 300 missiles are to be produced, then the maximum number of automobiles that can be made is 500,000 (point *D* in Figure 2-3). The economy is therefore operating efficiently only if it produces 500,000 automobiles rather than some smaller amount such as 300,000 (as at point *G*).

Point *D* is efficient, but point *G* is not, because the economy is capable of moving from *G* to *D*, thereby producing 200,000 more automobiles without giving up any missiles (or anything else). Clearly, failure to take advantage of the option of choosing point *D* rather than point *G* constitutes a wasted opportunity—an inefficiency.

Note that the concept of efficiency does not tell us which point on the production possibilities frontier is *best*. Rather, it tells us only that any point *below* the frontier cannot be best, because any such point represents wasted resources. For example, should society ever find itself at a point such as *G*, the necessity of making hard choices would (temporarily) disappear. It would be possible to increase production of *both* missiles *and* automobiles by moving to a point such as *E*.

Why, then, would a society ever find itself at a point below its production possibilities frontier? Why are resources wasted in real life? The most important reason in today's economy is *unemployment*. When many workers are unemployed, the economy must be at a point such as *G*, below the frontier, because by putting the unemployed to work, some in each industry, the economy could produce both more missiles *and* more automobiles. The economy would then move from point *G* to the right (more missiles) and upward (more automobiles) toward a point such as *E* on the production possibilities frontier. Only when no resources are wasted is the economy operating on the frontier.

Inefficiency occurs in other ways, too. A prime example is assigning inputs to the wrong task—as when wheat is grown on land best suited to soybean cultivation. Another important type of inefficiency occurs when large firms produce goods that smaller enterprises could make better because they can pay closer attention to detail, or when small firms produce outputs best suited to large-scale production. Some other examples are the outright waste that occurs because of favoritism (for example, promotion of an incompetent brother-in-law) or restrictive labor practices (for example, requiring a railroad to keep a fireman on a diesel-electric locomotive where there is nothing for him to do).

A particularly deplorable form of waste is caused by discrimination against African American, Hispanic, or female workers. When a job is given to a white male in preference to a more qualified African American woman, society sacrifices potential output and the entire community is apt to be affected adversely. Every one of these inefficiencies means that the community obtains less output than it could have, given the available inputs.

THE THREE COORDINATION TASKS OF ANY ECONOMY

Allocation of resources refers to the society's decisions on how to divide up its scarce input resources among the different outputs produced in the economy and among the different firms or other organizations that produce those outputs.

In deciding how to **allocate its scarce resources,** every society must somehow make three sorts of decisions:

- First, as we have emphasized, it must figure out *how to utilize its resources efficiently;* that is, it must find a way to reach its production possibilities frontier.
- Second, it must decide *which of the possible combinations of goods to produce*—how many missiles, automobiles, and so on; that is, it must select one specific point on the production possibilities frontier.

■ Third, it must decide *how much of the total output of each good to distribute to each person*, doing so in a sensible way that does not assign meat to vegetarians and wine to teetotalers.

Societies can and do make each of these decisions—which economists often refer to as *how, what,* and *to whom?*—in many ways. For example, a central planner may tell people how to produce, what to produce, and what to consume, as the authorities used to do, at least to some extent, in the former Soviet Union. But in a market economy, no one group or individual makes all such resource allocation decisions explicitly. Rather, consumer demands and production costs allocate resources *automatically* and *anonymously* through a system of prices and markets. As the formerly socialist countries learned, markets do an impressively effective job in carrying out these tasks. To see how markets can do all this, let's consider each task in turn.

SPECIALIZATION FOSTERS EFFICIENT RESOURCE ALLOCATION

Production efficiency is one of the economy's three basic tasks, and societies pursue it in many ways. But one source of efficiency is so fundamental that we must single it out for special attention: the tremendous productivity gains that stem from *specialization*.

The Wonders of the Division of Labor

Adam Smith, the founder of modern economics, first marveled at how **division of labor** raises efficiency and productivity when he visited a pin factory. In a famous passage near the beginning of his monumental book, *The Wealth of Nations* (1776), he described what he saw:

> One man draws out the wire, another straightens it, a third cuts it, a fourth points it, a fifth grinds it at the top for receiving the head. To make the head requires two or three distinct operations; to put it on is a peculiar business, to whiten the pins is another; it is even a trade by itself to put them into the paper.[1]

Division of labor means breaking up a task into a number of smaller, more *specialized* tasks so that each worker can become more adept at a particular job.

Smith observed that by dividing the work to be done in this way, each worker became quite skilled in a particular specialty, and the productivity of the group of workers as a whole was greatly enhanced. As Smith related it:

> I have seen a small manufactory of this kind where ten men only were employed. . . . Those ten persons . . . could make among them upwards of forty-eight thousand pins in a day. . . . But if they had all wrought separately and independently . . . they certainly could not each of them have made twenty, *perhaps not one pin in a day.*[2]

In other words, through the miracle of division of labor and specialization, ten workers accomplished what might otherwise have required thousands. This was one of the secrets of the Industrial Revolution, which helped lift humanity out of the abject poverty that had been its lot for centuries.

The Amazing Principle of Comparative Advantage

But specialization in production fosters efficiency in an even more profound sense. Adam Smith noticed that *how* goods are produced can make a huge difference to productivity. But so can *which* goods are produced. The reason is that people (and businesses, and nations) have different abilities. Some can repair automobiles,

---

[1] Adam Smith, *The Wealth of Nations* (New York: Random House, 1937), p. 4.

[2] Ibid., p. 5.

whereas others are wizards with numbers. Some are handy with computers, and others can cook. An economy will be most efficient if people specialize in doing what they do best and then trade with one another, so that the accountant gets her car repaired and the computer programmer gets to eat tasty and nutritious meals.

This much is obvious. What is less obvious—and is one of the great ideas of economics—is that two people (or two businesses, or two countries) can generally gain from trade *even if one of them is more efficient than the other in producing everything*. A simple example will help explain why.

Some lawyers can type better than their administrative assistants. Should such a lawyer fire her assistant and do her own typing? Not likely. Even though the lawyer may type better than the assistant, good judgment tells her to concentrate on practicing law and leave the typing to a lower-paid assistant. Why? Because the *opportunity cost* of an hour devoted to typing is an hour less time spent with clients, which is a far more lucrative activity.

> One country is said to have a **comparative advantage** over another in the production of a particular good *relative to other goods* if it produces that good less inefficiently than it produces other goods, as compared with the other country.

This example illustrates the principle of **comparative advantage** at work. The lawyer specializes in arguing cases despite her advantage as a typist because she has a *still greater* advantage as an attorney. She suffers some direct loss by leaving the typing to a less-efficient employee, but she more than makes up for that loss by the income she earns selling her legal services to clients.

Precisely the same principle applies to nations. As we shall learn in greater detail in Chapter 33, comparative advantage underlies the economic analysis of international trade patterns. A country that is particularly adept at producing certain items—such as aircraft manufacturing in the United States, coffee growing in Brazil, and oil extraction in Saudi Arabia—should specialize in those activities, producing more than it wants for its own use. The country can then take the money it earns from its exports and purchase from other nations items that it does not make for itself.

The underlying logic is precisely the same as in our lawyer-typist example. The United States might, for example, be better than Japan at manufacturing both computers and television sets. But if the United States is vastly more efficient at producing computers, but only slightly more efficient at making TV sets, it pays for the United States to specialize in computer manufacture, for Japan to specialize in TV production, and for the two countries to trade.[3]

This principle, called the *law of comparative advantage*, was discovered by David Ricardo, one of the giants in the history of economic analysis, almost 200 years ago. It is one of the *Ideas for Beyond the Final Exam* introduced in Chapter 1.

IDEAS FOR BEYOND THE FINAL EXAM

THE SURPRISING PRINCIPLE OF COMPARATIVE ADVANTAGE   Even if one country (or one worker) is worse than another country (or another worker) in the production of *every* good, it is said to have a *comparative advantage* in making the good at which it is *least inefficient*—compared to the other country. Ricardo discovered that two countries can gain by trading even if one country is more efficient than another in the production of *every* commodity. Precisely the same logic applies to individual workers or to businesses.

In determining the most efficient patterns of production and trade, it is comparative advantage that matters. Thus, a country can gain by importing a good from abroad even if that good can be produced more efficiently at home. Such imports make sense if they enable the country to specialize in producing those goods at which it is *even more efficient*.

SPECIALIZATION LEADS TO EXCHANGE

The gains from specialization are welcome, but they create a problem: With specialization, people no longer produce only what they want to consume themselves. The workers in Adam Smith's pin factory had no use for the thousands of pins they produced each day; they wanted to trade them for things like food, clothing, and shelter.

---

[3] This particular example is considered in detail in Chapter 33, which examines international trade.

Similarly, the administrative assistant has no personal use for the legal briefs she types. Thus, specialization requires some mechanism by which workers producing pins can *exchange* their wares with workers producing such things as cloth and potatoes, and office workers can turn their typing skills into things they want to consume.

Without a system of exchange, the productivity miracle achieved by comparative advantage and the division of labor would do society little good. With it, standards of living have risen enormously. As we observed in Chapter 1, such exchange benefits *all* participants.

IDEAS FOR BEYOND THE FINAL EXAM

TRADE IS A WIN-WIN SITUATION *Mutual Gains from Voluntary Exchange*   Unless someone is deceived or misunderstands the facts, a *voluntary* exchange between two parties must make both parties better off—or else why would each party agree? Trading increases production by permitting specialization, as we have just seen. But even if no additional goods are produced as a result of the act of trading, the welfare of society is increased because each individual acquires goods that are more suited to his or her needs and tastes. This simple but fundamental precept of economics is another of our *Ideas for Beyond the Final Exam.*

Although people can and do trade goods for other goods, a system of exchange works better when everyone agrees to use some common item (such as pieces of paper with unique markings printed on them) for buying and selling things. Enter *money.* Then workers in pin factories, for example, can be paid in money rather than in pins, and they can use this money to purchase cloth and potatoes. Textile workers and farmers can do the same.

These two phenomena—specialization and exchange (assisted by money)—working in tandem led to vast improvements in humanity's well-being. But what forces induce workers to join together so that society can enjoy the fruits of the division of labor? And what forces establish a smoothly functioning system of exchange so that people can first exploit their comparative advantages and then acquire what they want to consume? One alternative is to have a central authority telling people what to do. Adam Smith explained and extolled yet another way of organizing and coordinating economic activity—markets and prices can coordinate those activities.

MARKETS, PRICES, AND THE THREE COORDINATION TASKS

Smith noted that people are adept at pursuing their own self-interests, and that a **market system** harnesses this self-interest remarkably well. As he put it—with clear religious overtones—in doing what is best for themselves, people are "led by an invisible hand" to promote the economic well-being of society as a whole.

Those of us who live in a well-functioning market economy like that found in the United States tend to take the achievements of the market for granted, much like the daily rising and setting of the sun. Few bother to think about, say, what makes Florida oranges show up daily in South Dakota supermarkets. Although the process by which the market guides the economy in such an orderly fashion is subtle and complex, the general principles are well known.

The market deals with efficiency in production through the profit motive, which discourages firms from using inputs wastefully. Valuable resources (such as energy) command high prices, giving producers strong incentives to use them efficiently. The market mechanism also guides firms' output decisions, matching quantities produced to consumer preferences. A rise in the price of wheat because of increased demand for bread, for example, will persuade farmers to produce more wheat and devote less of their land to soybeans.

Finally, a price system distributes goods among consumers in accord with their tastes and preferences, using voluntary exchange to determine who gets what. Consumers spend their incomes on the things they like best (among those they can afford). But the ability to buy goods is hardly divided equally. Workers with valuable skills and owners of scarce resources can sell what they have at attractive prices. With the incomes they earn, they can purchase generous amounts of goods and services.

A **market system** is a form of economic organization in which resource allocation decisions are left to individual producers and consumers acting in their own best interests without central direction.

Those who are less successful in selling what they own receive lower incomes and so can afford to buy less. In extreme cases, they may suffer severe deprivation.

This, in broad terms, is how a market economy solves the three basic problems facing any society: how to produce any given combination of goods efficiently, how to select an appropriate combination of goods to produce, and how to distribute these goods sensibly among people. As we proceed through the following chapters, you will learn much more about these issues. You will see that they constitute the central theme that permeates not only this text, but the work of economists in general. As you progress through the book, keep in mind two questions:

- What does the market do well?
- What does it do poorly?

There are numerous answers to both questions, as you will learn in subsequent chapters.

Society has many important goals. Some of them, such as producing goods and services with maximum efficiency (minimum waste), can be achieved extraordinarily well by letting markets operate more or less freely.

Free markets will not, however, achieve all of society's goals. For example, they often have trouble keeping unemployment low. In fact, the unfettered operations of markets may even run counter to some goals, such as protection of the environment. Many observers also believe that markets do not necessarily distribute income in accord with ethical or moral norms.

But even in cases where markets do not perform well, there may be ways of harnessing the power of the market mechanism to remedy its own deficiencies, as you will learn in later chapters.

LAST WORD: DON'T CONFUSE ENDS WITH MEANS

Economic debates often have political and ideological overtones. So we will close this chapter by emphasizing that the central theme we have just outlined is neither a *defense of* nor an *attack on* the capitalist system. Nor is it a "conservative" position. One does not have to be a conservative to recognize that the market mechanism can be an extraordinarily helpful instrument for the pursuit of economic goals. Most of the formerly socialist countries of Europe have been working hard to "marketize" their economies, and even the communist People's Republic of China has made huge strides in that direction.

The point is not to confuse ends with means in deciding how much to rely on market forces. Liberals and conservatives surely have different goals. But the means chosen to pursue these goals should, for the most part, be chosen on the basis of how effective they are, not on some ideological prejudgments.

Even Karl Marx emphasized that the market is remarkably efficient at producing an abundance of goods and services that had never been seen in precapitalist history. Such wealth can be used to promote conservative goals, such as reducing tax rates, or to facilitate goals favored by liberals, such as providing more generous public aid for the poor.

Certainly, the market cannot deal with every economic problem. Indeed, we have just noted that the market is the *source* of a number of significant problems. Even so, the evidence accumulated over centuries leads economists to believe that most economic problems are best handled by market techniques. The analysis in this book is intended to help you identify both the objectives that the market mechanism can reliably achieve and those that it will fail to promote, or at least not promote very effectively. We urge you to forget the slogans you have heard—whether from the left or from the right—and make up your own mind after learning the material in this book.

SUMMARY

1. Supplies of all **resources** are limited. Because resources are **scarce**, a **rational decision** is one that chooses the best alternative among the options that are possible with the available resources.

2. With limited resources, a decision to obtain more of one item is also a decision to give up some of another. What we give up is called the **opportunity cost** of what we get. The opportunity cost is the true cost of any decision. This is one of the *Ideas for Beyond the Final Exam.*

3. When markets function effectively, firms are led to use resources efficiently and to produce the things that consumers want most. In such cases, opportunity costs and money costs (prices) correspond closely. When the market performs poorly, or when important costly items do not get price tags, opportunity costs and money costs can diverge.

4. A firm's **production possibilities frontier** shows the combinations of goods it can produce, given the current technology and the resources at its disposal. The frontier is usually bowed outward because resources tend to be specialized.

5. The **principle of increasing costs** states that as the production of one good expands, the opportunity cost of producing another unit of that good generally increases.

6. Like a firm, the economy as a whole has a production possibilities frontier whose position is determined by its technology and by the available resources of land, labor, capital, and raw materials.

7. A firm or an economy that ends up at a point below its production possibilities frontier is using its resources inefficiently or wastefully. This is what happens, for example, when there is unemployment.

8. Economists define **efficiency** as the absence of waste. It is achieved primarily by the gains in productivity brought about through **specialization** that exploits **division of labor** and **comparative advantage** and by a system of exchange.

9. Two countries (or two people) can gain by specializing in the activity in which each has a comparative advantage and then trading with one another. These gains from trade remain available even if one country is inferior at producing everything. This so-called principle of comparative advantage is one of our *Ideas for Beyond the Final Exam.*

10. If an exchange is voluntary, both parties must benefit, even if no additional goods are produced. This is another of the *Ideas for Beyond the Final Exam.*

11. Every economic system must find a way to answer three basic questions: How can goods be produced most efficiently? How much of each good should be produced? How should goods be distributed?

12. The **market system** works very well in solving some of society's basic problems, but it fails to remedy others and may, indeed, create some of its own. Where and how it succeeds and fails constitute the central theme of this book and characterize the work of economists in general.

KEY TERMS

Resources   20

Opportunity cost   21

Rational decision   21

Outputs   22

Inputs   22

Production possibilities frontier   22

Principle of increasing costs   23

Efficiency   26

Allocation of resources   26

Division of labor   27

Comparative advantage   28

Market system   29

QUESTIONS FOR REVIEW

1. Discuss the resource limitations that affect:
   a. the poorest person on earth
   b. Bill Gates, the richest person on earth
   c. a farmer in Kansas
   d. the government of Indonesia

2. If you were president of your college, what would you change if your budget were cut by 10 percent? By 25 percent? By 50 percent?

3. If you were to leave college, what things would change in your life? What, then, is the opportunity cost of your education?

4. A person rents a house for which she pays the landlord $12,000 per year. The house can be purchased for $100,000, and the tenant has this much money in a bank account that pays 4 percent interest per year. Is buying the house a good deal for the tenant? Where does opportunity cost enter the picture?

5. Graphically show the production possibilities frontier for the nation of Stromboli, using the data given in the following table. Does the principle of increasing cost hold in Stromboli?

Stromboli's 2002 Production Possibilities	
Pizzas per Year	Pizza Ovens per Year
75,000,000	0
60,000,000	6,000
45,000,000	11,000
30,000,000	15,000
15,000,000	18,000
0	20,000

6. Consider two alternatives for Stromboli in 2002. In case (a), its inhabitants eat 60 million pizzas and build 6,000 pizza ovens. In case (b), the population eats 15 million pizzas but builds 18,000 ovens. Which case will lead to a more generous production possibilities frontier for Stromboli in 2003?

7. Jasmine's Snack Shop sells two brands of potato chips. Brand X costs Jasmine 60 cents per bag, and Brand Y costs her $1. Draw Jasmine's production possibilities frontier if she has $60 budgeted to spend on potato chips. Why is it not "bowed out"?

8. Raising chickens requires several types of feed, such as corn and soy meal. Consider a farm in the former Soviet Union. Try to describe how decisions on the number of chickens to be raised, and the amount of each feed to use in raising them, were made under the old communist regime. If the farm is now privately owned, how does the market guide the decisions that used to be made by the central planning agency?

9. The United States is one of the world's wealthiest countries. Think of a recent case in which the decisions of the U.S. government were severely constrained by scarcity. Describe the trade-offs that were involved. What were the opportunity costs of the decisions that were actually made?

3

Supply and Demand: An Initial Look

The free enterprise system is absolutely too important to be left to the voluntary action of the marketplace.

FLORIDA CONGRESSMAN RICHARD KELLY, 1979

I n this chapter, we study the most basic tool for investigation of the central subjects of economics: supply and demand. Whether your course concentrates on macroeconomics or microeconomics, you will find that it uses the so-called law of supply and demand as a fundamental tool. Economists use supply and demand analysis to study issues as diverse as inflation and unemployment, the effects of taxes on prices, government regulation of business, and environmental protection. Supply and demand curves—graphs that relate price to quantity supplied and quantity demanded, respectively—show how prices and quantities are determined in a free market.[1]

A major theme of the chapter is that governments around the world and throughout recorded history have tampered with the price mechanism. As we will see, these bouts with Adam Smith's "invisible hand" have produced undesirable side effects that often surprised and dismayed the authorities. The invisible hand fights back!

CONTENTS

---

[1] This chapter, like much of the rest of this book, uses many graphs like those described in the appendix to Chapter 1. If you have difficulties with these graphs, we suggest that you review that material before proceeding.

❓ Puzzle: What in the World Happened to Those Asian Currencies?

A worldwide financial crisis began in the last half of 1997, when the currencies of several Asian economies, including Thailand, Indonesia, Malaysia, and South Korea, plummeted in value. The most spectacular example was the fall of the Indonesian rupiah. In July 1997, about 10,000 rupiahs could buy four U.S. dollars. By winter, this amount could pay for only a single dollar. This means that, relative to the dollar, the rupiah lost a stunning 75 percent of its value in just a few months.

What could have caused such a calamitous drop in the value of the rupiah? The answer is complicated, and not entirely rational. But the essence of the rupiah's problem, as we shall see in this chapter, involved nothing more complex than the rudimentary law of supply and demand.

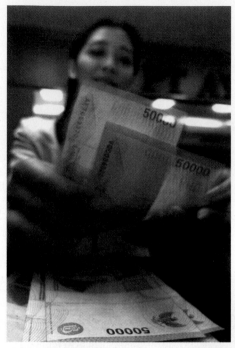

SOURCE: © AFP/Corbis

THE INVISIBLE HAND

The **invisible hand** is a phrase used by Adam Smith to describe how, by pursuing their own self-interests, people in a market system are "led by an invisible hand" to promote the well-being of the community.

Adam Smith greatly admired the price system. He marveled at its accomplishments—both as an efficient producer of goods and as a guarantor that consumers' preferences are obeyed. Although many people since Smith's time have shared his enthusiasm for the concept of the **invisible hand,** many have not. Smith's contemporaries in the American colonies, for example, were often unhappy with the prices produced by free markets and thought they could do better by legislative decree. Such attempts failed, as explained in the accompanying box, "Price Controls at Valley Forge." In countless other instances, the public was outraged by the prices charged on the open market, particularly in the case of housing rents, interest rates, and insurance rates.

Attempts to control interest rates (which are the price of borrowing money) go back hundreds of years before the birth of Christ, at least to the code of laws compiled under the Babylonian king Hammurabi in about 1800 B.C. Our historical legacy also includes a rather long list of price ceilings on foods and other products imposed in the reign of Diocletian, emperor of the declining Roman Empire. More recently, Americans have been offered the "protection" of a variety of price controls. Laws have placed ceilings on some prices (such as rents) to protect buyers, whereas legislation has placed floors under other prices (such as farm products) to protect sellers. Yet, somehow, everything such regulation touches seems to end up in even greater disarray than it was before. Despite rent controls, rents in New York City have soared. Despite laws against "scalping," tickets for popular shows and sports events sell at tremendous premiums—tickets to the Super Bowl, for example, often fetch thousands of dollars on the "gray" market. Taxis cost much more in New York City (where they are tightly regulated) than in Washington, D.C. (where they are not).

To understand what goes wrong when we tamper with markets, we must first learn how they operate unfettered. This chapter takes a first step in that direction by study-

Price Controls at Valley Forge

G eorge Washington, the history books tell us, was beset by many enemies during the winter of 1777–1778, including the British, their Hessian mercenaries, and the merciless winter weather. But he had another enemy that the history books ignore—an enemy that meant well but almost destroyed his army at Valley Forge. As the following excerpt explains, that enemy was the Pennsylvania legislature:

In Pennsylvania, where the main force of Washington's army was quartered . . . the legislature . . . decided to try a period of price control limited to those commodities needed for use by the army. . . . The result might have been anticipated by those with some knowledge of the trials and tribulations of other states. The prices of uncontrolled goods, mostly imported, rose to record heights. Most farmers kept back their produce, refusing to sell at what they regarded as an unfair price. Some who had large families to take care of even secretly sold their food to the British who paid in gold.

After the disastrous winter at Valley Forge when Washington's army nearly starved to death (thanks largely to these well-intentioned but misdirected laws), the ill-fated experiment in price controls was finally ended. The Continental Congress on June 4, 1778, adopted the following resolution:

"Whereas . . . it hath been found by experience that limitations upon the prices of commodities are not only ineffectual for the purposes proposed, but likewise productive of very evil consequences . . . resolved, that it be rec-

Valley Forge.

ommended to the several states to repeal or suspend all laws or resolutions within the said states respectively limiting, regulating or restraining the Price of any Article, Manufacture or Commodity."

SOURCE: Robert L. Schuettinger and Eamonn F. Butler, *Forty Centuries of Wage and Price Controls* (Washington, D.C.: Heritage Foundation, 1979), p. 41. Reprinted by permission.

ing the machinery of supply and demand. Then, at the end of the chapter, we return to the issue of price controls.

Every market has both buyers and sellers. We begin our analysis on the consumers' side of the market.

DEMAND AND QUANTITY DEMANDED

People commonly think of consumer demands as fixed amounts. For example, when product designers propose a new computer model, management asks: "What is its market potential?" That is, just how many are likely to be sold? Similarly, government bureaus conduct studies to determine how many engineers or doctors the United States will require (demand) in subsequent years.

Economists respond that such questions are not well posed—that there is no single answer to such a question. Rather, they say, the "market potential" for computers or the number of engineers that will be "required" depends on a great number of influences, including the price charged for each.

The **quantity demanded** of any product normally depends on its price. Quantity demanded also depends on a number of other determinants, including population size, consumer incomes, tastes, and the prices of other products.

Because prices play a central role in a market economy, we begin our study of demand by focusing on how quantity demanded depends on price. A little later, we will

The **quantity demanded** is the number of units of a good that consumers are willing and can afford to buy over a specified period of time.

bring the other determinants of quantity demanded back into the picture. For now, we consider all influences other than price to be fixed. This assumption, often expressed as "other things being equal," is used in much of economic analysis. As an example of the relationship between price and demand, let us think about the quantity of milk demanded. If the price of milk is very high, its "market potential" may be very small. People will find ways to get along with less milk, perhaps by switching to fruit juice or soda. If the price of milk declines, people will tend to drink more milk. They may give their children larger portions or switch away from juices and sodas. Thus:

There is no one demand figure for milk, for computers, or for engineers. Rather, there is a different quantity demanded at each possible price, all other influences being held constant.

The Demand Schedule

A **demand schedule** is a table showing how the quantity demanded of some product during a specified period of time changes as the price of that product changes, holding all other determinants of quantity demanded constant.

Table 3-1 shows how such information for milk can be recorded in a **demand schedule.** It indicates how much milk consumers in a particular area are willing and able to buy at different possible prices during a specified period of time, other things held equal. Specifically, the table shows the quantity of milk that will be demanded in a year at each possible price ranging from $1.50 to $0.90 per quart. At a relatively low price, such as $1 per quart, customers wish to purchase 70 billion quarts per year. But if the price were to rise to, say, $1.40 per quart, quantity demanded would fall to 50 billion quarts.

Common sense tells us why this happens.[2] First, as prices rise, some customers will reduce the quantity of milk they consume. Second, higher prices will induce some customers to drop out of the market entirely—for example, by switching to soda or juice. On both counts, quantity demanded will decline as the price rises.

TABLE 3-1
Demand Schedule for Milk

Price per Quart	Quantity Demanded	Label in Figure 3-1
$1.50	45	A
1.40	50	B
1.30	55	C
1.20	60	E
1.10	65	F
1.00	70	G
0.90	75	H

NOTE: Quantity is in billions of quarts per year.

As the price of an item rises, the quantity demanded normally falls. As the price falls, the quantity demanded normally rises, all other things held constant.

The Demand Curve

A **demand curve** is a graphical depiction of a demand schedule. It shows how the quantity demanded of some product will change as the price of that product changes during a specified period of time, holding all other determinants of quantity demanded constant.

The information contained in Table 3-1 can be summarized in a graph like Figure 3-1, which is called a **demand curve.** Each point in the graph corresponds to a line in the table. This curve shows the relationship between price and quantity demanded. For example, it tells us that to sell 70 billion quarts per year, the price must be $1.00. This relationship is shown at point *G* in Figure 3-1. If the price were $1.40, however, consumers would demand only 50 billion quarts (point *B*). Because the quantity demanded declines as the price increases, the demand curve has a negative slope.[3]

Notice the last phrase in the definitions of the demand schedule and the demand curve: "holding all other determinants of quantity demanded constant." What are some of these "other things," and how do they affect the demand curve?

Shifts of the Demand Curve

The quantity of milk demanded is subject to a variety of influences other than the price of milk. Changes in population size and characteristics, consumer incomes and

---

[2] This common-sense answer is examined more fully in later chapters.

[3] If you need to review the concept of slope, refer back to the appendix to Chapter 1.

tastes, and the prices of alternative beverages such as soda and orange juice presumably change the quantity of milk demanded, even if the price of milk does not change.

Because the demand curve for milk depicts only the relationship between the quantity of milk demanded and the price of milk, holding all other factors constant, a change in milk price moves the market for milk from one point on the demand curve to another point on the same curve. However, a change in any of these *other* influences on demand causes a **shift of the entire demand curve.** More generally:

A change in the price of a good produces a movement *along* a fixed demand curve. By contrast, a change in any other variable that influences quantity demanded produces a shift of the *entire* demand curve.

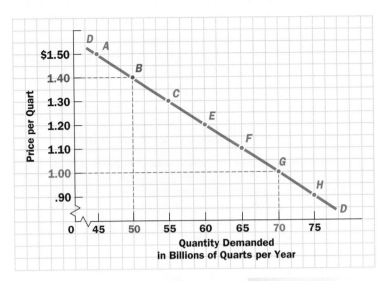

■ FIGURE 3-1
Demand Curve for Milk

If consumers want to buy more milk at every given price than they wanted previously, the demand curve shifts to the right (or outward). If they desire less at every given price, the demand curve shifts to the left (or inward toward the origin).

Figure 3-2 shows this distinction graphically. If the price of milk falls from $1.30 to $1.10 per quart, and quantity demanded rises accordingly, we move along demand curve D_0D_0 from point C to point F, as shown by the blue arrow. If, on the other hand, consumers suddenly decide that they like milk better than they did formerly, or if more children are born who need more milk, the entire demand curve shifts outward from D_0D_0 to D_1D_1, as indicated by the red arrows, meaning that at any given price consumers are now willing to buy more milk than before. To make this general idea more concrete, and to show some of its many applications, let us consider some specific examples of those "other things" that can shift demand curves.

A **shift in a demand curve** occurs when any relevant variable other than price changes. If consumers want to buy *more* at any given price than they wanted previously, the demand curve shifts to the right (or outward). If they desire *less* at any given price, the demand curve shifts to the left (or inward).

Consumer Incomes   If average incomes rise, consumers will purchase more of most goods, including milk, even if the prices of those goods remain the same. That is, increases in income normally shift demand curves outward to the right, as depicted in Figure 3-3(a), where the demand curve shifts outward from D_0D_0 to D_1D_1, establishing a new equilibrium price and quantity.

Population Population growth affects quantity demanded in more or less the same way as increases in average incomes. For instance, a larger population will presumably want to consume more milk, even if the price of milk and average incomes do not change, thus shifting the entire demand curve to the right, as in Figure 3-3(a). The equilibrium price and quantity both rise. Increases in particular population segments can also elicit shifts in demand—for example, the

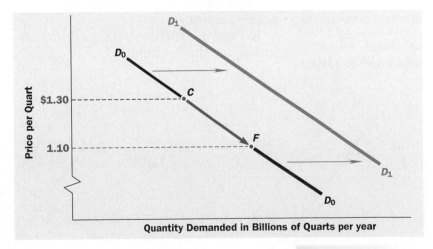

■ FIGURE 3-2
Movements along versus Shifts of a Demand Curve

United States in recent years has been experiencing a miniature population boom of people in their mid- to late 20s. Dubbed "Generation X," this fast-growing group has

Volatility in Electricity Prices

F or complex reasons, in 2000–2001 California experienced shocking jumps and declines in electricity prices. Two years earlier in Texas, volatile electricity prices were easier to understand. The following newspaper story shows the dramatic effect on prices that can sometimes result from a shift in a demand curve.

> Because no one can stockpile electricity . . . prices have proved to be extremely volatile at times of high demand like a recent summer's heat waves. Here is the *Cinergy-Power Markets Week* daily index, in dollars per megawatt hour. When heat waves blistered much of the country in June and July of 1998, utility customers in cities like Dallas ran fans and air conditioners nonstop, and power demand soared. So the price of electricity exploded, as the graph demonstrates.

NOTE: Price is in dollars per megawatt hour.

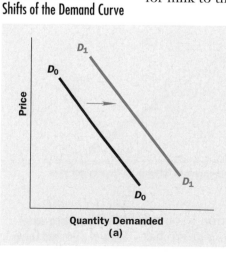

SOURCES: *New York Times,* Business Section, August 23, 1998, p. 4. (text). Scatter Graph showing power prices from July to August from "A 20,000% Bounce: Now That's Volatility" by A.R. Myerson, *The New York Times,* Business Section, August 8, 1998, p. 4. Copyright © 1998 by The New York Times. Reprinted by permission; Enron Corporation (graph).

sparked higher demand for big-ticket items such as sport-utility vehicles and contemporary furniture.

In Figure 3-3(b) we see that a decrease in population should shift the demand curve for milk to the left from D_0D_0 to D_2D_2.

■ **FIGURE 3-3**

Shifts of the Demand Curve

Consumer Preferences   If the dairy industry mounts a successful advertising campaign extolling the benefits of drinking milk, families may decide to buy more at any given price. If so, the entire demand curve for milk would shift to the right, as in Figure 3-3(a). Alternatively, a medical report on the dangers of kidney stones may persuade consumers to drink less milk, thereby shifting the demand curve to the left, as in Figure 3-3(b). Again, these are general phenomena:

If consumer preferences shift in favor of a particular item, its demand curve will shift outward to the right, as in Figure 3-3(a).

An example is the ever-shifting "rage" in children's toys—be it Beanie Babies, Pokemon cards, or new video games. These items become the object of desperate hunts as parents snap them up for their offspring, and stores are unable to keep up with the demand.

Prices and Availability of Related Goods   Because soda, orange juice, and coffee are popular drinks that compete with milk, a change in the price of any of these other beverages can be expected to shift the demand curve for milk. If any of these alternative drinks becomes cheaper, some consumers will switch away from milk. Thus, the demand curve for milk will shift to the left, as in Figure 3-3(b). Other price changes may shift the demand curve for milk in the opposite direction. For example, suppose that cookies, which are often consumed with milk, become less expensive. This may induce some consumers to drink more milk and thus shift the demand curve for milk to the right, as in Figure 3-3(a). In general:

Increases in the prices of goods that are substitutes for the good in question (as soda is for milk) move the demand curve to the right. Increases in the prices of goods that are normally used together with the good in question (such as cookies and milk) shift the demand curve to the left.

This is just what happened when a frost wiped out almost half of Brazil's coffee bean harvest in 1995. The three largest U.S. coffee producers raised their prices by 45 percent, and, as a result, the demand curve for alternative beverages such as tea shifted to the right. Then in 1998, coffee prices dropped about 34 percent, which in turn caused the demand curve for tea to shift toward the left (or toward the origin), all other things being equal.

Although the preceding list does not exhaust the possible influences on quantity demanded, we have said enough to suggest the principles followed by demand and shifts of demand. Let us therefore turn to the supply side of the market.

SUPPLY AND QUANTITY SUPPLIED

Like quantity demanded, the quantity of milk that is supplied by business firms such as dairy farms is not a fixed number; it also depends on many things. Obviously, we expect more milk to be supplied if there are more dairy farms or more cows per farm. Cows may give less milk if bad weather deprives them of their feed. As before, however, let's turn our attention first to the relationship between the price and quantity of milk supplied.

Economists generally suppose that a higher price calls forth a greater **quantity supplied.** Why? Remember our analysis of the principle of increasing cost in Chapter 2 (page 23). According to that principle, as more of any farmer's (or the nation's) resources are devoted to milk production, the opportunity cost of obtaining another quart of milk increases. Farmers will therefore find it profitable to increase milk production only if they can sell the milk at a higher price—high enough to cover the additional costs incurred to expand production.

In other words, it normally will take higher prices to persuade farmers to raise milk production. This idea is quite general and applies to the supply of most goods and

The **quantity supplied** is the number of units that sellers want to sell over a specified period of time.

A **supply schedule** is a table showing how the quantity supplied of some product changes as the price of that product changes during a specified period of time, holding all other determinants of quantity supplied constant.

services.[4] As long as suppliers want to make profits and the principle of increasing costs holds:

As the price of any commodity rises, the quantity supplied normally rises. As the price falls, the quantity supplied normally falls.

The Supply Schedule and the Supply Curve

TABLE 3-2		
Supply Schedule for Milk		
Price per Quart	Quantity Supplied	Label in Figure 3-4
$1.50	90	a
1.40	80	b
1.30	**70**	c
1.20	60	e
1.10	50	f
1.00	**40**	g
0.90	30	h

NOTE: Quantity is in billions of quarts per year.

Table 3-2 shows the relationship between the price of milk and its quantity supplied. Tables such as this one are called **supply schedules;** they show how much sellers are willing to provide during a specified period at alternative possible prices. This particular supply schedule asserts that a low price like $1.00 per quart will induce suppliers to provide only 40 billion quarts, whereas a higher price like $1.30 will induce them to provide much more—70 billion quarts.

As you might have guessed, when such information is plotted on a graph, it is called a **supply curve**. Figure 3-4 is the supply curve corresponding to the supply schedule in Table 3-2, showing the relationship between the price of milk and the quantity supplied. It slopes upward—it has a positive slope—because quantity supplied is higher when price is higher. Notice again the same phrase in the definition: "holding all other determinants of quantity supplied constant." What are these "other determinants"?

A **supply curve** is a graphical depiction of a supply schedule. It shows how the quantity supplied of some product will change as the price of that product changes during a specified period of time, holding all other determinants of quantity supplied constant.

Shifts of the Supply Curve

Like quantity demanded, the quantity supplied in a market typically responds to many influences other than price. The weather, the cost of feed, the number and size of dairy farms, and a variety of other factors all influence how much milk will be brought to market. Because the supply curve depicts only the relationship between the price of milk and the quantity of milk supplied, holding all other influences constant, a change in any of these other determinants of quantity supplied will cause the entire supply curve to shift. That is:

A change in the price of the good causes a movement _along_ a fixed supply curve. Price is not the only influence on quantity supplied, however. If any of these other influences change, the _entire_ supply curve shifts.

Figure 3-5 depicts this distinction graphically. A rise in price from $1.10 to $1.30 will raise quantity supplied by moving along supply curve S_0S_0 from point f to point c. Any rise in quantity supplied attributable to an influence other than price, however, will shift the _entire_ supply curve outward to the right from S_0S_0 to S_1S_1, as shown by the red arrows. Let us consider what some of these other influences are and how they shift the supply curve.

FIGURE 3-4
Supply Curve for Milk

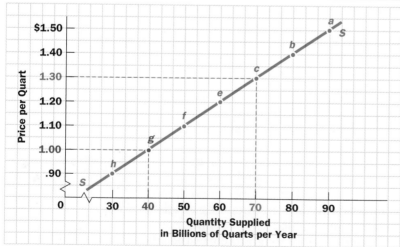

Size of the Industry   We begin with the most obvious influence. If more farmers enter the milk industry, the quantity supplied at any given price will increase. For example, if each farm provides 600,000 quarts

---

[4] This analysis is carried out in much greater detail in later chapters.

of milk per year at a price of $1.10 per quart, then 100,000 farmers would provide 60 billion quarts, but 130,000 farmers would provide 78 billion. Thus, when more farms are in the industry, the quantity of milk supplied will be greater at any given price—and hence the supply curve will move farther to the right.

Figure 3-6(a) illustrates the effect of an expansion of the industry from 100,000 farms to 130,000 farms—a rightward shift of the supply curve from S_0S_0 to S_1S_1. Figure 3-6(b) illustrates the opposite case: a contraction of the industry from 100,000 farms to 62,500 farms. The supply curve shifts inward to the left from S_0S_0 to S_2S_2. Even if no farmers enter or leave the industry, results like those depicted in Figure 3-6 can be produced by expansion or contraction of the *existing* farms.

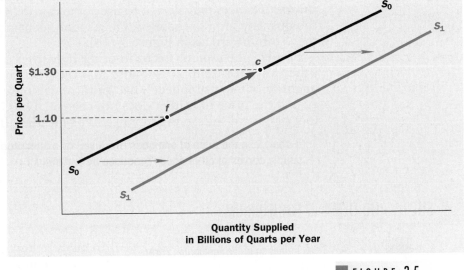

■ FIGURE 3-5
Movements along versus
Shifts of a Supply Curve

Technological Progress   Another influence that shifts supply curves is technological change. Suppose some enterprising farmer invents a new milking machine that uses much less electricity. Thereafter, at any given price, farms will be able to produce more milk; that is, the supply curve will shift outward to the right, as in Figure 3-6(a). This example, again, illustrates a general influence that applies to most industries:

Technological progress that reduces costs will shift the supply curve outward to the right.

Automakers, for example, have been able to reduce production costs since industrial technology invented robots that can be programmed to work on several different car models. This technological advance has shifted the supply curve outward.

Prices of Inputs   Changes in input prices also shift supply curves. Suppose a drought raises the price of animal feed. Farmers will have to pay more to keep their cows alive and healthy and consequently will no longer be able to provide the same quantity of milk at each possible price. This example illustrates that:

Increases in the prices of inputs that suppliers must buy will shift the supply curve inward to the left.

■ FIGURE 3-6
Shifts of the Supply Curve

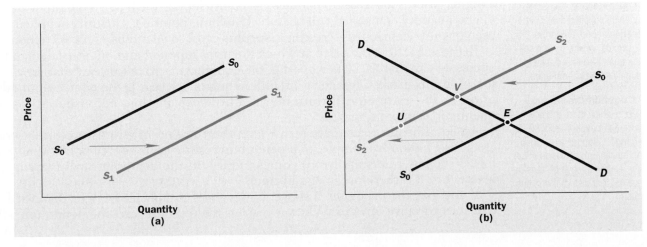

Prices of Related Outputs   Dairy farms sell products other than milk. If cheese prices rise sharply, farmers may decide to use some raw milk to make cheese, thereby reducing the quantity of milk supplied. On a supply-demand diagram, the supply curve would then shift inward, as in Figure 3-6(b).

Similar phenomena occur in other industries, and sometimes the effect goes the other way. For example, suppose that the price of beef goes up, which increases the quantity of meat supplied. That, in turn, will raise the number of cowhides supplied even if the price of leather does not change. Thus, a rise in the price of beef will lead to a rightward shift in the supply curve of leather. In general:

A change in the price of one good produced by a multiproduct industry may be expected to shift the supply curves of other goods produced by that industry.

SUPPLY AND DEMAND EQUILIBRIUM

TABLE 3-3   Determination of the Equilibrium Price and Quantity of Milk

Price per Quart	Quantity Demanded	Quantity Supplied	Surplus or Shortage?	Price Direction
$1.50	45	90	Surplus	Fall
1.40	50	80	Surplus	Fall
1.30	55	70	Surplus	Fall
1.20	60	60	Neither	Unchanged
1.10	65	50	Shortage	Rise
1.00	70	40	Shortage	Rise
0.90	75	30	Shortage	Rise

NOTE: Quantity is in billions of quarts per year.

A **supply-demand diagram** graphs the supply and demand curves together. It also determines the equilibrium price and quantity.

A **shortage** is an excess of quantity demanded over quantity supplied. When there is a shortage, buyers cannot purchase the quantities they desire at the current price.

A **surplus** is an excess of quantity supplied over quantity demanded. When there is a surplus, sellers cannot sell the quantities they desire to supply at the current price.

An **equilibrium** is a situation in which there are no inherent forces that produce change. Changes away from an equilibrium position will occur only as a result of "outside events" that disturb the status quo.

To analyze how the free market determines price, we must compare the desires of consumers (demand) with the desires of producers (supply) to see whether the two plans are consistent. Table 3-3 and Figure 3-7 help us do this.

Table 3-3 brings together the demand schedule from Table 3-1 and the supply schedule from Table 3-2. Similarly, Figure 3-7 puts the demand curve from Figure 3-1 and the supply curve from Figure 3-4 on a single graph. Such graphs are called **supply-demand diagrams**, and you will encounter many of them in this book. Notice that, for reasons already discussed, the demand curve has a negative slope and the supply curve has a positive slope. That is generally true of supply-demand diagrams.

In a free market, price and quantity are determined by the intersection of the supply and demand curves. At only one point in Figure 3-7, point *E*, do the supply curve and the demand curve intersect. At the price corresponding to point *E*, which is $1.20 per quart, the quantity supplied and the quantity demanded are both 60 billion quarts per year. This means that at a price of $1.20 per quart, consumers are willing to buy exactly what producers are willing to sell.

At a lower price, such as $1.00 per quart, only 40 billion quarts of milk will be supplied (point *g*) whereas 70 billion quarts will be demanded (point *G*). Thus, quantity demanded will exceed quantity supplied. There will be a **shortage** equal to 70 minus 40, or 30 billion quarts. Price will thus be driven up by unsatisfied demand. Alternatively, at a higher price, such as $1.50 per quart, quantity supplied will be 90 billion quarts (point *a*) and quantity demanded will be only 45 billion (point *A*). Quantity supplied will exceed quantity demanded—creating a **surplus** equal to 90 minus 45, or 45 billion quarts.

Because $1.20 is the price at which quantity supplied and quantity demanded are equal, we say that $1.20 per quart is the equilibrium price (or the "market clearing" price) in this market. Similarly, 60 billion quarts per year is the equilibrium quantity of milk. The term **equilibrium** merits a little explanation, because it arises so frequently in economic analysis.

An equilibrium is a situation in which there are no inherent forces that produce change. Think, for example, of a pendulum resting at its center point. If no outside force (such as a person's hand) comes to push it, the pendulum will remain exactly where it is; it is therefore in equilibrium.

If you give the pendulum a shove, however, its equilibrium will be disturbed and it will start to move upward. When it reaches the top of its arc, the pendulum will, for an instant, be at rest again. This point is not an equilibrium position, for the force of gravity will pull the pendulum downward. Thereafter, gravity and friction will govern its motion from side to side. Eventually, the pendulum will return to its original position. The fact that the pendulum tends to return to its original position is described by saying that this position is a *stable* equilibrium. That position is also the only equilibrium position of the pendulum. At any other point, inherent forces will cause the pendulum to move.

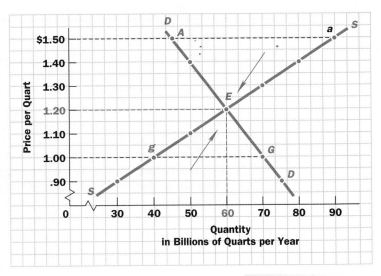

FIGURE 3-7
Supply-Demand Equilibrium

The concept of equilibrium in economics is similar and can be illustrated by our supply-and-demand example. Why is no price other than $1.20 an equilibrium price in Table 3-3 or Figure 3-7? What forces will change any other price?

Consider first a low price such as $1.00, at which quantity demanded (70 billion quarts) exceeds quantity supplied (40 billion quarts). If the price were this low, many frustrated customers would be unable to purchase the quantities they desired. In their scramble for the available supply of milk, some would offer to pay more. As customers sought to outbid one another, the market price would be forced up. Thus, a price below the equilibrium price cannot persist in a free market because a shortage sets in motion powerful economic forces that push the price upward.

Similar forces operate if the market price exceeds the equilibrium price. If, for example, the price should somehow reach $1.50, Table 3-3 tells us that quantity supplied (90 billion quarts) would far exceed the quantity demanded (45 billion quarts). Producers would be unable to sell their desired quantities of milk at the prevailing price, and some would undercut their competitors by reducing price. Such competitive price cutting would continue as long as the surplus remained—that is, as long as quantity supplied exceeded quantity demanded. Thus, a price above the equilibrium price cannot persist indefinitely.

We are left with a clear conclusion. The price of $1.20 per quart and the quantity of 60 billion quarts per year constitute the only price-quantity combination that does not sow the seeds of its own destruction. It is thus the only equilibrium for this market. Any lower price must rise, and any higher price must fall. It is as if natural economic forces place a magnet at point E that attracts the market, just as gravity attracts a pendulum.

The pendulum analogy is worth pursuing further. Most pendulums are more frequently in motion than at rest. However, unless they are repeatedly buffeted by outside forces (which, of course, is exactly what happens to economic equilibria in reality), pendulums gradually return to their resting points. The same is true of price and quantity in a free market. They are moved about by shifts in the supply and demand curves that we have already described. As a consequence, markets are not always in equilibrium. But, if nothing interferes with them, experience shows that they normally move toward equilibrium.

The Law of Supply and Demand

In a free market, the forces of supply and demand generally push the price toward its equilibrium level, the price at which quantity supplied and quantity demanded are equal. Like most economic "laws," some markets will occasionally disobey the **law of supply and demand.** Markets sometimes display shortages or surpluses for long periods of time. Prices sometimes fail to move toward equilibrium. But the "law" is a fair generalization that is right far more often than it is wrong.

The **law of supply and demand** states that in a free market the forces of supply and demand generally push the price toward the level at which quantity supplied and quantity demanded are equal.

EFFECTS OF DEMAND SHIFTS ON SUPPLY-DEMAND EQUILIBRIUM

Figure 3-3 showed how developments other than changes in price—such as increases in consumer income—can shift the demand curve. We saw that a rise in income, for example, will shift the demand curve to the right, meaning that at any given price, consumers—with their increased purchasing power—will buy more of the good than before. This, in turn, will move the equilibrium point, changing both market price and quantity sold.

This market adjustment is shown in Figure 3-8(a). It adds a supply curve to Figure 3-3(a) so that we can see what happens to the supply-demand equilibrium. In the example in the graph, the quantity demanded at the old equilibrium price of $1.20 increases from 60 billion quarts per year (point E on the demand curve D_0D_0) to 75 billion quarts per year (point R on the demand curve D_1D_1). We know that $1.20 is no longer the equilibrium price, because at this price quantity demanded (75 billion quarts) exceeds quantity supplied (60 billion quarts). To restore equilibrium, the price must rise. The new equilibrium occurs at point T, where the price is $1.30 per quart and both quantities demanded and supplied are 70 billion quarts per year. This example illustrates a general result, true when the supply curve slopes upward:

Any influence that makes the demand curve shift outward to the right, and does not affect the supply curve, will raise the equilibrium price and the equilibrium quantity.[5]

Everything works in reverse if consumer incomes fall. Figure 3-8(b) depicts a leftward (inward) shift of the demand curve that results from a decline in consumer incomes. For example, the quantity demanded at the previous equilibrium price ($1.20) falls from 60 billion quarts (point E) to 45 billion quarts (point L on the demand curve D_2D_2). The initial price is now too high and must fall. The new equilibrium will eventually be established at point M, where the price is $1.10 and both quantity demanded and quantity supplied are 50 billion quarts. In general:

Any influence that shifts the demand curve inward to the left, and that does not affect the supply curve, will lower both the equilibrium price and the equilibrium quantity.

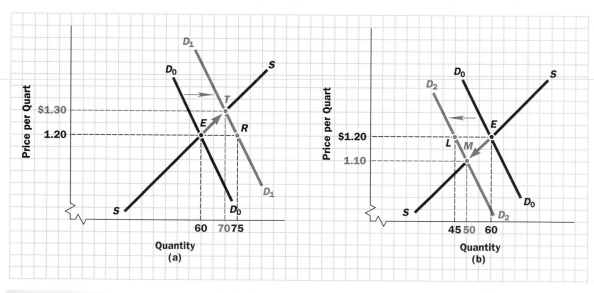

NOTE: Quantity is in billions of quarts per year.

■ FIGURE 3-8
The Effects of Shifts of the
Demand Curve

---

[5] For example, when incomes rise rapidly, in many developing countries the demand curves for a variety of consumer goods shift rapidly outward to the right. In Japan, for example, the demand for used Levi's jeans and Nike running shoes from the United States skyrocketed in the early 1990s as status-conscious Japanese consumers searched for outlets for their then rising incomes.

Puzzle Revisited: The Fall of the Rupiah

As we observed earlier in the chapter, sharp drops in the values of a number of Asian currencies, especially the Indonesian rupiah, stunned the world in 1997. What happened?

The basic problem was that people lost confidence in the rupiah—which translated into a sharp leftward shift in the demand curve, like that depicted in Figure 3-3(b). Specifically, foreigners became worried about the stability of the rupiah and decided to hold less of it. Similarly, Indonesians became concerned about the large losses they would suffer if the rupiah fell, and therefore they did the same.

As we know, when the demand curve in a market shifts inward, the price normally falls. In this case, the relevant price was the exchange rate—the price of a rupiah in terms of U.S. dollars—and it dropped precipitously as the market equilibrium moved from point E to point M.

SUPPLY SHIFTS AND SUPPLY-DEMAND EQUILIBRIUM

A story precisely analogous to that of the effects of a demand shift on equilibrium price and quantity applies to supply shifts. Figure 3-6 described the effects on the supply curve of milk if the number of farms increases. Figure 3-9(a) now adds a demand curve to the supply curves of Figure 3-6 so that we can see the supply-demand equilibrium. Notice that at the initial price of $1.20, the quantity supplied after the shift is 78 billion quarts (point I on the supply curve S_1S_1), which is 30 percent more than the original quantity demanded of 60 billion quarts (point E on the supply curve S_0S_0). We can see from the graph that the price of $1.20 is too high to be the equilibrium price; the price must fall. The new equilibrium point is J, where the price is $1.10 per quart and the quantity is 65 billion quarts per year. In general:

> **Any change that shifts the supply curve outward to the right, and does not affect the demand curve, will lower the equilibrium price and raise the equilibrium quantity.**

This must always be true if the industry's demand curve has a negative slope, because the greater quantity supplied can be sold only if the price is decreased so as to induce customers to buy more.[6] The cellular phone industry is a case in point.

FIGURE 3-9

Effects of Shifts of the Supply Curve

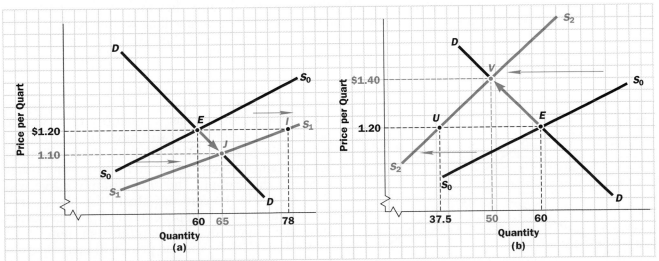

Quantity
(a)

Quantity
(b)

---

[6] Graphically, whenever a positively sloped curve shifts to the right, its intersection point with a negatively sloping curve must always move lower. Just try drawing it yourself.

As more providers have entered the industry, the cost of cellular service has plummeted. Some cellular carriers have even given away telephones as sign-up bonuses.

Figure 3-9(b) illustrates the opposite case: a contraction of the industry. The supply curve shifts inward to the left and equilibrium moves from point E to point V, where the price is $1.40 and quantity is 50 billion quarts per year. In general:

Any influence that shifts the supply curve to the left, and does not affect the demand curve, will raise the equilibrium price and reduce the equilibrium quantity.

Many outside forces can disturb equilibrium in a market by shifting the demand curve or the supply curve, either temporarily or permanently. In 1998, for example, gasoline prices dropped because recession in Asia reduced demand, and a reduction in use of petroleum resulted from a mild winter. In the summer of 1998, severely hot weather and lack of rain damaged the cotton crop in the United States. Often these outside influences change the equilibrium price and quantity by shifting either the supply curve or the demand curve. If you look again at Figures 3-8 and 3-9, you can see clearly that any event that causes either the demand curve or the supply curve to shift will also change the equilibrium price and quantity.

▌ Application: Who Really Pays That Tax?

Supply and demand analysis offers insights that may not be readily apparent. Here is an example. Suppose your state legislature raises the gasoline tax by 10 cents per gallon. Service station operators will then have to collect 10 additional cents in taxes on every gallon they pump. They will consider this higher tax as an addition to their costs and will shift it to you and other consumers by raising the price of gas by 10 cents per gallon. Right? No, wrong—or rather, partly wrong.

The gas station owners would certainly *like* to shift the entire tax to buyers, but the market mechanism will allow them to shift only *part* of it—perhaps 6 cents per gallon. They will then be stuck with the remainder—4 cents in our example. Figure 3-10, which is just another supply-demand graph, shows why.

The demand curve is the blue curve DD. The supply curve before the tax is the black curve S_0S_0. Before the new tax, the equilibrium point is E_0 and the price is $1.54. We can interpret the supply curve as telling us at what price sellers are willing to provide any given quantity. For example, they are willing to supply quantity $Q_1 = 50$ million gallons per year if the price is $1.54 per gallon.

So what happens as a result of the new tax? Because they must now turn 10 cents per gallon over to the government, gas station owners will be willing to supply any given quantity only if they get 10 cents more per gallon than they did before. Therefore, to get them to supply quantity $Q_1 = 50$ million gallons, a price of $1.54 per gallon will no longer suffice. Only a price of $1.64 per gallon will now induce them to supply 50 million gallons. Thus, at quantity $Q_1 = 50$, the point on the supply curve will move up by 10 cents, from point E_0 to point M. Because firms will insist on the same 10-cent price increase for any other quantity they supply, the *entire* supply curve will shift up by the 10-cent tax—from the black curve S_0S_0 to the new red supply curve S_1S_1. And, as a result, the supply-demand equilibrium point will move from E_0 to E_1 and the price will increase from $1.54 to $1.60.

The supply curve shift may give the impression that gas station owners have succeeded in passing the entire 10-cent increase on to consumers—the

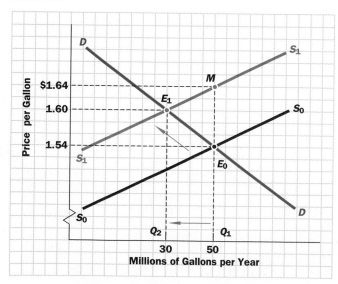

▌ FIGURE 3-10

Who Pays for a New Tax on Products?

distance from E_0 to M—but look again. The *equilibrium* price has only gone up from \$1.54 to \$1.60. That is, the price has risen by only 6 cents, not by the full 10-cent amount of the tax. The gas station will have to absorb the remaining 4 cents of the tax.

Now this really *looks* as though we have pulled a fast one on you—a magician's sleight of hand. After all, the supply curve has shifted upward by the full amount of the tax, and yet the resulting price increase has covered only part of the tax rise. However, a second look reveals that, like most apparent acts of magic, this one has a simple explanation. The explanation arises from the *demand* side of the supply-demand mechanism. The negative slope of the demand curve means that when prices rise, at least some consumers will reduce the quantity of gasoline they demand. That will force sellers to give up part of the price increase. In other words, firms must absorb the part of the tax— 4 cents—that consumers are unwilling to pay. But note that the equilibrium quantity Q_1 has fallen from 50 million gallons to $Q_2 = 30$ million gallons—so both consumers and suppliers lose out in some sense.

This example is not an oddball case. Indeed, the result is almost always true. The cost of any increase in a tax on any commodity will usually be paid partly by the consumer and partly by the seller. This is so no matter whether the legislature says that it is imposing the tax on the sellers or on the buyers. Whichever way it is phrased, the economics are the same: The supply-demand mechanism ensures that the tax will be shared by both of the parties.

FIGHTING THE INVISIBLE HAND: THE MARKET FIGHTS BACK

IDEAS FOR BEYOND THE FINAL EXAM

As we noted in our *Ideas for Beyond the Final Exam* in Chapter 1, lawmakers and rulers have often been dissatisfied with the outcomes of free markets. From Rome to Reno, and from biblical times to the space age, they have battled the invisible hand. Sometimes, rather than trying to adjust the workings of the market, governments have tried to raise or lower the prices of specific commodities by decree. In many such cases, the authorities felt that market prices were, in some sense, immorally low or immorally high. Penalties were therefore imposed on anyone offering the commodities in question at prices above or below those established by the authorities. Such legally imposed constraints on prices are called "price ceilings" and "price floors." To see their result, we will focus on the use of price ceilings.

Restraining the Market Mechanism: Price Ceilings

The market has proven itself a formidable foe that strongly resists attempts to get around its decisions. In case after case where legal **price ceilings** are imposed, virtually the same series of consequences ensues:

> A **price ceiling** is a maximum that the price charged for a commodity cannot legally exceed.

1. *A persistent shortage develops because quantity demanded exceeds quantity supplied.* Queuing (people waiting in lines), direct rationing, or any of a variety of other devices, usually inefficient and unpleasant, must substitute for the distribution process provided by the price mechanism. Example: Rampant shortages in Eastern Europe and the former Soviet Union helped precipitate the revolts that ended communism.
2. *An illegal, or "black," market often arises to supply the commodity.* Usually some individuals are willing to take the risks involved in meeting unsatisfied demands illegally. Example: Although most states ban the practice, ticket "scalping" occurs at most popular sporting events and rock concerts.
3. *The prices charged on illegal markets are almost certainly higher than those that would prevail in free markets.* After all, lawbreakers expect some compensation for the risk of being caught and punished. Example: Illegal drugs are

POLICY DEBATE   Economic Aspects of the War on Drugs

For years now, the U.S. government has engaged in a highly publicized "war on drugs." Billions of dollars have been spent on trying to stop illegal drugs at the country's borders. In some sense, interdiction has succeeded: Federal agents have seized literally tons of cocaine and other drugs. Yet these efforts have made barely a dent in the flow of drugs to America's city streets. Simple economic reasoning explains why.

When drug interdiction works, it shifts the supply curve of drugs to the left, thereby driving up street prices. But that, in turn, raises the rewards for potential smugglers and attracts more criminals into the "industry," which shifts the supply curve back to the right. The net result is that increased shipments of drugs to U.S. shores replace much of what the authorities confiscate. This is why many economists believe that any successful anti-drug program must concentrate on reducing demand, which would lower the street price of drugs, not on reducing supply, which can only raise it.

Some people suggest that the government should go even further and legalize many drugs. Although this idea remains a highly controversial position that few are ready to endorse, the reasoning behind it is straightforward. A stunningly high fraction of all the violent crimes committed in America—especially robberies and murders—are drug-related. One major reason is that street prices of drugs are so high that addicts must steal to get the money, and drug traffickers are all too willing to kill to protect their highly profitable "businesses."

How would things differ if drugs were legal? Because South American farmers earn pennies for drugs that sell for hundreds of dollars on the streets of Los Angeles and New York, we may safely assume that legalized drugs would be vastly cheaper. In fact, according to one estimate, a dose of cocaine would cost less than 50 cents. That, proponents point out, would reduce drug-related crimes dramatically. When, for example, was the last time you heard of a gang killing connected with the distribution of cigarettes or alcoholic beverages?

The argument against legalization of drugs is largely moral: Should the state sanction potentially lethal substances? But there is an economic aspect to this position as well: The vastly lower street prices of drugs that would surely follow legalization would increase drug use. Thus, while legalization would almost certainly reduce crime, it would also produce more addicts. The key question here is, How many more addicts? (No one has a good answer.) If you think the increase in quantity demanded would be large, you are unlikely to find legalization an attractive option.

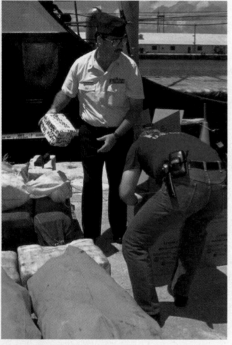

SOURCE: Chris Brown/Picturequest/Stock Boston

normally quite expensive. (See the accompanying Policy Debate box, "Economic Aspects of the War on Drugs.")

4. *A substantial portion of the price falls into the hands of the illicit supplier instead of going to those who produce the good or perform the service.* Example: A constant complaint during the public hearings that marked the history of theater-ticket price controls in New York City was that the "ice" (the illegal excess charge) fell into the hands of ticket scalpers rather than going to those who invested in, produced, or acted in the play.

5. *Investment in the industry generally dries up.* Because price ceilings reduce the monetary returns that investors can legally earn, less capital will be invested in industries that are subject to price controls. Even fear of impending price controls can have this effect. Example: Price controls on farm products in Zambia have prompted peasant farmers and large agricultural conglomerates alike to cut back production rather than grow crops at a loss. The result has been thousands of lost jobs and widespread food shortages.

Case Study: Rent Controls in New York City

These points and others are best illustrated by considering a concrete example involving price ceilings. New York is the only major city in the United States that has legislated rent controls continuously since World War II. Rent controls, of course, are intended to protect the consumer from high rents. But most economists believe that rent control does not help the cities or their residents and that, in the long run, it leaves almost everyone worse off. Elementary supply-demand analysis shows us why.

Figure 3-11 is a supply-demand diagram for rental units in New York. Curve *DD* is the demand curve and curve *SS* is the supply curve. Without controls, equilibrium would be at point *E*, where rents average $2,000 per month and 3 million housing units are occupied. If rent controls are effective, the ceiling price must be below the equilibrium price of $2,000. But with a low rent ceiling, such as $1,200, the quantity of housing demanded will be 3.5 million units (point *B*) whereas the quantity supplied will be only 2.5 million units (point *C*).

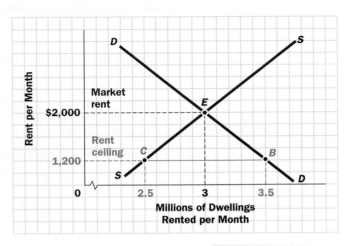

The diagram shows a shortage of 1 million apartments. This theoretical concept of a "shortage" manifests itself in New York City as an abnormally low vacancy rate—typically about half the national urban average. Naturally, rent controls have spawned a lively black market in New York. The black market raises the effective price of rent-controlled apartments in many ways, including bribes, so-called "key money" paid to move up on a waiting list, or the requirement that prospective tenants purchase worthless furniture at inflated prices.

According to Figure 3-11, rent controls reduce the quantity supplied from 3 million to 2.5 million apartments. How does this reduction show up in New York? First, some property owners, discouraged by the low rents, have converted apartment buildings into office space or other uses. Second, some apartments have been inadequately maintained. After all, rent controls create a shortage, which makes even dilapidated apartments easy to rent. Third, some landlords have actually abandoned their buildings rather than pay rising tax and fuel bills. These abandoned buildings rapidly become eyesores and eventually pose threats to public health and safety.

An important implication of these last observations is that rent controls—and price controls more generally—harm consumers in ways that offset part or all of the benefits to those who are fortunate enough to find and acquire at lower prices the product that the reduced prices has made scarce. Tenants must undergo long waits and undertake time-consuming searches to find an apartment, the apartment they obtain is likely to be poorly maintained or even decrepit, and normal landlord services are apt to disappear. Thus, even for the lucky beneficiaries, rent control is always far less of a bargain than the reduced monthly payments make them appear to be. The same problems generally apply with other forms of price control as well.

With all of these problems, why does rent control persist in New York City? And why do other cities sometimes move in the same direction?

Part of the explanation is that most people simply do not understand the problems that rent controls create. Another part is that landlords are unpopular politically. But a third, and very important, part of the explanation is that not everyone is hurt by rent controls—and those who benefit from controls fight hard to preserve them. In New York, for example, many tenants pay rents that are only a fraction of what their apartments would fetch on the open market. They are, naturally enough, quite happy with this situation. This last point illustrates another very general phenomenon:

FIGURE 3-11

Supply-Demand Diagram for Rental Housing

"If you leave me, you know, you'll never see this kind of rent again."

Virtually every price ceiling or floor creates a class of people that benefits from the regulations. These people use their political influence to protect their gains by preserving the status quo, which is one reason why it is so difficult to eliminate price ceilings or floors.

Restraining the Market Mechanism: Price Floors

Interferences with the market mechanism are not always designed to keep prices low. Agricultural price supports and minimum wages are two notable examples in which the law keeps prices *above* free-market levels. Such **price floors** are typically accompanied by a standard series of symptoms:

A **price floor** is a legal minimum below which the price charged for a commodity is not permitted to fall.

1. *A surplus develops as sellers cannot find enough buyers.* Example: Surpluses of various agricultural products have been a persistent—and costly—problem for the U.S. government. The problem is even worse in the European Union (EU), where the common agricultural policy holds prices even higher. One source estimates that this policy accounts for half of all EU spending.[7]
2. *Where goods, rather than services, are involved, the surplus creates a problem of disposal.* Something must be done about the excess of quantity supplied over quantity demanded. Example: The U.S. government has often been forced to purchase, store, and then dispose of large amounts of surplus agricultural commodities.
3. *To get around the regulations, sellers may offer discounts in disguised—and often unwanted—forms.* Example: Back when airline fares were regulated by the government, airlines offered more and better food and stylish uniforms for flight attendants instead of lowering fares. Today, the food is worse, but tickets cost much less.
4. *Regulations that keep prices artificially high encourage overinvestment in the industry.* Even inefficient businesses whose high operating costs would doom them in an unrestricted market can survive beneath the shelter of a generous price floor. Example: This is why the airline and trucking industries both went through painful "shakeouts" of the weaker companies in the 1980s, after they were deregulated and allowed to charge market-determined prices.

Once again, a specific example is useful for understanding how price floors work.

Case Study: Farm Price Supports and the Case of Sugar Prices

America's extensive program of farm price supports began in 1933 as a "temporary method of dealing with an emergency"—farmers were going broke in droves. These price supports are still with us today, even though farmers account for less than 3 percent of the U.S. workforce.[8]

One of the consequences of these price supports has been the creation of unsaleable surpluses—more output of crops such as grains than consumers were willing to buy at the inflated prices yielded by the supports. Warehouses were filled to overflowing. New storage facilities had to be built, and the government was forced to set up programs in which grain from the unmanageable surpluses was shipped to poor foreign countries to combat malnutrition and starvation in those nations. Realistically, if price supports are to be effective in keeping prices above the equilibrium level, then *someone* must be prepared to purchase the surpluses that invariably result. Otherwise, those surpluses will somehow find their way into the market and drive down prices, undermining the price support program. In the United States (and elsewhere), the buyer of the surpluses has usually turned out to be the government, which makes its purchases at the expense of taxpayers who are forced to pay twice—once through taxes to finance the government purchases, and a second time in the form of higher prices for the farm products bought by the American public.

---

[7] *The Economist*, Feb. 20, 1999.

[8] Under major legislation passed in 1996, many agricultural price supports were supposed to be phased out over a seven-year period. In reality, many support programs, especially that for sugar, have changed little.

One of the more controversial farm price supports involves the sugar industry. Sugar producers receive low-interest loans from the federal government and a guarantee that the price of sugar will not fall below a certain level.

In a market economy such as that found in the United States, Congress cannot simply set prices by decree; rather, it must take some action to enforce the price floor. In the case of sugar, that "something" is limiting both domestic production and foreign imports, thereby shifting the supply curve inward to the left. Figure 3-12 shows the mechanics involved in this price floor. Government policies shift the supply curve inward from S_0S_0 to S_1S_1 and drive the U.S. price up from $1 to $2 per pound. The more the supply curve shifts inward, the higher the price.

The sugar industry obviously benefits from the price-control program. But consumers pay for it in the form of higher prices for sugar and sugar-filled products such as soft drinks, candy bars, and cookies. Although estimates vary, the federal sugar price support program appears to cost consumers approximately $1.5 billion per year.

If all of this sounds a bit abstract to you, take a look at the ingredients in a U.S.-made soft drink. Instead of sugar, you will likely find "high-fructose corn syrup" listed as a sweetener. Foreign producers generally use sugar, but sugar is simply too expensive to be used for this purpose in the United States.

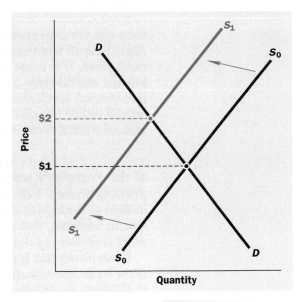

■ FIGURE 3-12
Supporting the Price of Sugar

■ A Can of Worms

Our two case studies—rent controls and sugar price supports—illustrate some of the major side effects of price floors and ceilings, but barely hint at others. Difficulties arise that we have not even mentioned, for the market mechanism is a tough bird that imposes suitable retribution on those who seek to evade it by government decree. Here is a partial list of other problems that may arise when prices are controlled.

Favoritism and Corruption   When price ceilings or floors create shortages or surpluses, someone must decide who gets to buy or sell the limited quantity that is available. This decision-making process can lead to discrimination along racial or religious lines, political favoritism, or corruption in government. For example, many prices were held at artificially low levels in the former Soviet Union, making queuing for certain goods quite common. Even so, Communist party officials and other favored groups were somehow able to purchase the scarce commodities that others could not get.

Unenforceability   Attempts to limit prices are almost certain to fail in industries with numerous suppliers, simply because the regulating agency must monitor the behavior of so many sellers. People will usually find ways to evade or violate the law, and something like the free-market price will generally reappear. But there is an important difference: Because the evasion process, whatever its form, will have some operating costs, those costs must be borne by someone. Normally, that someone is the consumer.

Auxiliary Restrictions   Fears that a system of price controls will break down invariably lead to regulations designed to shore up the shaky edifice. Consumers may be told when and from whom they are permitted to buy. The powers of the police and the courts may be used to prevent the entry of new suppliers. Occasionally, an intricate system of market subdivision is imposed, giving each class of firms a protected sphere in which others are not permitted to operate. For example, in New York City, there are laws banning conversion of rent-controlled apartments to condominiums.

Limitation of Volume of Transactions   To the extent that controls succeed in affecting prices, they can be expected to reduce the volume of transactions. Curiously, this is true regardless of whether the regulated price is above or below the free-market equilibrium price. If it is set above the equilibrium price, the quantity demanded will be below the equilibrium quantity. On the other hand, if the imposed price is set below the free-market level, the quantity supplied will be reduced. Because sales volume cannot exceed either the quantity supplied or the quantity demanded, a reduction in the volume of transactions is the result.[9]

Misallocation of Resources   Departures from free-market prices are likely to result in misuse of the economy's resources because the connection between production costs and prices is broken. For example, Russian farmers used to feed their farm animals bread instead of unprocessed grains because price ceilings kept the price of bread ludicrously low. In addition, just as more complex locks lead to more sophisticated burglary tools, more complex regulations lead to the use of yet more resources for their avoidance.

Economists put it this way. Free markets are capable of dealing efficiently with the three basic coordination tasks outlined in Chapter 2: deciding what to produce, how to produce it, and to whom the goods should be distributed. Price controls throw a monkey wrench into the market mechanism. Although the market is surely not flawless, and government interferences often have praiseworthy goals, good intentions are not enough. Any government that sets out to repair what it sees as a defect in the market mechanism runs the risk of causing even more serious damage elsewhere. As a prominent economist once quipped, societies that are too willing to interfere with the operation of free markets soon find that the invisible hand is nowhere to be seen.

A SIMPLE BUT POWERFUL LESSON

Astonishing as it may seem, many people in authority do not understand the law of supply and demand, or they act as if it does not exist. For example, a few years ago the *New York Times* carried a dramatic front-page picture of the president of Kenya setting fire to a large pile of elephant tusks that had been confiscated from poachers. The accompanying story explained that the burning was intended as a symbolic act to persuade the world to halt the ivory trade.[10] One may certainly doubt whether the burning really touched the hearts of criminal poachers, but one economic effect was clear: By reducing the supply of ivory on the world market, the burning of tusks forced up the price of ivory, which raised the illicit rewards reaped by those who slaughter elephants. That could only encourage more poaching—precisely the opposite of what the Kenyan government sought to accomplish.

SUMMARY

1. An attempt to use government regulations to force prices above or below their equilibrium levels is likely to lead to **shortages** or **surpluses,** to black markets in which goods are sold at illegal prices, and to a variety of other problems. The market always strikes back at attempts to repeal the law of supply and demand.

2. The quantity of a product that is demanded is not a fixed number. Rather, **quantity demanded** depends on such factors as the price of the product, consumer incomes, and the prices of other products.

3. The relationship between quantity demanded and price, holding all other things constant, can be displayed graphically on a **demand curve.**

4. For most products, the higher the price, the lower the quantity demanded. As a result, the demand curve usually has a negative slope.

[9] See Review Question 9 at the end of the chapter.
[10] *The New York Times,* July 19, 1989.

5. The quantity of a product that is supplied depends on its price and many other influences. A **supply curve** is a graphical representation of the relationship between **quantity supplied** and price, holding all other influences constant.

6. For most products, supply curves have positive slopes, meaning that higher prices lead to supply of greater quantities.

7. A change in quantity demanded that is caused by a change in the price of the good is represented by a movement *along* a fixed demand curve. A change in quantity demanded that is caused by a change in any other determinant of quantity demanded is represented by a **shift of the demand curve.**

8. This same distinction applies to the supply curve: Changes in price lead to movements along a fixed supply curve; changes in other determinants of quantity supplied lead to shifts of the entire supply curve.

9. A market is said to be in **equilibrium** when quantity supplied is equal to quantity demanded. The equilibrium price and quantity are shown by the point on the supply-demand graph where the supply and demand curves intersect. The **law of supply and demand** states that price and quantity tend to gravitate to this point in a free market.

10. Changes in consumer incomes, tastes, technology, prices of competing products, and many other influences lead to shifts in either the demand curve or the supply curve and produce changes in price and quantity that can be determined from **supply-demand diagrams.**

11. A tax on a good generally leads to a rise in the price at which the taxed product is sold. The rise in price is generally less than the tax, so consumers usually pay less than the entire tax.

12. Consumers generally pay only part of a tax because the resulting rise in price leads them to buy less and the cut in the quantity they demand helps to force price down.

KEY TERMS

Invisible hand 34	Quantity supplied 39	Surplus 42
Quantity demanded 35	Supply schedule 40	Equilibrium 42
Demand schedule 36	Supply curve 40	Law of supply and demand 43
Demand curve 36	Supply-demand diagram 42	Price ceiling 47
Shift in a demand curve 37	Shortage 42	Price floor 50

QUESTIONS FOR REVIEW

1. How often do you rent videos? Would you do so more often if a rental cost half as much? Distinguish between your demand curve for home videos and your "quantity demanded" at the current price.

2. What shapes would you expect for demand curves for the following:
   a. A medicine that means life or death for a patient
   b. French fries in a food court with kiosks offering many types of food

3. The following are the assumed supply and demand schedules for hamburgers in Collegetown:

Demand Schedule		Supply Schedule	
Price	Quantity Demanded per Year (thousands)	Price	Quantity Supplied per Year (thousands)
$2.25	12	$2.25	30
2.00	16	2.00	28
1.75	20	1.75	26
1.50	24	1.50	24
1.25	28	1.25	22
1.00	32	1.00	20

a. Plot the supply and demand curves and indicate the equilibrium price and quantity.

b. What effect would a decrease in the price of beef (a hamburger input) have on the equilibrium price and quantity of hamburgers, assuming all other things remained constant? Explain your answer with the help of a diagram.

c. What effect would an increase in the price of pizza (a substitute commodity) have on the equilibrium price and quantity of hamburgers, assuming again that all other things remain constant? Use a diagram in your answer.

4. Suppose the supply and demand schedules for bicycles are as they appear below.

a. Graph these curves and show the equilibrium price and quantity.

Price	Quantity Demanded per Year (millions)	Quantity Supplied per Year (millions)
$160	40	24
200	36	28
240	32	32
280	28	36
320	24	40
360	20	44

b. Now suppose that it becomes unfashionable to ride a bicycle, so that the quantity demanded at each price falls by 8 million bikes per year. What is the new equilibrium price and quantity? Show this solution graphically. Explain why the quantity falls by less than 8 million bikes per year.

c. Suppose instead that several major bicycle producers go out of business, thereby reducing the quantity supplied by 8 million bikes at every price. Find the new equilibrium price and quantity, and show it graphically. Explain again why quantity falls by less than 8 million.

d. What are the equilibrium price and quantity if the shifts described in Review Questions 4(b) and 4(c) happen at the same time?

5. The following table summarizes information about the market for principles of economics textbooks:

Price	Quantity Demanded per Year	Quantity Supplied per Year
$40	4,200	200
50	2,200	600
60	1,200	1,200
70	700	2,000
80	550	3,000

a. What is the market equilibrium price and quantity of textbooks?

b. To quell outrage over tuition increases, the college places a $50 limit on the price of textbooks. How many textbooks will be sold now?

c. While the price limit is still in effect, automated publishing increases the efficiency of textbook production. Show graphically the likely effect of this innovation on the market price and quantity.

6. Show how the following demand curves are likely to shift in response to the indicated changes:

a. The effect of a drought on the demand curve for umbrellas

b. The effect of higher popcorn prices on the demand curve for movie tickets

c. The effect on the demand curve for coffee of a decline in the price of Coca-Cola

7. Discuss the likely effects of the following:

a. Rent ceilings on the market for apartments

b. Floors under wheat prices on the market for wheat

Use supply-demand diagrams to show what may happen in each case.

8. U.S. government price supports for milk led to a chronic surplus of milk. In an effort to reduce the surplus about a decade ago, Congress offered to pay dairy farmers to slaughter cows. Use two diagrams, one for the milk market and one for the meat market, to illustrate how this policy should have affected the price of meat. (Assume that meat is sold in an unregulated market.)

9. It is claimed in this chapter that either price floors or price ceilings reduce the actual quantity exchanged in a market. Use a diagram or diagrams to test this conclusion, and explain the common sense behind it.

10. The same rightward shift of the demand curve may produce a very small or a very large increase in quantity, depending on the slope of the supply curve. Explain this conclusion with diagrams.

11. In 1981, when regulations were holding the price of natural gas below its free-market level, then-Congressman Jack Kemp of New York said the following in an interview with the *New York Times*: "We need to decontrol natural gas, and get production of natural gas up to a higher level so we can bring down the price."[11] Evaluate the congressman's statement.

12. From 1990 to 1997 in the United States, the number of working men grew by 6.7 percent; the number of working women grew by 11 percent. During this time, average wages for men grew by 20 percent, while average wages for women grew by 25 percent. Which of the following two explanations seems more consistent with the data?

a. Women decided to work more, raising their relative supply (relative to men).

b. Discrimination against women declined, raising the relative (to men) demand for female workers.

13. The two accompanying diagrams show supply and demand curves for two substitute commodities: tapes and compact discs (CDs).

a. On the right-hand diagram, show what happens when rising raw material prices make it costlier to produce tapes.

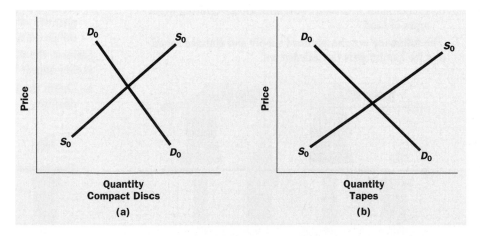

(a)

(b)

---

b. On the left-hand diagram, show what happens to the market for CDs.

14. Consider the market for milk discussed in this chapter (Tables 3-1 through 3-3 and Figures 3-1 and 3-8). Suppose that the government decides to fight kidney stones by levying a tax of 30 cents per quart on sales of milk. Follow these steps to analyze the effects of the tax:

   a. Construct the new supply schedule (to replace Table 3-2) that relates quantity supplied to the price that consumers pay.

   b. Graph the new supply curve constructed in Review Question 14(a) on the supply-demand diagram depicted in Figure 3-8. What are the new equilibrium price and quantity?

   c. Does the tax succeed in its goal of reducing the consumption of milk?

   d. How much does the equilibrium price increase? Is the price rise greater than, equal to, or less than the 30-cent tax?

   e. Who actually pays the tax, consumers or producers? (This may be a good question to discuss in class.)

15. (More difficult) The demand and supply curves for T-shirts in Touristtown, U.S.A., are given by the following equations:

$$Q = 24,000 - 500P \qquad Q = 6,000 + 1,000P$$

where P is measured in dollars and Q is the number of T-shirts sold per year.

   a. Find the equilibrium price and quantity algebraically.

   b. If tourists decide they do not really like T-shirts that much, which of the following might be the new demand curve?

$$Q = 21,000 - 500P \qquad Q = 27,000 - 500P$$

   Find the equilibrium price and quantity after the shift of the demand curve.

   c. If, instead, two new stores that sell T-shirts open up in town, which of the following might be the new supply curve?

$$Q = 3,000 + 1,000P \qquad Q = 9,000 + 1,000P$$

   Find the equilibrium price and quantity after the shift of the supply curve.

THE MACROECONOMY: AGGREGATE SUPPLY AND DEMAND

Macroeconomics is the headline-grabbing part of economics. When economic news appears on the front page of your daily newspaper or is reported on the nightly television news, you are most likely reading or hearing about some macroeconomic development in the national or world economy. The Federal Reserve has just raised interest rates. Inflation remains low. Jobs are plentiful in the United States, but scarce in Japan. The federal government's budget is in deficit. The euro or the Brazilian real is falling in value. These developments are all macroeconomic news stories. But what do they mean?

Part II is your introduction to macroeconomics. It will first acquaint you with some of the major concepts of macroeconomics—things that you hear about every day, such as gross domestic product (GDP), inflation, unemployment, and economic growth (Chapters 4 and 5). Next, it will introduce the basic theory that we use to interpret and understand macroeconomic events (Chapters 6 through 9). By the time you finish Chapter 9—which is only six chapters away—those newspaper articles should make a lot more sense.

The Realm of Macroeconomics

Where the telescope ends, the microscope begins.
Which of the two has the grander view?

VICTOR HUGO

By time-honored tradition, economics is divided into two fields: *microeconomics* and *macroeconomics.* These inelegant words are derived from the Greek, where *micro* means something small and *macro* means something large. Chapters 2 and 3 introduced you to microeconomics. This chapter does the same for macroeconomics.

How do the two branches of the discipline differ? It is *not* a matter of using different tools. Supply and demand provide the basic organizing framework for constructing macroeconomic models, just as they do for microeconomic models. Rather, the distinction is based on the issues addressed. An example of a macroeconomic question starts at the top of the next page.

CONTENTS

Issue: Why Did Growth Slow Down So Sharply in 2000 and 2001?

From early 1996 through the middle of 2000, the U.S. economy confounded economic experts by growing at an annual rate of 4.4 percent—a growth performance markedly superior to its average growth rate over the previous quarter-century. But then it slowed down abruptly, to an average annual growth rate of merely 0.2 percent from mid-2000 through the end of 2001. What happened?

As this chapter will show you, sharp fluctuations in the economy's growth rate are not unusual. They have been happening regularly for as long as we have data. It will be several chapters before we are in a position to offer a complete explanation of what happened in 2000–2001, but this chapter will sketch the theory that economists use to explain why our economy's growth rate goes up and down.

DRAWING A LINE BETWEEN MACROECONOMICS AND MICROECONOMICS

In microeconomics, the spotlight is on *how individual decision-making units behave.* For example, the dairy farmers of Chapter 3 are individual decision makers; so are the consumers who purchase the milk. How do they decide which actions are in their own best interests? How are these millions of decisions coordinated by the market mechanism, and with what consequences? Questions such as these lie at the heart of microeconomics.

Although Plato and Aristotle might wince at the abuse of their language, microeconomics applies to the decisions of some astonishingly large units. The annual sales of General Electric and General Motors, for example, exceed the total production of many nations. Yet someone who studies GE's pricing policies is a microeconomist, whereas someone who studies inflation in Monaco is a macroeconomist. The micro-versus-macro distinction in economics is thus certainly not based solely on size.

What, then, is the basis for this long-standing distinction? The answer is that, whereas microeconomics focuses on the decisions of individual units, no matter how large, macroeconomics concentrates on *the behavior of entire economies*, no matter how small. Microeconomists might look at a single company's pricing and output decisions; macroeconomists study the overall price level, unemployment rate, and other things that we call *economic aggregates.*

Aggregation and Macroeconomics

An "economic aggregate" is simply an *abstraction* that people use to describe some salient feature of economic life. For example, although we observe the prices of gasoline, telephone calls, and movie tickets every day, we never actually see "the price level." Yet many people—not just economists—find it meaningful to speak of "the cost of living." In fact, the government's attempts to measure it are widely publicized by the news media each month.

Among the most important of these abstract notions is the concept of *domestic product*, which represents the total production of a nation's economy. The process by which real objects such as software, baseballs, and theater tickets are combined into an abstraction called total domestic product is **aggregation,** and it is one of the foundations of macroeconomics. We can illustrate it by a simple example.

An imaginary nation called Agraria produces nothing but foodstuffs to sell to consumers. Rather than deal separately with the many markets for pizzas, candy bars, hamburgers, and so on, macroeconomists group them all into a single abstract "market for output." Thus, when macroeconomists announce that output in Agraria grew 10 percent last year, are they referring to more potatoes or hot dogs, more soybeans

Aggregation means combining many individual markets into one overall market.

or green peppers? The answer is: They do not care. In the aggregate measures of macroeconomics, output is output, no matter what form it takes.

The Foundations of Aggregation

Amalgamating many markets into one means ignoring distinctions among different products. Can we really believe that no one cares whether the national output of Agraria consists of $800,000 worth of pickles and $200,000 worth of ravioli rather than $500,000 each of lettuce and tomatoes? Surely this is too much to swallow. Macroeconomists certainly do not believe that no one cares; instead, they rest the case for aggregation on two foundations:

1. While the *composition* of demand and supply in the various markets may be terribly important for *some* purposes (such as how income is distributed and what kinds of diets the people enjoy), it may be of little consequence for the economy-wide issues of growth, inflation, and unemployment—the issues that concern macroeconomists.

2. During economic fluctuations, markets tend to move up or down together. When demand in the economy rises, there is more demand for potatoes *and* tomatoes, more demand for artichokes *and* pickles, more demand for ravioli *and* hot dogs.

Although there are exceptions to these two principles, both seem serviceable enough as approximations. In fact, if they were not, there would be no discipline called macroeconomics, and a full-year course in economics could be reduced to a half-year. Lest this cause you a twinge of regret, bear in mind that many people believe that unemployment and inflation would be far more difficult to control without macroeconomics—which would be a lot worse.

The Line of Demarcation Revisited

These two principles—that the composition of demand and supply may not matter for some purposes, and that markets normally move together—enable us to draw a different kind of dividing line between microeconomics and macroeconomics.

In macroeconomics, we typically assume that most details of resource allocation and income distribution are relatively unimportant to the study of the overall rates of inflation and unemployment. In microeconomics, we generally ignore inflation, unemployment, and growth, focusing instead on how individual markets allocate resources and distribute income.

To use a well-worn metaphor, a macroeconomist analyzes the size of the economic "pie," paying scant attention to what is inside it or to how it gets divided among the dinner guests. A microeconomist, on the other hand, assumes that the pie is of the right size and shape, and frets over its ingredients and who gets to eat it. If you have ever baked or eaten a pie, you will realize that either approach alone is a trifle myopic.

Economics is divided into macroeconomics and microeconomics largely for the sake of pedagogical clarity. In reality, the crucial interconnection between macroeconomics and microeconomics is with us all the time. There is, after all, only one economy.

SUPPLY AND DEMAND IN MACROECONOMICS

Whether you are taking a course that concentrates on macroeconomics or one that focuses on microeconomics, the discussion of supply and demand in Chapter 3 serves

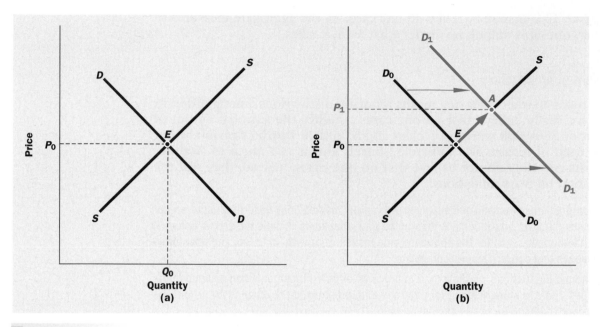

■ FIGURE 4-1

Two Interpretations of a Shift in the Demand Curve

as an invaluable introduction. Supply and demand analysis is just as fundamental to macroeconomics as it is to microeconomics.

■ A Quick Review

Figure 4-1 shows two diagrams that should look familiar from Chapter 3. In Figure 4-1(a), we find a downward-sloping demand curve, labeled DD, and an upward-sloping supply curve, labeled SS. Because the figure is a multipurpose diagram, the axes labeled "Price" and "Quantity" do not specify any particular commodity. To start on familiar terrain, first imagine that this graph depicts the market for milk, so the vertical axis measures the price of milk and the horizontal axis measures the quantity of milk demanded and supplied. As we know, if nothing interferes with the operation of a free market, equilibrium will be at point E with a price P_0 and a quantity of output Q_0.

Next, suppose something happens to shift the demand curve outward. For example, we learned in Chapter 3 that an increase in consumer incomes might have this effect. Figure 4-1(b) shows this shift as a rightward movement of the demand curve from D_0D_0 to D_1D_1. Equilibrium shifts from point E to point A, so both price and output rise.

■ Moving to Macroeconomic Aggregates

Now let's switch from microeconomics to macroeconomics. To do so, we reinterpret Figure 4-1 as representing the market for an abstract object called "domestic product"—one of those economic aggregates that we described earlier. No one has ever seen, touched, or eaten a unit of domestic product, but these kinds of abstractions provide a foundation for macroeconomic analysis.

Consistent with this reinterpretation, think of the price measured on the vertical axis as being another abstraction—the overall price index, or "cost of living."[1] Then the curve DD in Figure 4-1(a) is called an **aggregate demand curve,** and the curve

The **aggregate demand curve** shows the quantity of domestic product that is demanded at each possible value of the price level.

The **aggregate supply curve** shows the quantity of domestic product that is supplied at each possible value of the price level.

Inflation refers to a sustained increase in the general price level.

A **recession** is a period of time during which the total output of the economy declines.

---

[1] The appendix to Chapter 5 explains how such price indexes are calculated.

SS is called an **aggregate supply curve.** We will develop an economic theory to derive these curves explicitly in Chapters 6 through 9. As we shall see there, the curves are rather different from the microeconomic counterparts we encountered in Chapter 3.

Inflation

With this macroeconomic reinterpretation, Figure 4-1(b) depicts the problem of **inflation.** We see from the figure that the outward shift of the aggregate demand curve, whatever its cause, pushes the price level up. If aggregate demand keeps shifting out month after month, the economy will suffer from inflation—meaning a sustained increase in the general price level.

Recession and Unemployment

The second principal issue of macroeconomics, recession and unemployment, also can be illustrated on a supply-demand diagram, this time by shifting the demand curve in the opposite direction. Figure 4-2 repeats the supply and demand curves of Figure 4-1(a) and in addition depicts a leftward shift of the aggregate demand curve from D_0D_0 to D_2D_2. Equilibrium now moves from point E to point B so that domestic product (total output) declines. This is what we normally mean by a **recession**—a period of time during which production falls and people lose jobs.

Economic Growth

Figure 4-3 illustrates macroeconomists' third area of concern: the process of economic growth. Here the original aggregate demand and supply curves are, once again, D_0D_0 and S_0S_0, which intersect at point E. But now we consider the possibility that *both* curves shift to the right over time, moving to D_1D_1 and S_1S_1, respectively. The new intersection point is C, and the red arrow running from point E to point C shows the economy's growth path. Over this period of time, domestic product grows from Q_0 to Q_1.

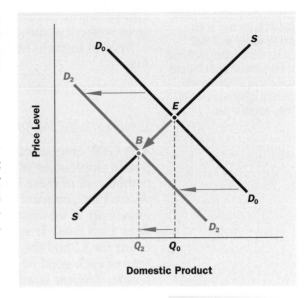

FIGURE 4-2
An Economy Slipping into a Recession

FIGURE 4-3
Economic Growth

GROSS DOMESTIC PRODUCT

Up to now, we have been somewhat cavalier in using the phrase "domestic product." Let's now get more specific. Of the various ways to measure an economy's total output, the most popular choice by far is the **gross domestic product,** or **GDP** for short—a term you have probably encountered in the news media. GDP is the most comprehensive measure of the output of all the factories, offices, and shops in the

Gross domestic product (GDP) is the sum of the money values of all final goods and services produced in the domestic economy and sold on organized markets during a specified period of time, usually a year.

United States. Specifically, it is the sum of the *money values* of all *final* goods and services *produced* in the *domestic* economy within the year.

Several features of this definition need to be underscored.[2] First, you will notice that:

> **We add up the money values of things.**

Money as the Measuring Rod: Real Versus Nominal GDP

The GDP consists of a bewildering variety of goods and services: computer chips and potato chips, tanks and textbooks, ballet performances and rock concerts. How can we combine all of these into a single number? To an economist, there is a natural way to do so: First, convert every good and service into *money* terms, and then add all the money up. If we want to add 10 apples and 20 oranges, we first ask: How much *money* does each cost? If apples cost 20 cents and oranges cost 25 cents, then the apples count for $2 and the oranges for $5, so the sum is $7 worth of "output." The market *price* of each good or service is used as an indicator of its *value* to society for a simple reason: *Someone* is willing to pay that much money for it.

Nominal GDP is calculated by valuing all outputs at current prices.

This decision raises the question of what prices to use in valuing different outputs. The official data offer two choices. Most obviously, we can value each good and service at the price at which it was actually sold. If we take this approach, the resulting measure is called **nominal GDP**, or *money GDP*, or *GDP in current dollars*. This seems like a perfectly sensible choice, but it has one serious drawback as a measure of output: Nominal GDP rises when prices rise, even if there is no increase in actual production. For example, if hamburgers cost $2.00 this year but cost only $1.50 last year, then 100 hamburgers will contribute $200 to this year's nominal GDP whereas they contributed only $150 to last year's nominal GDP. But 100 hamburgers are still 100 hamburgers—output has not grown.

For this reason, government statisticians have devised alternative measures that correct for inflation by valuing goods and services produced in *different* years at *the same* set of prices. For example, if the hamburgers were valued at $1.50 each in both years, $150 worth of hamburger output would be included in GDP *in each year*. In practice, such calculations can be quite complicated, but the details need not worry us in an introductory course. Suffice it to say that, when the calculations are done, we obtain **real GDP** or *GDP in constant dollars*. The news media often refer to this measure as "GDP corrected for inflation." Throughout most of this book, and certainly whenever we are discussing the nation's output, we will be concerned with *real* GDP.

Real GDP is calculated by valuing outputs of different years at common prices. Therefore, real GDP is a far better measure than nominal GDP of changes in total production.

The distinction between nominal and real GDP leads us to a working definition of a *recession* as a period in which *real* GDP declines. For example, between the first and third quarters of 2001, nominal GDP *rose* from $10,025 billion to $10,096 billion, but real GDP *fell* from $9,882 billion to $9,835 billion. In fact, it has become conventional to say that a recession occurs when real GDP declines for two or more consecutive quarters, as happened in 2001.

What Gets Counted in GDP?

The next important aspect of the definition of GDP is that:

> **The GDP for a particular year includes only goods and services produced within the year. Sales of items produced in previous years are explicitly excluded.**

For example, suppose you buy a perfectly beautiful 1980 Thunderbird next week and are overjoyed by your purchase. The national income statistician will not share your glee. She counted that car in the GDP of 1980, when it was first produced and

---

[2] Certain exceptions to the definition are dealt with in the appendix to Chapter 7. Some instructors may prefer to take up that material here.

sold, and will never count it again. The same is true of houses. The resale values of houses do not count in GDP because they were counted in the years they were built.

Next, you will note from the definition of gross domestic product that:

Only final goods and services count in the GDP.

The adjective *final* is the key word here. For example, when Dell buys computer chips from Intel, the transaction is not included in the GDP because Dell does not want the chips for itself. It buys them only to resell to consumers. Only when the chips are sold to consumers as components of computers are they considered a final product. When Dell buys them from Intel, economists consider the chips to be an **intermediate good.** The GDP excludes sales of intermediate goods and services because, if they were included, we would wind up counting the same outputs several times.[3] For example, if chips sold to computer manufacturers were included in GDP, we would count the same chip when it was sold to the computer maker and then again when the computer was sold to a consumer.

Next, note that:

The adjective *domestic* in the definition of GDP denotes production within the geographic boundaries of the United States.

Some Americans work abroad, and many American companies have offices or factories in foreign countries. All of these people and businesses produce valuable outputs, but none of it counts in the GDP of the United States. (It counts, instead, in the GDPs of the other countries.) On the other hand, a number of foreigners and foreign companies produce goods and services in the United States. All this activity does count in our GDP.[4]

Finally, the definition of GDP notes that:

For the most part, only goods and services that pass through organized markets count in the GDP.

This restriction, of course, excludes many economic activities. For example, illegal activities are not included in the GDP. Thus, gambling services in Atlantic City are part of GDP, but gambling services in Chicago are not. Garage sales, although sometimes lucrative, are not included either. The definition reflects the statisticians' inability to measure the value of many of the economy's most important activities, such as housework, do-it-yourself repairs, and leisure time. These activities certainly result in currently produced goods or services, but they all lack that important measuring rod—a market price.

This omission results in certain oddities. For example, suppose that each of two neighboring families hires the other to clean house, generously paying $1,000 per week for the services. Each family can easily afford such generosity because it collects an identical salary from its neighbor. Nothing real has changed, but GDP goes up by $104,000 per year. If this example seems trivial, you may be interested to know that, according to one estimate, America's GDP would be a stunning 44 percent higher if unpaid housework were valued at market prices.[5]

Limitations of the GDP: What GDP Is Not

Having seen in some detail what the GDP *is*, let's examine what it *is not*. In particular:

Gross domestic product is not a measure of the nation's economic well-being.

> **Final goods and services** are those that are purchased by their ultimate users.

> An **intermediate good** is a good purchased for resale or for use in producing another good.

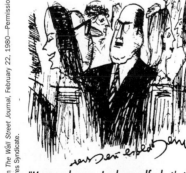

SOURCE: From *The Wall Street Journal*, February 22, 1980—Permission, Cartoon Features Syndicate.

"More and more, I ask myself what's the point of pursuing the meaning of the universe if you can't have a rising GNP."

---

[3] Actually, there is another way to add up the GDP by counting a portion of each intermediate transaction. This is explained in the appendix to Chapter 7.

[4] There is another concept, called gross *national* product, which counts the goods and services produced by all Americans, regardless of where they work. For consistency, the outputs produced by foreigners working in the United States are not included in GNP. In practice, the two measures—GDP and GNP—are very close.

[5] Ann Chadeau, "What Is Households' Non-Market Production Worth?" *OECD Economic Studies*, 18, 1992, pp. 85–103.

The GDP is not intended to measure economic well-being and does not do so for several reasons:

Only Market Activity Is Included in GDP   As we have just seen, a great deal of work done in the home contributes to the nation's well-being but is not counted in GDP because it has no price tag. One important implication of this exclusion arises when we try to compare the GDPs of developed and less developed countries. Americans are always amazed to hear that the per-capita GDPs of the poorest African countries are less than $250 per year. Surely, no one could survive in America on $5 per week. How can Africans do it? Part of the answer, of course, is that these people are terribly poor. But another part of the answer is that:

International GDP comparisons are vastly misleading when the two countries differ greatly in the fraction of economic activity that each conducts in organized markets.

This fraction is relatively large in the United States and relatively small in the less developed countries, so when we compare their respective measured GDPs, we are not comparing the same economic activities. Many things that get counted in the U.S. GDP are not counted in the GDPs of less developed nations because they do not pass through markets. It is ludicrous to think that these people, poor as they are, survive on what an American thinks of as $5 per week.

A second implication is that GDP statistics take no account of the so-called underground economy—a term that includes not just criminal activities, but also a great deal of legitimate business that is conducted in cash or by barter to escape the tax collector. Naturally, we have no good data on the size of the underground economy. Some observers, however, think that it may amount to 10 percent or more of U.S. GDP—and much more in some foreign countries.

GDP Places No Value on Leisure   As a country gets richer, its citizens normally take more and more leisure time. If that is true, a better measure of national well-being that includes the value of leisure would display faster growth than conventionally measured GDP. For example, the length of the typical workweek in the United States fell steadily for many decades, which means that growth in GDP systematically *underestimated* the growth in national well-being. But lately this trend has stopped, and may even have reversed. (See "Are Americans Working More?")

"Bads" as Well as "Goods" Get Counted in GDP   There are also reasons why the GDP *overstates* how well-off we are. Suppose there is a natural disaster—such as an earthquake or flood. Surely the well-being of the United States would be diminished by such a catastrophe. People would be injured; many homes and businesses would be destroyed. Yet the disaster would probably raise GDP. Consumers would spend more to clean up and replace lost homes and possessions. Businesses would spend more to rebuild and repair damaged buildings. The government would spend more for disaster relief and cleanup. Yet no one would think America was better off for this additional GDP.

Wars represent an extreme example. Mobilization for a war fought on some other nation's soil normally causes a country's GDP to rise rapidly. But men and women serving in the military could be producing civilian output instead. Factories assigned to produce armaments could instead be making cars, washing machines, and televisions. A country at war is surely worse off than a country at peace, but this fact will not be reflected in its GDP.

Ecological Costs Are Not Netted Out of the GDP   Many productive activities of a modern industrial economy have undesirable side effects on the environment. Automobiles provide an essential means of transportation, but they also despoil the atmosphere. Factories pollute rivers and lakes while manufacturing valuable commodities. Almost everything seems to produce garbage, which creates serious disposal problems. None of these ecological costs are deducted from the GDP in an effort to give us a truer measure of the *net* increase in economic welfare that our economy produces. Is this omission foolish? Not if

Are Americans Working More?

According to conventional wisdom, the workweek in the United States is steadily shrinking, leaving Americans with more and more leisure time to enjoy. But, in a 1991 book, economist Juliet Schor argued that this view is wrong: Americans are really working longer and longer hours. Her findings are both provocative and controversial.

In the last twenty years the amount of time Americans have spent at their jobs has risen steadily. . . . Americans report that they have only sixteen and a half hours of leisure a week, after the obligations of job and household are taken care of. . . . If present trends continue, by the end of the century Americans will be spending as much time at their jobs as they did back in the nineteen twenties.

The rise in worktime was unexpected. For nearly a hundred years, hours had been declining. . . . Equally surprising, but also hardly recognized, has been the deviation from Western Europe. After progressing in tandem for nearly a century, the United States veered off into a trajectory of declining leisure, while in Europe work has been disappearing. . . . U.S. manufacturing employees currently work 320 more hours [per year]—the equivalent of over two months—than their counterparts in West Germany or France. . . . We have paid a price for prosperity. . . . We are eating more, but we are burning up those calories at work. We have color televisions and compact disc players, but we need them to unwind after a stressful day at

SOURCE: © Photopia

the office. We take vacations, but we work so hard throughout the year that they become indispensable to our sanity.

SOURCE: Juliet B. Schor, *The Overworked American* (New York: Basic Books; 1991), pp. 1–2, 10–11.

"Green" GDP

GDP as conventionally measured does not net out the costs of pollution, nor does it "charge" for using up natural resources. The consequence, some critics argue, is that GDP *overstates* economic well-being. A few years ago, the U.S. government embarked on a project to develop experimental measures that would adjust for each of these factors—so-called green GDP. Unfortunately, this effort proved to be politically controversial. Although environmentalists supported it, the Republican Congress cut off funding for it in 1994.

Politics aside, the first phase of the research turned up a surprising result: Making an adjustment for the depletion of mineral resources hardly changed the official GDP numbers. Specifically, when government statisticians tabulated the U.S. stock of mineral resources to estimate how much had been consumed from 1958 to 1991, they found that proven supplies had barely declined.

How can this be? In a purely physical sense, of course, it cannot be. America certainly had fewer actual mineral deposits in the ground in 1991 than in 1958. However, new discoveries of minerals and new tech-

SOURCE: © Rob Badger/Getty Images

nologies compensated for all the mining, so that *proven* reserves barely fell over the 33-year period.

we remember that national income statisticians are trying to measure economic activity conducted through organized markets, not national welfare (but see the box on "'Green' GDP"). Having defined several of the basic concepts of macroeconomics, let us breathe some life into them by perusing the economic history of the United States.

THE ECONOMY ON A ROLLER COASTER

Growth, but with Fluctuations

The most salient fact about the U.S. economy has been its *growth*; it gets bigger almost every year. Nominal gross domestic product in 2003 was around $11 trillion, about 22 times as much as in 1959. In Figure 4-4, the black curve shows that extraordinary up-

FIGURE 4-4

Nominal GDP, Real GDP, and Real GDP per Capita Since 1959

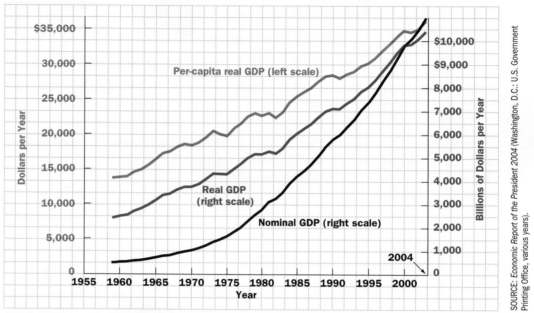

NOTE: Real GDP figures are in 1996 dollars.

SOURCE: *Economic Report of the President 2004* (Washington, D.C.: U.S. Government Printing Office, various years).

ward march. But, as the discussion of nominal versus real GDP suggests, a large part of this apparent growth was simply inflation. Because of higher prices, the *purchasing power* of each 2003 dollar was actually only about one-sixth of each 1959 dollar. Corrected for inflation, we see that *real GDP* (the blue curve in the figure) was only about four times greater in 2003 than in 1959.

Another reason for the growth of GDP is population growth. A nation becomes richer only if its GDP grows *faster* than its population. To see how much richer the United States has actually become since 1959, we must divide real GDP by the size of the population to obtain *real GDP per-capita*—which is the red line in Figure 4-4. It turns out that real output per person in 2003 was only about three times as much as in 1959. That is still not a bad performance.

If aggregate supply and demand grew smoothly from one year to the next, as was depicted in Figure 4-3, the economy would expand at some steady rate. But U.S. economic history displays a less regular pattern—of alternating periods of rapid and slow growth that are called *economic fluctuations*, or sometimes just *business cycles*. In some years—five since 1959, to be exact—real GDP actually declined.[6] Such *recessions*, and their attendant problem of rising unemployment, have been a persistent feature of American economic performance.

The bumps encountered along the American economy's historic growth path stand out more clearly in Figure 4-5, which displays the same data in a different way and extends the time period back to 1870. Here we plot not the *level* of real GDP each

---

[6] The 2001 recession was so mild that real GDP for the full year 2001 was actually higher than in 2000.

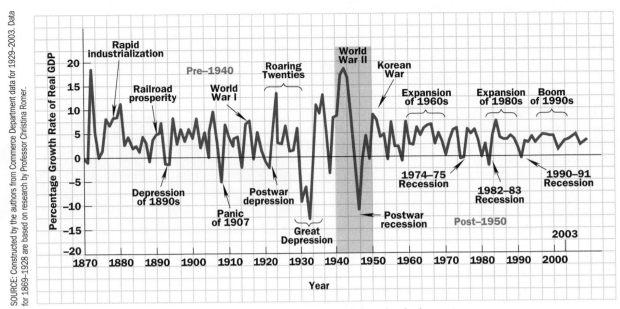

SOURCE: Constructed by the authors from Commerce Department data for 1929–2003. Data for 1869–1928 are based on research by Professor Christina Romer.

Does the growth rate look smoother to the right of the shaded area?

FIGURE 4-5

The Growth Rate of U.S. Real Gross Domestic Product, 1870–2003

Deflation refers to a sustained decrease in the general price level.

year, but rather its *growth rate*—the percentage change from one year to the next. Now the booms and busts that delight and distress people—and swing elections—stand out clearly. From 1983 to 1984, for example, real GDP grew by close to 7 percent, which helped ensure Ronald Reagan's landslide reelection. But from 1990 to 1991, real GDP actually fell by 1 percent, which helped Bill Clinton defeat George H. W. Bush. The growth spurt of the late 1990s is also clearly visible.

Inflation and Deflation

The history of the inflation rate depicted in Figure 4-6 also shows more positive numbers than negative ones—more inflation than **deflation**. Although the price level has risen more than 15-fold since 1869, the upward trend is of rather recent vintage. Prior to World War II, Figure 4-6 shows periods of inflation and deflation, with little or no tendency for one to be more common than the other. Indeed, prices in 1940 were barely higher than those at the close of the Civil War. However, the figure does show some large gyrations in the inflation rate, including sharp bursts of inflation during and immediately

FIGURE 4-6

The Inflation Rate in the United States, 1870–2003

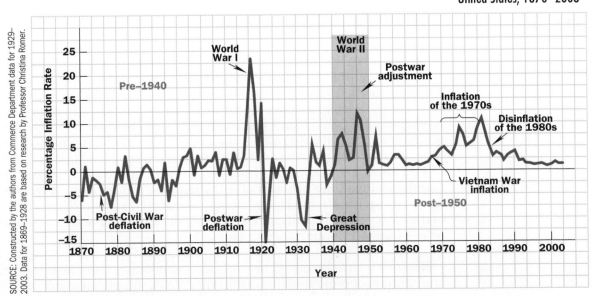

SOURCE: Constructed by the authors from Commerce Department data for 1929–2003. Data for 1869–1928 are based on research by Professor Christina Romer.

Life in "Hooverville"

D uring the worst years of the Great Depression, unemployed workers congregated in shantytowns on the outskirts of many major cities. With a heavy dose of irony, these communities were known as "Hoovervilles," in honor of Herbert Hoover, the president of the United States who preached rugged individualism. A contemporary observer described a Hooverville in New York City as follows:

It was a fairly popular "development" made up of a hundred or so dwellings, each the size of a dog house or chickencoop, often constructed with much ingenuity out of wooden boxes, metal cans, strips of cardboard or old tar paper. Here human beings lived on the margin of civilization by foraging for garbage, junk, and waste lumber. I found some . . . picking through heaps of rubbish they had gathered before their doorways or cooking over open fires or battered oilstoves. Still others spent their days improving their rent-free homes . . . Most of them, according to the police, lived by begging or trading in junk; when all else failed they ate at the soup kitchens or public canteens . . . They lived in fear of being forcibly removed by the authorities, though the neighborhood peo-

SOURCE: © Culver Pictures

ple in many cases helped them and the police tolerated them for the time being.

SOURCE: Mathew Josephson, *Infidel in the Temple* (New York: Knopf; 1967), pp. 82–83.

after the two world wars and dramatic deflations in the 1870s, the 1880s, 1921–1922, and 1929–1933. Recently, as you can see, inflation has been both low and stable.

In sum, although both real GDP, which measures the economy's output, and the price level have grown a great deal over the past 130 years, neither has grown smoothly. The ups and downs of both real growth and inflation have been important economic events that need to be explained. The remainder of Part II, which develops a model of aggregate supply and demand, and Part III, which addresses monetary and fiscal policy, will build a macroeconomic theory designed to do precisely that.

■ The Great Depression

As you look at these graphs, the Great Depression of the 1930s is bound to catch your eye. The decline in economic activity from 1929 to 1933 indicated in Figure 4-5 was the most severe in our nation's history, and the rapid deflation in Figure 4-6 was most unusual. The Depression is but a dim memory now, but those who lived through it—including some of your grandparents—will never forget it.

Human Consequences   Statistics usually conceal the human consequences and drama of economic events. But this is not so of the Great Depression—instead, they stand as bitter testimony to its severity. The production of goods and services dropped an astonishing 30 percent, business investment almost dried up entirely, and the unemployment rate rose ominously from about 3 percent in 1929 to 25 percent in 1933—one person in four was jobless! From the data alone, you can conjure up pictures of soup lines, beggars on street corners, closed factories, and homeless families. (See "Life in 'Hooverville.'")

The Great Depression was a worldwide event; no country was spared its ravages. It literally changed the histories of many nations. In Germany, it facilitated the ascendancy of Nazism. In the United States, it enabled Franklin Roosevelt to engineer one of the most dramatic political realignments in our history and to push through a host of political and economic reforms.

A Revolution in Economic Thought   The worldwide depression also caused a much-needed revolution in economic thinking. Until the 1930s, the prevailing economic theory held that a capitalist economy occasionally misbehaved but had a natural tendency to cure recessions or inflations by itself. The roller coaster bounced around but did not run off the tracks.

But the stubbornness of the Great Depression shook almost everyone's faith in the ability of the economy to correct itself. In Cambridge, England, this questioning attitude led John Maynard Keynes, one of the world's most renowned economists, to write *The General Theory of Employment, Interest, and Money* (1936). Probably the most important economics book of the 20th century, it carried a rather revolutionary message. Keynes rejected the idea that the economy naturally gravitated toward smooth growth and high levels of employment, asserting instead that if a pessimistic outlook led business firms and consumers to curtail their spending plans, the economy might be condemned to years of stagnation.

SOURCE: © Corbis

John Maynard Keynes

Thought of in terms of our aggregate demand–aggregate supply framework, Keynes suggested that there were times when the aggregate demand curve shifted inward—as depicted in Figure 4-2 on page 63. As that figure showed, the consequence would be declining output and deflation.

Although this doleful prognosis sounded all too realistic at the time, Keynes closed his book on a hopeful note, for he showed how government actions might prod the economy out of its depressed state. The lessons he taught the world then are among the lessons we will be learning in the rest of Part II and in Part III (along with many qualifications that economists have learned since the publication of Keynes's book). These lessons show how governments can manage their economies so that recessions will not turn into depressions and depressions will not last as long as the Great Depression.

While Keynes was working on *The General Theory*, he wrote his friend George Bernard Shaw that, "I believe myself to be writing a book on economic theory which will largely revolutionize . . . the way the world thinks about economic problems." In many ways, he was right.

From World War II to 1973

The Great Depression finally ended when the United States mobilized for war in the early 1940s. As government spending rose to extraordinarily high levels, it gave aggregate demand a big boost. The economy boomed, and the unemployment rate fell as low as 1.2 percent during the war.

Figure 4-1(b) on page 62 suggested that spending spurts such as this one should lead to inflation. But much of the potential inflation during World War II was contained by price controls. With prices held below the levels at which quantity supplied equaled quantity demanded, shortages of consumer goods were common. Sugar, butter, gasoline, cloth, and a host of other goods were strictly rationed. When controls were lifted after the war, prices shot up.

The period after the war was one of strong growth marred by several short recessions. Moderate but persistent inflation also became a fact of life. Then came the fabulous 1960s, a period of unprecedented—and noninflationary—growth that was credited to the success of the economic policies that Keynes had prescribed in the 1930s. For a while, it looked as if we could avoid both unemployment and inflation, as aggregate demand and aggregate supply expanded in approximate balance. (Refer back to Figure 4-3 on page 63.) But the optimistic verdicts were premature on both counts.

Inflation came first, beginning about 1966. Its major cause was high levels of wartime spending, as it had been so many times in the past. This time, the Vietnam War pushed aggregate demand up too fast. Unemployment then rose when the economy ground to a halt in 1969. Despite a short and mild recession, inflation continued at 5 to 6 percent per year. Faced with persistent inflation, President Richard Nixon stunned the nation by instituting wage and price controls in 1971, the first time this tactic had ever been employed in peacetime. The controls program held inflation in check for a while. But inflation worsened dramatically in 1973, mainly because of an explosion in food prices caused by poor harvests around the world.

The Great Stagflation, 1973–1980

In 1973 things began to get much worse, not only for the United States, but for all oil-importing nations. A 1973 war between Israel and the Arab nations precipitated a quadrupling of oil prices by the Organization of Petroleum Exporting Countries (OPEC). At the same time, continued poor harvests in many parts of the globe pushed world food prices higher. Prices of other raw materials also skyrocketed. Naturally, higher costs of fuel and other materials soon were reflected in the prices of manufactured goods.

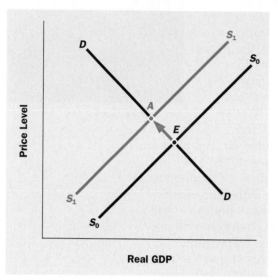

By unhappy coincidence, these events came just as the Nixon administration was lifting wage and price controls. Just as had happened after World War II, the elimination of controls led to a temporary acceleration of inflation as prices that had been held artificially below equilibrium levels were allowed to rise. For all of these reasons, the inflation rate in the United States soared above 12 percent during 1974.

Meanwhile, the U.S. economy was slipping into what was, up to then, its longest and most severe recession since the 1930s. Real GDP fell between late 1973 and early 1975, and the unemployment rate rose to nearly 9 percent. With both inflation and unemployment unusually virulent in 1974 and 1975, the press coined a new term—**stagflation**—to refer to the simultaneous occurrence of economic *stag*nation and rapid in*flation*. Conceptually, what was happening in this episode is that the economy's aggregate supply curve, which normally moves outward from one year to the next, shifted *inward* instead. When this happens, the economy moves from a point like *E* to a point like *A* in Figure 4-7. Real GDP declines as the price level rises.

FIGURE 4-7

The Effects of an Adverse Supply Shift

Stagflation is inflation that occurs while the economy is growing slowly ("stagnating") or in a recession.

Thanks partly to government actions, but mostly to natural economic forces, the economy recovered. Unfortunately, stagflation came roaring back in 1979 when the price of oil soared again. This time, inflation hit the astonishing rate of 16 percent and the economy sagged during the first half of 1980.

Reaganomics and Its Aftermath

Recovery was under way when President Ronald Reagan assumed office in January 1981, but the inflation rate seemed stuck near 10 percent. The new president promised to change things with a package of policies called "supply-side economics" that, he claimed, would boost growth and reduce inflation.[7]

At first, things did change dramatically—but not in the way President Reagan wanted. Although inflation fell, the economy slumped into its worst recession since the Great Depression. When the 1981–1982 recession hit bottom, the unemployment rate was approaching 11 percent, the financial markets were in disarray, and the word *depression* had reentered the American vocabulary. The U.S. government also had a huge budget deficit, bigger than anyone had dreamed possible only a few years before. This problem, as we will see in subsequent chapters, remained with us for about 15 years.

The recovery that began in the winter of 1982–1983 proved to be one of the most vigorous and long-lasting in U.S. history. Unemployment fell more or less steadily for about six years, eventually dropping below 5.5 percent. Meanwhile, inflation remained tame. These developments provided an ideal economic platform on which George H. W. Bush ran to succeed Reagan—and to continue his policies.

Unfortunately for President Bush, the good times did not keep rolling. Shortly after he took office, inflation began to accelerate a bit, and Congress enacted a deficit-reduction package (including a tax increase) not entirely to the president's liking. Then, in mid-1990, the U.S. economy slumped into another recession—precipitated by yet another spike in oil prices before the Persian Gulf War. When the recovery from the 1990–1991 recession proved to be sluggish, candidate Bill Clinton ham-

---

[7] Supply-side economics is discussed further in Chapter 10.

mered away at the lackluster economic performance of the Bush years. His message apparently resonated with American voters.

Clintonomics: Deficit Reduction and the "New Economy"[8]

While President Clinton ran on an economic platform that concentrated on spurring economic growth, the yawning budget deficit forced him to concentrate on deficit reduction instead. A politically contentious package of tax increases and spending cuts barely squeaked through Congress in August 1993 without a single Republican vote, and a second deficit-reduction package passed with bipartisan support in 1997. Indeed, turning the huge federal budget deficit into a large surplus was the crowning achievement of the Clinton economic policy.

Whether by cause or coincidence, the national economy improved dramatically during President Clinton's first term. Business perked up, unemployment fell rapidly, and inflation remained remarkably well contained. By the time of the 1996 election, macroeconomic conditions were the best in a generation—a wonderful backdrop for an incumbent running for reelection.

As we mentioned at the beginning of this chapter, economic growth then accelerated during Clinton's second term, surprising most forecasters. With such rapid growth, the unemployment rate fell to 3.9 percent, its lowest level since 1970. And, to top it all off, inflation dropped to less than 2 percent for a while before rising a bit. Why did all these wonderful things happen at once? Some optimists heralded the arrival of an exciting "New Economy"—a product of globalization and computerization—that naturally performs better than the economy of the past.

The new economy is certainly an alluring vision. But is it real? Most mainstream economists would answer: yes and no. On the one hand, advances in computer and information technology did seem to lead to faster growth in the second half of the 1990s. In that respect, we may well have a "New Economy." But something more mundane also happened: A variety of transitory factors pushed the economy's aggregate supply curve outward at an unusually rapid pace between 1996 and 1998. When this happens, the expected result is faster economic growth and lower inflation.

To see why, look at Figure 4-8—which takes the graphical analysis of economic growth from Figure 4-3 and adds a new aggregate supply curve, S_2S_2, which lies to the right of S_1S_1. With supply curve S_2S_2 instead of S_1S_1, the economy moves from point E not just to point C, as in the earlier figure, but all the way to point B. Comparing B to C, we see that the economy winds up both farther to the right (that is, it grows faster) and lower (that is, it experiences less inflation).

That, in a nutshell, is how our simple aggregate demand–aggregate supply framework explains at least part of recent U.S. economic history. There is much more to say about this episode, and we will return to it several times in subsequent chapters. But, in any case, the boom ended around the middle of 2000—just before the election of President George W. Bush.

The Bush Economy to Date

In the first year of the Bush presidency, Americans learned that their economy is not invulnerable to recessions. Real GDP grew very slowly in the second half of 2000 and then actually *declined* for three quarters in 2001. Ironically, it was the first recession in the U.S. in ten years—when President Bush's father was in office.

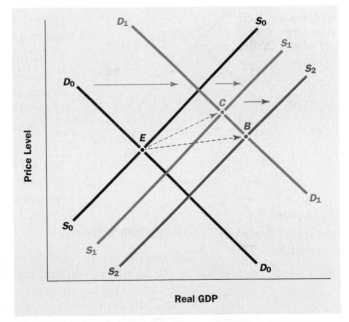

FIGURE 4-8
The Effects of a Favorable Supply Shift

---
[8] One of the authors of this book was a member of President Clinton's original Council of Economic Advisers.

The tax cut of 2001 turned out to be remarkably well timed, however, and the war on terrorism led to a burst of government spending. Both of these policies helped shift the aggregate demand curve outward, mitigating the recession. The recession ended late in 2001. But the recovery was extremely weak until the second half of 2003, when growth finally picked up. The weak economy was still an issue in the 2004 election campaign.

THE PROBLEM OF MACROECONOMIC STABILIZATION: A SNEAK PREVIEW

Stabilization policy is the name given to government programs designed to prevent or shorten recessions and to counteract inflation (that is, to *stabilize* prices).

This brief look at the historical record shows that our economy has not generally produced steady growth without inflation. Rather, it has been buffeted by periodic bouts of unemployment or inflation, and sometimes it has been plagued by both. There was also a hint that government policies may have had something to do with this performance. Let us now expand briefly upon this hint—a subject that we will be developing further in subsequent chapters.

To provide a preliminary analysis of **stabilization policy,** the name given to government programs designed to shorten recessions and to counteract inflation, we can once again use the basic tools of aggregate supply and demand analysis. To facilitate this discussion, we have reproduced as Figures 4-9 and 4-10 two diagrams found earlier in this chapter, but we now give them slightly different interpretations.

Combating Unemployment

Figure 4-9 offers a simplified view of government policy to fight unemployment. Suppose that, in the absence of government intervention, the economy would reach an equilibrium at point E, where the aggregate demand curve D_0D_0 crosses the aggregate supply curve SS. Now if the output corresponding to point E is too low, leaving many workers unemployed, *the government can reduce unemployment by increasing aggregate demand.* Chapter 10 will consider in detail how the government might do this. In the diagram, such an action would shift the demand curve outward to D_1D_1, causing equilibrium to move to point A. In general:

> Recessions and unemployment are often caused by insufficient aggregate demand. When such situations occur, government policies that successfully augment demand—such as increases in government spending—can be an effective way to increase output and reduce unemployment. But they also normally raise prices.

The most extreme example of such a policy came when military spending soared during World War II, adding greatly to aggregate demand. This surge in spending, as we noted earlier, brought the Great Depression to an end.

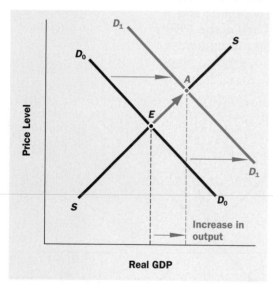

FIGURE 4-9
Stabilization Policy to Fight Unemployment

Combating Inflation

The opposite type of demand management is called for when inflation is the main macroeconomic problem. Figure 4-10 illustrates this case. Here again, point E, the intersection of aggregate demand curve D_0D_0 and aggregate supply curve SS, is the equilibrium the economy would reach in the absence of government policy. But now suppose the price level corresponding to point E is considered "too high," meaning that the price level would be rising too rapidly if the economy were to move to point E. A government program that reduces demand from D_0D_0 to D_2D_2 (for example, a reduction in government spending) can keep prices down and thereby reduce inflation. Thus:

> Inflation is frequently caused by aggregate demand racing ahead too fast. When this is the case, government policies that reduce aggregate demand can be effective anti-inflationary devices. But such policies also decrease real GDP and raise unemployment.

This, in brief, summarizes the intent of stabilization policy. When aggregate demand fluctuations are the source of economic instability, the government can limit both recessions and inflations by pushing aggregate demand ahead when it would otherwise lag, and restraining it when it would otherwise grow too quickly.

Does It Really Work?

Can the government actually stabilize the economy, as these simple diagrams suggest? That is a matter of some debate—a debate we will take up in Part III. But a look back at Figures 4-5 and 4-6 (page 69) may be enlightening right now. First, cover the portions of the two figures that deal with the period after 1940, the portions from the shaded area rightward in each figure. The picture that emerges for the 1870–1940 period is that of an economy with frequent and sometimes quite pronounced fluctuations.

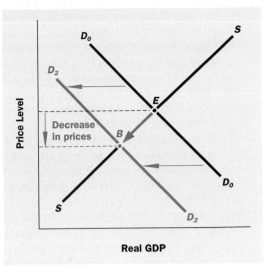

FIGURE 4-10
Stabilization Policy to Fight Inflation

Now do the reverse. Cover the data before 1950 and look only at the postwar period. There is indeed a difference. Instances of negative real GDP growth are less common and business fluctuations look less severe. Although government policies have not achieved perfection, things do look much better.

When we turn to inflation, however, matters look rather worse. Gone are the periods of deflation and price stability that occurred before World War II. Prices now seem only to rise or remain the same.

This quick tour through the data suggests that something *has* changed. The U.S. economy behaved differently from 1950 to 2003 than it did from 1870 to 1940. Although controversy over this point continues, many economists attribute this shift in the economy's behavior to lessons the government has learned about managing the economy—lessons you will be learning in Part III.

When you look at the prewar data, you see the fluctuations of an unmanaged economy that went through booms and recessions for "natural" economic reasons. The government did little about either. When you examine the postwar data, on the other hand, you see an economy that has been increasingly managed by government policy—sometimes successfully and sometimes unsuccessfully. Although the recessions are less severe, this improvement has come at a cost: The economy appears to be more inflation-prone than it was in the more distant past. These two changes in our economy may be connected. But to understand why, we will have to provide some relevant economic theory.

We have, in a sense, spent much of this chapter running before we have learned to walk—that is, we have been using aggregate demand and aggregate supply curves extensively before developing the theory that underlies them. That is the task for the rest of Part II.

SUMMARY

1. Microeconomics studies the decisions of individuals and firms, the ways in which these decisions interact, and their influence on the allocation of a nation's resources and the distribution of income. Macroeconomics looks at how entire economies behave and studies the pressing social problems of economic growth, inflation, and unemployment.

2. Although they focus on different subjects, microeconomics and macroeconomics rely on virtually identical tools. Both use the supply and demand analysis introduced in Chapter 3.

3. Macroeconomic models use abstract concepts like "the price level" and "gross domestic product" that are derived by combining many different markets into one. This

process is known as **aggregation;** it should not be taken literally but rather viewed as a useful approximation.

4. The best specific measure of the nation's economic output is **gross domestic product (GDP),** which is obtained by adding up the money values of all **final goods and services** produced in a given year. These outputs can be evaluated at current market prices (to get **nominal GDP**) or at some fixed set of prices (to get **real GDP**). Neither **intermediate goods** nor transactions that take place outside organized markets are included in GDP.

5. GDP measures an economy's production, not the increase in its well-being. For example, the GDP places no value on housework, other do-it-yourself activities, or leisure time.

On the other hand, even commodities that might be considered as "bads" rather than "goods" are counted in the GDP (for example, activities that harm the environment).

6. America's economic history shows steady growth punctuated by periodic **recessions**—that is, periods in which real GDP declined. Although the distant past included some periods of falling prices **(deflation)**, more recent history shows only rising prices **(inflation).**

7. The Great Depression of the 1930s was the worst in U.S. history. It profoundly affected both our nation and countries throughout the world. It also led to a revolution in economic thinking, thanks largely to the work of John Maynard Keynes.

8. From World War II to the early 1970s, the American economy exhibited steadier growth than in the past. Many observers attributed this more stable performance to the implementation of the **stabilization policies** that Keynes had suggested. At the same time, however, the price level seems only to rise—never to fall—in the modern economy. The economy seems to have become more "inflation-prone."

9. Between 1973 and 1991, the U.S. economy suffered through several serious recessions. In the first part of that period, inflation was also unusually virulent. This unhappy combination of economic stagnation with rapid inflation was nicknamed **"stagflation."** Since 1982, however, inflation has been low and has dropped recently.

10. U.S. economic performance was generally excellent after 1992—until a slowdown in 2000 and a recession in 2001. One possible explanation for this rapid growth is that the **aggregate supply curve** shifted out unusually rapidly.

11. One major cause of inflation is that aggregate demand may grow more quickly than does aggregate supply. In such a case, a government policy that reduces aggregate demand may be able to stem the inflation.

12. Recessions often occur because aggregate demand grows too slowly. In this case, a government policy that stimulates demand may be an effective way to fight the recession.

KEY TERMS

Aggregation 60

Aggregate demand curve 62

Aggregate supply curve 62

Inflation 62

Recession 62

Gross domestic product (GDP) 64

Nominal GDP 64

Real GDP 64

Final goods and services 65

Intermediate good 65

Deflation 69

Stagflation 72

Stabilization policy 74

QUESTIONS FOR REVIEW

1. Which of the following problems are likely to be studied by a microeconomist and which by a macroeconomist?

   a. The rapid growth of Microsoft

   b. Why unemployment in the United States rose from 2000 to 2001

   c. Why Japan's economy grew faster than the U.S. economy in the 1980s, but slower in the 1990s

   d. Why college tuition costs have risen so rapidly in recent years

2. You probably use "aggregates" frequently in everyday discussions. Try to think of some examples. (Here is one: Have you ever said, "The students at this college generally think . . ."? What, precisely, did you mean?)

3. Use an aggregate supply and demand diagram to study what would happen to an economy in which the aggregate demand curve never moved while the aggregate supply curve shifted outward year after year.

4. Try asking a friend who has not studied economics in which year he or she thinks prices were higher: 1870 or 1900? 1920 or 1940? (In both cases, prices were higher in the earlier year.) Most young people think that prices have always risen. Why do you think they have this opinion?

5. Which of the following transactions are included in gross domestic product, and by how much does each raise GDP?

   a. Smith pays a carpenter $15,000 to build a garage.

   b. Smith purchases $3,000 worth of materials and builds himself a garage, which is worth $15,000.

   c. Smith goes to the woods, cuts down a tree, and uses the wood to build himself a garage that is worth $15,000.

   d. The Jones family sells its old house to the Reynolds family for $100,000. The Joneses then buy a newly constructed house from a builder for $150,000.

   e. You purchase a used computer from a friend for $200.

   f. Your university purchases a new mainframe computer from IBM, paying $200,000.

   g. You win $1,000 in an Atlantic City casino.

   h. You make $1,000 in the stock market.

   i. You sell a used economics textbook to your college bookstore for $25.

   j. You buy a new economics textbook from your college bookstore for $50.

6. Give some reasons why gross domestic product is not a suitable measure of the well-being of the nation. (Have you noticed newspaper accounts in which journalists seem to use GDP for this purpose?)

The Goals of Macroeconomic Policy

When men are employed, they are best contented.
BENJAMIN FRANKLIN

Inflation is repudiation.
CALVIN COOLIDGE

S omeone once quipped that you could turn a parrot into an economist by teaching him just two words: supply and demand. And now that you have been through Chapter 3 and Chapter 4, you see what he meant. Sure enough, economists think of the process of *economic growth* as having two essential ingredients:

- The first ingredient is *aggregate supply.* Given the available **inputs** of labor and capital, and the technology at its disposal, the economy is able to produce a certain volume of **outputs,** measured by GDP. This *capacity to produce* normally increases from one year to the next as the supplies of inputs grow and the technology improves. The theory of aggregate supply will be our focus in Chapters 6 and 9.
- The second ingredient is *aggregate demand.* How much of the capacity to produce is actually *utilized* depends on how many of these goods and services people and businesses want to *buy.* We begin to construct a theory of aggregate demand in Chapters 7 and 8.

CONTENTS

Inputs are the labor, machinery, buildings, and other resources used to produce outputs.

Outputs are the goods and services that the economy produces.

Growth policy refers to government policies intended to make the economy grow faster in the long run.

Corresponding to these two ingredients, economists visualize a dual task for those who make macroeconomic policy. First, *policy should create an environment in which the economy can expand its productive capacity rapidly*, because that is the ultimate source of higher living standards. This first task is the domain of **growth policy**, which is taken up in the next chapter. Second, *policymakers should manage aggregate demand so that it grows in line with the economy's capacity to produce*—neither faster nor slower. We called this approach *stabilization policy* in the last chapter. As we noted there, inadequate growth of aggregate demand can lead to *unemployment*, while excessive growth of aggregate demand can lead to *inflation*. Both are to be avoided.

Thus the goals of macroeconomic policy can be summarized succinctly as *achieving rapid growth while keeping both unemployment and inflation low*. Unfortunately, that turns out to be a tall order. In chapters to come, we will explain why these goals cannot be attained with machine-like precision, and why improvement on one front often spells deterioration on another. Along the way, we will pay a great deal of attention to both the *causes* of and *cures* for high inflation, high unemployment, and sluggish growth.

But before getting involved in such weighty issues of theory and policy, we pause in this chapter to take a close look at the goals themselves. How fast can—or should—the economy grow? Why does a rise in unemployment cause such social distress? Why is inflation so loudly deplored? The answers to some of these questions may seem obvious at first. But, as you will see, there is more to them than meets the eye.

The chapter is divided into three parts: The first part deals with growth, the second part focuses on unemployment, and the third part is concerned with inflation. An appendix explains how inflation is measured.

PART 1: THE GOAL OF ECONOMIC GROWTH

To residents of a prosperous society like ours, economic growth—the notion that standards of living rise from one year to the next—seems like part of the natural order of things. But it is not. Historians tell us that living standards barely changed from the Roman Empire to the dawn of the Industrial Revolution—a period of some 16 centuries! Closer in time, per capita incomes have tragically declined in some of the poorest countries of Africa in recent decades. Economic growth is not automatic.

Growth is also a very *slow*, and therefore barely noticeable, process. The typical American will consume about 3 percent more goods and services in 2004 than he or she did in 2003. Can you perceive a difference that small? Perhaps not, but such tiny changes, when compounded for decades or even centuries, transform societies. During the 20th century, for example, living standards in the United States increased by a factor of more than seven—which means that your ancestors in the year 1900 consumed roughly 14 percent as much food, clothing, shelter, and other amenities as you do today. Try to imagine how your family would fare on one-seventh of its current income.

PRODUCTIVITY GROWTH: FROM LITTLE ACORNS . . .

Small differences in growth rates make an enormous difference—*eventually*. To illustrate this point, think about the relative positions of three major nations—the United States, the United Kingdom, and Japan—at two points in history: 1870 and 1979. In 1870, the United States was a young, upstart nation. Although already among the most prosperous countries on earth, the United States was in no sense yet a major power. The United Kingdom, by contrast, was the preeminent economic and military power of the world. The Victorian era was at its height, and the sun never set on the

The Wonders of Compound Interest

Growth rates, like interest rates, *compound* so that, for example, ten years of growth at 3 percent per year leaves the economy *more than* 30 percent larger. How much more? The answer is 34.4 percent. To see how we get this figure, start with the fact that $100 left in a bank account for one year at 3 percent interest grows to $103, which is 1.03 × $100. If left for a second year, that $103 will grow another 3 percent—to 1.03 × $103 = $106.09, which is already more than $106. Compounding has begun.

Notice that 1.03 × $103 is $(1.03)^2$ × $100. Similarly, after three years the original $100 will grow to $(1.03)^3$ × $100 = $109.27. As you can see, each additional year adds another 1.03 growth factor to the multiplication. Now returning to answer our original question, after ten years of compounding, the depositor will have $(1.03)^{10}$ × $100 = $134.39 in the bank. Thus her balance will have grown by 34.4 percent. By identical logic, an economy growing at 3 percent per year for ten years will expand 34.4 percent in total.

You may not be impressed by the difference between 30 percent and 34.4 percent. If so, follow the logic for longer periods. After 20 years of 3 percent growth, the economy will be 80.6 percent bigger (because $(1.03)^{20}$ = 1.806), not just 60 percent bigger. After 50 years, cumulative growth will be 338 percent, not 150 percent. And after a century, it will be 1,822 percent, not just 300 percent. Now we are talking about large discrepancies! No wonder Einstein once said, presumably in jest, that compounding was the most powerful force in the universe.

SOURCE: © CORBIS

The arithmetic of growth leads to a convenient "doubling rule" that you can do in your head. If something (the money in a bank account, the GDP of a country, and so on) grows at an annual rate of *g* percent, how long will it take to double? The approximate answer is 70/*g*, so the rule is often called "the Rule of 70." For example, at a 2 percent growth rate, something doubles in about 70/2 = 35 years. At a 3 percent growth rate, doubling takes roughly 70/3 = 23.33 years. Yes, small differences in growth rates can make a large difference.

British Empire. Meanwhile, somewhere across the Pacific was an inconsequential island nation called Japan. In 1870, Japan had only recently opened up to the West and was economically backward.

Now fast-forward 109 years. By 1979, the United States had become the world's preeminent economic power, Japan had emerged as the clear number two, and the United Kingdom had retreated into the second rank of nations. Obviously, the Japanese economy grew faster than the U.S. economy during this century while the British economy grew more slowly, or else this stunning transformation of relative positions would not have occurred. But the magnitudes of the differences in growth rates may astound you.

Over the 109-year period, GDP per capita in the United States grew at a 2.3 percent compound annual rate while the United Kingdom's growth rate was 1.8 percent—a difference of merely 0.5 percent per annum, but compounded for more than a century. And what of Japan? What growth rate propelled it from obscurity into the front rank of nations? The answer is just 3.0 percent, a mere 0.7 percent per year faster than the United States. These numbers show vividly what a huge difference a 0.5 or 0.7 percentage point change in the growth rate makes, *if sustained for a long time.*

Economists define the *productivity* of a country's labor force (or **"labor productivity"**) as the amount of output a typical worker turns out in an hour of work. For example, if output is measured by GDP, productivity would be measured by GDP divided by the total number of hours of work. It is the growth rate of productivity that determines whether living standards will rise rapidly or slowly.

Labor productivity is the amount of output a worker turns out in an hour (or a week, or a year) of labor. If output is measured by GDP, it is GDP per hour of work.

PRODUCTIVITY GROWTH IS (ALMOST) EVERYTHING IN THE LONG RUN   As we pointed out in our list of *Ideas for Beyond the Final Exam,* only rising productivity can raise standards of living in the long run. Over long periods of time, small differences in rates of productivity growth compound like interest in a bank account and can make an enormous difference to a society's prosperity. Nothing contributes more to material well-being, to the reduction of poverty, to increases in leisure time, and to a country's ability to finance education, public health, environmental improvement, and the arts than its productivity growth rate.

 Issue: Is Faster Growth Always Better?

How fast should the U.S. economy, or any economy, grow? At first, the question may seem silly. Isn't it obvious that we should grow as fast as possible? After all, that will make us all richer. For the most part, economists agree; faster growth is generally preferred to slower growth. But as we shall see in a few pages, further thought suggests that the apparently naive question is not quite as silly as it sounds. Growth comes at a cost.

THE CAPACITY TO PRODUCE: POTENTIAL GDP AND THE PRODUCTION FUNCTION

Potential GDP is the real GDP that the economy would produce if its labor and other resources were fully employed.

The labor force is the number of people holding or seeking jobs.

Questions like how fast our economy can or should grow require quantitative answers. Economists have invented the concept of **potential GDP** to measure the economy's normal capacity to produce goods and services. Specifically, potential GDP is the real gross domestic product (GDP) an economy *could* produce if its **labor force** were fully employed. Note the use of the word *normal* in describing capacity. Just as it is possible to push a factory beyond its normal operating rate (by, for example, adding a night shift), it is possible to push an economy beyond its normal full-employment level by working it very hard. For example, we observed in the last chapter that the unemployment rate dropped as low as 1.2 percent under abnormal conditions during World War II.

Conceptually, we estimate potential GDP in two steps. First, we count up the available supplies of labor, capital, and other productive resources. Then we estimate how much *output* these *inputs* could produce if they were fully utilized. This second step—the transformation of inputs into outputs—involves an assessment of the economy's *technology.* The more technologically advanced an economy, the more output it will be able to produce from any given bundle of inputs—as we emphasized in Chapter 2's discussion of the production possibilities frontier.

The economy's **production function** shows the volume of output that can be produced from given inputs (such as labor and capital), given the available technology.

To help us understand how technology affects the relationship between inputs and outputs, it is useful to introduce a tool called the **production function.** It is simply a mathematical or graphical depiction of the relationship between inputs and outputs. We will use a graph in our discussion.

For a given level of technology, Figure 5-1 shows how output (measured by real GDP) depends on labor input (measured by hours of work). To read this graph, and to relate it to the concept of potential GDP, begin with the black curve $0K$ in Panel (a), which shows how GDP depends on labor input, *holding both capital and technology constant.* Naturally, output rises as labor inputs increase as we move outward along the curve $0K$, just as you would expect. If the country's labor force can supply L_0 hours of work when it is fully employed, then *potential GDP is Y_0* (see point A). If the technology improves, the production function will shift upward—say, to the red curve labeled $0M$—meaning that the *same* amount of labor input now produces *more* output. The graph shows that potential GDP increases to Y_1.

Now what about capital? Panel (b) shows two production functions. The black curve $0K_0$ applies when the economy has some lower capital stock, K_0. The higher, red curve $0K_1$ applies when the capital stock is some higher number, K_1. Thus the production function tells us that potential GDP will be Y_0 if the capital stock is K_0 (see

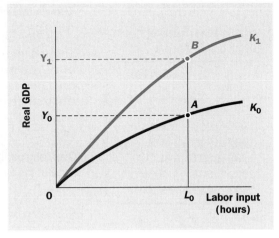

(a)

(b)

■ FIGURE 5-1
The Economy's Production Function

point A) but Y_1 if the capital stock is K_1 instead (see point B). Once again, this relationship is just what you expect: The economy can produce *more* output with the *same* amount of labor if workers have more capital to work with.

You can hardly avoid noticing the similarities between the two panels of Figure 5-1: Better technology, as in Panel (a), or more capital, as in Panel (b), affects the production function in more or less the same way:

Given the labor force, either more capital or better technology will shift the production function upward and therefore raise potential GDP.

THE GROWTH RATE OF POTENTIAL GDP

With this new tool, it is but a short jump to potential growth rates. If the *size* of potential GDP depends on the size of the economy's labor force, the amount of capital and other resources it has, and its technology, it follows that the *growth rate* of potential GDP must depend on:

- The growth rate of the labor force
- The growth rate of the nation's capital stock
- The rate of technical progress

To sharpen this point, observe that real GDP is, by definition, the product of the total hours of work in the economy times the amount of output produced per hour—what we have just called *labor productivity:*

GDP = Hours of work × Output per hour = Hours of work × Labor productivity.

For example, in the United States today, using very rough numbers, GDP is about $11 trillion and total hours of work per year are about 225 billion. Thus labor productivity is roughly $11 trillion/225 billion hours = $49 per hour.

How fast can the economy increase its productive capacity? By transforming the preceding equation into growth rates, we have our answer: The growth rate of potential GDP is the *sum* of the growth rates of labor input (hours of work) and labor productivity:[1]

[1] You may be wondering about what happened to capital. The answer, as we have just seen in our discussion of the production function, is that one of the main determinants of potential GDP, and thus of labor productivity, is the amount of capital that each worker has to work with. Accordingly, the role of capital is incorporated into the productivity number.

TABLE 5-1 Recent Growth Rates of Real GDP in the United States	
Years	Growth Rate per Year
1993–1995	3.2%
1995–1997	4.1
1997–1999	4.3
1999–2001	2.1
2001–2003	2.6
1993–2003	**3.3**

SOURCE: U.S. Department of Commerce.

Growth rate of potential GDP = Growth rate of labor input + Growth rate of labor productivity

In the U.S. in recent decades, labor input has been increasing at a rate of about 1 percent per year. But labor productivity growth, which was very slow until the mid-1990s, has leaped upward since then—averaging about 3 percent per annum from 1995 to 2003. Together, these two figures imply an estimated growth rate of potential GDP in the 4 percent range.

Do the growth rates of potential GDP and actual GDP match up? The answer is an important one to which we will return often in this book:

Over long periods of time, the growth rates of actual and potential GDP are normally quite similar. But the two often diverge sharply over short periods.

Table 5-1 illustrates this point with some recent U.S. data. Since 1995, GDP growth rates over two-year periods have ranged from as low as 2.1 percent per annum to as high as 4.3 percent. Over the entire ten-year period, GDP growth averaged 3.3 percent, which is probably a bit below current estimates of the growth rate of potential GDP.

ALTERNATIVE MEASURES OF ECONOMIC GROWTH

There are three basic measures of economic growth, two of which have already been mentioned. The right one to use depends on the purpose of the analysis.

Real GDP   If the objective is to track the *size* of an expanding economy, the growth rate of *real GDP* is the natural choice, and international growth comparisons normally focus on that measure. But increasing size *per se* may be of limited interest. For example, India's GDP is slightly bigger than Switzerland's. But with a population more than 140 times as large, India remains a poor country whereas the Swiss are rich.

Real GDP per Capita   If, instead, the objective is to indicate how rapidly a country's *standard of living* is rising, a different measure—the growth rate of **real GDP per capita,** or total GDP divided by the population—makes more sense because it automatically (by definition) ignores the growth that occurs simply because there are more people.

Real GDP per capita is the ratio of real GDP to the population.

Labor Productivity   Finally, if our interest is in how much more *productive* an economy is becoming, the natural choice is the measure we have just discussed—the growth rate of labor productivity, which is GDP per hour of work.

A simple bit of algebra will bring out the relationships among these three measures of economic progress. As before, let Y denote real GDP and L denote the number of hours of work. In addition, let N denote the population, Then it is obviously true that:

$$Y = N \times (L/N) \times (Y/L)$$

In this decomposition of GDP into its three components, the first term is population, the middle term is hours of work per person, and the last term is labor productivity—which is GDP per hour of work.

If we were to divide GDP by population (N) instead of by hours (L), we would obtain GDP per capita, Y/N, instead. The difference is apparent by dividing both sides of the previous equation by N:

$$Y/N = (L/N) \times (Y/L) .$$

These last two measures of economic progress differ only in their denominators, so they will disagree whenever hours of work per person (L/N) changes.

In fact, the ratio L/N has fallen slightly in the United States in recent decades as Americans have been working a bit less. So real GDP per capita has increased about 2 percent per year over the past 20 years while real GDP per hour has increased about 2.1 percent per year.

WHAT DETERMINES THE GROWTH RATE?

The next chapter is devoted to studying the *determinants* of economic growth and some *policies* that might speed it up. But we already know from the production function that there are two basic ways to boost a nation's growth rate—other than faster population growth and simply working harder. One is accumulating more capital. Other things being equal, a nation that builds more capital for its future will grow faster. The other way to increase the growth rate is by improving technology. When technological breakthroughs are coming at a fast and furious pace, an economy will grow more rapidly. We will discuss both of these factors in detail in the next chapter.

First, however, we should answer the more basic question posed earlier in this chapter.

Issue Revisited: Is Faster Growth Always Better?

It might seem that the answer to this question is obviously yes. After all, faster growth of either labor productivity or GDP per capita is the route to higher living standards. But exceptions have been noted.

For openers, some social critics have questioned the desirability of faster economic growth as an end in itself, at least in the rich countries. Faster growth surely brings more wealth, and to most people the desirability of wealth is beyond question. "I've been rich and I've been poor. Believe me, honey, rich is better," singer Sophie Tucker once told an interviewer. And most people seem to share her sentiment. To those who hold this belief, a healthy economy is one that is capable of producing vast quantities of jeans, pizzas, cars, and computers.

Yet the desirability of further economic growth for a society that is already quite wealthy has been questioned on several grounds. Environmentalists worry that the sheer increase in the volume of goods imposes enormous costs on society in the form of pollution, crowding, and proliferation of wastes that need disposal. It has, they argue, dotted our roadsides with junkyards, filled our air with pollution, and poisoned our food with dangerous chemicals.

Some psychologists and social critics argue that the never-ending drive for more and better goods has failed to make people happier. Instead, industrial progress has transformed the satisfying and creative tasks of the artisan into the mechanical and dehumanizing routine of the assembly-line worker. In some countries, such as the United States, it seems to be driving people to work longer and longer hours. The question is whether the vast outpouring of material goods is worth all the stress and environmental damage.

Most economists would answer: probably yes. For one thing, slower growth would make it extremely difficult to finance programs that improve the quality of life—including efforts to protect the environment. Such programs tend to be expensive, and growth is what makes available the additional resources needed to pay the bills. Second, it would be difficult to prevent further economic growth even if we were so inclined. Mandatory controls are abhorrent to most Americans; we cannot order people to stop being inventive and hard-working. Third, slower economic growth would seriously hamper efforts to eliminate poverty—both within our own country and throughout the world. Much of the earth's population still lives in a state of extreme want. These unfortunate people are far less interested in clean air and fulfillment in the workplace than they are in more food, better clothing, and sturdier shelters.

That said, economists concede that faster growth is not *always* better. One important reason will occupy our attention later in Parts II and III: An economy that grows too fast may generate inflation. Why? You were introduced to the answer at the end of the last chapter: Inflation arises when *aggregate demand* races ahead of *aggregate supply*. In plain English, an economy will become inflationary when people's demands for goods and services expand faster than its capacity to produce them. So we probably do not want to grow faster than the growth rate of potential GDP, at least not for long.

Should society then seek the maximum possible growth rate of *potential* GDP? Well, maybe not. After all, more rapid growth does not come for free. We have noted that building more capital is one good way to speed up the growth of potential GDP. But the resources used to manufacture jet engines and computer servers could have been used to make home air conditioners and video games instead. Building more capital imposes an obvious cost on a society: The citizens must consume less today. This point does not constitute a brief against investing for the future. Indeed, most economists believe we need to do more of that. But we must realize that faster growth through capital formation comes at a cost—an *opportunity cost*. Here, as elsewhere, you don't get something for nothing.

■ PART 2: THE COSTS OF UNEMPLOYMENT

We noted earlier that actual GDP growth can differ sharply from potential GDP growth over periods as long as several years. This fact has major implications for employment and unemployment.

When the economy grows more *slowly* than its potential, it fails to generate enough new jobs for its ever-growing labor force. Hence, *the unemployment rate* rises. Conversely, GDP growth *faster* than the economy's potential leads to a *falling unemployment rate*.

The **unemployment rate** is the number of unemployed people, expressed as a percentage of the labor force.

High unemployment is socially wasteful. When the economy does not create enough jobs to employ everyone who is willing to work, a valuable resource is lost. Potential goods and services that might have been produced and enjoyed by consumers are lost forever. This lost output is the central economic cost of high unemployment, and we can measure it by comparing actual and potential GDP.

That cost is considerable. Table 5-2 summarizes the idleness of workers and machines, and the resulting loss of national output, for some of the years of lowest economic activity in recent decades. The second column lists the civilian unemployment rate, and thus measures unused labor resources. The third lists the percentage of industrial capacity that U.S. manufacturers were actually using, which indicates the extent to which plant and equipment went unused. The fourth column estimates the shortfall between potential and actual real GDP. We see that unemployment has cost the people of the United States as much as an 8.1 percent reduction in their real incomes.

Although Table 5-2 shows extreme examples, our inability to utilize all of the nation's available resources was a persistent economic problem for decades. The blue line in Figure 5-2 shows actual real GDP in the United States from 1954 to 2003, while the black line shows potential GDP. The graph makes it clear that actual GDP has fallen short of potential GDP more often than it has exceeded it, especially during the 1973–1993 period. In fact:

■ TABLE 5-2　The Economic Costs of High Unemployment

Year	Civilian Unemployment Rate	Capacity Utilization Rate	Real GDP Lost Due to Idle Resources
1958	6.8%	75.0%	4.8%
1961	6.7	77.3	4.1
1975	8.5	73.4	5.4
1982	9.7	71.3	8.1
1992	7.5	79.4	2.6
2003	6.0	73.4	2.2

SOURCES: Bureau of Labor Statistics; Federal Reserve System; and the authors' calculation.

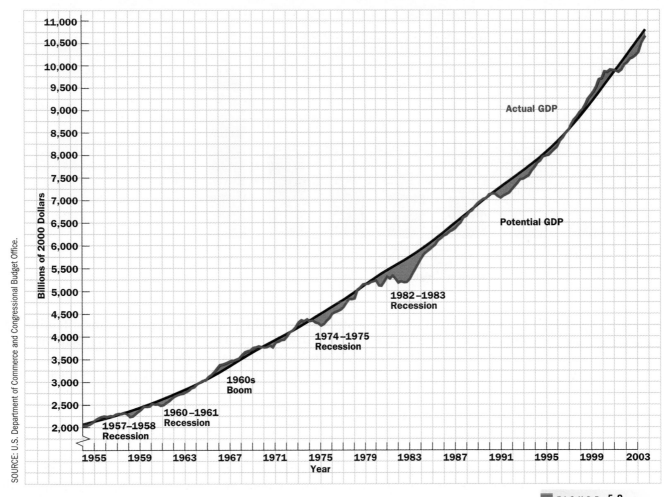

SOURCE: U.S. Department of Commerce and Congressional Budget Office.

■ FIGURE 5-2

Actual and Potential GDP in the United States, 1954–2003

A conservative estimate of the cumulative gap between actual and potential GDP over the years 1974 to 1993 (all evaluated in 2000 prices) is roughly $1,750 billion. At 2004 levels, this loss in output as a result of unemployment would be over two months worth of production. And there is no way to redeem those losses. The labor wasted in 1992 cannot be utilized in 2004.

THE HUMAN COSTS OF HIGH UNEMPLOYMENT

If these numbers seem a bit dry and abstract, think about the human costs of being unemployed. Years ago, job loss meant not only enforced idleness and a catastrophic drop in income, it often led to hunger, cold, ill health, even death. Here is how one unemployed worker during the Great Depression described his family's plight in a mournful letter to the governor of Pennsylvania:

> I have been out of work for over a year and a half. Am back almost thirteen months and the landlord says if I don't pay up before the 1 of 1932 out I must go, and where am I to go in the cold winter with my children? If you can help me please for God's sake and the children's sakes and like please do what you can and send me some help, will you, I cannot find any work. . . . Thanksgiving dinner was black coffee and bread and was very glad to get it. My wife is in the hospital now. We have no shoes to were [sic]; no clothes hardly. Oh what will I do I sure will thank you.[2]

---

[2] From *Brother, Can You Spare a Dime? The Great Depression 1929–1933*, by Milton Meltzer, p. 103. Copyright 1969 by Milton Meltzer. Reprinted by permission of Alfred A. Knopf, Inc.

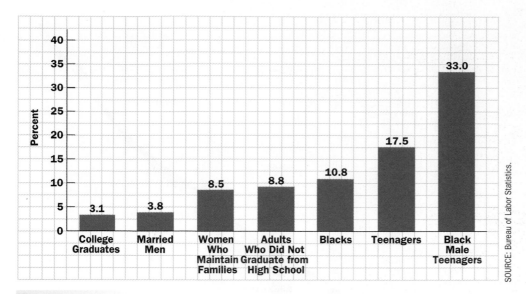

FIGURE 5-3

Unemployment Rates for
Selected Groups, 2003

Nowadays, unemployment does not hold quite such terrors for most families, although its consequences remain dire enough. Our system of unemployment insurance (discussed later in this chapter) has taken part of the sting out of unemployment, and other social welfare programs support the incomes of the poor. Yet most families still suffer painful losses of income and, often, severe noneconomic consequences when a breadwinner becomes unemployed.

Even families that are well protected by unemployment compensation suffer when joblessness strikes. Ours is a work-oriented society. A man's place has always been in the office or shop, and lately this has become true for women as well. A worker forced into idleness by a recession endures a psychological cost that is no less real for our inability to measure it. Martin Luther King, Jr., put it graphically: "In our society, it is murder, psychologically, to deprive a man of a job. . . . You are in substance saying to that man that he has no right to exist."[3] High unemployment has been linked to psychological and physical disorders, divorces, suicides, and crime.

It is important to realize that these costs, whether large or small in total, are distributed most unevenly across the population. In 2003, for example, the unemployment rate among all workers averaged 6.0 percent. But, as Figure 5-3 shows, 10.8 percent of black workers were unemployed, as were 8.5 percent of women who maintained families. For teenagers, the situation was worse still, with unemployment at 17.5 percent, and that of black male teenagers 33 percent. College graduates had the lowest rate—about 3 percent. Overall unemployment varies from year to year, but these relationships are typical:

In good times and bad, married men suffer the least unemployment and teenagers suffer the most; nonwhites are unemployed much more often than whites; blue-collar workers have above-average rates of unemployment; well-educated people have below-average unemployment rates.[4]

It is worth noting that unemployment in the United States has been much lower than in most other industrialized countries in recent years. For example, during 2002, when the U.S. unemployment rate averaged 5.8 percent, the comparable figures were 7.0 percent in Canada, 8.7 percent in France, 9.1 percent in Italy, and 8.4 percent in Germany.[5]

---

[3] Quoted in Coretta Scott King (ed.), *The Words of Martin Luther King* (New York: Newmarket Press; 1983), p. 45.

[4] These days, unemployment rates for men and women are about equal.

[5] The numbers for foreign countries are based (approximately) on U.S. unemployment concepts.

COUNTING THE UNEMPLOYED: THE OFFICIAL STATISTICS

We have been using unemployment figures without considering where they come from or how accurate they are. The basic data come from a monthly survey of about 60,000 households conducted for the U.S. Bureau of Labor Statistics (BLS). The census taker asks several questions about the employment status of each member of the household and, on the basis of the answers, classifies each person as *employed*, *unemployed*, or *not in the labor force*.

The Employed   The first category is the simplest to define. It includes everyone currently at work, including part-time workers. Although some part-timers work less than a full week by choice, others do so only because they cannot find suitable full-time jobs. Nevertheless, these workers are counted as employed, even though many would consider them "underemployed."

The Unemployed   The second category is a bit trickier. For persons not currently working, the BLS first determines whether they are temporarily laid off from a job to which they expect to return. If so, they are counted as unemployed. The remaining workers are asked whether they actively sought work during the previous four weeks. If they did, they are also counted as unemployed.

Out of the Labor Force   But if they failed to look for a job, they are classified as *out of the labor force* rather than unemployed. This seems a reasonable way to draw the distinction—after all, not *everyone* wants to work. Yet there is a problem: Research shows that many unemployed workers give up looking for jobs after a while. These so-called **discouraged workers** are victims of poor job prospects, just like the officially unemployed. But when they give up hope, the measured unemployment rate—which is the ratio of the number of unemployed people to the total labor force—declines.

Involuntary part-time work, loss of overtime or shortened work hours, and discouraged workers are all examples of "hidden" or "disguised" unemployment. People concerned about such phenomena argue that we should include them in the official unemployment rate because, if we do not, the magnitude of the problem will be underestimated. Others, however, argue that measured unemployment overestimates the problem because, to count as unemployed, potential workers need only *claim* to be looking for jobs, even if they are not really interested in finding them.

A **discouraged worker** is an unemployed person who gives up looking for work and is therefore no longer counted as part of the labor force.

SOURCE: © *The New Yorker Collection*, 1975, Ed Arno from cartoonbank.com. All Rights Reserved.

"The rise in unemployment, however, which was somewhat offset by an expanding job market, was countered by an upturn in part-time dropouts, which, in turn, was diminished by seasonal factors, the anticipated summer slump, and, over-all, a small but perceptible rise in actual employment."

TYPES OF UNEMPLOYMENT

Providing jobs for those willing to work is one principal goal of macroeconomic policy. How are we to define this goal?

One clearly *incorrect* answer would be "a zero measured unemployment rate." Ours is a dynamic, highly mobile economy. Households move from one state to another. Individuals quit jobs to seek better positions or retool for more attractive occupations. These and other decisions produce some minimal amount of unemployment—people who are literally between jobs. Economists call this **frictional unemployment.** The critical distinguishing feature of frictional unemployment, which is unavoidable in our market economy, is that it is short-lived. A frictionally unemployed person has every reason to expect to find a new job soon.

Frictional unemployment is unemployment that is due to normal turnover in the labor market. It includes people who are temporarily between jobs because they are moving or changing occupations, or are unemployed for similar reasons.

POLICY DEBATE   Does the Minimum Wage Cause Unemployment?

E lementary economic reasoning—summarized in the simple supply-demand diagram to the right—suggests that setting a minimum wage (*W* in the graph) above the free-market wage (*w* in the graph) must cause unemployment. In the graph, unemployment is the horizontal gap between the quantity of labor supplied (point *B*) and the quantity demanded (point *A*) at the minimum wage. Indeed, the conclusion seems so elementary that generations of economists took it for granted. Earlier editions of this book, for example, confidently told students that a higher minimum wage must lead to higher unemployment.

But some surprising economic research published in the 1990s cast serious doubt on this conventional wisdom.* For example, economists David Card and Alan Krueger compared employment changes at fast-food restaurants in New Jersey and nearby Pennsylvania after New Jersey, but not Pennsylvania, raised its minimum wage in 1992. To their surprise, the New Jersey stores did *more* net hiring than their Pennsylvania counterparts. Similar results were found for fast-food stores in Texas after the federal minimum wage was raised in 1991, and in California after the statewide minimum wage was increased in 1988.

In none of these cases did a higher minimum wage seem to reduce employment—in contrast to the implications of simple economic theory. Thus, a policy question previously deemed closed now seems to be open: Does the minimum wage cause unemployment?

Resolution of this debate is of more than academic interest. In 1996, President Clinton recommended and Congress passed an in-

*See David Card and Alan Krueger, *Myth and Measurement: The New Economics of the Minimum Wage* (Princeton, N.J.: Princeton University Press; 1995).

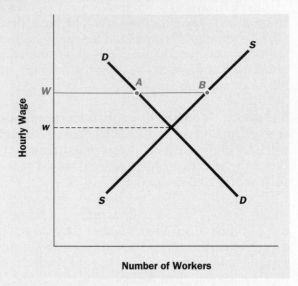

Number of Workers

crease in the federal minimum wage—justifying its action, in part, by the new research suggesting that unemployment would not rise as a result. In 2001, Congressional Democrats again proposed an increase in the minimum wage. But President Bush opposed the idea, and it was not passed. Research can have consequences.

Structural unemployment refers to workers who have lost their jobs because they have been displaced by automation, because their skills are no longer in demand, or because of similar reasons.

A second type of unemployment can be difficult to distinguish from frictional unemployment but has very different implications. **Structural unemployment** arises when jobs are eliminated by changes in the economy, such as automation or permanent changes in demand. The crucial difference between frictional and structural unemployment is that, unlike frictionally unemployed workers, structurally unemployed workers cannot realistically be considered "between jobs." Instead, their skills and experience may be unmarketable in the changing economy in which they live. They are thus faced with either prolonged periods of unemployment or the necessity of making major changes in their skills or occupations.

Cyclical unemployment is the portion of unemployment that is attributable to a decline in the economy's total production. Cyclical unemployment rises during recessions and falls as prosperity is restored.

The remaining type of unemployment, **cyclical unemployment,** will occupy most of our attention. Cyclical unemployment rises when the level of economic activity declines, as it does in a recession. Thus, when macroeconomists speak of maintaining "full employment," they do not mean achieving zero measured unemployment, but rather limiting unemployment to its frictional and structural components—which means, roughly, producing at potential GDP. A key question, therefore, is this: How much measured unemployment is frictional and structural?

HOW MUCH EMPLOYMENT IS "FULL EMPLOYMENT"?

President John F. Kennedy was the first to commit the federal government to a specific numerical goal for unemployment. He picked a 4 percent target, but that goal was subsequently rejected as too ambitious in the 1970s and 1980s for three major reasons.

First, some economists argued that the 4 percent target had to be raised because the composition of the labor force had changed. Specifically, a large wave of young workers entered the labor force in the 1970s, and teenagers always have higher rates of unemployment than adults.

Second, the economists suggested, the increased generosity of unemployment compensation (which is discussed next) had reduced the incentive to get off the unemployment rolls. The logic here is simple. Because unemployment insurance reduces the income gap between those who work and those who collect unemployment benefits, it must therefore dull the incentive to seek and accept a job. And the more generous the benefits, the weaker the incentive.

A third reason stems from the short-run *trade-off between inflation and unemployment*, a notion we mentioned in Chapter 1 and which we will study in depth in Chapter 15. Economic research suggested that the original 4 percent unemployment target was too low in a very specific sense: Inflation would rise if unemployment remained at such a low level.

When the government abandoned the 4 percent unemployment target, no new number was put in its place. Instead, we have experienced a long-running debate over exactly how much measured unemployment corresponds to **full employment**. In the early 1990s, some economists argued that full employment came at a measured unemployment rate above 6 percent. But others pointed out that the main factors that had raised the full-employment unemployment rate in the 1970s were reversed in the 1980s. For example, the teenage labor force dwindled, and unemployment benefits went to a smaller percentage of the unemployed.

Full employment is a situation in which everyone who is willing and able to work can find a job. At full employment, the measured unemployment rate is still positive.

As it happened, real-world events decisively rejected the notion that the full-employment unemployment rate was as high as 6 percent. The boom of the 1990s pushed the unemployment rate below 6 percent by the fall of 1994 and then below 5 percent by the summer of 1997. It remained below 5 percent every month until September 2001, falling as low as 3.9 percent twice in 2000. All this left economists guessing where full employment might be. Official government reports issued early in 2004 estimated the full-employment unemployment rate to be just above 5 percent, but no one was totally confident in such estimates.

UNEMPLOYMENT INSURANCE: THE INVALUABLE CUSHION

One major reason why America's unemployed workers no longer experience the complete loss of income that devastated so many during the 1930s is our system of **unemployment insurance**—one of the most valuable institutional innovations to emerge from the trauma of the Great Depression.

Each of the 50 states administers an unemployment insurance program under federal guidelines. Although the precise amounts vary, the average weekly benefit check in 2003 was about $262, which amounted to approximately 49 percent of average earnings. Although a 51 percent drop in earnings still poses serious problems, the importance of this 49 percent income cushion can scarcely be exaggerated, especially because it may be supplemented by funds from other welfare programs. Families that are covered by unemployment insurance rarely go hungry or are dispossessed from their homes when they lose their jobs.

Unemployment insurance is a government program that replaces some of the wages lost by eligible workers who lose their jobs.

Eligibility for benefits varies by state, but some criteria apply quite generally. Only experienced workers qualify, so persons just joining the labor force (such as recent college graduates) or reentering after prolonged absences (such as women returning to the job market after years of child rearing) cannot collect benefits. Neither can those who quit their jobs, except under unusual circumstances. Also, benefits end after a stipulated period of time, normally six months. For all of these reasons, only some 41 percent of the roughly 8.75 million people who were unemployed in an average week in 2003 actually received benefits.

The importance of unemployment insurance to the unemployed is obvious. But significant benefits also accrue to citizens who never become unemployed. During recessions, billions of dollars are paid out in unemployment benefits, and because recipients probably spend most of their benefits, unemployment insurance limits the severity of recessions by providing additional purchasing power when and where it is most needed.

The unemployment insurance system is one of several cushions built into our economy since 1933 to prevent another Great Depression. By giving money to those who become unemployed, the system helps prop up aggregate demand during recessions.

Although the U.S. economy is now probably "depression-proof," this should not be a cause for too much rejoicing, for the many recessions we have had since the 1950s amply demonstrate that we are far from "recession-proof."

The fact that unemployment insurance and other social welfare programs replace a significant fraction of lost income has led some skeptics to claim that unemployment is no longer a serious problem. But the fact is that unemployment insurance is just what the name says—an *insurance* program. And insurance can never prevent a catastrophe from occurring; it simply spreads the costs among many people instead of letting all of the costs fall on the shoulders of a few unfortunate souls. As we noted earlier, unemployment robs the economy of output it could have produced, and no insurance policy can insure society against such losses.

Our system of payroll taxes and unemployment benefits spreads the costs of unemployment over the entire population. But it does not eliminate the basic economic cost.

PART 3: THE COSTS OF INFLATION

Both the human and economic costs of inflation are less obvious than the costs of unemployment. But this does not necessarily make them any less real, for if one thing is crystal clear about inflation, it is that people do not like it.

Nowadays, inflation barely registers as a problem in national public opinion polls. But when inflation is high, it often heads the list—generally even ahead of unemployment. Surveys also show that inflation, like unemployment, makes people unhappy. Finally, studies of elections suggest that voters penalize the party that occupies the White House when inflation is high.

The fact is beyond dispute: People dislike inflation. The question is, why?

INFLATION: THE MYTH AND THE REALITY

At first, the question may seem ridiculous. During inflationary times, people pay higher prices for the same quantities of goods and services they had before. So more and more income is needed just to maintain the same standard of living. Is it not obvious that this erosion of **purchasing power**—that is, the decline in what money will buy—makes everyone worse off?

The **purchasing power** of a given sum of money is the volume of goods and services that it will buy.

Inflation and Real Wages

The **real wage rate** is the wage rate adjusted for inflation. It indicates the volume of goods and services that money wages will buy.

This would indeed be the case were it not for one very significant fact. The wages that people earn are also prices—prices for labor services. During a period of inflation, wages also rise. In fact, the average wage typically rises more or less in step with prices. Thus, contrary to popular myth, workers as a group are not usually victimized by inflation.

The purchasing power of wages—what is called the **real wage rate**—is not systematically eroded by inflation. Sometimes wages rise faster than prices, and sometimes prices rise faster than wages. In the long run, wages tend to outstrip prices as new capital equipment and innovation increase output per worker.

SOURCE: By Cochran from *The Wall Street Journal*—Permission, Cartoon Features Syndicate.

"Sure, you're raising my allowance. But am I actually gaining any purchasing power?"

Figure 5-4 illustrates this simple fact. The red line shows the rate of increase of prices in the United States for each year since 1948, and the black line shows the rate of increase of wages. The difference between the two, shaded in the diagram, indicates the rate of growth of *real* wages. Generally, wages rise faster than prices, reflecting the steady advance of labor productivity; therefore, real wages rise. (But this is not always the case; the graph shows that real wages fell several times in the 1970s and 1980s.)

The feature of Figure 5-4 that virtually jumps off the page is the way the two lines dance together. Wages normally rise rapidly when prices rise rapidly, and they rise slowly when prices rise slowly. But you should not draw any hasty conclusions from this association. It does not, for example, imply that rising prices *cause* rising wages or that rising wages *cause* rising prices. Remember the warnings given in Chapter 1 about trying to infer causation just by looking at data. But analyzing cause and effect is not our purpose right now. We merely want to dispel the myth that inflation inevitably erodes real wages.

Why is this myth so widespread? Imagine a world without inflation in which wages are rising 2 percent per year because of the increasing productivity of labor. Now imagine that, all of a sudden, inflation sets in and prices start rising 3 percent per year but nothing else changes. Figure 5-4 suggests that, with perhaps a small delay, wage increases will accelerate to 2 + 3 = 5 percent per year.

Will workers view this change with equanimity? Probably not. To each worker, the 5 percent wage increase will be seen as something he earned by the sweat of his brow. In his view, he *deserves* every penny of his 5 percent raise. In a sense, he is right because "the sweat of his brow" earned him a 2 percent increment in real wages that, when the inflation rate is 3 percent, can be achieved only by increasing his money wages by 5 percent. An economist would divide the wage increase in the following way:

Reason for Wages to Increase	Amount
Higher productivity	2%
Compensation for higher prices	3%
Total	5%

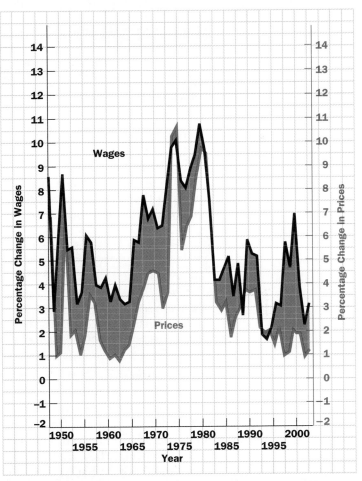

SOURCE: Bureau of Labor Statistics. Data pertain to the nonfarm business sector.

FIGURE 5-4

Rates of Change of Wages and Prices in the United States, 1948–2003

But the worker will probably keep score differently. Feeling that he earned the entire 5 percent raise by his own merits, he will view inflation as having "robbed" him of three-fifths of his just deserts. The higher the rate of inflation, the more of his raise the worker will feel has been stolen from him.

Of course, nothing could be farther from the truth. Basically, the economic system rewards the worker with *the same 2 percent real wage increment for higher productivity, regardless of the rate of inflation.* The "evils of inflation" are often exaggerated because people fail to understand this point.

The Illusion of Traditional "Fair" Prices

A second reason for misunderstanding the effects of inflation is that people tend to think in terms of the number of dollars it takes to buy something rather than in terms of the *purchasing power* of these dollars. For example, if both prices and wages double, people will have to work exactly the same amount of time as before to earn the price of a loaf of bread. But because they now pay $2 per loaf instead of $1, they feel that the price of bread is scandalously high. In fact, nothing has really changed, but people cling to an outmoded idea of what bread *should* cost.

The Importance of Relative Prices

An item's **relative price** is its price in terms of some other item rather than in terms of dollars.

A third misperception results from failure to distinguish between a *rise in the general price level* and a change in **relative prices,** which is a rise in one price relative to another. To see the distinction most clearly, imagine first a *pure inflation* in which *every* price rises by 10 percent during the year, so that relative prices do not change. Table 5-3 gives an example in which the price of movie tickets increases from $6.00 to $6.60, the price of candy bars from 50 cents to 55 cents, and the price of automobiles from $9,000 to $9,900. After the inflation, just as before, it will still take 12 candy bars to buy a movie ticket, 1,500 movie tickets to buy a car, and so on. A person who manufactures candy bars in order to purchase movie tickets is neither helped nor harmed by the inflation. Neither is a car dealer with a sweet tooth.

TABLE 5-3	Pure Inflation		
Item	Last Year's Price	This Year's Price	Increase
Candy bar	$0.50	$0.55	10%
Movie ticket	6.00	6.60	10
Automobile	9,000	9,900	10

But real inflations are not like this. When there is 10 percent general inflation—meaning that the "average price" rises by 10 percent—some prices may jump 20 percent or more while others actually fall.[6] Suppose that, instead of the price increases shown in Table 5-3, prices rise as shown in Table 5-4. Movie prices go up by 25 percent, but candy prices do not change. Surely, candy manufacturers who love movies will be disgruntled because it now costs 15 candy bars instead of 12 to get into the theater. They will blame inflation for raising the price of movie tickets, even though their real problem stems from the *increase in the price of movies relative to candy.* (They would have been hurt as much if movie tickets had remained at $6 while the price of candy fell to 40 cents.)

TABLE 5-4	Real-World Inflation		
Item	Last Year's Price	This Year's Price	Increase
Candy bar	$0.50	$0.50	0%
Movie ticket	6.00	7.50	25
Automobile	9,000	9,450	5

Because car prices have risen by only 5 percent, theater owners in need of new cars will be delighted by the fact that an auto now costs only 1,260 movie admissions—just as they would have cheered if car prices had fallen to $7,560 while movie tickets remained at $6. However, they are unlikely to attribute their good fortune to inflation. Indeed, they should not. What has actually happened is that *cars became cheaper relative to movies.*

Because real-world inflations proceed at uneven rates, relative prices are always changing. There are gainers and losers, just as some would gain and others lose if relative prices were to change without any general inflation. Inflation, however, gets a bad name because losers often blame inflation for their misfortune, whereas gainers rarely credit inflation for their good luck.

These three kinds of misconceptions help explain why respondents to public opinion polls often cite inflation as a major national issue, why higher inflation rates depress consumers, and why voters express their ire at the polls when inflation is high.

Inflation does not systematically erode the purchasing power of wages or lead to "unfair" prices. Nor is it usually to blame when some goods become more expensive relative to others.

---

[6] The way statisticians figure out "average" price increases is discussed in the appendix to this chapter.

But not all of the costs of inflation are mythical. Let us now turn to some of the real costs.

INFLATION AS A REDISTRIBUTOR OF INCOME AND WEALTH

We have just seen that the *average* person is neither helped nor harmed by inflation. But almost no one is exactly average! Some people gain from inflation and others lose. For example, senior citizens trying to scrape by on pensions or other fixed incomes suffer badly from inflation. Because they earn no wages, it is little solace to them that wages keep pace with prices. Their pension incomes do not.[7]

This example illustrates a general problem. Think of pensioners as people who "lend" money to an organization (the pension fund) when they are young and expect to be paid back with interest when they are old. Because of the rise in the price level during the intervening years, the unfortunate pensioners get back less valuable dollars than those they originally loaned. In general:

Those who lend money are apt to be victimized by inflation.

Although lenders may lose heavily, borrowers may do quite well. For example, homeowners who borrowed money from banks in the form of mortgages back in the 1950s, when interest rates were 3 or 4 percent, gained enormously from the surprisingly virulent inflation of the 1970s. They paid back dollars of much lower purchasing power than those that they borrowed. The same is true of other borrowers.

Borrowers often gain from inflation.

Because the redistribution caused by inflation generally benefits borrowers at the expense of lenders,[8] and because both lenders and borrowers can be found at every income level, we conclude that:

Inflation does not systematically steal from the rich to aid the poor, nor does it always do the reverse.

Why, then, is the redistribution caused by inflation so widely condemned? Because its victims are selected capriciously. No one legislates the redistribution. No one enters into it voluntarily. The gainers do not earn their spoils, and the losers do not deserve their fate. Moreover, inflation robs particular classes of people of purchasing power year after year—people living on private pensions, families who save money and "lend" it to banks, and workers whose wages and salaries do not adjust to higher prices. Even if the average person suffers no damage from inflation, that fact offers little consolation to those who are its victims. This is one fundamental indictment of inflation.

Inflation redistributes income in an arbitrary way. Society's income distribution should reflect the interplay of the operation of free markets and the purposeful efforts of government to alter that distribution. Inflation interferes with and distorts this process.

REAL VERSUS NOMINAL INTEREST RATES

But wait. Must inflation always rob lenders to bestow gifts upon borrowers? If both parties see inflation coming, won't lenders demand that borrowers pay a higher interest rate as compensation for the coming inflation? Indeed they will. For this reason, economists draw a sharp distinction between *expected* inflation and *unexpected* inflation.

What happens when inflation is fully expected by both parties? Suppose Diamond Jim wants to borrow $1,000 from Scrooge for one year, and both agree that, in the absence of inflation, a fair rate of interest would be 3 percent. This means that Diamond Jim would pay back $1,030 at the end of the year for the privilege of having $1,000 now.

---

[7] The same is not true of Social Security benefits, which are automatically increased to compensate recipients for changes in the price level.

[8] By the same token, *deflation* generally benefits lenders at the expense of borrowers, because the borrowers must pay back money of greater purchasing power.

If both men expect prices to increase by 6 percent, Scrooge may reason as follows: "If Diamond Jim pays me back $1,030 one year from today, that money will buy less than what $1,000 buys today. Thus, I'll really be *paying him* to borrow from me! I'm no philanthropist. Why don't I charge him 9 percent instead? Then he'll pay back $1,090 at the end of the year. With prices 6 percent higher, this will buy roughly what $1,030 is worth today. So I'll get the same 3 percent increase in purchasing power that we would have agreed on in the absence of inflation and won't be any worse off. That's the least I'll accept."

Diamond Jim may follow a similar chain of logic. "With no inflation, I was willing to pay $1,030 one year from now for the privilege of having $1,000 today, and Scrooge was willing to lend it. He'd be crazy to do the same with 6 percent inflation. He'll want to charge me more. How much should I pay? If I offer him $1,090 one year from now, that will have roughly the same purchasing power as $1,030 today, so I won't be any worse off. That's the most I'll pay."

This kind of thinking may lead Scrooge and Diamond Jim to write a contract with a 9 percent interest rate—3 percent as the increase in purchasing power that Diamond Jim pays to Scrooge and 6 percent as compensation for expected inflation. Then, if the expected 6 percent inflation actually materializes, neither party will be made better or worse off by inflation.

This example illustrates a general principle. The 3 percent increase in purchasing power that Diamond Jim agrees to turn over to Scrooge is called the **real rate of interest.** The 9 percent contractual interest charge that Diamond Jim and Scrooge write into the loan agreement is called the **nominal rate of interest.** The nominal rate of interest is calculated by adding the *expected rate of inflation* to the real rate of interest. Expected inflation is added to compensate the lender for the loss of purchasing power that the lender expects to suffer as a result of inflation. Because of this:

> **Inflation that is accurately predicted need not redistribute income between borrowers and lenders. If the *expected* rate of inflation that is embodied in the nominal interest rate matches the *actual* rate of inflation, no one gains and no one loses. However, to the extent that expectations prove incorrect, inflation will still redistribute income.[9]**

It need hardly be pointed out that errors in predicting the rate of inflation are the norm, not the exception. Published forecasts bear witness to the fact that economists have great difficulty in predicting the rate of inflation. The task is no easier for businesses, consumers, and banks. This is another reason why inflation is so widely condemned as unfair and undesirable. It sets up a guessing game that no one likes.

The real rate of interest is the percentage increase in purchasing power that the borrower pays to the lender for the privilege of borrowing. It indicates the increased ability to purchase goods and services that the lender earns.

The nominal rate of interest is the percentage by which the money the borrower pays back exceeds the money that she borrowed, making no adjustment for any decline in the purchasing power of this money that results from inflation.

INFLATION DISTORTS MEASUREMENTS

As we see, inflation imposes costs on society because it is difficult to predict. But other costs arise even when inflation is predicted accurately. Many such costs stem from the fact that people are simply unaccustomed to thinking in inflation-adjusted terms and so make errors in thinking and calculation. Many laws and regulations that were designed for an inflation-free economy malfunction when inflation is high. Here are some important examples.

Confusing Real and Nominal Interest Rates

People frequently confuse *real* and *nominal* interest rates. For example, most Americans viewed the 12 percent mortgage interest rates that banks charged in 1980 as scandalously high but saw the 6 percent mortgage rates of 2003 as a great bargain. In

---

[9] *Exercise:* Who gains and who loses if the inflation turns out to be only 4 percent instead of the 6 percent that Scrooge and Diamond Jim expected? What if the inflation rate is 8 percent?

truth, the real interest rate in 2003 (over 4 percent) was above the bargain-basement real rates in 1980 (about 2 percent).

Public Utility Regulation

A similar problem arose in regulating public utilities. When utilities asked their regulatory agencies to permit them to earn a rate of return closer to 11 percent—a *negative* real rate of return!—there was a public uproar. The companies frequently found that their "exorbitant" requests for rate hikes were rejected by the commissions. One consequence was that many utilities could no longer afford to borrow the money needed to build new generating capacity. Subsequent power shortages were among the predictable results.

The Malfunctioning Tax System

The tax system is probably the most important example of inflation illusion at work. The law does not recognize the distinction between *nominal* and *real* interest rates; it simply taxes nominal interest regardless of how much real interest it represents. Similarly, **capital gains**—the difference between the price at which an investor sells an asset and the price that she paid for it—are taxed in nominal, not real, terms. As a result, our tax system can do strange things when inflation is high. An example will show why.

A **capital gain** is the difference between the price at which an asset is sold and the price at which it was bought.

Between 1981 and 2003, the price level roughly doubled. Consider some stock that was purchased for $20,000 in 1981 and sold for $35,000 in 2003. The investor actually *lost* purchasing power while holding the stock because $35,000 in 2003 could purchase less than $20,000 in 1981. Yet because the law levies taxes on nominal capital gains, with no correction for inflation, the investor would be taxed on the $15,000 *nominal* capital gain.

Many economists have proposed that this (presumably unintended) feature of the law be changed by taxing only capital gains in excess of inflation. To date, Congress has not agreed. This little example illustrates a pervasive and serious problem:

> Because it fails to recognize the distinction between nominal and real capital gains, our tax system levies high, and presumably unintended, tax rates on capital income when there is high inflation. Similar problems arise in the taxation of interest, corporate profits, and other items. Thus the laws that govern our financial system can become counterproductive in an inflationary environment, causing problems that were never intended by the legislators. Some economists feel that the high tax rates caused by inflation discourage saving, lending, and investing—and therefore retard economic growth.

Thus, failure to understand that high *nominal* interest rates can still be low *real* interest rates has been known to make the tax code misfire, to impoverish savers, to inhibit borrowing and lending, and to make it nearly impossible for public utilities to raise capital. It is important to note that *these costs of inflation are not purely redistributive.* Society as a whole loses when mutually beneficial transactions are prohibited by dysfunctional legislation.

Why, then, do such harmful laws stay on the books? The main reason may be a lack of understanding of the difference between real and nominal interest rates. People fail to understand that it is normally the *real* rate of interest that matters in an economic transaction because only that rate reveals how much borrowers pay and lenders receive *in terms of the goods and services that money can buy.* They focus on the high *nominal* interest rates caused by inflation, even when these rates correspond to low real interest rates.

> The difference between real and nominal interest rates, and the fact that the real rate matters economically whereas the nominal rate is often politically significant, are matters that are of the utmost importance and yet are understood by very few people—including many who make public policy decisions.

OTHER COSTS OF INFLATION

Another cost of inflation is that rapidly changing prices make it risky to enter into long-term contracts. In an extremely severe inflation, the "long term" may be only a few days. But even moderate inflations can have remarkable effects on long-term loans. Suppose a corporation wants to borrow $1 million to finance the purchase of some new equipment and needs the loan for 20 years. If inflation averages 2 percent over this period, the $1 million it repays at the end of 20 years will be worth $672,971 in today's purchasing power. But if inflation averages 5 percent instead, it will be worth only $376,889.

Lending or borrowing for this long a period is obviously a big gamble. With the stakes so high, the outcome may be that neither lenders nor borrowers want to get involved in long-term contracts. But without long-term loans, business investment may become impossible. The economy may stagnate.

Inflation also makes life difficult for the shopper. You probably have a group of stores that you habitually patronize because they carry the items you want to buy at (roughly) the prices you want to pay. This knowledge saves you a great deal of time and energy. But when prices are changing rapidly, your list quickly becomes obsolete. You return to your favorite clothing store to find that the price of jeans has risen drastically. Should you buy? Should you shop around at other stores? Will they have also raised their prices? Business firms have precisely the same problem with their suppliers. Rising prices force them to shop around more, which imposes costs on the firms and, more generally, reduces the efficiency of the entire economy.

THE COSTS OF LOW VERSUS HIGH INFLATION

The preceding litany of the costs of inflation alerts us to one very important fact: *Predictable inflation is far less burdensome than unpredictable inflation.* When is inflation most predictable? When it proceeds year after year at a modest and more or less steady rate. Thus, the *variability of the inflation rate* is a crucial factor. Inflation of 3 percent per year for three consecutive years will exact lower social costs than inflation that is 2 percent in the first year, zero in the second year, and 7 percent in the third year. In general:

Steady inflation is more predictable than variable inflation and therefore has smaller social and economic costs.

But the *average level of inflation* also matters. Partly because of the inflation illusions mentioned earlier and partly because of the more rapid breakdown in normal customer relationships that we have just mentioned, steady inflation at 6 percent per year is more damaging than steady inflation at 3 percent per year.

Economists distinguish between *low inflation*, which is a modest economic problem, and *high inflation*, which can be a devastating one, partly on the basis of the average level of inflation and partly on its variability. If inflation remains steady and low, prices may rise for a long time, but at a moderate and fairly constant pace, allowing people to adapt. For example, prices in the United States climbed a total of 58 percent from 1982 to 1996, for an average annual inflation rate of 3.3 percent. And the pace of inflation was remarkably steady, never dropping below 2.1 percent nor rising above 4.4 percent.

Very high inflations typically last for short periods of time and are often marked by highly variable inflation rates from month to month or year to year. In recent decades, for example, countries ranging from Argentina to Israel to Russia have experienced bouts of inflation exceeding 100 percent or even 1,000 percent per year. (See "Hyperinflation and the Piggy Bank.") Each of these episodes severely disrupted the affected country's economy.

Hyperinflation and the Piggy Bank

Whereas mild inflations are barely noticeable in everyday life, hyperinflation makes all sorts of normal economic activities more difficult and transforms a society in strange and unexpected ways. This article, excerpted from *The New York Times,* illustrates some of the problems that hyperinflation created for Nicaraguans in 1989.

For generations, Nicaraguans have guarded their savings in piggy banks. . . . But no longer. In a country where inflation recently reached 161 percent for a 2-week period, a penny saved is a penny spent. "No one wants a bank now," said a potter who has given over his kilns to making beer mugs. "We've given up even making them."

The demise of the piggy bank is only the least of the complications that have vexed the public as inflation and government efforts to combat it have sent the value of the Nicaraguan córdoba fluctuating wildly . . .

That kind of uncertainty has left the banking system in shambles, despite savings accounts that offer up to 70 percent interest a month. . . . And it has left a legacy of quirks that now extends throughout the country's daily life. . . .

In many parts of the country, enterprising mechanics have converted the nation's once-precious stock of coins into something more valuable: metal washers to fit the nuts and bolts of rapidly deteriorating machinery. . . .

In Managua, it is still necessary to deposit a copper-colored 1-córdoba coin to make a pay phone call. But . . . not everybody even remembers what a 1-córdoba coin looks like, and fewer still actually own one. That is probably just as well for the phone system, because if anyone bothered to carry the coins, they could make about 26,250 phone calls for a dollar. . . .

SOURCE: © Mario Tapia/*The New York Times*

SOURCE: Mark A. Uhlig, "Is Nicaraguan Bank an Endangered Species?" *The New York Times,* June 22, 1989, p.2. Copyright © 1989 by the New York Times Company. Reprinted by permission.

The German hyperinflation after World War I is perhaps the most famous episode of runaway inflation. Between December 1922 and November 1923, when a hard-nosed reform program finally broke the spiral, wholesale prices in Germany increased by almost 100 million percent! But even this experience was dwarfed by the great Hungarian inflation of 1945–1946, the greatest inflation of them all. For a period of one year, the *monthly* rate of inflation averaged about 20,000 percent. In the final month, the price level skyrocketed 42 quadrillion percent!

If you review the costs of inflation that have been discussed in this chapter, you will see why the distinction between low and high inflation is so fundamental. Many economists think we can live rather nicely in an environment of steady, low inflation. No one believes we can survive very well under extremely high inflation.

When inflation is steady and low, the rate at which prices rise is relatively easy to predict. It can therefore be taken into account in setting interest rates. Under high inflation, especially if prices are rising at ever-increasing or highly variable rates, this is extremely difficult, and perhaps impossible, to do. The potential redistributions become monumental, and lending and borrowing may cease entirely.

Any inflation makes it difficult to write long-term contracts. Under low, creeping inflation, the "long term" may be 20 years, or 10 years, or 5 years. By contrast, under high, galloping inflation, the "long term" may be measured in days or weeks. Restaurant prices may change daily. Airfares may go up while you are in the

SOURCE: © Camera Press/Globe Photos, Inc.

These children in Germany during the hyperinflation of the 1920s are building a pyramid with cash, worth no more than the sand or sticks used by children elsewhere.

middle of your journey. When it is impossible to enter into contracts of any duration longer than a few days, economic activity becomes paralyzed. We conclude that:

The horrors of hyperinflation either are absent in low, steady inflations or are present in such muted forms that they can scarcely be considered horrors.

LOW INFLATION DOES NOT NECESSARILY LEAD TO HIGH INFLATION

We noted earlier that inflation is surrounded by a mythology that bears precious little relation to reality. It seems appropriate to conclude this chapter by disposing of one particularly persistent myth: that low inflation is a slippery slope that invariably leads to high inflation.

There is neither statistical evidence nor theoretical support for the belief that low inflation inevitably leads to high inflation. To be sure, inflations sometimes speed up. At other times, however, they slow down.

Although creeping inflations have many causes, runaway inflations have occurred only when the government has printed incredible amounts of money, usually to finance wartime expenditures. In the German inflation of 1923, the government finally found that its printing presses could not produce enough paper money to keep pace with the exploding prices. Not that it did not try—by the end of the inflation, the *daily* output of currency exceeded 400 quadrillion marks! The Hungarian authorities in 1945–1946 tried even harder: The average growth rate of the money supply was more than 12,000 percent *per month*. Needless to say, these are not the kind of inflation problems that are likely to face industrialized countries in the foreseeable future.

But that does not mean there is nothing wrong with low inflation. We have spent several pages analyzing the very real costs of even modest inflation. A case against moderate inflation can indeed be built, but it does not help this case to shout slogans like "Creeping inflation always leads to galloping inflation." Fortunately, it is simply not true.

SUMMARY

1. Macroeconomic policy strives to achieve rapid growth while keeping both unemployment and inflation low.

2. Only rising productivity can raise standards of living in the long run. And seemingly small differences in productivity growth rates can compound to enormous differences in living standards. This is one of our *Ideas for Beyond the Final Exam*.

3. The **production function** tells us how much output the economy can produce from the available supplies of labor and capital, given the state of technology.

4. The growth rate of **potential GDP** is the sum of two things: the growth rate of the **labor force** and the growth rate of **labor productivity**. The latter depends on, among other things, technological change and investment in new capital.

5. Over long periods of time, the growth rates of actual and potential GDP match up quite well. But the two can diverge sharply over short periods.

6. Although some psychologists, environmentalists, and social critics question the merits of faster economic growth, economists generally assume that faster growth of potential GDP is socially beneficial.

7. When GDP is below its potential, unemployment is above "**full employment.**" High unemployment exacts heavy financial and psychological costs from those who are its victims, costs that are borne quite unevenly by different groups in the population.

8. **Frictional unemployment** arises when people are between jobs for normal reasons. Thus, most frictional unemployment is desirable.

9. **Structural unemployment** is due to shifts in the pattern of demand or to technological change that makes certain skills obsolete.

10. **Cyclical unemployment** is the portion of unemployment that rises when real GDP grows more slowly than potential GDP and falls when the opposite is true.

11. Today, after years of extremely low unemployment, economists are unsure where full employment lies. Some think it may be at a measured unemployment rate between 5 and 5.5 percent.

12. **Unemployment insurance** replaces nearly one-half of the lost income of unemployed persons who are insured. But fewer than half of the unemployed actually collect benefits,

and no insurance program can bring back the lost output that could have been produced had these people been working.

13. People have many misconceptions about inflation. For example, many believe that inflation systematically erodes **real wages,** are appalled by rising prices even when wages are rising just as fast, and blame inflation for any unfavorable changes in relative prices. All of these ideas are myths.

14. Other costs of inflation are real, however. For example, inflation often redistributes income from lenders to borrowers.

15. This redistribution is ameliorated by adding the expected rate of inflation to the interest rate. But such expectations often prove to be inaccurate.

16. The **real rate of interest** is the **nominal rate of interest** minus the expected rate of inflation.

17. Because the real rate of interest indicates the command over real resources that the borrower surrenders to the lender, it is of primary economic importance. But public attention often is riveted on nominal rates of interest, and this confusion can lead to costly policy mistakes.

18. Because nominal—not real—**capital gains** and interest are taxed, our tax system levies heavy taxes on income from capital when inflation is high.

19. Low inflation that proceeds at moderate and fairly predictable rates year after year carries far lower social costs than does high or variable inflation. But even low, steady inflations entail costs.

20. The notion that low inflation inevitably accelerates into high inflation is a myth with no foundation in economic theory and no basis in historical fact.

KEY TERMS

Inputs 78	Real GDP per capita 82	Purchasing power 90
Outputs 78	Unemployment rate 84	Real wage rate 90
Economic growth 78	Discouraged workers 87	Relative prices 92
Growth policy 78	Frictional unemployment 87	Redistribution by inflation 93
Labor productivity 79	Structural unemployment 88	Real rate of interest 94
Potential GDP 80	Cyclical unemployment 88	Nominal rate of interest 94
Labor force 80	Full employment 89	Expected rate of inflation 94
Production function 80	Unemployment insurance 89	Capital gain 95

QUESTIONS FOR REVIEW

1. Two countries start with equal GDPs. The economy of Country A grows at an annual rate of 2 percent while the economy of Country B grows at an annual rate of 2.5 percent. After 25 years, how much larger is Country B's economy than Country A's economy? Why is the answer *not* 12.5 percent?

2. If output rises by 25 percent while hours of work increase by 30 percent, has productivity increased or decreased? By how much?

3. Most economists believe that from 1994 to 2000, actual GDP in the United States grew faster than potential GDP. What, then, should have happened to the unemployment rate? (Check the data on the inside back cover of this book to see what actually happened.)

4. If an earthquake destroys some of the factories in Poorland, what happens to Poorland's potential GDP? What happens to Poorland's potential GDP if it acquires some new advanced technology from Richland, and starts using it?

5. Country A and Country B have identical population growth rates of 1.5 percent per annum, and everyone in each country always works 40 hours per week. Labor productivity grows at a rate of 2 percent in Country A and a rate of 2.5 percent in Country B. What are the growth rates of potential GDP in the two countries?

6. Why may it not be as terrible to become unemployed nowadays as it was during the Great Depression?

7. "Unemployment is no longer a social problem because unemployed workers receive unemployment benefits and other benefits that make up for most of their lost wages." Comment.

8. Why is it so difficult to define *full employment?* What unemployment rate should the government be shooting for today?

9. Show why each of the following complaints is based on a misunderstanding about inflation:

   a. "Inflation must be stopped because it robs workers of their purchasing power."

   b. "Inflation is a terrible social disease. It leads to unconscionably high prices for basic necessities."

   c. "Inflation makes it impossible for working people to afford many of the things they were hoping to buy."

   d. "Inflation must be stopped today, for if we do not stop it, it will surely accelerate to ruinously high rates and lead to disaster."

10. What is the *real interest rate* paid on a credit-card loan bearing 18 percent nominal interest per year, if the rate of inflation is

   a. zero?

   b. 3 percent?

   c. 6 percent?

   d. 12 percent?

   e. 18 percent?

11. Suppose you agree to lend money to your friend on the day you both enter college at what you both expect to be a zero *real* rate of interest. Payment is to be made at graduation, with interest at a fixed *nominal* rate. If inflation proves to be *lower* during your college years than what you both had expected, who will gain and who will lose?

APPENDIX   How Statisticians Measure Inflation

INDEX NUMBERS FOR INFLATION

Inflation is generally measured by the change in some index of the general price level. For example, between 1973 and 2001 the Consumer Price Index (CPI), the most widely used measure of the price level, rose from 44.4 to 177.1—an increase of 299 percent. The meaning of the *change* is clear enough. But what are the meanings of the 44.4 figure for the price level of 1973 and the 177.1 figure for 2001? Both are **index numbers.**

An index number expresses the cost of a market basket of goods *relative to its cost in some "base" period,* which is simply the year used as a basis of comparison.

Because the CPI currently uses 1982–1984 as its base period, the CPI of 177.1 for 2001 means that it costs $177.10 to purchase the same basket of several hundred goods and services that cost $100 in 1982–1984.

Now, the particular list of consumer goods and services under scrutiny did not actually cost $100 in 1982–1984. When constructing index numbers, by convention the index is set at 100 in the base period. How is this conventional figure used in obtaining index numbers of other years? Very simply. Suppose that the budget needed to buy the roughly 350 items included in the CPI was $2,000 per month in 1982–1984 and $3,542 per month in 2001. Then the index is defined by the following rule:

$$\frac{\text{CPI in 2001}}{\text{CPI in 1982–1984}}$$

$$= \frac{\text{Cost of market basket in 2001}}{\text{Cost of the market basket in 1982–1984}}$$

Because the CPI in 1982–1984 is set at 100:

$$\frac{\text{CPI in 2001}}{100} = \frac{\$3,542}{\$2,000} = 1.771$$

or

$$\text{CPI in 2001} = 177.1$$

Exactly the same sort of equation enables us to calculate the CPI in any other year. We have the following rule:

$$\text{CPI in given year} = \frac{\begin{array}{c}\text{Cost of market basket}\\ \text{in given year}\end{array}}{\begin{array}{c}\text{Cost of market basket}\\ \text{in base year}\end{array}} \times 100$$

Of course, not every combination of consumer goods that cost $2,000 in 1982–1984 rose to $3,542 by 2001. For example, a color TV set that cost $400 in 1983 might still have cost $400 in 2001, but a $400 hospital bill in 1983 might have ballooned to $1,600.

The index number problem is the fact that there is no perfect cost-of-living index because no two families buy precisely the same bundle of goods and services, and hence no two families suffer precisely the same increase in prices. Economists refer to this phenomenon as the *index number problem.*

When relative prices are changing, there is no such thing as a "perfect price index" that is correct for every consumer. Any statistical index will understate the increase in the cost of living for some families and overstate it for others. At best, the index can represent the situation of an "average" family.

THE CONSUMER PRICE INDEX

The **Consumer Price Index (CPI),** which is calculated and announced each month by the Bureau of Labor Statistics (BLS), is surely the most closely watched price index. When you read in the newspaper or see on television that the "cost of living rose by 0.2 percent last month," chances are the reporter is referring to the CPI.

The Consumer Price Index (CPI) is measured by pricing the items on a list representative of a typical urban household budget.

To know which items to include and in what amounts, the BLS conducts an extensive survey of spending habits roughly once every decade. As a consequence, the *same*

TABLE 5-5 Results of Student Expenditure Survey, 1983

Item	Average Price	Average Quantity Purchased per Month	Average Expenditure per Month
Hamburger	$ 0.80	70	$56
Jeans	24.00	1	24
Movie ticket	5.00	4	20
Total			$100

TABLE 5-7 Cost of 1983 Student Budget in 2001 Prices

70 Hamburgers at $1.20	$84
1 pair of jeans at $30	30
4 movie tickets at $7	28
Total	$142

bundle of goods and services is used as a standard for ten years or so, whether or not spending habits change.[10] Of course, spending habits do change, and this variation introduces a small error into the CPI's measurement of inflation.

A simple example will help us understand how the CPI is constructed. Imagine that college students purchase only three items—hamburgers, jeans, and movie tickets—and that we want to devise a cost-of-living index (call it SPI, or "Student Price Index") for them. First, we would conduct a survey of spending habits in the base year. (Suppose it is 1983.) Table 5-5 represents the hypothetical results. You will note that the frugal students of that day spent only $100 per month: $56 on hamburgers, $24 on jeans, and $20 on movies.

Table 5-6 presents hypothetical prices of these same three items in 2001. Each price has risen by a different amount, ranging from 25 percent for jeans up to 50 percent for hamburgers. By how much has the SPI risen? Pricing the 1983 student budget at 2001 prices, we find that what once cost $100 now costs $142, as the calculation in Table 5-7 shows. Thus, the SPI, based on 1983 = 100, is

$$\text{SPI} = \frac{\text{Cost of budget in 2001}}{\text{Cost of budget in 1983}} \times 100 = \frac{\$142}{\$100} \times 100 = 142$$

So, the SPI in 2001 stands at 142, meaning that students' cost of living has increased 42 percent over the 18 years.

TABLE 5-6 Prices in 2001

Item	Price	Increase over 1983
Hamburger	$1.20	50%
Jeans	30.00	25
Movie ticket	7.00	40

---

[10] Economists call this a *base-period weight index* because the relative importance it attaches to the price of each item depends on how much money consumers actually chose to spend on the item during the base period.

HOW TO USE A PRICE INDEX TO "DEFLATE" MONETARY FIGURES

One of the most common uses of price indexes is in the comparison of monetary figures relating to two different points in time. The problem is that, if there has been inflation, the dollar is not a good measuring rod because it can buy less now than it did in the past.

Here is a simple example. Suppose the average student spent $100 per month in 1983 but $130 per month in 2001. If there was an outcry that students had become spendthrifts, how would you answer the charge?

The obvious answer is that a dollar in 2001 does not buy what it did in 1983. Specifically, our SPI shows us that it takes $1.42 in 2001 to purchase what $1 would purchase in 1983. To compare the spending habits of students in the two years, we must divide the 2001 spending figure by 1.42. Specifically, *real* spending per student in 2001 (where "real" is defined by 1983 dollars) is:

$$\text{Real spending in 2001} = \frac{\text{Nominal spending in 2001}}{\text{Price index of 2001}} \times 100$$

Thus:

$$\text{Real spending in 2001} = \frac{\$130}{142} \times 100 = \$91.55$$

This calculation shows that, despite appearances to the contrary, the change in nominal spending from $100 to $130 actually represented a *decrease* in real spending.

This procedure is called **deflating** by a price index, and it serves to translate noncomparable monetary figures into more directly comparable real figures.

Deflating is the process of finding the real value of some monetary magnitude by dividing by some appropriate price index.

A good practical illustration is the real wage, a concept we have discussed in this chapter. Average hourly earnings in the U.S. economy were $8.02 in 1983 and $14.33 in 2001. Since the CPI in 2001 was 177.1 (with 1982–1984 as the base period), the real wage in 2001 (expressed in 1982–1984 dollars) was:

$$\text{Real wage in 2001} = \frac{\text{Money wage in 2001}}{\text{Price index of 2001}}$$

$$= \frac{\$14.33}{177.1} \times 100 = \$8.09$$

Thus, by this measure, the real wage rose less than 1 percent over the 18 years.

THE GDP DEFLATOR

In macroeconomics, one of the most important of the monetary magnitudes that we have to deflate is the nominal gross domestic product (GDP).

The price index used to deflate nominal GDP is called the **GDP deflator**. It is a broad measure of economy-wide inflation; it includes the prices of all goods and services in the economy.

Our general principle for deflating a nominal magnitude tells us how to go from nominal GDP to real GDP:

$$\text{Real GDP} = \frac{\text{Nominal GDP}}{\text{GDP deflator}} \times 100$$

As with the CPI, the 100 simply serves to establish the base of the index as 100, rather than 1.00.

Some economists consider the GDP deflator to be a better measure of overall inflation than the Consumer Price Index. The main reason is that the GDP deflator is based on a broader market basket. As mentioned earlier, the CPI is based on the budget of a typical urban family. By contrast, the GDP deflator is constructed from a market basket that includes *every* item in the GDP—that is, every final good and service produced by the economy. Thus, in addition to prices of consumer goods, the GDP deflator includes the prices of airplanes, lathes, and other goods purchased by businesses—especially computers, which fall in price every year. It also includes government services.

For this reason, the two indexes rarely give the same measure of inflation. Usually the discrepancy is minor. But sometimes it can be substantial, as in 1990 when the CPI recorded a 6.1 percent inflation rate over 1989 while the GDP deflator recorded an inflation rate of only 4.3 percent.

SUMMARY

1. Inflation is measured by the percentage increase in an **index number** of prices, which shows how the cost of some basket of goods has changed over a period of time.

2. Because relative prices are always changing, and because different families purchase different items, no price index can represent precisely the experience of every family.

3. The **Consumer Price Index (CPI)** tries to measure the cost of living for an average urban household by pricing a typical market basket every month.

4. Price indexes such as the CPI can be used to **deflate** monetary figures to make them more comparable. Deflation amounts to dividing the monetary magnitude by the appropriate price index.

5. The **GDP deflator** is a broader measure of economy-wide inflation than the CPI because it includes the prices of all goods and services in the economy.

KEY TERMS

Index number   100

Index number problem   100

Consumer Price Index   100

Deflating   101

GDP deflator   102

QUESTIONS FOR REVIEW

1. At the right you will find the yearly average values of the Dow Jones Industrial Average, the most popular index of stock market prices, for five different years. The Consumer Price Index for each year (on a base of 1982–1984 = 100) can be found on the inside back cover of this book. Use these numbers to deflate all five stock market values. In which year were stocks worth the most?

Year	Dow Jones Industrial Average
1965	911
1972	951
1987	2,276
1994	3,794
2001	10,189

2. Below you will find nominal GDP and the GDP deflator for the years 1981, 1991, and 2001.

GDP Statistics	1981	1991	2001
Nominal GDP (Billions of dollars)	3,131	5,986	10,206
GDP deflator	62.4	89.7	109.4

a. Compute real GDP for each year.

b. Compute the percentage change in nominal and real GDP from 1981 to 1991, and from 1991 to 2001.

c. Compute the percentage change in the GDP deflator over these two periods.

3. Fill in the blanks in the following table of GDP statistics:

	1999	2000	2001
Nominal GDP	9,269		10,206
Real GDP	8,857	9,224	
GDP deflator		107.0	109.4

4. Use the following data to compute the College Price Index for 2001 using the base 1972 = 100.

Item	Price in 1972	Quantity per Month in 1972	Price in 2001
Button-down shirts	$10	1	$25
Loafers	25	1	55
Sneakers	10	3	35
Textbooks	12	12	40
Jeans	12	3	30
Restaurant meals	5	11	14

5. Average hourly earnings in the U.S. economy during several past years were as follows:

1970	1980	1990	2000
$3.23	$6.66	$10.01	$13.75

Use the CPI numbers provided on the inside back cover of this book to calculate the real wage (in 1982–1984 dollars) for each of these years. Which decade had the fastest growth of money wages? Which had the fastest growth of real wages?

6. The example in the appendix showed that the Student Price Index (SPI) rose by 42 percent from 1983 to 2001. You can understand the meaning of this better if you do the following:

a. Use Table 5-5 to compute the fraction of total spending accounted for by each of the three items in 1983. Call these values the "expenditure weights."

b. Compute the weighted average of the percentage increases of the three prices shown in Table 5-6, using the expenditure weights you just computed.

You should get 42 percent as your answer. This shows that "inflation," as measured by the SPI, is a weighted average of the percentage price increases of all the items that are included in the index.

6

Economic Growth: Theory and Policy

Once one starts to think about . . . [differences in growth rates across countries], it is hard to think about anything else.

ROBERT E. LUCAS, 1995 NOBEL PRIZE WINNER IN ECONOMICS

Why do some economies grow rapidly while others grow slowly—or not at all? There is perhaps no more important question in all of economics. Chapter 5's discussion of growth focused our attention on two crucial but distinct tasks for macroeconomic policymakers, both of which are quite difficult to achieve:

- *Growth policy:* Ensure that the economy sustains a high long-run growth rate of potential GDP (though not necessarily the *highest possible* growth rate).

- *Stabilization policy:* Keep actual GDP reasonably close to potential GDP in the short run, so that society is plagued by neither high unemployment nor high inflation.

This chapter is devoted to growth policy. We will study the factors that determine an economy's long-run growth rate, and we will ask how policymakers can speed it up.

As we learned in Chapter 5, the growth rate of potential GDP is the *sum* of the growth rates of *hours of work* and *labor productivity*. It is certainly no mystery that an economy will grow if its people keep working harder and harder, year after year. And a few societies have followed that recipe successfully for relatively brief periods of time. But, of course, there is a limit to how much people can work or, more importantly, to how much they want to work. In fact, people typically want more leisure time, not longer hours of work, as they get richer. So as a consequence, the focus of growth policy is, naturally, on enhancing productivity—on working *smarter* rather than working *harder*.

CONTENTS

Puzzle: Why Does College Education Keep Getting More Expensive?

SOURCES: © Jose L. Pelaez/corbisstockmarket

Have you ever wondered why the cost of a college education rises more rapidly than most other prices year after year? If you have not, your parents surely have! And it's not a myth. Between 1978 and 2003, the component of the Consumer Price Index (CPI) that measures college tuition costs rose by a cumulative 674 percent—compared to just 182 percent for the overall CPI. That is, the *relative* price of college tuition increased massively.

Economists understand at least part of the reason, and it has little, if anything, to do with the efficiency (or lack thereof) with which colleges are run. Rather, it is a natural accompaniment to the economy's long-run growth rate. Furthermore, there is good reason to expect the relative price of college tuition to rise more rapidly in faster-growing societies. Economists believe that the same explanation for the unusually rapid growth in the cost of attending college applies to services as diverse as visits to the doctor, theatrical performances, and restaurant meals—all of which have also grown relatively more expensive over time. Later in this chapter, we shall see precisely what this explanation is.

THE THREE PILLARS OF PRODUCTIVITY GROWTH

The last chapter introduced a tool called the *production function*, which tells us how much *output* the economy can produce from specified *inputs* of labor and capital, given the state of *technology*. The discussion there focused on two of the three main determinants of productivity growth:[1]

- The rate at which the economy builds up its stock of *capital*
- The rate at which *technology* improves

Before introducing the third determinant, let us review how these first two pillars work.

Capital

Figure 6-1 resembles Figure 5-1 (see page 81). The lower, black curve $0K_1$ is the production function when the capital stock is some low number, K_1. Its upward slope indicates, naturally enough, that larger quantities of labor input produce more output. (Remember, technology is held constant in this graph.) The middle, red curve $0K_2$ is the production function corresponding to some larger capital stock, K_2, and the upper, blue curve $0K_3$ pertains to an even larger capital stock, K_3.

To keep things simple at first, suppose hours of work do not grow over time, but rather remain fixed at L_1. However, the nation's businesses invest in new plant and equipment, so the capital stock grows from K_1 in the first year to K_2 in the second year and K_3 in the third year. Then the economy's capacity to produce will move up from point a in year 1 to point b in year 2 and point c in year 3. Potential GDP will therefore rise from Y_a to Y_b to Y_c. Because hours of work do not change in this example (by assumption), every bit of this growth comes from rising *productivity*.[2] In general:

---

[1] If you need review, see pages 80–82 of Chapter 5.

[2] Because productivity is the ratio Y/L, it is shown on the graph by the *slope* of the straight-line connecting the origin to point a, or point b, or point c. Clearly, that slope is rising over time.

For a given technology and labor force, labor productivity will be higher when the capital stock is larger.

This conclusion is hardly surprising. Employees who work with more capital can obviously produce more goods and services. Just imagine manufacturing a desk with (1) a hammer and saw, (2) power tools, or (3) all the equipment available in a modern furniture factory. Or think about selling books (1) from a sidewalk stand, (2) in a bookstore, or (3) over the Internet. Indeed, the volume of *capital per worker* is one of the main factors distinguishing rich countries from poor ones. Furthermore, workers with *more* capital are almost certainly blessed with *newer*—and hence *better*—capital as well. This advantage, too, makes them more productive. Again, compare one of Henry Ford's assembly-line workers of a century ago to an autoworker in a Ford plant today.

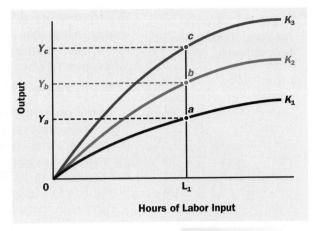

FIGURE 6-1

Production Functions Corresponding to Three Different Capital Stocks

Technology

In Chapter 5, we saw that the same graph can be used to depict the effects of *improvements in technology.* So now imagine that curves $0K_1$, $0K_2$, and $0K_3$ in Figure 6-1 all correspond to the *same* capital stock, but to *different* levels of technology. Specifically, the economy's technology improves as we move up from $0K_1$ to $0K_2$ to $0K_3$. The graphical (and common-sense) conclusion is exactly the same: Labor becomes more productive from year 1 to year 2 to year 3. In general:

For given inputs of labor and capital, labor productivity will be higher when the technology is better.

Once again, this conclusion hardly comes as a surprise—indeed, it is barely more than the definition of technical progress. When we say that a nation's technology improves, we mean, more or less, that firms in the country can produce more output from the same inputs. And of course, superior technology is the second major factor behind the vastly higher productivity of workers in rich countries versus poor ones. Textile plants in North Carolina, for example, use technologies that are far superior to those employed in Africa.

Labor Quality: Education and Training

It is now time to introduce the third pillar of productivity growth, the one not mentioned in Chapter 5: *workforce quality.* It is generally assumed—and supported by reams of evidence—that more highly educated workers can produce more goods and services in an hour than can less well-educated workers. And the same lesson applies to training that takes place outside the schools, such as on the job: Better-trained workers are more productive. The amount of education and training embodied in a nation's labor force is often referred to as its stock of **human capital.**

Conceptually, an increase in human capital has the same effect on productivity as does an increase in physical capital or an improvement in technology, that is, the same *quantity* of labor input becomes capable of producing more output. So we can use the ever-adaptable Figure 6-1 for yet a third purpose—to represent increasing *workforce quality* as we move up from $0K_1$ to $0K_2$ to $0K_3$. Once again, the general conclusion is obvious:

For a given capital stock and given technology, labor productivity will be higher when the workforce has more education and training.

This third pillar is another obvious source of large disparities between rich nations, which tend to have well-educated populations, and poor nations, which do not. Table 6-1 shows some data on average years of schooling in selected countries. The

Human capital is the amount of skill embodied in the workforce. It is most commonly measured by the amount of education and training.

TABLE 6-1 Average Educational Attainment in Selected Countries, 2000*

United States	12.3
Canada	11.4
South Korea	10.5
Japan	9.7
United Kingdom	9.4
Italy	7.0
Mexico	6.7
India	4.8
Brazil	4.6
Sudan	1.9

* For people older than 25 years of age.

SOURCE: Web site accompanying R. Barro and J.-W. Lee, "International Data on Educational Attainment: Updates and Implications," CID Working Paper No. 42, Harvard University, 2000, www.cid.harvard.edu/ciddata/ciddata.html

differences are dramatic—ranging from a high of 12.3 years in the United States to less than 5 years in India and less than 2 years in the Sudan. So we can add a third item to our list of the principal determinants of a nation's productivity growth rate:

■ The rate at which *workforce quality* (or "human capital") is improving

In the contemporary United States, where average educational attainment is high, workforce quality changes little from year to year. In some rapidly developing countries, however, this transformation can be an important engine of growth. For example, average years of schooling in South Korea soared from less than five in 1970 to more than nine in 1990, which contributed mightily to South Korea's remarkably rapid economic development.

Although there is no unique formula for growth, the most successful growth strategies of the post–World War II era, beginning with the Japanese "economic miracle," made ample use of all three pillars. Starting from a base of extreme deprivation after World War II, Japan showed the world how a combination of (1) very high rates of investment, (2) a well-educated workforce, and (3) the adoption of state-of-the-art technology could catapult a poor nation into the leading ranks within a few decades. The lessons were not lost on the so-called Asian Tigers—including Taiwan, South Korea, Singapore, and Hong Kong—which developed rapidly using their own versions of the Japanese model. Today, a number of other countries in Asia, Eastern Europe, and Latin America are trying to apply variants of this growth formula.

LEVELS, GROWTH RATES, AND THE CONVERGENCE HYPOTHESIS

Notice that, where productivity growth rates are concerned, it is the *rates of increase* of capital, technology, and workforce quality that matter, rather than their current *levels*. The distinction is an important one.

Productivity *levels* are vastly higher in the rich countries—which is precisely why they are rich. The wealthy nations have more bountiful supplies of capital, more highly skilled workers, and superior technologies. Naturally, they can produce more output per hour of work. Table 6-2 shows, for example, that an hour of labor in France and Germany in 1998 produced 98 percent and 77 percent as much output, respectively, as an hour of labor in the United States. But in Mexico and Brazil, the corresponding figures were only 29 percent and 23 percent, respectively.

But the *growth rates* of capital, workforce skills, and technology are not necessarily higher in the rich countries. For example, Country A might have abundant capital, but the amount may be increasing at a snail's pace, whereas in Country B capital may be scarce but growing rapidly. When it comes to determining the long-run growth rate, it is the *growth* rather than the current *levels* of these underpinnings of the country's well-being that matter most.

In fact, GDP per hour of work actually grew faster in several countries that have lower average incomes than those found in the United States. For example, Table 6-2 shows that Ireland, France, Germany, and the United Kingdom all grew faster than the U.S. Why? While a typical Irish worker in 1973 had less physical and human capital than a typical American worker, and used less advanced technology, the capital stock, average educational attainment, and level of technology probably all *increased* faster in Ireland than in the United States.

TABLE 6-2 Productivity Levels and Productivity Growth Rates in Selected Countries

Country	GDP per Hour of Work 1973 (as percentage of U.S. GDP)	GDP per Hour of Work 1998 (as percentage of U.S. GDP)	Growth Rate
United States	100	100	1.5
France	76	98	2.5
United Kingdom	67	79	2.2
Germany	62	77	2.4
Argentina	45	39	0.9
Ireland	41	78	4.1
Mexico	38	29	0.5
Peru	26	15	–0.7
Brazil	24	23	1.2

SOURCE: Angus Maddison, *The World Economy: A Millennial Perspective*, OECD, 2001, pp. 352–353.

The *level* of productivity in a nation depends on its supplies of human and physical capital and the state of its technology. But the *growth rate* of productivity depends on the *rates of increase* of these three factors.

The distinction between productivity levels and productivity growth rates may strike you as a bit of boring arithmetic, but it has many important practical applications. Here is a particularly striking one:

If the productivity growth rate is higher in poorer countries than in richer ones, then poor countries will close the gap on rich ones. The so-called **convergence hypothesis** suggests that this is what normally happens.

The Convergence Hypothesis: **The productivity growth rates of poorer countries tend to be higher than those of richer countries.**

The idea behind the convergence hypothesis, as illustrated in Figure 6-2, is that productivity growth will typically be faster where the initial level of productivity is lower. In this hypothetical example, the poorer country starts out with a per-capita GDP of $2,000, just one-fifth that of the richer country. But the poor country's real GDP per capita grows faster, so it gradually closes the relative income gap.

Why might we expect convergence to be the norm? In some poor countries, the supply of capital may be growing very rapidly. In others, educational attainment may be rising quickly, albeit from a low base. But the main reason to expect convergence in the long run is that *low-productivity countries should be able to learn from high-productivity countries* as scientific and managerial know-how spreads around the world.

A country that is operating at the technological frontier can improve its technology only by *innovating*. It must constantly figure out ways to do things better than it was doing them before. By comparison, a less advanced country can boost its productivity simply by *imitating*, by adopting technologies that are already in common use in the advanced countries. Not surprisingly, it is much easier to "look it up" than to "think it up."

Modern communications assist the convergence process by speeding the flow of information around the globe. The Internet was invented mainly in the United States, but it quickly spread to almost every corner of the world. Likewise, advances in human genomics and stem-cell research are originating in some of the most advanced countries these days, but they are communicated rapidly to scientists all over the world. A poor country that is skilled at importing scientific and engineering advances from the rich countries can achieve very rapid productivity growth.

Unfortunately, not all poor countries seem able to participate in the convergence process. For a variety of reasons (some of which will be mentioned later in this chapter), a number of developing countries seem incapable of adapting and adopting advanced technologies. Per-capita incomes in some of these nations are actually growing more slowly than in the rich countries, as Table 6-2 illustrates. Sadly, real incomes are stagnating or even falling in some of the poorest countries of the world, especially in Africa and many of the formerly communist countries (see Table 6-3). Convergence certainly cannot be taken for granted.

The **convergence hypothesis** holds that nations with low levels of productivity tend to have high productivity growth rates, so that international productivity differences shrink over time.

■ FIGURE 6-2

The Convergence Hypothesis

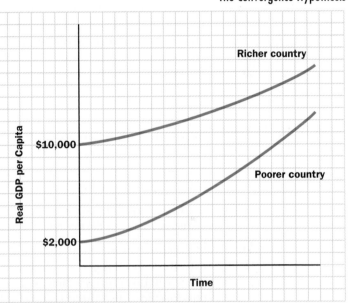

■ TABLE 6-3   GDP per Capita and GDP Growth Rates in Selected Poor Countries

Country	GDP per Capita, 1999*	GDP Growth Rate, 1990–1999
Belarus	$2,630	−4.3%
Russia	2,270	−6.1
Ukraine	750	−10.8
Ecuador	1,310	2.2
Haiti	460	−1.7
Cameroon	580	1.3
Rwanda	250	−1.5
Sierra Leone	130	−4.8

* In U.S. dollars.

SOURCE: World Bank, *World Development Report, 2000/2001,* September 2000.

Technological laggards can, and sometimes do, close the gap with technological leaders by imitating and adapting existing technologies. Within this "convergence club," productivity growth rates are higher where productivity levels are lower. Unfortunately, some of the world's poorest nations have been unable to join the club.

GROWTH POLICY: ENCOURAGING CAPITAL FORMATION

Let us now see how the government might spur growth by working on these three pillars, beginning with capital.

First, we need to clarify some terminology. We have spoken of the supply of **capital,** by which we mean the volume of plant (factories, office buildings, and so on), equipment (drill presses, computers, and so on), and software currently available. Businesses *add* to the existing supply of capital whenever they make **investment** expenditures—purchases of new plant, equipment, and software. In this way, the *growth* of the capital stock depends on how much businesses spend on investment. That is the process called **capital formation**—literally, forming new capital.

Now suppose the government wants the capital stock to grow faster. In a capitalist, market economy such as ours, private businesses make almost all investment decisions—how many factories and office buildings to build, how many drill presses and computers to purchase, and so on. To speed up the process of capital formation, the government must somehow persuade private businesses to invest more. But how?

Interest Rates   The most obvious way to increase investment by private businesses is to lower real interest rates. When real interest rates fall, investment normally rises. Why? Because businesses often borrow to finance their investments, and the real interest rate indicates how much firms must pay for that privilege. An investment project that looks unattractive at an interest rate of 10 percent may look highly profitable if the firm has to pay only 6 percent.

> The amount that businesses want to invest depends on the real interest rate they must pay to borrow funds. The lower the real rate of interest, the more investment spending there will be.

In subsequent chapters, we will learn how government policy can influence interest rates—which gives policymakers some leverage over private investment decisions. That relationship, in fact, is why interest rates will play such a crucial role in our discussions in subsequent chapters. But we might as well come clean right away: For reasons to be examined later, the government's ability to control interest rates is imperfect. In addition, the rate of interest is only one of several determinants of investment spending. So policymakers have only a limited ability to affect the level of investment by manipulating interest rates.

Tax Provisions   The government can also influence investment spending by altering various provisions of the tax code. For example, President George W. Bush and Congress agreed in 2003 to reduce the tax rate on *capital gains*—the profit earned by selling an asset for more than you paid for it. Perhaps the major argument for lowering capital gains taxes is the claim, which is disputed by critics, that it would lead to greater investment spending. In addition, the United States imposes a tax on *corporate profits* and can reduce that tax to spur investment. There are other, more complicated, tax provisions, as well. To summarize:

> The tax law gives the government several ways to influence business spending on investment goods. But influence is far different from total control.

Technical Change   Technology, which we have listed as a separate pillar of growth, also drives investment. New business opportunities suddenly appear when a new product

*A nation's **capital** is its available supply of plant, equipment, and software. It is the result of past decisions to make* investments *in these items.*

Investment *is the* flow *of resources into the production of new capital. It is the labor, steel, and other inputs devoted to the* construction *of factories, warehouses, railroads, and other pieces of capital during some period of time.*

Capital formation *is synonymous with investment. It refers to the process of building up the capital stock.*

such as the mobile telephone is invented, or when a technological breakthrough makes an existing product much cheaper or better, as happened with Internet services in the 1990s. In a capitalist system, entrepreneurs pounce on such opportunities—building new factories, stores, and offices, and buying new equipment. Thus, if the government can figure out how to spur technological progress (a subject discussed later in this chapter), those same policies will probably boost investment.

The Growth of Demand   High growth itself can induce businesses to invest more. When demand presses against capacity, executives are likely to believe that new factories and machinery can be employed profitably—and that creates strong incentives to build new capital. Thus it was no coincidence that investment soared in the United States during the boom years of the 1990s, collapsed when the economy slowed precipitously in 2000–2001, and then revived again in 2003. By contrast, if machinery and factories stand idle—as is common nowadays in recession-prone Japan—businesses may find new investments unattractive.[3] In summary:

High levels of sales relative to current capacity and expectations of rapid economic growth create an atmosphere conducive to investment.

As you can see, this situation creates a kind of virtuous circle in which high rates of investment boost economic growth, and rapid growth boosts investment. Of course, the same process can also operate in reverse—as a vicious circle: When the economy stagnates, firms do not want to invest much, which damages prospects for further growth.

Political Stability and Property Rights   There is one other absolutely critical determinant of investment spending that Americans simply take for granted.

A business thinking about committing funds to, say, build a factory faces any number of risks. Construction costs might run higher than estimates. Interest rates might rise. Demand for the product might prove weaker than expected. The list goes on and on. These risks are all among the normal hazards of entrepreneurship, an activity that is not for the faint-hearted. But, at a minimum, business executives contemplating a long-term investment want assurances that their property will not be taken from them for capricious or political reasons.

Republican businesspeople in the United States do not worry that their property will be seized if the Democrats win the next election. Nor do they worry that court rulings will deprive them of their **property rights** without due process. In contrast, in many less well-organized societies, the rule of law is regularly threatened by combinations of arbitrary government actions, political instability, anti-capitalist ideology, rampant corruption, or runaway crime.

Such problems have posed serious impediments to long-term investment in many poor countries throughout history. They are among the reasons these countries have remained poor. And the litany of problems that threaten property rights is not just a matter of history—these issues remain relevant in countries as different as Russia, much of Africa, and parts of Latin America today. Where businesses fear that their property may be expropriated, a drop in interest rates of, say, two percentage points will not encourage much investment.

Needless to say, the strength of property rights, adherence to the rule of law, the level of corruption, and the like are not easy to measure. Anyone who attempts to rank countries on such criteria must make many subjective judgments. Nevertheless, some results from one heroic attempt to do so are displayed in Table 6-4. The relative rankings of the various countries is roughly what you might expect.

Property rights are laws and/or conventions that assign owners the rights to use their property as they see fit (within the law)—for example, to sell the property and to reap the benefits (such as rents or dividends) while they own it.

■ **TABLE 6-4   Selected Countries Ranked by Respect for Property Rights**

Country	Rating*
Switzerland	100
Canada	98
United States	**95**
Japan	93
Italy	82
United Kingdom	78
South Korea	74
Brazil	68
Mexico	59
India	59
Sudan	31

* Average over the years 1986–1995.
SOURCE: Web site accompanying R. Hall and C. Jones, "Why Do Some Countries Produce So Much More Output per Worker Than Others?", *Quarterly Journal of Economics*, February 1999 elsa.berkeley.edu/~chad/HallJones400.asc. The index is constructed by a private company, Political Risk Services, and is based on the degree of law and order, the quality of the bureaucracy, the risk of expropriation, and the risk of government repudiation of contracts.

---

[3] This is one major reason why the economy of Japan, once a model of rapid growth, fell into stagnation in the 1990s.

To Grow Fast, Get the Institutions Right

T he World Bank recently surveyed the ways the governments of around 100 countries either encourage or discourage market activity. Its conclusion, as summarized in *The Economist*, was that "when poor people are allowed access to the institutions richer people enjoy, they can thrive and help themselves. A great deal of poverty, in other words, may be easily avoidable."

The World Bank study highlighted the importance of making simple institutions accessible to the poor—such as (1) protection of property rights (especially over land), (2) access to the judicial system, and (3) a free and open flow of information—as key ingredients in successful economic development. *The Economist* put it graphically:

If it is too expensive and time-consuming, for example, to open a bank account, the poor will stuff their savings under the mattress. When it takes

19 steps, five months and more than an average person's annual income to register a new business in Mozambique, it is no wonder that aspiring, cash-strapped entrepreneurs do not bother.

The Bank's conclusion reminded people of the central message of a best-selling 2000 book by Peruvian economist and businessman Hernando de Soto—who found to his dismay that, in his own country, it took 700 bureaucratic steps to obtain legal title to a house!

SOURCES: "Now, think small," *The Economist* September 15, 2001, pp. 40–42. Hernando de Soto, *The Mystery of Capital: Why Capitalism Triumphs in the West and Fails Everywhere Else* (New York: Basic Books), 2000.

GROWTH POLICY: IMPROVING EDUCATION AND TRAINING

Numerous studies of data from many countries support the view that more-educated and better-trained workers earn higher wages. Economists naturally assume that people who earn more are more productive. Thus more education and training contribute to higher productivity.

While private institutions play a role in the educational process, in most societies the state bears the primary responsibility for educating the population. So *educational policy* is an obvious and critical component of growth policy.

In most rich countries, universal primary education is mandated by law. But in many poor countries, completing grade school may be the exception rather than the rule, leaving even rudimentary skills such as reading, writing, and basic arithmetic in short supply. In such cases, expanding and improving primary education—including keeping children in school until they reach at least the age of 12—may be among the most cost-effective growth policies available. The problem is particularly acute in many traditional societies, where the education of girls may be considered unimportant or even inappropriate. In middle-income societies, where universal primary education is more or less a reality, access to secondary education may be the more pressing need.

Today, a modern industrial society is built more on brains than on brawn. Even ordinary blue-collar jobs often require a high school education. For this reason, policies that raise rates of high school attendance and completion and, perhaps more importantly, improve the *quality* of secondary education can make major contributions to growth. Unfortunately, such policies have proved difficult to devise and implement. In the United States, for example, the debate over how to improve our public schools goes on and on, with no resolution in sight.

Finally, if knowledge is power in the information age, then sending more young people to college and graduate school may be crucial to economic success. This is especially true in the rich countries, where universal primary education and high rates of high school completion are already realities.

It is well documented that the earnings gap between high school and college graduates in the United States has risen dramatically since the late 1970s. (One graphical depiction of this rising disparity is shown in Figure 6-3.) Clearly, the job market is rewarding the skills acquired in college more generously than ever before. To the extent that high wages reflect high productivity, low-cost tuition (such as that paid at many state colleges and universities), student loans to low-income families, and other policies to encourage college attendance may yield society rich dividends.

But education is no panacea for all of an economy's ills. Education in the former Soviet Union was, at least in some respects, probably outstanding. Ultimately, however, it proved insufficient to prevent the Soviet economy from falling ever further behind the capitalist economies in terms of economic growth.

On-the-job training may be just as important as formal education in raising productivity, but it is less amenable to influence by the government. For the most part, private businesses decide how much, and in what ways, to train their workers. Various public policy initiatives—ranging from government-run training programs, to subsidies for private-sector training, to mandated minimum training expenditures by firms—have been tried in various countries with mixed results. In the United States, mandates have been viewed as improper interferences with private business decisions, and government training programs (other than those in the Armed Forces) have not been terribly successful.

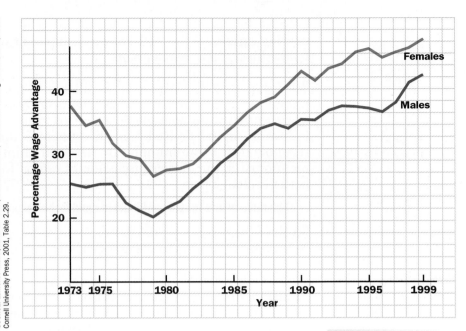

SOURCE: Lawrence Mishel, Jared Bernstein, and John Schmitt, *The State of Working America, 2000/2001.* Cornell University Press, 2001, Table 2.29.

■ FIGURE 6-3

Wage Premium for College Graduates over High School Graduates

On-the-job training refers to skills that workers acquire while at work, rather than in school or in formal vocational training programs.

GROWTH POLICY: SPURRING TECHNOLOGICAL CHANGE

Our third pillar of growth is *technology*, or getting more output from given supplies of inputs. Some of the most promising policies for speeding up the pace of technical progress have already been mentioned:

More Education   While some inventions and innovations are the product of dumb luck, most result from the sustained application of knowledge, resources, and brainpower to scientific, engineering, and managerial problems. We have just noted that more educated workers appear to be more productive *per se*. In addition, a society is likely to be more innovative if it has a greater supply of scientists, engineers, and skilled business managers who are constantly on the prowl for new opportunities. What is sometimes called the "new growth theory" emphasizes the pivotal role in the growth process of committing more human, physical, and financial resources to the acquisition of knowledge.

High levels of education, especially scientific, engineering, and managerial education, contribute to the advancement of technology.

There is little doubt that the United States leads the world in the quality of its graduate programs in business and in many of the scientific and engineering disciplines. As evidence of this superiority, one need only look at the tens of thousands of foreign students who flock to our graduate schools. It seems reasonable to suppose that America's unquestioned leadership in scientific and business education contributes to our leadership in productivity. On this basis, many economists endorse policies designed to induce more bright young people to pursue scientific and engineering careers. Some well-known examples of such incentives include scholarships, fellowships, and research grants.

More Capital Formation   We are all familiar with the fact that the latest versions of cell phones, PCs, personal digital assistants (PDAs), and even televisions embody new features that were unavailable a year or even six months ago. The same is true of industrial capital. Indeed, new investment is the principal way in which the latest technological breakthroughs are hard-wired into the nation's capital stock. As we mentioned in our earlier discussion of capital formation, newer capital is normally better capital. Thus:

High rates of investment contribute to rapid technical progress.

So all of the policies we discussed earlier as ways to bolster capital formation can also be thought of as ways to speed up technical progress.

Invention is the act of discovering new products or new ways of making products.

Innovation is the act of putting new ideas into effect by, for example, bringing new products to market, changing product designs, and improving the way in which things are done.

Research and development (R&D) refers to activities aimed at inventing new products or processes, or improving existing ones.

Research and Development   But there is an even more direct way to spur **invention** and **innovation:** devote more of society's resources to **research and development (R&D).**

Driven by the profit motive, American businesses have long invested heavily in industrial R&D. According to the old saying, "Build a better mousetrap, and the world will beat a path to your door." And innovative companies in the United States and elsewhere have been engaged in research on "better mousetraps" for decades. Polaroid invented instant photography, Xerox developed photocopying, and Apple pioneered the desktop computer. Boeing improved jet aircraft several times. Pharmaceutical companies have discovered many new, life-enhancing drugs. Intel has developed generation after generation of ever-faster microprocessors.

All these companies and others have spent untold billions of dollars on R&D to discover new products, to improve old ones, and to make their industrial processes more efficient. While many research dollars are inevitably "wasted" on false starts and experiments that don't pan out, numerous studies have shown that the average dollar invested in R&D has yielded high returns to society. Heavy spending on R&D is, indeed, one of the keys to high productivity growth.

The U.S. government supports and encourages R&D in several ways. First, it subsidizes private R&D spending through the tax code. Specifically, the Research and Experimentation Tax Credit reduces the taxes of companies that spend more money on R&D.

Second, the government sometimes joins with private companies in collaborative research efforts. The Human Genome Project is probably the best-known example of such a public–private partnership (some might call it a race!), but there are also cooperative ventures in new automotive technology, alternative energy sources, and other areas.

Last, and certainly not least, the federal government has over the years spent a great deal of taxpayer money directly on R&D. Much of this spending has been funneled through the Department of Defense. But the National Aeronautics and Space Administration (NASA), the National Science Foundation, the National Institutes of Health, and many other agencies have also played important roles. Inventions as diverse as atomic energy, advanced ceramic materials, and the Internet were originally developed in federal laboratories. Federal government R&D spending in fiscal year 2003 amounted to roughly $117 billion, roughly half of which went through the Pentagon.

THE PRODUCTIVITY SLOWDOWN AND SPEED-UP IN THE UNITED STATES

Around 1973, productivity growth in the United States suddenly and mysteriously slowed down—from the rate of about 2.8 percent per year that had characterized the 1948–1973 period to about 1.4 percent thereafter (see Figure 6-4). Hardly anyone anticipated this productivity slowdown. Then, starting around 1995, productivity growth suddenly speeded up again—from about 1.4 percent per year during the 1973–1995 period to about 2.8 percent since then (see Figure 6-4 again). Once again, the abrupt change in the growth rate caught most people by surprise.

Recall from Chapter 5's discussion of compounding that a change in the growth rate of 1.4 percentage points, if sustained for decades, makes an enormous difference in living standards. So understanding these two major events is of critical importance. Yet even now, some 30 years later, economists remain puzzled about the 1973 productivity slowdown, and the reasons behind the 1995 productivity speed-up are only partly understood. Let us see what economists know about these two episodes.

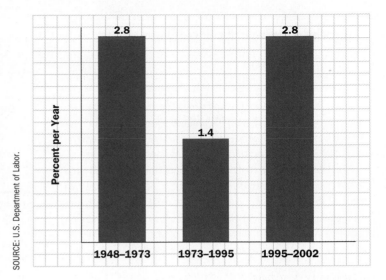

SOURCE: U.S. Department of Labor.

■ FIGURE 6-4
Average Productivity Growth Rates in the United States, 1948–2002
NOTE: Data pertain to the nonfarm business sector.

■ The Productivity Slowdown, 1973–1995

The productivity slowdown after 1973 was certainly a disconcerting development, and economists have been struggling to explain it ever since. Among the leading candidate explanations are:

Lagging Investment For years, many people suggested that inadequate investment was behind America's productivity problem. Countries such as Germany and Japan, these critics observed, saved and invested far more than Americans did, thereby equipping their workers with more modern equipment that boosted labor productivity. U.S. tax policy, they argued, should create stronger incentives for business to invest and households to save.

While the argument was logical, the facts have not treated it kindly. For example, the share of U.S. GDP accounted for by business investment did not actually decline during the period of slow productivity growth. Nor did the contribution of capital formation to growth (see the boxed insert on the next page).

High Energy Prices A second explanation begins with a tantalizing fact: The productivity slowdown started around 1973, just when the Organization of Petroleum Exporting Countries (OPEC) jacked up the price of oil. As a matter of logic, higher oil prices should reduce business use of energy, which should make labor less productive. Furthermore, energy prices rose just as productivity growth fell, not just in the United States but all over the world—which is quite a striking coincidence.

Once again, the argument sounds persuasive—until you remember another important fact: Energy prices dropped sharply in the mid-1980s but productivity growth did not revive. So the energy explanation of the productivity slowdown has many skeptics.

Inadequate Workforce Skills Could it be that after 1973 the skills of the U.S. labor force failed to keep pace with the demands of new technology? Although workforce skills are notoriously difficult to measure, there was and is a widespread feeling that the *quality* of education in the United States has declined. For example, SAT scores peaked in the late 1960s and then declined for about 20 years.[4] Yet standard measures such as school attendance rates, graduation rates, and average levels of educational attainment have all continued to register gains. Clearly, the proposition that the quality of the U.S. workforce declined is at least debatable.

---

[4] You may know that the SAT was rescaled about seven years ago to reflect this decline in average scores.

Growth Accounting in the United States

I n this chapter, we have learned that labor productivity (output per hour of work) rises because (1) more capital is accumulated, (2) technology improves, and (3) workforce quality rises. The last of these three pillars is quantitatively unimportant in the modern United States, where average educational attainment is already high. But the other two certainly are not.

The table breaks down the growth rate of labor productivity into its two main components over three different periods of time. We see that the productivity slowdown after 1973 was entirely accounted for by slower technological improvement; the contribution of capital formation did not decline.* The productivity speed-up after 1995, however, came from *both* faster capital formation and faster technical progress.

	1948–1973	1973–1995	1995–2001
Growth rate of labor productivity	2.8%	1.4%	2.4%
Contribution of capital formation	0.9	1.0	1.6
Contribution of technology	1.9	0.4	0.8

Note: Totals may not add up due to rounding.

SOURCE: Bureau of Labor Statistics.

*Changes in workforce quality, which are very small, are included in the technology component.

A Technological Slowdown?   Could the pace of innovation have slowed in the 1973–1995 period? Most people instinctively answer "no." After all, the microchip and the personal computer were invented in the 1970s, opening the door to what can only be called a revolution in computing and information technology (IT). Workplaces were transformed beyond recognition. Entirely new industries (such as those related to PCs and Internet services) were spawned. Why didn't these technological marvels raise productivity by an enormous amount?

The paradox of seemingly rapid technological advance coupled with sluggish productivity performance has puzzled economists for years. How could the contribution of technology to growth have *fallen*? One possibility is that the slowdown marked the end of the golden age of the 1950s and 1960s, when civilian innovation spurted after being suppressed during World War II. In any case, the data since 1995 may finally offer an answer: While it took a long time, the IT revolution seems finally to be paying rich productivity dividends.

The Productivity Speed-up, 1995–??

Figure 6-4 shows that productivity growth speeded up remarkably around 1995, rising from about 1.4 percent per annum before that year to about 2.8 percent since. This time, the causes are better understood—and most of them relate to the IT revolution.

Surging Investment   Bountiful new business opportunities in the IT sector and elsewhere, coupled with a strong national economy, led to a surge in business investment spending in the 1990s. Business investment as a percentage of real GDP rose from 9.1 percent in 1991 to 14.6 percent in 2000, and most of that increase was concentrated in computers, software, and telecommunications equipment. We have observed several times in this chapter that the productivity growth rate should rise when the capital stock grows faster—and it did.

Falling Energy Prices?   For part of this period, especially the years 1996–1998, energy prices were falling. By the same logic used earlier, falling energy prices should have boosted productivity growth. But, as we noted earlier, this argument did not seem to work so well when energy prices fell in the 1980s. Should we then believe it for the 1990s?

Advances in Information Technology   We seem to be on safer ground when we look to technological progress, especially in computers and semiconductors, to explain the speed-up in productivity growth. First, innovation seemed to explode in the 1990s. Computers became faster and much, much cheaper—as did telecommunications equipment and services. Corporate intranets became commonplace. The Internet grew from a scientific curiosity into a commercial reality. And so on. We truly entered the Information Age.

Second, it probably took American businesses some time to learn how to fully exploit the computer and telecommunications technologies that were invented between, say, 1980 and the early 1990s. It was only in the late 1990s, some observers argue, that U.S. industry was positioned to reap the benefits of these advances in the form of higher productivity. Such long delays are not unprecedented. Research has shown, for example, that it took a long time for the availability of electric power at the end of the nineteenth century to contribute much to productivity growth. Like electric power, computers were a novel input to production, and it may have taken years for prospective users to find the most productive ways to employ them.

In summary:

Two of the three main pillars of productivity growth—capital formation and technological change—seem to do a credible job of explaining why productivity accelerated in the United States after 1995.

 ## Puzzle Resolved: Why the Relative Price of College Tuition Keeps Rising

Earlier in this chapter, we observed that the relative prices of services such as college tuition, medical care, and theater tickets seem to rise year after year. And we suggested that one main reason for this perpetual increase is tied to the economy's long-run growth rate. We are now in a position to understand precisely how that mechanism works. The argument comes in three steps.

Step 1   It stands to reason, and is amply demonstrated by historical experience, that *real wages tend to rise at the same rate as labor productivity.* This relationship makes sense: When and where labor produces more, it normally gets paid more. Thus real wages will be rising most rapidly in those economies with the fastest productivity growth.

Step 2   Although average labor productivity in the economy increases from year to year, *there are a number of personally provided services for which productivity (output per hour) cannot or does not grow.* We have already mentioned several of them. Your college or university *can* increase the productivity of its faculty—by increasing class size. Most students and parents, however, would view that development as a decrease in the quality of the service. Similarly, a modern doctor takes roughly as long to examine a patient as his counterparts did 25 or 50 years ago. It also takes *exactly* the same time for an orchestra to play one of Beethoven's symphonies today as it did in Beethoven's time.

The common ingredient in each of these disparate examples is that the major sources of higher labor productivity that we have studied in this chapter—more capital and better technology—are completely or nearly irrelevant. It still takes one lecturer to teach a class, one doctor to examine a patient, and four musicians to play a string quartet—just as it did 100 years ago. Saving on labor by using more and better equipment is more or less out of the question.[5] These so-called *personal services* stand in stark contrast to, say, working on an automobile assembly line or in a semiconductor plant, or even to working in service industries such as telecommunications—all instances in which both capital formation and technical progress regularly raise labor productivity.

---

[5] However, some people foresee a world in which education and medical care are delivered long distance over the Internet.

Step 3 *Real wages in different occupations must, in the long run, rise at roughly similar rates.* This point may sound wrong at first: Haven't the wages of computer programmers risen faster than those of school teachers in recent years? Yes they have, and that is the market's way of attracting more young people into computer programming. But in the long run, these growth rates must (more or less) equilibrate, or else virtually no one would want to be a school teacher any more.

Now let's put the three steps together. College teachers are no more productive than they used to be, but autoworkers are (Step 2). But in the long run, the real wages of college teachers and autoworkers must grow at roughly the same rate (Step 3), which is the economy-wide productivity growth rate (Step 1). As a result, wages of college teachers and doctors will rise *faster* than their productivity does, and so their services must grow ever more expensive compared to, say, computers and phone calls.

That is, indeed, the way things seem to have worked out. Compared to the world in which your parents grew up, computers and telephone calls are now very cheap while college tuition and doctors' bills are very expensive. The same logic applies to the services of police officers (two per squad car), baseball players (nine per team), chefs, and many other occupations where productivity improvements are either impossible or undesirable. All of these services have grown much more expensive over the years. This phenomenon has been called the **cost disease of the personal services.**

According to the **cost disease of the personal services**, service activities that require direct personal contact tend to rise in price relative to other goods and services.

Ironically, the villain of the piece is actually the economy's productivity growth rate. If manufacturing and telecommunications workers did *not* become more productive over time, their real wages would not rise. In that case, the real wages of teachers and doctors would not *have to* keep pace, so their services would not have to grow ever more expensive. Paradoxically, the enormous productivity gains that have blessed our economy and raised our standard of living also account for the problem of rising tuition costs. In the most literal sense, we are the victims of our own success.

LINKING THE LONG RUN TO THE SHORT RUN

Most of this chapter has been devoted to explaining and evaluating the factors underlying the long-run growth rate of *potential* GDP. But, just like people, economies do not always live up to their full potential. As we observed in Chapter 5 (see especially Table 5-1 on page 82), the growth of *actual* GDP in the United States has often diverged markedly from the growth of *potential* GDP. Sometimes it has been higher, but sometimes it has been lower.

Why? What factors determine the rate at which the GDP of a particular country grows from one year to the next? Why does GDP occasionally *shrink* rather than grow—that is, why do countries sometimes experience *recessions?* And what can, or should, policymakers do when GDP either outstrips or falls short of potential? The answers to these difficult questions will have to wait until we have developed a theory of the determinants of actual (as opposed to potential) GDP—a task that begins in the next chapter.

SUMMARY

1. More **capital,** improved workforce quality (which is normally measured by the amount of education and training), and better technology all raise labor productivity and therefore shift the production function upward. They constitute the three main pillars of growth.

2. The growth rate of labor productivity depends on the rate of capital formation, the rate of improvement of workforce quality, and the rate of technical progress. So growth policy concentrates on speeding up these processes.

3. **Capital formation** can be encouraged by low real interest rates, favorable tax treatment, rapid technical change, rapid growth of demand, and a climate of political stability that respects **property rights.** Each of these factors is at least influenced by policy.

4. Policies that increase education and training—the second pillar of growth—can be expected to make a country's workforce more productive. They range from universal primary education to post-graduate fellowships in science and engineering.

5. Technological advances can be encouraged by more education, by higher rates of **investment,** and also by direct expenditures—both public and private—on **research and development.**

6. The **convergence hypothesis** holds that countries with lower productivity levels tend to have higher productivity growth rates, so that poor countries gradually close the gap on rich ones.

7. One major reason to expect convergence is that technological know-how can be transferred quickly from the leading nations to the laggards. Unfortunately, not all countries seem able to benefit from this information transfer.

8. Productivity growth slowed precipitously in the United States around 1973, and economists are still not sure why.

9. Productivity growth in the United States has speeded up again since 1995, probably mainly as a result of the information technology (IT) revolution and the large investments that accompanied it.

10. Because many personal services—such as education, medical care, and police protection—are essentially handicraft activities that are not amenable to labor-saving innovations, they suffer from a **cost disease** that makes them grow ever more expensive over time.

KEY TERMS

Human capital   107
Convergence hypothesis   109
Capital   110
Investment   110

Capital formation   110
Property rights   111
On-the-job training   113
Invention   114

Innovation   114
Research and development (R&D)   114
Cost disease of the personal services   118

QUESTIONS FOR REVIEW

1. Explain the different objectives of (long-run) growth policy versus (short-run) stabilization policy.

2. Show on a graph how capital formation shifts the production function. Use this graph to show that capital formation increases labor productivity. Explain in words *why* labor is more productive when the capital stock is larger.

3. The table below shows real GDP per hour of work in four imaginary countries in the years 1990 and 2000. By what percentage did labor productivity grow in each country? Is it true that productivity *growth* was highest where the initial *level* of productivity was the lowest? For which countries?

| | Output per Hour | |
	1990	2000
Country A	$40	$48
Country B	$25	$35
Country C	$ 2	$ 3
Country D	$ 0.50	$ 0.60

4. Explain why economic growth might be higher in a country with well-established property rights and a stable political system compared with a country where property rights are uncertain and the government is unstable.

5. Chapter 5 pointed out that, because faster capital formation comes at a cost (reduced current consumption), it is possible for a country to invest too much. Suppose the government of some country decides that its businesses are investing too much. What steps might it take to slow the pace of capital formation?

6. Explain why the best educational policies to promote faster growth might be different in the following countries.
   a. Tanzania
   b. Mexico
   c. Japan

7. Comment on the following: "Sharp changes in the volume of investment in the United States help explain both the productivity slowdown in 1973 and the productivity speed-up in 1995."

8. Imagine that new inventions in the computer industry affect the growth rate of productivity as follows:

Year of Invention	Following Year	5 Years Later	10 Years Later	20 Years Later
0%	−1%	0%	+2%	+4%

Would such a pattern help explain U.S. productivity performance since the mid-1970s?

9. Which of the following prices would you expect to rise rapidly? Why?
   a. cable television rates
   b. football tickets
   c. Internet access
   d. household cleaning services
   e. driving lessons

7

Aggregate Demand and the Powerful Consumer

Men are disposed, as a rule and on the average, to increase their consumption as their income increases, but not by as much as the increase in their income.

JOHN MAYNARD KEYNES

T he last chapter focused on the determinants of *potential GDP*—the economy's capacity to produce. We turn our attention now to the factors determining *actual GDP*—how much of that potential is actually utilized. Will the economy be pressing against its capacity, and therefore perhaps also having trouble with inflation? Or will there be a great deal of unused capacity, and therefore high unemployment?

The theory that economists use to answer such questions is based on the concepts of *aggregate demand and supply.* In this chapter and the next, we will construct a simplified model of aggregate demand and learn the origins of the *aggregate demand curve* that was introduced in Chapter 4. Chapter 9 will complete the model by adding the *aggregate supply curve.*

Chapter 4's whirlwind tour of U.S. economic history suggested that the strength of aggregate demand holds the key to the economy's condition in the short run. When aggregate demand grows briskly, the economy booms. When aggregate demand is weak, the economy stagnates. The first model we develop to understand aggregate demand will teach us much about this process. But it is too simple to deal with policy issues effectively, because the government and the financial system are largely ignored. We remedy these omissions in Part III, where we give government spending, taxation, and interest rates appropriately prominent roles. The influence of the exchange rate between the U.S. dollar and foreign currencies is considered in Part IV.

CONTENTS

Issue: Demand Management and the Ornery Consumer

In Chapter 4, we suggested that the government sometimes wants to shift the aggregate demand curve. It can do so a number of ways. One direct approach is to alter its own spending, becoming extravagant when private demand is weak or miserly when private demand is strong. Alternatively, the government can take a more indirect route, by using taxes and other policy tools to influence *private* spending decisions. Because consumer expenditures constitute more than two-thirds of gross domestic product, the consumer presents the most tempting target.

A case in point arose after the 2000 election, when the long boom of the 1990s ended abruptly and economic growth in the United States slowed to a crawl. President George W. Bush and his economic advisers decided that consumer spending needed a boost, and Congress passed a multiyear tax cut in 2001. One provision of the tax cut gave taxpayers an advance *rebate* on their 2001 taxes.[1] Checks ranging as high as $600 went out starting in July 2001. There should be no mystery about how changes in personal taxes are expected to affect consumer spending. Any reduction in personal taxes leaves consumers with more after-tax income to spend; any tax increase leaves them with less. The linkage from taxes to spendable income to consumer spending seems direct and unmistakable, and, in a certain sense, it is.

Yet the Congressional debate over the tax bill sent legislators and journalists scurrying to the scholarly evidence on a similar episode 26 years earlier. In the spring of 1975, as the U.S. economy hit a recessionary bottom, Congress enacted a tax rebate to spur consumer spending. But that time consumers did not follow the wishes of the president and Congress. They saved a substantial share of their tax cuts, rather than spending them. As a result, the economy did not receive the expected boost.

Perhaps the legislators should have taken the 1975 episode to heart. Early estimates of the effects of the 2001 rebates suggested that consumers spent relatively little of the money they received. Thus, in a sense, history repeated itself. But why? Why did these two temporary tax cuts seem to have so little effect? This chapter attempts to provide some answers. But before getting involved in such complicated issues, we must build some vocabulary and learn some basic concepts. Then we will see what went wrong in 1975 and 2001.

AGGREGATE DEMAND, DOMESTIC PRODUCT, AND NATIONAL INCOME

Aggregate demand is the total amount that all consumers, business firms, and government agencies spend on final goods and services.

First, the vocabulary. We have already introduced the concept of *gross domestic product* as the standard measure of the economy's total output.[2]

For the most part, firms in a market economy produce goods only if they think they can sell them. **Aggregate demand** is the total amount that all consumers, business firms, government agencies, and foreigners wish to spend on U.S. final goods and services. The downward-sloping aggregate demand curve of Chapter 4 alerted us to the fact that *aggregate demand is a schedule, not a fixed number*—the actual numerical value of aggregate demand depends on the price level. Several reasons for this dependence will emerge in coming chapters.

But the level of aggregate demand also depends on a variety of other factors—such as consumer incomes, various government policies, and events in foreign countries. To understand the nature of aggregate demand, it is best to break it up into its major components, as we do in this chapter.

Consumer expenditure (*C*) is the total amount spent by consumers on newly produced goods and services (excluding purchases of new homes, which are considered investment goods).

---

[1] In fact, Candidate George W. Bush had proposed a large tax cut during the 2000 presidential campaign, long before the U.S. economy weakened. The rebate was added by Congress in 2001.

[2] See Chapter 4, pages 63–71.

Consumer expenditure (*consumption* for short) is simply the total value of all consumer goods and services demanded. Because consumer spending constitutes more than two-thirds of total spending, it is the main focus of this chapter. We represent it by the letter *C*.

Investment spending, represented by the letter *I*, was discussed extensively in Chapter 6. It is the amount that firms spend on factories, machinery, software, and the like, plus the amount that families spend on new houses. Notice that this usage of the word *investment* differs from common parlance. Most people speak of *investing* in the stock market or in a bank account. But that kind of investment merely swaps one form of financial asset (such as money) for another form (such as a share of stock). When economists speak of *investment*, they mean instead the purchase of some *new, physical asset*, such as a drill press, a computer, or a house. The distinction is important here because it is only the economists' kinds of investments that constitute direct additions to the demand for newly-produced goods.

"When I refer to it as disposable income, don't get the wrong idea."

SOURCE: From *The Wall Street Journal*. Permission, Cartoon Features Syndicate.

The third major component of aggregate demand, **government purchases** of goods and services, includes items such as paper, computers, airplanes, ships, and labor bought by all levels of government. We use the symbol *G* for this variable.

The final component of aggregate demand, **net exports,** is simply defined as U.S. exports *minus* U.S. imports. The reasoning here is simple. Part of the demand for American goods and services originates beyond our borders—as when foreigners buy our wheat, software, and banking services. So to obtain total demand for U.S. products, these goods and services must be added to U.S. domestic demand. Similarly, some items included in *C* and *I* are made abroad. Think, for example, of German beer, Japanese cars, and Korean textiles. So these must be subtracted from the total amount demanded by U.S. consumers if we want to measure total spending *on U.S. products*. The addition of exports, *X*, and the subtraction of imports, *IM*, leads to the following shorthand definition of aggregate demand:

Aggregate demand is the sum *C* + *I* + *G* + (*X* − *IM*).

The last concept we need for our vocabulary is a way to measure the total *income* of all individuals in the economy. It comes in two versions: one for before-tax incomes, called **national income,** and one for after-tax incomes, called **disposable income.**[3] The term *disposable income*, which we will abbreviate *DI*, is meant to be descriptive—it tells us how much consumers actually have available to spend or to save. For that reason, it will play a prominent role in this chapter and subsequent discussions.

Investment spending (*I*) is the sum of the expenditures of business firms on new plant and equipment and households on new homes. Financial "investments" are not included, nor are resales of existing physical assets.

Government purchases (*G*) refer to the goods (such as airplanes and paper clips) and services (such as school teaching and police protection) purchased by all levels of government.

Net exports, or *X* − *IM*, is the difference between exports (*X*) and imports (*IM*). It indicates the difference between what we sell to foreigners and what we buy from them.

National income is the sum of the incomes that all individuals in the economy earned in the forms of wages, interest, rents, and profits. It excludes government transfer payments and is calculated before any deductions are taken for income taxes.

THE CIRCULAR FLOW OF SPENDING, PRODUCTION, AND INCOME

Enough definitions. How do these three concepts—domestic product, total expenditure, and national income—interact in a market economy? We can answer this best with a rather elaborate diagram (Figure 7-1 on the next page). For obvious reasons, Figure 7-1 is called a *circular flow diagram*. It depicts a large tube in which an imaginary fluid circulates in a clockwise direction. At several points along the way, some of the fluid leaks out or additional fluid is injected into the tube.

Disposable income (*DI*) is the sum of the incomes of all individuals in the economy after all taxes have been deducted and all transfer payments have been added.

---

[3] More detailed information on these and other concepts is provided in the appendix to this chapter.

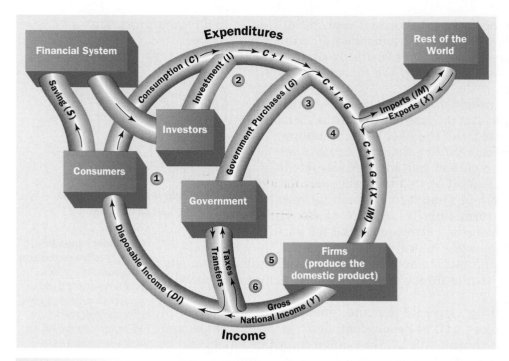

■ FIGURE 7-1

The Circular Flow of Expenditures and Income

Let's examine this system, beginning on the far left. At point 1 on the circle, we find consumers. Disposable income (*DI*) flows into their pockets, and two things flow out: consumption (*C*), which stays in the circular flow, and saving (*S*), which "leaks out." This outflow depicts the fact that consumers normally spend less than they earn and save the balance. The "leakage" to saving, of course, does not disappear; it flows into the financial system via banks, mutual funds, and so on. We defer consideration of what happens inside the financial system to Chapter 11.

The upper loop of the circular flow represents expenditures, and as we move clockwise to point 2, we encounter the first "injection" into the flow: investment spending (*I*). The diagram shows this injection as coming from "investors"—a group that includes both business firms and home buyers.[4] As the circular flow moves past point 2, it is bigger than it was before: Total spending has increased from *C* to *C* + *I*.

At point 3, there is yet another injection. The government adds its demand for goods and services (*G*) to those of consumers and investors (*C* + *I*). Now aggregate demand has grown to *C* + *I* + *G*.

The final leakage and injection come at point 4. Here we see export spending entering the circular flow from abroad and import spending leaking out. The net effect of these two forces may increase or decrease the circular flow, depending on whether net exports are positive or negative. In either case, by the time we pass point 4, we have accumulated the full amount of aggregate demand, *C* + *I* + *G* + (*X* − *IM*).

The circular flow diagram shows this aggregate demand for goods and services arriving at the business firms, which are located at point 5. Responding to this demand, firms produce the domestic product. As the circular flow emerges from the firms, however, we rename it *gross national income*. Why? The reason is that, except for some complications explained in the appendix:

National income and domestic product must be equal.

---

[4] You are reminded that expenditure on housing is part of *I*, not part of *C*.

Why is this so? When a firm produces and sells $100 worth of output, it pays most of the proceeds to its workers, to people who have lent it money, and to the landlord who owns the property on which the plant is located. All of these payments represent *income* to some individuals. But what about the rest? Suppose, for example, that the firm pays wages, interest, and rent totaling $90 million and sells its output for $100 million. What happens to the remaining $10 million? The firm's owners receive it as *profits*. Because these owners are citizens of the country, their incomes also count in national income.[5] Thus, when we add up all the wages, interest, rents, *and profits* in the economy to obtain the *national income*, we must arrive at the *value of output*.

The lower loop of the circular flow diagram shows national income leaving firms and heading for consumers. But some of the flow takes a detour along the way. At point 6, the government does two things. First, it siphons off a portion of the national income in the form of *taxes*. Second, it adds back government **transfer payments,** such as unemployment compensation and Social Security benefits, which government agencies give to certain individuals as outright *grants* rather than as payments for goods or services rendered.

By subtracting taxes from gross domestic product (GDP) and adding transfer payments, we obtain disposable income:[6]

$$DI = \text{GDP} - \text{Taxes} + \text{Transfer payments}$$
$$= \text{GDP} - (\text{Taxes} - \text{Transfers})$$
$$= Y - T$$

Transfer payments are sums of money that the government gives certain individuals as outright grants rather than as payments for services rendered to employers. Some common examples are Social Security and unemployment benefits.

where Y represents GDP and T represents taxes *net of transfers*. Disposable income flows unimpeded to consumers at point 1, and the cycle repeats.

Figure 7-1 raises several complicated questions, which we pose now but will not try to answer until subsequent chapters:

- Does the flow of spending and income grow larger or smaller as we move clockwise around the circle? Why?
- Is the output that firms produce at point 5 (the GDP) equal to aggregate demand? If so, what makes these two quantities equal? If not, what happens?

The next chapter provides the answers to these two questions.

- Do the government's accounts balance, so that what flows in at point 6 (taxes minus transfers) is equal to what flows out at point 3 (government purchases)? What happens if they do not balance?

This important question is first addressed in Chapter 10 and then recurs many times, especially in Chapter 14, which discusses budget deficits and surpluses.

- Is our international trade balanced, so that exports equal imports? More generally, what factors determine net exports and what consequences arise from trade deficits or surpluses?

We take up these questions in the next two chapters and then deal with them more fully in Part IV.

However, we cannot dig very deeply into any of these issues until we first understand what goes on at point 1, where consumers make decisions. So we turn next to the determinants of consumer spending.

---

[5] Some of the income paid out by American companies goes to noncitizens. Similarly, some Americans earn income from foreign firms. This complication is discussed in the appendix to this chapter.

[6] This definition omits a few minor details, which are explained in the appendix.

CONSUMER SPENDING AND INCOME: THE IMPORTANT RELATIONSHIP

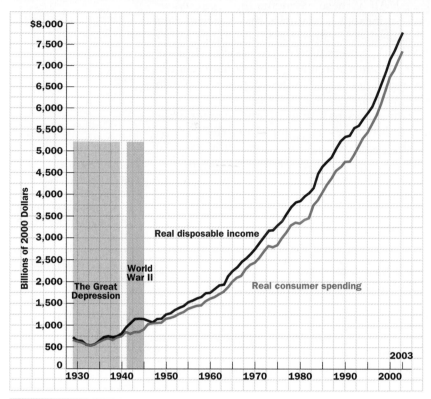

FIGURE 7-2

Consumer Spending and Disposable Income

A **scatter diagram** is a graph showing the relationship between two variables (such as consumer spending and disposable income). Each year is represented by a point in the diagram, and the coordinates of each year's point show the values of the two variables in that year.

Recall that we started the chapter with a puzzle: Why did consumers respond so weakly to tax rebates in 2001 and 1975? An economist interested in predicting how consumer spending will respond to a change in income taxes must first ask how consumption (*C*) relates to disposable income (*DI*), for a tax increase obviously decreases after-tax income, and a tax reduction increases it. This section, therefore, examines what we know about how consumer spending is influenced by changes in disposable income.

Figure 7-2 depicts the historical paths of *C* and *DI* for the United States since 1929. The association is extremely close, suggesting that consumption will rise whenever disposable income rises and fall whenever income falls. The vertical distance between the two lines represents personal saving. Notice how little saving consumers did during the Great Depression of the 1930s, where the two lines are very close together, and how much they did during World War II, when many consumer goods were either unavailable or rationed. The low volume of saving in recent years is also notable.

Of course, knowing that *C* will move in the same direction as *DI* is not enough for policy planners. They need to know *how much* one variable will go up when the other rises a given amount. Figure 7-3 presents the same data as in Figure 7-2, but in a way designed to help answer the "how much" question.

Economists call such pictures **scatter diagrams,** and they are very useful in predicting how one variable (in this case, consumer spending) will change in response to a change in another variable (in this case, disposable income). Each dot in the diagram represents the data on *C* and *DI* corresponding to a particular year. For example, the point labeled "1976" shows that real consumer expenditures in 1976 were $3,036 billion (which we read off the vertical axis), while real disposable incomes amounted to $3,432 billion (which we read off the horizontal axis). Similarly, each year from 1929 to 2003 is represented by its own dot in Figure 7-3.

To see how such a diagram can assist fiscal policy planners, imagine that it is 1963 and Congress is contemplating a tax cut. (In fact, Congress did cut taxes in 1964.) Legislators want to know how much additional consumer spending may be stimulated by tax cuts of various sizes. To assist your imagination, the scatter diagram in Figure 7-4 removes the points for 1964 through 2003 that appear in Figure 7-3; after all, these data were unknown in 1963. Years prior to 1947 have also been removed because, as Figure 7-2 showed, both the Great Depression and wartime rationing disturbed the normal relationship between *DI* and *C*. With no more training in economics than you have right now, what would you suggest?

One rough-and-ready approach is to get a ruler, set it down on Figure 7-4, and sketch a straight line that comes as close as possible to hitting all the points. That has been done for you in the figure, and you can see that the resulting line comes remarkably close to touching all of the points. The line summarizes, in a very rough way, the

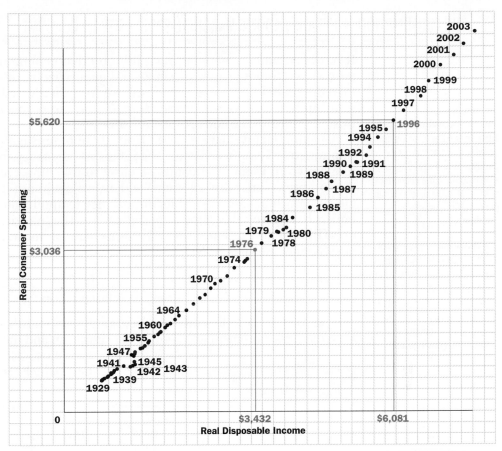

NOTE: Figures are in billions of 2000 dollars.

■ FIGURE 7-3

Scatter Diagram of Consumer Spending and Disposable Income

normal relationship between income and consumption. The two variables certainly appear to be closely related.

The *slope* of the straight line in Figure 7-4 is very important.[7] Specifically, we note that it is:

$$\text{Slope} = \frac{\text{Vertical change}}{\text{Horizontal change}} = \frac{\$180 \text{ billion}}{\$200 \text{ billion}} = 0.90$$

Because the horizontal change involved in the move from *A* to *B* represents a rise in disposable income of $200 billion (from $1,300 billion to $1,500 billion), and the corresponding vertical change represents the associated $180 billion rise in consumer spending (from $1,180 billion to $1,360 billion), the slope of the line indicates how consumer spending responds to changes in disposable income. In this case, we see that each additional $1 of income leads to 90 cents of additional spending.

Now let us return to tax policy. First, recall that each dollar of the tax cut increases disposable income by exactly $1. Next, apply the finding from Figure 7-4 that each additional dollar of disposable income increases consumer spending by about 90 cents. The conclusion is that a tax cut of, say, $9 billion—which is what happened in 1964—would be expected to increase consumer spending by about $9 × 0.9 = $8.1 billion.

■ FIGURE 7-4

Scatter Diagram of Consumer Spending and Disposable Income, 1947–1963

NOTE: Figures are in billions of 1996 dollars.

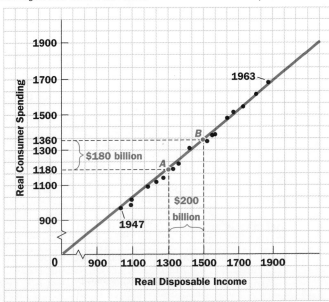

---

[7] To review the concept of *slope*, see the appendix to Chapter 1, pages 14–16.

THE CONSUMPTION FUNCTION AND THE MARGINAL PROPENSITY TO CONSUME

The consumption function shows the relationship between total consumer expenditures and total disposable income in the economy, holding all other determinants of consumer spending constant.

The marginal propensity to consume (MPC) is the ratio of changes in consumption relative to changes in disposable income that produce the change in consumption. On a graph, it appears as the slope of the consumption function.

It has been said (sometimes misleadingly) that economics is just systematized common sense. So let us now organize and generalize what has been a completely intuitive discussion up to now. One thing we have discovered is the apparently close relationship between consumer spending, *C*, and disposable income, *DI*. Economists call this relationship the **consumption function.**

A second fact we have gleaned from these figures is that the *slope* of the consumption function is quite constant. We infer this constancy from the fact that the straight line drawn in Figure 7-4 comes so close to touching every point. If the slope of the consumption function had varied widely, we could not have done so well with a single straight line.[8] Because of its importance in applications such as the tax cut, economists have given this slope a special name—the **marginal propensity to consume,** or **MPC** for short. The MPC tells us how much more consumers will spend if disposable income rises by $1.

$$MPC = \frac{\text{Change in } C}{\text{Change in } DI \text{ that produces the change in } C}$$

The MPC is best illustrated by an example, and for this purpose we turn away from U.S. data for a moment and look at consumption and income in a hypothetical country whose data come in nice round numbers, which facilitates computation.

Columns (1) and (2) of Table 7-1 show annual consumer expenditure and disposable income, respectively, from 1997 to 2002. These two columns constitute the consumption function, and they are plotted in Figure 7-5. Column (3) in the table shows the marginal propensity to consume (MPC), which is the slope of the line in Figure 7-5; it is derived from the first two columns. We can see that between 1999 and 2000, *DI* rose by $400 billion (from $4,000 billion to $4,400 billion) while *C* rose by $300 billion (from $3,300 billion to $3,600 billion). Thus, the MPC was:

TABLE 7-1   Consumption and Income in a Hypothetical Economy

Year	(1) Consumption, *C*	(2) Disposable Income, *DI*	(3) Marginal Propensity to Consume, MPC
1997	$2,700	$3,200	
1998	3,000	3,600	0.75
1999	3,300	4,000	0.75
2000	3,600	4,400	0.75
2001	3,900	4,800	0.75
2002	4,200	5,200	0.75

NOTE: Amounts are in billions of dollars.

$$MPC = \frac{\text{Change in } C}{\text{Change in } DI} = \frac{\$300}{\$400} = 0.75$$

As you can easily verify, the MPC between any other pair of years in Table 7-1 is also 0.75. This relationship explains why the slope of the line in Figure 7-4 was so crucial in estimating the effect of a tax cut. This slope, which we found there to be 0.90, is simply the MPC for the United States. The MPC tells us how much *additional* spending will be induced by each dollar *change* in disposable income. For each $1 of tax cut, economists expect consumption to rise by $1 times the marginal propensity to consume.

FIGURE 7-5

A Consumption Function

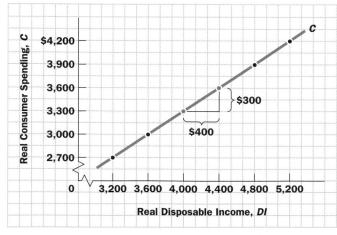

[8] Figure 7-4 is limited to 17 years of data, so try fitting a single straight line to all of the data in Figure 7-3. You will find that you can do remarkably well.

To estimate the *initial* effect of a tax cut on consumer spending, economists must first estimate the MPC and then multiply the amount of the tax cut by the estimated MPC. Because they never know the true MPC with certainty, their prediction is always subject to some margin of error.[9]

FACTORS THAT SHIFT THE CONSUMPTION FUNCTION

Unfortunately for policy planners, the consumption function does not always stand still. Recall from Chapter 3 the important distinction between a *movement along* a demand curve and a *shift* of the curve. A demand curve depicts the relationship between quantity demanded and *one* of its many determinants—price. Thus a change in price causes a *movement along the demand curve*. But a change in any other factor that influences quantity demanded causes a *shift of the entire demand curve*.

Because factors other than disposable income influence consumer spending, a similar distinction is vital to understanding real-world consumption functions. Look back at the definition of the consumption function in the margin of page 128. A change in disposable income leads to a *movement along the consumption function* precisely because the consumption function depicts the relationship between C and DI. Such movements, which are what we have been considering so far, are indicated by the red arrows in Figure 7-6.

But consumption also has other determinants, and a change in any of them will *shift the entire consumption function*—as indicated by the blue arrows in Figure 7-6. Such shifts account for many of the errors in forecasting consumption. To summarize:

Any change in disposable income moves us *along* a given consumption function. A change in any of the other determinants of consumption *shifts* the entire consumption schedule (see Figure 7-6).

Let us now see what some of these "other determinants" are.

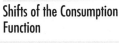

FIGURE 7-6

Shifts of the Consumption Function

Consumer Wealth   One factor affecting spending is consumers' *wealth*, which is a source of purchasing power in addition to income. Wealth and income are different things. For example, a wealthy retiree with a huge bank balance may earn little current *income*. But a high-flying investment banker who spends every penny of the high income she earns will not accumulate *wealth*.

To appreciate the importance of the distinction, think about two recent college graduates, each of whom earns $40,000 per year. If one of them has $100,000 in the bank, while the other has no assets at all, who do you think will spend more? Presumably the one with the big bank account. The general point is that current income is not the only source of spendable funds; households can also finance spending by cashing in some of the wealth they have previously accumulated.

One important implication of this analysis is that the stock market can exert a major influence on consumer spending. A stock market boom adds to wealth and thus raises the consumption function, as depicted in the shift from C_0 to C_1 in Figure 7-6. That is just what happened in the late 1990s, when the stock market soared and American consumers went on a spending spree. Correspondingly, a collapse of stock prices, like the one that occurred in 2000–2002, should shift the consumption function down (see the shift from C_0 to C_2).

The Price Level   Stocks are hardly the only form of wealth. People hold much wealth in forms that are fixed in money terms. Cash itself is the most obvious example, but

---

[9] The word *initial* in the first sentence is an important one. The next chapter will explain why the effects discussed in this chapter are only the beginning of the story.

A money-fixed asset is an asset whose value is a fixed number of dollars.

government bonds, bank accounts, and corporate bonds have fixed face values in money terms. The purchasing power of such **money-fixed assets** obviously declines whenever the price level rises, which means that the asset can buy less. For example, if the price level rises by 10 percent, a $1,000 government bond will buy about 10 percent less than it could when prices were lower. Consequently:

Higher prices decrease the demand for goods and services because they erode the purchasing power of consumer wealth.

This is no trivial matter. Consumers in the United States hold money-fixed assets worth well over $5 *trillion*, so that each 1 percent rise in the price level reduces the purchasing power of consumer wealth by more than $50 billion, a tidy sum. This process, of course, operates equally well in reverse, because a decline in the price level increases the purchasing power of money-fixed assets:

Lower prices increase the demand for goods and services by enhancing the purchasing power of consumer wealth.

For these reasons, a change in the price level will shift the entire consumption function. Specifically:

A higher price level leads to lower real wealth and therefore to less spending *at any given level of real income.* Thus, a higher price level leads to a lower consumption function (such as C_2 in Figure 7-6), and a lower price level leads to a higher consumption function (such as C_1 in Figure 7-6).

Because students often become confused by this point, it is worth repeating that the depressing effect of the price level on consumer spending works through real *wealth*, not through real *income*. The consumption function relates *real consumer income* to *real consumer spending*. Thus, any decline in real income, regardless of its cause, moves the economy leftward *along a fixed consumption function*; it does not shift the consumption function.[10] By contrast, any decline in *real wealth* will *shift the entire consumption function downward*, meaning that people spend less at any given level of real income.

The Real Interest Rate   A higher real rate of interest raises the rewards for saving. For this reason, many people believe it is "obvious" that higher real interest rates must encourage saving and therefore discourage spending. Surprisingly, however, statistical studies of this relationship suggest otherwise. With very few exceptions, they show that interest rates have virtually no effect on consumption decisions in the United States and other countries. Hence, in developing our model of the economy, we will assume that changes in real interest rates do not shift the consumption function. (See "Using the Tax Code to Spur Saving.")

Future Income Expectations   It is hardly earth-shattering to suggest that consumers' expectations about their *future* incomes may affect how much they spend today. This final determinant of consumer spending holds the key to resolving the puzzle posed at the beginning of the chapter: Why did tax policy designed to boost consumer spending apparently fail in 1975 and again in 2001?

 Issue Revisited: Why the Tax Rebates Failed in 1975 and 2001

To understand how expectations of future incomes affect current consumer expenditures, consider the abbreviated life histories of three consumers given in Table 7-2. (The reason for giving our three imaginary individuals such odd names will be apparent shortly.) The consumer named "No Change" earned $100 in each of the years considered in the table. The consumer named "Temporary Rise" earned $100 in three of the four years, but had a good year in 1975. The consumer named "Permanent Rise"

---

[10] This is true even if a rise in the price level lies behind the decline in real income. Because wages and prices normally move together, however, there is no reason to expect real wages to fall when the price level rises.

POLICY DEBATE   Using the Tax Code to Spur Saving

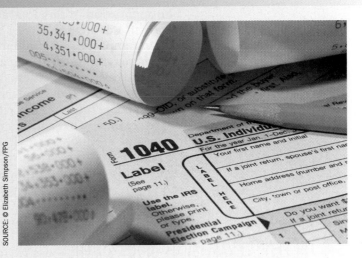

SOURCE: © Elizabeth Simpson/FPG

C ompared to the citizens of most industrial nations, Americans save rather little—only about 2 percent of disposable income in recent years. Many policymakers consider this lack of saving to be a serious problem, so they have proposed numerous changes in the tax laws to increase incentives to save. In 2001, for example, Congress expanded Individual Retirement Accounts (IRAs), which allow taxpayers to save tax-free, and made other changes to encourage saving.

These tax changes, and others like them, were designed to increase the after-tax return on saving. For example, if you put away money in a bank at a 5 percent rate of interest and your income is taxed at a 30 percent rate, your after-tax rate of return on saving is just 3.5 percent (70 percent of 5 percent). But if the interest is earned tax-free in an IRA, you get to keep the full 5 percent. Over long periods of time, this seemingly small interest differential compounds to make an enormous difference in returns. For example, $100 invested for 20 years at 3.5 percent interest grows to $199. But at 5 percent, it grows to $265. Members of Congress who advocate tax incentives for saving argue that lower tax rates will induce Americans to save more.

This idea seems reasonable and has many supporters. Unfortunately, the evidence runs squarely against it. Economists have conducted many studies of the effect of higher rates of return on saving. With very few exceptions, they detect little or no impact. Although the evidence fails to support the "common-sense" solution to the undersaving problem, the debate goes on. Many people, it seems, refuse to believe the evidence.

---

enjoyed a permanent increase in income in 1975 and was therefore clearly the richest.

Now let us use our common sense to figure out how much each of these consumers might have spent in 1975. Temporary Rise and Permanent Rise had the same income that year. Do you think they spent the same amount? Not if they had some ability to foresee their future incomes, because Permanent Rise was richer in the long run.

TABLE 7-2 Incomes of Three Consumers					
	Incomes in Each Year				
Consumer	1974	1975	1976	1977	Total Income
No Change	$100	$100	$100	$100	**$400**
Temporary Rise	100	120	100	100	**420**
Permanent Rise	100	120	120	120	**460**

Now compare No Change and Temporary Rise. Temporary Rise had 20 percent higher income in 1975 ($120 versus $100), but only 5 percent more over the entire four-year period ($420 versus $400). Do you think his spending in 1975 was closer to 20 percent above No Change's, or closer to 5 percent above it? Most people guess the latter.

The point of this example is that consumers very reasonably decide on their *current* consumption spending by looking at their *long-run* income prospects. This should come as no surprise to a college student. You are probably spending more than you earn this year, but that does not make you a foolish spendthrift. On the contrary, you know that your college education gives you a strong expectation of much higher incomes in the future, and you are spending with that idea in mind.

Now, to relate this example to the failure of the 1975 income tax cut, imagine that the three rows in Table 7-2 represent the entire economy under three different government policies. Recall that 1975 was the year of the temporary tax cut. The first row (No Change) shows the unchanged path of disposable income in the absence of any tax cut. The second (Temporary Rise) shows an increase in disposable income attributable to a tax cut *for one year only*. The bottom row (Permanent Rise) shows a policy that increases DI in *every future year* by cutting taxes permanently in 1975. Which of the two lower rows do you imagine would have generated more consumer spending in 1975? The bottom row (Permanent Rise), of course. What we have concluded, then, is this:

Permanent cuts in income taxes cause greater increases in consumer spending than do temporary cuts of equal magnitude.

The application of this analysis to the 1975 and 2001 tax rebates is immediate. The 1975 tax cut was advertised as a one-time increase in after-tax income, like that experienced by Temporary Rise in Table 7-2. No future income was affected, so consumers did not increase their spending as much as government officials had hoped. Ironically, the 2001 tax rebate checks actually represented the first installment of a projected ten-year program of tax reductions. But they were so widely advertised as a one-time event that most people receiving the checks probably viewed the income gain as temporary.

We have, then, what appears to be a general principle, backed up by both historical evidence and common sense. Permanent changes or changes of longer duration in income taxes have more significant effects on consumer spending than do temporary changes. This conclusion may seem obvious, but it is not a lesson you would have learned from an introductory textbook 30 years ago. It is one that we learned the hard way, through bitter experience.

THE EXTREME VARIABILITY OF INVESTMENT

Next, we turn to the most *volatile* component of aggregate demand: investment spending.[11] While consumer spending follows movements in disposable income quite closely, investment spending swings from high to low levels with astonishing speed. For example, when real GDP in the United States slowed from a rapid growth rate of 3.7 percent in 2000 to a sluggish 0.5 percent in 2001, a drop of over 3 percentage points, the growth rate of real investment spending dropped from 5.7 percent to −8.4 percent. What accounts for such dramatic changes in investment spending?

Several factors that influence how much businesses want to invest were discussed in the previous chapter, including interest rates, tax provisions, technical change, and the strength of the economy. Sometimes these determinants change abruptly, leading to dramatic variations in investment. But perhaps the most important factor accounting for the volatility of investment spending was not discussed in Chapter 6: the *state of business confidence*, which in turn depends on *expectations about the future*.

Though confidence is tricky to measure, it does seem obvious that businesses will build more factories and purchase more new machines when they are optimistic. Correspondingly, their investment plans will be very cautious if the economic outlook appears bleak. Keynes pointed out that psychological perceptions such as these are subject to abrupt shifts, so that fluctuations in investment can be a major cause of instability in aggregate demand.

Unfortunately, neither economists nor, for that matter, psychologists have many good ideas about how to *measure*—much less *control*—business confidence. So economists usually focus on several more objective determinants of investment that are easier to quantify and even influence—factors such as interest rates and tax provisions.

THE DETERMINANTS OF NET EXPORTS

Another highly variable source of demand for U.S. products is foreign purchases of U.S. goods—our *exports*. As we observed earlier in this chapter, we obtain the *net* contribution of foreigners to U.S. aggregate demand by subtracting *imports*, which is the portion of domestic demand that is satisfied by foreign producers.

---

[11] We repeat the warning given earlier about the meaning of the word *investment*. It *includes* spending by businesses and individuals on newly produced factories, machinery, and houses. But it *excludes* sales of used industrial plants, equipment, and homes as well as purely financial transactions, such as the purchases of stocks and bonds.

National Incomes

Although both exports and imports depend on many factors, the predominant one is *income levels in different countries*. When American consumers and firms spend more on consumption and investment, some of this new spending goes toward the purchase of foreign goods. Therefore:

Our imports rise when our GDP rises and fall when our GDP falls.

Similarly, because our *exports* are the *imports* of other countries, our exports depend on *their* GDPs, not on our own. Thus:

Our exports are relatively insensitive to our own GDP, but are quite sensitive to the GDPs of other countries.

Putting these two ideas together leads to a clear implication: When our economy grows faster than the economies of our trading partners, our net exports tend to shrink. Conversely, when foreign economies grow faster than ours, our net exports tend to rise. Events during the 1990s illustrated this point dramatically. The U.S. economy stagnated between 1990 and 1992, and our net exports rose from −$55 billion to −$16 billion. (Remember, −16 is a larger number than −55!) Then, when growth in the United States outstripped growth abroad from 1992 to 2000, U.S. net exports plummeted from −$16 billion to −$380 billion.

Relative Prices and Exchange Rates

Although GDP levels here and abroad are important influences on a country's net exports, they are not the only relevant factors. International price differences matter, too.

To make things concrete, let's focus on trade between the United States and Japan. Suppose American prices rise while Japanese prices fall, making U.S. goods more expensive *relative to Japanese goods*. If American consumers react to these new relative prices by buying more Japanese goods, U.S. *imports* rise. If Japanese consumers react to the same relative price changes by buying fewer American products, U.S. *exports fall*. Both reactions reduce America's *net* exports.

Naturally, a decline in American prices (or a rise in Japanese prices) does precisely the opposite. Thus:

A rise in the prices of a country's goods will lead to a reduction in that country's net exports. Analogously, a decline in the prices of a country's goods will raise that country's net exports. Similarly, price increases abroad raise the home country's net exports, whereas price decreases abroad have the opposite effect.

[handwritten margin note: Inflation in ~~affects~~ one country. is felt internationally. ~~felt~~.]

This simple idea holds the key to understanding how exchange rates among the world's currencies influence exports and imports—an important topic that we will consider in depth in Chapters 17 and 18. The reason is that exchange rates translate foreign prices into terms that are familiar to home country customers—their own currencies.

Consider, for example, Americans interested in buying Japanese cars that cost ¥3,000,000. If it takes ¥100 to buy a dollar, these cars cost American buyers $30,000. But if the dollar is worth ¥150, those same cars cost Americans just $20,000, and consumers in the United States are likely to buy more of them. These sorts of responses help explain why American automakers lost market share to Japanese imports when the dollar rose against the yen in the late 1990s.

HOW PREDICTABLE IS AGGREGATE DEMAND?

We have now learned enough to see why economists often have difficulty predicting aggregate demand. Consider the four main components, starting with consumer spending.

Because wealth affects consumption, forecasts of spending can be thrown off by unexpected movements of the stock market or by poor forecasts of future prices. It may also be difficult to anticipate how taxpayers will view changes in the income tax law. If the government says that a tax cut is permanent (as for example, in 1964 and 1981), will consumers take the government at its word and increase their spending accordingly? Perhaps not, if the government has a history of raising taxes after promising to keep them low. Similarly, when (as in 1975) the government explicitly announces that a tax cut is temporary, will consumers always believe the announcement? Or might they greet it with a hefty dose of skepticism? Such a reaction is quite possible if there is a history of "temporary" tax changes that stayed on the books indefinitely.

Swings in investment spending are even more difficult to predict, partly because they are tied so closely to business confidence and expectations. Developments abroad also often lead to surprises in the net export account. Even the final component of aggregate demand, government purchases (G), is subject to the vagaries of politics—which are not always predictable!

We could say much more about the determinants of aggregate demand, but it is best to leave the rest to more advanced courses. We are now ready to apply our knowledge of aggregate demand to the construction of the first model of the economy. Although it is true that income determines consumption, the consumption function in turn helps to determine the level of income. If that sounds like circular reasoning, read the next chapter!

SUMMARY

1. **Aggregate demand** is the total volume of goods and services purchased by consumers, businesses, government units, and foreigners. It can be expressed as the sum $C + I + G + (X - IM)$, where C is consumer spending, I is investment spending, G is **government purchases,** and $X - IM$ is **net exports.**

2. Aggregate demand is a schedule: The aggregate quantity demanded depends on (among other things) the price level. But, for any given price level, aggregate demand is a number.

3. Economists reserve the term **investment** to refer to purchases of newly produced factories, machinery, and houses.

4. Gross domestic product is the total volume of final goods and services produced in the country.

5. **National income** is the sum of the before-tax wages, interest, rents, and profits earned by all individuals in the economy. By necessity, it must be approximately equal to domestic product.

6. **Disposable income** is the sum of the incomes of all individuals in the economy after taxes and transfers. It is the chief determinant of **consumer expenditures.**

7. All of these concepts, and others, can be depicted in a circular flow diagram that shows expenditures on all four sources flowing into business firms and national income flowing out.

8. The close relationship between consumer spending (C) and disposable income (DI) is called the **consumption function.** Its slope, which is used to predict the change in consumption that will be caused by a change in income taxes, is called the **marginal propensity to consume (MPC).**

9. Changes in disposable income move us along a given consumption function. Changes in any of the other variables that affect C shift the entire consumption function. Among the most important of these other variables are total consumer wealth, the price level, and expected future incomes.

10. Because consumers hold so many **money-fixed assets,** they lose purchasing power when prices rise, which leads them to reduce their spending.

11. The government often tries to manipulate aggregate demand by influencing private consumption decisions, usually through changes in the personal income tax. But this policy did not work well in 1975 or 2001.

12. Future income prospects help explain why. The 1975 tax cut was temporary and therefore left future incomes unaffected. The 2001 tax cut was the first stage of a large permanent tax cut, which therefore affected both future and current incomes. But it was advertised as a one-time event.

13. Investment is the most volatile component of aggregate demand, largely because it is tied too closely to confidence and expectations.

14. Policymakers cannot influence confidence in any reliable way, so policies designed to spur investment focus on more objective, although possibly less important, determinants of investment—such as interest rates and taxes.

15. Net exports depend on GDPs and relative prices both domestically and abroad.

KEY TERMS

Aggregate demand   122

Consumer expenditure (*C*)   122

Investment spending (*I*)   123

Government purchases (*G*)   123

Net exports (*X* − *IM*)   123

C + *I* + *G* + (*X* − *IM*)   123

National income   123

Disposable income (*DI*)   123

Circular flow diagram   124

Transfer payments   125

Scatter diagram   126

Consumption function   128

Marginal propensity to consume (MPC)   128

Movements along versus shifts of the consumption function   129

Money-fixed assets   130

Temporary versus permanent tax changes   131

QUESTIONS FOR REVIEW

1. What are the four components of aggregate demand? Which is the largest? Which is the smallest?

2. What is the difference between *investment* as the term is used by most people and *investment* as defined by an economist? Which of the following acts constitute investment according to the economist's definition?

   a. Intel builds a new factory to manufacture semiconductors. *Yes*

   b. You buy 100 shares of Intel stock. *No* (*no stocks, bond AD spending on GDP*)

   c. A small chipmaker goes bankrupt, and Intel purchases its factory and equipment. *No*

   d. Your family buys a newly constructed home from a developer. *Yes,*

   e. Your family buys an older home from another family. (*Hint:* Are any *new* products demanded by this action?) (*No*)

3. What would the circular flow diagram (Figure 7-1) look like in an economy with no government? Draw one for yourself.

4. The marginal propensity to consume (MPC) for the United States as a whole is roughly 0.90. Explain in words what this means. What is your personal MPC at this stage in your life? How might that change by the time you are your parents' age?

5. Look at the scatter diagram in Figure 7-3. What does it tell you about what was going on in this country in the years 1942 to 1945?

6. What is a consumption function, and why is it a useful device for government economists planning a tax cut?

7. On a piece of graph paper, construct a consumption function from the data given below and determine the MPC.

Year	Consumer Spending	Disposable Income
1998	$1,200	$1,500 − .80
1999	1,440	1,800 .80
2000	1,680	2,100
2001	1,920	2,400
2002	2,160	2,700

8. In which direction will the consumption function shift if the price level rises? Show this on your graph from Review Question 7. *leftward*

9. Explain why permanent tax cuts are likely to lead to bigger increases in consumer spending than are temporary tax cuts. *Because 'temporary' would*

10. (**More difficult**) Between 1990 and 1991, real disposable income (in 1996 dollars) barely increased at all, owing to a recession. (It rose from $5,324 billion to $5,352 billion.) Use the data on real consumption expenditures given on the inside back cover of this book to compare the change in *C* to the $28 billion change in *DI*. Explain why dividing the two does *not* give a good estimate of the marginal propensity to consume.

11. In 1997 and again in 2001, Congress enacted several changes in the tax law designed to promote saving. If such saving incentives had been successful, how would the consumption function have shifted?

    right leftward — mean for a short period of time, and consumer would not change their spending habits for a short period of time

APPENDIX   National Income Accounting

The type of macroeconomic analysis presented in this book dates from the publication of John Maynard Keynes's *The General Theory of Employment, Interest, and Money* in 1936. But at that time, there was really no way to test Keynes's theories because the necessary data did not exist. It took some years for the theoretical notions used by Keynes to find concrete expression in real-world data.

The system of measurement devised for collecting and expressing macroeconomic data is called national income accounting.

The development of this system of accounts ranks as a great achievement in applied economics, perhaps as important in its own right as was Keynes's theoretical work. Without it, the practical value of Keynesian analysis would be severely limited. Economists spent long hours wrestling with the many difficult conceptual questions that arose as they translated the theory into numbers. Along the way, some more-or-less arbitrary decisions and conventions had to be made. You may not agree with all of them, but the accounting framework that was devised, though imperfect, is eminently serviceable.

DEFINING GDP: EXCEPTIONS TO THE RULES

We first encountered the concept of **gross domestic product (GDP)** in Chapter 4.

Gross domestic product (GDP) is the sum of the money values of all final goods and services produced during a specified period of time, usually one year.

However, the definition of GDP has certain exceptions that we have not yet noted.

First, the treatment of government output involves a minor departure from the principle of using market prices. Unlike private products, the "outputs" of government offices are not sold; indeed, it is sometimes even difficult to define what those outputs are. Lacking prices for outputs, national income accountants fall back on the only prices they have: prices for the inputs from which the outputs are produced. Thus:

Government outputs are valued at the cost of the inputs needed to produce them.

This means, for example, that if a clerk at the Department of Motor Vehicles earns $16 per hour and spends one-half hour torturing you with explanations of why you cannot get a driver's license, that particular government "service" increases GDP by $8.

Second, some goods that are produced during the year but not yet sold are nonetheless counted in that year's GDP. Specifically, goods that firms add to their *inventories* count in the GDP even though they do not pass through markets.

National income statisticians treat inventories as if they were "bought" by the firms that produced them, even though these "purchases" do not actually take place.

Finally, the treatment of investment goods runs slightly counter to the rule that GDP includes only final goods. In a broad sense, factories, generators, machine tools, and the like might be considered to be intermediate goods. After all, their owners want them only for use in producing other goods, not for any innate value that they possess. But this classification would present a real problem. Because factories and machines normally are never sold to consumers, when would we count them in GDP? National income statisticians avoid this problem by defining investment goods as final products demanded by the *firms* that buy them.

Now that we have a more complete definition of what the GDP is, let us turn to the problem of actually measuring it. National income accountants have devised three ways to perform this task, and we consider each in turn.

GDP AS THE SUM OF FINAL GOODS AND SERVICES

The first way to measure GDP seems to be the most natural, because it follows so directly from the circular flow diagram (Figure 7-1). It also turns out to be the most useful definition for macroeconomic analysis. We simply add up the final demands of all consumers, business firms, government, and foreigners. Using the symbols Y, C, I, G, and $(X - IM)$ as we did in the chapter, we have:

$$Y = C + I + G + (X - IM)$$

The I that appears in the actual U.S. national accounts is called **gross private domestic investment.** We will explain the word *gross* presently. *Private* indicates that government investment is considered part of G, and *domestic* means that machinery sold by American firms to foreign companies is included in exports rather than in I (investment). Gross private domestic investment in the United States has three components:

- Business investment in plant, equipment, and software

- Residential construction (home building)
- Inventory investment

Gross private domestic investment includes business investment in plant, equipment, and software; residential construction; and inventory investment.

We repeat again that *only* these three things are *investment* in national income accounting terminology.

As defined in the national income accounts, *investment* includes only newly produced capital goods, such as machinery, factories, and new homes. It does not include exchanges of existing assets.

The symbol *G*, for government purchases, represents the *volume of current goods and services purchased by all levels of government*. Thus, all government payments to its employees are counted in *G*, as are all of its purchases of goods.

Few citizens realize, however, that *the federal government spends most of its money, not for purchases of goods and services, but rather on transfer payments*—literally, giving away money—either to individuals or to other levels of government.

The importance of this conceptual distinction lies in the fact that *G* represents the part of the national product that government uses up for its own purposes—to pay for armies, bureaucrats, paper, and ink—whereas transfer payments merely shuffle purchasing power from one group of citizens to another. Except for the administrators needed to run these programs, real economic resources are not used up in this process.

In adding up the nation's total output as the sum of *C* + *I* + *G* + (*X* − *IM*), we sum the shares of GDP that are used up by consumers, investors, government, and foreigners, respectively. Because transfer payments merely give someone the capability to spend on *C*, it is logical to exclude transfers from our definition of *G*, including in *C* only the portion of these transfer payments that consumers spend. If we included transfers in *G*, the same spending would get counted twice: once in *G* and then again in *C*.

The final component of GDP is net exports, which are simply exports of goods and services minus imports of goods and services. Table 7-3 shows GDP for 2003, in both nominal and real terms, computed as the sum of *C* + *I* + *G* + (*X* − *IM*). Note that the numbers for net exports in the table are actually negative. We will say much more about America's trade deficit in Part IV.

GDP AS THE SUM OF ALL FACTOR PAYMENTS

We can count up the GDP another way: by *adding up all incomes in the economy*. Let's see how this method handles some typical transactions. Suppose General Electric

TABLE 7-3   Gross Domestic Product in 2003 as the Sum of Final Demands

Item	Nominal Amount*	Real Amount†
Personal consumption expenditures (*C*)	$ 7,752.3	$7,362.2
Gross private domestic investment (*I*)	1,667.5	1,635.7
Government purchases of goods and services (*G*)	2,055.7	1,899.5
Net exports (*X* − *IM*)	−491.5	−505.5
Exports (*X*)	1,048.1	1,033.9
Imports (*IM*)	1,539.6	1,539.4
Gross domestic product (*Y*)	**10,983.9**	**10,397.2**

*In billions of current dollars.
†In billions of 2000 dollars.

SOURCE: U.S. Department of Commerce. Totals do not add up precisely due to rounding and method of deflating.

builds a generator and sells it to General Motors for $1 million. The first method of calculating GDP simply counts the $1 million as part of *I*. The second method asks: What incomes resulted from producing this generator? The answer might be something like this:

Wages of GE employees	$400,000
Interest to bondholders	50,000
Rentals of buildings	50,000
Profits of GE stockholders	100,000

The total is $600,000. The remaining $400,000 is accounted for by inputs that GE purchased from other companies: steel, circuitry, tubing, rubber, and so on. But if we traced this $400,000 back even further, we would find that it is accounted for by the wages, interest, and rentals paid by these other companies, *plus* their profits, *plus* their purchases from other firms. In fact, for *every* firm in the economy, there is an accounting identity that says:

$$\text{Revenue from sales} = \begin{array}{l} \text{Wages paid } + \\ \text{Interest paid } + \\ \text{Rentals paid } + \\ \text{Profits earned } + \\ \text{Purchases from other firms} \end{array}$$

Why must this always be true? Because profits are the balancing item; they are what is *left over* after the firm has made all other payments. In fact, this accounting identity really reflects the definition of profits: sales revenue less all costs.

Now apply this accounting identity to *all firms in the economy*. Total purchases from other firms are precisely what we call *intermediate goods*. What, then, do we get if we subtract these intermediate transactions from both sides of the equation?

$$\text{Revenue from sales minus} \atop \text{Purchases from other firms} = \begin{array}{l} \text{Wages paid +} \\ \text{Interest paid +} \\ \text{Rentals paid +} \\ \text{Profits earned} \end{array}$$

On the right-hand side, we have the sum of all factor incomes: payments to labor, land, and capital. On the left-hand side, we have total sales minus sales of intermediate goods. This means that we have sales of *final goods*, which is precisely our definition of GDP. Thus, the accounting identity for the entire economy can be rewritten as follows:

GDP = Wages + Interest + Rents + Profits

This definition gives national income accountants another way to measure the GDP.

Table 7-4 shows how to obtain GDP from the sum of all incomes. Once again, we have omitted a few details in our discussion. By adding up wages, interest, rents, and profits, we obtain only $8,476 billion, whereas GDP in 2002 was $10,481 billion. When sales taxes, excise taxes, and the like are added to the sum of wages, interest, rents, and profits, we obtain what is called **national**

income—the sum of all factor payments, including indirect business taxes.

National income is the sum of the incomes that all individuals in the country earn in the forms of wages, interest, rents, and profits. It includes indirect business taxes, but excludes transfer payments and makes no deduction for income taxes.

Notice that national income is a measure of the factor incomes of all Americans, regardless of whether they work in this country or somewhere else. Likewise, incomes earned by foreigners in the United States are excluded from (our) national income. We will return to this distinction shortly.

But, reading down Table 7-4, we next encounter a new concept: **net national product (NNP),** a measure of *production*. For reasons explained in the chapter, NNP is conceptually identical to national income. However, in practice, national income accountants estimate *income* and *production* independently; and so the two measures are never precisely equal. The difference in 2002 was $77 billion, or just 0.8 percent of NNP; it is called the statistical discrepancy.

Moving further down the table, the only difference between NNP and **gross national product (GNP)** is **depreciation** of the nation's capital stock. Thus the adjective "net" means excluding depreciation and "gross" means including it. GNP is thus a measure of *all* final production, making no adjustment for the fact that some capital is "used up" each year, and thus needs to be replaced. NNP deducts the required replacements to arrive at a net production figure.

Depreciation is the value of the portion of the nation's capital equipment that is used up within the year. It tells us how much output is needed just to maintain the economy's capital stock.

From a conceptual point of view, most economists feel that NNP is a more meaningful indicator of the economy's output than is GNP. After all, the depreciation component of GNP represents the output that is needed just to repair and replace worn-out factories and machines; it is not available for anybody to consume.[12] Therefore, NNP seems to be a better measure of production than GNP.

Alas, GNP is much easier to measure because depreciation is a particularly tricky item. What fraction of his tractor did Farmer Jones "use up" last year? How much

■ TABLE 7-4
Gross Domestic Product in 2002 as the Sum of Incomes

Item	Amount
Compensation of employees (wages)	**$6,019.1**
plus	
Net interest	**582.4**
plus	
Rental income	**173.0**
plus	
Profits	**1,701.9**
Corporate profits	904.2
Proprietors' income	797.7
plus	
Indirect business taxes and misc. items	**814.5**
equals	
National income	**9,290.8**
plus	
Statistical discrepancy	**−77.2**
equals	
Net national product	**9,213.7**
plus	
Depreciation	1,288.6
equals	
Gross national product	**$10,502.3**
minus	
Income received from other countries	**299.1**
plus	
Income paid to other countries	**277.6**
equals	
Gross domestic product	**10,480.8**

NOTE: Amounts are in billions of dollars.

SOURCE: U.S. Department of Commerce. Totals do not add up precisely due to rounding.

---

[12] If the capital stock is used for consumption, it will decline, and the nation will wind up poorer than it was before.

did the Empire State Building depreciate during 2001? If you ask yourself these difficult questions, you will understand why most economists believe that we can measure GNP more accurately than NNP. For this reason, most economic models are based on GNP.

The final two adjustments that bring us to GDP return to a fact mentioned earlier. Some American citizens earn their incomes abroad, and some of the payments made by American companies are paid to foreign citizens. Thus, to obtain a measure of total production in the U.S. *domestic* economy (which is GDP) rather than a measure of the total production by U.S. *nationals* (which is GNP), we must *subtract* the income that Americans receive for factors supplied abroad and *add* the income that foreigners receive for factors supplied here. The net of these two adjustments is a very small number, as Table 7-4 shows. Thus, GDP and GNP are almost equal.

In Table 7-4, you can hardly help noticing the preponderant share of employee compensation in total factor payments—about 71 percent. Labor is by far the most important factor of production. The return on land is roughly 2 percent of factor payments, and interest accounts for almost 7 percent. Profits account for the remaining 20 percent, although the size of corporate profits (just 8.6 percent of GDP in 2002) is much less than the public thinks. If, by some magic stroke, we could convert all corporate profits into wages without upsetting the economy's performance, the average worker would get a raise of about 15 percent!

GDP AS THE SUM OF VALUES ADDED

It may strike you as strange that national income accountants include only *final* goods and services in GDP. Aren't *intermediate* goods part of the nation's product? Of course they are. The problem is that, if all intermediate goods were included in GDP, we would wind up double- and triple-counting certain goods and services and therefore get an exaggerated impression of the actual level of economic activity.

To explain why, and to show how national income accountants cope with this difficulty, we must introduce a new concept, called *value added*.

The **value added** by a firm is its revenue from selling a product minus the amount paid for goods and services purchased from other firms.

The intuitive sense of this concept is clear: If a firm buys some inputs from other firms, does something to them, and sells the resulting product for a price higher than it paid for the inputs, we say that the firm has "added value" to the product. If we sum up the values added by all firms in the economy, we must get the total value of all final products. Thus:

GDP can be measured as the sum of the values added by all firms.

To verify this fact, look back at the accounting identity at the top of the previous page. The left-hand side of this equation, sales revenue minus purchases from other firms, is precisely the firm's value added. Thus:

Value added = Wages + Interest + Rents + Profits

Because the second method we gave for measuring GDP is to add up wages, interest, rents, and profits, we see that the value-added approach must yield the same answer.

The value-added concept is useful in avoiding double-counting. Often, however, intermediate goods are difficult to distinguish from final goods. Paint bought by a painter, for example, is an intermediate good. But paint bought by a do-it-yourselfer is a final good. What happens, then, if the professional painter buys some paint to refurbish his own garage? The intermediate good becomes a final good. You can see that the line between intermediate goods and final goods is a fuzzy one in practice.

If we measure GDP by the sum of values added, however, we need not make such subtle distinctions. In this method, *every* purchase of a new good or service counts, but we do not count the entire selling price, only the portion that represents value added.

To illustrate this idea, consider the data in Table 7-5 and how they would affect GDP as the sum of final products. Our example begins when a farmer who grows soybeans sells them to a mill for $3 per bushel. This transaction does *not* count in the GDP, because the miller does not purchase the soybeans for her own use. The miller then grinds up the soybeans and sells the resulting bag of soy meal to a factory that produces soy sauce. The miller receives $4, but GDP still has not increased because the ground beans are also an intermediate product. Next, the factory turns the beans into soy sauce, which it sells to your favorite Chinese restaurant for $8. Still no effect on GDP.

But then the big moment arrives: The restaurant sells the sauce to you and other customers as a part of your meals, and you eat it. At this point, the $10 worth of soy sauce becomes a final product and *does* count in the GDP. Notice that if we had also counted the three intermediate transactions (farmer to miller, miller to fac-

TABLE 7-5 An Illustration of Final and Intermediate Goods

Item	Seller	Buyer	Price
Bushel of soybeans	Farmer	Miller	$3
Bag of soy meal	Miller	Factory	4
Gallon of soy sauce	Factory	Restaurant	8
Gallon of soy sauce used as seasoning	Restaurant	Consumers	10
		Total:	**$25**
Addendum: Contribution to GDP $10			

tory, factory to restaurant), we would have come up with $25—2½ times too much.

Why is it too much? The reason is straightforward. Neither the miller, the factory owner, nor the restaurateur values the product we have been considering *for its own sake*. Only the customers who eat the final product (the soy sauce) have increased their material well-being, so only this last transaction counts in the GDP. However, as we shall now see, value-added calculations enable us to come up with the right answer ($10) by counting only *part* of each transaction. The basic idea is to count at each step only the contribution to the value of the ultimate final product that is made at that step, excluding the values of items produced at other steps.

Ignoring the minor items (such as fertilizer) that the farmer purchases from others, the entire $3 selling price of the bushel of soybeans is new output produced by the farmer; that is, the whole $3 is value added. The miller then grinds the beans and sells them for $4. She has added $4 minus $3, or $1 to the value of the beans. When the factory turns this soy meal into soy sauce and sells it for $8, it has added $8 minus $4, or $4 more in value. Finally, when the restaurant sells it to hungry customers for $10, a further $2 of value is added.

The last column of Table 7-6 shows this chain of creation of value added. We see that the total value added by all four firms is $10, exactly the same as the restaurant's selling price. This is as it must be, for only the restaurant sells the soybeans as a final product.

TABLE 7-6   An Illustration of Value Added

Item	Seller	Buyer	Price	Value Added
Bushel of soybeans	Farmer	Miller	$3	$3
Bag of soy meal	Miller	Factory	4	1
Gallon of soy sauce	Factory	Restaurant	8	4
Gallon of soy sauce used as seasoning	Restaurant	Consumers	10	2
		Total:	$25	$10

Addendum: Contribution to GDP

Final Products	$10
Sum of values added	$10

SUMMARY

1. **Gross domestic product (GDP)** is the sum of the money values of all final goods and services produced during a year and sold on organized markets. There are, however, certain exceptions to this definition.

2. One way to measure the GDP is to add up the final demands of consumers, investors, government, and foreigners: GDP = $C + I + G + (X - IM)$.

3. A second way to measure the GDP is to start with all factor payments—wages, interest, rents, and profits—that consti-

tute the **national income** and then add indirect business taxes and **depreciation**.

4. A third way to measure the GDP is to sum up the **values added** by every firm in the economy (and then once again add indirect business taxes and depreciation).

5. Except for possible bookkeeping and statistical errors, all three methods must give the same answer.

KEY TERMS

National income accounting   136

Gross domestic product (GDP)   136

Gross private domestic investment (*I*)   137

National income   138

Net national product (NNP)   138

Net domestic product (NDP)   138

Depreciation   138

Value added   139

QUESTIONS FOR REVIEW

1. Which of the following transactions are included in the gross domestic product, and by how much does each raise GDP?

   a. You buy a new Honda, made in the United States, paying $18,000. Y

   b. You buy a new Toyota, imported from Japan, paying $18,000. N

   c. You buy a used Cadillac, paying $3,000.

   d. America Online spends $100 million to increase its Internet capacity.

   e. Your grandmother receives a Social Security check for $1,200.

f. Chrysler manufactures 1,000 automobiles at a cost of $12,000 each. Unable to sell them, the company holds the cars as inventories. N

g. Mr. Black and Mr. Blue, each out for a Sunday drive, have a collision in which their cars are destroyed. Black and Blue each hire a lawyer to sue the other, paying the lawyers $3,000 each for services rendered. The judge throws the case out of court. Y

h. You sell a used computer to your friend for $100. N

2. Explain the difference between final goods and intermediate goods. Why is it sometimes difficult to apply this distinction in practice? In this regard, why is the concept of value added useful?

3. Explain the difference between government spending and government purchases of goods and services (G). Which is larger?

4. Explain why national income and gross domestic product would be essentially equal if there were no depreciation and no indirect business taxes.

5. The following outline provides a complete description of all economic activity in Trivialand for 2001. Draw up versions of Tables 7-3 and 7-4 for Trivialand showing GDP computed in two different ways.[13]

i. There are thousands of farmers but only two big business firms in Trivialand: Specific Motors (an auto company) and Super Duper (a chain of food markets). There is no government and no depreciation.

ii. Specific Motors produced 1,000 small cars, which it sold at $6,000 each, and 100 trucks, which it sold at $8,000 each. Consumers bought 800 of the cars, and the remaining 200 cars were exported to the United States. Super Duper bought all the trucks.

iii. Sales at Super Duper markets amounted to $14 million, all of it sold to consumers.

iv. All farmers in Trivialand are self-employed and sell all of their wares to Super Duper.

v. The costs incurred by all of Trivialand's businesses were as follows:

	Specific Motors	Super Duper	Farmers
Wages	$3,800,000	$4,500,000	$ 0
Interest	100,000	200,000	700,000
Rent	200,000	1,000,000	2,000,000
Purchases of food	0	7,000,000	0

6. **(More difficult)** Now complicate Trivialand (see Review Question 5) in the following ways and answer the same questions. In addition, calculate national income and disposable income.[14]

a. The government bought 50 cars, leaving only 150 cars for export. In addition, the government spent $800,000 on wages and made $1,200,000 in transfer payments.

b. Depreciation for the year amounted to $600,000 for Specific Motors and $200,000 for Super Duper. (The farmers had no depreciation.)

c. The government levied sales taxes amounting to $500,000 on Specific Motors and $200,000 on Super Duper (but none on farmers). In addition, the government levied a 10 percent income tax on all wages, interest, and rental income.

d. In addition to the food and cars mentioned in Review Question 5, consumers in Trivialand imported 500 computers from the United States at $2,000 each.

---

[13] In Trivialand, net national product and net domestic product are the same. So there are no entries corresponding to "income received from other countries" or "income paid to other countries," as in Table 7-4.

[14] In this context, disposable income is *national income* plus transfer payments minus taxes.

8

Demand-Side Equilibrium:
Unemployment or Inflation?

A definite ratio, to be called the Multiplier, can be established between income and investment.

JOHN MAYNARD KEYNES

Let's briefly review where we have just been. In Chapter 4, we learned that the interaction of aggregate demand and aggregate supply determines whether the economy stagnates or prospers, whether our labor and capital resources are fully employed or unemployed. In Chapter 7, we learned that aggregate demand has four components: consumer expenditure (C), investment (I), government purchases (G), and net exports (X − IM). It is now time to start building a theory that puts all the pieces together so we can see where the aggregate demand and aggregate supply curves come from.

Our approach is sequential. Because it is best to walk before you try to run, we imagine for most of this chapter that the price level, the rate of interest, and the international value of the dollar are all constant. None of these assumptions is true, of course, and we will dispense with each in subsequent chapters. But we reap two important benefits from making these unrealistic assumptions now. First, they enable us to construct a simple but useful model of how the strength of aggregate demand influences the level of gross domestic product (GDP)—a model we will use to derive specific numerical solutions. Second, this model gives us an initial answer to a question of great importance to policymakers: Can we expect the economy to achieve full employment if the government does not intervene?

CONTENTS

Issue: Why Does the Market Permit Unemployment?

Economists are fond of pointing out, with some awe, the amazing achievements of free markets. Without central direction, they somehow get businesses to produce just the goods and services that consumers want—and to do so cheaply and efficiently. If consumers want less meat and more fish, markets respond. If people subsequently change their minds, markets respond again. Free markets seem able to coordinate literally millions of decisions effortlessly and seamlessly.

Yet for hundreds of years and all over the globe, market economies have stumbled over one particular coordination problem: the periodic bouts of mass unemployment that we call *recessions* and *depressions*. Widespread unemployment represents a failure to coordinate economic activity in the following sense. If the unemployed were hired, they would be able to buy the goods and services that businesses cannot sell. The revenues from those sales would, in turn, allow firms to pay the workers. So a seemingly straightforward "deal" offers jobs for the unemployed and sales for the firms. But somehow this deal is not made. Workers remain unemployed and firms get stuck with unsold output.

Thus free markets, which somehow manage to get rough diamonds dug out of the ground in South Africa and turned into beautiful rings that grooms buy for brides in Los Angeles, cannot seem to solve the coordination problem posed by unemployment. Why not? For centuries, economists puzzled over this question. By the end of the chapter, we will be well on the way toward providing an answer.

THE MEANING OF EQUILIBRIUM GDP

We begin by putting the four components of aggregate demand together to see how they interact, using as our organizing framework the circular flow diagram from the last chapter. In doing so, we initially ignore the possibility that the government might vary taxes and spending to steer the economy in some desired direction. Aside from pedagogical simplicity, there is an important reason for doing so. One of the crucial questions surrounding government stabilization policy is whether the economy would *automatically* gravitate toward full employment if the government simply left it alone. Contradicting the teachings of generations of economists before him, Keynes claimed it would not. But Keynes's views remain controversial to this day. We can study the issue best by imagining an economy in which the government never tried to manipulate aggregate demand, which is just what we do in this chapter.

To begin to construct a simple model of the size of the economy, we must first understand what we mean by *equilibrium GDP*. Figure 8-1, which repeats Figure 7-1 from the last chapter, is a circular flow diagram that will help us do this.

As explained in the last chapter, total *production* and total *income* must be equal. But the same need not be true of total spending. Imagine that, for some reason, the total expenditures made after point 4 in the figure, $C + I + G + (X - IM)$, exceed the output produced by the business firms at point 5. What happens then?

Because consumers, businesses, government, and foreigners together are buying more than firms are producing, businesses will start taking goods out of their warehouses to meet customer demand. Thus, inventory stocks will fall—which signals retailers that they need to increase their orders and manufacturers that they need to step up production. Consequently, output is likely to rise.

Equilibrium refers to a situation in which neither consumers nor firms have any incentive to change their behavior. They are content to continue with things as they are.

At some later date, if evidence indicates that the high level of spending is not just a temporary aberration, either manufacturers or retailers (or both) may also respond to buoyant sales performances by raising their prices. Economists therefore say that neither output nor the price level is in **equilibrium** when total spending exceeds current production.

The definition of *equilibrium* in the margin tells us that the economy cannot be in equilibrium when total spending exceeds production, because falling inventories

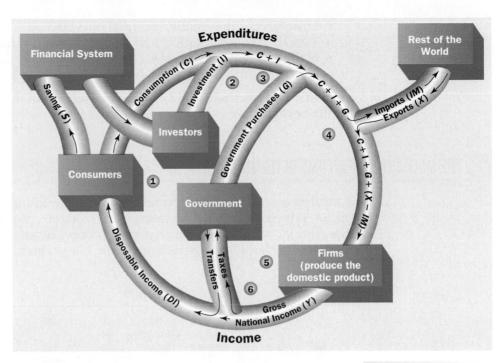

demonstrate to firms that their production and pricing decisions were not quite appropriate.[1] Thus, because we normally use GDP to measure output:

The equilibrium level of GDP on the demand side cannot be one at which total spending exceeds output because firms will notice that they are depleting their inventory stocks. Firms may first decide to increase production sufficiently to meet the higher demand. Later they may decide to raise prices.

Now imagine the other case, in which the flow of spending reaching firms falls short of current production. Unsold output winds up as additional inventories. The inventory pile-up signals firms that either their pricing or output decision was wrong. Once again, they will probably react first by cutting back on production, causing GDP to fall (at point 5 in Figure 8-1). If the imbalance persists, they may also lower prices to stimulate sales. But they certainly will not be happy with things as they are. Thus:

The equilibrium level of GDP on the demand side cannot be one at which total spending is less than output, because firms will not allow inventories to pile up. They may decide to decrease production, or they may decide to cut prices in order to stimulate demand.

We have now determined, by process of elimination, the only level of output that is consistent with people's desires to spend. We have reasoned that GDP will *rise* whenever it is less than total spending, $C + I + G + (X - IM)$, and that GDP will fall whenever it exceeds $C + I + G + (X - IM)$. Equilibrium can occur, then, only when there is just enough spending to absorb the current level of production. Under such circumstances, producers conclude that their price and output decisions are correct and have no incentive to change. We conclude that:

The *equilibrium level of GDP on the demand side* is the level at which total spending equals production. In such a situation, firms find their inventories remaining at desired levels, so they have no incentive to change output or prices.

Thus, the circular flow diagram has helped us to understand the concept of equilibrium GDP and has shown us how the economy is driven toward this equilibrium. It leaves unanswered, however, three important questions:

---

[1] All the models in this book assume, strictly for simplicity, that firms seek constant inventories. Deliberate inventory changes are treated in more advanced courses.

- How large is the equilibrium level of GDP?
- Will the economy suffer from unemployment, inflation, or both?
- Is the equilibrium level of GDP on the demand side also consistent with firms' desires to produce? That is, is it also an equilibrium on the *supply* side?

The first two questions will occupy our attention in this chapter; the third is reserved to the next chapter.

THE MECHANICS OF INCOME DETERMINATION

Our first objective is to determine precisely the equilibrium level of GDP on the demand side. To make the analysis more concrete, we turn to a numerical example. Specifically, we examine the relationship between total spending and GDP in the hypothetical economy we introduced in the last chapter.

TABLE 8-1   The Total Expenditure Schedule

(1) GDP (Y)	(2) Consumption (C)	(3) Investment (I)	(4) Government Purchases (G)	(5) Net Exports $(X - IM)$	(6) Total Expenditure
4,800	3,000	900	1,300	−100	5,100
5,200	3,300	900	1,300	−100	5,400
5,600	3,600	900	1,300	−100	5,700
6,000	3,900	900	1,300	−100	6,000
6,400	4,200	900	1,300	−100	6,300
6,800	4,500	900	1,300	−100	6,600
7,200	4,800	900	1,300	−100	6,900

Columns (1) and (2) of Table 8-1 repeat the consumption function that we first encountered in Table 7-1. They show how consumer spending, C, depends on GDP, which we symbolize by the letter Y. Columns (3) through (5) provide the other three components of total spending, I, G, and $X - IM$, through the simplifying assumptions that each is just a fixed number regardless of the level of GDP. Specifically, we assume that investment spending is $900 billion, government purchases are $1,300 billion, and net exports are −$100 billion—meaning that in this hypothetical economy, as in the United States at present, imports exceed exports.

By adding Columns (2) through (5), we calculate $C + I + G + (X - IM)$, or total expenditure, which appears in Column (6) of Table 8-1. Columns (1) and (6) are highlighted in blue to show how total expenditure depends on income. We call this relationship the **expenditure schedule**.

Figure 8-2 shows the construction of the expenditure schedule graphically. The black line labeled C is the consumption function; it plots on a graph the numbers given in Columns (1) and (2) of Table 8-1.

The blue line, labeled $C + I$, displays our assumption that investment is fixed at $900 billion. It lies a fixed distance (corresponding to $900 billion) above the C line. If investment were not always $900 billion, the two lines would either move closer together or grow farther apart. For example, our analysis of the determinants of investment spending suggested that I might be larger when GDP is higher. Such added investment as GDP rises—which is called **induced investment**—would give the resulting $C + I$ line a steeper slope than the C line. But we ignore that possibility here for simplicity.

The red line, labeled $C + I + G$, adds government purchases. Because they are assumed to be $1,300 billion regardless of the size of GDP, the red line is parallel to the blue line and $1,300 billion higher.

Finally, the gold line labeled $C + I + G + (X - IM)$ adds in net exports. It is parallel to the red line and $100 billion lower, reflecting our assumption that net exports are always −$100 billion. Once again, if imports depended on GDP, as the previous chapter suggested, the $C + I + G$ and $C + I + G + (X - IM)$ lines would

An **expenditure schedule** shows the relationship between national income (GDP) and total spending.

Induced investment is the part of investment spending that rises when GDP rises and falls when GDP falls.

not be parallel. We deal with this more complicated case in Appendix B to this chapter.

We are now ready to determine demand-side equilibrium in our hypothetical economy. Table 8-2 presents the logic of the circular flow argument in tabular form. The first two columns reproduce the expenditure schedule that we have just constructed. The other columns explain the process by which the economy approaches equilibrium. Let us see why a GDP of $6,000 billion must be the equilibrium level.

Consider first any output level below $6,000 billion. For example, at output level $Y = \$5,200$ billion, total expenditure is $5,400 billion, as shown in Column (2), which is $200 billion more than production. With spending greater than output, as noted in Column (3), inventories will fall (see Column (4)). As the table suggests in Column (5), this will signal producers to raise their output. Clearly, then, no output level below $Y = \$6,000$ billion can be an equilibrium, because output is too low.

A similar line of reasoning eliminates any output level above $6,000 billion. Consider, for example, $Y = \$6,800$ billion. The table shows that total spending would be $6,600 billion if output were $6,800 billion, so $200 billion would go unsold. This would raise producers' inventory stocks and signal them that their rate of production was too high.

Just as we concluded from our circular flow diagram, equilibrium will be achieved only when total spending, $C + I + G + (X - IM)$, exactly equals GDP, Y. In symbols, our condition for equilibrium GDP is:

$$Y = C + I + G + (X - IM)$$

Table 8-2 shows that this equation holds only at a GDP of $6,000 billion, which must be the equilibrium level of GDP.

Figure 8-3 depicts the same conclusion graphically, by adding a 45° line to Figure 8-2. Why a 45° line? Recall from the appendix to Chapter 1 that a 45° line marks all points on a graph at which the value of the variable measured on the horizontal axis (in this case,

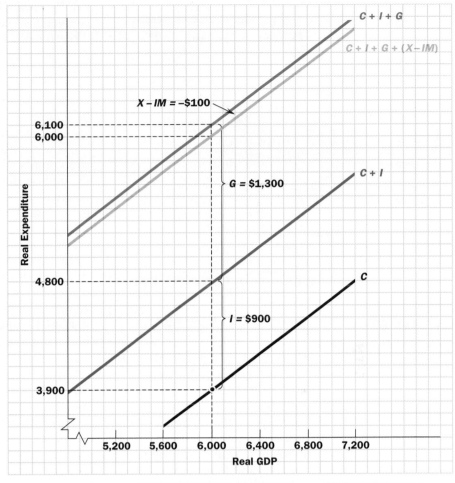

NOTE: Figures are in billions of dollars per year.

■ FIGURE 8-2

Construction of the Expenditure Schedule

■ TABLE 8-2   The Determination of Equilibrium Output

(1) Output (Y)	(2) Total Spending [C + I + G + (X − IM)]	(3) Balance of Spending and Output	(4) Inventory Status	(5) Producer Response
4,800	5,100	Spending exceeds output	Falling	Produce more
5,200	5,400	Spending exceeds output	Falling	Produce more
5,600	5,700	Spending exceeds output	Falling	Produce more
6,000	**6,000**	**Spending = output**	**Constant**	**No change**
6,400	6,300	Output exceeds spending	Rising	Produce less
6,800	6,600	Output exceeds spending	Rising	Produce less
7,200	6,900	Output exceeds spending	Rising	Produce less

NOTE: Amounts are in billions of dollars.

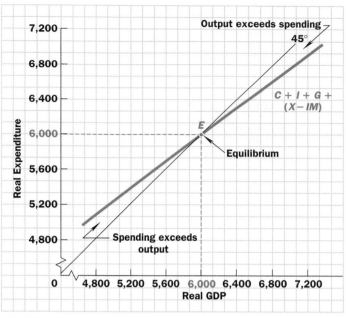

FIGURE 8-3

Income-Expenditure Diagram

An **income-expenditure diagram,** or **45° line diagram,** plots total real expenditure (on the vertical axis) against real income (on the horizontal axis). The 45° line marks off points where income and expenditure are equal.

GDP) equals the value of the variable measured on the vertical axis (in this case, total expenditure).[2] Thus the 45° line in Figure 8-3 shows all the points at which output and spending are equal—that is, where $Y = C + I + G + (X - IM)$. *The 45° line therefore displays all the points at which the economy can possibly be in demand-side equilibrium,* for firms will be content with current output levels only if total spending equals production.

Now we must compare these *potential* equilibrium points with the *actual* combinations of spending and output that are consistent with the current behavior of consumers and investors. That behavior is described by the $C + I + G + (X - IM)$ line in Figure 8-3, which shows how total expenditure varies as income changes. *The economy will always be on the expenditure line* because only points on the $C + I + G + (X - IM)$ line describe the spending plans of consumers and investors. Similarly, *if* the economy is in equilibrium, it *must* be on the 45° line. As Figure 8-3 shows, these two requirements imply that the only viable equilibrium is at point *E,* where the $C + I + G + (X - IM)$ line intersects the 45° line. Only this point is consistent with both equilibrium and people's actual desires to consume and invest.

Notice that to the left of the equilibrium point, *E,* the expenditure line lies *above* the 45° line. This means that total spending exceeds total output, as we have already noted. Hence, inventories will be falling and firms will conclude that they should increase production. Thus, production will rise toward the equilibrium point, *E.* The opposite is true to the right of point *E.* Here spending falls short of output, inventories rise, and firms will cut back production—thereby moving closer to *E.*

In other words, whenever production is *above* the equilibrium level, market forces will drive output *down.* And whenever production is *below* equilibrium, market forces will drive output *up.* In either case, deviations from demand-side equilibrium will gradually be eliminated.

Diagrams such as Figure 8-3 will recur so frequently in this and the next several chapters that it will be convenient to have a name for them. We call them **income-expenditure diagrams,** because they show how expenditures vary with income, or simply **45° line diagrams.**

THE AGGREGATE DEMAND CURVE

Chapter 4 introduced aggregate demand and aggregate supply curves relating aggregate quantities demanded and supplied to the price level. The expenditure schedule graphed in Figure 8-3 is certainly *not* the aggregate demand curve, for we have yet to bring the price level into our discussion. It is now time to remedy this omission and derive the aggregate demand curve.

Fortunately, we require no further mechanical apparatus. To bring the price level into the analysis, just recall something we learned in the last chapter: *At any given level of real income, higher prices lead to lower real consumer spending.* The reason, you will recall, is that consumers own many assets whose values are fixed in money terms, and which therefore lose purchasing power when prices rise.[3] With lower real wealth, consumers spend less. Therefore, total spending in the economy falls *even with no change in real income.*

---

[2] If you need review, see the appendix to Chapter 1, especially pages 16–17.

[3] The money in your bank account is a prime example. If prices rise, it will buy less.

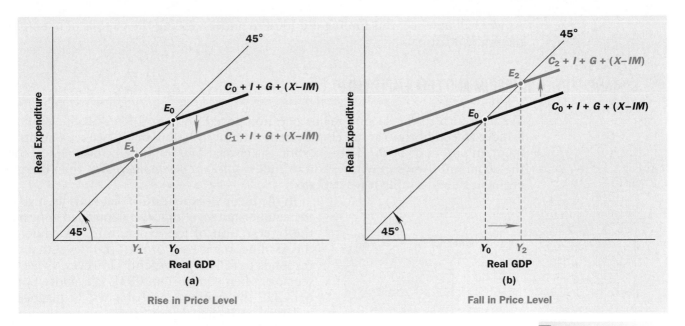

■ **FIGURE 8-4**
The Effect of the Price Level on Equilibrium Aggregate Quantity Demanded

In terms of the 45° line diagram, a rise in the price level will pull down the consumption function depicted in Figure 8-2 and, hence, will pull down the total expenditure schedule as well. Conversely, a fall in the price level will raise both the C and $C + I + G + (X - IM)$ schedules in the diagram. The two panels of Figure 8-4 illustrate both of these shifts.

How, then, do changes in the price level affect the equilibrium level of real GDP on the demand side? Common sense says that, with lower spending, equilibrium GDP should fall, and Figure 8-4 shows that this conclusion is correct. Panel (a) shows that a rise in the price level, by shifting the expenditure schedule downward, leads to a reduction in the equilibrium quantity of real GDP demanded from Y_0 to Y_1. Panel (b) shows that a fall in the price level, by shifting the expenditure schedule upward, leads to a rise in the equilibrium quantity of real GDP demanded from Y_0 to Y_2. In summary:

A rise in the price level leads to a lower equilibrium level of real aggregate quantity demanded. This relationship between the price level and real GDP (depicted in Figure 8-5) is precisely what we called the aggregate demand curve in earlier chapters. It comes directly from the 45° line diagrams in Figure 8-4. Thus, points E_0, E_1, and E_2 in Figure 8-5 correspond precisely to the points bearing the same labels in Figure 8-4.

■ **FIGURE 8-5**
The Aggregate Demand Curve

The effect of higher prices on consumer wealth is just one of several reasons why the aggregate demand curve slopes downward. A second reason comes from international trade. In Chapter 7's discussion of the determinants of net exports (see pages 132–133), we pointed out that higher U.S. prices will depress exports (X) and stimulate imports (IM), provided that foreign prices are held constant. That means that, other things equal, a higher U.S. price level will reduce the $(X - IM)$ component of total expenditure, thereby shifting the $C + I + G + (X - IM)$ line downward and lowering real GDP, as depicted in Figure 8-4(a).

Later in the book, after we have studied interest rates and exchange rates, we will encounter still more reasons for a downward-sloping aggregate demand curve. All of them imply that:

An income-expenditure diagram like Figure 8-3 can be drawn only for a *specific* price level. At different price levels, the $C + I + G + (X - IM)$ schedule will be different and, hence, the equilibrium quantity of GDP demanded will also differ.

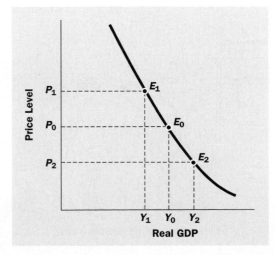

As we shall now see, this finding is critical to understanding the genesis of unemployment and inflation.

DEMAND-SIDE EQUILIBRIUM AND FULL EMPLOYMENT

We now turn to the second major question posed on page 146: Will the economy achieve an equilibrium at full employment without inflation, or will we see unemployment, inflation, or both? This question is a crucial one for stabilization policy, for if the economy always gravitates toward full employment *automatically*, then the government should simply leave it alone.

In the income-expenditure diagrams used so far, the equilibrium level of GDP demanded appears as the intersection of the expenditure schedule and the 45° line, regardless of the GDP level that corresponds to full employment. However, as we will see now, when equilibrium GDP falls above potential GDP, the economy probably will be plagued by inflation, and when equilibrium falls below potential GDP, unemployment and recession will result.

This remarkable fact was one of the principal messages of Keynes's *General Theory of Employment, Interest, and Money*. Writing during the Great Depression, it was natural for Keynes to focus on the case in which equilibrium falls short of full employment, leaving some resources unemployed. Figure 8-6 illustrates this possibility. A vertical line has been drawn at the level of *potential GDP*, which is here assumed to be $7,000 billion. We see that the $C + I + G + (X - IM)$ curve cuts the 45° line at point E, which corresponds to a GDP ($Y = $6,000 billion) below potential GDP. In this case, the expenditure curve is too low to lead to full employment. Such a situation has characterized the U.S. economy since the 2001 recession.

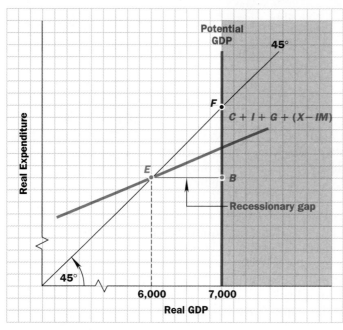

NOTE: Figures are in billions of dollars per year.

■ FIGURE 8-6
A Recessionary Gap

The **recessionary gap** is the amount by which the equilibrium level of real GDP falls short of potential GDP.

An equilibrium below potential GDP might arise because consumers or investors are unwilling to spend at normal rates, because government spending is low, because foreign demand is weak, or because the price level is "too high." Any of these events would depress the $C + I + G + (X - IM)$ curve. Unemployment must then occur because not enough output is demanded to keep the entire labor force at work.

The distance between the *equilibrium* level of output demanded and the *full-employment* level of output (that is, potential GDP) is called the **recessionary gap;** it is shown by the horizontal distance from E to B in Figure 8-6. Although the figure is entirely hypothetical, real-world gaps of precisely this sort were shown shaded in blue in Figure 5-2 (page 85). They have been a pervasive feature of U.S. economic history.

Figure 8-6 clearly shows that full employment can be reached only by raising the total spending schedule to eliminate the recessionary gap. Specifically, the $C + I + G + (X - IM)$ schedule must move upward until it cuts the 45° line at point F. Can this happen without government intervention? We know that a sufficiently large drop in the price level can do the job. But is that a realistic prospect? We will return to this question in the next chapter, after we bring the supply side into the picture, for we cannot discuss price determination without bringing in *both*

"Go home, I tell you! The recession is over!"

supply *and* demand. First, however, we will consider the other case—when equilibrium GDP exceeds full employment.

Figure 8-7 illustrates this possibility, which many people believe characterized the U.S. economy in the boom years of the late 1990s. Now the expenditure schedule intersects the 45° line at point E, where GDP is $8,000 billion. But this exceeds the full-employment level, Y = $7,000 billion. A case such as this can arise when consumer or investment spending is unusually buoyant, when foreign demand is particularly strong, when the government spends too much, or when a "low" price level pushes the $C + I + G + (X - IM)$ curve upward.

To reach an equilibrium at full employment, the price level would have to rise enough to drive the expenditure schedule *down* until it passed through point *F*. The horizontal distance *BE*—which indicates the amount by which the quantity of GDP demanded exceeds potential GDP—is called the **inflationary gap.** If there is an inflationary gap, a higher price level or some other means of reducing total expenditure is necessary to reach an equilibrium at full employment. Rising prices will eventually pull the $C + I + G + (X - IM)$ line down until it passes through point *F*. Real-world inflationary gaps were shown shaded in orange in Figure 5-2 on page 85. In sum:

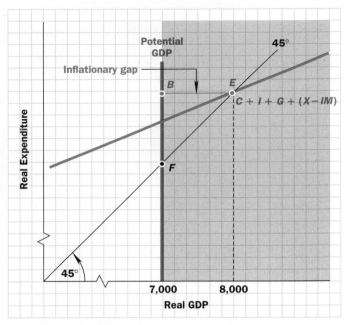

NOTE: Figures are in billions of dollars per year.

■ FIGURE 8-7
An Inflationary Gap

The **inflationary gap** is the amount by which equilibrium real GDP exceeds the full-employment level of GDP.

> **Only if the price level and spending plans are "just right" will the expenditure curve intersect the 45° line precisely at full employment, so that neither a recessionary gap nor an inflationary gap occurs.**

Are there reasons to expect this outcome? Does the economy have a self-correcting mechanism that automatically eliminates recessionary or inflationary gaps and propels it toward full employment? And why do inflation and unemployment sometimes rise or fall together?

We are not ready to answer these questions yet because we have not yet brought *aggregate supply* into the picture. However, it is not too early to get an idea about why things can go wrong during a recession.

■ THE COORDINATION OF SAVING AND INVESTMENT

To do so, it is useful to pose the following question: Must the full-employment level of GDP be a demand-side equilibrium? Decades ago, economists thought the answer was yes. Since Keynes, most economists believe the answer is "not necessarily."

To help us see why, Figure 8-8 offers a simplified circular flow diagram that ignores exports, imports, and the government. In this version, income can "leak out" of the circular flow only at point 1, where consumers save some of their income. Similarly, lost spending can be replaced only at point 2, where investment enters the circular flow.

What happens if firms produce exactly the full-employment level of GDP at point 3 in the diagram? Will this income level be maintained as we move around the circle, or will it shrink or grow? The answer is that full-employment income will be maintained *only* if the spending by investors at point 2 exactly balances the saving done by consumers at point 1. In other words:

> **The economy will reach an equilibrium at full employment on the demand side only if the amount that consumers wish to save out of their full-employment incomes happens to equal the amount that investors want to invest. If these two magnitudes are unequal, full employment will not be an equilibrium.**

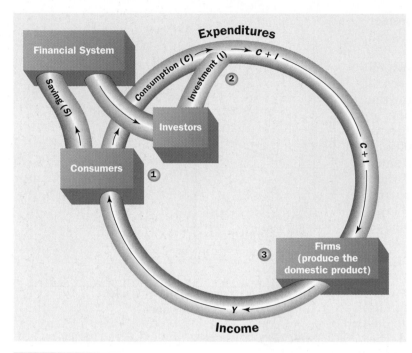

FIGURE 8-8
A Simplified Circular Flow

A **coordination failure** occurs when party A would like to change his behavior if party B would change hers, and vice versa, and yet the two changes do not take place because the decisions of A and B are not coordinated.

Specifically, the circular flow diagram shows that, if saving exceeds investment at full employment, the total demand received by firms at point 3 will fall short of total output because the added investment spending will not be enough to replace the leakage to saving. With demand inadequate to support production at full employment, GDP must fall below potential. There will be a recessionary gap. Conversely, if investment exceeds saving when the economy is at full employment, then total demand will exceed potential GDP and production will rise above the full-employment level. There will be an inflationary gap.

Now, this discussion does nothing but restate what we already know in different words.[4] But these words provide the key to understanding why the economy sometimes finds itself stuck above or below full employment, for *the people who invest are not the same as the people who save.* In a modern capitalist economy, investing is done by one group of individuals (primarily corporate executives and homebuyers), whereas saving is done by another group.[5] It is easy to imagine that their plans may not be well coordinated. If they are not, we have just seen how either unemployment or inflation can occur.

Neither of these problems would arise if the acts of saving and investing were perfectly coordinated. While perfection is never attainable, the analysis in the accompanying box, "Unemployment and Inflation as Coordination Failures," raises a tantalizing possibility. If both high unemployment and high inflation arise from **coordination failures**, might the government be able to do something about this problem? Keynes suggested that it could, and we will examine this idea in detail in later chapters. But the football analogy described in the box reminds us that a central authority may not find it easy to solve the coordination problem.

CHANGES ON THE DEMAND SIDE: MULTIPLIER ANALYSIS

The **multiplier** is the ratio of the change in equilibrium GDP (Y) divided by the original change in spending that causes the change in GDP.

We have just learned how demand-side equilibrium depends on the consumption function and the amounts spent on investment, government purchases, and net exports. But none of these is a constant of nature; they all change from time to time. How does equilibrium GDP change when the consumption function shifts or when I, G, or (X − IM) changes? As we will see now, the answer is simple: *by more!* A remarkable result called the **multiplier** says that a change in spending will bring about an *even larger* change in equilibrium GDP on the demand side. Let us see why.

The Magic of the Multiplier

Because it is subject to abrupt swings, investment spending often causes business fluctuations in the United States and elsewhere. So let us ask what would happen

---

[4] In symbols, our equilibrium condition without government or foreign trade is $Y = C + I$. If we note that Y is also the sum of consumption plus saving, $Y = C + S$, then it follows that $C + S = C + I$, or $S = I$, is a restatement of the equilibrium condition.

[5] In a modern economy, not only do households save, but businesses also save in the form of retained earnings. Nonetheless, households are the ultimate source of the saving needed to finance investment.

Unemployment and Inflation as Coordination Failures

The idea that unemployment stems from a *lack of coordination* between the decisions of savers and investors may seem abstract. But we encounter coordination failures in the real world quite frequently. The following familiar example may bring the idea down to earth.

Picture a crowd watching a football game. Now something exciting happens and the fans rise from their seats. People in the front rows begin standing first, and those seated behind them are forced to stand if they want to see the game. Soon everyone in the stadium is on their feet.

But with everyone standing, no one can see any better than when everyone was sitting. And the fans are enduring the further discomfort of being on their feet. (Never mind that stadium seats are uncomfortable!) Everyone in the stadium would be better off if everyone sat down. Sometimes this happens. But the crowd rises to its feet again on every exciting play. There is simply no way to coordinate the individual decisions of tens of thousands of football fans.

Unemployment poses a similar coordination problem. During a deep recession, workers are unemployed and businesses cannot sell their wares. Figuratively speaking, everyone is "standing" and unhappy about it. If only the firms could agree to hire more workers, those newly employed people could afford to buy more of the goods and services the firms want to produce. But, as at the football stadium, there is no central authority to coordinate these millions of decisions.

SOURCE: © Jonathan Nourok/PhotoEdit

The coordination failure idea also helps to explain why it is so difficult to stop inflation. Virtually everyone prefers stable prices to rising prices. But now think of yourself as the seller of a product. If all other participants in the economy would hold their prices steady, you would happily hold yours steady, too. But, if you believe that others will continue to raise their prices at a rate of, say, 5 percent per year, you may find it dangerous not to increase your prices apace. Hence, society may get stuck with 5 percent inflation even though everyone agrees that zero inflation is better.

---

if firms suddenly decided to spend more on investment goods. As we shall see, such a decision would have a *multiplied* effect on GDP; that is, each $1 of additional investment spending would add *more* than $1 to GDP.

Refer first to Table 8-3, which looks very much like Table 8-1. The only difference is that we assume here that firms now want to invest $200 billion more than previously—for a total of $1,100 billion. As indicated by the blue numbers, only income level $Y = \$6,800$ billion is an equilibrium on the demand side of the economy now, because only at this level is total spending, $C + I + G + (X - IM)$, equal to production (Y).

The *multiplier* principle says that GDP will rise by *more than* the $200 billion increase in investment. Specifically, the multiplier is defined as the ratio of the change in equilibrium GDP (Y) to the original change in spending that caused GDP to change. In shorthand, when we deal with the multiplier for investment (I), the formula is:

$$\text{Multiplier} = \frac{\text{Change in } Y}{\text{Change in } I}$$

Let us verify that the multiplier is, indeed, greater than 1. Table 8-3 shows how the new expenditure schedule is constructed by adding up C, I, G, and ($X - IM$) at each

TABLE 8-3   Total Expenditure after a $200 Billion Increase in Investment Spending

(1) Income (Y)	(2) Consumption (C)	(3) Investment (I)	(4) Government Purchases (G)	(5) Net Exports ($X - IM$)	(6) Total Expenditure
4,800	3,000	1,100	1,300	−100	5,300
5,200	3,300	1,100	1,300	−100	5,600
5,600	3,600	1,100	1,300	−100	5,900
6,000	3,900	1,100	1,300	−100	6,200
6,400	4,200	1,100	1,300	−100	6,500
6,800	**4,500**	**1,100**	**1,300**	**−100**	**6,800**
7,200	4,800	1,100	1,300	−100	7,100

NOTE: Figures are in billions of dollars per year.

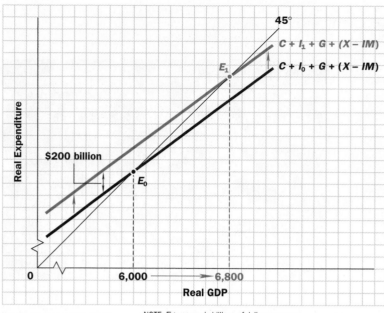

NOTE: Figures are in billions of dollars per year.

■ FIGURE 8-9
Illustration of the Multiplier

level of Y, just as we did earlier—only now $I = \$1,100$ billion rather than $\$900$ billion. If you compare the last columns of Tables 8-1 (page 146) and 8-3, you will see that the new expenditure schedule lies uniformly above the old one by $\$200$ billion.

Figure 8-9 depicts this change graphically. The curve marked $C + I_0 + G + (X - IM)$ is derived from the last column of Table 8-1, while the higher curve marked $C + I_1 + G + (X - IM)$ is derived from the last column of Table 8-3. The two expenditure lines are parallel and $\$200$ billion apart.

So far things look just as you might expect. But one more step will bring the multiplier rabbit out of the hat. Let us see what the upward shift of the expenditure line does to equilibrium income. In Figure 8-9, equilibrium moves outward from point E_0 to point E_1, or from $\$6,000$ billion to $\$6,800$ billion. The difference is an increase of $\$800$ billion in GDP. All this from a $\$200$ billion stimulus to investment? That is the magic of the multiplier.

Because the change in I is $\$200$ billion and the change in equilibrium Y is $\$800$ billion, by applying our definition, the multiplier is:

$$\text{Multiplier} = \frac{\text{Change in } Y}{\text{Change in } I} = \frac{\$800}{200} = 4$$

This tells us that, in our example, each additional $\$1$ of investment demand will add $\$4$ to equilibrium GDP!

This result does, indeed, seem mysterious. Can something be created from nothing? Let's first check that the graph has not deceived us. The first and last columns of Table 8-3 (page 153) show in numbers what Figure 8-9 shows graphically. Notice that equilibrium now comes at $Y = \$6,800$ billion, because only at that point is total expenditure equal to production (Y). This equilibrium level of GDP is $\$800$ billion higher than the $\$6,000$ billion level found when investment was only $\$900$ billion. Thus, a $\$200$ billion rise in investment does indeed lead to an $\$800$ billion rise in equilibrium GDP; the multiplier really *is* 4.

■ Demystifying the Multiplier: How It Works

The multiplier result seems strange at first, but it loses its mystery once we recall the circular flow of income and expenditure and the simple fact that one person's spending is another person's income. To illustrate the logic of the multiplier and see why it is exactly 4 in our example, think about what happens when businesses decide to spend $\$1$ million on investment goods.

Suppose that Microhard—a major corporation in our hypothetical country—decides to spend $\$1$ million on a new office building. Its $\$1$ million expenditure goes to construction workers and owners of construction companies as wages and profits. That is, the $\$1$ million becomes their *income.*

But the construction firm's owners and workers will not keep all of their $\$1$ million in the bank; instead, they will spend most of it. If they are "typical" consumers, their spending will be $\$1$ million times the marginal propensity to consume (MPC). In our example, the MPC is 0.75, so assume they spend $\$750,000$ and save the rest. *This*

$750,000 expenditure is a net addition to the nation's demand for goods and services, just as Microhard's original $1 million expenditure was. So, at this stage, the $1 million investment has already pushed GDP up by some $1.75 million. But the process is by no means over.

Shopkeepers receive the $750,000 spent by construction workers, and they in turn also spend 75 percent of their new income. This activity accounts for $562,500 (75 percent of $750,000) in additional consumer spending in the "third round." Next follows a fourth round in which the recipients of the $562,500 spend 75 percent of this amount, or $421,875, and so on. At each stage in the spending chain, people spend 75 percent of the additional income they receive, and the process continues—with consumption growing in every round.

Where does it all end? Does it all end? The answer is that, yes, it does eventually end—with GDP being a total of $4 million higher than it was before Microhard built the original $1 million office building. The multiplier is, indeed, 4.

Table 8-4 displays the basis for this conclusion. In the table, "Round 1" represents Microhard's initial investment, which creates $1 million in income for construction workers. "Round 2" represents the construction workers' spending, which creates $750,000 in income for shopkeepers. The rest of the table proceeds accordingly; each entry in Column (2) is 75 percent of the previous entry. Column (3) tabulates the running sum of Column (2).

We see that after 10 rounds of spending, the initial $1 million investment has mushroomed to $3.77 million—and the sum is still growing. After 20 rounds, the total increase in GDP is over $3.98 million—near its eventual value of $4 million. Although it takes quite a few rounds of spending before the multiplier chain nears 4, we see from the table that it hits 3 rather quickly. If each income recipient in the chain waits, say, two months before spending his new income, the multiplier will reach 3 in only about ten months.

Figure 8-10 provides a graphical presentation of the numbers in the last column of Table 8-4. Notice how the multiplier builds up rapidly at first and then tapers off to approach its ultimate value (4 in this example) gradually.

Although this is only a hypothetical example, the same thing occurs every day in the real world. For instance, a burst of new housing creates a multiplier effect on everything from appliances and furniture to carpeting and insulation. Similarly, when a large company such as Ford makes an investment in a developing country, the multiplier effect boosts business activity in many sectors.

■ Algebraic Statement of the Multiplier

Figure 8-10 and Table 8-4 probably make a persuasive case that the multiplier eventually reaches 4. But for the remaining skeptics, we offer a simple algebraic proof.[6] Most of you learned about something

■ TABLE 8-4	The Multiplier Spending Chain	
(1) Round Number	(2) Spending in This Round	(3) Cumulative Total
1	$1,000,000	$1,000,000
2	750,000	1,750,000
3	562,500	2,312,500
4	421,875	2,734,375
5	316,406	3,050,781
6	237,305	3,288,086
7	177,979	3,466,065
8	133,484	3,599,549
9	100,113	3,699,662
10	75,085	3,774,747
⋮	⋮	⋮
20	4,228	3,987,317
⋮	⋮	⋮
"Infinity"	0	4,000,000

■ FIGURE 8-10
How the Multiplier Builds

NOTE: Amounts are in millions of dollars.

---

[6] Students who blanch at the sight of algebra should not be put off. Anyone who can balance a checkbook (even many who cannot!) will be able to follow the argument.

called an *infinite geometric progression* in high school. This term refers to an infinite series of numbers, each one of which is a fixed fraction of the previous one. The fraction is called the *common ratio*. A geometric progression beginning with 1 and having a common ratio of 0.75 would look like this:

$$1 + 0.75 + (0.75)^2 + (0.75)^3 + \ldots$$

More generally, a geometric progression beginning with 1 and having a common ratio R would be:

$$1 + R + R^2 + R^3 + \ldots$$

A simple formula enables us to sum such a progression as long as R is less than 1.[7] The formula is:[8]

$$\textbf{Sum of infinite geometric progression} = \frac{1}{1 - R}$$

Now we can recognize that the multiplier chain in Table 8-4 is just an infinite geometric progression with 0.75 as its common ratio. That is, each \$1 that Microhard spends leads to a $(0.75) \times \$1$ expenditure by construction workers, which in turn leads to a $(0.75) \times (0.75 \times \$1) = (0.75)^2 \times \$1$ expenditure by the shopkeepers, and so on. Thus, for each initial dollar of investment spending, the progression is:

$$1 + 0.75 + (0.75)^2 + (0.75)^3 + (0.75)^4 + \ldots$$

Applying the formula for the sum of such a series, we find that:

$$\text{Multiplier} = \frac{1}{1 - 0.75} = \frac{1}{0.25} = 4$$

Notice how this result can be generalized. If we did not have a specific number for the marginal propensity to consume, but simply called it MPC, the geometric progression in Table 8-4 would have been:

$$1 + \text{MPC} + (\text{MPC})^2 + (\text{MPC})^3 + \ldots$$

This progression uses the MPC as its common ratio. Applying the same formula for summing a geometric progression to this more general case gives us the following general result:

$$\textbf{Oversimplified Multiplier Formula}$$

$$\text{Multiplier} = \frac{1}{1 - \text{MPC}}$$

We call this formula "oversimplified" because it ignores many factors that are important in the real world. You can begin to appreciate just how unrealistic the oversimplified formula is by considering some real numbers for the U.S. economy. The MPC is about 0.9. From our oversimplified formula, then, it would seem that the multiplier should be:

---

[7] If R exceeds 1, no one can possibly sum it—not even with the aid of a modern computer—because the sum is not a finite number.

[8] The proof of the formula is simple. Let the symbol S stand for the (unknown) sum of the series:

$$S = 1 + R + R^2 + R^3 + \ldots$$

Then, multiplying by R,

$$RS = R + R^2 + R^3 + R^4 + \ldots$$

By subtracting RS from S, we obtain:

$$S - RS = 1 \text{ or } S = \frac{1}{1 - R}$$

$$\text{Multiplier} = \frac{1}{1 - 0.9} = \frac{1}{0.1} = 10$$

In fact, the actual multiplier for the U.S. economy is less than 2. That is quite a discrepancy!

This disagreement does not mean that anything we have said about the multiplier so far is incorrect. Our story is simply incomplete. As we progress through this and subsequent chapters, you will learn why the multiplier in the U.S. is less than 2 even though the country's MPC is close to 0.9. One such reason relates to *international trade*—in particular, the fact that a country's imports depend on its GDP. We deal with this complication in Appendix B to this chapter. A second factor is *inflation*, a complication we will address in the next chapter. A third factor is *income taxation*, a point we will elaborate in Chapter 10. The last important reason arises from the *financial system* and, after we discuss money and banking in Chapters 11 and 12, we will explain how the financial system influences the multiplier in Chapter 13. As you will see, each of these factors *reduces* the size of the multiplier. So:

Although the multiplier is larger than 1 in the real world, it cannot be calculated with any degree of accuracy from the oversimplified formula. The actual multiplier is much lower than the formula suggests.

An **induced increase in consumption** is an increase in consumer spending that stems from an increase in consumer incomes. It is represented on a graph as a movement along a fixed consumption function.

THE MULTIPLIER IS A GENERAL CONCEPT

We have used business investment to illustrate the workings of the multiplier, but it should be clear from the logic that *any* increase in spending can kick off a multiplier chain. To see how the multiplier works when the process is initiated by an upsurge in consumer spending, we must distinguish between two types of change in consumer spending. To do so, it is helpful to bring back Figure 7-6, which we repeat here as Figure 8-11.

When C rises because income rises—that is, when consumers move outward *along a fixed consumption function*—we call the increase in C an **induced increase in consumption.** (See the red arrows in the figure.) When C rises because the entire consumption function *shifts upward* (such as from C_0 to C_1 in the figure), we call it an **autonomous increase in consumption.** The name indicates that consumption changes *independently* of income. Chapter 7's discussion of the consumption function pointed out that a number of events, such as a change in the value of the stock market, can initiate such a shift.

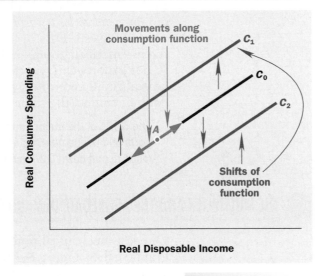

FIGURE 8-11
Shifts of the Consumption Function

If consumer spending were to rise autonomously by $200 billion, we would revise our table of aggregate demand to look like Table 8-5. Comparing this new table to Table 8-3, we note that each entry in Column (2) is $200 billion *higher* than the corresponding entry in Table 8-3 (because consumption is higher), and each entry in Column (3) is $200 billion *lower* (because in this case investment is only $900 billion).

Column (6), the expenditure schedule, is identical in both tables, so the equilibrium level of income is clearly $Y = \$6,800$ billion once again. The initial rise of $200 billion in consumer spending leads to an eventual rise of $800 billion in GDP, just as it did in the case of higher investment spending. In fact, Figure 8-9 (page 154) applies directly to this case once we note that the upward shift is now caused by an autonomous change in C rather than in I. The multiplier for autonomous changes in consumer spending, then, is also 4 (= $800/$200).

An **autonomous increase in consumption** is an increase in consumer spending without any increase in consumer incomes. It is represented on a graph as a shift of the entire consumption function.

TABLE 8-5   Total Expenditure after Consumers Decide to Spend $200 Billion More

(1) Income (Y)	(2) Consumption (C)	(3) Investment (I)	(4) Government Purchases (G)	(5) Net Exports (X − IM)	(6) Total Expenditure
4,800	3,200	900	1,300	−100	5,300
5,200	3,500	900	1,300	−100	5,600
5,600	3,800	900	1,300	−100	5,900
6,000	4,100	900	1,300	−100	6,200
6,400	4,400	900	1,300	−100	6,500
6,800	**4,700**	**900**	**1,300**	**−100**	**6,800**
7,200	5,000	900	1,300	−100	7,100

NOTE: Figures are in billions of dollars per year.

The reason is straightforward. It does not matter who injects an additional dollar of spending into the economy—business investors or consumers. Whatever the source of the extra dollar, 75 percent of it will be respent if the MPC is 0.75, and the recipients of this second round of spending will, in turn, spend 75 percent of their additional income, and so on. That continued spending constitutes the multiplier process. Thus a $200 billion increase in government purchases (G) or in net exports (X − IM) would have the same multiplier effect as depicted in Figure 8-9. The multipliers are identical because the logic behind them is identical.

The idea that changes in G have multiplier effects on GDP will play a central role in the discussion of government stabilization policy that begins in Chapter 10. So it is worth noting here that:

Changes in the volume of government purchases of goods and services will change the equilibrium level of GDP on the demand side in the same direction, but by a multiplied amount.

This is, more or less, what the Japanese government has been trying to accomplish for years: to give its economy a boost by spending more money on road building and other public works. But to date, this effort has not been very effective.[9] Applying the multiplier to exports and imports also teaches us an important lesson: *Booms and recessions tend to be transmitted across national borders.* Why is that? Suppose a boom abroad raises GDPs in foreign countries. With rising incomes, foreigners will buy more American goods—which means that U.S. exports will increase. But an increase in our exports will, via the multiplier, raise GDP in the United States. By this mechanism, rapid economic growth abroad contributes to rapid economic growth here. And, of course, the same mechanism also operates in reverse. Thus:

The GDPs of the major economies are linked by trade. A boom in one country tends to raise its imports and hence push up exports and GDP in other countries. Similarly, a recession in one country tends to pull down GDP in other countries.

THE MULTIPLIER AND THE AGGREGATE DEMAND CURVE

One last mechanical point about the multiplier: Recall that income-expenditure diagrams such as Figure 8-3 (page 148) can be drawn only for a given price level. Different price levels lead to different total expenditure curves. This means that our oversimplified multiplier formula indicates *the increase in real GDP demanded that would occur if the price level were fixed.* Graphically, this means that it measures the *horizontal shift* of the economy's aggregate demand curve.

Figure 8-12 illustrates this conclusion by supposing that the price level that underlies Figure 8-3 is P = 100. The top panel simply repeats Figure 8-9 (page 154) and shows how an increase in investment spending from $900 to $1,100 billion leads to an increase in GDP from $6,000 to $6,800 billion.

The bottom panel shows two downward-sloping aggregate demand curves. The first, labeled D_0D_0, depicts the situation when investment is $900 billion. Point E_0 on this curve indicates that, at the given price level (P = 100), the equilibrium quantity of GDP demanded is $6,000 billion. It corresponds exactly to point E_0 in the top panel. The second aggregate demand curve, D_1D_1, depicts the situation after invest-

[9] You may be wondering why it didn't work. So are many economists! The inability of Japan to spend its way out of its long slump is a puzzling phenomenon.

ment has risen to $1,100 billion. Point E_1 on this curve indicates that the equilibrium quantity of GDP demanded when $P = 100$ has risen to $6,800 billion, which corresponds exactly to point E_1 in the top panel.

As Figure 8-12 shows, the horizontal distance between the two aggregate demand curves is exactly equal to the increase in real GDP shown in the income-expenditure diagram—in this case, $800 billion. Thus:

An autonomous increase in spending leads to a horizontal shift of the aggregate demand curve by an amount given by the oversimplified multiplier formula.

So everything we have learned about the multiplier applies to *shifts of the economy's aggregate demand curve.* If businesses decide to increase their investment spending, if the consumption function shifts upward, or if the government or foreigners decide to buy more goods, then the aggregate demand curve moves horizontally to the right—as indicated in Figure 8-12. If any of these variables move downward instead, the aggregate demand curve moves horizontally to the left.

Thus, the economy's aggregate demand curve cannot be expected to stand still for long. Autonomous changes in one or another of the four components of total spending will cause it to move around. But to understand the *consequences* of such shifts of aggregate demand, we must bring the *aggregate supply* curve into the picture. That is the task we take up in the next chapter.

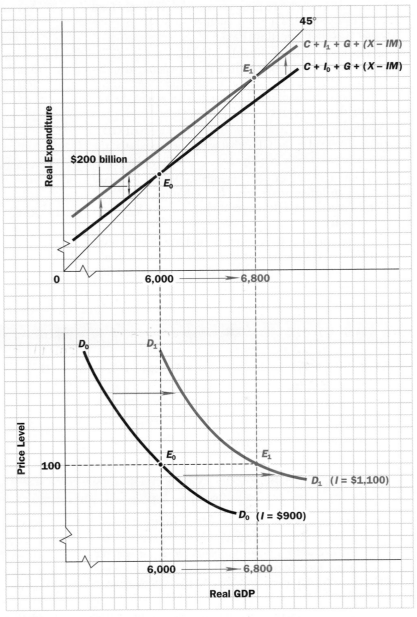

NOTE: Figures are in billions of dollars per year.

■ **FIGURE 8-12**
Two Views of the Multiplier

SUMMARY

1. The **equilibrium level of GDP on the demand side** is the level at which total spending just equals production. Because total spending is the sum of consumption, investment, government purchases, and net exports, the condition for equilibrium is $Y = C + I + G + (X - IM)$.

2. Income levels below **equilibrium** are bound to rise because, when spending exceeds output, firms will see their inventory stocks being depleted and will react by stepping up production.

3. Income levels above equilibrium are bound to fall because, when total spending is insufficient to absorb total output,

inventories will pile up and firms will react by curtailing production.

4. The determination of the equilibrium level of GDP on the demand side can be portrayed on a convenient **income-expenditure diagram** as the point at which the **expenditure schedule**—defined as the sum of $C + I + G + (X - IM)$—crosses the 45° line. The 45° line is significant because it marks off points at which spending and output are equal—that is, at which $Y = C + I + G + (X - IM)$, which is the basic condition for equilibrium.

5. An income-expenditure diagram can be drawn only for a specific price level. Thus, the equilibrium GDP so determined depends on the price level.

6. Because higher prices reduce the purchasing power of consumers' wealth and hence reduce their spending, equilibrium real GDP demanded is lower when prices are higher. This downward-sloping relationship is known as the **aggregate demand curve.**

7. Equilibrium GDP can be above or below **potential GDP,** which is defined as the GDP that would be produced if the labor force were fully employed.

8. If equilibrium GDP exceeds potential GDP, the difference is called an **inflationary gap.** If equilibrium GDP falls short of potential GDP, the resulting difference is called a **recessionary gap.**

9. Such gaps can occur because of the problem of **coordination failure:** The saving that consumers want to do at full-employment income levels may differ from the investing that investors want to do.

10. Any **autonomous increase in expenditure** has a multiplier effect on GDP; that is, it increases GDP by more than the original increase in spending.

11. The **multiplier** effect occurs because one person's additional expenditure constitutes a new source of income for another person, and this additional income leads to still more spending, and so on.

12. The multiplier is the same for an autonomous increase in consumption, investment, government purchases, or net exports.

13. A simple formula for the multiplier says that its numerical value is $1/(1 - MPC)$. This formula is too simple to give accurate results, however.

14. Rapid (or sluggish) economic growth in one country contributes to rapid (or sluggish) growth in other countries because one country's imports are other countries' exports.

KEY TERMS

Equilibrium   144

Expenditure schedule   146

Induced investment   146

$Y = C + I + G + (X - IM)$ 147

Income-expenditure (or 45° line) diagram   148

Aggregate demand curve   148

Full-employment level of GDP
   (or potential GDP)   150

Recessionary gap   150

Inflationary gap   151

Coordination of saving and investment   151

Coordination failure   152

Multiplier   152

Induced increase in consumption   157

Autonomous increase in consumption   157

QUESTIONS FOR REVIEW

1. For almost 20 years now, imports have consistently exceeded exports in the U.S. economy. Many people consider this imbalance to be a major problem. Does this chapter give you any hints about why? (You may want to discuss this issue with your instructor. You will learn more about it in later chapters.)

2. Look back at the income-expenditure diagram in Figure 8-3 (page 148) and explain why some level of real GDP other than $6,000 (say, $5,000 or $7,000) is *not* an equilibrium on the demand side of the economy. Do not give a mechanical answer to this question. Explain the economic mechanism involved.

3. From the following data, construct an expenditure schedule on a piece of graph paper. Then use the income-expenditure (45° line) diagram to determine the equilibrium level of GDP.

Income	Consumption	Investment	Government Purchases	Net Exports
$3,600	$3,220	$240	$120	$40
3,700	3,310	240	120	40
3,800	3,400	240	120	40
3,900	3,490	240	120	40
4,000	3,580	240	120	40

Now suppose investment spending rises to $260, and the price level is fixed. By how much will equilibrium GDP increase? Derive the answer both numerically and graphically.

4. From the following data, construct an expenditure schedule on a piece of graph paper. Then use the income-expenditure (45° line) diagram to determine the equilibrium level of GDP. Compare your answer with your answer to Review Question 3.

Income	Consumption	Investment	Government Purchases	Net Exports
$3,600	$3,280	$180	$120	$40
3,700	3,340	210	120	40
3,800	3,400	240	120	40
3,900	3,460	270	120	40
4,000	3,520	300	120	40

5. Suppose that investment spending is always $250, government purchases are $100, net exports are always $50, and consumer spending depends on the price level in the following way:

Price Level	Consumer Spending
$ 90	$740
95	720
100	700
105	680
110	660

On a piece of graph paper, use these data to construct an aggregate demand curve. Why do you think this example supposes that consumption declines as the price level rises?

6. Does the economy this year seem to have an inflationary gap or a recessionary gap? (If you do not know the answer from reading the newspaper, ask your instructor.)

7. **(More difficult)**[10] Consider an economy in which the consumption function takes the following simple algebraic form:

$$C = 300 + 0.75DI$$

and in which investment (I) is always $900 and net exports are always −$100. Government purchases are fixed at $1,300 and taxes are fixed at $1,200. Find the equilibrium level of GDP, and then compare your answer to Table 8-1 and Figure 8-2. (*Hint:* Remember that disposable income is GDP minus taxes: $DI = Y - T = Y - 1,200$.)

8. **(More difficult)** Keep everything the same as in Review Question 7 *except* change investment to $I = \$1,100$. Use the equilibrium condition $Y = C + I + G + (X - IM)$ to find the equilibrium level of GDP on the demand side. (In working out the answer, assume the price level is fixed.) Compare your answer to Table 8-3 and Figure 8-9. Now compare your answer to the answer to Review Question 7. What do you learn about the multiplier?

9. **(More difficult)** An economy has the following consumption function:

$$C = 200 + 0.8DI$$

The government budget is balanced, with government purchases and taxes both fixed at $1,000. Net exports are $100. Investment is $600. Find equilibrium GDP.

What is the multiplier for this economy? If G rises by $100, what happens to Y? What happens to Y if both G and T rise by $100 at the same time?

10. Try to remember where you last spent a dollar. Explain how this dollar will lead to a multiplier chain of increased income and spending. (Who received the dollar? What will he or she do with it?)

11. Use both numerical and graphical methods to find the multiplier effect of the following shift in the consumption function in an economy in which investment is always $220, government purchases are always $100, and net exports are always −$40. (*Hint:* What is the marginal propensity to consume?)

Income	Consumption before Shift	Consumption after Shift
$1,080	$ 880	$ 920
1,140	920	960
1,200	960	1,000
1,260	1,000	1,040
1,320	1,040	1,080
1,320	1,080	1,120
1,380	1,120	1,160
1,440	1,120	1,160
1,500	1,160	1,200

[10] The answer to this question is provided in Appendix A to this chapter.

APPENDIX A   The Simple Algebra of Income Determination and the Multiplier

The model of demand-side equilibrium that the chapter presented graphically and in tabular form can also be handled with some simple algebra. Written as an equation, the consumption function in our example is

$$C = 300 + 0.75DI$$

$$= 300 + 0.75(Y - T)$$

because, by definition, $DI = Y - T$. This is simply the equation of a straight line with a slope of 0.75 and an intercept of $300 - 0.75T$. Because $T = 1,200$ in our example, the intercept is −600 and the equation can be written more simply as follows:

$$C = -600 + 0.75Y$$

Investment in the example was assumed to be 900, regardless of the level of income, government purchases were 1,300, and net exports were −100. So the sum C 1 I 1 G 1 (X 2 IM) is

$$C + I + G + (X - IM) = -600 + 0.75Y + 900 + 1,300 - 100$$

$$= 1,500 + 0.75Y$$

This equation describes the expenditure curve in Figure 8-3. Because the equilibrium quantity of GDP demanded is defined by

$$Y = C + I + G + (X - IM)$$

we can solve for the equilibrium value of Y by substituting 1,500 + 0.75Y for $C + I + G + (X - IM)$ to get

$$Y = 1,500 + 0.75Y$$

To solve this equation for Y, first subtract $0.75Y$ from both sides to get

$$0.25Y = 1,500$$

Then divide both sides by 0.25 to obtain the answer:

$$Y = 6,000$$

This, of course, is precisely the solution we found by graphical and tabular methods in the chapter.

We can easily generalize this algebraic approach to deal with any set of numbers in our equations. Suppose that the consumption function is as follows:

$$C = a + bDI = a + b(Y - T)$$

(In the example, $a = 300$, $T = 1,200$, and $b = 0.75$.) Then the equilibrium condition that $Y = C + I + G + (X - IM)$ implies that

$$Y = a + bDI + I + G + (X - IM)$$

$$= a - bT + bY + I + G + (X - IM)$$

Subtracting bY from both sides leads to

$$(1 - b)Y = a - bT + I + G + (X - IM)$$

and dividing through by $1 - b$ gives:

$$Y = \frac{a - bT + I + G + (X - IM)}{1 - b}$$

This formula is valid for any numerical values of a, b, T, G, I, and $(X - IM)$ (so long as b is between zero and 1).

From this formula, it is easy to derive the oversimplified multiplier formula algebraically and to show that it applies equally well to a change in investment, autonomous consumer spending, government purchases, or net exports. To do so, suppose that *any* of the symbols in the numerator of the multiplier formula increases by one unit. Then GDP would rise from the previous formula to:

$$Y = \frac{a - bT + I + G + (X - IM) + 1}{1 - b}$$

By comparing this expression with the previous expression for Y, we see that a one-unit change in any component of spending changes equilibrium GDP by

$$\text{Change in } Y = \frac{a - bT + I + G + (X - IM) + 1}{1 - b}$$

$$- \frac{a - bT + I + G + (X - IM)}{1 - b}$$

or

$$\text{Change in } Y = \frac{1}{1 - b}$$

Recalling that b is the marginal propensity to consume, we see that this is precisely the oversimplified multiplier formula.

QUESTIONS FOR REVIEW

1. Find the equilibrium level of GDP demanded in an economy in which investment is always $300, net exports are always $-$50, the government budget is balanced with purchases and taxes both equal to $400, and the consumption function is described by the following algebraic equation:

$$C = 150 + 0.75DI$$

(*Hint:* Do not forget that $DI = Y - T$.)

2. Referring to Review Question 1, do the same for an economy in which investment is $250, net exports are zero, government purchases and taxes are both $400, and the consumption function is as follows:

$$C = 250 + 0.5DI$$

3. In each of these cases, how much saving is there in equilibrium? (*Hint:* Income not consumed must be saved.) Is saving equal to investment?

4. Imagine an economy in which consumer expenditure is represented by the following equation:

$$C = 50 + 0.75DI$$

Imagine also that investors want to spend $500 at every level of income ($I = $500), net exports are zero ($X - IM = 0$), government purchases are $300, and taxes are $200.

a. What is the equilibrium level of GDP?

b. If potential GDP is $3,000, is there a recessionary or inflationary gap? If so, how much?

c. What will happen to the equilibrium level of GDP if investors become optimistic about the country's future and raise their investment to $600?

d. After investment has increased to $600, is there a recessionary or inflationary gap? How much?

5. Fredonia has the following consumption function:

$$C = 100 + 0.8DI$$

Firms in Fredonia always invest $700 and net exports are zero, initially. The government budget is balanced with spending and taxes both equal to $500.

a. Find the equilibrium level of GDP.

b. How much is saved? Is saving equal to investment?

c. Now suppose that an export-promotion drive succeeds in raising net exports to $100. Answer (a) and (b) under these new circumstances.

APPENDIX B   The Multiplier with Variable Imports

In the chapter, we assumed that net exports were a fixed number. In fact, a nation's imports depend on its GDP for a simple reason: Higher GDP leads to higher incomes, some of which is spent on foreign goods. Thus:

Our imports rise as our GDP rises and fall as our GDP falls.

Similarly, our *exports* are the *imports* of other countries, so it is natural to assume that our exports depend on *their* GDPs, not on our own. Thus:

Our exports are relatively insensitive to our own GDP, but are quite sensitive to the GDPs of other countries.

This appendix derives the implications of these rather elementary observations. In particular, it shows that once we recognize the dependence of a nation's imports on its GDP:

International trade lowers the value of the multiplier.

To see why, we begin with Table 8-6, which adapts the example of our hypothetical economy to allow imports to depend on GDP. Columns (2) through (4) are the same as in Table 8-1; they show C, I, and G at alternative levels of GDP. Columns (5) and (6) record revised assumptions about the behavior of exports and imports. Exports are fixed at $650 billion regardless of GDP. But imports are assumed to rise by $60 billion for every $400 billion rise in GDP, which is a simple numerical example of the idea that imports depend on GDP. Column (7) subtracts imports from exports to get net exports, $(X - IM)$, and Column (8) adds up the four components of total expenditure, $C + I + G + (X - IM)$. The equilibrium, you can see, occurs at $Y = \$6{,}000$ billion, just as it did in the chapter.

Figures 8-13 and 8-14 display the same conclusion graphically. The upper panel of Figure 8-13 shows that exports are fixed at $650 billion regardless of GDP, whereas imports increase as GDP rises, just as in Table 8-6. The difference between exports and imports, or net exports, is positive until GDP approaches $5,300 billion and negative once GDP surpasses that amount. The bottom panel of Figure 8-13 shows the subtraction explicitly and makes it clear that:

Net exports decline as GDP rises.

Figure 8-14 carries this analysis over to the 45° line diagram. We begin with the familiar $C + I + G + (X - IM)$ line in black. Previously, we simply assumed that net exports were fixed at $-\$100$ billion regardless of GDP. Now that we have amended our model to note that net exports decline as GDP rises, the sum $C + I + G + (X - IM)$ rises more slowly than we previously assumed. This change is shown by the red line. Note that it is less steep than the black line.

Let us now consider what happens if exports rise by $160 billion while imports remain as in Table 8-6. Table 8-7 shows that equilibrium now occurs at a GDP of $Y = \$6{,}400$ billion. Naturally, higher exports have raised domestic GDP. But consider the magnitude. A $160 billion increase in exports (from $650 billion to $810 billion) leads to an increase of $400 billion in GDP (from $6,000 billion to $6,400 billion). So the multiplier is 2.5 $(= \$400/\$160)$.[11]

This same conclusion is shown graphically in Figure 8-15, where the line $C + I + G + (X_0 - IM)$ represents

[11] *Exercise:* Construct a version of Table 8-6 to show what would happen if imports rose by $160 billion at every level of GDP while exports remained at $650 billion. You should be able to show that the new equilibrium would be $Y = \$5{,}600$.

TABLE 8-6   Equilibrium Income with Variable Imports

(1) Gross Domestic Product (Y)	(2) Consumer Expenditures (C)	(3) Investment (I)	(4) Government Purchases (G)	(5) Exports (X)	(6) Imports (IM)	(7) Net Exports (X − IM)	(8) Total Expenditure [C + I + G + (X − IM)]
4,800	3,000	900	1,300	650	570	+80	5,280
5,200	3,300	900	1,300	650	630	+20	5,520
5,600	3,600	900	1,300	650	690	−40	5,760
6,000	**3,900**	**900**	**1,300**	**650**	**750**	**−100**	**6,000**
6,400	4,200	900	1,300	650	810	−160	6,240
6,800	4,500	900	1,300	650	870	−220	6,480
7,200	4,800	900	1,300	650	930	−280	6,720

NOTE: Figures are in billions of dollars per year.

■ FIGURE 8-13   The Dependence of Net Exports on GDP

NOTE: Figures are in billions of dollars per year.

the original expenditure schedule and the line $C + I + G + (X_1 - IM)$ represents the expenditure schedule after the $160 billion increase in exports. Equilibrium shifts from point E to point A, and GDP rises by $400 billion.

Notice that the multiplier in this example is 2.5, whereas in the chapter, with net exports taken to be a fixed number, it was 4. This simple example illustrates a general result: *International trade lowers the numerical value of the multiplier.* Why is this so? Because, in an open economy, any autonomous increase in spending is partly dissipated in purchases of foreign goods, which creates additional income for *foreigners* rather than for domestic citizens.

Thus, international trade gives us the first of what will eventually be several reasons why the oversimplified multiplier formula overstates the true value of the multiplier.

■ FIGURE 8-14   Equilibrium GDP with Variable Imports   ■ FIGURE 8-15   The Multiplier with Variable Imports

TABLE 8-7   Equilibrium Income after a $160 Billion Increase in Exports

(1) Gross Domestic Product (Y)	(2) Consumer Expenditures (C)	(3) Investment (I)	(4) Government Purchases (G)	(5) Exports (X)	(6) Imports (IM)	(7) Net Exports (X − IM)	(8) Total Expenditure [C + I + G + (X − IM)]
4,800	3,000	900	1,300	810	570	+240	5,440
5,200	3,300	900	1,300	810	630	+180	5,680
5,600	3,600	900	1,300	810	690	+120	5,920
6,000	3,900	900	1,300	810	750	+60	6,160
6,400	**4,200**	**900**	**1,300**	**810**	**810**	**0**	**6,400**
6,800	4,500	900	1,300	810	870	−60	6,640
7,200	4,800	900	1,300	810	930	−120	6,800

NOTE: Figures are in billions of dollars per year.

SUMMARY

1. Because imports rise as GDP rises, while exports are insensitive to (domestic) GDP, net exports decline as GDP rises.

2. If imports depend on GDP, international trade reduces the value of the multiplier.

QUESTIONS FOR REVIEW

1. Suppose exports and imports of a country are given by the following:

GDP	Exports	Imports
$2,500	$400	$250
3,000	400	300
3,500	400	350
4,000	400	400
4,500	400	450
5,000	400	500

Calculate net exports at each level of GDP.

2. If domestic expenditure (the sum of $C + I + G$ in the economy described in Review Question 1) is as shown in the following table, construct a 45° line diagram and locate the equilibrium level of GDP.

GDP	Domestic Expenditures
$2,500	$3,100
3,000	3,400
3,500	3,700
4,000	4,000
4,500	4,300
5,000	4,600

3. Now raise exports to $650 and find the equilibrium again. How large is the multiplier?

9

Supply-Side Equilibrium: Unemployment *and* Inflation?

We might as well reasonably dispute whether it is the upper or the under blade of a pair of scissors that cuts a piece of paper, as whether value is governed by [demand] or [supply].

ALFRED MARSHALL

C hapter 8 taught us that the position of the economy's total expenditure ($C + I + G + (X - IM)$) schedule governs whether the economy will experience a recessionary or an inflationary gap. Too little spending leads to a *recessionary gap.* Too much leads to an *inflationary gap.* Which sort of gap actually occurs is of considerable practical importance, because a recessionary gap translates into *unemployment,* whereas an inflationary gap leads to *inflation.*

But the tools provided in Chapter 8 cannot tell us which sort of gap will arise because the position of the expenditure schedule depends on the price level. And the price level is determined by *both* aggregate demand *and* aggregate supply. So this chapter has a clear task: to bring the supply side of the economy into the picture.

Doing so will put us in a position to deal with the crucial question raised in earlier chapters: Does the economy have an efficient self-correcting mechanism? We shall see that the answer is "yes, but . . .": Yes, but it works slowly. The chapter will also enable us to explain the vexing problem of *stagflation*—the simultaneous occurrence of high unemployment *and* high inflation—which plagued the economy in the 1980s.

CONTENTS

Puzzle: Why Did Inflation Fall While the Economy Boomed?

For years, economists talked about the agonizing trade-off between inflation and un-employment—a notion that made its first appearance in Chapter 1's list of *Ideas for Beyond the Final Exam*. Very low unemployment was supposed to make the inflation rate rise. Yet the stunning success of the U.S. economy from 1996 through the mid-dle of 2000 seemed to belie this idea. The unemployment rate fell to about 4 percent of the labor force, which was the lowest rate recorded in 30 years. But inflation did not rise; in fact, it *fell* for part of this period. How can we explain this marvelous con-junction of events—extremely low unemployment coupled with falling inflation? Does it mean—as many critics said at the time—that standard economic theory did not apply to the "New Economy" of the late 1990s? Before this chapter is over, we shall have some answers.

THE AGGREGATE SUPPLY CURVE

In earlier chapters, we noted that aggregate demand is a schedule, not a fixed number. The quantity of real gross domestic product (GDP) that will be de-manded depends on the price level, as summarized in the economy's *aggregate de-mand curve*. The same point applies to *aggregate supply*: The concept of aggregate supply does not refer to a fixed number, but rather to a schedule (an *aggregate sup-ply curve*).

The volume of goods and services that profit-seeking enterprises will provide depends on the prices they obtain for their outputs, on wages and other produc-tion costs, on the state of technology, and on other things. The relationship be-tween the price level and the quantity of real GDP supplied, *holding all other deter-minants of quantity supplied constant*, is called the economy's **aggregate supply curve.**

The **aggregate supply curve** shows, for each possi-ble price level, the quantity of goods and services that all the nation's businesses are willing to produce during a specified period of time, hold-ing all other determinants of aggregate quantity supplied constant.

Figure 9-1 shows a typical aggregate supply curve. It slopes upward, meaning that, as prices rise, more output is produced, *other things held constant*. Let's see why.

Why the Aggregate Supply Curve Slopes Upward

Producers are motivated mainly by profit. The profit made by producing a unit of output is simply the difference between the price at which it is sold and the unit cost of production:

Profit per unit = Price − Cost per unit

So the response of output to a rising price level—which is what the slope of the aggregate supply curve shows—depends on the response of costs.

Many of the prices that firms pay for labor and other in-puts remain fixed for periods of time—although certainly not forever. For example, workers and firms often enter into long-term labor contracts that set money wages one to three years in advance. Even where no explicit contracts ex-ist, wage rates typically adjust only annually. Similarly, a va-riety of material inputs are delivered to firms under long-term contracts at prearranged prices.

Why is this fact significant? Because firms decide how much to produce by comparing their selling prices with their costs of production. If the selling prices of the firm's

■ FIGURE 9-1

An Aggregate Supply Curve

products rise while its wages and other factor costs are fixed, production becomes more profitable, and firms will presumably produce more.

A simple example will illustrate the idea. Suppose a firm uses one hour of labor to manufacture a gadget that sells for $9. If workers earn $8 per hour, and the firm has no other costs, its profit per unit is:

$$\text{Profit per unit} = \text{Price} - \text{Cost per unit}$$
$$= \$9 - \$8 = \$1$$

If the price of a gadget rises to $10 but wage rates remain constant, the firm's profit per unit becomes:

$$\text{Profit per unit} = \text{Price} - \text{Cost per unit}$$
$$= \$10 - \$8 = \$2$$

With production more profitable, the firm will likely supply more gadgets.

The same process also operates in reverse. If selling prices fall while input costs remain relatively fixed, profit margins will be squeezed and production cut back. This behavior is summarized by the upward slope of the aggregate supply curve: Production rises when the price level (henceforth, P) rises, and falls when P falls. In other words:

The aggregate supply curve slopes upward because firms normally can purchase labor and other inputs at prices that are fixed for some period of time. Thus, higher selling prices for output make production more attractive.[1]

The phrase "for some period of time" alerts us to an important fact: The aggregate supply curve may not stand still for long. If wages or prices of other inputs change, as they surely will during inflationary times, then the aggregate supply curve will shift.

▮ Shifts of the Aggregate Supply Curve

We have concluded so far that, for given levels of wages and other input prices, there will be an upward-sloping aggregate supply curve relating the price level to aggregate quantity supplied. Now let's consider what happens when these input prices change.

The Money Wage Rate   The most obvious determinant of the aggregate supply curve's position is the *money wage rate*. Wages are the major element of cost in the economy, accounting for more than 70 percent of all inputs. Because higher wage rates mean higher costs, they spell lower profits at any given prices. That relationship explains why companies have been known to dig in their heels when unions demand large wage increases. For example, Verizon, the giant telephone company serving most of the northeastern United States, took a well-publicized strike in the summer of 2000 rather than give in to its workers' demands.

Returning to our example, consider what would happen to a gadget producer if the money wage rose to $8.75 per hour while the gadget's price remained $9. Profit per unit would decline from:

$$\$9 - \$8 = \$1$$

to

$$\$9.00 - \$8.75 = \$0.25$$

With profits squeezed, the firm would probably cut back on production.

---

[1] There are both differences and similarities between the *aggregate* supply curve and the *microeconomic* supply curves studied in Chapter 3. Both are based on the idea that quantity supplied depends on how output prices move relative to input prices. The aggregate supply curve pertains to the behavior of *the overall price level*, however, whereas a microeconomic supply curve pertains to the *price of some particular commodity*.

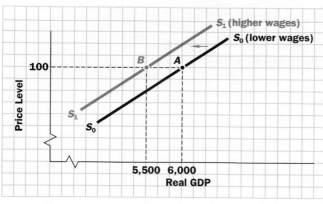

NOTE: Amounts are in billions of dollars per year.

■ FIGURE 9-2
A Shift of the Aggregate Supply Curve

Thus a wage increase leads to a decrease in aggregate quantity supplied at current prices. Graphically, the aggregate supply curve *shifts to the left* (or inward), as shown in Figure 9-2. In this diagram, firms are willing to supply $6,000 billion in goods and services at a price level of 100 when wages are low (point *A*). But after wages increase, the same firms are willing to supply only $5,500 billion at this price level (point *B*). By similar reasoning, the aggregate supply curve will shift to the right (or outward) if wages fall.

An increase in the money wage rate shifts the aggregate supply curve *inward*, meaning that the quantity supplied at any price level *declines*. A decrease in the money wage rate shifts the aggregate supply curve *outward*, meaning that the quantity supplied at any price level *increases*.

Prices of Other Inputs   In this regard, wages are hardly unique. An increase in the price of *any* input that firms buy will shift the aggregate supply curve in the same way. That is:

The aggregate supply curve is shifted *inward* by an increase in the price of any input to the production process, and it is shifted *outward* by any decrease.

Although producers use many inputs other than labor, the one that has attracted the most attention in recent decades is energy. Increases in the prices of imported energy, such as those that took place most recently in 2003 and 2004, push the aggregate supply curve inward as shown in Figure 9-2. By the same token, decreases in the price of imported oil, such as the ones we enjoyed in 2001, shift the aggregate supply curve in the opposite direction—outward.

Productivity is the amount of output produced by a unit of input.

Technology and Productivity   Another factor that can shift the aggregate supply curve is the state of technology. The idea that technological progress increases the **productivity** of labor is already familiar to us from earlier chapters. If wages do not change, higher productivity will *decrease* business costs, improve profitability, and encourage more production.

Once again, our gadget company will help us understand how this process works. Suppose the price of a gadget stays at $9 and the hourly wage rate stays at $8, but gadget workers become more productive. Specifically, suppose the labor input required to manufacture a gadget decreases from one hour (which costs $8) to three-quarters of an hour (which costs $6). Then profit per unit rises from

$$\$9 - \$8 = \$1$$

to

$$\$9 - \$6 = \$3$$

The lure of higher profits should induce gadget manufacturers to increase production—which is, of course, why companies are constantly striving to raise their productivity. In brief, we have concluded that:

Improvements in productivity shift the aggregate supply curve outward.

We can therefore interpret Figure 9-2 as illustrating a *decline* in productivity. As we mentioned in Chapter 6, a slowdown in productivity growth was a persistent problem for the United States for more than two decades (roughly, 1973–1995).

Available Supplies of Labor and Capital   The last determinant of the position of the aggregate supply curve is obvious. The bigger the economy—as measured by its available supplies of labor and capital—the more it is capable of producing. The conclusion should be familiar from Chapter 6:

As the labor force grows or improves in quality, and as investment increases the capital stock, the aggregate supply curve shifts *outward* to the right, meaning that more output can be produced at any given price level.

So, for example, the investment boom of the 1990s, by boosting the supply of capital, left the U.S. economy with a greater capacity to produce goods and services—that is, it shifted the aggregate supply curve outward.

These factors, then, are the major "other things" that we hold constant when drawing an aggregate supply curve: wage rates, prices of other inputs (such as energy), technology, labor force, and capital stock. A change in the price level moves the economy *along a given supply curve*, but a change in any of the other determinants of aggregate quantity supplied *shifts the entire supply schedule*.

EQUILIBRIUM OF AGGREGATE DEMAND AND SUPPLY

Chapter 8 taught us that the price level is a crucial determinant of whether equilibrium GDP falls below full employment (a "recessionary gap"), precisely at full employment, or above full employment (an "inflationary gap"). We can now analyze which type of gap, if any, will occur in any particular case by combining the aggregate supply analysis we just completed with the aggregate demand analysis from the last chapter.

Figure 9-3 displays the simple mechanics. In the figure, the aggregate demand curve *DD* and the aggregate supply curve *SS* intersect at point *E*, where real GDP (*Y*) is $6,000 billion and the price level (*P*) is 100. As can be seen in the graph, at any higher price level, such as 120, aggregate quantity supplied would exceed aggregate quantity demanded. In such a case, a glut would appear in the market as firms found themselves unable to sell all their output. As inventories piled up, firms would compete more vigorously for the available customers, thereby forcing prices down. Both the price level and production would fall.

At any price level lower than 100, such as 80, quantity demanded would exceed quantity supplied. There would be a shortage of goods on the market. With inventories disappearing and customers knocking on their doors, firms would be encouraged to raise prices. The price level would rise, and so would output. Only when the price level is 100 are the quantities of real GDP demanded and supplied equal. Therefore, only the combination of *P* = 100, *Y* = $6,000 is an equilibrium.

Table 9-1 illustrates the same conclusion in another way, by using a tabular analysis similar to the one in Chapter 8 (refer back to Table 8-2 on page 147). Columns (1) and (2) constitute an aggregate

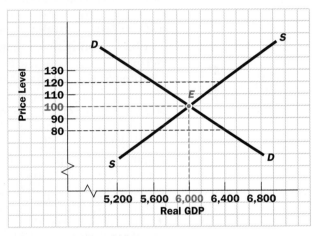

NOTE: Amounts are in billions of dollars per year.

■ FIGURE 9-3

Equilibrium of Real GDP and the Price Level

■ TABLE 9-1   Determination of the Equilibrium Price Level

(1) Price Level	(2) Aggregate Quantity Demanded	(3) Aggregate Quantity Supplied	(4) Balance of Supply and Demand	(5) Prices will be:
80	$6,400	$5,600	Demand exceeds supply	Rising
90	6,200	5,800	Demand exceeds supply	Rising
100	**6,000**	**6,000**	**Demand equals supply**	**Unchanged**
110	5,800	6,200	Supply exceeds demand	Falling
120	5,600	6,400	Supply exceeds demand	Falling

NOTE: Quantities are in billions of dollars.

demand schedule corresponding to curve *DD* in Figure 9-3. Columns (1) and (3) constitute an aggregate supply schedule corresponding to aggregate supply curve *SS*.

The table clearly shows that equilibrium occurs only at $P = 100$ and $Y = \$6,000$. At any other price level, aggregate quantities supplied and demanded would be unequal, with consequent upward or downward pressure on prices. For example, at a price level of 90, customers demand \$6,200 billion worth of goods and services, but firms wish to provide only \$5,800 billion. In this case, the price level is too low and will be forced upward. Conversely, at a price level of 110, quantity supplied (\$6,200 billion) exceeds quantity demanded (\$5,800 billion), implying that the price level must fall.

RECESSIONARY AND INFLATIONARY GAPS REVISITED

Let us now reconsider the question we have been deferring: Will equilibrium occur at, below, or beyond potential GDP?

We could not answer this question completely in Chapter 8 because we had no way to determine the equilibrium price level, and therefore no way to tell which type of gap, if any, would arise. The aggregate supply and demand analysis summarized in Figure 9-3 and Table 9-1 now gives us what we need. But we find that our answer is still the same: Anything can happen.

The reason is that Figure 9-3 tells us nothing about where *potential* GDP falls. The factors determining the economy's capacity to produce were discussed extensively in Chapter 6. But this analysis might leave potential GDP above the \$6,000 billion equilibrium level or below it. Depending on the locations of the aggregate demand and aggregate supply curves, then, we can reach equilibrium *beyond* potential GDP (an inflationary gap), *at* potential GDP, or *below* potential GDP (a recessionary gap).

All three possibilities are illustrated in Figure 9-4. The three upper panels are familiar from Chapter 8. (Recall that each income-expenditure diagram considers *only* the demand side of the economy by holding the price level fixed.) As we move from left to right, the expenditure schedule rises from $C + I_0 + G + (X - IM)$ to $C + I_1 + G + (X - IM)$ to $C + I_2 + G + (X - IM)$, leading respectively to a recessionary gap, an equilibrium exactly at potential GDP, and an inflationary gap. In fact, the upper-left diagram looks just like Figure 8-6 (page 150), and the upper-right diagram duplicates Figure 8-7 (page 151). In Chapter 8, we emphasized that any one of the three cases is possible, depending on the price level and other determinants of the position of the expenditure schedule.[2]

The three lower panels consider *both* aggregate demand *and* aggregate supply, and therefore determine *both* the equilibrium price level *and* the equilibrium GDP at point *E*—the intersection of the aggregate supply curve *SS* and the aggregate demand curve *DD*. But the same three possibilities emerge nonetheless.

In the lower-left panel, aggregate demand is too low to provide jobs for the entire labor force, so we have a recessionary gap equal to distance *EB*, or \$1,000 billion. This situation corresponds precisely to the one depicted on the income-expenditure diagram immediately above it.

In the lower-right panel, aggregate demand is so high that the economy reaches an equilibrium well beyond potential GDP. An inflationary gap equal to *BE*, or \$1,000 billion, arises, just as in the diagram immediately above it.

In the lower-middle panel, the aggregate demand curve D_1D_1 is at just the right level to produce an equilibrium at potential GDP. Neither an inflationary gap nor a recessionary gap occurs, as in the diagram just above it.

It may seem, therefore, that we have simply restated our previous conclusions. But, in fact, we have done much more. Now that we have studied the determination of the equilibrium price level, we are able to examine how the economy adjusts to either a

---

[2] These three diagrams hold potential GDP at \$7,000 billion and vary the expenditure schedule. You can draw equivalent diagrams by holding the $C + I + G + (X - IM)$ line constant and changing the presumed level of potential GDP. Try it as an exercise.

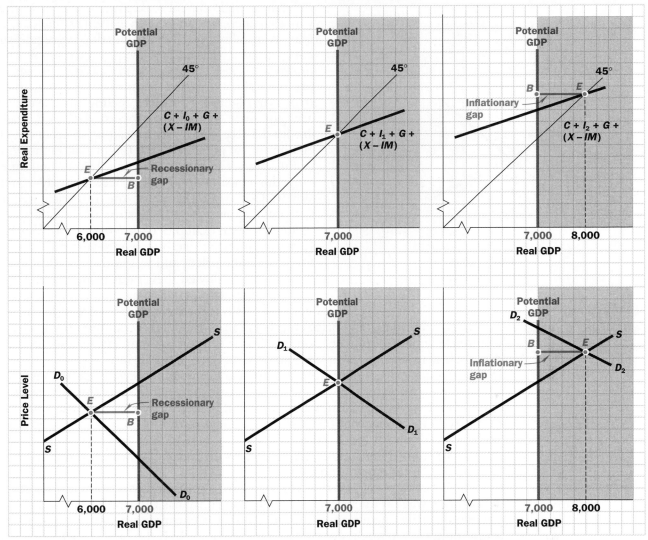

NOTE: Real GDP is in billions of dollars per year.

FIGURE 9-4

Recessionary and Inflationary Gaps Revisited

recessionary gap or an inflationary gap. Specifically, because wages are fixed in the short run, any one of the three cases depicted in Figure 9-4 can occur. But, in the long run, wages will adjust to labor market conditions, which will shift the aggregate supply curve. It is to that adjustment that we now turn.

ADJUSTING TO A RECESSIONARY GAP: DEFLATION OR UNEMPLOYMENT?

Suppose the economy starts with a recessionary gap—that is, an equilibrium *below* potential GDP—as depicted in the lower-left panel of Figure 9-4. Such a situation might be caused, for example, by inadequate consumer spending or by anemic investment spending. In 2001 and 2002, many observers were saying that the United States was in just such straits—for the first time in years. In Japan, however, recessionary gaps have been the norm for years. What happens when an economy experiences a recessionary gap?

With equilibrium GDP below potential, jobs will be difficult to find. The ranks of the unemployed will exceed the number of people who are jobless because of moving, changing occupations, and so on. In the terminology of Chapter 5, the economy will experience a considerable amount of *cyclical unemployment*. Businesses, on the other hand, will have little trouble finding workers, and their current employees will be eager to hang on to their jobs.

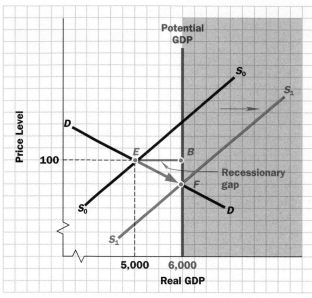

FIGURE 9-5

The Elimination of a Recessionary Gap

NOTE: Amounts are in billions of dollars per year.

Such an environment makes it difficult for workers to win wage increases. Indeed, in extreme situations, wages may even fall—thereby shifting the aggregate supply curve *outward*. (Recall that an aggregate supply curve is drawn for a *given* money wage.) But as the aggregate supply curve shifts outward—eventually moving from S_0S_0 to S_1S_1 in Figure 9-5—prices decline and the recessionary gap shrinks. By this process, deflation gradually erodes the recessionary gap—leading the economy to an equilibrium at potential GDP (point F in Figure 9-5).

But there is an important catch. In our modern economy, this adjustment process proceeds slowly—painfully slowly. Our brief review of the historical record in Chapter 4 showed that the history of the United States includes several examples of *deflation* before World War II but none since then. Not even severe recessions have forced average prices and wages down—although they have certainly slowed their rates of increase. The only protracted episode of deflation in an advanced economy since the 1930s is the recent experience of Japan.

Exactly why wages and prices rarely fall in our modern economy remains a subject of intense debate among economists. Some economists emphasize institutional factors such as minimum wage laws, union contracts, and a variety of government regulations that place legal floors under particular wages and prices. Because most of these institutions are of recent vintage, this theory successfully explains why wages and prices fall less frequently now than they did before World War II. But only a small minority of the U.S. economy is subject to legal restraints on wage and price cutting. So it seems doubtful that legal restrictions can take us very far in explaining sluggish wage-price adjustments in the United States. In Europe, however, these institutional factors may be far more important.

Other observers suggest that workers have a profound psychological resistance to accepting a wage reduction. This theory certainly has the ring of truth. Think how you would react if your boss announced he was cutting your hourly wage rate. You might quit, or you might devote less care to your job. If the boss suspects you will react this way, he may be reluctant to cut your wage. Nowadays, genuine wage reductions are rare enough to be newsworthy. But although no one doubts that wage cuts can damage morale, this psychological theory has one major drawback: It fails to explain why the psychological resistance to wage cuts apparently started only after World War II. Until a satisfactory answer to this question is provided, many economists will remain skeptical of this hypothesis.

A third explanation is based on a fact we emphasized in Chapter 4—that business cycles have been less severe in the postwar period than they were in the prewar period. As workers and firms came to realize that recessions would not turn into depressions, the argument goes, they decided to wait out the bad times rather than accept wage or price reductions that they would later regret.

Yet another theory is based on the old adage, "You get what you pay for." The idea is that workers differ in productivity, but that the productivities of individual employees are difficult to identify. Firms therefore worry that they will lose their best employees if they reduce wages—because these workers have the best opportunities elsewhere in the economy. Rather than take this chance, the argument goes, firms prefer to maintain high wages even in recessions.

Other theories have also been proposed, none of which commands a clear majority of professional opinion. But regardless of the cause, we may as well accept it as a fact that wages fall only sluggishly when demand is weak.

The implications of this rigidity are quite serious, for a recessionary gap cannot cure itself without some deflation. And if wages and prices will not fall, recessionary gaps like *EB* in Figure 9-5 will linger for a long time. That is:

When aggregate demand is low, the economy may get stuck with a recessionary gap for a long time. If wages and prices fall very slowly, the economy will endure a prolonged period of production below potential GDP.

Does the Economy Have a Self-Correcting Mechanism?

Now a situation like that described above would, presumably, not last forever. As the recession lengthened and perhaps deepened, more and more workers would be unable to find jobs at the prevailing "high" wages. Eventually, their need to be employed would overwhelm their resistance to wage cuts.

Firms, too, would become increasingly willing to cut prices as the period of weak demand persisted and managers became convinced that the slump was not merely a temporary aberration. Prices and wages did, in fact, fall in many countries during the Great Depression of the 1930s, and they are falling now (albeit slightly) in Japan.

Nowadays, however, political leaders of both parties believe that it is folly to wait for falling wages and prices to eliminate a recessionary gap. They agree that government action is both necessary and appropriate under recessionary conditions. Nevertheless, vocal—and highly partisan—debate continues over how much and what kind of intervention is warranted. One reason for the disagreement is that the **self-correcting mechanism** does operate—if only weakly—to cure recessionary gaps.

The economy's **self-correcting mechanism** refers to the way money wages react to either a recessionary gap or an inflationary gap. Wage changes shift the aggregate supply curve and therefore change equilibrium GDP and the equilibrium price level.

An Example from Recent History: Deflation in Japan

Fortunately for us, recent U.S. history offers no examples of long-lasting recessionary gaps. But the world's second-largest economy does. The Japanese economy has been consistently weak since the early 1990s—including several recessions. As a result, Japan has experienced persistent recessionary gaps for about a decade. Unsurprisingly, Japan's modest inflation rate evaporated and turned into a small *deflation* rate. Qualitatively, this is just the sort of behavior the theoretical model of the self-correcting mechanism predicts. But it took a very long time! Hence, the practical policy question is: How long can a country afford to wait?

ADJUSTING TO AN INFLATIONARY GAP: INFLATION

Let us now turn to what happens when the economy finds itself *beyond* full employment—that is, with an *inflationary* gap like that shown in Figure 9-6. When the aggregate supply curve is S_0S_0 and the aggregate demand curve is DD, the economy will initially reach equilibrium (point E) with an inflationary gap, shown by the segment BE.

According to many economists, this situation prevailed in the United States in 1999. What should happen under such circumstances? As we shall see now, the supertight labor market produces an inflation that eventually eliminates the inflationary gap, though perhaps in a slow and painful way. Let us see how.

When equilibrium GDP exceeds potential GDP, jobs are plentiful and labor is in great demand. Firms are likely to have trouble recruiting new workers or even holding onto their old ones as other firms try to lure workers away with higher wages.

Rising wages add to business costs, which shift the aggregate supply curve *inward*. As the aggregate supply curve moves from S_0S_0 to S_1S_1 in Figure 9-6, the inflationary gap shrinks. In other words, inflation eventually erodes the inflationary gap and brings the economy to an equilibrium at potential GDP (point F).

■ FIGURE 9-6

The Elimination of an Inflationary Gap

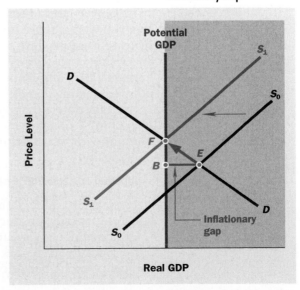

There is a straightforward way of looking at the economics underlying this process. Inflation arises because buyers are demanding more output than the economy is capable of producing at normal operating rates. To paraphrase an old cliché, there is too much demand chasing too little supply. Such an environment encourages price hikes.

Ultimately, rising prices eat away at the purchasing power of consumers' wealth, forcing them to cut back on consumption, as explained in Chapter 7. In addition, exports fall and imports rise, as we learned in Chapter 8. Eventually, aggregate quantity demanded is scaled back to the economy's capacity to produce—graphically, the economy moves back along curve DD from point E to point F. At this point the self-correcting process stops. In brief:

> If aggregate demand is exceptionally high, the economy may reach a short-run equilibrium above full employment (an *inflationary gap*). When this occurs, the tight situation in the labor market soon forces wages to rise. Because rising wages increase business costs, prices increase; there is inflation. As higher prices cut into consumer purchasing power and net exports, the inflationary gap begins to close.

> As the inflationary gap closes, output falls and prices continue to rise. When the gap is finally eliminated, a long-run equilibrium is established with a higher price level and with GDP equal to potential GDP.

This scenario was precisely what many economists expected in 1998 and 1999. Because they believed that the U.S. economy had an inflationary gap in 1997 and 1998, they expected inflation to rise. But it did not. Why not? We will have the answer in just a few more pages.

But first we repeat an important caveat: *The self-correcting mechanism takes time* because wages and prices do not adjust quickly. Thus, while an inflationary gap sows the seeds of its own destruction, the seeds germinate slowly. So, once again, policymakers may want to speed up the process.

▌ Demand Inflation and Stagflation

Simple as it is, this model of how the economy adjusts to an inflationary gap teaches us a number of important lessons about inflation in the real world. First, Figure 9-6 reminds us that the real culprit is *excessive aggregate demand*—relative to potential GDP. The aggregate demand curve is initially so high that it intersects the aggregate supply curve well beyond full employment. The resulting intense demand for goods and labor pushes prices and wages higher. Although aggregate demand in excess of potential GDP is not the only possible cause of inflation, it certainly is the cause in our example.

However, business managers and journalists may blame inflation on rising wages. In a superficial sense, of course, they are right, because higher wages do indeed lead firms to raise product prices. But in a deeper sense they are wrong. Both rising wages and rising prices are symptoms of the same underlying malady: too much aggregate demand. Blaming labor for inflation in such a case is a bit like blaming high doctor bills for making you ill.

Second, notice that output *falls* while prices *rise* as the economy adjusts from point E to point F in Figure 9-6. This is our first (but not our last) explanation of the phenomenon of **stagflation**—the conjunction of in*flation* and economic *stag*nation. Specifically:

Stagflation is inflation that occurs while the economy is growing slowly or having a recession.

> A period of stagflation is part of the normal aftermath of a period of excessive aggregate demand.

It is easy to understand why. When aggregate demand is excessive, the economy will temporarily produce beyond its normal capacity. Labor markets tighten and wages rise. Machinery and raw materials may also become scarce and so start rising in price. Faced with higher costs, business firms quite naturally react by producing less and charging higher prices. That is stagflation.

A Tale of Two Graduating Classes: 2000 Versus 2002

Timing matters in life. The college graduates of 2000 could hardly have asked for better luck. The unemployment rate dropped to 4.1 percent in May 2000—roughly, the lowest level in a generation—and employers were literally scrambling for new hires. Starting salaries rose, many graduating seniors had numerous job offers, and some firms even offered $10,000–$20,000 bonuses to students who signed on the dotted line!

Just two years later, the job market for the Class of 2002 was rather different. U.S. economic growth had slowed to a crawl, and then to a halt. Companies that had stocked up on recent college grads in the tight labor markets of 1998–2000 suddenly found themselves with more employees than they knew what to do with. Bonuses and other "perks" disappeared; job offers became scarcer. With the unemployment rate still under 6 percent, the job market of 2002 was far from the worst ever. But it was nothing like the glory days of 2000.

SOURCE: © Felicia Martinez/PhotoEdit

A Recent Example

The stagflation that follows a period of excessive aggregate demand is, you will note, a rather benign form of the dreaded disease. After all, while output is falling, it nonetheless remains above potential GDP, and unemployment is low. The U.S. economy last experienced such an episode at the end of the 1980s.

The long economic expansion of the 1980s brought the unemployment rate down to a 15-year low of 5 percent by March 1989. Almost all economists believe that 5 percent was below the full-employment unemployment rate at the time; that is, that the U.S. economy had an *inflationary gap* in 1989. As the theory suggests, inflation began to accelerate—from 4.4 percent in 1988 to 4.6 percent in 1989 and then to 6.1 percent in 1990.

In the meantime, the economy was stagnating. Real GDP growth fell from 3.5 percent during 1989 to 1.8 percent in 1990 and −0.5 percent in 1991. Inflation was eating away at the inflationary gap, which had virtually disappeared by mid-1990, when the recession started. Yet inflation remained high through the early months of the recession. The U.S. economy was in a *stagflation* phase.

Our overall conclusion about the economy's ability to right itself seems to run something like this:

The economy does, indeed, have a self-correcting mechanism that tends to eliminate either unemployment or inflation. But this mechanism works slowly and unevenly. In addition, its beneficial effects on either inflation or unemployment are sometimes swamped by strong forces (such as rapid increases or decreases in aggregate demand) pushing in the opposite direction. Thus, the self-correcting mechanism is not always reliable.

STAGFLATION FROM A SUPPLY SHOCK

We have just discussed the type of stagflation that follows in the wake of an inflationary boom. However, that is not what happened when unemployment and inflation both soared in the 1970s and early 1980s. What caused this more virulent strain of stagflation? Several things, though the principal culprit was rising energy prices.

In 1973, the Organization of Petroleum Exporting Countries (OPEC) quadrupled the price of crude oil. American consumers soon found the prices of gasoline and

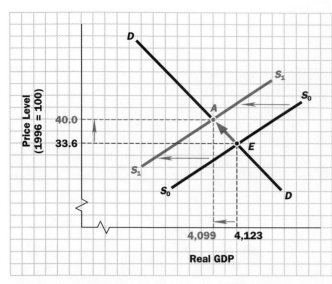

FIGURE 9-7

Stagflation from an Adverse Shift in Aggregate Supply

NOTE: Amounts are in billions of dollars per year.

home heating fuels increasing sharply, and U.S. businesses saw an important cost of doing business—energy prices—rising drastically. OPEC struck again in the period 1979–1980, this time doubling the price of oil. Then the same thing happened again, albeit on a smaller scale, when Iraq invaded Kuwait in 1990. Most recently, oil prices surged briefly in early 2003 on fears that the upcoming war in Iraq might disrupt oil supplies.

Higher energy prices, we observed earlier, shift the economy's aggregate supply curve *inward* in the manner shown in Figure 9-7. If the aggregate supply curve shifts inward, as it surely did following each of these "oil shocks," production will decline. To reduce demand to the available supply, prices will have to rise. The result is the worst of both worlds: falling production and rising prices.

This conclusion is shown graphically in Figure 9-7, which superimposes an aggregate demand curve, *DD*, on the two aggregate supply curves of Figure 9-2. The economy's equilibrium shifts upward to the left, from point *E* to point *A*. Thus, output falls while prices rise—exactly our definition of stagflation. In brief:

Stagflation is the typical result of adverse shifts of the aggregate supply curve.

The numbers used in Figure 9-7 are roughly indicative of what happened in the United States after the big "energy shock" of late 1973. Between 1973 (represented by supply curve S_0S_0 and point *E*) and 1975 (represented by supply curve S_1S_1 and point *A*), real GDP fell by about ½ percent, while the price level rose a stunning 19 percent. Thus, inflation soared and the economy weakened. The general lesson to be learned from the U.S. experience with supply shocks is both clear and important:

The typical results of an adverse supply shock are lower output and higher inflation. This is one reason why the world economy was plagued by stagflation in the mid-1970s and early 1980s. And it can happen again if another series of supply-reducing events takes place.

Puzzle Resolved: Explaining the Roaring Nineties

Of course, the aggregate supply curve can shift in the other direction as well. Therein lies the key to understanding why the U.S. economy performed so marvelously in the late 1990s. As we observed at the beginning of this chapter, inflation *fell* while unemployment was extremely low, leading many observers to proclaim that some of the most basic precepts of macroeconomics no longer applied.

What really happened? Several things, but one of them was a favorable oil shock. The world oil market weakened in 1997 and 1998, and oil prices plummeted from about $26 per barrel to just $11 per barrel. This sharp drop in the price of oil constituted a supply shock that shifted the aggregate supply curve *outward*, thereby stimulating U.S. economic growth and curbing inflation. In addition, productivity growth speeded up in the late 1990s—as we discussed in Chapter 6. Thus we enjoyed the happy combination of falling unemployment and declining inflation at the same time.

Lucky? Yes. But mysterious? No. What was happening was that the economy's aggregate supply curve was shifting outward much faster than it normally does. As we know from turning our previous analysis of supply shocks in the opposite direction:

Favorable supply shocks tend to push output up and reduce inflation.

It was mainly favorable supply shocks, plus a speedup in productivity growth that may reflect a "New Economy," that accounted for the surprisingly good news in the late 1990s.

INFLATION AND THE MULTIPLIER

When we introduced the concept of the multiplier in Chapter 8, we noted that its actual value is smaller than suggested by the oversimplified multiplier formula for several reasons. One of these factors—variable imports—emerged in an appendix to the previous chapter. We are now in a position to understand the second reason:

Inflation reduces the size of the multiplier.

The basic idea is simple. In Chapter 8, we described a multiplier process in which one person's spending becomes another person's income, which leads to further spending by the second person, and so on. But this story was confined to the *demand* side of the economy. Let us therefore consider what is likely to be happening on the *supply* side as the multiplier process unfolds. Will the additional demand be taken care of by firms without raising prices?

If the aggregate supply curve slopes upward, the answer is no. More goods will be provided only at *higher* prices. Thus, as the multiplier chain progresses, pulling income and employment up, prices will rise in tandem. This development, as we know from earlier chapters, will reduce net exports and dampen consumer spending because rising prices erode the purchasing power of consumers' wealth. As a consequence, the multiplier chain will not proceed as far as it would have in the absence of inflation.

How much inflation results from the rise in demand? How much is the multiplier chain muted by inflation? The answers to these questions depend on the slope of the economy's aggregate supply curve.

For a concrete example, let us return to the $200 billion increase in investment spending used early in Chapter 8. There we found (see especially Figure 8-9 on page 154) that $200 billion in additional investment spending will eventually lead to $800 billion in additional spending *if the price level does not rise.* But that scenario, as we now see, is unlikely to happen. To determine the actual quantity that will ultimately be produced and the actual price level, we must bring the aggregate supply curve into the picture.

Figure 9-8 does precisely that. Here we show the $800 billion rightward shift of the aggregate demand curve, from $D_0 D_0$ to $D_1 D_1$, that we derived from the oversimplified multiplier formula in Chapter 8. Recall that this calculation ignored rising prices—that is, *it tacitly assumed that the aggregate supply curve was horizontal.* But that is not so. The slope of the aggregate supply curve, SS, tells us how any expansion of aggregate demand is apportioned between higher output and higher prices.

We see in this example that, as the economy's equilibrium moves from point E_0 to point E_1, real GDP does not rise by $800 billion. Instead, prices rise, which cancels out part of the increase in quantity demanded. As a result, output rises from $6,000 billion to $6,600 billion—an increase of only $600 billion. Thus, in our example, inflation reduces the multiplier from $800/$200 = 4 to $600/$200 = 3. In general:

As long as the aggregate supply curve slopes upward, any increase in aggregate demand will push up the price level. Higher prices, in turn, will drain off some of the higher real demand by eroding the purchasing power of consumer wealth and by reducing net exports. Thus, inflation reduces the value of the multiplier below that suggested by the oversimplified formula.

Notice also that the price level in this example has been pushed up (from 100 to 120, or 20 percent) by the rise in investment demand. This, too, is a general result:

As long as the aggregate supply curve slopes upward, any outward shift of the aggregate demand curve will cause some rise in prices.

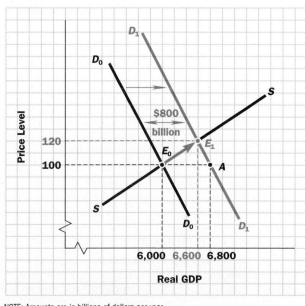

■ FIGURE 9-8

Inflation and the Multiplier

NOTE: Amounts are in billions of dollars per year.

The economic behavior behind these results is certainly not surprising. Firms faced with large increases in quantity demanded at their original prices respond to these changed circumstances in two natural ways: (1) They raise production (so real GDP rises), and (2) they raise prices (so the price level rises). But this rise in the price level, in turn, reduces the purchasing power of the bank accounts and bonds held by consumers, and they, too, react in the natural way: They cut down on their spending. Such a reaction amounts to a movement *along* aggregate demand curve D_1D_1 in Figure 9-8 from point A to point E_1.

Figure 9-8 also shows us exactly where the oversimplified multiplier formula goes wrong. By ignoring the effects of the higher price level, the oversimplified formula erroneously supposes that the economy moves horizontally from point E_0 to point A—which it would do only if the aggregate supply curve was horizontal. As the diagram clearly shows, output does not actually rise this much, which is one reason why the oversimplified formula exaggerates the size of the multiplier.

A ROLE FOR STABILIZATION POLICY

Chapter 7 emphasized the volatility of investment spending, and Chapter 8 noted that changes in investment have multiplier effects on aggregate demand. This chapter took the next step by showing how shifts in the aggregate demand curve cause fluctuations in *both* real GDP *and* prices—fluctuations that are widely decried as undesirable. It also suggested that the economy's self-correcting mechanism works, but slowly, thereby leaving room for government stabilization policy to improve the workings of the free market. Can the government really accomplish this goal? If so, how? These are some of the important questions for Part III.

SUMMARY

1. The economy's **aggregate supply curve** relates the quantity of goods and services that will be supplied to the price level. It normally slopes upward to the right because the costs of labor and other inputs remain relatively fixed in the short run, meaning that higher selling prices make input costs relatively cheaper and therefore encourage greater production.

2. The position of the aggregate supply curve can be shifted by changes in money wage rates, prices of other inputs, technology, or quantities or qualities of labor and capital.

3. The **equilibrium price level** and the **equilibrium level of real GDP** are jointly determined by the intersection of the economy's aggregate supply and aggregate demand schedules. This intersection may come at full employment, below full employment (a **recessionary gap**), or above full employment (an **inflationary gap**).

4. The economy has a **self-correcting mechanism** that erodes a recessionary gap. Specifically, a weak labor market reduces wage increases and, in extreme cases, may even drive wages down. Lower wages shift the aggregate supply curve outward. But it happens very slowly.

5. If an inflationary gap occurs, the economy has a similar mechanism that erodes the gap through a process of inflation. Unusually strong job prospects push wages up, which

shifts the aggregate supply curve to the left and reduces the inflationary gap.

6. One consequence of this self-correcting mechanism is that, if a surge in aggregate demand opens up an inflationary gap, the economy's subsequent natural adjustment will lead to a period of **stagflation**—that is, a period in which prices are rising while output is falling.

7. An inward shift of the aggregate supply curve will cause output to fall while prices rise—that is, it will produce stagflation. Among the events that have caused such a shift are abrupt increases in the price of foreign oil.

8. Adverse supply shifts like this plagued the U.S. economy when oil prices skyrocketed in 1973–1974, in 1979–1980, and again in 1990, leading to stagflation each time.

9. But things reversed in 1997–1998, when falling oil prices and rising productivity shifted the aggregate supply curve out more rapidly than usual, thereby boosting real growth and reducing inflation simultaneously.

10. Among the reasons why the oversimplified multiplier formula is wrong is the fact that it ignores the inflation that is caused by an increase in aggregate demand. Such **inflation decreases the multiplier** by reducing both consumer spending and net exports.

KEY TERMS

Aggregate supply curve 168

Productivity 170

Equilibrium of real GDP and the price level 171

Recessionary gap 173

Inflationary gap 175

Self-correcting mechanism 175

Stagflation 176

Inflation and the multiplier 179

QUESTIONS FOR REVIEW

1. In an economy with the following aggregate demand and aggregate supply schedules, find the equilibrium levels of real output and the price level. Graph your solution. If full employment comes at $2,800 billion, is there an inflationary or a recessionary gap?

Aggregate Quantity Demanded	Price Level	Aggregate Quantity Supplied
$3,200	85	$2,600
3,100	90	2,750
3,000	95	2,850
2,900	100	2,900
2,800	105	2,925

NOTE: Amounts are in billions of dollars.

2. Suppose a worker receives a wage of $18 per hour. Compute the real wage (money wage deflated by the price index) corresponding to each of the following possible price levels: 85, 95, 100, 110, 120. What do you notice about the relationship between the real wage and the price level? Relate your finding to the slope of the aggregate supply curve.

3. Explain why a decrease in the price of foreign oil shifts the aggregate supply curve outward to the right. What are the consequences of such a shift?

4. Comment on the following statement: "Inflationary and recessionary gaps are nothing to worry about because the economy has a built-in mechanism that cures either type of gap automatically."

5. Give two different explanations of how the economy can suffer from stagflation.

6. Why do you think wages tend to be rigid in the downward direction?

7. Add the following aggregate supply and demand schedules to the example in Review Question 3 of Chapter 8 (page 160) to see how inflation affects the multiplier.

(1) Price Level	(2) Aggregate Demand When Investment Is $240	(3) Aggregate Demand When Investment Is $260	(4) Aggregate Supply
90	$3,860	$4,060	$3,660
95	3,830	4,030	3,730
100	3,800	4,000	3,800
105	3,770	3,970	3,870
110	3,740	3,940	3,940
115	3,710	3,910	4,010

Draw these schedules on a piece of graph paper.

a. Notice that the difference between Columns (2) and (3), which show the aggregate demand schedule at two different levels of investment, is always $200. Discuss how this constant gap of $200 relates to your answer in the previous chapter.

b. Find the equilibrium GDP and the equilibrium price level both before and after the increase in investment. What is the value of the multiplier? Compare that to the multiplier you found in Review Question 3 of Chapter 8.

8. Explain in words why rising prices reduce the multiplier effect of an autonomous increase in aggregate demand.

9. Use an aggregate supply and demand diagram to show that multiplier effects are smaller when the aggregate supply curve is steeper. Which case gives rise to more inflation—the steep aggregate supply curve or the flat one? What happens to the multiplier if the aggregate supply curve is vertical?

FISCAL AND
MONETARY POLICY

Part II developed a framework for understanding the macroeconomy. The basic theory came in three pieces: long-run growth of potential GDP (Chapter 6), short-run aggregate demand (Chapters 7 and 8), and short-run aggregate supply (Chapter 9). Part III *uses* that framework to consider a variety of public policy issues—the sorts of things that make headlines in the newspapers and on television.

At several points in earlier chapters, we suggested that the government might be able to manage aggregate demand by using *fiscal and monetary policies.* Chapters 10–12 pick up and develop that suggestion. You will learn how the government tries to promote rapid growth and low unemployment while simultaneously limiting inflation—and why its efforts do not always succeed. Then, in Chapters 13–15, we turn explicitly to a number of important controversies related to the government's *stabilization policy.* How should the Federal Reserve do its job? Why is preserving the budget surplus considered to be so important? Is there a tradeoff between inflation and unemployment?

By the end of Part III, you will be in an excellent position to understand some of the most important debates over national economic policy—not only today, but also in the years to come.

10

Managing Aggregate Demand: Fiscal Policy

Next, let us turn to the problems of our fiscal policy. Here the myths are legion and the truth hard to find.

JOHN F. KENNEDY

In the model of the economy we constructed in Part II, the government played a passive role. It did some spending and collected taxes, but that was about it. We concluded that such an economy has only a weak tendency to move toward an equilibrium with high employment and low inflation. Furthermore, we hinted that well-designed government policies might enhance that tendency and improve the economy's performance. It is now time to develop that hint—and to learn about some of the difficulties that must be overcome if stabilization policy is to succeed.

We begin in this chapter with **fiscal policy.** The next three chapters take up the government's other main tool for managing aggregate demand: *monetary policy.*

CONTENTS

The government's **fiscal policy** is its plan for spending and taxation. It is designed to steer aggregate demand in some desired direction.

 Issue: How to Stimulate Japan's Economy

The Japanese economy has grown at a crawl—or worse—for more than a decade, opening up a huge recessionary gap. For years, the Japanese government tried to stimulate its economy with massive doses of government spending (G)—but with little success. The government budget deficit grew, but the economy did not. Then, in 2001, a new Prime Minister took office, vowing to reduce the budget deficit by cutting spending. Many observers applauded this new approach. After all, the old one had not worked.

But a number of economists voiced skepticism that *reducing* government spending would *stimulate* Japan's economy. On the contrary, the analysis in Chapter 8 suggests that cutbacks in G should have multiplier effects that would pull GDP *down*. Some of these economists suggested that, after years of wasteful government spending, the Japanese government should try cutting taxes instead—rather than reducing the budget deficit while the economy was so weak.

Japanese officials resisted this suggestion. They argued that income tax cuts would have unusually small multiplier effects in such depressed circumstances—even smaller than the multiplier effects of additional government spending. In this chapter, we will learn the basis for the Japanese claim that a tax cut would have a smaller multiplier than an equal amount of government spending. And we will also investigate other aspects of the choice between spending and taxes as stabilization tools.

INCOME TAXES AND THE CONSUMPTION SCHEDULE

To understand how taxes affect equilibrium gross domestic product (GDP), we must first distinguish between *fixed taxes*, which are the only kind we have considered so far, and *variable taxes*, which are much more important in practice.

Most of the taxes collected by both the Japanese and U.S. governments—indeed, by all national governments—rise and fall with GDP. In some cases, the reason is obvious: *Personal* and *corporate income tax* collections, for example, depend on how much income there is to be taxed. *Sales tax* receipts depend on GDP because consumer spending is higher when GDP is higher. However, other types of tax receipts—such as property taxes—do not vary with GDP. We call the first kind of tax **variable taxes** and the second kind **fixed taxes.**

Variable taxes are taxes that vary with the level of GDP.

Fixed taxes are taxes that do not vary with the level of GDP.

Why is this distinction important? Recall that taxes (T) are the difference between gross domestic product (Y) and disposable income (DI):

$$DI = Y - T$$

Thus, when taxes rise, disposable income falls—and hence so does consumption—*even if GDP remains unchanged*. As a result:

An increase in taxes shifts the consumption schedule in the 45° line diagram *downward*. Similarly, a tax reduction shifts the consumption schedule *upward*.

But precisely *how* the consumption schedule shifts depends on the nature of the tax change. If a fixed tax is increased, disposable income falls by the *same* amount regardless of the level of GDP. Hence, the decline in consumer spending is the same at every income level. In other words, the C schedule shifts downward in a parallel manner, as shown in Figure 10-1(a).

But many tax policies actually change disposable income by larger amounts when incomes are higher. That is true, for example, whenever Congress alters the bracket rates in the personal income tax code, as it did in 2001 and 2003. Because higher tax rates decrease disposable income *more* when GDP is *higher*, the C schedule shifts down more sharply at higher income levels than at lower ones, as shown in Figure 10-1(b). The same relationships apply for tax decreases, as the upward shifts in both panels of the figure show.

Figure 10-2 illustrates the second reason why the distinction between fixed and variable taxes is important. This figure shows two different consumption lines. C_1 is the consumption schedule used in previous chapters; it reflects the assumption that taxes are fixed at $1,200 billion regardless of GDP. C_2 depicts a more realistic case in which the government collects taxes equal to 20 percent of GDP. Notice that C_2 is flatter than C_1. This is no accident. In fact:

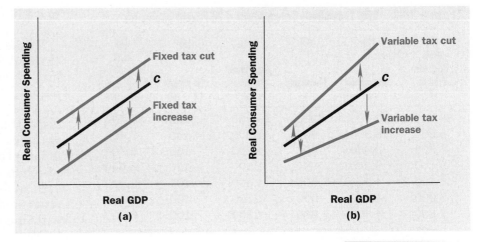

■ FIGURE 10-1

How Tax Policy Shifts the Consumption Schedule

Variable taxes such as the income tax flatten the consumption schedule in a 45° line diagram.

We can easily understand why. Column (1) of Table 10-1 shows alternative values of GDP ranging from $4.5 trillion to $7.5 trillion. Column (2) then indicates that taxes are always one-fifth of this amount. Column (3) subtracts Column (2) from Column (1) to arrive at disposable income (*DI*). Column (4) then gives the amount of consumer spending corresponding to each level of *DI*. The schedule relating C to Y, which we need for our 45° line diagram, is therefore found in Columns (1) and (4).

Notice that, in Table 10-1, each $500 billion increase in GDP leads to a $300 billion rise in consumer spending. Thus, the slope of line C_2 in Figure 10-2 is $300/$500, or 0.60. But, in our examples in Chapter 8, consumption rose by $300 billion each time GDP increased $400 billion—making the slope $300/$400, or 0.75. (See the steeper line C_1 in Figure 10-2.) Table 10-2 compares the two cases explicitly. In Chapter 8, taxes were fixed at $1,200 billion and each $400 billion rise in Y led to a $300 billion rise in C—as in the left-hand panel of Table 10-2. But now, with taxes variable (equal to 20 percent of GDP), each $500 billion increment to Y gives rise

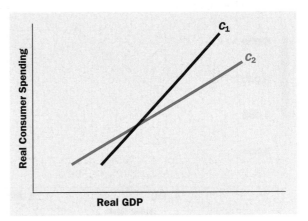

■ FIGURE 10-2

The Consumption Schedule with Fixed and Variable Taxes

■ TABLE 10-1   The Effects of an Income Tax on the Consumption Schedule

(1) Gross Domestic Product	(2) Taxes	(3) Disposable Income (GDP minus taxes)	(4) Consumption
$4,500	$ 900	$3,600	$3,000
5,000	1,000	4,000	3,300
5,500	1,100	4,400	3,600
6,000	1,200	4,800	3,900
6,500	1,300	5,200	4,200
7,000	1,400	5,600	4,500
7,500	1,500	6,000	4,800

NOTE: Figures are in billions of dollars per year.

■ TABLE 10-2   The Relationship between Consumption and GDP

With Fixed Taxes ($T = $1,200$) (from Table 8-1)		With a 20 Percent Income Tax (from Table 10-1)	
Y	C	Y	C
$4,800	$3,000	$4,500	$3,000
5,200	3,300	5,000	3,300
5,600	3,600	5,500	3,600
6,000	3,900	6,000	3,900
6,400	4,200	6,500	4,200
6,800	4,500	7,000	4,500
7,200	4,800	7,500	4,800
Line C_1 in Figure 10-2		**Line C_2 in Figure 10-2**	

TABLE 10-3   Total Expenditure Schedule with a 20 Percent Income Tax

(1) Gross Domestic Product Y	(2) Consumption C	(3) Investment I	(4) Government Purchases G	(5) Net Exports (X − IM)	(6) Total Expenditures C + I + G + (X − IM)
$4,500	$3,000	$900	$1,300	−$100	$5,100
5,000	3,300	900	1,300	−100	5,400
5,500	3,600	900	1,300	−100	5,700
6,000	3,900	900	1,300	−100	6,000
6,500	4,200	900	1,300	−100	6,300
7,000	4,500	900	1,300	−100	6,600
7,500	4,800	900	1,300	−100	6,900

NOTE: Figures are in billions of dollars per year.

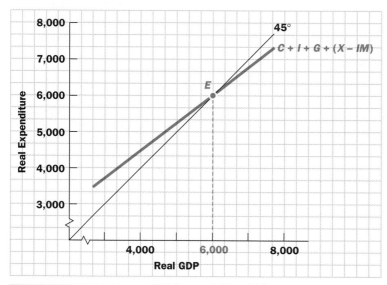

FIGURE 10-3

Income Determination with a Variable Income Tax

NOTE: Figures are in billions of dollars per year.

to a $300 billion increase in *C*—as in the right-hand panel of Table 10-2.

These differences sound terribly mechanical, but the economic reasoning behind them is vital to understanding tax policies. When taxes are fixed, as in line C_1, each additional dollar of GDP raises disposable income (*DI*) by $1. Consumer spending then rises by $1 times the marginal propensity to consume (MPC), which is 0.75 in our example. Hence, each additional dollar of GDP leads to 75 cents more spending. But when taxes vary with income, each additional dollar of GDP raises *DI* by less than $1 because the government takes a share in taxes. In our example, taxes are 20 percent of GDP, so each additional $1 of GDP generates just 80 cents more *DI*. With an MPC of 0.75, then, spending rises by only 60 cents (75 percent of 80 cents) each time GDP rises by $1. Thus, the slope of line C_2 in Figure 10-2 is only 0.60, instead of 0.75.

Table 10-3 and Figure 10-3 take the next step by replacing the old consumption schedule with this new one in both the tabular presentation of income determination and the 45° line diagram. We see immediately that the equilibrium level of GDP is at point *E*. Here gross domestic product is $6,000 billion, consumption is $3,900 billion, investment is $900 billion, net exports are −$100 billion, and government purchases are $1,300 billion. As we know, full employment may occur above or below *Y* = $6,000 billion. If it is below this level, an inflationary gap arises. Prices will probably start to rise, pulling the expenditure schedule down and reducing equilibrium GDP. If it is above this level, a recessionary gap results, and history suggests that prices will fall only slowly. In the interim, the economy will suffer a period of high unemployment.

In short, once we adjust the expenditure schedule for variable taxes, the determination of national income proceeds exactly as before. The effects of government spending and taxation, therefore, are fairly straightforward and can be summarized as follows:

> Government purchases of goods and services add to total spending *directly* through the G component of C + I + G + (X − IM). Taxes reduce total spending *indirectly* by lowering disposable income and thus reducing the C component of C + I + G + (X − IM). On balance, then, the government's actions may raise or lower the equilibrium level of GDP, depending on how much spending and taxing it does.

However, there is more to the story. As we will see next:

> The multiplier is smaller in the presence of an income tax.

THE MULTIPLIER REVISITED

In Chapter 8, we learned that the multiplier works through a chain of spending and respending, as one person's expenditure becomes another's income. But, if income is taxed, some of the additional income leaks out of the circular flow at each stage. Suppose the income tax rate is 20 percent. When Microhard spends $1 million on salaries, workers actually receive only $800,000 in *after-tax* (that is, disposable) income. If workers spend 75 percent of this amount (because the MPC is 0.75), spending in the next round will be only $600,000. Notice that this is only *60 percent* of the original expenditure, not *75 percent*—just as we observed in the last section.

Thus, the multiplier chain for each original dollar of spending shrinks from:

$$1 + 0.75 + (0.75)^2 + (0.75)^3 + \ldots = \frac{1}{(1 - 0.75)} = \frac{1}{0.25} = 4$$

to

$$1 + 0.6 + (0.6)^2 + (0.6)^3 + \ldots = \frac{1}{(1 - 0.6)} = \frac{1}{0.4} = 2.5$$

This is clearly a large reduction in the multiplier. We thus have a third reason why the oversimplified multiplier formula of Chapter 8 exaggerates the size of the multiplier: It ignores income taxes.

REASONS WHY THE OVERSIMPLIFIED MULTIPLIER FORMULA IS WRONG:

1. It ignores variable imports, which reduce the size of the multiplier (see Appendix B to Chapter 8).

2. It ignores price-level changes, which reduce the multiplier (see Chapter 9).

3. It ignores income taxes, which also reduce the size of the multiplier (this chapter).

The last of these three reasons is the most important in practice.

This conclusion about the multiplier is shown graphically in Figure 10-4, where we have drawn our $C + I + G + (X - IM)$ schedules with a slope of 0.6 rather than the 0.75 slope we used in earlier chapters. This new slope reflects an MPC of 0.75 and a tax rate of 20 percent. Figure 10-4 illustrates the effect of a $400 billion increase in government purchases of goods and services, which shifts the $C + I + G + (X - IM)$ schedule from $C + I + G_0 + (X - IM)$ to $C + I + G_1 + (X - IM)$. Equilibrium moves from point E_0 to point E_1—a GDP increase from $Y = \$6,000$ billion to $Y = \$7,000$ billion. Thus, if we ignore for the moment any increases in the price level (which would further reduce the multiplier), a $400 billion increment in government spending leads to a $1,000 billion increment in GDP. So, when taxes are included in our model, the multiplier is only $\$1,000/\$400 = 2.5$, just as we concluded before.

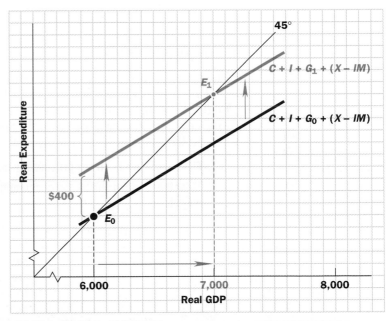

NOTE: Figures are in billions of dollars per year.

FIGURE 10-4
The Multiplier in the Presence of an Income Tax

Automatic Stabilizers

The size of the multiplier may seem to be a rather abstract notion with little practical importance. But such is not the case. Fluctuations in one or another of the components of total spending—C, I, G, or $X - IM$—happen all the time. Some come unexpectedly; some are even difficult to explain after the fact. We know from Chapter 8 that any such fluctuation will move GDP up or down by a multiplied amount. If the multiplier is smaller, GDP will be less sensitive to such shocks—that is, the economy will be less volatile.

An **automatic stabilizer** is a feature of the economy that reduces its sensitivity to shocks, such as sharp increases or decreases in spending.

Features of the economy that reduce its sensitivity to shocks are called **automatic stabilizers.** The most obvious example is the one we have just been discussing: the personal income tax. This tax acts as a shock absorber because it makes disposable income, and thus consumer spending, less sensitive to fluctuations in GDP. As we have just seen, when GDP rises, disposable income (*DI*) rises less because part of the increase in GDP is siphoned off by the U.S. Treasury. This leakage helps limit any increase in consumption spending. When GDP falls, *DI* falls less sharply because part of the loss is absorbed by the Treasury rather than by consumers. So consumption does not drop as much as it otherwise might. Thus, the much-maligned personal income tax is one of several features of our modern economy that helps ensure against a repeat performance of the Great Depression.

Our economy features many other automatic stabilizers. For example, Chapter 5 discussed the U.S. system of unemployment insurance. This program serves as an automatic stabilizer as well: When GDP drops and people lose their jobs, unemployment benefits prevent disposable incomes from falling as dramatically as earnings do. As a result, unemployed workers can maintain their spending better, and consumption fluctuates less than employment does.

The list could continue, but the basic principle remains the same: Each automatic stabilizer serves, in one way or another, as a shock absorber, thereby lowering the multiplier. And each does so quickly, without the need for any decision maker to take action. In a word, such stabilizers work *automatically*.

A case in point arose when the U.S. economy sagged in 2001. The budget surplus naturally shrank as tax receipts came in lower than had been expected. While there was much hand-wringing over the decline in what was then a budget surplus, most economists viewed it as a good thing: The automatic stabilizers were propping up spending, as they should. (Taxes were also cut *permanently* in 2001, which was much more controversial.)

◼ Multipliers for Tax Policy

Now let us turn our attention to multipliers for tax changes. They are more complicated than multipliers for spending because they work indirectly via consumption. For this reason, we will restrict ourselves to the multiplier for fixed taxes, leaving the more complicated case of variable taxes to more advanced courses. Tax multipliers must be worked out in two steps:

1. **Figure out how much any proposed or actual changes in the tax law will affect consumer spending.**

2. **Enter this vertical shift of the consumption schedule in the 45° line diagram and see how it affects output.**

To create a simple and familiar numerical example, suppose income taxes fall by a fixed amount at each level of GDP—say, by $400 billion. Step 1 instructs us to multiply the $400 billion tax cut by the marginal propensity to consume (MPC), which is 0.75, to get $300 billion as the decrease in consumer spending—that is, as the vertical shift of the consumption schedule.

Next, Step 2 instructs us to multiply this $300 billion increase in consumption by the multiplier—which is 2.5 in our example—giving $750 billion as the rise in GDP. Figure 10-5 verifies that this result is correct by depicting a $300 billion vertical shift of the consumption function in the 45° line diagram and noting that GDP does indeed rise by $750 billion as a consequence—from $6,000 billion to $6,750 billion.

Notice something interesting here. The $400 billion tax cut raises GDP by $750 billion, whereas the multiplier effect of the $400 billion increase in

◼ **FIGURE 10-5**

The Multiplier for a Reduction in Fixed Taxes

government purchases depicted in Figure 10-4 raised GDP by $1,000 billion. What's going on here? Apparently:

The multiplier for changes in fixed taxes is smaller than the multiplier for changes in government purchases.

The reason is no mystery. Although G is a direct component of total expenditure, taxes are not. Taxes work indirectly, by *first* changing disposable income, which *then* changes C according to the MPC. Because some of the change in disposable income affects *saving* rather than *spending*, a $1 tax cut does not pack as much punch as $1 of G. That is why we multiplied the $400 billion change in taxes by 0.75 to get the $300 billion shift of the C schedule shown in Figure 10-5.

The fact that the multiplier for taxes is smaller than the multiplier for G has several interesting implications.

Issue Revisited: The Japanese Economy

The first implication pertains to the debate over Japanese fiscal policy mentioned at the beginning of this chapter. It really is true that a tax cut should pack less punch than a spending increase of equal dollar (or yen) amount. How much less? That depends on the marginal propensity to consume. Some people believed that the MPC in Japan in 2001 was extremely low because consumers were insecure. If so, the tax-cut multiplier would have been much smaller than the expenditure multiplier—as the government of Japan claimed.

Second, different multipliers for government purchases and taxes imply that if the government raises G and T by equal amounts, the effects do not cancel out. Instead, the equilibrium level of GDP on the demand side rises. For example, we have seen that a $400 billion increase in G raises GDP by $1,000 billion, whereas a $400 billion cut in T raises GDP by just $750 billion. Thus, if *both* G and T are *raised* by $400 billion, GDP will go up by $250 billion.

The moral of the story is that fiscal policies that seem to keep the *deficit*, $G - T$, the same do not necessarily keep *aggregate demand* the same. A cut in government spending balanced by an equal cut in tax revenues can be expected to reduce Y—a lesson that policymakers frequently forget.

Government Transfer Payments

The last major tool of fiscal policy is *government transfer payments*. Transfers, as you will remember, are payments to individuals that do not compensate them for any direct contribution to production. How are transfers treated in our models of income determination—like purchases of goods and services (G) or like taxes (T)?

The answer to this question follows readily from the circular flow diagram on page 124 or the accounting identity on page 125. The important thing to understand about transfer payments is that they intervene between gross domestic product (Y) and disposable income (DI) in precisely the *opposite* way from income taxes.

Specifically, starting with the wages, interest, rents, and profits that constitute national income, we *subtract* income taxes to calculate disposable income. We do so because these taxes represent the portion of incomes that consumers *earn* but never *receive*. But then we must *add* transfer payments because they represent sources of income that are *received* although they were not *earned* in the process of production. Thus:

Transfer payments are basically negative taxes.

For this reason, giving consumers $400 billion in the form of transfer payments is treated in the 45° line diagram as a $400 billion decrease in taxes. Thus, Figure 10-5, which we devised to illustrate a tax cut, also illustrates a rise in unemployment benefits, or in Social Security benefits, or any other such transfer payment.

PLANNING EXPANSIONARY FISCAL POLICY

SOURCE: © R. J. Matson, *Roll Call*

Now imagine you were a member of the U.S. Congress (or the Japanese Diet) trying to decide whether to use fiscal policy to stimulate the economy in 2001—and, if so, by how much. Suppose the economy would have a GDP of $6,000 billion if the government simply reenacted last year's budget. Suppose further that your goal is to achieve a fully employed labor force and that staff economists tell you that reaching this milestone would require a GDP of approximately $7,000 billion. Finally, just to keep the calculations manageable, imagine that the price level is fixed. What sort of budget should you vote for?

This chapter has taught us that the government has three ways to raise GDP by $1,000 billion. Congress can close the recessionary gap between actual and potential GDP by:

- Raising government purchases
- Reducing taxes
- Increasing transfer payments

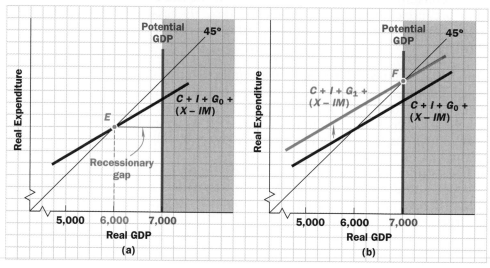

Figure 10-6 illustrates the problem, and its cure through higher government spending, on our 45° line diagram. Figure 10-6(a) shows the equilibrium of the economy if no changes are made in the budget. Except for the full-employment line at $Y = \$7,000$ and the corresponding recessionary gap, it looks just like Figure 10-3. With an expenditure multiplier of 2.5, you can figure out that an additional $400 billion of government spending will be needed to push GDP up by $1,000 billion and eliminate the gap ($400 × 2.5 = $1,000).

NOTE: Figures are in billions of dollars per year.

■ FIGURE 10-6
Fiscal Policy to Eliminate a Recessionary Gap

So you might vote to raise G from $G_0 = \$1,300$ billion to $G_1 = \$1,700$ billion, hoping to move the $C + I + G + (X - IM)$ line in Figure 10-6(a) up to the position indicated in Figure 10-6(b), thereby achieving full employment. Or you might prefer to achieve this fiscal stimulus by lowering income taxes. Or you might opt for more generous transfer payments. The point is that a variety of budgets are capable of increasing GDP by $1,000 billion. Figure 10-6 applies equally well to any of them. President George W. Bush favored tax cuts, which is the tool the U.S government relied upon in 2001. Especially after September 11th, encouraging consumers to spend more via tax cuts became a national priority.

PLANNING CONTRACTIONARY FISCAL POLICY

The preceding example assumed that the basic problem of fiscal policy is to close a recessionary gap. But only two years before, in 1999, many economists believed that the major macroeconomic problem in the United States was just the opposite: Real GDP exceeded potential GDP, leading to an inflationary gap. In such a case, government would wish to adopt more restrictive fiscal policies to reduce aggregate demand.

It does not take much imagination to run our previous analysis in reverse. If an inflationary gap would arise from a continuation of current budget policies, contractionary fiscal policy tools can eliminate it. By cutting spending, raising taxes, or by some combination of the two, the government can pull the $C + G + I + (X - IM)$ schedule down to a noninflationary position and achieve an equilibrium at full employment.

Notice the difference between this way of eliminating an inflationary gap and the natural self-correcting mechanism that we discussed in the last chapter. There we observed that, if the economy were left to its own devices, a cumulative but self-limiting process of inflation would eventually eliminate the inflationary gap and return the economy to full employment. Here we see that we need not put the economy through the inflationary wringer. Instead, a restrictive fiscal policy can avoid inflation by limiting aggregate demand to the level that the economy can produce at full employment.

THE CHOICE BETWEEN SPENDING POLICY AND TAX POLICY

In principle, fiscal policy can nudge the economy in the desired direction equally well by changing government spending or by changing taxes. For example, if the government wants to expand the economy, it can raise G or lower T. Either policy would shift the total expenditure schedule upward, as depicted in Figure 10-6, thereby raising the equilibrium GDP on the demand side.

In terms of our aggregate demand and supply diagram, either policy shifts the aggregate demand curve outward, from D_0D_0 to D_1D_1 in Figure 10-7. As a result, the economy's equilibrium moves from point E to point A. Both real GDP and the price level rise. As this diagram points out:

Any combination of higher spending and lower taxes that produces the same aggregate demand curve leads to the same increases in real GDP and prices.

How, then, do policymakers decide whether to raise spending or to cut taxes? The answer depends mainly on how large a public sector they want to create—a major issue in the long-running debate in the United States over the proper size of government.

The small-government point of view, typically advocated by conservatives, says that we are foolish to rely on the public sector to do what private individuals and businesses can do better on their own. Conservatives believe that the growth of government interferes too much in our everyday lives, thereby curtailing our freedom. Those who hold this view can argue for *tax cuts* when macroeconomic considerations call for expansionary fiscal policy (as President Bush has done), and for *lower public spending* when contractionary policy is required.

An opposing opinion, expressed most often by liberals, holds that something is amiss when a country as wealthy as the United States has such an impoverished public sector. In this view, America's most pressing needs are not for more fast food and video games but rather for better schools, more efficient public transportation systems, and cleaner and safer city streets. People on this side of the debate believe that we should *increase* spending when the economy needs stimulus and pay for

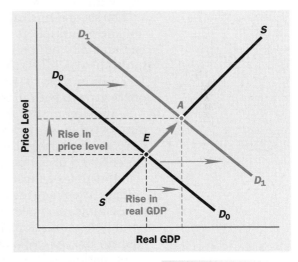

■ FIGURE 10-7
Expansionary Fiscal Policy

"Free gifts to every kid in the world? Are you a Keynesian or something?"

SOURCE: From *The Wall Street Journal*—Permission, Cartoon Features Syndicate

these improved public services by *increasing taxes* when it is necessary to rein in the economy.

The use of fiscal policy for economic stabilization is sometimes erroneously associated with a large and growing public sector—that is, with "big government." This need not be the case.

Individuals favoring a smaller public sector can advocate an active fiscal policy just as well as those who favor a larger public sector. Advocates of bigger government should seek to expand demand (when appropriate) through higher government spending and contract demand (when appropriate) through tax increases. By contrast, advocates of smaller government should seek to expand demand by cutting taxes and reduce demand by cutting expenditures.

SOME HARSH REALITIES

The mechanics outlined so far in this chapter make the fiscal policy planner's job look much simpler than it really is. The elementary diagrams suggest, rather misleadingly, that policymakers can drive GDP to any level they please simply by manipulating spending and tax programs. It seems they should be able to hit the full-employment bull's eye every time. In fact, a better analogy is to a poor rifleman shooting through dense fog at an erratically moving target with an inaccurate gun and slow-moving bullets.

The target is moving because, in the real world, the investment, net exports, and consumption schedules constantly shift about as expectations, technology, events abroad, and other factors change. For all of these reasons and others, the policies decided on today, which will take effect at some future date, may no longer be appropriate by the time that future date rolls around.

The second misleading feature of our diagrams (the "inaccurate gun") is that we do not know multipliers with the precision of our examples. Although our best guess may be that a $20 billion cut in government purchases will reduce GDP by $35 billion (a multiplier of 1.75), the actual outcome may be as little as $20 billion or as much as $50 billion. It is therefore impossible to "fine-tune" every wobble out of the economy's growth path. Economic science is simply not that precise.

A third complication is that our target—full-employment GDP—may be only dimly visible, as if through a fog. For example, a lively debate has raged in recent years over whether the unemployment rate that corresponds to full employment is closer to 4.5 or 5.5 percent.

A fourth complication is that fiscal policy "bullets" travel slowly: Tax and spending policies affect aggregate demand only after some time elapses. Consumer spending, for example, may take months to react to an income tax cut. Because of these *time lags*, fiscal policy decisions must be based on *forecasts* of the future state of the economy. And no one has yet discovered a foolproof method of economic forecasting. The combination of long lags and poor forecasts may occasionally leave the government fighting the last inflation just as the new recession gets under way.

And finally, the people aiming the fiscal "rifle" are politicians, not economic technicians. Sometimes political considerations lead to policies far different from what textbook economics would suggest. And even when they do not, the wheels of Congress grind slowly.

In addition to all of these operational problems, legislators trying to decide whether to push the unemployment rate lower would like to know how large the inflation cost is likely to be. As we know, an expansionary fiscal policy that reduces a recessionary gap by increasing aggregate demand will lower unemployment. But it also tends to be inflationary. This undesirable side effect may make the government hesitant to use fiscal policy to combat recessions.

Is there a way out of this dilemma? Can we carry on the battle against unemployment without aggravating inflation? For about 25 years, a small but influential minority of economists, journalists, and politicians have argued that we can. They call their approach "supply-side economics." The idea helped sweep Ronald Reagan to smashing electoral victories in 1980 and 1984 and was revived in the 2000 presidential campaign by candidate George W. Bush. Just what is supply-side economics?

THE IDEA BEHIND SUPPLY-SIDE TAX CUTS

The central idea of supply-side economics is that certain types of tax cuts will increase aggregate supply. For example, taxes can be cut in ways that raise the rewards for working, saving, and investing. *If people actually respond to these incentives*, such tax cuts will increase the total labor and capital supplies in the economy, thereby increasing aggregate supply.

Figure 10-8 illustrates the idea on an aggregate supply and demand diagram. If policy measures can shift the economy's aggregate supply to position $S_1 S_1$, then prices will be lower and output higher than if the aggregate supply curve remained at $S_0 S_0$. Policymakers will have reduced inflation and raised real output at the same time—as shown by point B in the figure. The trade-off between inflation and unemployment will therefore have been defeated. This is the goal of supply-side economics.

What sorts of policies do supply-siders advocate? Here is a small sample of their long list of recommended tax cuts:

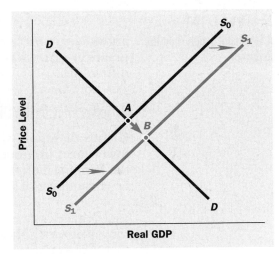

■ FIGURE 10-8
The Goal of Supply-Side Tax Cuts

Lower Personal Income Tax Rates   Sharp cuts in personal taxes were the cornerstone of the economic strategies of Presidents Reagan and George W. Bush. Tax rates on individuals were reduced in stages between 1981 and 1984, and we are now in the process of doing so again. The 2001 and 2003 tax acts reduced the four upper tax bracket rates (which were 39.6 percent, 36 percent, 31 percent, and 28 percent) to 35 percent, 33 percent, 28 percent, and 25 percent respectively. In addition, some very-low-income taxpayers have seen their tax rate fall from 15 percent to 10 percent. Lower tax rates, supply-siders argue, augment the supplies of both labor and capital.

Reduce Taxes on Income from Savings   One extreme form of this proposal would simply exempt from taxation all income from interest and dividends. Because income must be either consumed or saved, doing this would, in effect, change our present personal income tax into a tax on consumer spending. Several such proposals for radical tax reform have been considered in Washington over the years, but never adopted. However, Congress did reduce the tax rate on dividends to just 15 percent in 2003.

Reduce Taxes on Capital Gains   When investors sell assets for a profit, that profit is called a *capital gain* on their investments. Supply-siders argue that the government can encourage more investment by taxing capital gains at lower rates than ordinary income. This proposal was last acted upon in 2003, when the top rate on capital gains was cut to 15 percent.

Reduce the Corporate Income Tax   By reducing the tax burden on corporations, proponents argue, the government can provide both greater investment incentives (by raising the profitability of investment) and more investable funds (by letting companies keep more of their earnings). This advice was followed in 1986.

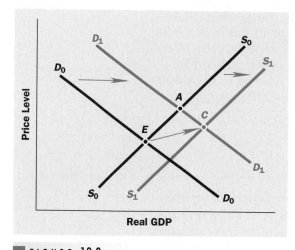

FIGURE 10-9

A Successful Supply-Side Tax Reduction

Let us suppose, for the moment, that a successful supply-side tax cut is enacted. Because *both* aggregate demand *and* aggregate supply increase simultaneously, the economy may be able to avoid the painful inflationary consequences of an expansionary fiscal policy shown in Figure 10-7 (page 193).

Figure 10-9 illustrates this conclusion. The two aggregate demand curves and the initial aggregate supply curve S_0S_0 carry over directly from Figure 10-7. But now we have introduced an additional supply curve, S_1S_1, to reflect the successful supply-side tax cut depicted in Figure 10-8. The equilibrium point for the economy moves from E to C, whereas with a conventional demand-side tax cut it would have moved from E to A. As compared with point A, which reflects only the demand-side effects of a tax cut, output is higher and prices are lower at point C.

A good deal, you say! And indeed it is. The supply-side argument is extremely attractive in principle. The question is: Does it work in practice? Can we actually do what is depicted in Figure 10-9? Let us consider some difficulties.

Some Flies in the Ointment

Critics of supply-side economics rarely question its goals or the basic idea that lower taxes improve incentives. They argue, instead, that supply-siders exaggerate the beneficial effects of tax cuts and ignore some undesirable side effects. Here is a brief rundown of some of their main objections.

Small Magnitude of Supply-Side Effects   The first objection is that supply-siders are simply too optimistic: No one knows how to do what Figure 10-9 shows. Although it is easy, for example, to design tax incentives that make saving more *attractive* financially, people may not actually respond to these incentives. In fact, most of the statistical evidence suggests that we should not expect much from tax incentives for saving. As economist Charles Schultze once quipped: "There's nothing wrong with supply-side economics that division by 10 couldn't cure."

Demand-Side Effects   The second objection is that supply-siders ignore the effects of tax cuts on aggregate demand. If you cut personal taxes, for example, individuals *may possibly* work more. But they *will certainly* spend more.

The joint implications of these two objections appear in Figure 10-10. This figure depicts a *small* outward shift of the aggregate supply curve (which reflects the first objection) and a *large* outward shift of the aggregate demand curve (which reflects the second objection). The result is that the economy's equilibrium moves from point E (the intersection of S_0S_0 and D_0D_0) to point C (the intersection of S_1S_1 and D_1D_1). Prices rise as output expands. The outcome differs only a little from the straight "demand-side" fiscal stimulus depicted in Figure 10-7.

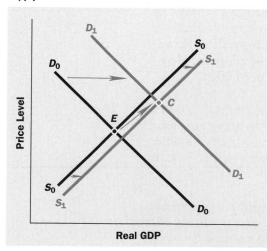

FIGURE 10-10

A More Pessimistic View of Supply-Side Tax Cuts

Problems with Timing   Investment incentives are the most promising type of supply-side tax cuts. But the benefits from greater investment do not arrive by overnight mail. In particular, the *expenditures* on investment goods almost certainly come before any *expansion of capacity*. Thus supply-side tax cuts have their primary short-run effects on aggregate demand. Effects on aggregate supply come later.

Supply-Side Economics and Presidential Elections

A s we have mentioned, Ronald Reagan won landslide victories in 1980 and 1984 by running on a supply-side platform. But in 1992, candidate Bill Clinton attacked supply-side economics as "trickle-down economics," arguing that it had failed. He emphasized the last two drawbacks of such a fiscal policy mentioned in our assessment: the effects on income inequality and on the budget deficit. The voters apparently agreed with his analysis.

The hallmark of Clintonomics was, first, reducing the budget deficit that Clinton had inherited from the first President George Bush, and second, building up a large surplus. This policy succeeded. The huge budget deficit turned into a large surplus, the economy boomed, and Clinton, like Reagan before him, was elected twice.

In the 2000 presidential election, the voters once again switched their allegiance. During the campaign, it was candidate Al Gore who promised to continue the "fiscal responsibility" of the Clinton years, while candidate George W. Bush echoed Reagan by offering large tax cuts. Bush won.[1]

So which approach do American voters really prefer? They appear to be fickle! But one thing is clear: The debate over fiscal policy played a major role in determining each of the last six presidential elections.

SOURCE: (a) © CORBIS; (b) and (c) © Wally McNamee/CORBIS; (d) © AFP/Corbis

[1] To those who would interpret the election of 2000 as a vote for the tax cut, cynics will point out that Gore won the popular vote.

Effects on Income Distribution   The preceding objections all pertain to the likely effects of supply-side policies on aggregate supply and demand. But a different problem bears mentioning: Most supply-side initiatives increase income inequality. Indeed, some tilt toward the rich is an almost inescapable corollary of supply-side logic. The basic aim of supply-side economics is to increase the incentives for working and investing—that is, to increase the gap between the rewards of those who succeed in the economic game (by working hard, investing well, or just plain being lucky) and those who fail. It can hardly be surprising, therefore, that supply-side policies tend to increase economic inequality.

Losses of Tax Revenue   You can hardly help noticing that most of the policies suggested by supply-siders involve cutting one tax or another. Thus supply-side tax cuts are bound to raise the government budget deficit. This problem proved to be the Achilles' heel of supply-side economics in the United States in the 1980s. It left behind a legacy of budget deficits that took 15 years to overcome. Opponents argued against George W. Bush's proposals for large income-tax reductions on similar grounds: They would use up the surplus, and turn it into a deficit. And they have.

Toward an Assessment of Supply-Side Economics

On balance, most economists have reached the following conclusions about supply-side tax initiatives:

1. **The likely effectiveness of supply-side tax cuts depends on what kinds of taxes are cut. Tax reductions aimed at stimulating business investment are likely to pack more punch than tax reductions aimed at getting people to work longer hours or to save more.**

2. Such tax cuts probably will increase aggregate supply much more slowly than they increase aggregate demand. Thus, supply-side policies should not be regarded as a substitute for short-run stabilization policy, but rather as a way to promote (slightly) faster economic growth in the long run.

3. Demand-side effects of supply-side tax cuts are likely to overwhelm supply-side effects in the short run.

4. Supply-side tax cuts are likely to widen income inequalities.

5. Supply-side tax cuts are almost certain to lead to smaller budget surpluses or larger deficits.

Some people will look over this list and decide that they favor supply-side tax cuts; others, perusing the same facts, will reach the opposite conclusion. We cannot say that either group is wrong because, like almost every economic policy, supply-side economics has its pros and cons and involves value judgments that color people's conclusions.

Why, then, did so many economists and politicians react so negatively to supply-side economics as preached and practiced in the early 1980s and again in recent years? The main reason seems to be that the claims made by the most ardent supply-siders were clearly excessive. Naturally, these claims proved wrong. But showing that wild claims are wild does not eliminate the kernel of truth in supply-side economics: Reductions in marginal tax rates *do* improve economic incentives. Any specific supply-side tax cut must be judged on its individual merits.

SUMMARY

1. The government's **fiscal policy** is its plan for managing aggregate demand through its spending and taxing programs. This policy is made jointly by the president and Congress.

2. The government's net effect on aggregate demand—and hence on equilibrium output and prices—depends on whether the expansionary effects of its spending are greater or smaller than the contractionary effects of its taxes.

3. Because consumer spending (*C*) depends on disposable income (*DI*), and *DI* is GDP minus taxes, any change in taxes will shift the consumption schedule on a 45° line diagram. The nature of this shift depends on whether **fixed taxes** or **variable taxes** are changed.

4. Such shifts in the consumption function caused by tax policy are subject to the same multiplier as autonomous shifts in *G*, *I*, or *X − IM*.

5. An income tax reduces the size of this common multiplier.

6. The multiplier for changes in taxes is smaller than the multiplier for changes in government purchases, because each $1 of tax cuts leads to less than $1 of increased spending.

7. Government transfer payments act like negative taxes, rather than like government purchases of goods and services, because they influence total spending only indirectly through their effect on consumption.

8. If the multipliers were known precisely, it would be possible to plan any of a variety of fiscal policies to eliminate either a recessionary gap or an inflationary gap. Recessionary gaps can be cured by raising *G*, cutting taxes, or increasing transfers. Inflationary gaps can be cured by cutting *G*, raising taxes, or reducing transfers.

9. Active stabilization policy can be carried out either by means that tend to expand the size of government (by raising either *G* or *T* when appropriate) or by means that reduce the size of government (by reducing either *G* or *T* when appropriate).

10. Expansionary fiscal policy can cure recessions, but it normally exacts a cost in terms of higher inflation. This dilemma has led to a great deal of interest in "supply-side" tax cuts designed to stimulate aggregate supply.

11. **Supply-side tax cuts** aim to push the economy's aggregate supply curve outward to the right. When successful, they can expand the economy and reduce inflation at the same time—a highly desirable outcome.

12. But critics point out at least five serious problems with supply-side tax cuts: They also stimulate aggregate demand; the beneficial effects on aggregate supply may be small; the demand-side effects occur before the supply-side effects; they make the income distribution more unequal; and large tax cuts lead to large budget deficits.

KEY TERMS

Fiscal policy 186	Fixed taxes 186	Automatic stabilizer 190
Variable taxes 186	Effect of income taxes on the multiplier 189	Supply-side tax cuts 195

QUESTIONS FOR REVIEW

1. The U.S. defense budget shrank from the end of the Cold War until the 9/11 attacks. How would GDP in the United States have been affected if the reduced defense spending were used to:

   a. Reduce the budget deficit, so that government purchases fell?

   b. Free funds for other public purposes, so that government purchases remained the same?

2. Consider an economy in which tax collections are always $800 and in which the four components of aggregate demand are as follows:

GDP	Taxes	DI	C	I	G	(X − IM)
$1,360	$800	$560	$420	$200	$800	$30
1,480	800	680	510	200	800	30
1,600	800	800	600	200	800	30
1,720	800	920	690	200	800	30
1,840	800	1,040	780	200	800	30

Find the equilibrium of this economy graphically. What is the marginal propensity to consume? What is the multiplier? What would happen to equilibrium GDP if government purchases were reduced by $60 and the price level remained unchanged?

3. Consider an economy similar to that in Review Question 2 in which investment is also $200, government purchases are also $800, net exports are also $30, and the price level is also fixed. But taxes now vary with income, and as a result the consumption schedule looks like the following:

GDP	Taxes	DI	C
$1,360	$720	$640	$510
1,480	760	720	570
1,600	800	800	630
1,720	840	880	690
1,840	880	960	750

Find the equilibrium graphically. What is the marginal propensity to consume? What is the tax rate? Use your diagram to show the effect of a decrease of $60 in govern-

ment purchases. What is the multiplier? Compare this answer to your answer to Review Question 2. What do you conclude?

4. Explain why G has the same multiplier as I, but taxes have a different multiplier.

5. Return to the hypothetical economy in Review Question 2 and suppose that *both* taxes and government purchases are increased by $120. Find the new equilibrium under the assumption that consumer spending continues to be exactly three-quarters of disposable income (as it is in Review Question 2).

6. If the government today decides that aggregate demand is excessive and is causing inflation, what options are open to it? What if the government decides that aggregate demand is too weak instead?

7. Suppose that you are in charge of the fiscal policy for the economy described in Review Question 2. There is an inflationary gap, and you want to reduce income by $120. What specific actions can you take to achieve this goal?

8. Now put yourself in charge of the economy in Review Question 3, and suppose that full employment comes at a GDP of $1,840. How can you push income up to that level?

9. Which of the proposed supply-side tax cuts appeals to you most? Draw up a list of arguments for and against enacting such a cut right now.

10. **(More difficult)** Advocates of lower taxes on capital gains argue that this type of tax cut will raise aggregate supply by spurring business investment. But, of course, any increase in investment spending will also raise aggregate demand. Compare the effects on aggregate supply, aggregate demand, and tax revenues of three different ways to cut the capital gains tax:

    a. Reduce capital gains taxes on *all* investments, including those that were made before tax rates were cut.

    b. Reduce capital gains taxes only on investments made after tax rates are cut.

    c. Reduce capital gains taxes only on certain types of investments, such as corporate stocks and bonds.

    Which of the three options seems most desirable to you? Why?

APPENDIX Algebraic Treatment of Fiscal Policy and Aggregate Demand

In this appendix, we explain the simple algebra behind the fiscal policy multipliers discussed in Chapter 10. In so doing, we deal only with a simplified case in which prices do not change. Although it is possible to work out the corresponding algebra for the more realistic aggregate demand—aggregate supply analysis with variable prices—the

analysis is rather complicated and is best left to more advanced courses.

We start with the example used in the chapter (especially on pages 189–191). The government spends $1,300 billion on goods and services (G = 1,300) and levies an income tax equal to 20 percent of GDP. So, if the symbol T denotes tax receipts,

$$T = 0.20Y$$

Because the consumption function we have been working with is

$$C = 300 + 0.75DI$$

where DI is disposable income, and because disposable income and GDP are related by the accounting identity

$$DI = Y - T$$

it follows that the C schedule used in the 45° line diagram is described by the following algebraic equation:

$$C = 300 + 0.75(Y - T)$$
$$= 300 + 0.75(Y - 0.20Y)$$
$$= 300 + 0.75(0.80Y)$$
$$= 300 + 0.60Y$$

We can now apply the equilibrium condition:

$$Y = C + I + G + (X - IM)$$

Because investment in this example is $I = 900$ and net exports are -100, substituting for C, I, G, and $(X - IM)$ into this equation gives:

$$Y = 300 + 0.60Y + 900 + 1,300 - 100$$
$$0.40Y = 2,400$$
$$\mathbf{Y = 6,000}$$

This is all there is to finding equilibrium GDP in an economy with a government.

To find the multiplier for government spending, increase G by 1 and solve the problem again:

$$Y = C + I + G + (X - IM)$$
$$Y = 300 + 0.60Y + 900 + 1,301 - 100$$
$$0.40Y = 2,401$$
$$\mathbf{Y = 6,002.5}$$

Thus the multiplier is $6,002.5 - 6,000 = 2.5$, as stated in the text.

To find the multiplier for an increase in fixed taxes, change the tax schedule as follows:

$$T = 0.20Y + 1$$

Disposable income is then

$$DI = Y - T = Y - (0.20Y + 1) = 0.80Y - 1$$

so the consumption function is

$$C = 300 + 0.75DI$$
$$= 300 + 0.75(0.80Y - 1)$$
$$= 299.25 + 0.60Y$$

Solving for equilibrium GDP as usual gives:

$$Y = C + I + G + (X - IM)$$
$$Y = 299.25 + 0.60Y + 900 + 1,300 - 100$$
$$0.40Y = 2,399.25$$
$$\mathbf{Y = 5,998.125}$$

So a \$1 increase in fixed taxes lowers Y by \$1.875. The tax multiplier is -1.875.

Now let us proceed to a more general solution, using symbols rather than specific numbers. The equations of the model are as follows:

$$Y = C + I + G + (X - IM) \tag{1}$$

is the usual equilibrium condition.

$$C = a + bDI \tag{2}$$

is the same consumption function we used in Appendix A of Chapter 8.

$$DI = Y - T \tag{3}$$

is the accounting identity relating disposable income to GDP.

$$T = T_0 + tY \tag{4}$$

is the tax function, where T_0 represents fixed taxes (which are zero in our numerical example) and t represents the tax rate (which is 0.20 in the example). Finally, I, G, and $(X - IM)$ are just fixed numbers.

We begin the solution by substituting Equations (3) and (4) into Equation (2) to derive the consumption schedule relating C to Y:

$$C = a + bDI$$
$$C = a + b(Y - T)$$
$$C = a + b(Y - T_0 - tY)$$
$$C = a - bT_0 + b(1 - t)Y \tag{5}$$

Notice that a change in fixed taxes (T_0) *shifts the intercept* of the C schedule, whereas a change in the tax rate (t) changes its *slope*, as explained in the chapter (pages 186–188).

Next, substitute Equation (5) into Equation (1) to find equilibrium GDP:

$$Y = C + I + G + (X - IM)$$
$$Y = a - bT_0 + b(1 - t)Y + I + G + (X - IM)$$
$$[1 - b(1 - t)]\, Y = a - bT_0 + I + G + (X - IM)$$

or

$$\mathbf{Y = \dfrac{a - bT_0 + I + G + (X - IM)}{1 - b(1 - t)}} \tag{6}$$

Equation (6) shows us that the multiplier for G, I, a, or $(X - IM)$ is

$$\mathbf{Multiplier = \dfrac{1}{1 - b(1 - t)}}$$

To see that this is, in fact, the multiplier, raise any of G, I, a, or $(X - IM)$ by one unit. In each case, Equation (6) would be changed to read:

$$Y = \frac{a - bT_0 + I + G + (X - IM) + 1}{1 - b(1 - t)}$$

Subtracting Equation (6) from this expression gives the change in Y stemming from a one-unit change in G, I, or a:

$$\text{Change in } Y = \frac{1}{1 - b(1 - t)}$$

In Chapter 8 (page 157), we noted that if there were no income tax ($t = 0$), a realistic value for b (the marginal propensity to consume) would yield a multiplier of 10, which is much bigger than the true multiplier. Now that we have added taxes to the model, our multiplier formula produces much more realistic numbers. Approximate values for these parameters for the U.S. economy are $b = 0.90$ and $t = \frac{1}{3}$. The multiplier formula then gives

$$\text{Multiplier} = \frac{1}{1 - 0.90(1 - \frac{1}{3})}$$
$$= \frac{1}{1 - \frac{3}{5}} = \frac{1}{\frac{2}{5}} = 2.50$$

which is not far from its actual estimated value—between 1.5 and 2.

Finally, we can see from Equation (6) that the multiplier for a change in fixed taxes (T_0) is:

$$\textbf{Tax Multiplier} = \frac{-b}{1 - b(1 - t)}$$

For the example considered in the text and earlier in this appendix, $b = 0.75$ and $t = 0.20$, so the formula gives:

$$\frac{-0.75}{1 - 0.75(1 - 0.20)} = \frac{-0.75}{1 - 0.75(0.80)}$$

$$= \frac{-0.75}{1 - 0.60} = \frac{-0.75}{0.40} = -1.875$$

According to these figures, each \$1 *increase* in T_0 *reduces* Y by \$1.875.

QUESTIONS FOR REVIEW

1. Consider an economy described by the following set of equations:

$$C = 120 + 0.80DI$$
$$I = 320$$
$$G = 480$$
$$(X - IM) = -80$$
$$T = 200 + 0.25Y$$

Find the equilibrium level of GDP. Next, find the multipliers for government purchases and for fixed taxes. If full employment comes at $Y = 1,800$, what are some policies that would move GDP to that level?

2. This question is a variant of the previous problem that approaches things in the way that a fiscal policy planner might. In an economy whose consumption function and tax function are as given in Review Question 1, with investment fixed at 320 and net exports fixed at −80, find the value of G that would make GDP equal to 1,800.

3. You are given the following information about an economy:

$$C = 0.90DI$$
$$I = 100$$
$$G = 540$$
$$(X - IM) = -40$$
$$T = (\tfrac{1}{3})Y$$

a. Find equilibrium GDP and the budget deficit.

b. Suppose the government, unhappy with the budget deficit, decides to cut government spending by precisely the amount of the deficit you found in Review Question 3(a). What actually happens to GDP and the budget deficit, and why?

4. **(More difficult)** In the economy considered in Review Question 3, suppose the government, seeing that it has not wiped out the deficit, keeps cutting G until it succeeds in balancing the budget. What level of GDP will then prevail?

11

Money and the Banking System

[Money] is a machine for doing quickly and commodiously what would be done, though less quickly and commodiously, without it.

JOHN STUART MILL

The circular flow diagrams of earlier chapters had a "financial system" in the upper-left corner. (Look back, for example, at Figure 8-1 on page 145.) Savings flowed into this system and investment flowed out. Something obviously goes on *inside* the financial system to channel the savings back into investment, and it is time we learned just what this something is.

There is another, equally important, reason for studying the financial system. The government exercises significant control over aggregate demand by manipulating *monetary policy* as well as fiscal policy. Indeed, most observers nowadays see monetary policy as the more important stabilization tool. To understand how monetary policy works (the subject of Chapters 12 and 13), we must first acquire some understanding of the banking and financial system. By the end of this chapter, you will have that understanding.

CONTENTS

Issue: Why Are Banks so Heavily Regulated?

Banking has long been one of the most heavily regulated industries in America. But the pendulum of bank regulation has swung back and forth.

In the late 1970s and early 1980s, the United States eased several restrictions on interest rates and permissible bank activities. Then, after a number of banks and savings institutions went bankrupt in the 1980s, Congress and the bank regulatory agencies cracked down with stiffer regulation and closer scrutiny. Later, the pendulum swung back in the deregulatory direction, with two landmark banking laws in the 1990s. Most restrictions on banking across state lines were lifted in 1994. And the once-strict separation of banking from insurance and investment banking was more or less ended in 1999.

So how much bank regulation is enough—or too much? To answer this question, we must first address a more basic one: Why were banks so heavily regulated in the first place?

A first reason is that the major "output" of the banking industry—the nation's money supply—is *an important determinant of aggregate demand,* as we will learn in the next chapter. Bank managers are paid to do what is best for their stockholders. But as we will see, what is best for bank stockholders may not be best for the economy as a whole. Consequently, the government does not allow bankers to determine the money supply strictly on profit considerations.

A second reason for the extensive web of bank regulation is concern for the *safety of depositors.* In a free-enterprise system, new businesses are born and die every day; and no one other than the people immediately involved takes much notice. When a firm goes bankrupt, stockholders lose money and employees may lose their jobs. But, except for the case of very large firms, that is about all that happens.

But banking is different. If banks were treated like other firms, depositors would lose money whenever one went bankrupt. That outcome is bad enough by itself, but the real danger emerges in the case of a **run on a bank.** When depositors get jittery about the security of their money, they may all rush to cash in their accounts. For reasons we will learn about in this chapter, most banks cannot survive such a "run" and would be forced to shut their doors.

> A **run on a bank** occurs when many depositors withdraw cash from their accounts all at once.

Worse yet, this disease is highly *contagious.* If one family hears that their neighbors just lost their life savings because their bank went broke, they are likely to rush to their own bank to withdraw their funds. In fact, that is precisely what happened in Argentina when people lost confidence in the local banks in January and February 2002.[1]

Without modern forms of bank regulation, therefore, one bank failure might lead to another. Indeed, bank failures were common throughout most of U.S. history. (See Figure 11-1.) But since the 1930s, bank failures have been less common. And they have rarely been precipitated by runs because the government has taken steps to ensure that such an infectious disease will not spread. It has done so in several ways that we will mention in this chapter.

THE NATURE OF MONEY

Money is so much a part of our daily existence that we take it for granted and fail to appreciate all that it accomplishes. But money is in no sense "natural." Like the wheel, it had to be invented.

The most obvious way to trade commodities is not by using money, but by **barter**—a system in which people exchange one good directly for another. And the best way to appreciate what monetary exchange accomplishes is to imagine a world without it.

> **Barter** is a system of exchange in which people directly trade one good for another, without using money as an intermediate step.

---

[1] As will be explained in Chapter 17, the Argentine crisis had much to do with worries about the exchange rate between the Argentine peso and the U.S. dollar.

SOURCE: Federal Deposit Insurance Corporation.

FIGURE 11-1

Bank Failures in the United States, 1915–2002

Barter versus Monetary Exchange

Under a system of direct barter, if Farmer Jones grows corn and has a craving for peanuts, he has to find a peanut farmer, say, Farmer Smith, with a taste for corn. If he finds such a person (a situation called the *double coincidence of wants*), the two farmers make the trade. If that sounds easy, try to imagine how busy Farmer Jones would be if he had to repeat the sequence for everything he consumed in a week. For the most part, the desired double coincidences of wants are more likely to turn out to be double wants of coincidence. (See the accompanying cartoon.) Jones gets no peanuts and Smith gets no corn. Worse yet, with so much time spent looking for trading partners, Jones would have far less time to grow corn. In brief:

Money greases the wheels of exchange, and thus makes the whole economy more productive.

Under a monetary system, Farmer Jones gives up his corn for money. He does so not because he wants the money per se, but because of what that money can buy. Now

SOURCE: By permission of Johnny Hart and Creators Syndicate, Inc.

Dealing by Wheeling on Yap

Primitive forms of money still exist in some remote places, as this extract from an old newspaper article shows.

Yap, Micronesia—On this tiny South Pacific Island . . . the currency is as solid as a rock. In fact, it is rock. Limestone to be precise.

For nearly 2,000 years the Yapese have used large stone wheels to pay for major purchases, such as land, canoes and permission to marry. Yap is a U.S. trust territory, and the dollar is used in grocery stores and gas stations. But reliance on stone money . . . continues.

Buying property with stones is "much easier than buying it with U.S. dollars," says John Chodad, who recently purchased a building lot with a 30-inch stone wheel. "We don't know the value of the U.S. dollar."

Stone wheels don't make good pocket money, so for small transactions, Yapese use other forms of currency, such as beer. . . .

Besides stone wheels and beer, the Yapese sometimes spend *gaw*, consisting of necklaces of stone beads strung together around a whale's tooth. They also can buy things with *yar*, a currency made from large seashells. But these are small change.

The people of Yap have been using stone money ever since a Yapese warrior named Anagumang first brought the huge stones over from limestone caverns on neighboring Palau, some 1,500 to 2,000 years ago. Inspired by the moon, he fashioned the stone into large circles. The rest is history. . . .

By custom, the stones are worthless when broken. You never hear people on Yap musing about wanting a piece of the rock.

SOURCE: University of Pennsylvania Museum (58-21338)

SOURCE: Excerpted from Art Pine, "Hard Assets, or Why a Loan in Yap Is Hard to Roll Over," *The Wall Street Journal*, March 29, 1984, p. 1.

---

he need simply locate a peanut farmer who wants money. And what peanut farmer does not? For these reasons, monetary exchange replaced barter at a very early stage of human civilization, and only extreme circumstances, such as massive wars and runaway inflations, have been able to bring barter (temporarily) back.

The Conceptual Definition of Money

> **Money** is the standard object used in exchanging goods and services. In short, money is the **medium of exchange.**
>
> The **medium of exchange** is the object or objects used to buy and sell other items such as goods and services.
>
> The **unit of account** is the standard unit for quoting prices.
>
> A **store of value** is an item used to store wealth from one point in time to another.

Under monetary exchange, people trade **money** for goods when they purchase something, and they trade goods for money when they sell something, but they do not trade goods directly for other goods. This practice defines money's principal role as the **medium of exchange.** But once it has become accepted as the medium of exchange, whatever serves as money is bound to serve other functions as well. For one, it will inevitably become the **unit of account**—that is, the standard unit for quoting prices. Thus, if inhabitants of an idyllic tropical island use coconuts as money, they would be foolish to quote prices in terms of seashells.

Money may also come to be used as a **store of value.** If Farmer Jones's corn sales bring in more value than he wants to spend right away, he may find it convenient to store the difference temporarily in the form of money. He knows that money can be "sold" easily for goods and services at a later date, whereas land, gold, and other stores of value might not be. Of course, if inflation is substantial, he may decide to forgo the convenience of money and store his wealth in some other form rather than see its purchasing power eroded. So money's role as a store of value is far from inevitable.

Because money may not always serve as a store of value, and because other commodities may act as stores of value, we will not include the store-of-value function as part of our conceptual definition of money. Instead, we simply label as "money" whatever serves as the medium of exchange.

What Serves as Money?

Anthropologists and historians can testify that a bewildering variety of objects have served as money in different times and places. Cattle, stones, candy bars, cigarettes, woodpecker scalps, porpoise teeth, and giraffe tails provide a few of the more colorful examples. (For another example, see the box at the top of this page.)

Remaking America's Paper Money

Over the last few years, the U.S. Treasury has replaced much of America's paper money with new notes designed to be much more difficult to counterfeit. Several of the new anticounterfeiting features are visible to the naked eye. By inspecting one of the new $20 bills—the ones with the big picture of Andrew Jackson that looks like it's been through a washing machine—you can easily see several of them. (Others are harder to detect.)

Most obvious are the various shades of coloration, including the silver blue eagle to Jackson's left. Next, hold the bill up to a light, with Jackson facing you. Near the left edge, you will find some small type set vertically, rather than horizontally. If your eyesight is good, you will be able to read what it says. But, if you were a counterfeiter, you would find this line devilishly difficult to duplicate. Third, twist the bill and see how the gold numeral "20" in the lower-right corner glistens and changes color. An optical illusion? No, a clever way to make life hard on counterfeiters.

© 2003 The Department of the Treasury Bureau of Engraving and Printing

In primitive or less organized societies, the commodities that served as money generally held value in themselves. If not used as money, cattle could be slaughtered for food, cigarettes could be smoked, and so on. But such **commodity money** generally runs into several severe difficulties. To be useful as a medium of exchange, a commodity must be divisible. This criterion makes cattle a poor choice because it's difficult to keep the other 15/16ths of a cow fresh enough. It must also be of uniform, or at least readily identifiable, quality so that inferior substitutes are easy to recognize. This shortcoming may be why woodpecker scalps never achieved great popularity. The medium of exchange must also be storable and durable, which presents a serious problem for candy-bar money. Finally, because people will carry and store commodity money, it is helpful if the item is compact—that is, if it has high value per unit of volume and weight.

All of these traits make it natural that gold and silver have circulated as money since the first coins were struck about 2,500 years ago. Because they have high value in nonmonetary uses, a lot of purchasing power can be carried without too much weight. Pieces of gold are also storable, divisible (with a little trouble), and of identifiable quality (with a little more trouble).

The same characteristics suggest that paper would make an even better money. The Chinese invented paper money in the 11th century, and Marco Polo brought the idea to Europe. Because we can print any number on it that we please, we can make paper money as divisible as we like. People can also carry a large value of paper money in a lightweight and compact form. Paper is easy to store and, with a little cleverness, we can make counterfeiting challenging, though never impossible. (See the box above.)

Paper cannot, however, serve as commodity money because its value per square inch in alternative uses is so low. A paper currency that is repudiated by its issuer can, perhaps, be used as wallpaper or to wrap fish, but these uses will surely represent only a small fraction of the paper's value as money.[2] Contrary to the popular expression,

> A **commodity money** is an object in use as a medium of exchange, but which also has a substantial value in alternative (nonmonetary) uses.

---

[2] The first paper money issued by the U.S. federal government, the Continental dollar, was essentially repudiated. (Actually, the new government of the United States redeemed the Continentals for 1 cent on the dollar in the 1790s.) This event gave rise to the derisive expression, "It's not worth a Continental."

Fiat money is money that is decreed as such by the government. It is of little value as a commodity, but it maintains its value as a medium of exchange because people have faith that the issuer will stand behind the pieces of printed paper and limit their production.

such a currency literally *is* worth the paper it is printed on—which is to say that it is not worth much. Thus, paper money is always **fiat money**. ✳

Money in the contemporary United States is almost entirely fiat money. Look at a dollar bill. Next to George Washington's picture it states: "This note is legal tender for all debts, public and private." Nowhere on the certificate is there a promise, stated or implied, that the U.S. government will exchange it for anything else. A dollar bill is convertible into, say, four quarters or 10 dimes—but not into gold, chocolate, or any other commodity.

Why do people hold these pieces of paper? Because they know that others are willing to accept them for things of intrinsic value—food, rent, shoes, and so on. If this confidence ever evaporated, dollar bills would cease serving as a medium of exchange and, given that they make ugly wallpaper, would become virtually worthless.

But don't panic. This series of events is hardly likely to occur. Our current monetary system has evolved over hundreds of years, during which *commodity money* was first replaced by *full-bodied paper money*—paper certificates that were backed by gold or silver of equal value held in the issuer's vaults. Then the full-bodied paper money was replaced by certificates that were only partially backed by gold and silver. Finally, we arrived at our present system, in which paper money has no "backing" whatsoever. Like a hesitant swimmer who first dips her toes, then her legs, then her whole body into a cold swimming pool, we have "tested the water" at each step of the way—and found it to our liking. It is unlikely that we will ever take a step back in the other direction.

HOW THE QUANTITY OF MONEY IS MEASURED

Because the amount of money in circulation is important for the determination of national product and the price level, the government must know how much money there is. Thus we must devise some *measure* of the money supply.

Our conceptual definition of money as the medium of exchange raises difficult questions about just which items to include and which items to exclude when we count up the money supply. Such questions have long made the statistical definition of money a subject of dispute. In fact, the U.S. government has several official definitions of the money supply, two of which we will meet shortly.

Some components are obvious. All of our coins and paper money—the small change of our economic system—clearly should count as money. But we cannot stop there if we want to include the main vehicle for making payments in our society, for the lion's share of our nation's payments are made neither in metal nor in paper money, but by check.

Checking deposits are actually no more than bookkeeping entries in bank ledgers. Many people think of checks as a convenient way to pass coins or dollar bills to someone else. But that is not so. For example, when you pay the grocer $50 by check, dollar bills rarely change hands. Instead, that check normally travels back to your bank, where $50 is deducted from the bookkeeping entry that records your account and $50 is added to the bookkeeping entry for your grocer's account. (If you and the grocer hold accounts at different banks, more books get involved, but still no coins or bills will likely move.) The volume of money held in the form of checkable deposits far exceeds the volume of currency.

M1

So it seems imperative to include checkable deposits in any useful definition of the money supply. Unfortunately, this is not an easy task nowadays, because of the wide variety of ways to transfer money by check. Traditional checking accounts in commercial banks are the most familiar vehicle. But many people can also write checks on their savings accounts, on their deposits at credit unions, on their mutual funds, on their accounts with stockbrokers, and so on.

One popular definition of the money supply draws the line early and includes only coins, paper money, traveler's checks, conventional checking accounts, and certain other checkable deposits in banks and savings institutions. In the official U.S. statistics, this narrowly defined concept of money is called **M1.** The upper part of Figure 11-2 shows the composition of M1 as of January 2004.

M2

But other types of accounts allow withdrawals by check, so they are also candidates for inclusion in the money supply. Most notably, *money market deposit accounts* allow their owners to write only a few checks per month but pay market-determined interest rates. Consumers have found these accounts attractive, and balances in them now exceed all the checkable deposits included in M1.

In addition, many mutual fund organizations and brokerage houses offer *money market mutual funds*. These funds sell shares and use the proceeds to purchase a variety of short-term securities. But the important point for our purposes is that owners of shares in money market mutual funds can withdraw their funds by writing checks. Thus depositors can use their holdings of fund shares just like checking accounts.

Finally, although you cannot write a check on a *savings account*, modern banking procedures have blurred the distinction between checking balances and savings balances. For example, most banks these days offer convenient electronic transfers of funds from one account to another, either by telephone or by pushing a button on an automated teller. Consequently, savings balances can become checkable almost instantly. For this reason, savings accounts are included—along with money market deposit accounts and money market mutual fund shares—in the broader definition of the money supply known as **M2.**

The composition of M2 as of January 2004 is shown on the lower part of Figure 11-2. You can see that savings deposits predominate, dwarfing M1. Figure 11-2 illustrates that our money supply comes not only from banks, but also from savings institutions, brokerage houses, and mutual fund organizations. Even so, banks still play a predominant role.

Other Definitions of the Money Supply

Some economists do not want to stop counting at M2; they prefer still broader definitions of money (M3, and so on), which include more types of bank deposits and other closely related assets. The inescapable problem, however, is that there is no obvious place to stop, no clear line of demarcation between those assets that *are* money and those that are merely *close substitutes* for money—so-called **near moneys.**

If we define an asset's **liquidity** as the ease with which its holder can convert it into cash, there is a spectrum of assets of varying degrees of liquidity. Everything in M1 is completely "liquid," the money market fund shares and passbook savings accounts included in M2 are a bit less so, and so on, until we encounter items such as short-term government bonds, which, while still quite liquid, would not normally be included in the money supply. Any number of different *M*s can be defined—and have been—by drawing the line in different places.

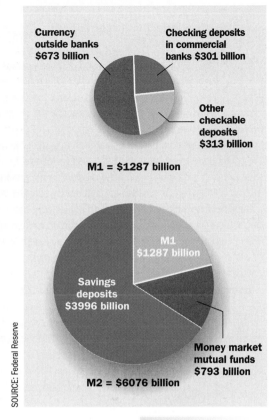

SOURCE: Federal Reserve

M1 = $1287 billion

Currency outside banks $673 billion

Checking deposits in commercial banks $301 billion

Other checkable deposits $313 billion

M1 $1287 billion

Savings deposits $3996 billion

Money market mutual funds $793 billion

M2 = $6076 billion

▪ FIGURE 11-2

Two Definitions of the Money Supply, January 2004

The narrowly defined money supply, usually abbreviated **M1,** is the sum of all coins and paper money in circulation, plus certain checkable deposit balances at banks and savings institutions.[3]

The broadly defined money supply, usually abbreviated **M2,** is the sum of all coins and paper money in circulation, plus all types of checking account balances, plus most forms of savings account balances, plus shares in money market mutual funds.

Near moneys are liquid assets that are close substitutes for money.

An asset's **liquidity** refers to the ease with which it can be converted into cash.

---

[3] This amount includes travelers' checks and NOW (negotiable order of withdrawal) accounts.

Is There a Smart Card in Your Future?

In the 1990s, several banks and other companies began test-marketing new forms of high-tech electronic currency, or "e-cash." One proposed form uses encrypted electronic messages to send balances from one computer to another, possibly bypassing banks entirely.

But the most commonly discussed form of e-cash—at least so far—is the so-called stored-value card. It works as follows. First, you buy a "smart card" (which looks much like a credit card) with an embedded memory chip on which your initial payment is recorded. At this point, your conventional money is transformed into electronic currency. Thereafter, you can use the cash stored on the card to make purchases simply by inserting your card into specially designed slots in vending machines and stores. When the stored value on your card is depleted, you can replenish it at an ATM.

Electronic currency raises several novel issues. For one thing, the federal government has long held a monopoly over currency issue; e-cash may erode that monopoly. For another, consumers and businesses may have privacy and safety concerns: Will their electronic transactions be safe from system errors and computer snoopers and hackers? Law enforcement agencies are also worried that large, untraceable electronic transfers of funds may prove attractive to criminals and tax evaders.

SOURCE: AP/Wide World Photos

Although futurists confidently predict that these new products represent the money of the future, skeptics note that we have heard such claims before—and they have never come true. Only time will tell if the new technologies will catch on. So far, they have not.

And yet more complexities arise. For example, credit cards clearly serve as a medium of exchange. Should they be included in the money supply? Of course, you say. But how much *money* does your credit card represent? Is it the amount you currently owe on the card, which may well be zero? Or is it your entire line of credit, even though you may never use it all? Neither choice seems sensible, which is one reason why economists have so far ignored credit cards in their definitions of money. And soon Americans may start using electronic money instead of cash. Money will be transferred via computer hookups or by so-called smart cards with memory chips (see "Is There a Smart Card in Your Future?").

We could mention further complexities, but an introductory course in economics is not the place to get bogged down in complex definitional issues. So we will simply adhere to the convention that:

"Money" consists only of coins, paper money, and checkable deposits.

THE BANKING SYSTEM

Now that we have defined money and seen how to measure it, we turn our attention to the principal creators of money—the banks. Banking is a complicated business—and getting more so. If you go further in your study of economics, you will probably learn more about the operations of banks. But for present purposes, a few simple principles will suffice. Let's start at the beginning.

How Banking Began

When Adam and Eve left the Garden of Eden, they did not encounter an ATM. Banking had to be invented. With a little imagination, we can see how the first banks must have begun.

When money was made of gold or other metals, it was inconvenient for consumers and merchants to carry it around and weigh and assay its purity every time they made a transaction. So the practice developed of leaving gold in a goldsmith's safe storage facilities and carrying in its place a receipt stating that John Doe did indeed own 5 ounces of gold. When people began trading goods and services for the goldsmiths' receipts, rather than for the gold itself, the receipts became an early form of paper money.

At this stage, paper money was fully backed by gold. Gradually, however, the goldsmiths began to notice that the amount of gold they were actually required to pay out in a day was but a small fraction of the total gold they had stored in their warehouses. Then one day some enterprising goldsmith hit upon a momentous idea that must have made him fabulously wealthy.

His thinking probably ran something like this: "I have 2,000 ounces of gold stored away in my vault, for which I collect storage fees from my customers. But I am never called upon to pay out more than 100 ounces on a single day. What harm could it do if I lent out, say, half the gold I now have? I'll still have more than enough to pay off any depositors who come in for withdrawals, so no one will ever know the difference. And I could earn 30 additional ounces of gold each year in interest on the loans I make (at 3 percent interest on 1,000 ounces). With this profit, I could lower my service charges to depositors and so attract still more deposits. I think I'll do it."

With this resolution, the modern system of **fractional reserve banking** was born. This system has three features that are crucially important to this chapter.

Fractional reserve banking is a system under which bankers keep as reserves only a fraction of the funds they hold on deposit.

Bank Profitability

By getting deposits at zero interest and lending some of them out at positive interest rates, goldsmiths made profits. The history of banking as a profit-making industry was begun and has continued to this date. *Banks, like other enterprises, are in business to earn profits.*

Bank Discretion over the Money Supply

When goldsmiths decided to keep only fractions of their total deposits on reserve and lend out the balance, they acquired the ability to *create money*. As long as they kept 100 percent reserves, each gold certificate represented exactly 1 ounce of gold. So whether people decided to carry their gold or leave it with their goldsmiths did not affect the money supply, which was set by the volume of gold.

With the advent of fractional reserve banking, however, new paper certificates appeared whenever goldsmiths lent out some of the gold they held on deposit. The loans, in effect, created new money. In this way, the total amount of money came to depend on the amount of gold that each goldsmith felt compelled to keep in his vault. For any given volume of gold on deposit, the lower the reserves the goldsmiths kept, the more loans they could make, and therefore the more money would circulate.

Although we no longer use gold to back our money, this principle remains true today. *Bankers' decisions on how much to hold in reserves influence the supply of money.* A substantial part of the rationale for modern monetary policy is, as we have mentioned, that profit-seeking bankers might not create the amount of money that is best for society.

Exposure to Runs

A goldsmith who kept 100 percent reserves never had to worry about a run on his vault. Even if all his depositors showed up at the door at once, he could always convert their paper receipts back into gold. But as soon as the first goldsmith decided to get by with only fractional reserves, the possibility of a run on the vault became a real concern. If that first goldsmith who lent out half his gold had found 51 percent of his customers at his door one unlucky day, he would have had a lot of explaining to do. Similar problems have worried bankers for centuries. *The danger of a run on the bank has induced bankers to keep prudent reserves and to lend out money carefully.*

As we observed earlier, this danger is one of the main rationales for bank regulation.

▌ Principles of Bank Management: Profits versus Safety

Bankers have a reputation for conservatism in politics, dress, and business affairs. From what has been said so far, the economic rationale for this conservatism should be clear. Checking deposits are pure fiat money. Years ago, these deposits were "backed" by nothing more than a particular bank's promise to convert them into currency on demand. If people lost trust in a bank, it was doomed.

Thus, bankers have always relied on a reputation for prudence, which they achieved in two principal ways. First, they maintained a sufficiently generous level of reserves to minimize their vulnerability to runs. Second, they were cautious in making loans and investments, because any large losses on their loans would undermine their depositors' confidence.

It is important to realize that banking under a system of fractional reserves is an inherently risky business that is rendered safe only by cautious and prudent management. America's long history of bank failures (see Figure 11-1) bears sober testimony to the fact that many bankers were neither cautious nor prudent. Why not? Because caution is not the route to high profits. Bank profits are maximized by keeping reserves as low as possible, and by making at least some loans to borrowers with questionable credit standing who will pay higher interest rates.

The art of bank management is to strike the appropriate balance between the lure of profits and the need for safety. If a banker errs by being too stodgy, his bank will earn inadequate profits. If he errs by taking unwarranted risks, his bank may not survive at all.

▌ Bank Regulation

Governments in virtually every society have decided that profit-minded bankers may not strike the balance between profits and safety exactly where society wants it struck. So they have thrown up a web of regulations designed to ensure depositors' safety and to control the money supply.

Deposit insurance is a system that guarantees that depositors will not lose money even if their bank goes bankrupt.

Deposit Insurance   The principal innovation that guarantees the safety of bank deposits is **deposit insurance.** Today, most U.S. bank deposits are insured against loss by the *Federal Deposit Insurance Corporation (FDIC)*—an agency of the federal government. If your bank belongs to the FDIC, as almost all do, your account is insured for up to $100,000 regardless of what happens to the bank. Thus, while bank failures may spell disaster for the bank's stockholders, they do not create concern for many depositors. Deposit insurance eliminates the motive for customers to rush to their bank just because they hear some bad news about the bank's finances. Many observers give this innovation much of the credit for the pronounced decline in bank failures after the FDIC was established in 1933—which is apparent in Figure 11-1.

Bank Supervision   In addition to insuring depositors against loss, the government takes steps to see that banks do not get into financial trouble. For one thing, various regulatory authorities conduct periodic *bank examinations* to keep tabs on the financial conditions and business practices of the banks under their purview. After a rash of bank failures in the late 1980s and early 1990s (visible in Figure 11-1), U.S. bank supervision was tightened by legislation that permits the authorities to intervene early in the affairs of financially troubled banks. Other laws and regulations *limit the kinds and quantities of assets in which banks may invest.* For example, banks are permitted to own only limited amounts of common stock. Both of these forms of regulation are clearly aimed at keeping banks safe.

Reserve Requirements   A final type of regulation also has some bearing on safety but is motivated primarily by the government's desire to control the money supply. We have seen that the amount of money any bank will issue depends on the amount of reserves it elects to keep. For this reason, most banks are subject by law to minimum **required reserves.** Although banks may (and sometimes do) keep reserves in excess of these legal minimums, they may not keep less. This regulation places an upper limit on the money supply. The rest of this chapter is concerned with the details of this mechanism.

Required reserves are the minimum amount of reserves (in cash or the equivalent) required by law. Normally, required reserves are proportional to the volume of deposits.

THE ORIGINS OF THE MONEY SUPPLY

Our objective is to understand how the money supply is determined. But before we can fully understand the process by which money is "created," we must acquire at least a nodding acquaintance with the mechanics of modern banking.

How Bankers Keep Books

The first thing to know is how to distinguish assets from liabilities. An **asset** of a bank is something of value that the bank *owns.* This "thing" may be a physical object, such as the bank building or a computer, or it may be a piece of paper, such as an IOU from a customer to whom the bank has made a loan. A **liability** of a bank is something of value that the bank *owes.* Most bank liabilities take the form of bookkeeping entries. For example, if you have an account in the Main Street Bank, your bank balance is a liability of the bank. (It is, of course, an asset to you.)

An **asset** of an individual or business firm is an item of value that the individual or firm owns.

An easy test shows whether some piece of paper or bookkeeping entry is a bank's *asset* or *liability.* Ask yourself whether, if this paper were converted into cash, the bank would receive the cash (if so, it is an asset) or pay it out (if so, it is a liability). This test makes it clear that loans to customers are bank assets (when loans are repaid, the bank collects), whereas customers' deposits are bank liabilities (when deposits are cashed in, the bank must pay). Of course, things are just the opposite to the bank's customers: The loans are liabilities and the deposits are assets.

A **liability** of an individual or business firm is an item of value that the individual or firm owes. Many liabilities are known as *debts.*

When accountants draw up a complete list of all the bank's assets and liabilities, the resulting document is called the bank's **balance sheet.** Typically, the value of all the bank's assets exceeds the value of all its liabilities. (On the rare occasions when this is not so, the bank is in serious trouble.) In what sense, then, do balance sheets "balance"?

A **balance sheet** is an accounting statement listing the values of all assets on the left side and the values of all liabilities and *net worth* on the right side.

They balance because accountants have invented the concept of **net worth** to balance the books. Specifically, they define the net worth of a bank to be the difference between the value of all its assets and the value of all its liabilities. Thus, by definition, when accountants add net worth to liabilities, the sum they get must be equal to the value of the bank's assets:

Net worth is the value of all assets minus the value of all liabilities.

$$\text{Assets} = \text{Liabilities} + \text{Net worth}$$

Table 11-1 illustrates this point with the balance sheet of a fictitious bank, Bank-a-mythica, whose finances are extremely simple. On December 31, 2003, it had only two kinds of assets (listed on the left side of the balance sheet)—$1 million in cash reserves, and $4.5 million in outstanding loans to its customers, that is, in customers' IOUs. And it had only one type of liability (listed on the right side)—$5 million in checking deposits. The difference between total assets ($5.5 million) and total liabilities ($5.0 million) was the bank's net worth ($500,000), also shown on the right side of the balance sheet.

TABLE 11-1   Balance Sheet of Bank-a-mythica, December 31, 2003

Assets		Liabilities and Net Worth	
Assets		**Liabilities**	
Reserves	$1,000,000	Checking deposits	$5,000,000
Loans outstanding	$4,500,000		
Total	**$5,500,000**	**Net Worth**	
Addendum: Bank Reserves		Stockholders' equity	$500,000
Actual reserves	$1,000,000	Total	**$5,500,000**
Required reserves	1,000,000		
Excess reserves	0		

BANKS AND MONEY CREATION

Let us now turn to the process of deposit creation. Many bankers will deny that they have any ability to "create" money. The phrase itself has a suspiciously hocus-pocus sound to it. But the protesting bankers are not quite right. Although any individual bank's ability to create money is severely limited, the banking system as a whole can achieve much more than the sum of its parts. Through the modern alchemy of **deposit creation,** it can turn one dollar into many dollars. But to understand this important process, we had better proceed in steps, beginning with the case of a single bank, our hypothetical Bank-a-mythica.

Deposit creation refers to the process by which a fractional reserve banking system turns $1 of bank reserves into several dollars of bank deposits.

The Limits to Money Creation by a Single Bank

According to the balance sheet in Table 11-1, Bank-a-mythica holds cash reserves of $1 million, equal to 20 percent of its $5 million in deposits. Assume that this is the reserve ratio prescribed by law and that the bank strives to keep its reserves down to the legal minimum; that is, it strives to keep its **excess reserves** at zero.

Excess reserves are any reserves held in excess of the legal minimum.

Now let us suppose that on January 2, 2004, an eccentric widower comes into Bank-a-mythica and deposits $100,000 in cash in his checking account. The bank now has $100,000 more in cash reserves, and $100,000 more in checking deposits. But because deposits are up by $100,000, *required* reserves rise by only $20,000, leaving $80,000 in *excess* reserves. Table 11-2 illustrates the effects of this transaction on Bank-a-mythica's balance sheet. Tables such as this one, which show *changes* in balance sheets rather than the balance sheets themselves, will help us follow the money-creation process.[4]

Bank-a-mythica is unlikely to be happy with the situation illustrated in Table 11-2, for it is holding $80,000 in excess reserves on which it earns no interest. So as soon as possible, it will lend out the extra $80,000—let us say to Hard-Pressed Construction Company. This loan leads to the balance sheet changes shown in Table 11-3: Bank-a-mythica's loans rise by $80,000 while its holdings of cash reserves fall by $80,000.

By combining Tables 11-2 and 11-3, we arrive at Table 11-4, which summarizes the bank's transactions for the week. Reserves are up $20,000, loans are up $80,000, and, now that the bank has had a chance to adjust to the inflow of deposits, it no longer holds excess reserves.

Looking at Table 11-4 and keeping in mind our specific definition of money, it appears at first that the chairman of Bank-a-mythica is right when he claims not to have engaged in the nefarious practice of "money creation." All that happened was that, in exchange for the $100,000 in cash it received, the bank issued the widower a checking balance of $100,000. This transaction does not change M1; it merely converts one form of money (currency) into another (checking deposits).

But wait. What happened to the $100,000 in cash that the eccentric

TABLE 11-2   Changes in Bank-a-mythica's Balance Sheet, January 2, 2004

Assets		Liabilities	
Reserves	+$100,000	Checking deposits	+$100,000
Addendum: Changes in Reserves			
Actual reserves	+$100,000		
Required reserves	+$ 20,000		
Excess reserves	**+$ 80,000**		

TABLE 11-3   Changes in Bank-a-mythica's Balance Sheet, January 3–6, 2004

Assets		Liabilities	
Loans outstanding	+$80,000	No change	
Reserves	−$80,000		
Addendum: Changes in Reserves			
Actual reserves	−$80,000		
Required reserves	No change		
Excess reserves	**−$80,000**		

[4] In all such tables, which are called *T accounts,* the two sides of the ledger must balance. This balance is required because changes in assets and changes in liabilities must be equal if the balance sheet is to balance both before and after the transaction.

man brought to the bank? The table shows that Bank-a-mythica retained $20,000 in its vault. Because this currency is no longer in circulation, it no longer counts in the official money supply, M1. (Notice that Figure 11-2 included only "currency outside banks.") But the other $80,000, which the bank lent out, is still in circulation. It is held by Hard-Pressed Construction Company, which probably will redeposit it in some other bank. But even

TABLE 11-4   Changes in Bank-a-mythica's Balance Sheet, January 2–6, 2004

Assets		Liabilities	
Reserves	+$20,000	Checking deposits	+$100,000
Loans outstanding	+$80,000		
Addendum: Changes in Reserves			
Actual reserves	+$20,000		
Required reserves	+$20,000		
Excess reserves	**No change**		

before this new deposit is made, the original $100,000 in cash has supported an increase in the money supply. There is now $100,000 in checking deposits and $80,000 of cash in circulation, making a total of $180,000—whereas prior to the original deposit there was only the $100,000 in cash. The money creation process has begun.

Multiple Money Creation by a Series of Banks

Let us now trace the $80,000 in cash and see how the process of money creation gathers momentum. Suppose that Hard-Pressed Construction Company, which banks across town at the First National Bank, deposits the $80,000 into its bank account. First National's reserves increase by $80,000. But because its deposits rise by $80,000, its *required* reserves increase by only 20 percent of this amount, or $16,000. If First National Bank behaves like Bank-a-mythica, it will lend out the $64,000 of excess reserves.

Table 11-5 shows the effects of these events on First National Bank's balance sheet. (We do not show the preliminary steps corresponding to Tables 11-2 and 11-3 separately.) At this stage in the chain, the original $100,000 in cash has led to $180,000 in deposits—$100,000 at Bank-a-mythica and $80,000 at First National Bank—and $64,000 in cash, which is still in circulation (in the hands of the recipient of First National's loan—Al's Auto Shop). Thus, instead of the original $100,000, a total of $244,000 worth of money ($180,000 in checking deposits plus $64,000 in cash) has been created.

But, to coin a phrase, the bucks do not stop here. Al's Auto Shop will presumably deposit the proceeds from its loan into its own account at Second National Bank, leading to the balance sheet adjustments shown in Table 11-6 when Second National makes an additional loan of $51,200 rather than hold on to excess reserves. You can see how the money creation process continues.

Figure 11-3 summarizes the balance sheet changes of the first five banks in the chain (from Bank-a-mythica through the Fourth National Bank) graphically, based on the assumptions that (1) each bank holds exactly the 20 percent required reserves, and (2) each loan recipient redeposits the proceeds in the next bank. But the chain does not end there. The Main Street Movie Theatre, which received the $32,768 loan from the Fourth

TABLE 11-5   Changes in First National Bank's Balance Sheet

Assets		Liabilities	
Reserves	+$16,000	Checking deposits	+$80,000
Loans outstanding	+$64,000		
Addendum: Changes in Reserves			
Actual reserves	+$16,000		
Required reserves	+$16,000		
Excess reserves	**No change**		

TABLE 11-6   Changes in Second National Bank's Balance Sheet

Assets		Liabilities	
Reserves	+$12,800	Checking deposits	+$64,000
Loans outstanding	+$51,200		
Addendum: Changes in Reserves			
Actual reserves	+$12,800		
Required reserves	+$12,800		
Excess reserves	**No change**		

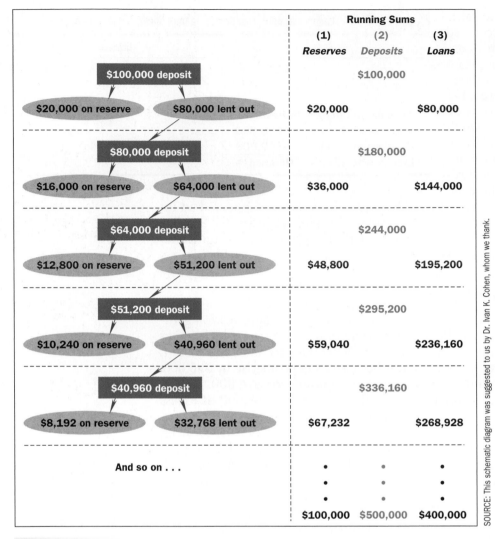

Running Sums

	(1) Reserves	(2) Deposits	(3) Loans
$100,000 deposit		$100,000	
$20,000 on reserve / $80,000 lent out	$20,000		$80,000
$80,000 deposit		$180,000	
$16,000 on reserve / $64,000 lent out	$36,000		$144,000
$64,000 deposit		$244,000	
$12,800 on reserve / $51,200 lent out	$48,800		$195,200
$51,200 deposit		$295,200	
$10,240 on reserve / $40,960 lent out	$59,040		$236,160
$40,960 deposit		$336,160	
$8,192 on reserve / $32,768 lent out	$67,232		$268,928
And so on . . .	• • •	• • •	• • •
	$100,000	$500,000	$400,000

SOURCE: This schematic diagram was suggested to us by Dr. Ivan K. Cohen, whom we thank.

■ FIGURE 11-3
The Chain of Multiple Deposit Creation

National Bank, deposits these funds into the Fifth National Bank. Fifth National has to keep only 20 percent of this deposit, or $6,553.60, on reserve and will lend out the balance. And so the chain continues.

Where does it all end? The running sums on the right side of Figure 11-3 show what eventually happens to the entire banking system. The initial deposit of $100,000 in cash is ultimately absorbed in bank reserves, Column (1), leading to a total of $500,000 in new deposits, Column (2), and $400,000 in new loans, Column (3). The money supply rises by $400,000 because the non-bank public eventually holds $100,000 *less* in currency and $500,000 *more* in checking deposits.

As we see, there really is some hocus-pocus. Somehow, an initial deposit of $100,000 leads to $500,000 in new bank deposits—a multiple expansion of $5 for every original dollar—and a net increase of $400,000 in the money supply. We need to understand *why* this is so. But first let us verify that the calculations in Figure 11-3 are correct.

If you look carefully at the numbers, you will see that each column forms a *geometric progression*; specifically, each entry is equal to exactly 80 percent of the entry before it. Recall that in our discussion of the multiplier in Chapter 8 we learned how to sum an *infinite geometric progression*, which is just what each of these chains is. In particular, if the common ratio is R, the sum of an infinite geometric progression is:

$$1 + R + R^2 + R^3 + \ldots = \frac{1}{1 - R}$$

By applying this formula to the chain of checking deposits in Figure 11-3, we get:

$$\$100,000 + \$80,000 + \$64,000 + \$51,200 + \ldots$$
$$= \$100,000 \times (1 + 0.80 + 0.64 + 0.512 + \ldots)$$
$$= \$100,000 \times (1 + 0.80 + 0.80^2 + 0.80^3 + \ldots)$$
$$= \$100,000 \times \frac{1}{1 - 0.80} = \frac{\$100,000}{0.20} = \$500,000$$

Proceeding similarly, we can verify that the new loans sum to $400,000 and that the new required reserves sum to $100,000. (Check these figures as exercises.) Thus the numbers in Figure 11-3 are correct. Let us, therefore, think through the logic behind them.

The chain of deposit creation ends only when there are no more *excess* reserves to be loaned out—that is, when the entire $100,000 in cash is tied up in *required* reserves. That explains why the last entry in Column (1) of Figure 11-3 must be $100,000. But, with a reserve ratio of 20 percent, excess reserves disappear only when checking deposits expand by $500,000—which is the last entry in Column (2). Finally, because balance sheets must balance, the sum of all newly created assets (reserves plus loans) must equal the sum of all newly created liabilities ($500,000 in deposits). That leaves $400,000 for new loans—which is the last entry in Column (3).

More generally, if the reserve ratio is some number m (rather than the one-fifth in our example), each dollar of deposits requires only a fraction m of a dollar in reserves. The common ratio in the preceding formula is, therefore, $R = 1 - m$, and deposits must expand by $1/m$ for each dollar of new reserves that are injected into the system. This suggests the general formula for multiple money creation when the required reserve ratio is some number m:

OVERSIMPLIFIED MONEY MULTIPLIER FORMULA

If the required reserve ratio is some fraction, m, the banking system as a whole can convert each $1 of reserves into $1/m$ in new money. That is, the so-called **money multiplier** is given by:

Change in money supply = $(1/m) \times$ Change in reserves

The **money multiplier** is the ratio of newly created bank deposits to new reserves.

While this formula correctly describes what happens in our example, it leaves out an important detail. The initial deposit of $100,000 in cash at Bank-a-mythica constitutes $100,000 in new reserves (see Table 11-2 on page 214). Applying a multiplier of $1/m = 1/0.20 = 5$ to this $100,000, we conclude that bank deposits will rise by $500,000—which is just what happens. But remember that the process started when the eccentric widower took $100,000 in cash and deposited it in his bank account. Thus the public's holdings of *money*—which includes both checking deposits *and* cash—increase by only $400,000 in this case: There is $500,000 *more* in deposits, but $100,000 *less* in cash.

The Process in Reverse: Multiple Contractions of the Money Supply

Let us now briefly consider how this deposit creation mechanism operates in reverse—as a system of deposit *destruction*. In particular, suppose that our eccentric widower returned to Bank-a-mythica to withdraw $100,000 from his checking account and return it to his mattress, where it rightfully belongs. Bank-a-mythica's *required* reserves would fall by $20,000 as a result of this transaction (20 percent of $100,000), but its *actual* reserves would fall by $100,000. The bank would be $80,000 short, as indicated in Table 11-7(a).

TABLE 11-7 Changes in the Balance Sheet of Bank-a-mythica

(a) Assets		Liabilities		(b) Assets		Liabilities	
Reserves	−$100,000	Checking deposits	−$100,000	Reserves	+$80,000	No change	
				Loans outstanding	−$80,000		
Addendum: Changes in Reserves				**Addendum: Changes in Reserves**			
Actual reserves	−$100,000			Actual reserves	+$80,000		
Required reserves	−$20,000			Reserves required	No change		
Excess reserves	**−$80,000**			Excess reserves	**+$80,000**		

■ TABLE 11-8   Changes in the Balance Sheet of First National Bank

| (a) | | | (b) | | |
Assets		Liabilities	Assets		Liabilities
Reserves	−$80,000	Checking deposits −$80,000	Reserves	+$64,000	No change
			Loans outstanding	−$64,000	
Addendum: Changes in Reserves			**Addendum: Changes in Reserves**		
Actual reserves	−$80,000		Actual reserves	+$64,000	
Required reserves	−$16,000		Reserves required	No change	
Excess reserves	**−$64,000**		Excess reserves	**+$64,000**	

How would the bank react to this discrepancy? As some of its outstanding loans are routinely paid off, it will cease granting new ones until it has accumulated the necessary $80,000 in required reserves. The data for Bank-a-mythica's contraction are shown in Table 11-7(b), assuming that borrowers pay off their loans in cash.[5]

But where did the borrowers get this money? Probably by making withdrawals from other banks. In this case, assume that the funds all came from First National Bank, which loses $80,000 in deposits and $80,000 in reserves. It finds itself short some $64,000 in reserves, as shown in Table 11-8(a), and therefore must reduce its loan commitments by $64,000, as in Table 11-8(b). This reaction, of course, causes some other bank to suffer a loss of reserves and deposits of $64,000, and the whole process repeats just as it did in the case of deposit expansion.

After the entire banking system had become involved, the picture would be just as shown in Figure 11-3, except that all the numbers would have *minus signs* in front of them. Deposits would shrink by $500,000, loans would fall by $400,000, bank reserves would be reduced by $100,000, and the M1 money supply would fall by $400,000. As suggested by our money multiplier formula with $m = 0.20$, the decline in the bank deposit component of the money supply is $1/0.20 = 5$ times as large as the decline in reserves.

One of the authors of this book was a student in Cambridge, Massachusetts, during the height of the radical student movement of the late 1960s. One day a pamphlet appeared urging citizens to withdraw all funds from their checking accounts on a prescribed date, hold them in cash for a week, and then redeposit them. This act, the circular argued, would wreak havoc upon the capitalist system. Obviously, some of these radicals were well schooled in modern money mechanics, for the argument was basically correct. The tremendous multiple contraction of the banking system and subsequent multiple expansion that a successful campaign of this sort could have caused might have seriously disrupted the local financial system. But history records that the appeal met with little success. Checking-account withdrawals are not the stuff of which revolutions are made.

WHY THE MONEY CREATION FORMULA IS OVERSIMPLIFIED

So far, our discussion of the process of money creation has seemed rather mechanical. If everything proceeds according to formula, each $1 in new reserves injected into the banking system leads to a $1/m$ increase in new deposits. But in reality, things are not

---

[5] In reality, the borrowers would probably pay with checks drawn on other banks. Bank-a-mythica would then cash these checks to acquire the reserves.

quite this simple. Just as in the case of the expenditure multiplier, the oversimplified money multiplier is accurate only under very particular circumstances. These circumstances require that:

1. Every recipient of cash must redeposit the cash into another bank rather than hold it.
2. Every bank must hold reserves no larger than the legal minimum.

The "chain" diagram in Figure 11-3 can teach us what happens if either of these assumptions is violated.

Suppose first that the business firms and individuals who receive bank loans decide to redeposit only a fraction of the proceeds into their bank accounts. Then, for example, the first $80,000 loan would lead to a deposit of less than $80,000—and similarly down the chain. The whole chain of deposit creation would therefore be reduced. Thus:

If individuals and business firms decide to hold more cash, the multiple expansion of bank deposits will be curtailed because fewer dollars of cash will be available for use as reserves to support checking deposits. Consequently, the money supply will be smaller.

The basic idea here is simple. Each $1 of cash held by a bank can support several dollars (specifically, $1/m$) of money. But $1 of cash held by an individual is exactly $1 of money; it supports no bank deposits. Hence, whenever cash moves from the banking system to a household or business, the money supply will decline. And whenever cash enters the banking system, the money supply will rise.

Next, suppose bank managers become more conservative or that the outlook for loan repayments worsens because of a recession. In such an environment, banks might decide to keep more reserves than the legal requirement and lend out less than the amounts assumed in Figure 11-3. If this happens, banks further down the chain receive smaller deposits and, once again, the chain of deposit creation is curtailed. Thus:

If banks wish to keep excess reserves, the multiple expansion of bank deposits will be restricted. A given amount of cash will support a smaller supply of money than would be the case if banks held no excess reserves.

The latter problem has afflicted Japan for several years. Because they have so many bad loans on their books, Japanese bankers have become super-cautious about lending money to any but their most creditworthy borrowers. So many Japanese businesses have been starved for credit even though bank reserves have soared.

THE NEED FOR MONETARY POLICY

If we pursue these two points a bit farther, we will see why the government must regulate the money supply in an effort to maintain economic stability. We have just suggested that banks will prefer to keep excess reserves when they do not foresee profitable and secure opportunities to make loans. This scenario is most likely to arise when business conditions are depressed. At such times, the propensity of banks to hold excess reserves can turn the deposit creation process into one of deposit destruction, as happened recently in both Japan and Argentina. In addition, if depositors become jittery, they may decide to hold on to more cash. Thus:

During a recession, profit-oriented banks would be prone to reduce the money supply by increasing their excess reserves and declining to lend to less creditworthy applicants—if the government did not intervene. As we will learn in subsequent chapters, the money supply is an important influence on aggregate demand, so such a contraction of the money supply would aggravate the recession.

This is precisely what happened—with a vengeance—during the Great Depression of the 1930s. Although total bank reserves grew, the money supply contracted violently because banks preferred to hold excess reserves rather than make loans that might not be repaid. And something similar is going on in Japan right now: The supply of reserves is expanding much more rapidly than the money supply because nervous bankers are holding on to their excess reserves.

On the other hand, banks will want to squeeze the maximum money supply possible out of any given amount of cash reserves by keeping their reserves at the bare minimum when the demand for bank loans is buoyant, profits are high, and secure investment opportunities abound. This reduced incentive to hold excess reserves in prosperous times means that:

During an economic boom, profit-oriented banks will likely make the money supply expand, adding undesirable momentum to the booming economy and paving the way for inflation. The authorities must intervene to prevent this rapid money growth.

Regulation of the money supply, then, is necessary because profit-oriented bankers might otherwise provide the economy with a money supply that dances to and amplifies the tune of the business cycle. Precisely how the authorities control the money supply is the subject of the next chapter.

SUMMARY

1. It is more efficient to exchange goods and services by using **money** as a medium of exchange than by **bartering** them directly.

2. In addition to being the **medium of exchange,** whatever serves as money is likely to become the standard **unit of account** and a popular **store of value.**

3. Throughout history, all sorts of items have served as money. **Commodity money** gave way to full-bodied paper money (certificates backed 100 percent by some commodity, such as gold), which in turn gave way to partially backed paper money. Nowadays our paper money has no commodity backing whatsoever; it is pure **fiat money.**

4. One popular definition of the U.S. money supply is **M1,** which includes coins, paper money, and several types of checking deposits. Most economists actually prefer the **M2** definition, which adds to M1 other types of checkable accounts and most savings deposits. Much of M2 is held outside of banks by investment houses, credit unions, and other financial institutions.

5. Under our modern system of fractional reserve banking, banks keep cash reserves equal to only a fraction of their total deposit **liabilities.** This practice is the key to their profitability, because the remaining funds can be loaned out at interest. But it also leaves banks potentially vulnerable to **runs.**

6. Because of this vulnerability, bank managers are generally conservative in their investment strategies. They also keep a prudent level of reserves. Even so, the government keeps a watchful eye over banking practices.

7. Before 1933, bank failures were common in the United States. They declined sharply when **deposit insurance** was instituted.

8. Because it holds only fractional reserves, the banking system as a whole can create several dollars of deposits for each dollar of reserves it receives. Under certain assumptions, the ratio of new bank deposits to new reserves will be $\$1/m$, where m is the **required reserve** ratio.

9. The same process works in reverse, as a system of money destruction, when cash is withdrawn from the banking system.

10. Because banks and individuals may want to hold more cash when the economy is shaky, the money supply would probably contract under such circumstances if the government did not intervene. Similarly, the money supply would probably expand rapidly in boom times if it were unregulated.

KEY TERMS

Run on a bank   204

Barter   204

Money   206

Medium of exchange   206

Unit of account   206

Store of value   206

Commodity money   207

Fiat money   208

M1   209

M2   209

Near moneys   209

Liquidity   209

Fractional reserve banking   211

Deposit insurance   212

Federal Deposit Insurance Corporation (FDIC)   212

Required reserves   213

Asset   213

Liability   213

Balance sheet   213

Net worth   213

Deposit creation   214

Excess reserves   214

Money multiplier   217

QUESTIONS FOR REVIEW

1. If ours were a barter economy, how would you pay your tuition bill? What if your college did not want the goods or services you offered in payment?

2. How is "money" defined, both conceptually and in practice? Does the U.S. money supply consist of commodity money, full-bodied paper money, or fiat money?

3. What is fractional reserve banking, and why is it the key to bank profits? (*Hint:* What opportunities to make profits would banks lose if reserve requirements were 100 percent?) Why does fractional reserve banking give bankers discretion over how large the money supply will be? Why does it make banks potentially vulnerable to runs?

4. During the 1980s and early 1990s, a rash of bank failures occurred in the United States. Explain why these failures did not lead to runs on banks.

5. Suppose banks keep no excess reserves and no individuals or firms hold on to cash. If someone suddenly discovers $12 million in buried treasure, explain what will happen to the money supply if the required reserve ratio is 10 percent.

6. How would your answer to Review Question 5 differ if the reserve ratio were 25 percent? If the reserve ratio were 100 percent?

7. Each year during Christmas shopping season, consumers and stores increase their holdings of cash. Explain how this development could lead to a multiple contraction of the money supply. (As a matter of fact, the authorities prevent this contraction from occurring by methods explained in the next chapter.)

8. Excess reserves make a bank less vulnerable to runs. Why, then, don't bankers like to hold excess reserves? What circumstances might persuade them that it would be advisable to hold excess reserves?

9. Use tables such as Tables 11-2 and 11-3 to illustrate what happens to bank balance sheets when each of the following transactions occurs:

    a. You withdraw $50 from your checking account to buy concert tickets.

    b. Sam finds a $50 bill on the sidewalk and deposits it into his checking account.

    c. Mary Q. Contrary withdraws $1,000 in cash from her account at Hometown Bank, carries it to the city, and deposits it into her account at Big City Bank.

10. For each of the transactions listed in Review Question 9, what will be the ultimate effect on the money supply if the required reserve ratio is one-eighth (12.5 percent)? Assume that the oversimplified money multiplier formula applies.

11. If the government takes over a failed bank with liabilities (mostly deposits) of $2 billion, pays off the depositors, and sells the assets for $1.5 billion, where does the missing $500 million come from? Why?

12

Monetary Policy and the National Economy

Victorians heard with grave attention that the Bank Rate had been raised. They did not know what it meant. But they knew that it was an act of extreme wisdom.

JOHN KENNETH GALBRAITH

Armed with our understanding of the rudiments of banking, we are now ready to bring money and interest rates into our model of income determination and the price level. Up to now, we have taken investment (*I*) to be a fixed number. But this is a poor assumption. Not only is investment highly variable, but it also depends on interest rates—which are, in turn, heavily influenced by *monetary policy.* The main task of this chapter is to explain how monetary policy affects interest rates, investment, and aggregate demand. By the end of the chapter, we will have constructed a complete macroeconomic model, which we will use in subsequent chapters to investigate a variety of important policy issues.

CONTENTS

? Issue: Just Why Is Alan Greenspan so Important?

ALAN GREENSPAN PONDERS HIS GROCERY LIST...

Alan Greenspan, the chairman of the Federal Reserve Board since 1987, is something of an American institution. Many people consider him the most powerful person in the world, at least where economic policy is concerned.

Greenspan is a taciturn and not very charismatic economist. But when he speaks, people in financial markets around the world listen. Listen? They scrutinize his remarks for nuances with an intensity that was once reserved for utterances from behind the Kremlin walls. Why? Because, in the view of many economists, the Federal Reserve's decisions on interest rates are the single most important influence on aggregate demand—and hence on economic growth, unemployment, and inflation.

Greenspan heads America's central bank, the *Federal Reserve System.* The "Fed," as it is called, is a bank—but a very special kind of bank. Its customers are banks rather than individuals, and it performs some of the same services for them as your bank performs for you. Although it makes enormous profits, profit is not its goal. Instead, the Fed tries to manage interest rates according to what it perceives to be the national interest. This chapter will teach you how the Fed does its job, and why its decisions affect our economy so profoundly. In brief, it will teach you why people listen so intently when Alan Greenspan speaks.

MONEY AND INCOME: THE IMPORTANT DIFFERENCE

But first we must get some terminology straight. The words *money* and *income* are used almost interchangeably in common parlance. Here, however, we must be more precise.

Money is a snapshot concept. It answers questions such as "How much money do you have right now?" or "How much money did you have at 3:32 P.M. on Friday, November 5?" To answer these questions, you would add up the cash you are (or were) carrying and whatever checkable balances you have (or had), and answer something like: "I have $126.33," or "On Friday, November 5, at 3:32 P.M., I had $31.43."

Income, by contrast, is more like a motion picture; it comes to you over a period of time. If you are asked, "What is your income?" you must respond by saying "$200 *per week,*" or "$800 *per month,*" or "$10,000 *per year,*" or something like that. Notice the unit of time attached to each of these responses. If you just answer, "My income is $4,500," without indicating whether it is per week, per month, or per year, no one will understand what you mean.

That the two concepts are very different is easy to see. A typical American family has an *income* of about $40,000 per year, but its *money* holdings at any point in time (using the M1 definition) may be less than $2,000. Similarly, at the national level, nominal GDP at the end of 2003 was more than $11 trillion, while the money stock (M1) was under $1.3 trillion.

Although money and income are very different, they are certainly related. This chapter focuses on that relationship. Specifically, we will look at how the stock of *money* in existence at any moment of time influences the rate at which people earn *income*—that is, *how money affects GDP.*

AMERICA'S CENTRAL BANK: THE FEDERAL RESERVE SYSTEM

When Congress established the *Federal Reserve System* in 1914, the United States joined the company of most other advanced industrial nations. Until then, the United States, distrustful of centralized economic power, was almost the only important nation without a **central bank.** Great Britain's central bank, the Bank of England, for example, dates from 1694.

A **central bank** is a bank for banks. The United States' central bank is the *Federal Reserve System.*

▌ Origins and Structure

Some painful experiences with economic reality, not the power of economic logic, provided the impetus to establish a central bank for the United States. Four severe banking panics between 1873 and 1907, in which many banks failed, convinced legislators and bankers alike that a central bank that would regulate credit conditions was not a luxury but a necessity. The 1907 crisis led Congress to study the shortcomings of the banking system and, eventually, to establish the Federal Reserve System.

Although the basic ideas of central banking came from Europe, the United States made some changes when it imported the idea, making the Federal Reserve System a uniquely American institution.[1] Owing to the vastness of our country, the extraordinarily large number of commercial banks, and our tradition of shared state-federal responsibilities, Congress decided that the United States should have not one central bank but 12.

Technically, each Federal Reserve bank is a corporation; its stockholders are its member banks. But your bank, if it is a member of the system, does not enjoy the privileges normally accorded to stockholders: It receives only a token share of the Federal Reserve's immense profits (the bulk is turned over to the U.S. Treasury), and it has virtually no say in corporate decisions. In many ways, the private banks are more like customers of the Fed than owners.

Who, then, controls the Fed? Most of the power resides in the seven-member Board of Governors of the Federal Reserve System in Washington, especially in its chairman. The governors are appointed by the president of the United States, with the advice and consent of the Senate, for 14-year terms. The president also designates one of the members to serve a four-year term as chairman of the board, and thus to be the most powerful central banker in the world.

The Federal Reserve stands independent of the rest of the government. As long as it stays within its statutory authority as delineated by Congress, it alone has responsibility for determining the nation's monetary policy. The power of appointment, however, gives the president some long-run influence over Federal Reserve policy.

Closely allied with the board of governors is the powerful Federal Open Market Committee (FOMC), which meets eight times a year in Washington. For reasons to be explained shortly, FOMC decisions largely determine short-term interest rates and the size of the U.S. money supply. This 12-member committee consists of the seven governors of the Federal Reserve System, the president of the Federal Reserve Bank of New York, and, on a rotating basis, four of the other 11 district bank presidents.[2]

"I'm sorry, sir, but I don't believe you know us well enough to call us the Fed."

---

[1] Ironically, when the European Central Bank was established in 1999, its structure was patterned on that of the Federal Reserve.

[2] Alan Blinder was the vice chairman of the Federal Reserve Board and thus a member of the Federal Open Market Committee from 1994 to 1996.

A Meeting of the Federal Open Market Committee

Meetings of the Federal Open Market Committee are serious and formal affairs. All 19 members—7 governors and 12 reserve bank presidents—sit around a mammoth table in the Fed's cavernous but austere board room. A limited number of top Fed staffers join them at and around the table, for access to FOMC meetings is strictly controlled.

At precisely 9 A.M.—for punctuality is a high virtue at the Fed—the doors are closed and the chairman calls the meeting to order. No press is allowed and, unlike most important Washington meetings, nothing will leak. Secrecy is another high virtue at the Fed.

After hearing a few routine staff reports, the chairman calls on each of the members in turn to give their views of the current economic situation. Although he knows them all well, he addresses each member formally as "Governor X" or "President Y." District bank presidents offer insights into their local economies, and all members comment on the outlook for the national economy. Disagreements are raised, but voices are not. There are no interruptions while people talk. Strikingly, in this most political of cities, politics is almost never mentioned.

Once he has heard from all the others, the chairman offers his own views of the economic situation. Then he usually recommends a course of action. Members of the committee, in their turn, comment on the chairman's proposal. Most agree, though some note differences of opinion. After hearing all this, the chairman announces what he per-

SOURCE: Courtesy of the Federal Reserve Board

ceives to be the committee's consensus and asks the secretary to call the roll. Only the 12 voting members answer, saying yes or no. Negative votes are rare, for the FOMC tries to operate by consensus and a dissent is considered a loud objection.

The meeting adjourns, and at 2:15 P.M. a Fed spokesman announces the decision to the public. Within minutes, financial markets around the world react.

▌ Central Bank Independence

Central bank independence refers to the central bank's ability to make decisions without political interference.

There has been a longstanding debate over the pros and cons of **central bank independence,** both in the United States and in other countries.

Some people look upon the institutional independence of the Federal Reserve and other central banks as a source of pride. Proponents of central bank independence argue that it enables the central bank to make monetary policy decisions on objective, technical criteria and keeps monetary policy out of the "political thicket." Without this independence, they argue, politicians might try to force the Fed to expand the money supply too rapidly, thereby contributing to chronic inflation and undermining faith in America's financial system. They point to historical evidence showing that countries with more independent central banks have, on average, experienced lower inflation.

Opponents of this view counter that there is something profoundly undemocratic about letting a group of unelected bankers and economists make decisions that affect every citizen's well-being. Monetary policy, they argue, should be formulated by the elected representatives of the people, just as fiscal policy is. Those who argue for political control over the Fed and other central banks can point to historical instances in which monetary and fiscal policy were at loggerheads—with the central bank undermining or even overwhelming the effects of fiscal policy decisions.

In recent years, however, the debate over central bank independence has become increasingly "academic" as one country after another has made its central bank independent—and no major country has moved in the other direction. Why? The main reason seems to have been the desire to fight inflation.

Under the terms of the Maastricht Treaty, which committed members of the European Union to move toward a single currency (the euro), each member-state was re-

A Central Bank Is Born

The Maastricht Treaty, which provides for a common currency for all members of the European Union, requires all member nations to follow the same monetary policy. That meant that authority over monetary policy had to be assigned to a single European-wide central bank. This new institution—called the European Central Bank (ECB)—officially opened for business on January 1, 1999.

The structure of the ECB is patterned on that of the Federal Reserve: monetary policy is made by a committee consisting of six ECB officials headquartered in Frankfurt plus the heads of the 12 national central banks.* They meet monthly in Frankfurt to determine Europe's monetary policy.

After a nasty international squabble in 1998, the honor of being the first person selected to head the ECB was granted to Wim Duisenberg, a widely respected veteran central banker from the Netherlands. Under an informal agreement reached at the time, he was succeeded by

*Until May 2004, the European Union had 15 members. But the United Kingdom, Sweden, and Denmark are not part of the monetary union. Nor are any of the 10 new members.

SOURCE: © AFP/Corbis

Jean-Claude Trichet, the former Governor of the Bank of France, in 2003. Because the ECB is not a creature of any national government, it is arguably the most independent central bank in the world.

quired to make its central bank independent. All did so, even though several have not yet joined the monetary union. Japan also decided to make its central bank independent in 1998. In Latin America, several formerly high-inflation countries like Brazil and Mexico have found that giving their central banks more independence helped them control inflation. And some of the formerly socialist countries in Europe, finding themselves saddled with high inflation and "unsound" currencies, made their central banks more independent for similar reasons.

The worldwide trend toward greater central bank independence is clear. Whether it will last forever is anyone's guess.

IMPLEMENTING MONETARY POLICY: OPEN-MARKET OPERATIONS

When it wants to change the money supply and interest rates, the Fed normally relies on **open-market operations.** Open-market operations either give banks more reserves or take reserves away from them, thereby triggering a multiple expansion or contraction of the money supply, as described in the previous chapter.

How does this process work? If the Federal Open Market Committee decides that interest rates are too high, it can issue instructions to expand the money supply through open-market operations. The Federal Reserve System would then *purchase* U.S. government securities (generally short-term securities called *Treasury bills*) from any individual or bank that wished to sell them, thus putting more reserves in the hands of the banks.

An example will illustrate the mechanics. Suppose the FOMC orders a purchase of $100 million worth of securities in the open market and that commercial banks sell those securities. *The Fed makes payment by giving the banks $100 million in new reserves.* As a result, if they held only their required reserves initially, the banks now have $100 million in *excess reserves.* The relevant transactions are shown in Table 12-1.

When the Fed buys $100 million worth of securities from the banks, the ownership of these securities shifts from the banks to the Fed. (See the black arrows in

Open-market operations refer to the Fed's purchase or sale of government securities through transactions in the open market.

TABLE 12-1   Effects of an Open-Market Purchase of Securities on the Balance Sheets of Banks and the Fed

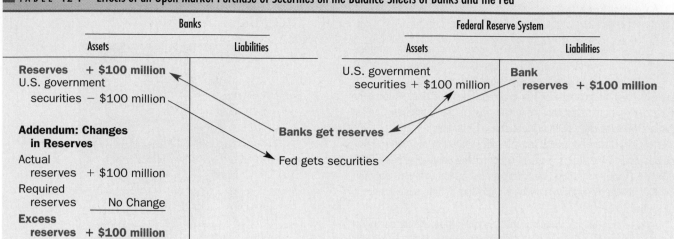

Table 12-1.) The Fed makes payment by adding $100 million to the bookkeeping entries that represent the banks' accounts at the Fed—called "bank reserves" in the table. These reserves (shown in blue in the table) are liabilities of the Fed and assets of the banks. Because deposits have not increased at all, *required* reserves remain unchanged by this transaction. But *actual* reserves are increased by $100 million, so there are now $100 million in *excess* reserves. This excess, we know from the previous chapter, will trigger a multiple expansion of the banking system.

Where does the Fed get the money that it turns over to the banks in exchange for the securities? It could pay in cash, but normally does not. Instead, it manufactures the funds out of thin air or, more literally, by punching the keyboard of a computer terminal. Specifically, the Fed pays the banks for the securities by adding the appropriate sums to the reserve accounts that the banks maintain at the Fed. Balances held in these accounts constitute bank reserves, just like cash in bank vaults.

Although this process of creating bookkeeping entries at the Federal Reserve is commonly referred to as "printing money," the Fed does not literally run any printing presses. Instead, it simply trades its IOUs for an existing asset (a government security). But unlike other IOUs, the Fed's IOUs constitute bank reserves and thus can support a multiple expansion of the money supply in the same way that cash does. The banks—not the Fed—actually increase the money supply; the Fed's actions, however, give the banks the ability to lend the additional funds that fuel the expansion.

Once excess reserves are created, multiple expansion of the banking system proceeds in the usual way. It is not difficult for the Fed to estimate the ultimate increase in the money supply that will result from its actions. As we saw in the previous chapter, each dollar of newly created bank reserves can support $1/m$ dollars of checking deposits, if m is the required reserve ratio. In our example, $m = 0.20$; hence, $100 million in new reserves can support $100 million ÷ 0.2 = $500 million in new money.

But *estimating* the ultimate monetary expansion is a far cry from *knowing it* with certainty. As we know from the previous chapter, the simple money multiplier formula is predicated on two assumptions: that people will want to hold no more cash and that banks will want to hold no more excess reserves, as the monetary expansion proceeds. In practice, these assumptions are unlikely to be literally true. So to predict the eventual effect of its action on the money supply, the Fed must *estimate* both the amount that firms and individuals will add to their currency holdings and the amount that banks will add to their excess reserves. Neither of these quantities can be estimated with utter precision. In summary:

When the Federal Reserve System wants to increase the money supply, it purchases U.S. government securities in the open market. It pays for these securities by creating new bank reserves, and these additional reserves lead to a multiple expansion of the money supply. However, because of fluctuations in people's desires to hold cash and banks' desires to hold excess reserves, the Fed cannot predict the consequences of these actions with perfect accuracy. Thus, over short periods, control over the money supply must of necessity be imperfect.

The procedures followed when the FOMC wants to *contract* the money supply are just the opposite of those we have just explained. In brief, it *sells* government securities in the open market. This takes reserves *away* from banks, because banks pay for the securities by drawing down their deposits at the Fed.[3] A multiple *contraction* of the banking system ensues. The principles are exactly the same as when the process operates in reverse—and so are the uncertainties.

Open-Market Operations, Bond Prices, and Interest Rates

The *expansionary monetary policy* action used as an example in the previous section began with the Fed deciding to buy more government bonds. When it goes into the open market to purchase more bonds, the Federal Reserve normally drives up bond prices. This process is illustrated in Figure 12-1, which shows a *leftward shift* of the (vertical) supply curve of bonds *available to private investors*—from $S_0 S_0$ to $S_1 S_1$—indicating that the Fed's action has taken some of the bonds off the private market. With an unchanged (private) demand curve, DD, the price of bonds rises from P_0 to P_1 as equilibrium in the bond market shifts from point A to point B.

Rising bond prices translate directly into falling interest rates. Why? Most bonds pay a fixed number of dollars of interest per year. For concreteness, consider a bond that pays $60 each year. If the bond sells for $1,000, bondholders earn a 6 percent return on their investment (the $60 interest payment is 6 percent of $1,000). We say that *the interest rate on the bond is 6 percent.* Now suppose that the price of the bond rises to $1,200. The annual interest payment is still $60, so bondholders now earn just 5 percent on their money ($60 is 5 percent of $1,200). *The effective interest rate on the bond has fallen to 5 percent.* This relationship between bond prices and interest rates is completely general:

FIGURE 12-1
Open-Market Sales and Bond Prices

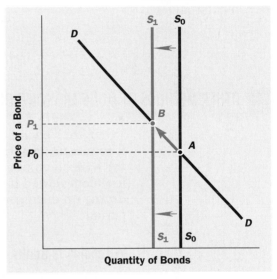

When bond prices rise, interest rates fall because the purchaser of a bond spends more money than before to earn a given number of dollars of interest per year. Similarly, when bond prices fall, interest rates rise.

In fact, the relationship amounts to nothing more than two ways of saying the same thing. Higher interest rates *mean* lower bond prices; lower interest rates *mean* higher bond prices.[4]

We see, therefore, that the Fed exercises direct influence over interest rates through its open-market operations. Specifically:

An open-market purchase of bonds by the Fed not only raises the money supply but also drives up bond prices and pushes interest rates down. Conversely, an open-market sale of bonds, which reduces the money supply, lowers bond prices and raises interest rates.

---

[3] It is not important that *banks* be the buyers. Review Question 5 at the end of the chapter shows that the effect on the money supply is the same if bank *customers* purchase the securities.

[4] For further discussion and examples, see Review Question 6 at the end of the chapter.

You Now Belong to a Distinctive Minority Group

A s the stock market sagged from 2000 to early 2003, more and more investors became attracted to bonds as a safer alternative. But an amazing number of investors do not understand even the elementary facts about bond investing—including the relationship between bond prices and interest rates.

The Wall Street Journal reported in November 2001 that "One of the bond basics about which many investors are clueless, for instance, is the fundamental seesaw relationship between interest rates and bond prices. Only 31% of 750 investors participating in the American Century [a mutual fund company] telephone survey knew that when interest rates rise, bond prices generally fall."* Imagine how many fewer, then, could explain *why* this is so.

*Karen Damato, "Investors Love Their Bond Funds—Too Much?," *The Wall Street Journal*, November 9, 2001, page C1.

SOURCE: © Sidney Harris

"When interest rates go up, bond prices go down. When interest rates go down, bond prices go up. But please don't ask me why."

OTHER METHODS OF MONETARY CONTROL

When the Federal Reserve System was first established, its founders did not intend it to pursue an active monetary policy designed to stabilize the economy. Indeed, the basic ideas of stabilization policy were unknown at the time. Instead, the Fed's founders viewed it as a means of preventing the supplies of money and credit from drying up during economic contractions, as had often happened in the pre-1914 period.

Lending to Banks

One of the principal ways in which Congress intended the Fed to provide such insurance against financial panics was to act as a "lender of last resort." When risky business prospects made commercial banks hesitant to extend new loans, or when banks were in trouble, the Fed would step in by lending money to the banks, thus inducing the banks to lend more to their customers. The Fed most recently performed this role on a large scale in September 2001, when the terrorist attack on New York City literally disabled several large financial institutions. Mammoth amounts of lending to banks kept the financial system functioning and averted a panic.

When the Fed extends borrowing privileges to a bank in need of reserves, that bank receives a credit in its deposit account at the Fed (see the blue entries in Table 12-2). Because bank deposits, and hence required reserves, have not increased, this addition to bank reserves creates *excess reserves*—$5 million in the example. This excess may lead to an expansion of the money supply; alternatively, it may eliminate a reserve deficiency and thereby prevent a multiple contraction of the banking system. In either case, the Fed eases monetary conditions by lending to banks.

The **discount rate** is the interest rate the Fed charges on loans that it makes to banks.

Federal Reserve officials can influence the amount banks borrow by manipulating the *rate of interest charged on these loans*, which is known as the **discount rate**. If the Fed wants banks to have more reserves, it can reduce the interest rate that it charges on loans, thereby tempting banks to borrow more. Alternatively, it can soak up reserves by raising its rate and persuading the banks to reduce their borrowings.

But when it changes its discount rate, the Fed cannot know for sure how banks will react. Sometimes they may respond vigorously to a cut in the rate, borrowing a great deal from the Fed and lending a correspondingly large amount to their customers. At

What Is the Federal Funds Rate?

If you read or listen to the financial press the next time the FOMC changes monetary policy, you will probably hear that the Fed has raised or lowered "the Federal funds rate." What in the world is that?

As we mentioned in the previous chapter, banks sometimes find themselves with either insufficient or excess reserves. Neither situation is satisfactory. Reserve deficiencies (actual reserves below required reserves) are not allowed. Excess reserves (actual reserves above requirements) are perfectly legal but earn the bank no interest. So an active market has developed in which banks with excess reserves lend their surpluses to banks with reserve deficiencies. The interest rate charged on such loans is called the *federal funds rate.*

When the Fed conducts an open-market operation, the federal funds rate reacts almost instantly. Why? Because the Fed's action alters the supply-demand balance in the federal funds market. An open-market purchase bolsters reserve *supply,* and therefore lowers the federal funds rate. An open-market sale adds new reserve *demand,* and so pushes the funds rate higher. Although changes in the federal funds rate affect only certain banks *directly,* the effects soon ripple through the economy's entire interest rate structure.

SOURCE: AP/Wide World Photos

Think of the federal funds market as the Archimedean lever that the Fed uses to move the giant U.S. economy.

TABLE 12-2   Balance Sheet Changes for Borrowings from the Fed

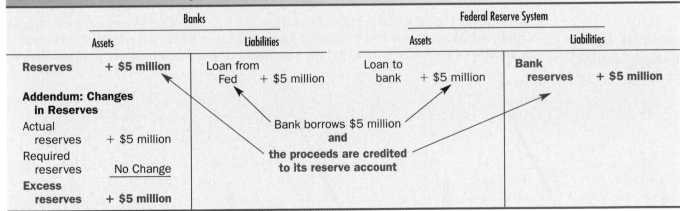

Banks				Federal Reserve System			
Assets		**Liabilities**		**Assets**		**Liabilities**	
Reserves	+ $5 million	Loan from Fed	+ $5 million	Loan to bank	+ $5 million	**Bank reserves**	+ $5 million
Addendum: Changes in Reserves							
Actual reserves	+ $5 million						
Required reserves	No Change						
Excess reserves	+ $5 million						

Bank borrows $5 million **and** the proceeds are credited to its reserve account

other times they may essentially ignore the change in the discount rate. So the link between the discount rate and the money supply is apt to be quite loose.

Some foreign central banks *actively* use their versions of the discount rate as the centerpiece of monetary policy. But in the United States, the Fed lends infrequently and normally in very small amounts. Instead, it relies on open-market operations to conduct monetary policy. The Fed typically adjusts its discount rate *passively*, to keep it in line with market interest rates.

Changing Reserve Requirements

In principle, the Fed has another way to conduct monetary policy: varying the minimum required reserve ratio. To see how this process works, imagine that banks hold reserves that just match their required minimums. In other words, excess reserves are zero. If the Federal Reserve decides that the money supply needs to be increased, it can lower the required reserve ratio, thereby transforming some previously *required* reserves into *excess* reserves. No new money is created directly by this action. But we know from the previous chapter that this change will set in motion the wheels of a multiple expansion of the banking system. Similarly, raising the required reserve ratio will set off a multiple contraction.

In point of fact, however, the Fed no longer uses the reserve ratio as a weapon of monetary control. Current law and regulations provide for a reserve ratio of 10 percent against most transaction deposits—a figure that has not changed since 1992.

SUPPLY-DEMAND ANALYSIS OF THE MONEY MARKET

This completes our discussion of the Fed's three methods of controlling the money supply—open-market operations, lending policy, and reserve requirements—and the limitations of each. One point, however, merits further emphasis. We have noted that the Fed's control of the money supply is imperfect because banks can and do vary their excess reserve holdings. Because reserves earn no interest, banks will hold substantial *excess* reserves only when they feel that funds cannot be put to profitable use without excessive risk. This situation may happen if shaky business conditions make loans to customers look unusually risky or if interest rates are very low. Conversely, banks will work hard to keep reserves down to the legal minimum when loans to customers look safe and when interest rates are high. Thus:

> **As interest rates rise, banks normally find it more profitable to expand their volume of loans and deposits, thus increasing the money supply. However, the Fed can shift the relationship between the money supply and interest rates by employing any of its principal weapons of monetary control: open-market operations, changes in reserve requirements, or changes in lending policy to banks.**

▌ The Money Supply Mechanism

These ideas are depicted graphically in Figure 12-2. Panel (a) shows a typical money supply schedule, labeled *MS*, illustrating the fact that banks will supply more money as interest rates rise.[5] Notice that the sensitivity of the money supply to interest rates

FIGURE 12-2
The Supply Schedule for Money

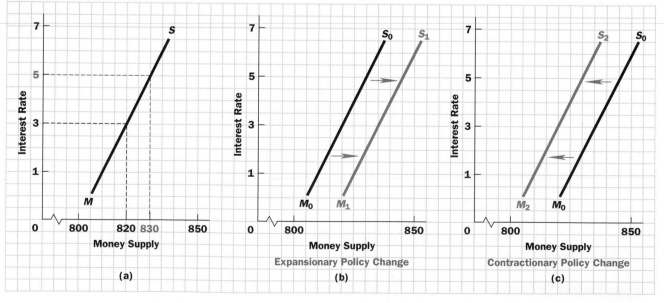

---

[5] There are many interest rates in the economy, but they all tend to move up and down together. Hence, for present purposes, we can speak of "the" rate of interest.

is rather weak in the diagram—a large increase in the rate of interest (from 3 percent to 5 percent) induces only a small increase in the money supply (from $820 billion to $830 billion). The drawing is deliberately constructed that way because that is what the statistical evidence suggests.

The *MS* line in Panel (a) shows the money supply schedule corresponding to some specific monetary policy. Panel (b) portrays how the money supply schedule responds to an *expansionary change in monetary policy*, such as an open-market purchase of government bonds. The money supply schedule shifts *outward* from the black line $M_0 S_0$ to the red line $M_1 S_1$, as indicated by the arrows. After banks have adjusted to the change, the money supply is greater at any given interest rate.

Panel (c) shows what happens in the reverse case—a *contractionary monetary policy*, such as an open-market sale of securities. The money supply shifts inward from the black line $M_0 S_0$ to the red line $M_2 S_2$.

As we have emphasized, the diagrams make things look rather more precise than they actually are. Because the Fed's control over the money supply schedule is imperfect in the short run, the actual *MS* schedule is obscured by a bit of fog. In what follows, we portray all the graphs as clean straight lines only for pedagogical simplicity. The Fed wishes things were so simple in the real world!

The Demand for Money

Just as we must know something about both the supply of and the demand for milk before we can predict how much will be sold and at what price, we must know something about the demand for money if we are to understand the amount of money actually in existence and the prevailing interest rate.

The definition of *money* given in Chapter 11 suggests the most important reason why people hold money balances: The medium of exchange is needed to carry out purchases and sales of goods and services conveniently. If more purchases and sales are made, more dollars are needed to conduct the nation's business. And real gross domestic product (Y) is normally used to measure the volume of goods and services traded in the economy. Similarly, if the average price per transaction—that is, the price level, P— rises, more dollars will be needed to conduct the nation's business. Hence it seems safe to assume that the demand for money will rise as Y and/or P rises. And an impressive amount of statistical evidence supports this hypothesis.

But real GDP and prices are not the only factors affecting the demand for money; interest rates matter, too. At first, that may seem surprising, because many forms of money pay either no interest or a fixed interest rate. Why, then, are interest rates relevant? They are relevant because money is only one of a variety of forms in which individuals can store wealth. Holders of money give up the opportunity to hold one of these other assets, such as government bonds, to gain the convenience of money. In so doing, they give up the interest that they could have earned on one of these alternative assets. Thus, while people hold money to facilitate transactions, this benefit comes at a cost— the potential interest they could earn by investing the funds in, say, government bonds.

This case is another example of the concept of opportunity cost at work.[6] On the surface, it seems virtually costless to hold money. But, *compared to the next best alternative*, this action is not costless at all. If the best alternative to holding $100 in cash is to put those funds into a government bond that pays 6 percent interest, then the opportunity cost of holding that cash is $6 per year (6 percent of $100). Because higher interest rates raise the opportunity cost of holding idle money balances, they should induce households and firms to hold less money. In a word, the demand to hold money should *decline* as the interest rate *rises*. Once again, careful analysis of the data shows this to be true. To summarize:

People and businesses hold money primarily to finance transactions. Therefore, the quantity of money demanded *increases* as output and/or prices rise. However, the quantity of money demanded

[6] If you need to review this concept, see Chapter 2.

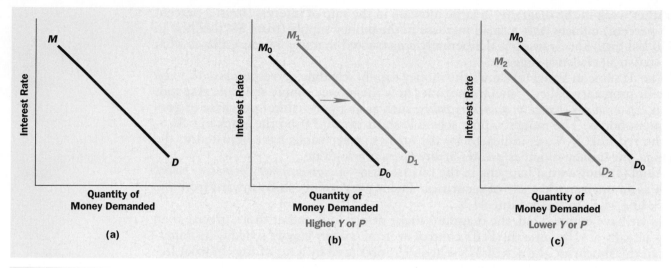

■ FIGURE 12-3
The Demand Schedule for Money

■ FIGURE 12-4
Equilibrium in the Money Market

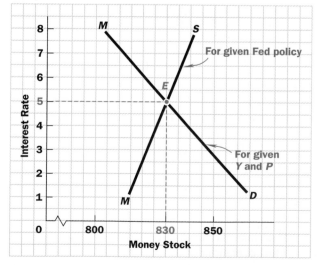

NOTE: Interest rates are in percent; money stock figures are in billions of dollars.

decreases as the rate of interest rises because the rate of interest is the opportunity cost of holding money balances.

We can portray the demand for money by a graphical device, as shown in the three panels of Figure 12-3. Panel (a) depicts a downward-sloping demand schedule for money (the curve labeled *MD*)—the quantity of money demanded decreases as the rate of interest rises. But because the quantity of money demanded also depends on real GDP (Y) and the price level (P), we must hold Y and P *constant* in drawing such a curve. Changes in either of these variables will *shift* the *MD* curve in the manner indicated in the other two panels. At higher levels of Y and P, as illustrated in Panel (b), the demand for money is greater at any interest rate because more transactions occur and because the average transaction requires more money. At lower levels of Y and P, as shown in Panel (c), the demand for money is smaller.

■ Equilibrium in the Money Market

As is usual in supply and demand analysis, it is useful to put both sides of the market together on a single graph. Figure 12-4 combines the money supply schedule of Figure 12-2(a) (labeled MS) with the money demand schedule of Figure 12-3(a) (labeled MD). Point E is the equilibrium of the money market. The diagram thus shows that *given* real GDP and the price level (which locate the MD curve) and *given* the Federal Reserve's monetary policy (which locates the MS curve), the money market is in equilibrium at an interest rate of 5 percent and a money stock of $830 billion. At any interest rate above 5 percent, the quantity of money supplied would exceed the quantity demanded and the interest rate—which is the price for renting money—would therefore decline. At any interest rate below 5 percent, more money would be demanded than supplied, and so the interest rate would rise. This is familiar ground.

Because the Fed can shift the MS curve, it can alter this equilibrium through its **monetary policy.** Purchasing government securities in the open market will provide additional excess reserves to the banking system, thus encouraging banks to increase their loans and deposits. As money becomes more plentiful, interest rates drop.

Our supply-demand analysis of the money market illustrates such an *expansionary monetary policy* in Figure 12-5(a). By shifting the money supply schedule outward from M_0S_0 to M_1S_1, the Fed moves the market equilibrium from point E to point A—thus forcing the interest rate down and the money supply up. *Contractionary monetary policy* actions, or "monetary tightenings," such as selling securities in the open market, have the opposite effect. They push interest rates up and the money supply down, as Figure 12-5(b) shows. Thus:

Monetary policies that expand the money supply normally lower interest rates. Monetary policies that reduce the money supply normally raise interest rates.

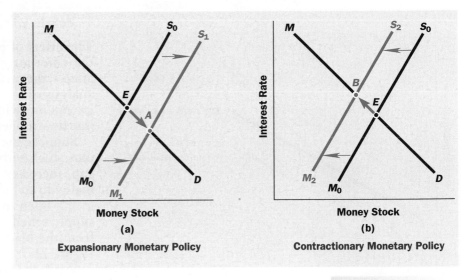

(a)
Expansionary Monetary Policy

(b)
Contractionary Monetary Policy

■ FIGURE 12-5
The Effects of Monetary Policy on the Money Market

HOW MONETARY POLICY WORKS

We are now ready to see precisely how the Federal Reserve's monetary policy decisions affect unemployment, inflation, and the overall state of the economy. To begin, we go back to the analysis of Chapters 6 through 10, where we learned that aggregate demand is the sum of consumption spending (C), investment spending (I), government purchases of goods and services (G), and net exports ($X - IM$). We know that *fiscal policy* controls G directly and influences both C and I through the tax laws. We now want to find out how *monetary policy* affects total spending.

Most economists agree that, of the four components of aggregate demand, investment and net exports are the most sensitive to monetary policy. We will study the effects of monetary and fiscal policy on net exports in Chapter 18, after we have learned about international exchange rates. For now, we will assume that net exports ($X - IM$) are *fixed* and focus on monetary policy's influence on investment (I).

Investment and Interest Rates

Business investment in new factories and machinery is sensitive to interest rates for reasons that have been explained in earlier chapters.[7] Because the rate of interest that must be paid on borrowings is part of the cost of an investment, business executives will find investment prospects less attractive as interest rates rise. Therefore, they will spend less. Similarly, because the interest cost of a home mortgage is the major component of the total cost of owning a home, fewer families will want to buy new houses when interest rates rise. Thus higher interest rates will deter some individuals from *investment in housing*. We conclude that:

Higher interest rates lead to lower investment spending. But investment (I) is a component of total spending, $C + I + G + (X - IM)$. Therefore, when interest rates rise, total spending falls. In terms of the 45° line diagram of previous chapters, a higher interest rate leads to a lower expenditure schedule. Conversely, a lower interest rate leads to a higher expenditure schedule.

This situation is depicted graphically in Figure 12-6 on the next page.

---

[7] See, for example, Chapter 6, page 110.

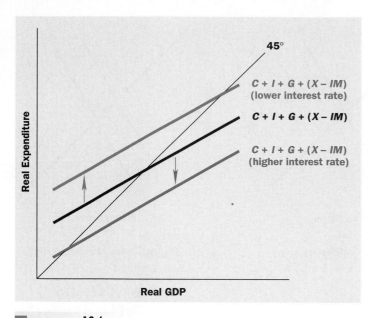

FIGURE 12-6
The Effect of Interest Rates on Total Expenditure

Monetary Policy and Total Expenditure

The effect of interest rates on spending provides the chief mechanism by which monetary policy affects the macroeconomy. We know from our analysis of the money market that monetary policy can move interest rates. Let us, therefore, outline how monetary policy works.

Suppose the Federal Reserve, seeing the economy stuck with unemployment and a recessionary gap, increases the money supply. It would normally do so by purchasing government securities in the open market, thereby shifting the money supply schedule outward—as shown by the shift from the black line $M_0 S_0$ to the red line $M_1 S_1$ in Figure 12-7.

With the demand schedule for money, MD, temporarily fixed, such a shift in the supply curve for money has the effect that an increase in supply always has in a free market: It lowers the price, as Figure 12-7 shows. In this case, the price of renting money is the rate of interest, r, so r falls from 5 percent to 3 percent in the example.

Next, for reasons we have just outlined, investment spending (I) rises in response to the lower interest rates. But, as we learned in Chapter 8, such an autonomous rise in investment kicks off a multiplier chain of increases in output and employment. Finally, we have completed the links from the money supply to the level of aggregate demand. In brief, monetary policy works as follows:

A higher money supply (M) leads to lower interest rates (r), and these lower interest rates encourage investment (I), which has multiplier effects on aggregate demand.

This process operates equally well in reverse. By contracting the money supply, the Fed can force interest rates up, causing investment spending to fall and pulling down aggregate demand via the multiplier mechanism. This, in outline form, is how monetary policy operates in the Keynesian model. Because the chain of causation is fairly long, the following schematic diagram may help clarify it:

FIGURE 12-7
The Effect of Expansionary Monetary Policy on the Money Supply and Rate of Interest

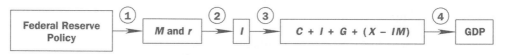

In this causal chain, Link 1 indicates that the Federal Reserve's actions affect money and interest rates. Link 2 stands for the effect of interest rates on investment. Link 3 simply notes that investment is one component of total spending. Link 4 is the multiplier, relating an autonomous change in investment to the ultimate change in aggregate demand. Let us review what we know about each of these links and fill in some illustrative numbers. In the process, we will see what economists must study if they are to estimate the effects of monetary policy.

Link 1 is the subject of this chapter. It was just depicted in Figure 12-7, which shows the money stock rising from $830 billion to $880 billion while the interest rate declines from 5 percent to 3 percent. Thus, the first thing an economist must know is how sensitive interest rates are to changes in the supply of money.

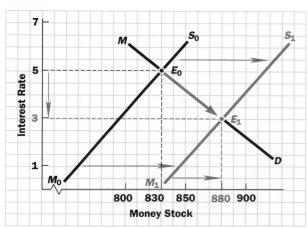

NOTE: Interest rates are in percent; money stock figures are in billions of dollars.

Link 2 translates the lower interest rate into higher investment spending. In this example, we assume that I rises by $200 billion. To estimate this effect in practice, economists must study the sensitivity of investment to interest rates—a topic we took up in Chapter 8.

Link 3 instructs us to enter this $200 billion rise in I as an autonomous shift in the $C + I + G + (X - IM)$ schedule of a 45° line diagram. Figure 12-8 carries out this step. The expenditure schedule rises from $C + I_0 + G + (X - IM)$ to $C + I_1 + G + (X - IM)$.

Finally, Link 4 applies multiplier analysis to this vertical shift in the expenditure schedule to predict the eventual increase in real GDP demanded. We have been using a multiplier of 2.5 in our examples, so multiplying $200 billion by 2.5 gives the final effect on aggregate demand—a rise of $500 billion. This change is shown in Figure 12-8 as a shift in equilibrium from E_0 (where GDP is $6,000 billion) to E_1 (where GDP is $6,500 billion). Of course, the size of the multiplier itself must also be estimated. To summarize:

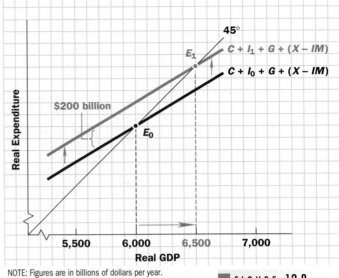

NOTE: Figures are in billions of dollars per year.

■ FIGURE 12-8

The Effect of Expansionary Monetary Policy on Total Expenditure

The effect of monetary policy on aggregate demand depends on the sensitivity of interest rates to the money supply, on the responsiveness of investment spending to the rate of interest, and on the size of the multiplier.

MONEY AND THE PRICE LEVEL IN THE KEYNESIAN MODEL

Our analysis up to this point leaves one important question unanswered: What happens to the price level? To find the answer, we must simply recall that aggregate demand *and* aggregate supply jointly determine prices and output. Our analysis of monetary policy so far has shown us how an increase in the money supply boosts total spending—that is, it increases the *aggregate quantity demanded at any given price level*. But to learn what happens to the price level and to real output, we must consider *aggregate supply* as well.

Specifically, when considering shifts in aggregate demand caused by *fiscal* policy in Chapter 10, we noted that an upsurge in total spending normally induces firms to increase output somewhat *and* to raise prices somewhat. This is just what an aggregate supply curve shows. Whether prices or real output responds more dramatically depends on the slope of the aggregate supply curve.

Because this analysis of output and price responses applies equally well to monetary policy or, for that matter, to any other factor that raises aggregate demand, we conclude that:

Expansionary monetary policy causes some inflation under normal circumstances. But exactly how much inflation it causes depends on the slope of the aggregate supply curve.

The effect of a rise in the money supply on the price level appears graphically on an aggregate supply and demand diagram in Figure 12-9. In the example we have been using, the Fed's actions raise the money supply by $50 billion, which in turn increases aggregate demand

■ FIGURE 12-9

The Inflationary Effects of Expansionary Monetary Policy

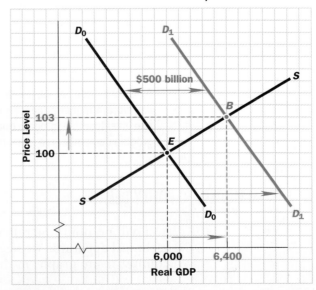

NOTE: GDP figures are in billions of dollars per year.

(through the multiplier) by $500 billion. We enter this increase as a horizontal shift of $500 billion in the aggregate demand curve of Figure 12-9, from D_0D_0 to D_1D_1. The diagram shows that this expansionary monetary policy pushes the economy's equilibrium from point E to point B—the price level therefore rises from 100 to 103, or 3 percent. The diagram also shows that real GDP rises by only $400 billion, which is less than the $500 billion stimulus to aggregate demand. The reason, as we know from earlier chapters, is that rising prices stifle real aggregate demand.

By taking account of the effect of an increase in the money supply on the price level, we have completed our story about the role of monetary policy in the Keynesian model. We can thus expand our schematic diagram of monetary policy as follows:

The last link now recognizes that both output and prices normally are affected by changes in the money supply.

Application: Why the Aggregate Demand Curve Slopes Downward

This analysis of the effect of money on the price level puts us in a better position to understand why higher prices reduce aggregate quantity demanded—that is, why the aggregate demand curve slopes downward. In earlier chapters, we explained this phenomenon in two ways. First, we observed that rising prices reduce the purchasing power of certain assets held by consumers, especially money and government bonds, and that falling real wealth in turn retards consumption spending. Second, we noted that higher domestic prices depress exports and stimulate imports.

There is nothing wrong with this analysis; it is just incomplete. Higher prices have another important effect on aggregate demand, through a channel that we are now in a position to understand.

Money is demanded primarily to conduct transactions. As we have noted in this chapter, an increase in the *average money cost* of each transaction—that is, a rise in the price level—will increase the quantity of money demanded. Thus, when expansionary policy of any kind raises the price level, more money will be demanded at any given interest rate.

But if the money supply is *not* increased, an increase in the quantity of money demanded at any given interest rate must force the cost of borrowing money—the rate of interest—to rise. As we know, increases in interest rates reduce investment and, hence, reduce aggregate demand. This is the main reason why the economy's aggregate demand curve has a negative slope, meaning that aggregate quantity demanded is lower when prices are higher. In sum:

At higher price levels, the quantity of money demanded is greater. Given a fixed supply schedule, therefore, a higher price level must lead to a higher interest rate. Because high interest rates discourage investment, aggregate quantity demanded is lower when the price level is higher. That is, the aggregate demand curve has a negative slope.

FROM MODELS TO POLICY DEBATES

You will no doubt be relieved to hear that we have now provided just about all the technical apparatus we need to analyze stabilization policy. To be sure, you will encounter many graphs in the next few chapters. Most of them, however, repeat diagrams with which you are already familiar. Our attention now turns from *building* a theory to *using* that theory to understand important policy issues.

The next three chapters address a trio of important and controversial policy debates that surface regularly in the newspapers: the debate over the conduct of stabilization policy (Chapter 13), the continuing debate over budget deficits and surpluses and the effects of fiscal and monetary policy on growth (Chapter 14), and the controversy over the trade-off between inflation and unemployment (Chapter 15).

"Ray Brown on bass, Elvin Jones on drums, and Alan Greenspan on interest rates."

SUMMARY

1. A **central bank** is a bank for banks.

2. The Federal Reserve System is America's central bank. There are 12 Federal Reserve banks, but most of the power is held by the Board of Governors in Washington and by the Federal Open Market Committee.

3. The Federal Reserve acts independently of the rest of the government. While there is some controversy over whether **central bank independence** is a good idea, many countries have moved in this direction over the past 10 to 15 years.

4. The Fed has three major monetary policy weapons: **open-market operations,** reserve requirements, and its lending policy to banks. But only open-market operations are used frequently.

5. The Fed increases the money supply by purchasing government securities in the open market. When it pays banks for such purchases, the Fed provides banks with new reserves, which in turn lead to a larger money supply. Conversely, open-market sales of securities take reserves from banks and lead to a smaller money supply.

6. When the Fed buys bonds, bond prices rise and interest rates fall. When the Fed sells bonds, bond prices fall and interest rates rise.

7. The Fed can also pursue a more expansionary monetary policy by allowing banks to borrow more reserves, perhaps by reducing the interest rate it charges on such loans, or by reducing reserve requirements.

8. None of these weapons, however, gives the Fed perfect control over the money supply in the short run, because it cannot predict perfectly how far the process of deposit creation or destruction will go.

9. The upward-sloping money supply schedule shows that more money is supplied at higher interest rates because, as interest rates rise, banks find it more profitable to expand their loans and saving account deposits. This schedule can be shifted by Federal Reserve policy.

10. The downward-sloping money demand schedule shows that less money is demanded at higher interest rates because interest is the opportunity cost of holding money. This schedule shifts when output or the price level changes—that is, when nominal GDP changes.

11. The equilibrium money stock (M) and the equilibrium interest rate (r) are determined by the intersection of the money supply and money demand schedules.

12. Federal Reserve policy can shift this equilibrium. Expansionary policies cause M to rise and r to fall. Contractionary policies reduce M and increase r.

13. Investment spending (I), including business investment and investment in new homes, is sensitive to interest rates (r). Specifically, I is lower when r is higher.

14. **Monetary policy** works in the following way in the Keynesian model: Raising the money supply (M) leads to lower r; the lower interest rates stimulate investment spending; and this investment stimulus, via the multiplier, then raises aggregate demand.

15. Prices are likely to rise as output rises. The amount of inflation caused by increasing the money supply depends on the slope of the aggregate supply curve. Much inflation will occur if the supply curve is steep, but little inflation if it is flat.

16. The main reason why the aggregate demand curve slopes downward is that higher prices increase the demand to hold money so as to finance transactions. Given a fixed money supply, higher money demand pushes interest rates up, which, in turn, discourages investment.

KEY TERMS

QUESTIONS FOR REVIEW

1. Why does a modern industrial economy need a central bank?

2. What are some reasons behind the worldwide trend toward greater central bank independence? Are there arguments on the other side?

3. Suppose there is $120 billion of cash and that half of this cash is held in bank vaults as *required* reserves (that is, banks hold no *excess* reserves). How large will the money supply be if the required reserve ratio is 10 percent? 12½ percent? 16⅔ percent?

4. Show the balance sheet changes that would take place if the Federal Reserve Bank of New York purchased an office building from Citibank for a price of $100 million. Compare this effect to the effect of an open-market purchase of securities shown in Table 12-1. What do you conclude?

5. Suppose the Fed purchases $5 billion worth of government bonds from Bill Gates, who banks at the Bank of America in San Francisco. Show the effects on the balance sheets of the Fed, the Bank of America, and Gates. (*Hint:* Where will Gates get the $5 billion to pay the Fed?) Does it make any difference if the Fed sells bonds to a bank or to an individual?

6. Treasury bills have a fixed face value and pay interest by selling "at a discount." For example, if a one-year bill with a $1,000 face value sells today for $950, it will pay $1,000 − $950 = $50 in interest over its life. The interest rate on the bill is therefore $50/$950 = 0.0526, or 5.26 percent.

   a. Suppose the price of the Treasury bill falls to $925. What happens to the interest rate?

   b. Suppose, instead, that the price rises to $975. What is the interest rate now?

   c. **(More difficult)** Now generalize this example. Let *P* be the price of the bill and *r* be the interest rate. Develop an algebraic formula expressing *r* in terms of *P*. (*Hint:* The interest earned is $1,000 − *P*. What is the percentage interest rate?) Show that this formula illustrates the point made in the text: Higher bond prices mean lower interest rates.

7. Explain why the quantity of money supplied normally is higher and the quantity of money demanded normally is lower at higher interest rates.

8. Throughout 2001, the Fed decided that interest rates were too high and took steps to lower them. How did the Fed cut interest rates? Illustrate your answer on a diagram.

9. Explain why both business investments and purchases of new homes rise when interest rates decline.

10. Explain what a $50 billion increase in the money supply will do to real GDP under the following assumptions:

    a. Each $10 billion increase in the money supply reduces the rate of interest by 0.5 percentage point.

    b. Each 1 percentage point decline in interest rates stimulates $30 billion worth of new investment.

    c. The expenditure multiplier is 2.

    d. The aggregate supply curve is so flat that prices do not rise noticeably when demand increases.

11. Explain how your answers to Review Question 10 would differ if each of the assumptions changed. Specifically, what sorts of changes in the assumptions would make monetary policy very weak?

12. Use graphs like those in Figures 12-4 and 12-6 to explain why the aggregate demand curve has a negative slope.

13. In the late 1990s, the federal government eliminated its budget deficit by reducing its spending. If the Federal Reserve wanted to maintain the same level of aggregate demand in the face of large-scale deficit reduction, what should it have done? What would you expect to happen to interest rates?

14. **(More difficult)** Consider an economy in which government purchases, taxes, and net exports are all zero, the consumption function is

$$C = 300 + 0.75Y$$

and investment spending (*I*) depends on the rate of interest (*r*) in the following way:

$$I = 1,000 − 100r$$

Find the equilibrium GDP if the Fed makes the rate of interest (a) 2 percent (*r* = 0.02), (b) 5 percent, and (c) 10 percent.

13

The Debate over Monetary and Fiscal Policy

The love of money is the root of all evil.
THE NEW TESTAMENT

Lack of money is the root of all evil.
GEORGE BERNARD SHAW

Up to now, our discussion of stabilization policy has been almost entirely objective and technical. In seeking to understand how the national economy works and how government policies affect it, we have mostly ignored the intense economic and political controversies that surround the actual conduct of monetary and fiscal policy. Chapters 13 through 15 cover precisely these issues.

We begin this chapter by introducing an alternative theory of how monetary policy affects the economy, known as *monetarism*. Although the monetarist and Keynesian *theories* seem to contradict one another, we will see that the conflict is more apparent than real. However, important differences *do* arise among economists over the appropriate design and execution of monetary *policy*. These differences are the central concern of the chapter. We will learn about the continuing debates over the nature of aggregate supply, over the relative virtues of monetary versus fiscal policy, and over whether the Federal Reserve should try to control the money stock or interest rates. As we will see, the resolution of these issues is crucial for the proper conduct of stabilization policy and, indeed, to the decision of whether the government should attempt to conduct any stabilization policy at all.

CONTENTS

Issue: Should We Forsake Stabilization Policy?

We have suggested several times in this book that well-timed changes in fiscal or monetary policy can mitigate fluctuations in inflation and unemployment. For example, when the U.S. economy sagged after the terrorist attacks in September 2001, *both* fiscal policy *and* monetary policy turned more expansionary. These might be called "textbook responses," reflecting the lessons you have learned in Chapters 10 and 12.

But some economists argue that these lessons are best forgotten. In practice, they claim, attempts at macroeconomic stabilization are likely to do more harm than good. Policymakers are therefore best advised to follow fixed *rules* rather than use their best judgment on a case-by-case basis.

Nothing we have said so far leads to this conclusion. But we have not yet told the whole story. By the end of the chapter you will have encountered several arguments in favor of rules, and so you will be in a better position to make up your own mind on this important issue.

VELOCITY AND THE QUANTITY THEORY OF MONEY

In the previous chapter, we studied the *Keynesian* view of how money influences real output and the price level. But another, older model provides a different way to look at these matters. This model, known as the *quantity theory of money*, is easy to understand once we have introduced one new concept: **velocity.**

Velocity indicates the number of times per year that an "average dollar" is spent on goods and services. It is the ratio of nominal gross domestic product (GDP) to the number of dollars in the money stock. That is:

$$Velocity = \frac{Nominal\ GDP}{Money\ stock}$$

In Chapter 11, we learned that because barter is so cumbersome, virtually all economic transactions in advanced economies use money. Thus, if there are $5,000 billion worth of transactions in an economy during a particular year, and there is an average money stock of $1,000 billion during that year, then each dollar of money must have been used an average of five times during the year.

The number 5 in this example is called the *velocity of circulation*, or *velocity* for short, because it indicates the *speed* at which money circulates. For example, a particular dollar bill might be used to buy a haircut in January; the barber might use it to purchase a sweater in March; the storekeeper might then use it to pay for gasoline in May; the gas station owner could pay it out to a house painter in October; and the painter might spend it on a Christmas present in December. In this way, the same dollar is used five times during the year. If it were used only four times during the year, its velocity would be 4, and so on.

No one has data on every transaction in the economy. To make velocity an operational concept, economists need a workable definition of transactions—one they can actually measure. The most popular choice is nominal gross domestic product (GDP), even though it ignores many transactions that use money, such as the huge volume of activity in financial markets. If we accept nominal GDP as our measure of the money value of transactions, we are led to a concrete definition of velocity as the ratio of nominal GDP to the number of dollars in the money stock. Because nominal GDP is the product of real GDP times the price level, we can write this definition in symbols as follows:

$$Velocity = \frac{Value\ of\ transactions}{Money\ stock} = \frac{Nominal\ GDP}{M} = \frac{P \times Y}{M}$$

By multiplying both sides of the equation by M, we arrive at an identity called the **equation of exchange,** which relates the money supply and nominal GDP:

The **equation of exchange** states that the money value of GDP transactions must be equal to the product of the average stock of money times velocity. That is:

$$M \times V = P \times Y$$

Money supply × Velocity = Nominal GDP

Alternatively, stated in symbols, we have:

$$M \times V = P \times Y$$

Here we have an obvious link between the stock of money, M, and the nominal value of the nation's output. This connection is merely an arithmetic link, however—not an economic one. For example, it does not imply that the Fed can raise nominal GDP by increasing M. Why not? Because V might simultaneously fall enough to prevent $M \times V$ from rising. In other words, if more dollar bills circulated than before, but each bill changed hands more slowly, total spending might not rise. Thus, we need an auxiliary assumption to change the arithmetic identity into an economic theory:

> The **quantity theory of money** transforms the equation of exchange from an arithmetic identity into an economic model by assuming that changes in velocity are so minor that velocity can be taken to be virtually constant.

The **quantity theory of money** assumes that velocity is (approximately) constant. In that case, nominal GDP is proportional to the money stock.

You can see that if V never changed, the equation of exchange would be a marvelously simple model of the determination of nominal GDP—far simpler than the Keynesian model that took several chapters to develop. To see this, it is convenient to rewrite the equation of exchange in growth-rate form:

$$\%\Delta M + \%\Delta V = \%\Delta P + \%\Delta Y$$

If V was constant (so that its percentage change was always zero), this equation would say, for example, that if the Federal Reserve wanted to make nominal GDP grow by 4.7 percent per year, it need merely raise the money supply by 4.7 percent per year. In such a simple world, economists could use the equation of exchange to *predict* nominal GDP growth by predicting the growth rate of money. And policymakers could *control* nominal GDP growth by controlling growth of the money supply.

In the real world, things are not so simple because velocity is not a fixed number. But variable velocity does not necessarily destroy the usefulness of the quantity theory. As we explained in Chapter 1, all economic models make assumptions that are at least mildly unrealistic. Without such assumptions, they would not be models at all, just tedious descriptions of reality. The question is really whether the assumption of constant velocity is a useful abstraction from annoying detail or a gross distortion of the facts.

Figure 13-1 sheds some light on this question by showing the behavior of velocity since 1929. Note that the figure includes two different measures of velocity, labeled V_1 and V_2. Why? Recall from Chapter 11 that we can measure money in several ways,

■ FIGURE 13-1
Velocity of Circulation, 1929–2002

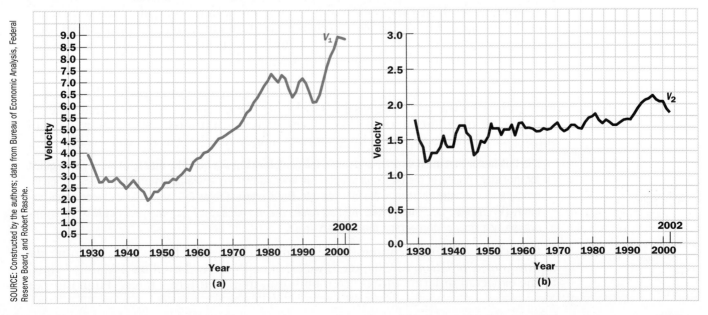

SOURCE: Constructed by the authors; data from Bureau of Economic Analysis, Federal Reserve Board, and Robert Rasche.

the most popular of which are M1 and M2. Because velocity (V) is simply nominal GDP divided by the money stock (M), we get a different measure of V for each measure of M. Figure 13-1 shows the velocities of both M1 and M2.

You will undoubtedly notice the stark difference in the behavior of V_1 versus V_2. V_1 is nowhere near constant; it displays a clear downward trend from 1929 until 1946, a pronounced upward trend until 1981, and quite erratic behavior since then. V_2 is much closer to constant, but it has risen noticeably since the 1980s. Furthermore, closer examination of monthly or quarterly data reveals rather substantial fluctuations in velocity, by either measure. Because velocity is not constant in the short run, predictions of nominal GDP growth based on assuming constant velocity have not fared well, regardless of how M is measured. In a word, the strict quantity theory of money is not an adequate model of aggregate demand.

▌ Some Determinants of Velocity

Because it is abundantly clear that velocity is a variable, not a constant, the equation of exchange is useful as a model of GDP determination only if we can explain movements in velocity. What factors decide whether a dollar will be used to buy goods and services four or five or six times per year? While numerous factors are relevant, two are important enough to merit discussion here.

Efficiency of the Payments System   Money is convenient for conducting transactions, which is why people hold it. But money has one important *dis*advantage: Cash pays no interest, and ordinary checking accounts pay very little. Thus, if it were possible to convert interest-bearing assets into money on short notice and at low cost, a rational individual might prefer to use, say, credit cards for most purchases, making periodic transfers to her checking account as necessary. That way, the same volume of transactions could be accomplished with lower money balances. By definition, velocity would rise.

The incentive to limit cash holdings thus depends on the ease and speed with which it is possible to exchange money for other assets—which is what we mean by the "efficiency of the payments system." As computerization has speeded up banks' bookkeeping procedures, as financial innovations have made it possible to transfer funds rapidly between checking accounts and other assets, and as credit cards have come to be used instead of cash, the need to hold money balances has declined and velocity has increased.

In practice, improvements in the payments system have posed severe practical problems for analysts interested in predicting velocity. A host of financial innovations, beginning in the 1970s and continuing to the present day (some of which were mentioned in Chapter 11's discussion of the definitions of money), have transformed forecasting velocity into a hazardous occupation. In fact, many economists believe the task is impossible and should not even be attempted.

Interest Rates   A second key determinant of velocity is the rate of interest. The reason is implicit in what we have already said: The higher the rate of interest, the greater the *opportunity cost* of holding money. Therefore, as interest rates rise, people want to hold smaller cash balances. So the existing stock of money circulates faster, and velocity rises.

> It is this factor that most directly undercuts the usefulness of the quantity theory of money as a guide for monetary policy. In the previous chapter, we learned that expansionary monetary policy, which increases *M,* normally decreases the interest rate. But if interest rates fall, other things being equal, velocity (*V*) will also fall. Thus, *when the Fed raises the money supply* (M), *the product* M × V *may increase by a smaller percentage than does* M *itself.*

One component of the interest rate is worth singling out for special attention: *the expected rate of inflation.* In Chapter 5, we explained why an "inflation premium" equal to the expected inflation rate is often built into market interest rates.[1] High rates of

---

[1] If you need a review of this idea, turn back to page 94.

inflation, which erode the purchasing power of money, therefore raise nominal interest rates and lead both individuals and businesses to hold as little money as they can get by on—actions that increase velocity. To summarize:

Velocity is not a strict constant but depends on such things as the efficiency of the financial system, the rate of interest, and the rate of inflation. Only by studying these determinants of velocity can we hope to predict the growth rate of nominal GDP from knowledge of the growth rate of the money supply.

Monetarism: The Quantity Theory Modernized

Adherents to a school of thought called **monetarism** try to do precisely that. Monetarists realize that velocity changes, but they claim that such changes are fairly *predictable*—certainly in the long run and perhaps even in the short run. As a result, they conclude that the best way to study economic activity is to start with the equation of exchange in growth-rate form:

$$\%\Delta M + \%\Delta V = \%\Delta P + \%\Delta Y$$

Monetarism is a mode of analysis that uses the equation of exchange to organize and analyze macroeconomic data.

From here, careful study of the determinants of money growth (which we provided in the previous two chapters) and of changes in velocity (which we just completed) can be used to *predict* the growth rate of nominal GDP. Similarly, given an understanding of movements in V, control over M gives the Fed *control* over nominal GDP. These ideas are the central tenets of monetarism.

Let us compare the monetarist approach with the Keynesian approach that we described in earlier chapters. Each is a theory of aggregate demand.

Keynesians divide economic knowledge into four neat compartments marked C, I, G, and $(X - IM)$ and unite them all with the equilibrium condition that $Y = C + I + G + (X - IM)$. In Keynesian analysis, money affects the economy by first affecting interest rates. Monetarists, on the other hand, organize their knowledge into two alternative boxes labeled M and V, and then use the identity $M \times V = P \times Y$ to predict aggregate demand. In the monetarist model, the role of money is not necessarily limited to working through interest rates.

The bit of arithmetic that multiplies M and V to get $P \times Y$ is neither more nor less profound than the one that adds up C, I, G and $(X - IM)$ to get Y, and certainly both are correct. The real question is which framework is more *useful* in practice. That is, which approach works better as a model of aggregate demand?

While there is no generally correct answer for all economies in all periods of time, a glance back at Figure 13-1 (page 243) will show you why most economists had abandoned monetarism by the 1990s. During the 1960s and 1970s, velocity (at least V_2) was fairly stable. That constancy helped monetarism win many converts—in the United States and around the world. Since then, however, velocity has behaved so erratically here and in many other countries that there are few real monetarists left. Nonetheless, as we will see later in this chapter, some echoes of the debate between Keynesians and monetarists can still be heard.

FISCAL POLICY, INTEREST RATES, AND VELOCITY

As we learned in the previous chapter, Keynesian economics provides a powerful and important role for *monetary* policy: An increase in the money supply reduces interest rates, which, in turn, stimulates the demand for investment. But *fiscal* policy also exerts a powerful influence on interest rates.

To see how, think about what happens to real output and the price level following, say, a rise in government spending. We learned in Chapter 10 that both real GDP (Y) and the price level (P) rise, so nominal GDP certainly rises. But Chapter 12's analysis of the demand for money taught us that rising prices and output pushes the demand curve for money outward to the right. With no change in the supply curve for money, the rate of interest must rise. *So expansionary fiscal policy raises interest rates.*

POLICY DEBATE Does Money Growth Always Cause Inflation?

Monetarists have long claimed that, in the famous words of Milton Friedman, "inflation is always and everywhere a monetary phenomenon." By this statement, Friedman means that changes in the growth rate of the money supply (%ΔM) are far and away the principal cause of changes in the inflation rate (%ΔP)—in all places and at all times.

Few economists question the dominant role of rapid money growth in accounting for extremely high rates of inflation. During the German hyperinflation of the 1920s, for example, money was being printed so fast that the printing presses had a difficult time keeping up the pace! But most economists question the words "always and everywhere" in Friedman's dictum. Aren't many cases of moderate inflation driven by factors other than the growth rate of the money supply?

The answer appears to be "yes." The accompanying charts use recent U.S. history as an illustration. In the scatter diagram on the left,

each point records both the growth rate of the M2 money supply and the inflation rate (as measured by the Consumer Price Index) for a particular year between 1979 and 2003. Because of the years 1979–1981, there seems to be a weak positive relationship between the two variables. But no relationship at all appears for the years 1982–2003.

Monetarists often argue that this comparison is unfair because the effect of money supply growth on inflation operates with a lag of perhaps two years. So the right hand scatter diagram compares inflation with money supply growth *two years earlier*. It tells a pretty similar story. More sophisticated versions of scatter plots like these have led most economists to reject the monetarist claim that inflation and money supply growth are tightly linked.

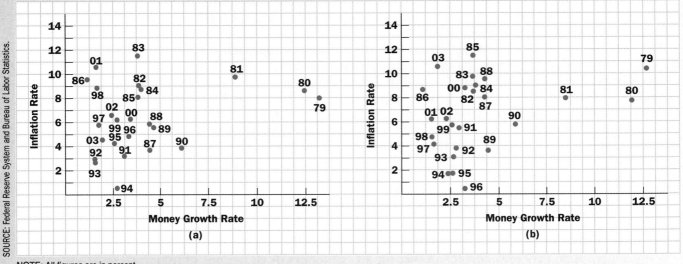

SOURCE: Federal Reserve System and Bureau of Labor Statistics.

NOTE: All figures are in percent.

If the government uses its spending and taxing weapons in the opposite direction, the same process works in reverse. Falling output and (possibly) falling prices shift the demand curve for money inward to the left. With a fixed supply curve for money, equilibrium in the money market leads to a lower interest rate. Thus:

Monetary policy is not the only type of policy that affects interest rates. Fiscal policy also affects interest rates. Specifically, increases in government spending or tax cuts normally push interest rates up, whereas restrictive fiscal policies normally pull interest rates down.

The apparently banal fact that changes in fiscal policy move interest rates up and down has several important consequences. Here are two:

Application: The Multiplier Formula Revisited

We have just noted that expansionary fiscal policy raises interest rates. We also know that higher interest rates deter private investment spending. So when the government raises the G component of $C + I + G + (X - IM)$, one notable side effect will probably be a reduction in the *I* component. Consequently, total spending will rise by *less* than simple multiplier analysis might suggest. The fact that a surge in government demand (*G*) discourages some private demand (*I*) provides another reason why the oversimplified multiplier formula of earlier chapters, $1/(1 - \text{MPC})$, exaggerates the size of the multiplier:

> **Because a rise in *G* (or, for that matter, an autonomous rise in any component of total expenditure) pushes interest rates higher, and hence deters some investment spending, the increase in the sum *C* + *I* + *G* + (*X* − *IM*) is smaller than what the oversimplified multiplier formula predicts.**

Combining this observation with our previous analysis of the multiplier, we now have the following complete list:

REASONS WHY THE OVERSIMPLIFIED MULTIPLIER FORMULA IS WRONG

1. It ignores variable imports, which reduce the size of the multiplier (see Appendix B to Chapter 8).
2. It ignores price-level changes, which reduce the size of the multiplier (see Chapter 9).
3. It ignores the income tax, which reduces the size of the multiplier (see Chapter 10).
4. It ignores the rising interest rates that accompany any autonomous increase in spending, which also reduce the size of the multiplier (this chapter).

Notice that all four of these adjustments point to a *reduction* of the multiplier. No wonder the actual multiplier, which is estimated to be less than 2 for the U.S. economy, is so much less than the oversimplified formula suggests.

Application: The Government Budget and Investment

We will discuss government budget deficits and surpluses in great detail in the next chapter. But one major argument for reducing a deficit or building up a surplus is that lower deficits or bigger surpluses should lead to higher levels of private investment spending. We can now see why. The government reduces its deficit (or raises its surplus) by engaging in *contractionary* fiscal policies—lower spending or higher taxes. As we have just seen, any such measure should *reduce* real interest rates. These lower real interest rates should spur investment spending. This simple insight will play a major role in the next chapter.

DEBATE: SHOULD WE RELY ON FISCAL OR MONETARY POLICY?

While the Keynesian and monetarist approaches are more like two different languages than two different theories, it is well known that language influences attitudes in many subtle ways. For example, the Keynesian language biases things subtly toward thinking first about fiscal policy simply because *G* is a part of *C* + *I* + *G* + (*X* − *IM*). By contrast, the monetarist approach, working through the equation of exchange, $M \times V = P \times Y$, puts the spotlight on *M*. In fact, years ago economists engaged in a spirited debate in which extreme monetarists claimed that fiscal policy was futile, whereas extreme Keynesians argued that monetary policy was useless. Today, such arguments are rarely heard.

Instead of arguing over which type of policy is more *powerful*, economists nowadays debate which type of medicine—fiscal or monetary—cures the patient more *quickly*. Until now, we have ignored questions of timing and pretended that the authorities noticed the need for stabilization policy instantly, decided on a course of action right away, and administered the appropriate medicine at once. In reality, each of these steps takes time.

First, delays in data collection mean that the most recent data describe the state of the economy a few months ago. Second, one of the prices of democracy is that the government often takes a distressingly long time to decide what should be done, to muster the necessary political support, and to put its decisions into effect. Finally, our

$10 trillion economy is a bit like a sleeping elephant that reacts rather sluggishly to moderate fiscal and monetary prods. As it turns out, these *lags in stabilization policy*, as they are called, play a pivotal role in the choice between fiscal and monetary policy. Here's why.

The main policy tool for manipulating consumer spending (*C*) is the personal income tax, and Chapter 7 documented why the fiscal policy planner can feel fairly confident that each $1 of tax reduction will lead to about 90 to 95 cents of additional spending *eventually*. But not all of this extra spending happens at once.

First, consumers must learn about the tax change. Then they may need to be convinced that the change is permanent. Finally, there is simple force of habit: Households need time to adjust their spending habits when circumstances change. For all these reasons, consumers may increase their spending by only 30 to 50 cents for each $1 of additional income within the first few months after a tax cut. Only gradually will they raise their spending up to about 90 to 95 cents for each additional dollar of income.

Lags are much longer for investment (*I*), which provides the main vehicle by which monetary policy affects aggregate demand. Planning for capacity expansion in a large corporation is a long, drawn-out process. Ideas must be submitted and approved, plans must be drawn up, funding acquired, orders for machinery or contracts for new construction placed. And most of this activity occurs *before* any appreciable amount of money is spent. Economists have found that much of the response of investment to changes in interest rates or tax provisions takes several *years* to develop.

The fact that *C* responds more quickly than *I* has important implications for the choice among alternative stabilization policies. The reason is that the most common varieties of fiscal policy either affect aggregate demand directly—*G* is a component of $C + I + G + (X - IM)$—or work through consumption with a relatively short lag, whereas monetary policy primarily affects investment. Therefore:

Conventional types of fiscal policy actions, such as changes in *G* or in personal taxes, probably affect aggregate demand much more promptly than do monetary policy actions.

So is fiscal policy a superior stabilization tool? Not quite. The lags we have just described, which are beyond policymakers' control, are not the only ones affecting the timing of stabilization policy. Additional lags stem from the behavior of the policymakers themselves! We refer here to the delays that occur while policymakers study the state of the economy, contemplate which steps they should take, and finally put their decisions into effect. Here monetary policy has a huge advantage:

Policy lags are normally much shorter for monetary policy than for fiscal policy.

The reasons are apparent. The Federal Open Market Committee (FOMC) meets eight times each year, and more often if necessary. So monetary policy decisions are made frequently. Once the Fed decides on a course of action, it normally executes its plan immediately by buying or selling bonds on the open market.

In contrast, federal budgeting procedures operate on an annual budget cycle. Except in unusual cases, major fiscal policy initiatives can occur only at the time of the annual budget. In principle, tax laws can be changed at any time, but the wheels of Congress grind slowly and are often gummed up by partisan politics. For these reasons, it may take many months for Congress to change fiscal policy. President George W. Bush's tax cut proposal in 2001 was in some sense the proverbial exception that proves the rule. Congress passed it in record time—but that meant it took about four months. In sum, only in rare circumstances can the government take important fiscal policy actions on short notice.

So where does the combined effect of expenditure lags and policy lags leave us? With nothing very conclusive, we are afraid. In practice, most students of stabilization policy have come to believe that the unwieldy and often partisan nature of our political system make active use of fiscal policy for stabilization purposes difficult, if not impossible. Monetary policy, they claim, is the only realistic game in town, and therefore must bear the entire burden of stabilization policy. The failure of Congress to pass an economic stimulus package until long after September 11, 2001, was widely interpreted as supporting this view.

DEBATE: SHOULD THE FED CONTROL THE MONEY SUPPLY OR INTEREST RATES?

Another major controversy that raged for decades focused on how the Federal Reserve should conduct monetary policy. Some economists argued that the Fed should use its open-market operations to control the rate of interest (r); others, especially monetarists, insisted that the Fed should concentrate on controlling some measure of the money supply (M). This debate echoes even now in Europe, where the European Central Bank (ECB), unlike the Fed, pays close attention to the growth of the money supply—or, at least, claims to.

To understand the nature of this debate, we must first understand why the Fed cannot control both M and r at the same time. Figure 13-2 will help us see why. It shows an initial equilibrium in the money market at point E, where money demand curve M_0D_0 crosses money supply curve MS. Here the interest rate is $r = 5$ percent and the money stock is $M = \$830$ billion. We assume that these are the Fed's targets: It wants to keep the money supply and interest rates just where they are.

If the demand curve for money holds still, everything works out fine. But suppose the demand for money is not so obliging. Suppose, instead, that the demand curve shifts outward to the position indicated by the red line M_1D_1 in Figure 13-2. We learned in the previous chapter that such a shift might occur because output increases, prices rise, or simply because people decide to hold more money. Whatever the reason, the Fed can no longer achieve both of its previous targets.

If the Fed does nothing, the outward shift in the demand curve will push up both the quantity of money (M) and the rate of interest (r). Figure 13-2 shows these changes graphically as the move from point E to point A. If the demand curve for money shifts outward from M_0D_0 to M_1D_1, and monetary policy does not change

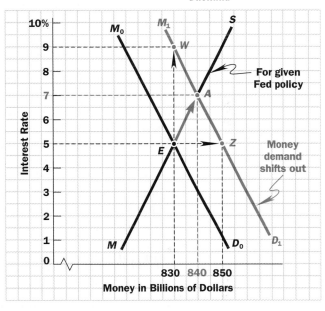

(so the supply schedule does not move), the money stock rises to $840 billion and the interest rate rises to 7 percent.

Now suppose the Fed is targeting the money supply and is unwilling to let M rise. In that case, it must use *contractionary* open-market operations to prevent M from rising. But in so doing, it will push r up even higher, as Figure 13-2 shows. After the demand curve for money shifts outward, point E is unattainable. The Fed must choose from among the points on the red line M_1D_1, and point W is the point on this line that keeps the money supply at $830 billion. By pushing the supply curve *inward* so that it passes through point W, the Fed can hold M at $830 billion. (Pencil this shift in for yourself on the diagram.) But the interest rate will skyrocket to 9 percent.

Alternatively, if the Fed is pursuing an interest rate target, it might decide that a rise in r is to be avoided. In this case, the Fed would be forced to engage in *expansionary* open-market operations to prevent the outward shift of the demand curve for money from pushing r up. In terms of Figure 13-2, the interest rate can be held at 5 percent by shifting the supply curve *outward* to pass through point Z. But to do this, the Fed will have to let the money supply rise to $850 billion. (Again, try penciling in the requisite shift of the money supply schedule.) To summarize this discussion:

When the demand curve for money shifts outward, the Fed must tolerate a rise in interest rates, a rise in the money stock, or both. It simply cannot control *both* the supply of money *and* the interest rate. If it tries to keep *M* steady, then *r* will rise sharply. Conversely, if it tries to stabilize *r*, then *M* will shoot up.

Two Imperfect Alternatives

For years, economists have debated how a central bank should deal with its inability to control both the money supply and the rate of interest. Should it adhere rigidly to its target growth path for the money supply, regardless of the consequences for interest rates—which is the monetarist policy? Should it hold interest rates steady, even if that causes sharp gyrations in the money stock—which is roughly what the Fed does now? Or is some middle ground, perhaps like the ECB's approach, more appropriate? Let us explore the issues first and then consider what has actually been done.

The main problem with imposing rigid targets on the *supply* of money is that the *demand* for money does not cooperate by growing smoothly and predictably from month to month; instead it dances about quite a bit in the short run. This variability presents the recommendation to control the money supply with two problems:

1. It is almost impossible to achieve. Because the volume of money in existence depends on *both* the demand *and* the supply curves, keeping M on target in the face of significant fluctuations in the demand for money would require exceptional dexterity.
2. For reasons just explained, rigid adherence to money-stock targets might lead to wide fluctuations in interest rates, which could create an unsettled atmosphere for business decisions.

But powerful objections can also be raised against exclusive concentration on interest rate movements. Because increases in output and prices shift the demand schedule for money outward (as shown in Figure 13-2), a central bank determined to keep interest rates from rising would have to expand the money supply in response. Conversely, when GDP sagged, it would have to contract the money supply to keep rates from falling. Thus, interest rate pegging would make the money supply expand in boom times and contract in recessions, with potentially grave consequences for the stability of the economy. Ironically, this is precisely the sort of monetary behavior the Federal Reserve System was designed to prevent. Hence, if the Fed is to control interest rates, it had better formulate flexible targets, not fixed ones.

What Has the Fed Actually Done?

For most of U.S. post–World War II history, the predominant view held that the interest rate was much more important of the two targets. The rationale was that gyrating interest rates would cause abrupt and unsettling changes in investment spending, which in turn would make the entire economy fluctuate. Stabilizing interest rates was therefore believed to be the best way to stabilize GDP. If doing so required fluctuations in the money supply, so be it. Consequently, the Fed focused on interest rates and paid little attention to the money supply. That is more or less the Fed's view today.

In the 1960s, this prevailing view came under attack by Milton Friedman and other monetarists. These economists argued that the Fed's obsession with stabilizing interest rates actually *destabilized* the economy by making the money supply fluctuate too much. For this reason, they urged the Fed to stop worrying about fluctuations in interest rates and make the money supply grow at a constant rate from month to month and year to year.

Monetarism made important inroads at the Fed during the inflationary 1970s, especially in October 1979 when then-Chairman Paul Volcker announced a major change in the conduct of monetary policy. Henceforth, he asserted, the Fed would stick more closely to its target for money-stock growth regardless of the implications for interest rates. Interest rates would go wherever the law of supply and demand took them.

According to our analysis, this change in policy should have led to wider fluctuations in interest rates—and it certainly did. Unfortunately, the Fed ran into some bad luck. The ensuing three years were marked by unusually severe gyrations in the demand for money, so the ups and downs of interest rates were far more extreme than anyone had expected. Figure 13-3 shows just how volatile interest rates were between late 1979 and late 1982. As you might imagine, this erratic performance provoked some heavy criticism of the Fed.

Then, in October 1982, Chairman Volcker announced that the Fed was temporarily abandoning its attempts to stick to a target growth path for the money supply. Although he did not say so, his announcement presumably meant that the Fed went back to paying more attention to interest rates. As you can see in Figure 13-3, interest rates did become much more stable after the change in policy. Most observers think this stability was no coincidence.

After 1982, the Fed gradually distanced itself from the position that the money supply should grow at a constant rate. Finally, in 1993, Chairman Alan Greenspan officially confirmed what many people already knew: that the Fed was no longer using the various Ms to guide policy. He strongly hinted that the Fed was targeting interest rates, especially *real* interest rates, instead—a hint that has been repeated many times since then. In truth, the Fed had little choice. The demand curve for money behaved so erratically and so unpredictably in the 1980s and 1990s that stabilizing the money stock was probably impossible and certainly undesirable. And at least so far, the Fed has shown little interest in the Ms.

FIGURE 13-3
The Behavior of Interest Rates, 1979–1985

DEBATE: THE SHAPE OF THE AGGREGATE SUPPLY CURVE

Another lively debate over stabilization policy revolves around the shape of the economy's aggregate supply curve. Many economists think of the aggregate supply curve as quite flat, as in Figure 13-4(a), so that large increases in output can be achieved with little inflation. But other economists envision the supply curve as steep, as shown in Figure 13-4(b), so that prices respond strongly to changes in output. The differences for public policy are substantial.

If the aggregate supply curve is flat, expansionary fiscal or monetary policy that raises the aggregate demand curve can buy large gains in real GDP at low cost in terms of inflation. In Figure 13-5(a), stimulation of demand pushes the aggregate demand curve outward from D_0D_0 to D_1D_1, thereby moving the economy's equilibrium from point E to point A. The substantial rise in output ($400 billion in the diagram) is accompanied by only a pinch of inflation (1 percent). So the antirecession policy is quite successful.

FIGURE 13-4
Alternative Views of the Aggregate Supply Curve

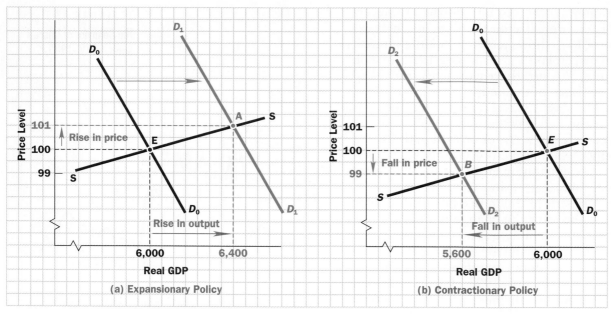

NOTE: Real GDP in billions of dollars per year.

◼ FIGURE 13-5

Stabilization Policy with a Flat Aggregate Supply Curve

Conversely, when the supply curve is flat, a restrictive stabilization policy is not a very effective way to bring inflation down. Instead, it serves mainly to reduce real output, as Figure 13-5(b) shows. Here a leftward shift of the aggregate demand curve from D_0D_0 to D_2D_2 moves equilibrium from point E to point B, lowering real GDP by $400 billion but cutting the price level by merely 1 percent. Fighting inflation by contracting aggregate demand is obviously quite costly in this example.

Things are just the reverse if the aggregate supply curve is steep. In that case, expansionary fiscal or monetary policies will cause a good deal of inflation without boosting real GDP much. This situation is depicted in Figure 13-6(a), where expansionary policies shift the aggregate demand curve outward from D_0D_0 to D_1D_1, thereby moving the economy's equilibrium from E to A. Output rises by only $100 billion, but prices shoot up 10 percent.

Similarly, contractionary policy is an effective way to bring down the price level without much sacrifice of output, as shown by the shift from E to B in Figure 13-6(b). Here it takes only a $100 billion loss of output (from $6,000 billion to $5,900 billion) to "buy" 10 percent less inflation.

As we see, deciding whether the aggregate supply curve is steep or flat is clearly of fundamental importance to the proper conduct of stabilization policy. If the supply curve is flat, stabilization policy is much more effective at combating recession than inflation. If the supply curve is steep, precisely the reverse is true.

But why does the argument persist? Why can't economists determine the shape of the aggregate supply curve and stop arguing? The answer is that supply conditions in the real world are far more complicated than our simple diagrams suggest. Some industries may have flat supply curves, whereas others have steep ones. For reasons explained in Chapter 9, supply curves shift over time. And, unlike laboratory scientists, economists cannot perform controlled experiments that would reveal the shape of the aggregate supply curve directly. Instead, they must use statistical inference to make educated guesses.

Although empirical research continues, our understanding of aggregate supply remains less settled than our understanding of aggregate demand. Nevertheless, many economists believe that the outline of a consensus view has emerged. This view holds that *the steepness of the aggregate supply schedule depends on the time period under consideration.*

"Daddy's not mad at you, dear— Daddy's mad at the Fed."

SOURCE: By Baloo from The Wall Street Journal, January 19, 1994. Permission, Cartoon Features Syndicate

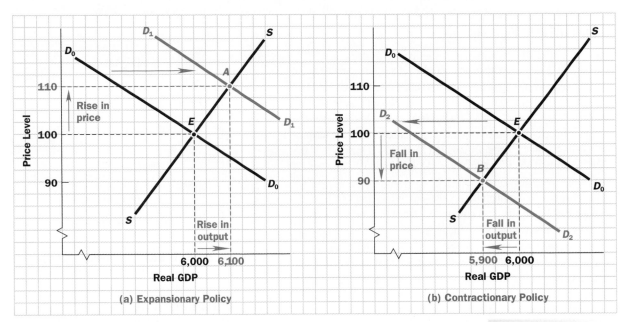

NOTE: Real GDP in billions of dollars per year.

FIGURE 13-6
Stabilization Policy with a Steep Aggregate Supply Curve

In the very short run, the aggregate supply curve is quite flat, making Figure 13-5 the more relevant picture of reality. Over short time periods, therefore, fluctuations in aggregate demand have large effects on output but only minor effects on prices. In the long run, however, the aggregate supply curve becomes quite steep, perhaps even vertical. In that case, Figure 13-6 is a better representation of reality, so that changes in demand affect mainly prices, not output.[2] The implication is that:

Any change in aggregate demand will have most of its effect on *output* in the short run but on *prices* in the long run.

DEBATE: SHOULD THE GOVERNMENT INTERVENE?

We have yet to consider what may be the most fundamental and controversial debate of all—the issue posed at the beginning of the chapter. Is it likely that government policy can successfully stabilize the economy? Or are even well-intentioned efforts likely to do more harm than good?

This controversy has raged for several decades, with no end in sight. The debate is partly political or philosophical because economists, like other people, come in both liberal and conservative stripes. Liberal economists tend to be more intervention-minded and hence more favorably disposed toward an activist stabilization policy. Conservative economists are more inclined to keep the government's hands off the economy and hence advise adhering to fixed rules. Such political differences are not surprising. More than ideology propels the debate, however. We need to understand the economics.

Critics of stabilization policy point to the lags and uncertainties that surround the operation of both fiscal and monetary policies—lags and uncertainties that we have stressed repeatedly in this and earlier chapters. Will the Fed's actions have the desired effects on the money supply? What will these actions do to interest rates and spending? Can fiscal policy actions be taken promptly? How large is the expenditure multiplier? The list could go on and on.

These skeptics look at this formidable catalog of difficulties, add a dash of skepticism about our ability to forecast the future state of the economy, and worry that stabilization policy may fail. They therefore advise both the fiscal and monetary authorities to pursue

---

[2] The reasoning behind the view that the aggregate supply curve is flat in the short run but steep in the long run will be developed in Chapter 15.

The Fed Fights Recession

T he great American economic boom of the 1990s ended about midway through 2000, and the U.S. growth rate plummeted. By January 2001, the Federal Open Market Committee was alarmed enough to start cutting interest rates in an attempt to give the economy a boost. By late summer, the Fed had shaved three full percentage points off the Federal funds rate, and several members of the FOMC were beginning to think they had done enough to stimulate growth.

Then came the horrific terrorist attacks of September 11, which changed everything. The Fed quickly concluded that the shock of the attacks would not just disrupt economy activity, but also damage consumer and business confidence. Six days later, at a hastily arranged telephonic meeting, it reduced the Federal funds rate by one-half percentage point; and it continued to cut the rate for the rest of the year, bringing it all the way down to 1.75 percent—the lowest since 1961. But when the economy did not snap back, the Fed started cutting rates again, lowering the Federal funds rate to an astonishing 1 percent in June 2003, where it remains as this book goes to press.

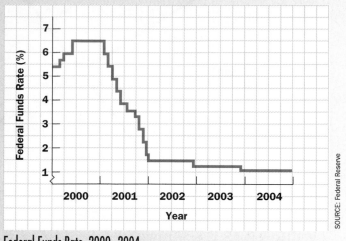

SOURCE: Federal Reserve

Federal Funds Rate, 2000–2004

a passive policy rather than an active one—adhering to fixed rules that, although incapable of ironing out every bump in the economy's growth path, will at least keep it roughly on track in the long run.

Advocates of active stabilization policies admit that perfection is unattainable. But they are much more optimistic about the prospects for success, and they are much *less* optimistic about how smoothly the economy would function in the absence of demand management. They therefore advocate discretionary increases in government spending (or decreases in taxes) and lower interest rates when the economy has a recessionary gap—and the reverse when the economy has an inflationary gap. Such policies, they believe, will help keep the economy closer to its full-employment growth path.

Each side can point to evidence that buttresses its own view. Activists look back with pride at the tax cut of 1964 and the sustained period of economic growth that it helped to introduce. They also point to the tax cut of 1975 (which was quickly enacted at just about the trough of a severe recession), the Federal Reserve's switch to "easy money" in 1982, the Fed's expert steering of the economy between 1992 and 2000, and its quick response to the threat to the economy after September 11, 2001. Advocates of rules remind us of the government's refusal to curb what was obviously a situation of runaway demand during the 1966–1968 Vietnam buildup, its over-expansion of the economy in 1972, the monetary overkill that helped bring on the sharp recession of 1981–1982, and the inadequate antirecession policies of the early 1990s.

The historical record of fiscal and monetary policy is far from glorious. Although the authorities have sometimes taken appropriate and timely actions to stabilize the economy, at other times they clearly either took inappropriate steps or did nothing at all. The question of whether the government should adopt passive rules or attempt an activist stabilization policy therefore merits a closer look. As we shall see, the *lags* in the effects of policy discussed earlier in this chapter play a pivotal role in the debate.

▮ Lags and the Rules-versus-Discretion Debate

Lags lead to a fundamental difficulty for stabilization policy—a difficulty so formidable that it has prompted some economists to conclude that attempts to stabilize economic activity are likely to do more harm than good. To see why, refer to Figure 13-7, which charts the behavior of both actual and potential GDP over the course of a business cycle in a hypothetical economy with no stabilization policy. At point *A*, the economy begins to slip into a recession and does not recover to full employment until point *D*. Then, between points D and *E*, it overshoots potential GDP and enters an inflationary boom.

The argument in favor of stabilization policy runs something like this: Policymakers recognize that the recession is a serious problem at point *B*, and they take appropriate actions. These actions have their major effects around point *C* and therefore limit both the depth and the length of the recession.

But suppose the lags are really longer and less predictable than those just described. Suppose, for example, that actions do not come until point *C* and that stimulative policies do not have their major effects until after point *D*. Then policy will be of little help during the recession and will actually do harm by overstimulating the economy during the ensuing boom. Thus:

In the presence of long lags, attempts at stabilizing the economy may actually succeed in destabilizing it.

For this reason, some economists argue that we are better off leaving the economy alone and relying on its natural self-corrective forces to cure recessions and inflations. Instead of embarking on periodic programs of monetary and fiscal stimulus or restraint, they advise policymakers to stick to fixed rules that ignore current economic events.

For monetary policy, we have already mentioned the monetarist policy rule: The Fed should keep the money supply growing at a constant rate. For fiscal policy, proponents of rules often recommend that the government resist the temptation to manage aggregate demand actively and rely instead on the economy's automatic stabilizers, which we discussed in Chapter 10 (see page 189).

FIGURE 13-7
A Typical Business Cycle

DIMENSIONS OF THE RULES-VERSUS-DISCRETION DEBATE

Are the critics right? Should we forget about discretionary policy and put the economy on autopilot—relying on automatic stabilizers and the economy's natural, self-correcting mechanisms? As usual, the answer depends on many factors.

How Fast Does the Economy's Self-Correcting Mechanism Work?

In Chapter 9, we emphasized that the economy has a self-correcting mechanism. If recessions and inflations will go away quickly by themselves, the case for intervention is weak. That is, if such problems typically last only a short time, then lags in discretionary stabilization policy mean that the medicine will often have its major effects only after the disease has run its course. In fact, a number of economists (albeit a distinct minority) used precisely this reasoning to argue against a fiscal stimulus after the September 11, 2001, terrorist attacks. In terms of Figure 13-7, this is a case in which point *D* comes very close to point *A*.

Although extreme advocates of rules argue that this is indeed what happens, most economists agree that the economy's self-correcting mechanism is slow and not terribly reliable, even when supplemented by the automatic stabilizers. On this count, then, a point is scored for discretionary policy.

How Long Are the Lags in Stabilization Policy?

We just explained why long and unpredictable lags in monetary and fiscal policy make it unlikely that stabilization policy can do much good. Short, reliable lags point in the opposite direction. Thus advocates of fixed rules emphasize the length of lags while proponents of discretion discount them.

Who is right depends on the circumstances. Sometimes policymakers take action promptly, and the economy receives at least some stimulus from expansionary policy within a year after slipping into a recession. The tax cut of 2001 and the Fed's sharp monetary stimulus in the fall of 2001 are the most recent examples. Although far from perfect, the effects of such timely actions are felt soon enough to do some good. But, as we have seen, very slow policy responses may actually prove destabilizing. Because history offers examples of each type, we can draw no general conclusion.

How Accurate Are Economic Forecasts?

One way to dramatically compress the policymaking lag is to forecast economic events accurately. If we could see a recession coming a full year ahead of time (which we certainly *cannot* do), even a rather sluggish policy response would still be timely. In terms of Figure 13-7, this would be a case where the recession is predicted well before point *A*.

Over the years, economists in universities, government agencies, and private businesses have developed a number of techniques to assist them in predicting what the economy will do. Unfortunately, none of these methods is terribly accurate. To give a rough idea of magnitudes, forecasts of either the inflation rate or the real GDP growth rate for the year ahead typically err by ± ¾ to 1 percentage point. But, in a bad year for forecasters, errors of 2 or 3 percentage points are common.

Is this record good enough? That depends on how the forecasts are used. It is certainly not good enough to support *fine tuning*—that is, attempts to keep the economy always within a hair's breadth of full employment. But it probably is good enough for policymakers interested in using discretionary stabilization policy to close persistent and sizable gaps between actual and potential GDP.

The Size of Government

One bogus argument that is nonetheless sometimes heard is that active fiscal policy must inevitably lead to a growing public sector. Because proponents of fixed rules tend also to oppose big government, they view this growth as undesirable. Of course, others think that a larger public sector is just what society needs.

This argument, however, is completely beside the point because, as we pointed out in Chapter 10: *One's opinion about the proper size of government should have nothing to do with one's view on stabilization policy.* For example, President Ronald Reagan was as conservative as they come and devoted to shrinking the size of the public sector. But his tax-cutting initiatives in the early 1980s constituted an extremely activist fiscal policy to spur the economy. Furthermore, most stabilization policy these days consists of monetary policy, which neither increases nor decreases the size of government.

Uncertainties Caused by Government Policy

Advocates of rules are on stronger ground when they argue that frequent changes in tax laws, government spending programs, or monetary conditions make it difficult for firms and consumers to formulate and carry out rational plans. They argue that the authorities can provide a more stable environment for the private sector by adhering to fixed rules, so that businesses and consumers will know exactly what to expect.

No one disputes that a more stable environment is better for private planning. Even so, supporters of discretionary policy emphasize that *stability in the economy* is more important than *stability in the government budget* (or in Federal Reserve operations). The whole idea of stabilization policy is to *prevent* gyrations in the pace of economic activity by *causing* timely gyrations in the government budget (or in monetary policy). Which atmosphere is better for business, they ask: one in which fiscal and monetary rules keep things peaceful on Capitol Hill and at the Federal Reserve while recessions and inflations wrack the economy, or one in which government changes its

Between Rules and Discretion

I n recent years, a number of economists and policymakers have sought a middle ground between saddling monetary policymakers with rigid rules and giving them complete discretion, as the Federal Reserve has in the United States.

One such approach is called "inflation targeting." As practiced in the United Kingdom, inflation targeting starts when an elected official (the Chancellor of the Exchequer, who is roughly equivalent to the U.S. Secretary of the Treasury) chooses a numerical target for the inflation rate—currently, this target is 2 percent for consumer prices. The United Kingdom's central bank, the Bank of England, is then bound by law to try to reach this target within two years. In that sense, the system functions somewhat like a *rule*. However, monetary policymakers are given complete *discretion* as to how they go about trying to achieve this goal. Neither the Chancellor nor Parliament interferes with day-to-day monetary policy decisions.

Another approach is called the "Taylor rule," after Professor John Taylor of Stanford, who is currently serving as President Bush's Undersecretary of the Treasury for International Affairs. Almost a decade ago, Taylor noticed that the Fed's interest rate decisions in the Greenspan era could be described by a simple algebraic equation. This equation, now called the Taylor rule, starts with a 2 percent *real* interest rate, and then instructs the Fed to *lower* the rate of interest in proportion to any

SOURCE: NewsCast

The Bank of England's Monetary Policy Committee

recessionary gap, and to *raise* the interest rate in proportion to any excess of inflation above 2 percent (which is the Fed's presumed inflation goal). No central bank uses the Taylor rule as a mechanical rule; nor did Taylor intend it to be used as such. But many central banks around the world, including the Fed, find the Taylor rule useful as a benchmark to guide their decision making.

policy abruptly on occasion but the economy grows more steadily? They think the answer is self-evident. The question, of course, is whether stabilization policy can succeed in practice.

◼ A Political Business Cycle?

A final argument put forth by advocates of rules is political rather than economic. Fiscal policy decisions are made by elected politicians: the president and members of Congress. When elections are on the horizon (and for members of the House of Representatives, they *always* are), these politicians may be as concerned with keeping their jobs as with doing what is right for the economy. This situation leaves fiscal policy subject to "political manipulation"—lawmakers may take inappropriate actions to attain short-run political goals. A system of purely automatic stabilization, its proponents argue, would eliminate this peril.

It is certainly *possible* that politicians could deliberately *cause* economic instability to help their own reelection. Indeed, some observers of these "political business cycles" have claimed that several American presidents have taken full advantage of the opportunity. Furthermore, even without any insidious intent, politicians may take the wrong actions for perfectly honorable reasons. Decisions in the political arena are never clear-cut, and it certainly is easy to find examples of grievous errors in the history of U.S. fiscal policy.

Taken as a whole, then, the political argument against discretionary fiscal policy seems to have a great deal of merit. But what are we to do about it? It is unrealistic to believe that fiscal decisions could or should be made by a group of objective and nonpartisan technicians. Tax and budget policies require inherently *political* decisions that, in a democracy, should be made by elected officials.

This fact may seem worrisome in view of the possibilities for political chicanery. But it should not bother us any more (or any less!) than similar maneuvering in other areas of policy making. After all, the same problem besets international relations, national defense, formulation and enforcement of the law, and so on. Politicians make all these decisions, subject only to sporadic accountability at elections. Is there really any reason why fiscal decisions should be different?

But monetary policy *is* different. Because Congress was concerned that elected officials focused on the short run would pursue monetary policies that are too inflationary, it long ago gave day-to-day decision-making authority over monetary policy to the unelected technocrats at the Federal Reserve System. Politics influences monetary policy only indirectly: The Fed must report to Congress, and the president has the power to appoint Federal Reserve governors to his liking.

 ### Issue Revisited: What Should Be Done?

So where do we come out on the question posed at the start of this chapter? On balance, is it better to pursue the best discretionary policy we can, knowing full well that we will never achieve perfection? Or is it wiser to rely on fixed rules and the automatic stabilizers?

In weighing the pros and cons, your basic view of the economy is crucial. Some economists believe that the economy, if left unmanaged, would generate a series of ups and downs that would be difficult to predict, but that it would correct each of them by itself in a relatively short time. They conclude that, because of long lags and poor forecasts, our ability to anticipate whether the economy will need stimulus or restraint by the time policy actions have their effects is quite limited. Consequently, they advocate fixed rules.

Other economists liken the economy to a giant glacier with a great deal of inertia. Under this view, if we observe an inflationary or recessionary gap today, it will likely still be there a year or two from now because the self-correcting mechanism works slowly. In such a world, accurate forecasting is not imperative, even if policy lags are long. If we base policy on a forecast of a 4 percent gap between actual and potential GDP a year from now, and the gap turns out to be only 2 percent, we still will have done the right thing despite the inaccurate forecast. So holders of this view of the economy tend to support discretionary policy.

There is certainly no consensus on this issue, either among economists or politicians. After all, the question touches on political ideology as well as economics. And liberals often look to government to solve social problems, whereas conservatives consistently point out that many efforts of government fail despite the best intentions. A prudent view of the matter might be that:

The case for active discretionary policy is strong when the economy has a serious deficiency or excess of aggregate demand. However, advocates of fixed rules are right that it is unwise to try to iron out every little wiggle in the growth path of GDP.

But one thing seems certain: The rules-versus-discretion debate is likely to go on for quite some time.

SUMMARY

1. **Velocity** (V) is the ratio of nominal GDP to the stock of money (M). It indicates how quickly money circulates.

2. One important determinant of velocity is the rate of interest (r). At higher interest rates, people find it less attractive

to hold money because money pays zero or little interest. Thus, when r rises, money circulates faster, and V rises.

3. **Monetarism** is a type of analysis that focuses attention on velocity and the money supply (M). Although monetarists

realize that V is not constant, they believe that it is predictable enough to make it a useful tool for policy analysis and forecasting.

4. Because it raises output and prices, and hence increases the demand for money, expansionary fiscal policy pushes interest rates higher. Higher interest rates reduce the multiplier by deterring some types of spending, especially investment.

5. Because fiscal policy actions affect aggregate demand either directly through G or indirectly through C, the expenditure lags between fiscal actions and their effects on aggregate demand are probably fairly short. By contrast, monetary policy operates mainly on investment, I, which responds slowly to changes in interest rates.

6. However, the policy-making lag normally is much longer for fiscal policy than for monetary policy. Hence, when the two lags are combined, it is not clear which type of policy acts more quickly.

7. Because it cannot control the demand curve for money, the Federal Reserve cannot control both M and r. If the demand for money changes, the Fed must decide whether it wants to hold M steady, hold r steady, or adopt some compromise position.

8. Monetarists emphasize the importance of stabilizing the growth path of the money supply, whereas the predominant Keynesian view puts more emphasis on keeping interest rates on target.

9. In practice, the Fed has changed its views on this issue several times. For decades, it attached primary importance to interest rates. Between 1979 and 1982, it stressed its commitment to stable growth of the money supply. But lately, the focus has clearly turned to interest rates again.

10. When the aggregate supply curve is very flat, changes in aggregate demand will have large effects on the nation's real output but small effects on the price level. Under those circumstances, stabilization policy works well as an antirecession device, but it has little power to combat inflation.

11. When the aggregate supply curve is steep, changes in aggregate demand have small effects on real output but large effects on the price level. In such a case, stabilization policy can do much to fight inflation but is not a very effective way to cure unemployment.

12. The aggregate supply curve is likely to be relatively flat in the short run but relatively steep in the long run. Hence, stabilization policy affects mainly output in the short run, but mainly prices in the long run.

13. When the lags in the operation of fiscal and monetary policy are long and unpredictable, attempts to stabilize economic activity may actually destabilize it.

14. Some economists believe that our imperfect knowledge of the channels through which stabilization policy works, the long lags involved, and the inaccuracy of forecasts make it unlikely that discretionary stabilization policy can succeed.

15. Other economists recognize these difficulties but do not believe they are quite as serious. They also place much less faith in the economy's ability to cure recessions and inflations on its own. They therefore think that discretionary policy is not only advisable, but essential.

16. Stabilizing the economy by fiscal policy need not imply a tendency toward "big government."

KEY TERMS

Velocity 242

Equation of exchange 242

Quantity theory of money 243

Effect of interest rate on velocity 244

Monetarism 245

Effect of fiscal policy on interest rates 245

Lags in stabilization policy 248

Controlling M versus controlling r 249

Rules versus discretionary policy 253

QUESTIONS FOR REVIEW

1. How much money (including cash and checking account balances) do you typically have at any particular moment? Divide this amount into your total income over the past 12 months to obtain your own personal velocity. Are you typical of the nation as a whole?

2. The following table provides data on nominal gross domestic product and the money supply (M1 definition) for selected years. Compute velocity in each year. Can you see any trend?

Year	End-of-Year Money Supply (M1)	Nominal GDP
1999	$1,124	$9,269
2000	1,089	9,873
2001	1,178	10,206

NOTE: Amounts are in billions.

3. Use the concept of opportunity cost to explain why velocity is higher at higher interest rates.

4. How does monetarism differ from the quantity theory of money?

5. Given the behavior of velocity shown in Figure 13-1, would it make more sense for the Federal Reserve to formulate targets for M1 or M2?

6. Distinguish between the expenditure lag and the policy lag in stabilization policy. Does monetary or fiscal policy have the shorter expenditure lag? What about the policy lag?

7. Explain why their contrasting views on the shape of the aggregate supply curve lead some economists to argue much more strongly for stabilization policies to fight unemployment and other economists to argue much more strongly for stabilization policies to fight inflation.

8. Use a supply and demand diagram similar to Figure 13-2 to show the choices open to the Fed following an unexpected *decline* in the demand for money. If the Fed is following a monetarist policy, what will happen to the rate of interest?

9. Explain why lags make it possible that policy actions intended to stabilize the economy will actually destabilize it.

10. Which of the following events would strengthen the argument for the use of discretionary policy, and which would strengthen the argument for rules?

a. Structural changes make the economy's self-correcting mechanism work more quickly and reliably than before.

b. New statistical methods are found that improve the accuracy of economic forecasts.

c. A Republican president is elected when there is an overwhelmingly Democratic Congress. Congress and the president differ sharply on what should be done about the national economy.

11. Many observers think that the Federal Reserve succeeded in using deft applications of monetary policy to "fine-tune" the U.S. economy into the full-employment zone in the 1990s without worsening inflation. Use the data on money supply, interest rates, real GDP, unemployment, and the price level given on the inside back cover of this book to evaluate this claim.

12. After 2000, U.S. economic performance deteriorated. (See the data on the inside back cover of this book.) Can this decline be blamed on inferior monetary or fiscal policy? (You may want to ask your instructor about this question.)

Fiscal Policy, Monetary Policy, and Growth

*Blessed are the young, for they shall
inherit the national debt.*

HERBERT HOOVER

Monetary policy and fiscal policy are typically thought of as tools for short-run economic *stabilization*—that is, as ways to combat either inflation or unemployment. Debates over the Federal Reserve's next interest-rate decision, or over this year's federal budget, are normally dominated by short-run considerations such as: Does the economy need to be stimulated or restrained *right now*?

But the monetary and fiscal choices the government makes today also have profound effects on our economy's ability to produce goods and services *in the future*. We began Part II by emphasizing long-run growth, and especially the role of capital formation (see Chapters 5 and 6). But for most of Part III we have been preoccupied with the shorter-run issues of inflation, unemployment, and recession. This chapter integrates the two perspectives by considering both the long-run and short-run implications of fiscal and monetary policy decisions. What differences does it make if we stimulate (or restrain) the economy with fiscal or monetary policy? Should we strive to balance the budget? What are the economic virtues of large budget surpluses, both now and in the future?

CONTENTS

Issue: Did the September 2001 Terrorist Attack Warrant Fiscal Stimulus?

Several of these questions were brought into sharp relief by the debate over the proper macroeconomic response to the September 11, 2001, terrorist attacks. Almost immediately, many economists and politicians began calling for a fiscal stimulus that would boost spending right away. Their reasoning was that the U.S. economy, which —we now know—was in recession even before the attack, might be pushed over the brink by the blow to consumer confidence and spending.

But others disagreed. Some claimed that the economy needed no further stimulus. Others argued that monetary policy was better suited to the task than fiscal policy, which should be devoted to maintaining the budget surplus. Even many supporters of fiscal stimulus worried that Congress would use the banner of "short-run stimulus" to enact tax cuts and new spending programs that would damage long-run prospects for budget surpluses.

The debate quickly grew partisan and raged on for months. Republicans wanted sizable tax cuts, especially for business. Democrats wanted greatly-improved benefits for the unemployed. While the two parties dickered, spending on defense and homeland security surged and the indomitable American consumer kept on spending. So the economy held up far better than most people thought likely on September 11, 2001.

So which side was right? Did voting to reduce the budget surplus in 2001 help or hurt the U.S. economy? By the end of the chapter, you will be in an excellent position to answer this important question for yourself.

SHOULD THE BUDGET BE BALANCED? THE SHORT RUN

Americans have long been attracted by the idea of balancing the government budget year after year—so much so that they stuck to this belief both before and after Congress made a major change in the *definition* of budget balance in 1999 and then changed back just a few years later. (See "Balance the Budget? By What Definition?" on page 269.) Let us begin our examination of this idea by reviewing the basic principles of fiscal policy that we have learned so far (especially in Chapter 10) and by seeing what they say about the goal of balancing the budget.

In brief, these principles certainly do *not* imply that we should always maintain a balanced budget, much as that notion may appeal to our intuitive sense of good financial management. Rather, they instruct fiscal policymakers to focus on *balancing aggregate supply and aggregate demand* instead of on balancing the budget. They point to the desirability of budget *deficits* when private demand, $C + I + (X - IM)$, is too weak and of budget *surpluses* when private demand is too strong. The budget should be balanced, according to these principles, only when $C + I + G + (X - IM)$ under a balanced-budget policy approximately equals full-employment levels of output. This situation may sometimes occur, but it will not necessarily be the norm.

The reason why a balanced budget is not always advisable should be clear from our earlier discussion of stabilization policy. Consider the fiscal policy that the government would follow if its goal were to maintain a balanced budget every year. Suppose the budget was initially balanced and private spending sagged for some reason, as it did in 2000–2001. The multiplier would pull GDP down. Because personal and corporate tax receipts fall sharply when GDP declines, the budget would automatically start swinging into the red. To restore budget balance, the government would then be forced either to lower spending or to raise taxes—exactly the opposite of the appropriate policy response. Thus:

Attempts to balance the budget during recessions—as was done, say, during the Great Depression—will prolong and deepen slumps.

This is precisely what many observers feel happened to Japan when it raised taxes in a weak economy in 1997. In fact, Ryutaro Hashimoto, Japan's prime minister from 1996 to 1998, was once disparagingly called the "Herbert Hoover of Japan" because he sought to reduce the budget deficit despite Japan's sinking economy.

Budget balancing can also lead to inappropriate fiscal policy under boom conditions. If rising tax receipts induce a budget-balancing government to spend more or to cut taxes, then fiscal policy will "boom the boom"—with unfortunate inflationary consequences. This possibility is one reason why few economists thought cutting taxes was a wise policy during the U.S. election campaign in 2000, despite the fact that the federal government was running a large surplus.[1]

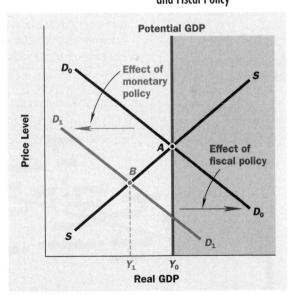

SOURCE: From The Wall Street Journal—Permission, Cartoon Features Syndicate

"The 'Twilight Zone' will not be seen tonight, so that we may bring you the following special on the federal budget."

The Importance of the Policy Mix

Actually, the issue is even more complicated than we have indicated so far. As we know, fiscal policy is not the only way that government affects aggregate demand. The government also influences aggregate demand through its monetary policy. For this reason:

The appropriate fiscal policy depends, among other things, on the current monetary policy stance. Although a balanced budget may be appropriate under one monetary policy, a deficit or a surplus may be appropriate under another monetary policy.

An example will illustrate the point. Suppose Congress and the president believe that the aggregate supply and demand curves will intersect approximately at full employment if the budget is balanced. Then a balanced budget would seem to be the appropriate fiscal policy.

Now suppose monetary policy turns contractionary, pulling the aggregate demand curve inward to the left, as shown by the red arrow in Figure 14-1, and thereby creating a recessionary gap. If the fiscal authorities wish to restore GDP to its original level, they must shift the aggregate demand curve back to its original position, D_0D_0, as indicated by the blue arrow. To do so, they must either raise spending or cut taxes, thereby opening up a budget deficit. Thus, the tightening of *monetary* policy changes the appropriate *fiscal* policy from a balanced budget to a deficit, because both monetary and fiscal policies affect aggregate demand.

By the same token, a given target for aggregate demand implies that any change in *fiscal* policy will alter the appropriate *monetary* policy. For example, we can reinterpret Figure 14-1 as indicating the effects of reducing the budget deficit by cutting government spending. Then, if the Fed does not want real GDP to fall, it must expand the money supply sufficiently to restore the aggregate demand curve to D_0D_0.

It is precisely this change in the *mix* of policy—a smaller budget deficit balanced by easier money—that the U.S. government managed to engineer with great success in the 1990s. Congress and the Clinton administration raised taxes and cut spending, which reduced aggregate demand. But the Federal Reserve pursued a sufficiently expansionary policy to return this "lost" aggregate demand to the economy by lowering interest rates.

So we should not expect a balanced budget to be the norm. How, then, can we tell whether any particular deficit is too large or too small? From the discussion so far, it

FIGURE 14-1

The Interaction of Monetary and Fiscal Policy

[Figure: graph of Price Level vs Real GDP showing curves D_0, D_1, S, points A and B, Potential GDP, Effect of monetary policy, Effect of fiscal policy, Y_1, Y_0]

[1] This campaign promise of then-candidate George W. Bush began to look much better timed when economic activity sagged after the election.

would appear that the answer depends on the strength of private-sector aggregate demand and the stance of monetary policy. But those are not the only considerations.

SURPLUSES AND DEFICITS: THE LONG RUN

One implication of what we have just said is that various *combinations* of fiscal and monetary policy can lead to the *same* level of aggregate demand, and hence to the same real GDP and price level, in the short run. For example, the government could reduce aggregate demand by raising taxes, but the Fed could make up for it by cutting interest rates. Or the reverse could happen: The government could cut taxes while the Fed raises interest rates, leaving aggregate demand unchanged. The long-run consequences of these alternative mixes of monetary and fiscal policy may be quite different, however.

In previous chapters, we learned that more expansionary fiscal policy (tax cuts or higher government spending) and tighter money should produce *higher* real interest rates and therefore *lower* investment. Thus such a policy mix should shift the composition of total expenditure, $C + I + G + (X - IM)$, toward more G, more C (from tax cuts), and less I.[2] The expected result is less capital formation, and therefore slower growth of potential GDP. As we shall see shortly, it was precisely that policy mix—large tax cuts and very tight money—that the U.S. government inadvertently chose in the early 1980s.

But the opposite policy mix—tighter budgets and looser monetary policy—should produce the opposite outcomes: lower real interest rates, more investment, and hence faster growth of potential GDP. That, fortunately, was the direction U.S. macroeconomic policy took in the 1990s—with excellent results.

Lowering the budget deficit and then turning it into a surplus, economists believe, was an effective way to increase the investment share of GDP, which rose from 13.2 percent in 1992 to 19.2 percent in 2000. The general point is:

The composition of aggregate demand is a major determinant of the rate of economic growth. If a larger fraction of GDP is devoted to investment, the nation's capital stock will grow faster and the aggregate supply schedule will shift more quickly to the right, accelerating growth.

■ FIGURE 14-2

Growth and Investment in 24 Countries

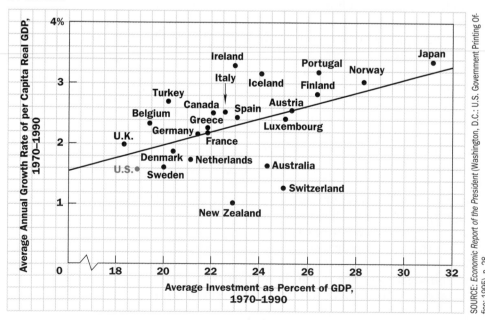

SOURCE: *Economic Report of the President* (Washington, D.C.: U.S. Government Printing Office; 1995), p. 28.

International data likewise show a positive relationship between growth and the share of GDP invested. Figure 14-2 shows, for a set of 24 countries on four continents, both investment as a share of GDP and growth in per-capita output over two decades (the 1970s and 1980s). Countries with higher investment rates clearly experienced higher growth, on average.

So it appears that when we ask whether the budget should be balanced, in deficit, or in surplus, we have posed a good question, but a complicated one. Before attempting to answer it, we need to get some facts straight.

---

[2] We will deal with the consequences of fiscal and monetary policy on $X - IM$ in Chapter 18.

DEFICITS AND DEBT: TERMINOLOGY AND FACTS

First, some critical terminology. People frequently confuse two terms that have different meanings: *budget deficits* and the *national debt*. We must learn to distinguish between the two.

The **budget deficit** is the amount by which the government's expenditures exceed its receipts during some specified period of time, usually a year. If, instead, receipts exceed expenditures, we have a **budget surplus.** For example, during fiscal year 2003, the government raised $1783 billion in taxes and spent $2158 billion, resulting in a deficit of $375 billion.[3]

The **national debt,** also called the *public debt*, is the total value of the government's indebtedness at a moment in time. Thus, for example, the U.S. national debt at the end of fiscal year 2003 was about $6.8 trillion.

These two concepts—deficit and debt—are closely related because the government accumulates *debt* by running *deficits* or reduces its debt by running *surpluses*. The relationship between the debt and the deficit or surplus can be explained by a simple analogy. As you run water into a bathtub ("run a deficit"), the accumulated volume of water in the tub ("the debt") rises. Alternatively, if you let water out of the tub ("run a surplus"), the level of the water ("the debt") falls. Analogously, budget deficits raise the national debt, whereas budget surpluses lower it.

But, of course, getting rid of the deficit (shutting off the flow of water) does not eliminate the accumulated debt (drain the tub). The U.S. government is a prime example. Although it has lately been running small annual deficits or surpluses, it still has a very large accumulated debt.

Having made this distinction, let us look first at the size and nature of the accumulated public debt and then at the annual budget deficit.

Some Facts about the National Debt

How large a public debt do we have? How did we get it? Who owes it? Is it growing or shrinking?

To begin with the simplest question, the public debt is enormous. At the end of 2003, it amounted to about $23,200 for every man, woman, and child in America. But more than half of this outstanding debt was owned by agencies of the U.S. government—in other words, one branch of the government owed it to another. If we deduct this portion, the net national debt was just about $3.3 trillion, or approximately $11,200 per person.

Furthermore, when we compare the debt with the gross domestic product—the volume of goods and services our economy produces in a year—it does not seem so large after all. With a GDP of over $11 trillion in late 2003, the net debt was roughly one-third of the nation's yearly income. By contrast, many families who own homes owe *several years'* worth of income to the banks that granted them mortgages. Many U.S. corporations also owe their bondholders much more than one-third of a year's sales.

But before these analogies make you feel too comfortable, we should point out that simple analogies between public and private debt are almost always misleading. A family with a large mortgage debt also owns a home with a value that presumably exceeds the mortgage. A solvent business firm has assets (factories, machinery, inventories, and so forth) that far exceed its outstanding debt in value.

Is the same thing true of the U.S. government? No one knows for sure. How much is the White House worth? Or the national parks? And what about military bases,

The **budget deficit** is the amount by which the government's expenditures exceed its receipts during a specified period of time, usually a year. If receipts exceed expenditures, it is called a **budget surplus** instead.

The **national debt** is the federal government's total indebtedness at a moment in time. It is the result of previous deficits.

[3] *Reminder:* The fiscal year of the U.S. government ends on September 30. Thus, fiscal year 2003 ran from October 1, 2002, to September 30, 2003.

SOURCE: Constructed by the authors from data in *Historical Statistics of the United States* and *Economic Report of the President*.

FIGURE 14-3

The U.S. National Debt Relative to GDP, 1915–2003

both here and abroad? Simply because these government assets are *not* sold on markets, no one really knows their true value.

Figure 14-3 charts the path of the *net* national debt from 1915 to 2003, expressing each year's net debt as a fraction of that year's nominal GDP. Looking at the debt *relative to GDP* is important for two reasons. First, we must remember that everything grows in a growing economy. Given that private debt has expanded greatly since 1915, it would be surprising indeed if the public debt had not grown as well. In fact, federal debt grew more slowly than did either private debt or GDP for most of the period since World War II. The years from 1980 to about 1995 stand out as an aberration in Figure 14-3.

Second, the debt is measured in dollars and, as long as there is any inflation, the amount of purchasing power that each dollar represents declines each year. Dividing the debt by nominal GDP, as is done in Figure 14-3, adjusts for both real growth and inflation, and so puts the debt numbers in better perspective.

Figure 14-3 shows us how and when the U.S. government acquired all this debt. Notice the sharp increases in the ratio of debt to GDP during World War I, the Great Depression, and especially World War II. Thereafter, you see an unmistakable downward trend until the recession of 1974–1975. In 1945, the national debt was the equivalent of 13 months' national income. By 1974, this figure had been whittled down to just two months' worth.

Thus, until the 1980s, the U.S. government had acquired most of its debt either to finance wars or during recessions. As we will see later, the *cause* of the debt is quite germane to the question of whether the debt is a burden. So it is important to remember that:

Until about 1983, almost all of the U.S. national debt stemmed from financing wars and from the losses of tax revenues that accompany recessions.

But then things changed. From the early 1980s until 1993, the national debt grew faster than nominal GDP, reversing the pattern that had prevailed since 1945. This growth spurt happened with no wars and only one recession. By 1993, the debt exceeded five months' GDP—nearly triple its value in 1974. This disturbing development alarmed many economists and public figures.

At that point, the government took decisive actions to reduce the budget deficit. The ratio of debt to GDP then fell for years until President Bush's tax cuts reversed the trend.

INTERPRETING THE BUDGET DEFICIT OR SURPLUS

We have observed that the federal government ran extremely large budget deficits from the early 1980s until the mid 1990s. As Figure 14-4 shows, the budget deficit ballooned from the $79 billion range in fiscal year 1981 to $208 billion by fiscal year 1983—setting a record that was subsequently eclipsed several times. As late as fiscal year 1995, the deficit was still $164 billion. These are enormous, even mind-boggling, numbers. But what do they mean? How should we interpret them?

The Structural Deficit or Surplus

First, it is important to understand that the same fiscal program can lead to a deficit or surplus, depending on the state of the economy. Failure to appreciate this point has led many people to assume that a larger deficit always signifies a more expansionary fiscal policy—but that is not always true.

Think, for example, about what happens to the budget during a recession. As GDP falls, the government's most important sources of tax revenue—income taxes, corporate taxes, and payroll taxes—all shrink because firms and people pay lower taxes when they earn less. Similarly, some types of government spending, notably transfer payments such as unemployment benefits, rise when GDP falls, because more people are out of work.

Recall that the deficit is the difference between government expenditures, which are either purchases or transfer payments, and tax receipts:

$$\text{Deficit} = G + \text{Transfers} - \text{Taxes} = G - (\text{Taxes} - \text{Transfers}) = G - T$$

■ FIGURE 14-4

Official Fiscal-Year Budget Deficits, 1981–2003

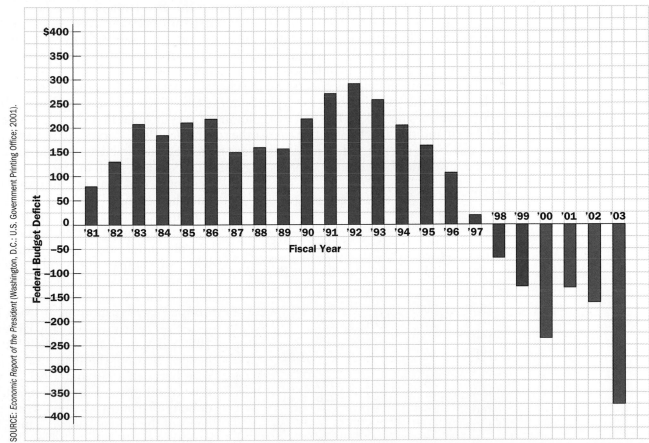

SOURCE: *Economic Report of the President* (Washington, D.C.: U.S. Government Printing Office; 2001).

NOTE: Amounts are in billions of dollars.

Because a falling GDP leads to higher expenditures and lower tax receipts:

The deficit rises in a recession and falls in a boom, even with no change in fiscal policy.

The **structural budget deficit or surplus** is the hypothetical deficit or surplus we *would have* under current fiscal policies if the economy were operating near full employment.

Figure 14-5 depicts the relationship between GDP and the budget deficit. The government's fiscal program is summarized by the blue and red lines. The horizontal blue line labeled *G* indicates that federal purchases of goods and services are approximately unaffected by GDP. The rising red line labeled *T* (for taxes minus transfers) indicates that taxes rise and transfer payments fall as GDP rises. Notice that the same fiscal policy (that is, the same two lines) leads to a large deficit if GDP is Y_1, a balanced budget if GDP is Y_2, or a surplus if GDP is as high as Y_3. Clearly, the deficit itself is not a good measure of the government's fiscal policy.

To seek a better measure, many economists pay more attention to what is called the **structural budget deficit or surplus.** This hypothetical measure replaces both the spending and taxes in the *actual* budget by estimates of how much the government *would be* spending and receiving, given current tax rates and expenditure rules, if the economy were operating at some fixed, high-employment level. For example, if the high-employment benchmark in Figure 14-5 was Y_2, although actual GDP was only Y_1, the structural deficit would be zero even though the actual deficit would be *AB*.

Because it is based on the spending and taxing the government *would be* doing at some fixed level of GDP, rather than on *actual* expenditures and receipts, the structural deficit is insensitive to the state of the economy. It changes *only* when policy changes, *not* when the GDP changes. That is why most economists view it as a better measure of the thrust of fiscal policy than the actual deficit.

This new concept helps us understand the changing nature of the large budget deficits of the 1980s, the stunning turn to surpluses in the late 1990s, and the rapid swing back to large deficits since 2001. The first two columns of data in Table 14-1 show both the actual deficit and the structural deficit every other year since 1981. Because of recessions in 1983 and 1991, the actual deficit was far larger than the structural deficit in those years. But the difference between the two was negligible in 1987 and small in 1995, when the economy was near full employment, and then changed sign (the structural surplus was substantially smaller than the actual surplus) in 1999 and 2001.

Four interesting facts stand out when we compare the numbers in the first and second columns. First, even though the *official* deficit was smaller in fiscal 1995 than in fiscal 1983, the *structural* deficit was actually larger in 1995—despite years of budget "stringency." Second, the structural deficit rose between 1989 and 1993. It was this trend toward larger structural deficits that most alarmed keen students of the federal budget. Third, the stunning $381 billion swing in the budget deficit from 1993 to 1999 (from a deficit of $255 billion to a sur-

■ **TABLE 14-1   Alternative Budget Concepts, 1981–2003**

Fiscal Year	Total Surplus (1)	Structural Surplus (2)	On-Budget Surplus (3)	Off-Budget Surplus (4)
1981	−79	−13	−74	−5
1983	−208	−109	−208	0
1985	−212	−178	−222	+10
1987	−150	−157	−169	+19
1989	−152	−121	−205	+53
1991	−269	−148	−322	+53
1993	−255	−188	−300	+45
1995	−164	−147	−226	+62
1997	−22	−83	−103	+81
1999	+126	+12	+2	+124
2001	+127	+106	−33	+160
2003	−375	−313	−536	+161

NOTE: Amounts in billions of dollars.

SOURCE: Congressional Budget Office

POLICY DEBATE   Balance the Budget? By What Definition?

A s mentioned in the text, American citizens have long favored a balanced federal budget. It just *sounds* right. After all, don't most families balance their budgets? (*Answer*: No. Many families borrow to buy a house or a car.) And don't state and city governments have to balance their budgets? (*Answer*: Not by the definitions used by the federal government.)

Almost totally unnoticed by the public, Congress made a major change in the *definition* of what a balanced budget means in November 1999. Traditionally, payments of Social Security benefits and the payroll tax revenues collected to finance them were segregated from other expenditures and receipts—and called *off-budget* items. But, when calculating the overall budget deficit or surplus, they were *included* in a budget concept called (for obvious reasons) the *unified budget*. "Balancing the budget" meant balancing the unified budget.

But under revised accounting rules adopted in November 1999, funds flowing into and out of Social Security were *excluded* from the calculation of the budget surplus or deficit—leaving only so-called *on-budget* expenditures and receipts. Because the Social Security System was then (as now) running a sizable surplus, this change made "balancing the budget" much harder. Thus, two amazing things happened: Congress actually "raised the bar" for itself, and hardly anyone noticed! For example, in fiscal year 2001, the unified budget (old concept) showed a $127 billion *surplus,* but the new on-budget accounts showed a $33 billion *deficit.* (The difference, $160 billion, was the Social Security surplus.)

SOURCE: © Bettmann/CORBIS

Seeing that it could no longer keep the budget in balance, and wanting to cut taxes, Congress changed the scorekeeping rules once again in 2001. And again, nobody seemed to notice. Now we are back to the old unified budget concept, which *includes* the Social Security surplus. For example, the fiscal year 2003 books closed with an official deficit of $375 billion, the largest ever. But had Congress adhered to its 1999 decision to disregard Social Security, the *on-budget* deficit would have been a stunning $536 billion. Confused? That may be the idea.

plus of $126 billion) far exceeds the change in the structural deficit, which fell by "only" $200 billion. This last number, which is still impressive, is a better indicator of how much fiscal policy changed during this period. Fourth, the swing from a small structural surplus in 2001 to a large structural deficit in 2003 was both rapid and huge.

On-Budget versus Off-Budget Surpluses

When you read about the budget in the newspapers, you may see references to the "off-budget" surplus and the "on-budget" surplus or deficit. What do those terms mean?

Because Social Security benefits are financed by an earmarked revenue source—the payroll tax—Social Security has traditionally been segregated in the federal fiscal accounts. Specifically, both Social Security expenditures and the payroll tax receipts that finance them are treated as off-budget items, while all other expenditures and receipts are classified as on-budget.[4] Thus:

Overall budget surplus = off-budget surplus + on-budget surplus

Because the Social Security System has been running sizable surpluses in recent years, the difference between the overall and on-budget balances has been substantial. For example, in fiscal year 2003, the overall budget showed a $375 billion deficit (Column 1). But this was composed of a whopping $536 billion on-budget *deficit* (Column 3) plus a $161 billion Social Security *surplus* (Column 4). For more on this accounting issue, see the box "Balance the Budget? By What Definition?" above.

---

[4] This statement is not quite true; a few other minor items are also treated as off-budget. Social Security is the only major off-budget item, however.

▌Conclusion: What Happened after 1981?

Table 14-1 helps us understand the remarkable rise, fall, and rise of the federal budget deficit since the 1980s. Column (1) shows the overall surplus (if positive) or deficit (if negative) every other year from 1981 to 2003, and Column (2) shows the corresponding *structural* surplus. Finally, Columns (3) and (4) break the overall surplus into its *on-budget* and *off-budget* components. The table tells the following story about the evolution of the budget deficit.

The large Reagan tax cuts in the early 1980s ballooned the budget deficit from $79 billion to $212 billion, and more than 100% of this deterioration was structural [see Column (2)]. Late in the 1980s, the deficit started rising again—even though Social Security began to run sizable surpluses [see Column (4)]. The overall deficit reached $269 billion in 1991, but then began to shrink. One reason was the burgeoning Social Security surplus, which increased by $115 between 1993 and 2001. And the strong economy helped, too—notice that the actual surplus rose more than the structural surplus. But most of the "work" was on-budget and structural, as tax increases and expenditure restraint during the Clinton years finally got the budget under control. Briefly, as it turned out. By 2003, a combination of large tax cuts, a burst of spending, and weaker economic growth had pushed the deficit up to a record $375 billion—a record that will be shattered when the books close on fiscal year 2004.

▌BOGUS ARGUMENTS ABOUT THE BURDEN OF THE DEBT

Having gained some perspective on the facts, let us now turn to some of the arguments advanced by those who claim that budget deficits place an intolerable burden on future generations.

Argument 1   Our children and grandchildren will be burdened by heavy interest payments, which will necessitate higher taxes.

Answer   It is certainly true that a higher debt means higher interest payments and, therefore, higher taxes on our children and grandchildren. But think who will own the bonds and therefore receive the higher interest payments as income: our children and grandchildren! Thus, one group of future Americans will be making interest payments to another group of future Americans. So we conclude that:

> **As long as the national debt is owned by domestic citizens, as the majority of the U.S. debt is, future interest payments transfer money from one group of Americans to another. These transfers may or may not be desirable, but they hardly constitute a burden on the nation as a whole.**

However, this argument *is* valid—and worrisome—for the portion of our debt that is held by foreigners, a share that has been growing rapidly and is now over 40 percent. Paying interest on this portion of the debt will burden future Americans in a concrete way: For years to come, a portion of America's GDP will have to be sent abroad to pay interest on the debts we incurred in the 1980s, 1990s, and 2000s. For this reason, many thoughtful observers are becoming concerned that the United States is borrowing too much from abroad.[5]

Another valid element of this argument is that the taxes that will have to be raised to pay interest even to U.S. citizens may reduce the efficiency of the economy.

Argument 2   Repaying the enormous debt will ruin the nation.

Answer   A first answer to this argument merely rephrases the answer to the previous one: Most of America's debt is owed to Americans. But this argument raises an even more fundamental point. *Unlike a private family, the nation need never pay off its debt.* Instead, each time the principal is due, the U.S. Treasury can simply "roll it over" by floating more debt. Indeed, that was done routinely for decades.

---

[5] We will discuss the linkages between the federal budget deficit and foreign borrowing in greater detail in Chapter 18.

Was this a bit of chicanery? How could the U.S. government get away with making loans that it never intended to pay back? The answer lies in the fallacy of comparing the U.S. government to a family or an individual. People cannot borrow in perpetuity, because they will not live that long. Sensible lenders will not extend long-term credit to very old people because their heirs cannot be forced to pay up. But the U.S. government will never "die"—at least, we hope not! So this problem does not arise. In this respect, the government is in much the same position as a large corporation. GE never pays off its debt. It, too, rolls it over by floating new debt all the time.

Argument 3   Like any family or any business firm, a nation has a limited capacity to borrow. If it exceeds this limit, it is in danger of being unable to pay its creditors. It may go bankrupt with calamitous consequences for everyone.

Answer   This is another false analogy. While private debtors and many foreign governments have to worry about defaulting on their debt, the U.S. government does not. Why not? First, because it has enormous power to raise revenues by taxation. If you had such power, you would never have to fear bankruptcy either.

But once again, the statement raises a more fundamental point—one that distinguishes the U.S. debt from that of most other nations. *The American national debt is an obligation to pay U.S. dollars:* Each debt certificate obligates the Treasury to pay the holder so many U.S. dollars on a prescribed date. But the U.S. government is the source of these dollars. It prints them! *No nation need default on debts that call for repayment in its own currency.*[6] If worse comes to worse, it can always print whatever money it needs to pay off its creditors. This option is not open to countries whose debts call for payment in U.S. dollars, as a number of Southeast Asian countries learned in 1997 and Argentina learned in 2001.

It does not, of course, follow that acquiring more debt through budget deficits is necessarily a good idea. Sometimes it is a very bad idea. As we know, printing money to pay the debt will expand aggregate demand and cause inflation. In addition, as we will learn in Chapter 18, printing more dollars should make the international value of the dollar fall. We may not relish either of these outcomes. The point is not that budget deficits are either good or bad; they can be either under the appropriate circumstances. Rather, the point is that worrying about a possible default on the national debt is unnecessary and even foolish.

Having cleared the air of these fallacious arguments about the national debt, we are now in a position to explore some genuine problems that may arise when the government spends more than it raises through taxation—that is, when it runs budget deficits.

BUDGET DEFICITS AND INFLATION

One indictment of deficit spending that certainly *is* valid under some circumstances—especially in developing countries—is the charge that it is inflationary. Why? Because when government policy pushes up aggregate demand, it may cause inflation.

The aggregate supply and demand diagram in Figure 14-6 on the next page reminds us why. Initially, equilibrium is at point A, where demand curve D_0D_0 and supply curve SS intersect. Output is \$7,000 billion, and the price index is 100. In the diagram, the aggregate demand and supply curves intersect precisely at potential GDP, indicating that the economy is operating at full employment.

If the government now raises spending or cuts taxes enough to shift the aggregate demand schedule outward from D_0D_0 to D_1D_1, equilibrium shifts from point A to point B. The graph shows the equilibrium price level rising from 100 to 106, or 6 percent. But that is not the end of the story, because point B represents an inflationary gap. We know from previous chapters that inflation will continue until the aggregate supply curve shifts far enough inward that it passes through point C, at which point the inflationary gap is

---

[6] Russia astounded the financial world by defaulting on ruble-denominated debt in August 1998.

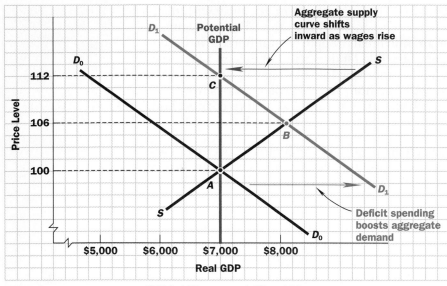

FIGURE 14-6

The Inflationary Effects of Deficit Spending

NOTE: Real GDP amounts are in billions of dollars.

gone. In this example, deficit spending will eventually raise the price level 12 percent.

Thus the cries that budget deficits are inflationary have the ring of truth. Such concerns were raised when candidate George W. Bush first proposed large income tax cuts in a fully employed economy in 1999. How much truth they hold, however, depends on several factors. One factor is the slope of the aggregate supply curve. Figure 14-6 clearly shows that a steep supply curve would lead to more inflation than a flat one. A second factor is the degree of resource utilization. Deficit spending is more inflationary in a fully employed economy (like that depicted in Figure 14-6) than in an economy with lots of slack.

Finally, we must remember that the Federal Reserve's monetary policy can always cancel out the potential inflationary effects of deficit spending by pulling the aggregate demand curve back to its original position. Once again, the *policy mix* is crucial.

The Monetization Issue

But will the Federal Reserve always neutralize the expansionary effect of a higher budget deficit? This question brings up another reason why some people worry about the inflationary consequences of deficits. They fear that the Federal Reserve may feel compelled to "monetize" part of the deficit by purchasing some of the newly issued government debt. Let us explain, first, why the Fed might make such purchases, and second, why these purchases are called **monetizing the deficit.**

> The central bank is said to **monetize the deficit** when it purchases bonds issued by the government.

Deficit spending, we have just noted, normally drives up both real GDP and the price level. As we have emphasized, such an economic expansion shifts the demand curve for money outward to the right—as depicted by the movement from $M_0 D_0$ to $M_1 D_1$ in Figure 14-7. The diagram shows that, if the Federal Reserve takes no action to shift the money supply curve, interest rates will rise as equilibrium moves from point A to point B.

Suppose now that the Fed does not want interest rates to rise. What can it do? To prevent the incipient rise in r, it would have to engage in *expansionary monetary policies* that shift the supply curve for money outward to the right—as indicated in Figure 14-8. With the blue money supply curve $M_1 S_1$, equilibrium would be at point C rather than at point B, leaving interest rates unchanged. Because the Fed usually pursues expansionary monetary policies by purchasing government bonds in the open market, deficit spending might induce the Federal Reserve to buy more government debt.

But why is this process called *monetizing* the deficit? The reason is simple. As we learned in Chapter 12, open-market purchases of bonds by the Fed give banks more reserves, which leads, eventually, to an increase in the money supply. This outcome is also shown in Figure 14-8: The outward shift of the money supply schedule from $M_0 S_0$ to $M_1 S_1$ leads to an increase in the quantity

FIGURE 14-7

Fiscal Expansion and Interest Rates

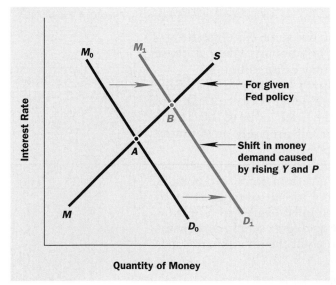

of money. By this indirect route, then, larger budget deficits may lead to a larger money supply. To summarize:

> If the Federal Reserve takes no countervailing actions, an expansionary fiscal policy that increases the budget deficit will raise real GDP and prices, thereby shifting the demand curve for money outward and driving up interest rates. If the Fed does not want interest rates to rise, it can engage in expansionary open-market operations; that is, it can purchase more government debt. If the Fed does so, the money supply will increase. In this case, we say that part of the deficit is *monetized*.

Monetized deficits are more inflationary than non-monetized deficits for a simple reason: Expansionary monetary and fiscal policies *together* are more inflationary than expansionary fiscal policy *alone*. But is this a real worry? Does the Fed actually monetize any substantial portion of the deficit? Normally, it does not. The clearest evidence is the fact that the Fed has managed to *reduce* inflation since the 1980s while the government ran unprecedented deficits. But monetization of deficits *has* been a serious cause of inflation in many other countries, ranging from Latin America to Russia, Israel, and elsewhere.

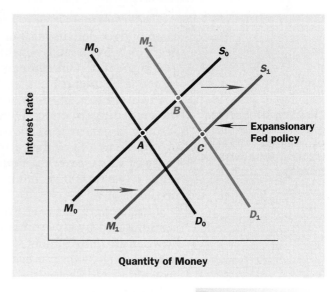

■ FIGURE 14-8
Monetization and Interest Rates

DEBT, INTEREST RATES, AND CROWDING OUT

So far, we have looked for possible problems that the national debt might cause on the *demand* side of the economy. But the real case for cutting the deficit or raising the surplus in the United States comes on the *supply* side. In brief, large budget deficits discourage investment and therefore retard the growth of the nation's capital stock. Conversely, budget surpluses speed up capital formation and growth.

The mechanism is easy to understand by presuming (as is generally the case) that the Fed does not engage in any substantial monetization. We have just seen that budget *deficits* tend to *raise* interest rates. By the same logic, budget *surpluses* tend to *reduce* interest rates. But we know from earlier chapters that the rate of interest (*r*) is a major determinant of investment spending (*I*). In particular, higher *r* leads to less *I*, and lower *r* leads to more *I*. The volume of investment made today will, in turn, determine how much capital we have tomorrow—and thus influence the size of our potential GDP. This, according to most economists, is the true sense in which a larger national debt may burden future generations and a smaller national debt may help them:

> A larger national debt may lead a nation to bequeath less physical capital to future generations. If they inherit less plant and equipment, these generations will be burdened by a smaller productive capacity—a lower potential GDP. In other words, large deficits may retard economic growth. By the same logic, budget surpluses can stimulate capital formation and economic growth.

Phrasing this point another way explains why this result is often called the **crowding-out** effect. Consider what happens in financial markets when the government engages in deficit spending. When it spends more than it takes in, the government must borrow the rest. It does so by selling bonds, which compete with corporate bonds and other financial instruments for the available supply of funds. As some savers decide to buy government bonds, the funds remaining to invest in private bonds must shrink. Thus, some private borrowers get "crowded out" of the financial markets as the government claims an increasing share of the economy's total saving.

Some critics of deficit spending have taken this lesson to its illogical extreme by arguing that each $1 of government spending crowds out exactly $1 of private spending, leaving "expansionary" fiscal policy with no net effect on total demand. In their view, when *G* rises, *I* falls by an equal amount, leaving the total of $C + I + G + (X - IM)$ unchanged.

Crowding out occurs when deficit spending by the government forces private investment spending to contract.

Under normal circumstances, we would not expect this to occur. Why? First, moderate budget deficits push up interest rates only slightly. Second, private spending appears only moderately sensitive to interest rates. Even at the higher interest rates that government deficits cause, most corporations will continue to borrow to finance their capital investments.

Furthermore, in times of economic slack, a counterforce arises that we might call the **crowding-in** effect. Deficit spending presumably quickens the pace of economic activity. That, at least, is its purpose. As the economy expands, businesses find it profitable to add to their capacity so as to meet the greater consumer demands. Because of this *induced investment*, as we called it in earlier chapters, any increase in *G* tends to *increase* investment, rather than *decrease* it as the crowding-out hypothesis predicts.

The strength of the crowding-in effect depends on how much additional real GDP is stimulated by government spending (that is, on the size of the multiplier) and on how sensitive investment spending is to the improved profit opportunities that accompany rapid growth. It is even conceivable that the crowding-in effect can dominate the crowding-out effect in the short run, so that *I* rises, on balance, when *G* rises.

But how can this be true in view of the crowding-out argument? Certainly, if the government borrows more *and the total volume of private saving is fixed*, then private industry must borrow less. That's just arithmetic. The fallacy in the strict crowding-out argument lies in supposing that the economy's flow of saving is really fixed. If government deficits succeed in raising output, we will have more income and therefore more saving. In that way, *both* government *and* industry can borrow more.

Which effect dominates—crowding out or crowding in? Crowding *out* stems from the increases in interest rates caused by deficits, whereas crowding *in* derives from the faster real economic growth that deficits sometimes produce. In the short run, the crowding-in effect—which results from the outward shift of the aggregate demand curve—is often the more powerful, especially when the economy is at less than full employment.

In the long run, however, the supply side dominates because, as we have learned, the economy's self-correcting mechanism pushes the growth rate of actual GDP toward the growth rate of potential GDP. With the economy approximately at full employment, the crowding-out effect takes over: Higher interest rates lead to less investment, so the capital stock and potential GDP grow more slowly. Turned on its head, this is the basic long-run argument for running budget surpluses: They speed up investment and growth.

Crowding in occurs when government spending, by raising real GDP, induces increases in private investment spending.

SOURCE: From *The Wall Street Journal*— Permission, Cartoon Features Syndicate

"Would you mind explaining again how high interest rates and the national deficit affect my allowance?"

▌ The Bottom Line

Let us summarize what we have learned so far about the crowding-out controversy.

- The basic argument of the crowding-out hypothesis is sound: *Unless the economy produces enough additional saving,* more government borrowing will force out some private borrowers, who are discouraged by the higher interest rates. This process will reduce investment spending and cancel out some of the expansionary effects of higher government spending.

- But crowding out is rarely strong enough to cancel out the *entire* expansionary thrust of government spending. Some net stimulus to the economy remains.

- If deficit spending induces substantial GDP growth, then the crowding-in effect will lead to more saving—perhaps so much more that private industry can borrow *more* than it did previously, despite the increase in government borrowing.

- The crowding-out effect is likely to dominate in the long run or when the economy is operating near full employment. The crowding-in effect is likely to dominate in the short run, especially when the economy has a great deal of slack.

- Surpluses have just the opposite effects. When slack exists, they are likely to slow growth by reducing aggregate demand. But in the long run, budget surpluses are likely to foster capital formation and speed up growth.

THE TRUE BURDEN OF THE NATIONAL DEBT: SLOWER GROWTH

This analysis of crowding out versus crowding in helps us understand whether or not the national debt imposes a burden on future generations:

When government budget deficits take place in a high-employment economy, the crowding-out effect will probably dominate. So deficits will exact a toll by leaving a smaller capital stock, and hence lower potential GDP to future generations. However, deficits in an economy with high unemployment may well lead to more investment rather than less. In this case, where the crowding-in effect dominates, deficit spending increases growth and the new debt is a blessing rather than a burden.

Which case applies to the U.S. national debt? To answer this question, let us go back to the historical facts and recall how we accumulated all that debt prior to the 1980s. The first cause was the financing of wars, especially World War II. Because this debt was contracted in a fully employed economy, it undoubtedly constituted a burden in the formal sense of the term. After all, the bombs, ships, and planes that it financed were used up in the war, not bequeathed as capital to future generations.

Yet today's Americans may not feel terribly burdened by the decisions of those in power in the 1940s, for consider the alternatives. We could have financed the entire war by taxation and thus placed the burden on consumption rather than on investment. But that choice would truly have been ruinous, and probably impossible, given the colossal wartime expenditures. Alternatively, we could have printed money, which would have unleashed an inflation that nobody wanted. Finally, the government could have spent much less money and perhaps not have won the war. Compared to these alternatives, today's Americans may not feel unduly burdened by the massive deficit spending undertaken in the 1940s.

A second major contributor to the national debt prior to 1983 was a series of recessions. But these are precisely the circumstances under which increasing the national debt might prove to be a blessing rather than a burden. So it was only in the 1980s that we began to have the type of deficits to which the valid burden-of-the-debt argument applies—deficits acquired in a fully employed, peacetime economy.

This sharp departure from historical norms is what made those budget deficits worrisome. The tax cuts of 1981–1984 blew a large hole in the government budget, and the recession of 1981–1982 ballooned the deficit even further. By the late 1980s, the U.S. economy had recovered to full employment, but a structural deficit of $100–$150 billion per year remained. This persistent deficit was something that had never happened before. Such large structural deficits posed a real threat of crowding out and constituted a serious potential burden on future generations. After a brief interlude of budget surpluses, large structural deficits re-emerged a few years ago, caused by a combination of large tax cuts coupled with rapid growth of spending. Current projections foresee very large deficits "as far as the eye can see," which worries economists and budget analysts.

Let us now summarize our evaluation of the burden of the national debt:

- **The arguments that a large national debt may lead the nation into bankruptcy, or unduly burden future generations who have to make onerous payments of interest and principal, are mostly bogus.**

- **The national debt *will* be a burden if it is sold to foreigners or contracted in a fully employed, peacetime economy. In the latter case, it will reduce the nation's capital stock.**

- **Under some circumstances, budget deficits are appropriate for stabilization-policy purposes.**

- **Until the 1980s, the actual public debt of the U.S. government was mostly contracted as a result of wars and recessions—precisely the circumstances under which the valid burden-of-the-debt argument does not apply. However, the large deficits since the 1980s have not been mainly attributable to recessions, and are therefore worrisome.**

■ The shift from budget surpluses back to deficits in this decade may retard capital formation and economic growth.

Issue Revisited: Was Fiscal Stimulus Warranted in 2001?

■FIGURE 14-9

The Short-Run Effect of Larger Deficits or Smaller Surpluses

We are now in a position to answer the question posed at the beginning of this chapter: Was it a good or bad idea to reduce the budget surplus in an effort to stimulate the U.S. economy after the September 2001 terrorist attacks? We can understand the nature of the debate that took place then by distinguishing between the short-run (demand side) and long-run (supply side) effects of smaller budget surpluses.

The terrorist attacks immediately set up fears that the U.S. economy, which was already in a mild recession, might slide downhill rapidly if consumers and businesses pulled in their horns. (Fortunately, those fears proved ill-founded.) As a short-run response, an expansionary fiscal policy consisting of both higher spending (for example, on national security and assisting New York) and tax cuts (for example, tax breaks for business investment) would push the aggregate demand curve outward—as shown in Figure 14-9. Shrinking the surplus in this way would cushion the recession by boosting real GDP as the economy's equilibrium moved from point *A* to point *B*. That was why advocates of fiscal stimulus argued for quick action.

There was a long-run cost, however—as critics of fiscal stimulus reminded us. Smaller budget surpluses, or even deficits, would lead to higher real interest rates and hence to lower levels of private investment. That would make the nation's capital stock grow more slowly, thereby retarding the growth rate of potential GDP. This case is depicted in Figure 14-10, which shows a smaller surplus leading to a potential GDP of Y_1 instead of Y_0. With the same aggregate demand curve, *DD*, the result is lower real GDP.

■FIGURE 14-10

The Long-Run Effect of Larger Deficits or Smaller Surpluses

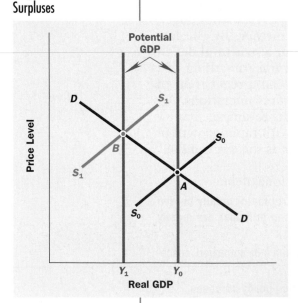

Notice that this case was precisely the argument behind calls for sharp deficit reduction in the 1990s, a period of time that was still fresh in people's minds when the terrorists struck.

In the end, Congress argued for months and then finally passed something called a "stimulus package" in March 2002—after the recession was over. One wag observed that this action was like taking Viagra the morning after. However, the emergency spending that followed September 11, 2001, and the first phase of the Bush tax cut (which had been enacted *before* the terrorist attacks) did stimulate the economy.

So which view was correct? Paradoxically, they both were! In the short run, aggregate demand factors dominate economic performance, and what fiscal stimulus there was did provide an expansionary force just when the economy badly needed one. But in the long run, output gravitates toward potential GDP, no matter what happens to aggregate demand, so aggregate supply rules the roost. And because smaller surpluses deter some investment spending, they slow down the economy's potential growth rate, which explains why thoughtful proponents of fiscal stimulus in 2001 urged the government to make any increases in spending or reductions in taxes *temporary*. We should *reduce* the surplus in the short run, they argued, but *maintain* it in the long run.

THE ECONOMICS AND POLITICS OF THE U.S. BUDGET DEFICIT

Given what we have learned in this chapter about the theory and facts of budget deficits, we can now address some of the issues that have been debated in the political arena for more than a decade.

1. *Have the deficits of the 1980s, 1990s, and 2000s been a problem?* In 1981–1982, 1990–1991, and again in 2001, the U.S. economy suffered through recessions. Under such circumstances, crowding out is not a serious concern, and actions to close the deficit during or right after these recessions would have threatened the subsequent recoveries. According to the basic principles of fiscal policies, growing deficits were appropriate in each case.

   But in each case, as the economy recovered toward full employment, crowding out became a more serious issue. Budget deficits should fall in such circumstances—as they did in the 1990s, but not in the 1980s or (at least so far) in this decade. But instead, the structural deficit rose. Worries about the burden of the national debt, once mostly myths, became all too realistic.

2. *How did we get rid of the deficit in the 1990s?* In part, we did it the old-fashioned way: by raising taxes and reducing spending in three not-so-easy steps. There was a contentious but bipartisan budget agreement in 1990, a highly partisan deficit-reduction package in 1993 (which passed without a single Republican vote), and a smaller budget deal in 1997.

   Taxing more and spending less produces a contractionary fiscal policy that reduces aggregate demand. This effect did not pose a problem for the United States in the 1990s because fiscal and monetary policies were well coordinated. If fiscal policy turns contractionary to reduce the deficit, monetary policy can turn expansionary to counteract the effects on aggregate demand. In this way, we can hope to shrink the deficit without shrinking the economy. Such a change in the *policy mix* should also bring down interest rates, because both tighter budgets and easier money tend to push interest rates down. That, indeed, was what happened in the 1990s. Interest rates fell, and the Fed made sure that aggregate demand was sufficient to keep the economy growing.

   In addition, surprisingly rapid economic growth in the late 1990s generated much more tax revenue than anyone thought likely only a few years before. And the so-called off-budget surplus also increased. Both of these developments helped the federal budget turn rapidly from deficit into surplus.

3. *How did the surplus give way to such large deficits so rapidly?* The answer comes in three parts. First, a recession in 2001 depressed revenues. Second, the terrorist attacks of September 11, 2001, and then the wars in Afghanistan (2001) and Iraq (2003) led to a burst of spending on national defense and homeland security. Third, President Bush pushed large, multi-year tax cuts through Congress in 2001 and 2003—and has urged Congress to make them permanent. It is hardly a mystery that sharply rising expenditures and rapidly falling revenue push the budget from the black into the red.

SUMMARY

1. Rigid adherence to budget balancing would make the economy less stable, by reducing aggregate demand (via tax increases and reductions in government spending) when private spending is low and by raising aggregate demand when private spending is high.

2. Because both monetary and fiscal policy influence aggregate demand, the appropriate **budget deficit or surplus** depends on monetary policy. Similarly, the appropriate monetary policy depends on budget policy.

3. The same level of aggregate demand can be generated by different mixes of fiscal and monetary policy. But the composition of GDP will be different in each case. Larger budget deficits and tighter money tend to produce higher interest rates, a smaller share of investment in GDP, and

slower growth. Smaller budget deficits (or surpluses) and looser monetary policy lead to a larger investment share and faster growth.

4. One major reason for the large budget deficits of the early 1980s and early 1990s was the fact that the economy operated well below full employment. In those years, the **structural deficit,** which uses estimates of what the government's receipts and outlays would be at full employment to correct for business-cycle fluctuations, was much smaller than the official deficit.

5. Arguments that the public debt will burden future generations, who will have to make huge payments of interest and principal, are mostly based on false analogies. In fact, most of these payments are simply transfers from one group of Americans to another. However, taxes must be raised to pay the interest, and there is a legitimate worry about the portion of the national debt that is owned by foreigners.

6. The bogus argument that a large **national debt** can bankrupt a country like the United States ignores the fact that our national debt consists entirely of obligations to pay U.S. dollars—a currency that the government can raise by increasing taxes or create by simply printing money.

7. Under many circumstances, budget deficits are inflationary because they expand aggregate demand. They are even more inflationary if they are **monetized**—that is, if the central bank buys some of the newly issued government debt in the open market.

8. Unless the deficit is substantially monetized, deficit spending forces interest rates higher and discourages private investment spending. This process is called the **crowding-out effect.** If a great deal of crowding out occurs, then deficits really do impose a burden on future generations by leaving them a smaller capital stock with which to work.

9. But higher government spending (G) also produces a **crowding-in effect.** If expansionary fiscal policy succeeds in raising real output (Y), more investment will be induced by the higher Y.

10. Whether crowding out or crowding in dominates largely depends on the time horizon. In the short run, and especially when unemployment is high, crowding in is probably the stronger force, so higher G does not cause lower investment. But, in the long run, the economy will be near full employment, and the proponents of the crowding-out hypothesis will be right: High government spending will mainly displace private investment.

11. Larger deficits may spur growth (via aggregate demand) in the short run but deter growth (via aggregate supply and potential GDP) in the long run.

12. Whether or not deficits create a burden depends on how and why the government incurred the deficits in the first place. If the government runs deficits to fight recessions, more investment may be crowded in by rising output than is crowded out by rising interest rates. Deficits contracted to carry on wars certainly impair the future capital stock, although they may not be considered a burden for noneconomic reasons. Because these two cases account for most of the debt the U.S. government contracted until the mid-1980s, that debt cannot reasonably be considered a serious burden. However, the deficits since 1984 are more worrisome on this score.

KEY TERMS

Mix of monetary and fiscal policy 263	National debt 265	Crowding out 273
Budget deficit 265	Structural deficit or surplus 267	Crowding in 274
Budget surplus 265	Monetization of deficits 272	Burden of the national debt 275

QUESTIONS FOR REVIEW

1. Explain the difference between the budget deficit and the national debt. If the deficit gets turned into a surplus, what happens to the debt?

2. Explain how the U.S. government managed to accumulate a debt of nearly $7 trillion. To whom does it owe this debt? Can the debt be considered a burden on future generations?

3. Comment on the following: "Deficit spending paves the road to ruin. If we keep it up, the whole nation will go bankrupt. Even if things do not go this far, what right have we to burden our children and grandchildren with these debts while we live high on the hog?"

4. Explain in words why the *structural* budget might show a surplus while the *actual* budget is in deficit. Illustrate your answer with a diagram like Figure 14-5 (page 268).

5. If the Federal Reserve begins to raise interest rates, what will happen to the government budget deficit? (*Hint:* What will happen to tax receipts and interest expenses?) If the government wants to offset the effects of the Fed's actions on aggregate demand, what might it do? How will this action affect the deficit?

6. Newspaper reports frequently suggest that the administration (regardless of who is president) is pressuring the Fed to lower interest rates. In view of your answer to Review Question 5, why do you think that might be?

7. Explain the difference between crowding out and crowding in. Given the current state of the economy, which effect would you expect to dominate today?

8. Given the current state of the economy, what sort of fiscal-monetary policy mix seems most appropriate to you now? (*Note:* There is no one correct answer to this question. It is a good question to discuss in class.)

15

Inflation and Growth: The Phillips Curve

We must seek to reduce inflation at a lower cost in lost output and unemployment.

JIMMY CARTER

As early as Chapter 1, we noted in our list of *Ideas for Beyond the Final Exam* that there is a bothersome *trade-off between inflation and unemployment*: High-growth policies that lower unemployment tend to raise inflation, and slow-growth policies that reduce inflation tend to raise unemployment. We also observed, in Chapter 13, that the trade-off looks rather different in the short run than in the long run because the aggregate supply curve is fairly flat in the short run but quite steep (perhaps even vertical) in the long run. But we did not really explain why. It is now time to fill in this gap.

A statistical relationship called the *Phillips curve* seeks to summarize the quantitative dimensions of the trade-off between inflation and unemployment in both the short and long runs. This chapter is about the Phillips curve.

CONTENTS

Issue: Is the Trade-Off between Inflation and Unemployment a Relic of the Past?

In the late 1990s, unemployment in the United States fell to extremely low levels—the lowest in 30 years. Yet, in stark contrast to prior experience, inflation did not rise. In fact, it fell slightly. This pleasant conjunction of extremely low unemployment and falling inflation, nearly unprecedented in U.S. history, set many people talking about a glorious "New Economy" in which there was no longer any trade-off between inflation and unemployment. The soaring stock market, especially for technology stocks, added to the euphoria.

Is the long-feared trade-off really just a memory now? Can the modern U.S. economy speed along without fear of rising inflation? Or does faster growth eventually have inflationary consequences? These are the central questions for this chapter. Our answers, in brief, are: no, no, and yes. And we devote most of this chapter to explaining them.

DEMAND-SIDE INFLATION VERSUS SUPPLY-SIDE INFLATION: A REVIEW

We begin by reviewing some of what we learned about inflation in earlier chapters. One major cause of inflation, although certainly not the only one, is *excessive growth of aggregate demand*. We know that any autonomous increase in spending—whether by consumers, investors, the government, or foreigners—will have a multiplier effect on aggregate demand. So each additional $1 of C or I or G or $(X - IM)$ will lead to more than $1 of additional demand. We also know that firms normally find it profitable to supply additional output only at higher prices. Hence, a stimulus to aggregate demand will normally pull up both real output and prices.

■ FIGURE 15-1

Inflation from the Demand Side

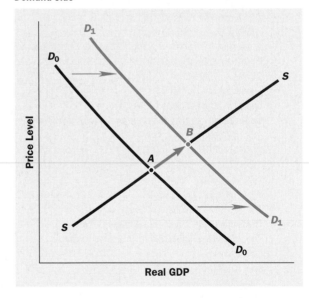

Real GDP

Figure 15-1, which is familiar from earlier chapters, reviews this conclusion. Initially, the economy is at point A, where aggregate demand curve D_0D_0 intersects aggregate supply curve SS. Then something happens to increase spending, and the aggregate demand curve shifts horizontally to D_1D_1. The new equilibrium is at point B, where both prices and output are higher than they were at A. Thus the economy experiences both inflation and increased output. The slope of the aggregate supply curve measures the amount of inflation that accompanies any specified rise in output and therefore encapsulates the trade-off between inflation and economic growth.

But we have also learned in this book (especially in Chapter 9) that inflation does not always originate from the demand side. Anything that retards the growth of aggregate supply—for example, an increase in the price of foreign oil—can shift the economy's aggregate supply curve inward. This sort of inflation is illustrated in Figure 15-2, where the aggregate supply curve shifts inward from S_0S_0 to S_1S_1, and the economy's equilibrium consequently moves from point A to point B. Prices rise as output falls. We have *stagflation*.

Demand-side inflation is a rise in the price level caused by rapid growth of aggregate demand.

Supply-side inflation is a rise in the price level caused by slow growth (or decline) of aggregate supply.

Thus, although inflation can emanate from either the demand side or the supply side of the economy, a crucial difference arises between the two sources. **Demand-side inflation** is normally accompanied by rapid growth of real GDP (see Figure 15-1), whereas **supply-side inflation** may well be accompanied by falling GDP (see Figure 15-2). This distinction has major practical importance, as we shall see in this chapter.

APPLYING THE MODEL TO A GROWING ECONOMY

You may have noticed that ever since Chapter 4 we have been using the simple aggregate supply and aggregate demand model to determine the equilibrium *price level* and the equilibrium *level of real GDP*. But in the real world, neither the price level nor real GDP remains constant for long. Instead, both normally rise from year to year.

The growth process is illustrated in Figure 15-3, which is a scatter diagram of the U.S. price level and the level of real GDP for every year from 1972 to 2003. The labeled points show the clear upward march of the economy through time—toward higher prices and higher levels of output.

This upward trend is hardly a mystery. As we have observed repeatedly, *both* the aggregate demand curve *and* the aggregate supply curve normally shift to the right each year. Aggregate supply grows because more workers join the workforce each year and because investment and technology improve productivity. Aggregate demand grows because a growing population generates more demand for both consumer and investment goods, because the government increases its spending, and because the Federal Reserve increases the money supply. We can think of each point in Figure 15-3 as the intersection of an aggregate supply curve and an aggregate demand curve for that particular year. To help you visualize this idea, the curves for 1984 and 1993 are sketched in the diagram.

Figure 15-4 is a more realistic version of a graph that we have been using since Chapter 4. It illustrates how our theoretical model of aggregate supply and demand applies to a growing economy. We have chosen the numbers so that the black curves $D_0 D_0$ and $S_0 S_0$ roughly represent the year 1999, and the red curves

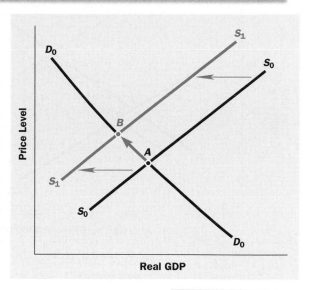

■ FIGURE 15-2
Inflation from the Supply Side

■ FIGURE 15-3
The Price Level and Real GDP Output in the United States, 1972–2003

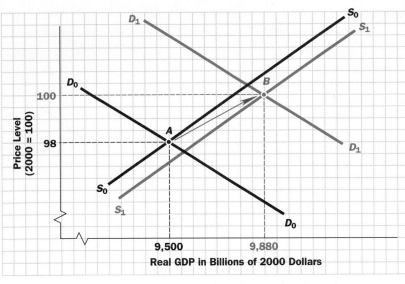

Aggregate Supply and Demand Analysis of a
Growing Economy

D_1D_1 and S_1S_1 roughly represent 2000—except that we use nice round numbers to facilitate computations. Thus, the equilibrium in 1999 was at point *A*, with a real GDP of $9,500 billion (in 2000 dollars) and a price level of 98. A year later, the equilibrium was at point *B*, with real GDP at $9,880 billion and the price level at 100. The blue arrow in the diagram shows how equilibrium moved from 1999 to 2000. It points upward and to the right, meaning that both prices and output increased. In this case, the economy grew by 4 percent and prices rose about 2 percent, which is roughly what happened in the United States.

DEMAND-SIDE INFLATION AND THE PHILLIPS CURVE

■ FIGURE 15-5

The Effects of Faster Growth of Aggregate Demand

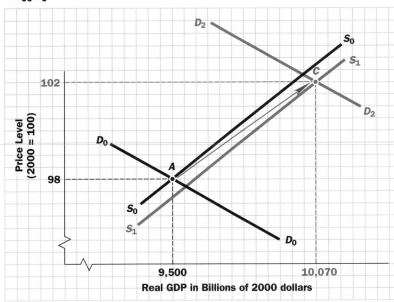

Let us now use our theoretical model to rewrite history. Suppose that aggregate demand grew *faster* than it actually did between 1999 and 2000. What difference would this change have made for the performance of the national economy? Figure 15-5 provides the answers. Here the black demand curve D_0D_0 is exactly the same as in the previous diagram, as are the two supply curves, indicating a given rate of aggregate supply growth. But the red demand curve D_2D_2 lies farther to the right than the demand curve D_1D_1 in Figure 15-4. Equilibrium is at point *A* in 1999 and point *C* in 2000. Comparing point *C* in Figure 15-5 with point *B* in Figure 15-4, we see that output would have increased more over the year ($570 billion versus $380 billion) and prices would also have increased more (to 102 instead of to 100)—that is, the economy would have experienced more *inflation*. This is generally what happens when the growth rate of aggregate demand speeds up.

For any given rate of growth of aggregate supply, a faster rate of growth of aggregate demand will lead to more inflation and faster growth of real output.

Figure 15-6 illustrates the opposite case. Here, we imagine that the aggregate demand curve shifted out *less* than in Figure 15-4. That is, the red demand curve D_3D_3 in Figure 15-6 lies to the left of the demand curve D_1D_1 in Figure 15-4. The consequence, we see, is that the shift of the economy's equilibrium from 1999 to 2000 (from point *A* to point *E*) would have entailed *less inflation* and *slower growth* of real output than actually took place. Again, that is generally the case when aggregate demand grows more slowly.

For any given rate of growth of aggregate supply, a slower rate of growth of aggregate demand will lead to less inflation and slower growth of real output.

If we put these two findings together, we have a clear prediction from our theory:

If fluctuations in the economy's real growth rate from year to year arise primarily from variations in the rate at which *aggregate demand* increases, then the data should show the most rapid inflation occurring when output grows most rapidly and the slowest inflation occurring when output grows most slowly.

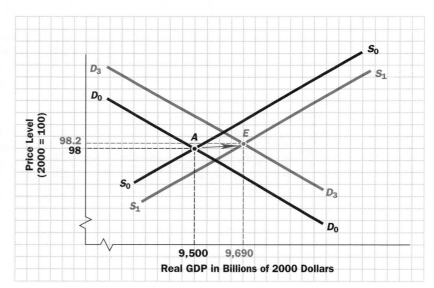

Does the theory fit the facts? We will put it to the test in a moment, but first let us translate this trade-off between inflation and *growth* into a corresponding trade-off between inflation and *unemployment*. Faster growth of real output naturally means faster growth in the number of jobs and, hence, *lower unemployment*. Conversely, slower growth of real output means slower growth in the number of jobs and, hence, *higher unemployment*. We conclude that, if business fluctuations emanate from the demand side, unemployment and inflation should move in opposite directions: Unemployment should be *low* when inflation is *high*, and inflation should be *low* when unemployment is *high*.

Figure 15-7 illustrates the idea. The unemployment rate in the United States in 2000 averaged 4 percent, and the inflation rate in Figure 15-4 was about 2 percent. Point *b* in Figure 15-7, which corresponds to equilibrium point *B* in Figure 15-4, records these two numbers. The faster growth rate of demand depicted by point *C* in Figure 15-5 would have led to higher inflation and lower unemployment. For the sake of concreteness, we suppose that unemployment would have been 3 percent and inflation would have been the 4.1 percent rate shown in Figure 15-5. This is denoted by point *c* in Figure 15-7. Point *E* in Figure 15-6 summarized the results of slower growth of aggregate demand: Unemployment would have been higher and inflation lower. In Figure 15-7, these facts are represented by point *e*, with an unemployment rate of 5 percent and an inflation rate barely above zero (just 0.2 percent). This figure shows graphically the principal empirical implication of our theoretical model:

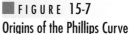
FIGURE 15-6
The Effects of Slower Growth of Aggregate Demand

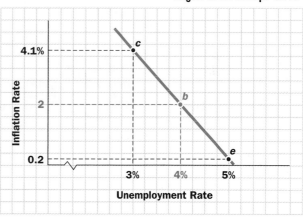
FIGURE 15-7
Origins of the Phillips Curve

If fluctuations in economic activity are primarily caused by variations in the rate at which the aggregate demand curve shifts outward from year to year, then the data should show an inverse relationship between unemployment and inflation, as in Figure 15-7.

Now we are ready to look at real data. Do we actually observe such an inverse relationship between inflation and unemployment? More than 40 years ago, economist A. W. Phillips plotted data on unemployment and the rate of change of money *wages* (not prices) for several extended periods of British history on a series of scatter diagrams, one of which is reproduced as Figure 15-8. He then sketched in a curve that seemed to "fit" the data well. This type of curve, which we now call a **Phillips curve,**

A **Phillips curve** is a graph depicting the rate of unemployment on the horizontal axis and either the rate of inflation or the rate of change of money wages on the vertical axis. Phillips curves are normally downward sloping, indicating that higher inflation rates are associated with lower unemployment rates.

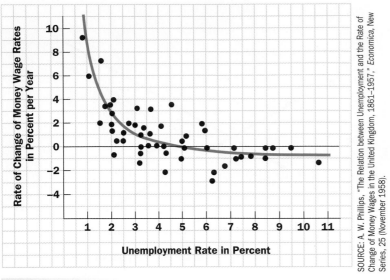

SOURCE: A. W. Phillips, "The Relation between Unemployment and the Rate of Change of Money Wages in the United Kingdom, 1861–1957," *Economica*, New Series, 25 (November 1958).

■ **FIGURE 15-8**
The Original Phillips Curve

■ **FIGURE 15-9**
A Phillips Curve for the United States, 1954–1969

shows that wage inflation normally is high when unemployment is low and is low when unemployment is high. So far, so good. These data illustrate the short run trade-off between inflation and unemployment, one of our *Ideas for Beyond the Final Exam*.

Phillips curves are more commonly constructed for *price* inflation; Figure 15-9 shows one such diagram for the post-World War II United States. The curve appears to fit the data well. As viewed through the eyes of our theory, these facts suggest that economic fluctuations in Great Britain between 1861 and 1913 and in the United States between 1954 and 1969 probably arose primarily from changes in the growth of aggregate demand. The simple model of demand-side inflation really does seem to describe what happened.

During the 1960s and early 1970s, economists often thought of the Phillips curve as a "menu" of choices available to policymakers. In this view, policymakers could opt for low unemployment and high inflation—as in 1969. Alternatively, they might prefer higher unemployment coupled with lower inflation—as, for example, in 1961. The Phillips curve, it was thought, described the quantitative trade-off between inflation and unemployment. And for a number of years it seemed to work.

Then something happened. The economy in the 1970s and early 1980s behaved far worse than the Phillips curve led economists to expect. In particular, given the unemployment rates in each of those years, inflation was astonishingly high by historical standards. This fact is shown in Figure 15-10, which simply adds to Figure 15-9 the points for 1970 to 1984. Clearly, something went wrong with the old view of the Phillips curve as a menu for policy choices. But what?

SUPPLY-SIDE INFLATION AND THE COLLAPSE OF THE PHILLIPS CURVE

There are two major answers to this question, and a full explanation contains elements of each. We begin with the simpler answer, which is that much of the inflation in the years from 1972 to 1982 did not emanate from the demand side. Instead, the 1970s and early 1980s were full of adverse "supply shocks"—events such as the crop failures of 1972–1973 and the oil price increases of 1973–1974 and 1979–1980. These events pushed the economy's aggregate supply curve inward to the left. What kind of Phillips curve will be generated when economic fluctuations come from the supply side?

To find out, let us take the events of 1979 and 1980 as an example. In Figure 15-11, the black aggregate demand curve D_0D_0 and aggregate supply curve S_0S_0 represent the economic situation in 1979. Equilibrium was at point A, with a price level of 50 and real output of $5,173 billion. By 1980, the aggregate demand curve had shifted out to the position indicated by the red curve D_1D_1, and, under normal conditions, the aggregate supply curve would have shifted out as well. But 1979 to 1980 was anything but normal. The Iranian revolution led to a long shutdown of Iran's oil fields, and the price of oil doubled.

Thus, instead of shifting *outward* as it normally does from one year to the next, the aggregate supply curve shifted *inward* from 1979 to 1980, to the red curve S_1S_1. The equilibrium for 1980 (point B in the figure) therefore wound up to the left of the equilibrium point for 1979. Real output declined slightly and prices—led by energy costs—rose rapidly.

Now, in a growing population with more people looking for jobs each year, a stagnant economy that does not generate new jobs suffers a rise in the unemployment rate. That is precisely what happened in the United States; the unemployment rate rose from 5.8 percent in 1979 to 7.1 percent in 1980. Thus, inflation and unemployment increased at the same time: The Phillips curve basically shifted upward. The general conclusion is:

If fluctuations in economic activity emanate from the supply side, higher rates of inflation will be associated with higher rates of unemployment, and lower rates of inflation will be associated with lower rates of unemployment.

The major supply shocks of the 1970s stand out clearly in Figure 15-10. (Remember—these are real data, not textbook examples.) Food prices soared from 1972 to 1974, and again in 1978. Energy prices skyrocketed in 1973–1974, and again in 1979–1980. Clearly, the inflation and unemployment data generated by the U.S. economy in 1972–1974 and in 1978–1980 are consistent with our model of supply-side inflation. Many economists believe that supply shocks, rather than abrupt changes in aggregate demand, made the Phillips curve shift.

Explaining the Fabulous 1990s

Now let's stand this analysis of supply shocks on its head. Suppose the economy experiences a *favorable* supply shock, rather than an adverse one, so that the aggregate supply curve shifts *outward* at an unusually rapid rate. Any number of factors—such as a drop in oil prices, bountiful harvests, or exceptionally rapid technological advance—can have this effect.

Whatever the cause, Figure 15-12 depicts the consequences. The aggregate demand curve shifts out from D_0D_0 to D_1D_1 as usual, but the aggregate supply curve shifts all the way out to S_1S_1. (The dotted line indicates what would happen in a "normal" year.) So the economy's equilibrium winds up at point B rather than at point C.

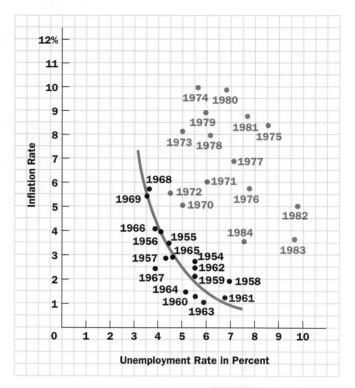

■ FIGURE 15-10

A Phillips Curve for the United States?

■ FIGURE 15-11

Stagflation from an Adverse Supply Shock

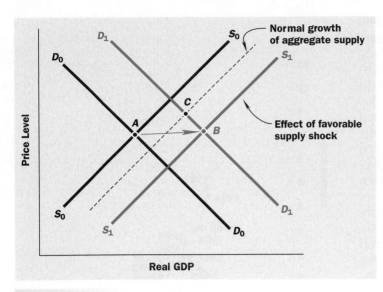

FIGURE 15-12
The Effects of a Favorable Supply Shock

Compared to C, point B represents *faster economic growth* (B is to the right of C) and *lower inflation* (B is lower than C). In brief, the economy wins on both fronts: Inflation falls while rapid growth reduces unemployment.

Figure 15-12 more or less characterizes the experience of the U.S. economy from 1996 to 1998. Oil prices plummeted, lowering costs to American businesses and households. Stunning advances in technology made computer prices drop even more rapidly than usual. Also, the rising value of the U.S. dollar made imported goods cheaper to Americans.[1] Thus, we benefited from a series of favorable supply shocks, and the effects were just as depicted in Figure 15-12. The U.S. economy grew rapidly, and both inflation and unemployment fell at the same time.

Issue Resolved: Why Inflation and Unemployment Both Declined

So we now have the answer to the question posed at the start of this chapter. We need nothing particularly new or mysterious to explain the marvelous economic performance of the second half of the 1990s. According to the basic macroeconomic theory taught in this book, favorable supply shocks should produce rapid economic growth with falling inflation. The U.S. economy did so well, in part, because we were so fortunate.[2]

WHAT THE PHILLIPS CURVE IS NOT

So one view is that adverse supply shocks caused the stagflation of the 1970s and 1980s. But there is another view of what went wrong. It holds that policymakers misinterpreted the Phillips curve and tried to pick combinations of inflation and unemployment that were simply unsustainable.

Specifically, the Phillips curve is a *statistical relationship* between inflation and unemployment that we expect to emerge *if business cycle fluctuations arise mainly from changes in the growth of aggregate demand*. But in the 1970s and 1980s, the curve was widely misinterpreted as depicting a number of *alternative equilibrium points* that the economy could achieve and from which policymakers could choose.

To understand the flaw in this reasoning, let us quickly review an earlier lesson. We know from Chapter 9 that the economy has a *self-correcting mechanism* that will cure both inflations and recessions *eventually*, even if the government does nothing. Why is this point relevant here? Because it tells us that many combinations of output and prices cannot be maintained indefinitely. Some will self-destruct. Specifically, if the economy finds itself far from the normal full-employment level of unemployment, forces will be set in motion that tend to erode the inflationary or recessionary gap.

Figure 15-13 depicts the case of a recessionary gap where aggregate supply curve S_0S_0 intersects aggregate demand curve DD at point A. With equilibrium output well below potential GDP, the economy has unused industrial capacity and unsold output,

---

[1] The dollar and imports will be discussed in detail in Chapter 18.

[2] For more on the story of the success of the U.S. economy in the 1990s, see Alan S. Blinder and Janet L. Yellen, *The Fabulous Decade: Macroeconomic Lessons from the 1990s* (New York: The Century Foundation; 2001).

so inflation will be tame. At the same time, the availability of unemployed workers eager for jobs limits the rate at which labor can push up wage rates. But wages are the main component of business costs, so when they decline (relative to what they would have been without a recession) so do costs. The lower costs, in turn, stimulate greater production. Figure 15-13 illustrates this process by an outward shift of the aggregate supply curve—from S_0S_0 to the red curve S_1S_1.

As the figure shows, the outward shift of the aggregate supply curve brought on by the recession pushes equilibrium output up as the economy moves from point A to point B. Thus, the size of the recessionary gap begins to shrink. This process continues until the aggregate supply curve reaches the position indicated by the blue curve S_2S_2 in Figure 15-13. Here wages have fallen enough to eliminate the recessionary gap, and the economy has reached a full-employment equilibrium at point C.[3]

We can relate this sequence of events to our discussion of the origins of the Phillips curve with the help of Figure 15-14, which is a hypothetical Phillips curve. Point a in Figure 15-14 corresponds to point A in Figure 15-13: It shows the initial recessionary gap with unemployment (assumed to be 6.5 percent) above full employment, which we assume to occur at 5 percent.

But we have just seen that point A in Figure 15-13—and therefore also point a in Figure 15-14—is not sustainable. The economy tends to rid itself of the recessionary gap through the disinflation process we have just described. The adjustment path from A to C depicted in Figure 15-13 would appear on our Phillips curve diagram as a movement toward less inflation and less unemployment—something like the blue arrow from point a to point c in Figure 15-14.

Similarly, points representing inflationary gaps—such as point d in Figure 15-14—are also not sustainable. They, too, are gradually eliminated by the self-correcting mechanism that we studied in Chapter 9. Wages are forced up by the abnormally low unemployment, which in turn pushes prices higher. Higher prices deter investment spending by forcing up interest rates, and they deter consumer spending by lowering the purchasing power of consumer wealth. The inflationary process continues until the amount people want to spend is brought into balance with the amount firms want to supply at normal full employment. During such an adjustment period, unemployment and inflation both rise—as indicated by the blue arrow from point d to point f in Figure 15-14.

Putting these two conclusions together, we see that:

On a Phillips curve diagram such as Figure 15-14, neither points corresponding to an inflationary gap (like point *d*) nor points corresponding to a recessionary gap (like point *a*) can be maintained

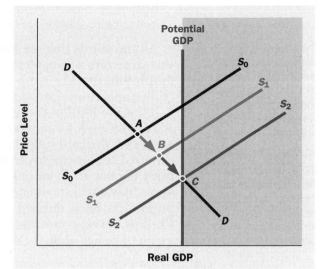

FIGURE 15-13
The Elimination of a Recessionary Gap

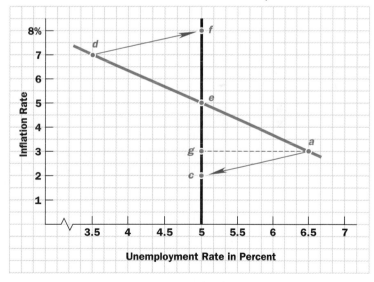

FIGURE 15-14
The Vertical Long-Run Phillips Curve

---

[3] This simple analysis assumes that the aggregate demand curve does not move during the adjustment period. If it is shifting to the right, the recessionary gap will disappear even faster, but inflation will not slow down as much. (*Exercise:* Construct the diagram for this case by adding a shift of the aggregate demand curve to Figure 15-13.)

indefinitely. Inflationary gaps lead to rising unemployment and rising inflation. Recessionary gaps lead to falling inflation and falling unemployment.

The economy's self-correcting mechanism always tends to push the unemployment rate back toward a specific rate of unemployment that we call the **natural rate of unemployment**.

The **vertical (long-run) Phillips curve** shows the menu of inflation/unemployment choices available to society in the long run. It is a vertical straight line at the natural rate of unemployment.

All the points that are sustainable in the long run (such as *c*, *e*, and *f*) correspond to the same rate of unemployment, which is therefore called the **natural rate of unemployment.** The natural rate corresponds to what we have so far been calling the "full-employment" unemployment rate.

Thus the Phillips curve connecting points *d*, *e*, and *a* is not a menu of policy choices at all. Although we can move from a point such as *e* to a point such as *d* by stimulating aggregate demand sufficiently, the economy will not be able to remain at point *d*. We cannot keep unemployment at such a low level indefinitely. Instead, policymakers must choose from among points such as *c*, *e*, and *f*, all of which correspond to the same "natural" rate of unemployment. For obvious reasons, the line connecting these points has been dubbed the **vertical long-run Phillips curve.** It is this vertical Phillips curve, connecting points such as *e* and *f*, that represents the true long-run menu of policy choices. We thus conclude:

IDEAS FOR BEYOND THE FINAL EXAM

THE TRADE-OFF BETWEEN INFLATION AND UNEMPLOYMENT   In the short run, it is possible to "ride up the Phillips curve" toward lower levels of unemployment by stimulating aggregate demand. (See, for example, point *d* in Figure 15-14.) Conversely, by restricting the growth of demand, it is possible to "ride down the Phillips curve" toward lower rates of inflation (such as point *a* in Figure 15-14). Thus, there is a *trade-off between unemployment and inflation in the short run*. Stimulating demand will improve the unemployment picture but worsen inflation; restricting demand will lower inflation but aggravate the unemployment problem.

However, there is no such trade-off in the long run. The economy's self-correcting mechanism ensures that unemployment will eventually return to the "natural rate" no matter what happens to aggregate demand. In the long run, faster growth of demand leads only to higher inflation, not to lower unemployment; and slower growth of demand leads only to lower inflation, not to higher unemployment.

FIGHTING UNEMPLOYMENT WITH FISCAL AND MONETARY POLICY

Now let us apply this analysis to a concrete policy problem—one that has troubled many U.S. presidents and the leaders of many foreign countries as well. Should the government's ability to manage aggregate demand through fiscal and monetary policy be used to combat unemployment? If so, how? To focus the discussion, we will deal with a recent, real-world example.

The unemployment rate in the United States bottomed out at 3.9 percent in the fall of 2000, a rate that most economists thought was well below the natural rate of unemployment (something like point *d* in Figure 15-14). It then began to creep up gradually, and a year later it stood at 4.9 percent—which may be close to the natural rate (see point *e* in the figure). After that, however, the U.S. economy slipped into a mild recession. Within a few months unemployment had risen to 5.8 percent. By December 2001, the economy was in a position resembling point *a* in Figure 15-14, with a recessionary gap.

Even if fiscal and monetary policymakers did nothing, the economy's self-correcting mechanism would have gradually eroded the recessionary gap. Both unemployment and inflation would have declined gradually as the economy moved along the blue arrow from point *a* to point *c* in Figure 15-14. Eventually, as the diagram shows, the economy would have returned to its natural rate of unemployment (assumed here to be 5 percent) and inflation would have fallen—in the example, from 3 percent to 2 percent.

This eventual outcome is quite satisfactory: Both unemployment and inflation are lower at the end of the adjustment period (point *c*) than at the beginning (point *a*). But it may take an agonizingly long time to get there. And American policymakers in 2001 did not view patience as a virtue. The Federal Reserve moved almost immediately after the terrorist attacks of September 11, 2001, cutting interest rates several times by year end. Fiscal policy reacted as well. Spending on defense and security was increased immediately after the attacks, the first phase of the 2001 tax cut kicked in, and after a six-month delay Congress passed a small fiscal stimulus package.

According to the theory we have learned, such a large dose of expansionary fiscal and monetary policy should have pushed the economy up the short-run Phillips curve from a point like *a* toward a point like *e* in Figure 15-14. Compared to simply relying on the self-correcting mechanism, then, the strong stabilization policy response presumably led to a faster recovery from the 2001 recession. That was certainly the intent of the president, Congress, and the Fed. But Figure 15-14 points out that it also probably left us with a higher inflation rate (5 percent in the figure, about 2 percent in reality).

This example illustrates the range of choices open to policymakers: They can wait patiently while the economy's self-correcting mechanism pulls unemployment down to the natural rate—leading to a long-run equilibrium like point *c* in Figure 15-14. Alternatively, they can rush the process along with expansionary monetary and fiscal policy—and wind up with the same unemployment rate but higher inflation (point *e*). In what sense, then, do policymakers face a *trade-off* between inflation and unemployment? The answer is:

The cost of reducing unemployment more rapidly by expansionary fiscal and monetary policies is a permanently higher inflation rate.

WHAT SHOULD BE DONE?

Should the government pay the inflationary costs of fighting unemployment? When the transitory benefit (lower unemployment for a while) is balanced against the permanent cost (higher inflation), have we made a good bargain?

We have noted that the U.S. government opted for a strong policy response in 2001. Thus two forces were at work simultaneously: The self-correcting mechanism was pulling the economy toward point *c* in Figure 15-14, even as the expansionary monetary and fiscal policies were pushing it toward point *e*. But the net result should be an intermediate path—shown as the dotted line leading to point *g* in Figure 15-14. As this book went to press in 2004, the recovery was progressing nicely.

How do policymakers make such decisions? Our analysis highlights three critical issues on which the answer depends.

The Costs of Inflation and Unemployment

In Chapter 5, we examined the social costs of inflation and unemployment. Most of the benefits of lower unemployment, we concluded, translate easily into dollars and cents. Basically, we need only estimate the higher real GDP each year. However, the costs of the permanently higher inflation rate are more difficult to measure. So there is considerable controversy over the costs and benefits of using demand management to fight unemployment.

Economists and political leaders who believe that inflation is extremely costly may deem it unwise to accept the inflationary consequences of reducing unemployment faster. And indeed, a few dissenters in 2001 were worried about future inflation. Most U.S. policymakers apparently disagreed with that view, however. They decided that reducing unemployment was more important. But things do not always work out that way. In the 1980s and 1990s, many European governments avoided expansionary stabilization policies rather than accept higher inflation.

The Slope of the (Short-Run) Phillips Curve

The shape of the short-run Phillips curve is also critical. Look back at Figure 15-14, and imagine that the Phillips curve connecting points *a* and *e* was much steeper. In that case, the inflationary costs of using expansionary policy to reduce unemployment would be more substantial. On the other hand, if the short-run Phillips curve was

Inflation Targeting and the Phillips Curve

In Chapter 13, we mentioned *inflation targeting* as a new approach to monetary policy that is gaining adherents in many countries. In practice, inflation targeting requires monetary policymakers to rely heavily on the Phillips curve. Why? Because a central bank with, say, a 2 percent inflation target is obligated to pursue a monetary policy that it believes will drive the inflation rate to 2 percent after, say, a year or two. But how does the central bank know which policy will accomplish this goal?

Knowing the proper policy with certainty is, of course, out of the question. But a central bank can use a model similar to the aggregate supply/demand model we have learned in earlier chapters to *estimate* how its policy choices will affect the unemployment rate, say, this year and next. Then it can use a Phillips curve to *estimate* how that unemployment path will affect inflation. In fact, that is more or less what inflation-targeting central banks from New Zealand to Sweden do.

much flatter than the one shown in Figure 15-14, unemployment could be reduced with little inflationary cost.

The Efficiency of the Economy's Self-Correcting Mechanism

We have emphasized that, once a recessionary gap opens, the economy's natural self-correcting mechanism will eventually close it—even in the absence of any policy response. The obvious question is: How long must we wait? If the self-correcting mechanism—which works through reductions in wage inflation—is fast and reliable, high unemployment will not last very long. So the costs of waiting will be small. But if wage inflation responds only slowly to unemployment, the costs of waiting may be enormous. That has evidently been true in much of Europe, where unemployment has remained persistently high for years.

The efficacy of the self-correcting mechanism is also surrounded by controversy. Most economists believe that the weight of the evidence points to extremely sluggish wage behavior: Wage inflation appears to respond slowly to economic slack. In terms of Figure 15-14, this lag means that the economy will traverse the path from *a* to *c* at an agonizingly slow pace, so that a long period of weak economic activity will be necessary to bring down inflation.

But a significant minority opinion finds this assessment far too pessimistic. Economists in this group argue that the costs of reducing inflation are not nearly so severe and that the key to a successful anti-inflation policy is how it affects people's *expectations* of inflation. To understand this argument, we must first understand why expectations are relevant to the Phillips curve.

INFLATIONARY EXPECTATIONS AND THE PHILLIPS CURVE

Recall from Chapter 9 that the main reason why the economy's aggregate supply curve slopes upward—that is, why output increases as the price level rises—is that businesses typically purchase labor and other inputs under long-term contracts that fix input costs in money terms. (The money wage rate is the clearest example.) With such contracts in force, *real* wages fall when prices of goods rise. Labor therefore becomes cheaper in real terms, which persuades businesses to expand employment and output. Buying low and selling high is, after all, the mantra for higher profits.

Table 15-1 illustrates how this principle works in a concrete example. We suppose that workers and firms agree today that the money wage to be paid a year from now will be $10 per hour. The table then shows the real wage corresponding to each alternative inflation rate. For example, if inflation is 4 percent, the real wage a year from now will be $10.00/1.04 = $9.62. Clearly, the higher the inflation rate, the higher the price level at the end of the year and the lower the real wage.

Lower real wages provide an incentive for firms to increase output, as we have just noted. But lower real wages also impose losses of purchasing power on workers. Thus, workers are, in some sense, "cheated" by inflation if they sign a contract specifying a fixed money wage in an inflationary environment.

Many economists doubt that workers will sign such contracts *if they can see inflation coming*. Would it not be wiser, these economists ask, to insist on being compensated for inflation? After all, firms should be willing to offer higher money wages if they expect inflation, because they realize that higher money wages need not imply higher *real* wages.

Table 15-2 illustrates how such a deal can be arranged. For example, if people expect 4 percent inflation, the contract could stipulate that the wage rate be increased to $10.40 (which is 4 percent more than $10) at the end of the year. That would keep the real wage at $10 (because $10.40/1.04 = $10.00), the same as it would be under zero inflation. The other money wage figures in Table 15-2 are derived similarly.

If workers and firms behave this way, and if they forecast inflation accurately, then the real wage will not decline as the price level rises. Instead, prices and wages will go up together, leaving the real wage unchanged. Workers will not lose from inflation, and firms will not gain. (In Table 15-2, the expected future real wage is $10 per hour regardless of the expected inflation rate.) But then there would be no reason for firms to raise production when the price level rises. In a word, the aggregate supply curve would become vertical. In general:

If workers can see inflation coming, and if they receive compensation for it, inflation does not erode *real* wages. But if real wages do not fall, firms have no incentives to increase production. In such a case, the economy's aggregate supply curve will not slope upward, but rather will be a vertical line at the level of output corresponding to potential GDP.

Such a curve is shown in Panel (a) of Figure 15-15 on the next page. Because we derived the Phillips curve from the aggregate supply curve earlier in the chapter, it follows that even the *short-run* Phillips curve would be vertical under these circumstances, as in Panel (b) of Figure 15-15.[4]

If this analysis is correct, it has profound implications for the costs and benefits of fighting inflation. To see this, refer once again to Figure 15-14 (page 287), but now use the graph to depict the strategy of fighting inflation by causing a recession. Suppose we start at point *e*, with 5 percent inflation. To move to point *c* (representing 2 percent inflation), the economy must take a long and unpleasant detour through point *a*. Specifically, contractionary policies must push the economy down the Phillips curve toward point *a* before the self-correcting mechanism takes over and moves the economy from *a* to *c*. In words, we must endure a recession to reduce inflation.

But what if even the *short-run* Phillips curve were *vertical* rather than downward sloping? In this case, the unpleasant recessionary detour would not be necessary. It would be possible for inflation to fall without unemployment rising. The economy could jump directly from point *e* to point *c*.

Is this analysis correct? Can we really slay the inflationary dragon so painlessly? Not necessarily, for our discussion of expectations so far has made at least one unrealistic assumption: that businesses and workers can predict inflation accurately. Under this assumption, as Table 15-2 shows, real wages are unaffected by inflation—leaving the aggregate supply curve vertical, even in the short run.

TABLE 15-1 Money and Real Wages under Unexpected Inflation

Inflation Rate	Price Level 1 Year from Now	Wage per Hour 1 Year from Now	Real Wage per Hour 1 Year from Now
0%	100	$10.00	$10.00
2	102	10.00	9.80
4	104	10.00	9.62
6	106	10.00	9.43

NOTE: Each real wage figure is obtained by dividing the $10 nominal wage by the corresponding price level a year later and multiplying by 100. Thus, for example, when the inflation rate is 4 percent, the real wage at the end of the year is ($10.00/104) × 100 = $9.62.

TABLE 15-2 Money and Real Wages under Expected Inflation

Expected Inflation Rate	Expected Price Level 1 Year from Now	Wage per Hour 1 Year from Now	Expected Real Wage per Hour 1 Year from Now
0%	100	$10.00	$10.00
2	102	10.20	10.00
4	104	10.40	10.00
6	106	10.60	10.00

---

[4] See Review Question 7 at the end of the chapter.

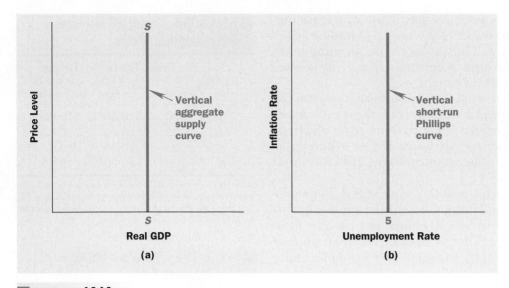

FIGURE 15-15

A Vertical Aggregate Supply Curve and the Corresponding Vertical Phillips Curve

But forecasts of inflation are often inaccurate. Suppose workers underestimate inflation. For example, suppose they expect 4 percent inflation but actually get 6 percent. Then real wages will decline by 2 percent. More generally, real wages will fall if workers underestimate inflation at all. The effects of inflation on real wages will be somewhere in between those shown in Tables 15-1 and 15-2.[5] So firms will retain some incentive to raise production as the price level rises. The aggregate supply curve will retain its upward slope. We thus conclude that:

> **The short-run aggregate supply curve is *vertical* when inflation is predicted accurately but *upward sloping* when inflation is underestimated. Thus, only *unexpectedly* high inflation will raise output, because only unexpected inflation reduces real wages. (To see this point, compare Tables 15-1 and 15-2.) Similarly, only an *unexpected* decline in inflation will lead to a recession.**

Because people often fail to anticipate changes in inflation correctly, this analysis seems to leave our earlier analysis of the Phillips curve almost intact. Indeed, most economists nowadays believe that the Phillips curve slopes downward in the short run but is vertical in the long run.

THE THEORY OF RATIONAL EXPECTATIONS

Rational expectations are forecasts that, while not necessarily correct, are the best that can be made given the available data. Rational expectations, therefore, cannot err systematically. If expectations are rational, forecasting errors are pure random numbers.

However, a vocal minority of economists disagrees with this hypothesis. This group, believers in the hypothesis of **rational expectations,** insists that the Phillips curve is vertical even in the short run. To understand their point of view, we must first explain what rational expectations are. Then we will see why rational expectations have such radical implications for the trade-off between inflation and unemployment.

What Are Rational Expectations?

In many economic contexts, people must formulate expectations about what the future will bring. For example, those who invest in the stock market need to forecast the future prices of the stocks they buy and sell. Likewise, as we have just discussed, workers and businesses may want to forecast future prices before agreeing on a money wage. Rational expectations is a controversial hypothesis about how such forecasts are made.

As used by economists, a forecast (an "expectation") of a future variable is considered rational if the forecaster makes *optimal* use of all relevant information that is *available* at the time of the forecast. Let us elaborate on the two italicized words in this definition, using as an example a hypothetical stock market investor who has rational expectations.

First, proponents of rational expectations recognize that *information is limited*. An investor interested in buying Coca-Cola stock would like to know how much profit

---

[5] To make sure you understand why, construct a version of Table 15-2 based on the assumption that workers expect 4 percent inflation (and hence set next year's wage at $10.40 per hour), regardless of what the actual rate of inflation is. If you create this table correctly, it will show that higher inflation leads to lower real wages, as in Table 15-1.

the company will make in the coming years. Armed with such information, she could predict the future price of Coke stock more accurately. But that information is simply not available. The investor's forecast of the future price of Coke stock is not "irrational" just because she cannot foresee the future. On the other hand, if Coke stock normally goes down on Fridays and up on Mondays, she should be aware of this fact.

Next, we have the word *optimal*. As used by economists, it means using proper statistical inference to process all the relevant information that is available before making a forecast. In brief, to have rational expectations, your forecasts do not have to be correct, but they cannot have systematic errors that you could avoid by applying better statistical methods. This requirement, although exacting, is not quite as outlandish as it may seem. A good billiards player makes expert use of the laws of physics even without understanding the theory. Similarly, an experienced stock market investor may make good use of information even without formal training in statistics.

Rational Expectations and the Trade-Off

Let us now see how some economists have used the hypothesis of rational expectations to deny any trade-off between inflation and unemployment—even in the short run.

Although they recognize that inflation cannot always be predicted accurately, proponents of rational expectations insist that workers will not make *systematic* errors. Our argument leading to a sloping short-run Phillips curve tacitly assumed that workers tend to be slow to recognize changes. They thus *underestimate* inflation when it is rising and *overestimate* inflation when it is falling. Many observers see such errors as a realistic description of human behavior. But advocates of rational expectations disagree, claiming that it is fundamentally illogical. Workers, they argue, will always make the best possible forecast of inflation, using all the latest data and the best available economic models. Such forecasts will sometimes be too high and sometimes too low, but they will not err systematically in one direction or the other. Consequently:

If expectations are rational, the difference between the *actual* rate of inflation and the *expected* rate of inflation (the forecasting error) must be a pure random number, that is:

Inflation = Expected inflation + A random number

Now recall that the argument in the previous section concluded that employment is affected by inflation only to the extent that inflation *differs* from what was expected. But, under rational expectations, no *predictable* change in inflation can make the *expected* rate of inflation deviate from the *actual* rate of inflation. The difference between the two is simply a random number. Hence, according to the rational expectations hypothesis, unemployment will always remain at the natural rate—except for random, and therefore totally unpredictable, gyrations due to forecasting errors. Thus:

If expectations are rational, inflation can be reduced without a period of high unemployment because the short-run Phillips curve, like the long-run Phillips curve, will be vertical.

According to the rational expectations view, the government's ability to manipulate aggregate demand gives it no ability to influence real output and unemployment because the aggregate supply curve is vertical—even in the short run. (To see why, experiment by moving an aggregate demand curve when the aggregate supply curve is vertical, as in Panel (a) of Figure 15-15.) The government's manipulations of aggregate demand are planned ahead and are therefore predictable, and any *predictable* change in aggregate demand will change the *expected* rate of inflation. It will therefore leave real wages unaffected.

The government can influence output only by making *unexpected* changes in aggregate demand. But unexpected changes are not easy to engineer if expectations are rational, because people will understand what policymakers are up to. For example, if the authorities typically react to high inflation by reducing aggregate demand, people will soon come to anticipate this reaction. And *anticipated* reductions in aggregate demand do not cause *unexpected* changes in inflation.

An Evaluation

Believers in rational expectations are optimistic that we can reduce inflation without losing any output, even in the short run. Are they right?

As a piece of pure logic, the rational expectations argument is impeccable. But as is common in economic policy, controversy arises over how well the idea applies in practice. Although the theory has attracted some adherents, the evidence to date leads most economists to reject the extreme rational expectationist position in favor of the view that a trade-off between inflation and unemployment does exist in the short run. Here are some of the reasons.

Contracts May Embody Outdated Expectations   Many contracts for labor and other raw materials cover such long periods of time that the expectations on which they were based, although rational at the time, may appear quite irrational from today's point of view. For example, some three-year labor contracts were drawn up in 1996, when inflation had been running near 3 percent for years. It might have been rational then to expect the 1999 price level to be about 9 percent higher than the 1996 price level, and to have set 1999 wages accordingly. By 1998, inflation had tumbled to barely over 1.5 percent, and such an expectation would have been plainly irrational—but it might already have been written into contracts. If so, real wages wound up much higher than intended, giving firms an incentive to reduce output and therefore employment—even though no one behaved irrationally.

Expectations May Adjust Slowly   Many people believe that inflationary expectations do not adapt as quickly to changes in the economic environment as the rational expectations theory assumes. If, for example, the government embarks on an anti-inflation policy, workers may continue to expect high inflation for a while. Thus, they may continue to insist on rapid money wage increases. Then, if inflation actually slows down, real wages will rise faster than anyone expected, and unemployment will result. Such behavior may not be strictly rational, but it may be realistic.

When Do Workers Receive Compensation for Inflation?   Some observers question whether wage agreements typically compensate workers for expected inflation *in advance*, as assumed by the rational expectations theory. More typically, they argue, wages catch up to actual inflation *after the fact*. If so, real wages will be eroded by inflation, as in the conventional view.

What the Facts Show   The facts have not been kind to the rational expectations hypothesis. The theory suggests that unemployment should hover around the natural rate most of the time, with random gyrations in one direction or the other. Yet this is not what the data show. The theory also predicts that preannounced (and thus expected) anti-inflation programs should be relatively painless. Yet, in practice, fighting inflation has proved very costly in virtually every country. Finally, many direct tests of the rationality of expectations have cast doubt on the hypothesis. For example, survey data on people's expectations rarely meet the exacting requirements of rationality.

But all these problems with rational expectations should not obscure a basic truth. In the long run, the rational expectations viewpoint should be more or less correct because people will not cling to incorrect expectations indefinitely. As Abraham Lincoln pointed out with characteristic wisdom, you cannot fool all the people all the time.

WHY ECONOMISTS (AND POLITICIANS) DISAGREE

This chapter has now taught us some of the reasons why economists often disagree about the proper conduct of stabilization policy. It also helps us understand some of the related political debates.

Should the government take strong actions to prevent or reduce inflation? You will say *yes* if you believe that (1) inflation is more costly than unemployment, (2) the short-run Phillips curve is steep, (3) expectations react quickly, and (4) the economy's self-correcting mechanism works smoothly and rapidly. These views on the economy tend to be held by monetarists and rational expectationists and by the (generally conservative) politicians who sympathize with them.

But you will say *no* if you believe that (1) unemployment is more costly than inflation, (2) the short-run Phillips curve is flat, (3) expectations react sluggishly, and (4) the self-correcting mechanism is slow and unreliable. These views are held by many Keynesian economists, so it is not surprising that the (generally liberal) politicians who share their views often oppose using recession to fight inflation.

The tables turn, however, when the question becomes whether to use demand management to bring a recession to a rapid end. The Keynesian view of the world—that unemployment is costly, that the short-run Phillips curve is flat, that expectations adjust slowly, and that the self-correcting mechanism is unreliable—leads to the conclusion that the benefits of fighting unemployment are high and the costs are low. Keynesians are therefore eager to fight recessions. The monetarist and rational expectationist positions on these four issues are precisely the reverse, and so are the policy conclusions.

THE DILEMMA OF DEMAND MANAGEMENT

We have seen that the makers of monetary and fiscal policy face an unavoidable trade-off. If they stimulate aggregate demand to reduce unemployment, they will aggravate inflation. If they restrict aggregate demand to fight inflation, they will cause higher unemployment.

But wait. Early in the chapter we learned that when inflation comes from the supply side, inflation and unemployment are *positively* correlated: We suffer from more of both or enjoy less of each. Does this mean that monetary and fiscal policymakers can escape the trade-off between inflation and unemployment? Certainly not.

IDEAS FOR BEYOND THE FINAL EXAM

Shifts of the aggregate supply curve can cause inflation and unemployment to rise or fall together, and thus can destroy the statistical Phillips curve relationship. Nevertheless, anything that monetary and fiscal policy can do will make unemployment and inflation move in *opposite* directions because monetary and fiscal policies influence only the *aggregate demand* curve, not the *aggregate supply* curve.

Thus, no matter what the source of inflation, and no matter what happens to the Phillips curve, the monetary and fiscal policy authorities still face the disagreeable trade-off between inflation and unemployment. Many policymakers have failed to understand this principle, and it is one of the *Ideas* that we hope you will remember well *Beyond the Final Exam*.

Naturally, the unpleasant nature of this trade-off has led both economists and public officials to search for a way out of the dilemma. We conclude this chapter by considering some of these ideas—none of which is a panacea.

ATTEMPTS TO REDUCE THE NATURAL RATE OF UNEMPLOYMENT

One highly desirable approach—if only we knew how to do it—would be to reduce the natural rate of unemployment. Then we could enjoy lower unemployment without higher inflation. The question is: How?

The most promising approaches have to do with education, training, and job placement. The data clearly show that more educated workers are unemployed less frequently than less educated ones are. Vocational training and retraining programs, if successful, help unemployed workers with obsolete skills acquire abilities that are currently in demand. By so doing, they both raise employment and help alleviate upward pressures on wages in jobs where qualified workers are in short supply.

Why Did the Natural Rate of Unemployment Fall?

I n 1995, most economists believed that the natural rate of unemployment in the United States was approximately 6 percent—and certainly not lower than 5.5 percent. If unemployment fell below that critical rate, they said, inflation would start to rise. Experience in the late 1990s belied that view. The unemployment rate dipped below 5.5 percent in the summer of 1996—and kept falling. By the end of 1998, it was below 4.5 percent. By the winter of 1999–2000, it hovered around 4 percent. And there were still no signs of rising inflation.

One reason for such incredible macroeconomic performance was discussed in this chapter: A series of favorable supply shocks pushed the aggregate supply curve outward at an unusually rapid pace. But it also appears that the natural rate of unemployment fell in the 1990s. Why?

Economists do not have a complete answer to this question, but a few pieces of the puzzle are understood. For one thing, the U.S. working population aged—and mature workers are normally unemployed less often than are young workers. The rise of temporary-help agencies and Internet job searching capabilities helped match workers to jobs better. Ironically, record-high levels of incarceration probably reduced unemployment, because many of those in jail would otherwise probably have been unemployed. It is also believed (though difficult to prove) that the weak labor markets of the early 1990s left labor more docile, thereby driving down the unemployment rate consistent with constant inflation.

Whatever the reasons, it does appear that the United States can now sustain a lower unemployment than it could a decade ago.

Government and private job placement and counseling services play a similar role. Such programs try to match workers to jobs better by funneling information from prospective employers to prospective employees.

These ideas sound promising and sensible, but two big problems arise in implementation. First, training and placement programs often look better on paper than they do in practice, where they achieve only modest successes. Too often, people are trained for jobs that do not exist by the time they finish their training—if, indeed, the jobs ever existed.

Second, the high cost of these programs restricts the number of workers who can be accommodated, even when they work. For this reason, publicly supported job training is done on a very small scale in the United States—much less, say, than in most European countries. Small expenditures can hardly be expected to make a large dent in the natural rate of unemployment.

But many observers believe the natural rate of unemployment has fallen in the United States despite these problems. Why? One reason is that *work experience* has much in common with formal training—workers become more productive by learning on the job. As the American workforce has aged, the average level of work experience has increased, which, according to many economists, has lowered the natural rate of unemployment. (For some other possible reasons, see "Why Did the Natural Rate of Unemployment Fall?")

INDEXING

Indexing refers to provisions in a law or a contract whereby monetary payments are automatically adjusted whenever a specified price index changes. Wage rates, pensions, interest payments on bonds, income taxes, and many other things can be indexed in this way, and have been. Sometimes such contractual provisions are called *escalator clauses*.

Indexing—which refers to provisions in a law or contract that automatically adjust monetary payments whenever a specific price index changes—presents a very different approach to the inflation-unemployment dilemma. Instead of trying to improve the terms of the trade-off, *indexing seeks to reduce the social costs of inflation*.

The most familiar example of indexing is an *escalator clause* in a wage agreement. Escalator clauses provide for automatic increases in money wages—without the need for new contract negotiations—whenever the price level rises by more than a specified amount. Such agreements thus act to protect workers partly from inflation. Nowadays, with inflation so low and stable, relatively few workers are covered by escalator clauses.

Interest payments on bonds or bank accounts can also be indexed, and the U.S. government began doing so with a small fraction of its bonds in 1997. The most extensive indexing to be found in the United States today, however, appears in government transfer payments. Social Security benefits, for instance, are indexed so that retirees are not victimized by inflation.

Some economists believe that the United States should follow the example of several foreign countries and adopt a more widespread indexing system. Why? Because, they argue, it would take most of the sting out of inflation. To see how, let us review some of the social costs of inflation that we enumerated in Chapter 5.

One important cost is the capricious redistribution of income caused by unexpected inflation. We saw that borrowers and lenders normally incorporate an *inflation premium* equal to the *expected rate of inflation* into the nominal interest rate. Then, if inflation turns out to be higher than expected, the borrower has to pay the lender only the agreed-upon nominal interest rate, including the premium for *expected* inflation; he does not have to compensate the lender for the (higher) *actual* inflation. Thus, the borrower enjoys a windfall gain and the lender loses out. The opposite happens if inflation turns out to be lower than expected.

But if interest rates on loans were indexed, none of this would occur. Borrowers and lenders would agree on a fixed *real* rate of interest, and the borrower would compensate the lender for whatever actual inflation occurred. No one would have to guess what the inflation rate would be.[6]

A second social cost mentioned in Chapter 5 stems from the fact that our tax system levies taxes on nominal interest and nominal capital gains. As we learned, this flaw in the tax system leads to extremely high effective tax rates in an inflationary environment. But indexing can cure this problem. We need only rewrite the tax code so that only *real* interest payments and *real* capital gains are taxed.

In the face of all these benefits, why does our economy not employ more indexing? One obvious reason is that inflation has been low for years. Indexing received much more attention in the 1970s and early 1980s, when inflation was high. A second reason is that some economists fear that indexing will erode society's resistance to inflation. With the costs of inflation so markedly reduced, they ask, what will stop governments from inflating more and more? They fear that the answer is: Nothing. Voters who stand to lose nothing from inflation are unlikely to pressure their legislators into stopping it. Opponents of indexing worry that a mild inflationary disease could turn into a ravaging epidemic in a highly indexed economy.

SUMMARY

1. Inflation can be caused either by rapid growth of aggregate demand or by sluggish growth of aggregate supply.

2. When fluctuations in economic activity emanate from the **demand side**, prices will rise rapidly when real output grows rapidly. Because rapid growth means more jobs, unemployment and inflation will be inversely related.

3. This inverse relationship between unemployment and inflation is called the **Phillips curve.** U.S. data for the 1950s and 1960s display a clear Phillips-curve relation, but data for the 1970s and 1980s do not.

4. The Phillips curve is not a menu of long-run policy choices for the economy, because the self-correcting mechanism guarantees that neither an inflationary gap nor a recessionary gap can last indefinitely.

5. Because of the self-correcting mechanism, the economy's true long-run choices lie along a **vertical long-run Phillips curve,** which shows that the so-called **natural rate of unemployment** is the only unemployment rate that can persist indefinitely.

6. In the short run, the economy can move up or down along its short-run Phillips curve. Temporary reductions in unemployment can be achieved at the cost of higher inflation, and temporary increases in unemployment can be used to fight inflation.

7. Whether it is advisable to use unemployment to fight inflation depends on four principal factors: the relative social costs of inflation versus unemployment, the efficiency of the economy's self-correcting mechanism, the shape of the short-run Phillips curve, and the speed at which inflationary expectations are adjusted.

8. If workers expect inflation to occur, and if they demand (and receive) compensation for inflation, output will be independent of the price level. Both the aggregate supply curve and the short-run Phillips curve are vertical in this case.

---

[6] For example, an indexed loan with a 2 percent real interest rate would require a 5 percent nominal interest payment if inflation were 3 percent, a 7 percent nominal interest payment if inflation were 5 percent, and so on.

9. Errors in predicting inflation will change real wages and therefore the quantity of output that firms wish to supply. Thus, unpredicted movements in the price level will lead to a normal, upward-sloping aggregate supply curve.

10. According to the **rational expectations** hypothesis, errors in predicting inflation are purely random. As a consequence, except for some random gyrations, the aggregate supply curve is vertical even in the short run.

11. Many economists reject the rational expectations view. Some deny that expectations are "rational" and believe instead that people tend, for example, to underpredict inflation when it is rising. Others point out that contracts signed years ago cannot possibly embody expectations that are "rational" in terms of what we know today.

12. When fluctuations in economic activity are caused by shifts of the aggregate supply curve, output will grow slowly (causing unemployment to rise) when inflation rises. Hence, the rates of unemployment and inflation will be positively correlated. Many observers feel that this sort of stagflation is why the Phillips curve collapsed in the 1970s. Similarly, a series of favorable supply shocks help explain the 1990s combination of low inflation and strong economic growth.

13. Even if inflation is initiated by supply-side problems, so that inflation and unemployment occur together, the monetary and fiscal authorities still face this trade-off: Anything they do to improve unemployment is likely to worsen inflation, and anything they do to reduce inflation is likely to aggravate unemployment. The reason is that monetary and fiscal policy mainly influence the aggregate demand curve, not the aggregate supply curve—one of our *Ideas for Beyond the Final Exam*.

14. Policies that improve the functioning of the labor market—including retraining programs and employment services—can, in principle, lower the natural rate of unemployment. To date, however, the U.S. government has enjoyed only modest success with these measures.

15. **Indexing** is another way to approach the trade-off problem. Instead of trying to improve the trade-off, it concentrates on reducing the social costs of inflation. Opponents of indexing worry, however, that the economy's resistance to inflation may be lowered by indexing.

KEY TERMS

Demand-side inflation   280

Supply-side inflation   280

Phillips curve   283

Stagflation caused by supply shocks   285

Self-correcting mechanism   286

Natural rate of unemployment   288

Vertical (long-run) Phillips curve   288

Trade-off between unemployment and inflation in the short run and in the long run   288

Rational expectations   292

Indexing (escalator clauses)   296

Real versus nominal interest rates   297

QUESTIONS FOR REVIEW

1. When inflation and unemployment fell together in the 1990s, some observers claimed that policymakers no longer faced a trade-off between inflation and unemployment. Were they correct?

2. "There is no sense in trying to shorten recessions through fiscal and monetary policy because the effects of these policies on the unemployment rate are sure to be temporary." Comment on both the truth of this statement and its relevance for policy formulation.

3. Why is it said that decisions on fiscal and monetary policy are, at least in part, political decisions that cannot be made on "objective" economic criteria?

4. What is a Phillips curve? Why did it seem to work so much better in the period from 1954 to 1969 than it did in the 1970s?

5. Explain why expectations of inflation affect the wages that result from labor-management bargaining.

6. What is meant by "rational" expectations? Why does the hypothesis of rational expectations have such stunning implications for economic policy? Would believers in rational expectations want to shorten a recession by expanding aggregate demand? Would they want to fight inflation by reducing aggregate demand?

7. Show that, if the economy's aggregate supply curve is vertical, fluctuations in the growth of aggregate demand produce only fluctuations in inflation with no effect on output. Relate this analysis to your answer to Review Question 6.

8. Long-term government bonds now pay approximately 5 percent nominal interest. Would you prefer to trade yours in for an indexed bond that paid a 3 percent real rate of interest? What if the real interest rate offered were 2 percent? What if it were 1 percent? What do your answers to these questions reveal about your personal attitudes toward inflation?

9. It is said that the Federal Reserve Board typically cares more about inflation and less about unemployment than the administration. If this is true, why might President Bush have been worried about what Fed Chairman Alan Greenspan would do in 2001?

10. The year 2001 closed with the unemployment rate nearly 6.8 percent, real GDP barely rising, inflation less than 3 percent, and the federal budget in deficit (slightly).

   a. Make an argument for engaging in expansionary monetary or fiscal policies under these circumstances.

   b. Make an argument for engaging in contractionary monetary or fiscal policies under these circumstances.

   c. Which argument do you find more persuasive?

THE UNITED STATES IN THE WORLD ECONOMY

"**G**lobalization" became a buzzword in the 1990s—and it remains one today. Some people extoll its virtues and view it as something to be encouraged. Others deplore its (real or imagined) costs and seek to stop globalization in its tracks. We will examine several aspects of the globalization debate in Part IV. But love it or hate it, one thing is clear: The United States is thoroughly integrated into a broader world economy.

What happens in the United States influences other countries, and events abroad reverberate back here. Trillions of dollars' worth of goods and services—American computers, German machine tools, Japanese cars—are traded across international borders each year. A vastly larger dollar volume of financial transactions—trade in stocks, bonds, and bank deposits, for example—takes place in the global economy at lightning speed.

While we have mentioned these subjects before, we have not emphasized them. Part IV brings international factors from the wings to center stage. Chapter 16 studies the factors that underlie *international trade,* and Chapter 17 takes up the determination of *exchange rates*—the prices at which the world's currencies are bought and sold. Then Chapter 18 integrates these international influences fully into our model of the macroeconomy.

If you want to understand why so much economic turmoil has occurred in Southeast Asia, Russia, and Latin America in recent years, why our international trade policy is so controversial, or why many thoughtful observers think we need to overhaul the international monetary system, read these three chapters with care.

16

International Trade and Comparative Advantage

No nation was ever ruined by trade.

BENJAMIN FRANKLIN

Economists emphasize international trade as the source of many of the benefits of "globalization." The world's major nations have always been linked in various ways. In recent decades, however, dramatic improvements in transportation, telecommunications, and international relations have drawn the nations of the world ever closer together economically. This process of globalization is often portrayed as something new. But in fact, it is not, as "Is Globalization Something New?" on page 302 points out.

Economic events in other countries affect the United States for both macroeconomic and microeconomic reasons. For example, we learned in Parts II and III that the level of net exports is an important determinant of a nation's output and employment. But we did not delve very deeply into the factors that determine a nation's exports and imports. Chapters 17 and 18 will take up these macroeconomic linkages in greater detail. First, however, this chapter studies some of the microeconomic linkages among nations: How are patterns and prices of world trade determined? How and why do governments interfere with foreign trade? The central idea of this chapter is one we have encountered before (in Chapters 1 and 2): the *principle of comparative advantage*.

CONTENTS

Is Globalization Something New?

Few people realize that the industrialized world was, in fact, highly globalized prior to World War I, before the ravages of two world wars and the Great Depression severed many international linkages. Furthermore, as the British magazine *The Economist* points out, globalization has not gone nearly as far as many people imagine.

Despite much loose talk about the "new" global economy, today's international economic integration is not unprecedented. The 50 years before the first world war saw large cross-border flows of goods, capital and people. That period of globalisation, like the present one, was driven by reductions in trade barriers and by sharp falls in transport costs, thanks to the development of railways and steamships. The present surge of globalisation is in a way a resumption of that previous trend. . . .

Two forces have been driving [globalization]. The first is technology. With the costs of communication and computing falling rapidly, the natural barriers of time and space that separate national markets have been falling too. The cost of a three-minute telephone call between New York and London has fallen from $300 (in 1996 dollars) in 1930 to $1 today . . .

The second driving force has been liberalisation. . . . Almost all countries have lowered barriers to trade. . . . [T]he ratio of trade to output . . . has increased sharply in most countries since 1950. But by this measure Britain and France are only slightly more open to trade today than they were in 1913. . . .

Product markets are still nowhere near as integrated across borders as they are within nations. Consider the example of trade between the United States and Canada, one of the least restricted trading borders in the world. On average, trade between a Canadian province and an American state is

SOURCE: Bettmann/CORBIS

20 times smaller than domestic trade between two Canadian provinces, after adjusting for distance and income levels.

The financial markets are not yet truly integrated either. Despite the newfound popularity of international investing, capital markets were by some measures more integrated at the start of this century than they are now. . . . [And] labour is less mobile than it was in the second half of the 19th century, when some 60m people left Europe for the New World.

SOURCE: "Schools Brief: One World?" *The Economist,* October 18, 1997. © The Economist Newspaper Group, Inc. Reprinted with permission. Further reproduction prohibited. www.economist.com

---

❓ Issue: How Can Americans Compete with "Cheap Foreign Labor"?

Why do Americans (and the citizens of many other nations) often want their government to limit or prevent import competition? One major reason is the common belief that imports take bread out of American workers' mouths. According to this view, "cheap foreign labor" steals jobs from Americans and pressures U.S. businesses to lower wages. Such worries underpinned President Bush's decision to protect the steel industry in March 2002.

Oddly enough, the facts are grossly inconsistent with this story. For one thing, wages in industrialized countries that export to the United States have risen spectacularly in recent decades—faster than wages here. Table 16-1 shows that hourly compensation in seven leading countries rose from an average of only 46 percent of American wages in 1970 to 95 percent by 2000. By 2000, labor costs in Japan and (western) Germany exceeded our own, and costs in the Netherlands and Sweden were about equal. Yet American imports of Toyotas from Japan, Volkswagens from Germany, and Volvos from Sweden grew while wages in those countries rose relative to U.S. wages.

By comparison, when European and Japanese wages were far below those in the United States in the 1950s, American industries had no trouble marketing our products abroad. In fact, the main problem then was to raise our imports up to the level of our bountiful exports. Ironically, the United States' dominant position in the inter-

■ TABLE 16-1   Labor Costs in Industrialized Countries as a Percentage of U.S. Labor Costs

	1970	2000
France	41%	83%
United Kingdom	35	80
Italy	42	74
Japan	24	111
Netherlands	51	96
Sweden	70	101
(West) Germany	56	121

SOURCE: U.S. Bureau of Labor Statistics.

NOTE: Data are compensation estimates per hour, converted at exchange rates, and relate to production workers in the manufacturing sector.

national marketplace *deteriorated* as wage levels in Europe and Japan began to approach our own.

Clearly, then, cheap foreign labor must not be a major obstacle to U.S. sales abroad, as a "common sense" view of the matter suggests. In this chapter, we will see precisely what is wrong with that view.

WHY TRADE?

The earth's resources are not equally distributed across the planet. Although the United States can produce its own coal and wheat, it depends almost *entirely* on the rest of the world for such items as rubber and coffee. Similarly, the Persian Gulf states have little land that is suitable for farming but sit atop huge pools of oil—something we are constantly reminded of by geopolitical events. Because of the seemingly whimsical distribution of vital resources, every nation must trade with others to acquire what it lacks.

Even if countries had all the resources they needed, other differences in natural endowments such as climate, terrain, and so on would lead them to engage in trade. Americans *could*, with great difficulty, grow their own bananas and coffee in hothouses. But these crops are grown much more efficiently in Honduras and Brazil, where the climates are appropriate.

The skills of a nation's labor force also play a role. If New Zealand has a large group of efficient farmers and few workers with industrial experience, while the opposite is true in Japan, it makes sense for New Zealand to specialize in agriculture and let Japan concentrate on manufacturing.

Finally, a small country that tried to produce every product would end up with many industries that are simply too small to utilize modern mass-production techniques or to take advantage of other economies of large-scale operations. For example, some countries operate their own international airlines for reasons that can only be described as political, not economic.

To summarize, the main reason why nations trade with one another is to exploit the many advantages of **specialization,** some of which were discussed in Chapter 2. International trade greatly enhances living standards for all parties involved because:

> **Specialization** means that a country devotes its energies and resources to only a small proportion of the world's productive activities.

1. **Every country lacks some vital resources that it can get only by trading with others.**

2. **Each country's climate, labor force, and other endowments make it a relatively efficient producer of some goods and an inefficient producer of other goods.**

3. **Specialization permits larger outputs and can therefore offer economies of large-scale production.**

Mutual Gains from Trade

Many people have long believed that one nation gains from trade only at the expense of another. After all, nothing new is produced by the mere act of trading. So if one country gains from a swap, it is argued, the other country must necessarily lose. One consequence of this mistaken belief was and continues to be a policy prescription calling for each country to try to take advantage of its trading partners on the (fallacious) grounds that one nation's gain must be another's loss.

Yet, as Adam Smith emphasized, and as we learned in Chapter 2, both parties must expect to gain something from any *voluntary exchange*. Otherwise, why would they agree to trade?

But how can mere exchange of goods leave both parties better off? The answer is that although trade does not increase the total output of goods, it does allow each party to acquire items better suited to its tastes. Suppose Scott has four cookies and nothing to drink, while Malcolm has two glasses of milk and nothing to eat. A trade of two of Scott's cookies for one of Malcolm's glasses of milk will not increase the total supply of either milk or cookies, but it almost certainly will make both boys better off.

By exactly the same logic, both the United States and Mexico must reap gains when Mexico voluntarily ships tomatoes to the United States in return for chemicals. In general, as we emphasized in Chapter 2:

IDEAS FOR BEYOND THE FINAL EXAM

TRADE IS A WIN-WIN SITUATION   Both parties must expect to gain from any *voluntary exchange.* Trade brings about mutual gains by redistributing products so that both parties end up holding more preferred combinations of goods than they held before. This principle, which is one of our *Ideas for Beyond the Final Exam,* applies to nations just as it does to individuals.

INTERNATIONAL VERSUS INTRANATIONAL TRADE

The 50 states of the United States may be the most eloquent testimony to the gains that can be realized from specialization and free trade. Florida specializes in growing oranges, Michigan builds cars, California makes computers and chips, and New York specializes in finance. All of these states trade freely with one another and enjoy great prosperity. Try to imagine how much lower your standard of living would be if you consumed only items produced in your own state.

The essential logic behind international trade is no different from that underlying trade among different states; the basic reasons for trade are equally applicable within a country or among countries. Why, then, do we study international trade as a special subject? There are at least three reasons.

Political Factors in International Trade

First, domestic trade takes place under a single national government, whereas foreign trade always involves at least two governments. But a nation's government is normally much less concerned about the welfare of other countries' citizens than it is about its own. So, for example, the U.S. Constitution prohibits tariffs on trade among states, but it does not prohibit the United States from imposing tariffs on imports from abroad. One major issue in the economic analysis of international trade is the use and misuse of impediments to free international trade.

The Many Currencies Involved in International Trade

Second, all trade within the borders of the United States is carried out in U.S. dollars, whereas trade across national borders almost always involves at least two currencies. Rates of exchange between different currencies can and do change. In 1985, it took about 250 Japanese yen to buy a dollar; now it takes only about 110. Variability in exchange rates brings with it a host of complications and policy problems.

Impediments to Mobility of Labor and Capital

Third, it is much easier for labor and capital to move about within a country than to move from one nation to another. If jobs are plentiful in California but scarce in West Virginia, workers can move freely to follow the job opportunities. Of course, personal costs such as the financial burden of moving and the psychological cost of leaving friends and familiar surroundings may discourage mobility. But such relocations are not inhibited by immigration quotas, by laws restricting the employment of foreigners, or by the need to learn a new language.

There are also greater impediments to the transfer of capital across national boundaries than to its movement within a country. For example, many countries have rules limiting foreign ownership; even the United States limits foreign ownership of broadcast outlets and airlines. Foreign investment is also subject to special political risks, such as the danger of outright expropriation or nationalization after a change in government.

But even if nothing as extreme as expropriation occurs, capital invested abroad faces significant risks from exchange rate variations. An investment valued at 250 million yen is worth $1 million to American investors when the dollar is worth 250 yen, but it is worth $2 million when it takes just 125 yen to buy a dollar.

THE LAW OF COMPARATIVE ADVANTAGE

The gains from international specialization and trade are clear and intuitive when one country is better at producing one item and its trading partner is better at producing another. For example, no one finds it surprising that Brazil sells coffee to the United States and the United States exports software to Brazil. We know that coffee can be produced using less labor and other inputs in Brazil than in the United States. Likewise, the United States can produce software at a lower resource cost than can Brazil.

In such a situation, we say that Brazil has an **absolute advantage** in coffee production, and the United States has an absolute advantage in software production. In such cases, it is obvious that both countries can gain by producing the item in which they have an absolute advantage and then trading with one another.

What is much less obvious, but equally true, is that these gains from international trade still exist *even if one country is more efficient than the other in producing everything*. This lesson, the principle of **comparative advantage,** is one we first learned in Chapter 2.[1] It is, in fact, one of the most important of our *Ideas for Beyond the Final Exam*, so we repeat it here for convenience.

> One country is said to have an **absolute advantage** over another in the production of a particular good if it can produce that good using smaller quantities of resources than can the other country.
>
> One country is said to have a **comparative advantage** over another in the production of a particular good relative to other goods if it produces that good less inefficiently as compared with the other country.

IDEAS FOR BEYOND THE FINAL EXAM

THE SURPRISING PRINCIPLE OF COMPARATIVE ADVANTAGE Even if one country is at an absolute *dis*advantage relative to another country in the production of every good, it is said to have a *comparative advantage* in making the good at which it is *least inefficient* (compared with the other country).

The great classical economist David Ricardo (1772–1823) discovered almost 200 years ago that two countries can still gain from trade, even if one is more efficient than the other in every industry—that is, even if one has an absolute advantage in producing *every* commodity.

In determining the most efficient patterns of production, it is *comparative* advantage, not *absolute* advantage, that matters. Thus, a country can gain by importing a good even if that good can be produced more efficiently at home. Such imports make sense if they enable the country to specialize in producing goods at which it is *even more* efficient.

The Arithmetic of Comparative Advantage

Let's see precisely how comparative advantage works using a hypothetical example first suggested in Chapter 2. Table 16-2 gives a somewhat exaggerated impression of the trading positions of the United States and Japan a few years ago. We imagine that labor is the only input used to produce computers and television sets in the two countries and that the United States has an absolute advantage in manufacturing both goods. In this example, one year's worth of labor can produce either 50 computers or 50 TV sets in the United States but only 10 computers or 40 televisions in Japan. So the United States is the more efficient producer of both goods. Nonetheless, as we will now show, it pays for the United States to specialize in producing computers and trade with Japan to get the TV sets it wants.

To demonstrate this point, we begin by noting that the United States has a comparative advantage in *computers*, whereas Japan has a comparative advantage in producing *TVs*. Specifically, the numbers in Table 16-2 show that the United States can

TABLE 16-2 Alternative Outputs from One Year of Labor Input

	In the U.S.	In Japan
Computers	50	10
Televisions	50	40

---

[1] To review, see pages 27–28.

produce 50 televisions with one year's labor whereas Japan can produce only 40; so the United States is 25 percent more efficient than Japan in producing TV sets. However, the United States is five times as efficient as Japan in producing computers: It can produce 50 per year of labor rather than 10. Because America's competitive edge is far greater in computers than in televisions, we say that the United States has a *comparative advantage* in computers.

From the Japanese perspective, these same numbers indicate that Japan is only slightly less efficient than the United States in TV production but drastically less efficient in computer production. So Japan's comparative advantage is in the television industry. According to Ricardo's law of comparative advantage, then, the two countries can gain if the United States specializes in producing computers, Japan specializes in producing TVs, and the two countries trade.

Let's verify that this conclusion is true. Suppose Japan transfers 1,000 years of labor out of the computer industry and into TV manufacturing. According to the figures in Table 16-2, its computer output will fall by 10,000 units while its TV output will rise by 40,000 units. (See the middle column of Table 16-3.) Suppose, at the same time, the United States transfers 500 years of labor out of television manufacturing (thereby losing 25,000 TVs) and into computer making (thereby gaining 25,000 computers). Table 16-3 shows us that these transfers of resources between the two countries increase the world's production of both outputs. Together, the two countries now have 15,000 additional TVs and 15,000 additional computers—surely a nice outcome.

■ TABLE 16-3	Example of the Gains from Trade		
	U.S.	Japan	Total
Computers	+25,000	−10,000	**+15,000**
Televisions	−25,000	+40,000	**+15,000**

Was there some sleight of hand here? How did *both* the United States *and* Japan gain *both* computers *and* TVs? The explanation is that the process we have just described involves more than just a swap of a fixed bundle of commodities—it is also *a change in the production arrangements.* Some of Japan's inefficient computer production is taken over by more efficient American makers. And some of America's TV production is taken over by Japanese television companies, which are *less inefficient* at making TVs than Japanese computer manufacturers are at making computers. The underlying principle is both simple and fundamental:

When every country does what it can do best, all countries can benefit because more of every commodity can be produced without increasing the amounts of labor and other resources used.

■ The Graphics of Comparative Advantage

The gains from trade can also be displayed graphically, and doing so helps us understand whether such gains are large or small.

The lines *US* and *JN* in Figure 16-1 are closely related to the production possibilities frontiers of the two countries, but they differ in that they pretend that each country has the same amount of labor available.[2] In this case, we assume that each has 1 million person-years of labor. For example, Table 16-2 tells us that for each 1 million years of labor, the United States can produce 50 million TVs and no computers (point *U* in Figure 16-1), 50 million computers and no TVs (point *S*), or any combination between (the line *US*). Similar reasoning leads to line *JN* for Japan.

America's *actual* production possibilities frontier would be even higher, relative to Japan's, than shown in Figure 16-1 because the U.S. population is larger. But Figure 16-1 is more useful because it highlights the differences in efficiency that determine both absolute and comparative advantage. Let's see how.

The fact that line *US* lies *above* line *JN* means that the United States can manufacture more televisions and more computers than Japan *with the same amount of labor.* This difference reflects our assumption that the United States has an *absolute* advantage in both commodities.

---

[2] To review the concept of the production possibilities frontier, see Chapter 2.

America's comparative advantage in computer production and Japan's comparative advantage in TV production are shown in a different way: by the relative *slopes* of the two lines. Look back to Table 16-2, which shows that the United States can acquire a computer on its own by giving up one TV. Thus, the *opportunity cost* of a computer in the United States is one television set. This opportunity cost is depicted graphically by the slope of the U.S. production possibilities frontier in Figure 16-1, which is $OU/OS = 50/50 = 1$.

Table 16-2 also tells us that the opportunity cost of a computer in Japan is four TVs. This relationship is depicted in Figure 16-1 by the slope of Japan's production possibilities frontier, which is $OJ/ON = 40/10 = 4$.

FIGURE 16-1
Production Possibilities
Frontiers for Two Countries
(per million years of labor)

A country's *absolute* advantage in production over another country is shown by its having a higher per-capita production possibilities frontier. The difference in the *comparative* advantages between the two countries is shown by the difference in the slopes of their frontiers.

Because opportunity costs differ in the two countries, gains are possible if the two countries specialize and trade with one another. Specifically, it is cheaper, in terms of real resources forgone, for *either* country to acquire its computers in the United States. By a similar line of reasoning, the opportunity cost of TVs is higher in the United States than in Japan, so it makes sense for both countries to acquire their televisions in Japan.[3]

Notice that if the slopes of the two production possibilities frontiers, *JN* and *US*, were equal, then opportunity costs would be the same in each country. In that case, no potential gains would arise from trade. Gains from trade arise from *differences* across countries, not from similarities. This is an important point about which people are often confused. Some argue that two very different countries, such as the United States and Mexico, cannot gain much by trading with one another. In fact:

Two very similar countries may gain little from trade. Large gains from trade are most likely when countries are very different.

How the two countries divide the gains from trade depends on the prices that emerge from world trade, which is the subject of the next section. But we already know enough to see that world trade must, in our example, leave a computer costing more than one TV and less than four. Why? Because, if a computer bought less than one TV (its opportunity cost in the United States) on the world market, the United States would produce its own TVs rather than buying them from Japan. And if a computer cost more than four TVs (its opportunity cost in Japan), Japan would prefer to produce its own computers rather than buy them from the United States.

We therefore conclude that, if both countries are to trade, the rate of exchange between TVs and computers must end up somewhere between 4:1 and 1:1. Generalizing:

If two countries voluntarily trade two goods with one another, the rate of exchange between the goods must fall in between the price ratios that would prevail in the two countries in the absence of trade.

To illustrate the gains from trade in our concrete example, suppose the world price ratio settles at 2:1—meaning that one computer costs as much as two televisions. How much, precisely, do the United States and Japan gain from world trade in this case?

Figure 16-2 is designed to help us visualize the answers. The blue production possibilities frontiers, *US* in Panel (b) and *JN* in Panel (a), are the same as in Figure 16-1.

---

[3] As an exercise, provide this line of reasoning.

NOTE: Quantities are in millions.

■ FIGURE 16-2
The Gains from Trade

But the United States can do better than line *US*. Specifically, with a world price ratio of 2:1, the United States can buy two TVs for each computer it gives up, rather than just one (which is the opportunity cost of a computer in the United States). Hence, if the United States produces only computers—point *S* in Figure 16-2(b)—and buys its TVs from Japan, America's *consumption possibilities* will be as indicated by the red line that begins at point *S* and has a slope of 2—that is, each computer sold brings the United States two television sets. Because trade allows the United States to choose a point on *AS* rather than on *US*, trade opens up consumption possibilities that were simply not available before.

A similar story applies to Japan. If the Japanese produce only television sets—point *J* in Figure 16-2(a)—they can acquire a computer from the United States for every two TVs they give up as they move along the red line *JP* (whose slope is 2). This result is better than they can achieve on their own, because a sacrifice of two TVs in Japan yields only one-half of a computer. Hence, world trade enlarges Japan's consumption possibilities from *JN* to *JP*.

Figure 16-2 shows graphically that gains from trade arise to the extent that world prices (2:1 in our example) differ from domestic opportunity costs (4:1 and 1:1 in our example). So it is a matter of some importance to understand how prices in international trade are established. We shall do so shortly.

? Issue Resolved: Comparative Advantage Exposes the "Cheap Foreign Labor" Fallacy

But first let us observe that the principle of comparative advantage takes us a long way toward understanding the fallacy in the "cheap foreign labor" argument described at the beginning of this chapter. Given the assumed productive efficiency of American labor, and the inefficiency of Japanese labor, we would expect wages to be much higher in the United States.

In these circumstances, one might expect American workers to be apprehensive about an agreement to permit trade between the two countries: "How can we hope to meet the unfair competition of those underpaid Japanese workers?" Japanese laborers might also be concerned: "How can we hope to meet the competition of those Americans, who are so efficient in producing everything?"

The principle of comparative advantage shows us that both fears are unjustified. As we have just seen, when trade opens up between Japan and the United States, *workers in both countries will be able to earn higher real wages than before* because of the increased productivity that comes through specialization.

As Figure 16-2 shows, once trade opens, Japanese workers should end up with more TVs and more computers than they had before. As a consequence, their living standards should rise, even though they have been left vulnerable to competition from "super-efficient" Americans. Workers in the United States should also end up with more TVs and with more computers, so their living standards should also rise even though they have been exposed to competition from "cheap" Japanese labor. These higher standards of living, of course, reflect the higher real wages earned by workers in both countries.

The lesson to be learned here is elementary:

Nothing helps raise living standards more than a greater abundance of goods.

SUPPLY, DEMAND, AND PRICING IN WORLD TRADE

How the two countries share the gains from world trade depends on the prices that emerge. As usual, price determination in a free market depends on supply and demand.

When applied to international trade, however, the supply-demand model runs into several new complications. First, it involves at least *two demand curves:* that of the exporting country and that of the importing country. Second, it may also involve *two supply curves*, because the importing country may produce part of its own consumption. Third, equilibrium does *not* take place at the intersection point of *either* pair of supply-demand curves. Why? Because if the two countries trade at all, the exporting nation must supply more than it demands, whereas the importing nation must demand more than it supplies.

All three of these complications are illustrated in Figure 16-3, which shows the supply and demand curves of a country that *exports* wheat in Panel (a) and of a country that *imports* wheat in Panel (b). For simplicity, we assume that these countries do not deal with anyone else. Where will the two-country wheat market reach equilibrium?

■ **FIGURE 16-3**
Supply-Demand Equilibrium in the International Wheat Trade

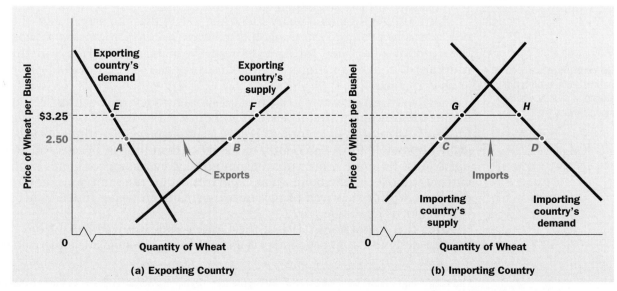

(a) Exporting Country

(b) Importing Country

Under free trade, the equilibrium price must satisfy two requirements:

1. **The quantity of wheat *exported* by one country must equal the quantity of wheat *imported* by the other country.**

2. **The price of wheat must be the *same* in both countries.[4]**

In Figure 16-3, these two conditions are met at a price of $2.50 per bushel. At that price, the distance *AB* between what the exporting country produces and what it consumes equals the distance *CD* between what the importing country consumes and what it produces. This means that the amount the exporting country wants to sell at $2.50 per bushel exactly equals the amount the importing country wants to buy at that price.

At any higher price, producers in both countries will want to sell more and consumers in both countries will want to buy less. For example, if the price rises to $3.25 per bushel, the exporter's quantity supplied will rise from *B* to *F*, whereas its quantity demanded will fall from *A* to *E*, as shown in Figure 16-3(a). As a result, more wheat will be available for export—*EF* rather than *AB*. For exactly the same reason, the price increase will cause higher production and lower sales in the importing country, leading to a reduction in imports from *CD* to *GH* in Panel (b).

But this means that the higher price, $3.25 per bushel, cannot be sustained in a free and competitive international market. With export supply *EF* far greater than import demand *GH*, there is pressure on price to fall back toward the $2.50 equilibrium price. Similar reasoning shows that no price below $2.50 can be sustained. Thus:

In international trade, the equilibrium price is the one that makes the exporting country want to export exactly the amount that the importing country wants to import. Equilibrium will thus occur at a price at which the horizontal distance *AB* in Figure 16-3(a) (the excess of the exporter's quantity supplied over its quantity demanded) is equal to the horizontal distance *CD* in Figure 16-3(b) (the excess of the importer's quantity demanded over its quantity supplied). At this price, the *world's* quantity demanded equals the *world's* quantity supplied.

TARIFFS, QUOTAS, AND OTHER INTERFERENCES WITH TRADE

Despite the mutual gains from international trade, nations often interfere with the operation of free markets. In fact, until the rise of the free-trade movement about 200 years ago (with such economists as Adam Smith and David Ricardo as its vanguard), it was taken for granted that one of the essential tasks of government was to *impede* trade, presumably in the national interest.

Many argued then (and many still argue today) that the proper aim of government policy was to promote exports and discourage imports, for doing so would increase the amount of money foreigners owed the nation. According to this so-called **mercantilist** view, a nation's wealth consists of the amount of gold or other monies at its command.

Mercantilism is a doctrine that holds that exports are good for a country, whereas imports are harmful.

Obviously, governments can pursue such a policy only within certain limits. A country *must* import vital foodstuffs and critical raw materials that it cannot supply for itself. Moreover, mercantilists ignore a simple piece of arithmetic: It is mathematically impossible for *every* country to sell more than it buys, because one country's exports must be some other country's imports. If everyone competes in this game by cutting imports to the bone, then exports must go the same way. The result is that everyone will be deprived of the mutual gains from trade. Indeed, that is precisely what happens in a trade war.

After the protectionist 1930s, the United States moved away from mercantilist policies designed to impede imports and gradually assumed a leading role in promot-

---

[4] To keep things simple, we ignore such details as the costs of shipping wheat from one country to the other.

Liberalizing World Trade: The Doha Round

T he time and place were not auspicious: an international gathering in the Persian Gulf just two months after the September 11, 2001, terrorists attacks. Nerves were frayed, security was extremely tight, and memories of a trade meeting in Seattle that failed in 1999 lingered on. Yet representatives of more than 140 nations, meeting in Doha, Qatar, in November 2001, managed to hammer out the outlines of a new round of comprehensive trade negotiations—one that will take years to complete.

The so-called Doha Round will focus on bringing down tariffs, subsidies, and other restrictions on world trade in agriculture, services, and a variety of manufactured goods. It will also seek greater protection for intellectual property rights, while making sure that poor countries have access to modern pharmaceuticals at prices they can afford. Reform of the World Trade Organization's own rules and procedures is also on the agenda. Perhaps most surprisingly, the United States even promised to consider changes in its antidumping laws, which are used to keep many foreign goods out of U.S. markets. (Dumping is explained at the end of this chapter.)

SOURCE: © AFP/Corbis

Large-scale trade negotiations such as this one, involving more than 100 countries and many different issues, take years to complete. (The last one, the Uruguay Round, took seven years.) And this round almost collapsed in 2003 at an acrimonious negotiating session in Mexico. So expect the Doha Round to be around for a while.

ing free trade. Over the past 50 years, tariffs and other trade barriers have come down dramatically.

In 1995, the United States led the world to complete the Uruguay Round of tariff reductions and, just before that, the country joined Canada and Mexico in the North American Free Trade Agreement (NAFTA). The latter caused a political firestorm in the United States in 1993 and 1994, with critic (and 1992 presidential candidate) Ross Perot predicting a "giant sucking sound" as American workers lost their jobs to competition from "cheap Mexican labor." (Does that argument sound familiar?) Today, most of the world's trading nations are engaged in a new multiyear round of trade talks, under guidelines adopted at an important meeting in Doha, Qatar, in November 2001. (See "Liberalizing World Trade: The Doha Round.")

Modern governments use three main devices when seeking to control trade: tariffs, quotas, and export subsidies. A **tariff** is simply a tax on imports. An importer of wheat, for example, may be charged $1 for each bushel brought into the country. The United States is generally a low-tariff country, with only a few notable exceptions, such as the recently-imposed tariffs on steel products of as much as 30 percent. However, many other countries rely on heavy tariffs to protect their industries. Indeed, tariff rates of 100 percent or more are not uncommon.

A **quota** is a legal limit on the amount of a good that may be imported. For example, the government might allow no more than 25 million bushels of wheat to be imported in a year. In some cases, governments ban the importation of certain goods outright—a quota of zero. The United States now imposes quotas on a smattering of goods, including textiles, meat, and sugar. Most imports, however, are not subject to quotas.

An **export subsidy** is a government payment to an exporter. By reducing the exporter's costs, such subsidies permit exporters to lower their selling prices and compete more effectively in world trade. Overt export subsidies are minor in the United States, but some foreign governments use them extensively to assist their domestic industries—a practice that provokes bitter complaints from American manufacturers about "unfair competition." For example, years of heavy government subsidies helped

A **tariff** is a tax on imports.

A **quota** specifies the maximum amount of a good that is permitted into the country from abroad per unit of time.

An **export subsidy** is a payment by the government to exporters to permit them to reduce the selling prices of their goods so they can compete more effectively in foreign markets.

the European Airbus consortium take a sizable share of the world commercial aircraft market away from U.S. manufacturers like Boeing and McDonnell-Douglas. More recently, the Europeans have argued that certain aspects of the U.S. tax code amount to an unfair export subsidy.

How Tariffs and Quotas Work

Both tariffs and quotas restrict supplies coming from abroad and drive up prices. A tariff works by raising prices, which in turn cuts the demand for imports. The sequence associated with a quota is just the reverse—a restriction in supply forces prices up.

The supply and demand curves in Figure 16-4 illustrate how tariffs and quotas work. Just as in Figure 16-3, the equilibrium price of wheat under free trade is $2.50 per bushel (in both countries). At this price, the exporting country produces 125 million bushels—point B in Panel (a)—and consumes 80 million (point A). So its exports are 45 million bushels—the distance AB. Similarly, the importing country consumes 95 million bushels—point D in Panel (b)—and produces only 50 million (point C), so its imports are also 45 million bushels—the distance CD.

Now suppose the government of the importing nation imposes a *quota* limiting imports to 30 million bushels. The free-trade equilibrium with imports of 45 million bushels is now illegal. Instead, the market must equilibrate at a point where both exports and imports are only 30 million bushels. As Figure 16-4 indicates, this requirement leads to different prices in the two countries.

Imports in Panel (b) will be 30 million bushels—the distance QT—only when the price of wheat in the importing nation is $3.25 per bushel, because only at this price will quantity demanded exceed domestic quantity supplied by 30 million bushels. Similarly, exports in Panel (a) will be 30 million bushels—the distance RS—only when the price in the exporting country is $2.00 per bushel. At this price, quantity supplied exceeds quantity demanded in the exporting country by 30 million bushels. Thus, the quota *raises* the price in the importing country to $3.25 and *lowers* the price in the exporting country to $2.00. In general:

An import quota on a product normally reduces the volume of that product traded, raises the price in the importing country, and reduces the price in the exporting country.

■ FIGURE 16-4
Quotas and Tariffs in International Trade

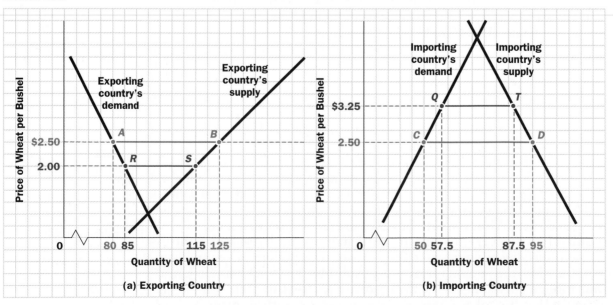

(a) Exporting Country

(b) Importing Country

NOTE: Quantities are in millions of bushels.

A tariff can accomplish exactly the same restriction of trade. In our example, a quota of 30 million bushels led to a price that was $1.25 higher in the importing country than in the exporting country ($3.25 versus $2.00). Suppose that, instead of a quota, the importing nation imposes a $1.25 per bushel *tariff.* International trade equilibrium then must satisfy the following two requirements:

1. The quantity of wheat *exported* by one country must equal the quantity of wheat *imported* by the other.

2. The price that consumers in the importing country pay for wheat must *exceed* the price that suppliers in the exporting country receive by the amount of the *tariff* ($1.25 in this example).

By consulting the graphs in Figure 16-4, you can see exactly where these two requirements are met. If the exporter produces at S and consumes at R, while the importer produces at Q and consumes at T, then exports and imports are equal (at 30 million bushels), and the two domestic prices differ by exactly $1.25. (They are $3.25 and $2.00.) What we have just discovered is a general result of international trade theory:

Any restriction of imports that is accomplished by a quota normally can also be accomplished by a tariff.

In this case, the tariff corresponding to an import quota of 30 million bushels is $1.25 per bushel.

Tariffs versus Quotas

Although tariffs and quotas can accomplish the same reduction in international trade and lead to the same domestic prices in the two countries, there are some important differences between the two types of restrictions.

First, under a quota, profits from the price increases in the importing country usually go into the pockets of the foreign and domestic sellers of the product. Because supplies are limited by quotas, customers in the importing country must pay more for the product. So the suppliers, whether foreign or domestic, receive more for every unit they sell. For example, the right to sell sugar in the United States under the tight sugar quota has been extremely valuable for decades. Privileged foreign and domestic firms can make a lot of money.

On the other hand, when trade is restricted by a tariff, some of the profits go instead as tax revenues to the *government* of the importing country. In effect, the government increases its tax revenues partly at its own citizens' expense and partly at the expense of foreign exporters, which must accept a reduced price for their wares. (Domestic producers again benefit, because they are exempt from the tariff.) In this respect, a tariff is certainly a better proposition than a quota from the viewpoint of the country that enacts it.

Another important distinction between the two measures arises from their different implications for productive efficiency. Because a tariff handicaps all foreign suppliers equally, it awards sales to those firms and nations that can supply the goods most cheaply—presumably because they are more efficient. A quota, by contrast, necessarily awards its import licenses more or less capriciously—perhaps in proportion to past sales or even based on political favoritism. There is no reason to expect the most efficient suppliers to get the import permits. For example, the U.S. sugar quota was for years suspected of being a source of corruption in the Caribbean.

If a country must inhibit imports, two important reasons support a preference for tariffs over quotas:

1. Some of the revenues resulting from tariffs go to the government of the importing country rather than to foreign and domestic producers.

2. Unlike quotas, tariffs offer special benefits to more efficient exporters.

WHY INHIBIT TRADE?

To state that tariffs provide a better way to inhibit international trade than quotas leaves open a far more basic question: Why limit trade in the first place? It has been estimated that trade restrictions cost American consumers more than $70 billion per year in the form of higher prices. Why should they be asked to pay these higher prices?

A number of answers are commonly given. Let's examine each in turn.

Gaining a Price Advantage

A tariff forces foreign exporters to sell more cheaply by restricting their market access. If they do not cut their prices, they will be left with unsold goods. Suppose, as in Figure 16-4(b), that a $1.25 tariff on wheat raises the price in the importing country from $2.50 to $3.25 per bushel. This higher price drives down imports from an amount represented by the length of the red line *CD* to the smaller amount represented by the blue line *QT*. In the exporting country, this change means an equal reduction in exports, as illustrated by the change from *AB* to *RS* in Figure 16-4(a).

As a result, the price at which the exporting country can sell its wheat is driven down—from $2.50 to $2.00 in the example. Meanwhile, producers in the importing country, which are exempt from the tariff, can charge $3.25 per bushel. So in effect, the tariff amounts to government intervention to rig prices in favor of domestic producers.

Not bad, you say. However, this technique works only as long as foreigners accept the tariff exploitation passively—which they rarely do. More often, they retaliate by imposing tariffs or quotas of their own on imports from the country that first began the tariff game. Such tit-for-tat behavior can easily lead to a trade war in which no one gains more favorable prices but everyone loses through the resulting reductions in trade. Something like this happened to the world economy in the 1930s, and it helped prolong the worldwide depression. Preventing such trade wars is one main reason why nations that belong to the World Trade Organization (WTO) pledge not to raise their tariffs.

Tariffs or quotas can benefit particular domestic industries in a country that is able to impose them without fear of retaliation. But when every country uses them, everyone is likely to lose in the long run.

Protecting Particular Industries

The second, and probably more frequent, reason why countries restrict trade is to protect particular industries from foreign competition. If foreigners can produce steel or shoes more cheaply, domestic businesses and unions in these industries are quick to demand protection. And their governments may be quite willing to grant it—as the recent steel case illustrates.

The "cheap foreign labor" argument is most likely to arise in this context. Protective tariffs and quotas are explicitly designed to rescue firms that are too inefficient to compete with foreign exporters in an open world market. But it is precisely this harsh competition that gives consumers the chief benefits of international specialization: better products at lower prices.

In our numerical example of comparative advantage, we can well imagine the indignant complaints from Japanese computer makers as the opening of trade with the United States leads to increased imports of American-made computers. At the same time, American TV manufacturers would probably express outrage over the flood of imported TVs from Japan. Yet Japanese specialization in televisions and U.S. specialization in computers is precisely what enables citizens of both countries to enjoy higher standards of living. If governments interfere with this process, consumers in both countries will lose out.

Industries threatened by foreign competition often argue that some form of protection against imports is needed to prevent job losses. For example, the U.S. steel industry has made exactly this argument time and time again since the 1960s—most recently in 2001, when world steel prices plummeted and imports surged. (And the U.S. government has usually delivered some protection in response.) Basic macroeconomics teaches us, however, that there are better ways to stimulate employment, such as raising aggregate demand.

A program that limits foreign competition will be more effective at preserving employment *in the particular protected industry*, but such job gains typically come at a high cost to consumers and to the economy. Table 16-4 estimates some of the costs to American consumers of using tariffs and quotas to save jobs in selected industries. In every case, the costs far exceed the wages of the workers in the protected industries—ranging as high as $600,000 per job for the sugar quota.

Nevertheless, complaints over proposals to reduce tariffs or quotas are justified unless something is done to ease the cost to individual workers of switching to the product lines that trade makes profitable.

■ **TABLE 16-4** Estimated Costs of Protectionism to Consumers	
Industry	Cost per Job Saved
Apparel	$139,000
Costume jewelry	97,000
Shipping	415,000
Sugar	600,000
Textiles	202,000
Women's footwear	102,000

SOURCE: Gary C. Hufbauer and Kimberly Ann Elliott, *Measuring the Costs of Protectionism in the United States* (Washington, D.C.: Institute for International Economics; January 1994), Table 1.3, pp. 12–13.

The argument for free trade between countries cannot be considered airtight if governments do not assist the citizens in each country who are harmed whenever patterns of production change drastically—as would happen, for example, if governments suddenly reduced tariff and quota barriers.

Owners of television factories in the United States and of computer factories in Japan may see large investments suddenly rendered unprofitable. Workers in those industries may see their special skills and training devalued in the marketplace. Displaced workers also pay heavy intangible costs—they may need to move to new locations and/or new industries, uprooting their families, losing old friends and neighbors, and so on. Although the *majority* of citizens undoubtedly gain from free trade, that is no consolation to those who are its victims.

To mitigate these problems, the U.S. government follows two basic approaches. First, our trade laws offer temporary protection from sudden surges of imports, on the grounds that unexpected changes in trade patterns do not give businesses and workers enough time to adjust.

Second, the government has set up **trade adjustment assistance** programs to help workers and businesses that lose their jobs or their markets to imports. Firms may be eligible for technical assistance, government loans or loan guarantees, and permission to delay tax payments. Workers may qualify for retraining programs, longer periods of unemployment compensation, and funds to defray moving costs. Each form of assistance is designed to ease the burden on the victims of free trade so that the rest of us can enjoy its considerable benefits.

Trade adjustment assistance provides special unemployment benefits, loans, retraining programs, and other aid to workers and firms that are harmed by foreign competition.

OTHER ARGUMENTS FOR PROTECTION

▌National Defense and Other Noneconomic Considerations

A third rationale for trade protection is the need to maintain national defense. For example, even if the United States were not the most efficient producer of aircraft, it might still be rational to produce our own military aircraft so that no foreign government could ever cut off supplies of this strategic product.

How Popular Is Protectionism?

A lthough the world has been moving gradually toward freer trade, its citizens are not entirely persuaded that this trend is desirable. In 1998, a Canadian polling company asked almost 13,000 people in 22 countries the following question: "Which of the following two broad approaches do you think would be the best way to improve the economic and employment situation in this country—protecting our local industries by restricting imports, or removing import restrictions to increase our international trade?" By this measure, protectionists outnumbered free traders by a narrow margin—47 percent to 42 percent, with the rest undecided. Protectionist sentiment was even stronger in the United States, where the margin was 56 percent to 37 percent.

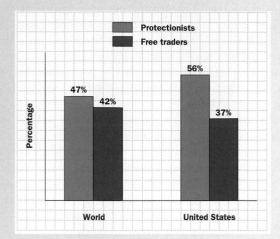

The national defense argument is fine as far as it goes, but it poses a clear danger: Even industries with the most peripheral relationship to defense are likely to invoke this argument on their behalf. For instance, for years the U.S. watchmaking industry argued for protection on the grounds that its skilled craftsmen would be invaluable in wartime!

Similarly, the United States has occasionally banned either exports to or imports from nations such as Cuba, Iran, and Iraq on political grounds. Such actions may have important economic effects, creating either bonanzas or disasters for particular American industries. But they are justified by politics, not by economics. Noneconomic reasons also explain quotas on importation of whaling products and on the furs of other endangered species.

▌ The Infant-Industry Argument

Yet a fourth common rationale for protectionism is the so-called *infant-industry argument.* Promising new industries often need breathing room to flourish and grow. If we expose these infants to the rigors of international competition too soon, the argument goes, they may never develop to the point where they can survive on their own in the international marketplace.

This argument, although valid in certain instances, is less defensible than it seems at first. Protecting an infant industry is justifiable only if the prospective future gains are sufficient to repay the up-front costs of protectionism. But if the industry is likely to be so profitable in the future, why doesn't private capital rush in to take advantage of the prospective net profits? After all, the annals of business are full of cases in which a new product or a new firm lost money at first but profited handsomely later on.

The infant-industry argument for protection stands up to scrutiny only if private funds are unavailable for some reason, despite an industry's glowing profit prospects. Even then it may make more sense to provide a government loan than to provide trade protection.

In an advanced economy such as ours, with well-developed capital markets to fund new businesses, it is difficult to think of legitimate examples where the infant-industry argument applies. Even if such a case were found, we would have to be care-

Can Protectionism Save Free Trade?

I n this 1983 column, William Safire shook off his long-standing attachment to free trade and argued eloquently for retaliation against protectionist nations.

Free trade is economic motherhood. Protectionism is economic evil incarnate. . . . Never should government interfere in the efficiency of international competition.

Since childhood, these have been the tenets of my faith. If it meant that certain businesses in this country went belly-up, so be it. . . . If it meant that Americans would be thrown out of work by overseas companies paying coolie wages, that was tough. . . .

The thing to keep in mind, I was taught, was the Big Picture and the Long Run. America, the great exporter, had far more to gain than to lose from free trade; attempts to protect inefficient industries here would ultimately cost more American jobs.

While playing with my David Ricardo doll and learning nursery rhymes about comparative advantage, I was listening to another laissez-fairy tale: Government's role in the world of business should be limited to keeping business honest and competitive. In God we antitrusted. Let businesses operate in the free marketplace.

Now American businesses are no longer competing with foreign companies. They are competing with foreign governments who help their local businesses. That means the world arena no longer offers a free marketplace; instead, most other governments are pushing a policy that can be called *helpfulism*.

Helpfulism works like this: A government like Japan decides to get behind its baseball-bat industry. It pumps in capital, knocks off marginal operators, finds subtle ways to discourage imports of Louisville Sluggers, and selects target areas for export blitzes. Pretty soon, the favored Japanese companies are driving foreign competitors batty.

How do we compete with helpfulism? One way is to complain that it is unfair; that draws a horselaugh. Another way is to demand a "Reagan Round" of trade negotiations under GATT, the Gentlemen's Agreement To Talk, which is equally laughable. Yet another way is to join the helpfuls by

SOURCE: © David Barnett/Contact Press Images

subsidizing our exports and permitting our companies to try monopolistic tricks abroad not permitted at home. But all that makes us feel guilty, with good reason.

The other way to deal with helpfulism is through—here comes the dreadful word—*protection.* Or, if you prefer a euphemism, *retaliation.* Or if that is still too severe, *reciprocity.* Whatever its name, it is a way of saying to the cutthroat cartelists we sweetly call our trading partners: "You have bent the rules out of shape. Change your practices to conform to the agreed-upon rules, or we will export a taste of your own medicine."

A little balance, then, from the free trade theorists. The demand for what the Pentagon used to call "protective reaction" is not demagoguery, not shortsighted, not self-defeating. On the contrary, the overseas pirates of protectionism and exemplars of helpfulism need to be taught the basic lesson in trade, which is: tit for tat.

SOURCE: William Safire, "Smoot-Hawley Lives," *The New York Times,* March 17, 1983. Copyright © 1983 by The New York Times Company. Reprinted by permission.

ful that the industry not remain in diapers forever. In too many cases, industries are awarded protection when young and, somehow, never mature to the point where protection can be withdrawn. We must be wary of infants that never grow up.

Strategic Trade Policy

A stronger argument for (temporary) protection has substantially influenced U.S. trade policy. Proponents of this line of thinking agree that free trade for all is the best system. But they point out that we live in an imperfect world in which many nations refuse to play by the rules of the free-trade game. And they fear that a nation that pursues free trade in a protectionist world is likely to lose out. It therefore makes sense, they argue, to *threaten* to protect your markets unless other nations agree to open theirs.

The United States has followed this strategy in trade negotiations with several countries in recent years. In one prominent recent case, the U.S. government threatened to impose high tariffs on a variety of European luxury goods unless

Europe opened its markets to imported bananas from the Americas. A dangerous trade war was narrowly averted when an agreement was struck at the eleventh hour.

The strategic argument for protection is a difficult one for economists to counter. Although it recognizes the superiority of free trade, it argues that *threatening* protectionism is the best way to achieve that end. (See "Can Protectionism Save Free Trade?") Such a strategy might work, but it clearly involves great risks. If threats that the United States will turn protectionist induce other countries to scrap their existing protectionist policies, then the gamble will have succeeded. But if the gamble fails, protectionism increases.

CAN CHEAP IMPORTS HURT A COUNTRY?

Dumping means selling goods in a foreign market at lower prices than those charged in the home market.

One of the most curious—and illogical—features of the protectionist position is the fear of low import prices. Countries that subsidize their exports are accused of **dumping**—of getting rid of their goods at unjustifiably low prices.

Economists find this argument strange. As a nation of consumers, we should be indignant when foreigners charge us *high* prices, not *low* ones. That common-sense rule guides every consumer's daily life. Only from the topsy-turvy viewpoint of an industry seeking protection are low prices seen as being against the public interest.

Ultimately, the best interests of any country are served when its imports are as cheap as possible. It would be ideal for the United States if the rest of the world were willing to provide us with goods at no charge. We could then live in luxury at the expense of other countries.

But, of course, benefits to the United States as a whole do not necessarily inure to every single American. If quotas on, say, sugar imports were dropped, American consumers and industries that purchase sugar would gain from lower prices. At the same time, however, owners of sugar fields and their employees would suffer serious losses in the form of lower profits, lower wages, and lost jobs—losses they would fight fiercely to prevent. For this reason, politics often leads to the adoption of protectionist measures that we would likely reject on strictly economic criteria.

A Last Look at the "Cheap Foreign Labor" Argument

The preceding discussion reveals the fundamental fallacy in the argument that U.S. workers should fear cheap foreign labor. The average American worker's living standard must *rise* if other countries willingly supply their products to us more cheaply. As long as the government's monetary and fiscal policies succeed in maintaining high levels of employment, how can we possibly lose by getting world products at bargain prices? This is precisely what happened to the U.S. economy in the late 1990s and into 2000—imports poured in at low prices while unemployment in the United States was at its lowest rate in a generation.

We must add some important qualifications, however. First, our macroeconomic policy may not always be effective. If workers displaced by foreign competition cannot find new jobs, they will indeed suffer from international trade. But high unemployment reflects a shortcoming of the government's monetary and fiscal policies, not of its international trade policies.

Second, we have noted that an abrupt stiffening of foreign competition can hurt U.S. workers by not allowing them adequate time to adapt to the new conditions. If change occurs fairly gradually, workers can be retrained and move on to the industries that now require their services. Indeed, if the change is slow enough, normal attrition may suffice. But competition that inflicts its damage overnight is certain to impose real costs on the affected workers—costs that are no less painful for being

Unfair Foreign Competition

S atire and ridicule are often more persuasive than logic and statistics. Exasperated by the spread of protectionism under the prevailing mercantilist philosophy, French economist Frédéric Bastiat decided to take the protectionist argument to its illogical conclusion. The fictitious petition of the French candlemakers to the Chamber of Deputies, written in 1845 and excerpted below, has become a classic in the battle for free trade.

> We are subject to the intolerable competition of a foreign rival, who enjoys, it would seem, such superior facilities for the production of light, that he is enabled to inundate our national market at so exceedingly reduced a price, that, the moment he makes his appearance, he draws off all custom for us; and thus an important branch of French industry, with all its innumerable ramifications, is suddenly reduced to a state of complete stagnation. This rival is no other than the sun.
>
> Our petition is, that it would please your honorable body to pass a law whereby shall be directed the shutting up of all windows, dormers, skylights, shutters, curtains, in a word, all openings, holes, chinks, and fissures through which the light of the sun is used to penetrate our dwellings, to the prejudice of the profitable manufactures which we flatter ourselves we have been enabled to bestow upon the country. . . .
>
> We foresee your objections, gentlemen; but there is not one that you can oppose to us . . . which is not equally opposed to your own practice and the principle which guides your policy. . . . Labor and nature concur in different proportions, according to country and climate, in every article of production.

SOURCE: © Culver Pictures

> . . . If a Lisbon orange can be sold at half the price of a Parisian one, it is because a natural and gratuitous heat does for the one what the other only obtains from an artificial and consequently expensive one. . . .
>
> Does it not argue the greatest inconsistency to check as you do the importation of coal, iron, cheese, and goods of foreign manufacture, merely because and even in proportion as their price approaches *zero*, while at the same time you freely admit, and without limitation, the light of the sun, whose price is during the whole day at *zero*?

SOURCE: F. Bastiat, *Economic Sophisms* (New York: G. P. Putnam's Sons; 1922).

temporary. That is why our trade laws make provisions for people and industries damaged by import surges.[5]

But these are, after all, only qualifications to an overwhelming argument. They call for intelligent monetary and fiscal policies and for transitional assistance to unemployed workers, not for abandonment of free trade. In general, the nation as a whole need not fear competition from cheap foreign labor.

In the long run, labor will be "cheap" only where it is not very productive. Wages will be high in countries with high labor productivity, and this high productivity will enable those countries to compete effectively in international trade despite high wages. It is thus misleading to say that the United States held its own in the international marketplace until recently *despite* high wages. Rather, it is much more accurate to note that the higher wages of American workers were a result of higher worker productivity, which gave the United States a major competitive edge.

Remember, in this matter it is *absolute* advantage, not *comparative* advantage, that counts. The country that is most efficient in producing every output can pay its workers more in every industry.

---

[5] It was precisely these provisions that President Bush used to justify the steel tariffs in 2002.

SUMMARY

1. Countries trade for two reasons: because differences in their natural resources and other inputs create discrepancies in the efficiency with which they can produce different goods, and because specialization may offer them greater economies of large-scale production.

2. Voluntary trade will generally be advantageous to both parties in an exchange. This concept is one of our *Ideas for Beyond the Final Exam*.

3. International trade is more complicated than trade within a nation because of political factors, differing national currencies, and impediments to the movement of labor and capital across national borders.

4. Two countries will gain from trade with each other if each nation exports goods in which it has a **comparative advantage.** Even a country that is inefficient across the board will benefit by exporting the goods in whose production it is *least inefficient*. This concept is another of the *Ideas for Beyond the Final Exam*.

5. When countries specialize and trade, each can enjoy consumption possibilities that exceed its production possibilities.

6. The prices of goods traded between countries are determined by supply and demand, but one must consider explicitly the demand curve and the supply curve of *each* country involved. Thus the equilibrium price must make the excess of quantity supplied over quantity demanded in the exporting country equal to the excess of quantity demanded over quantity supplied in the importing country.

7. The "cheap foreign labor" argument ignores the principle of comparative advantage, which shows that real wages (which determine living standards) can rise in both importing and exporting countries as a result of **specialization.**

8. **Tariffs** and **quotas** aim to protect a country's industries from foreign competition. Such protection may sometimes be advantageous to that country, but not if foreign countries adopt tariffs and quotas of their own in retaliation.

9. Although the same trade restrictions can be accomplished by either a tariff or a quota, tariffs offer at least two advantages to the country that imposes them: some of the gains go to the government rather than to foreign producers, and they provide greater incentive for efficient production.

10. When a nation eliminates protection in favor of free trade, some industries and their workers will lose out. Equity then demands that these people and firms be compensated in some way. The U.S. government offers protection from import surges and various forms of **trade adjustment assistance** to help those workers and industries adapt to the new conditions.

11. Several arguments for protectionism can, under the right circumstances, have validity. They include the national defense argument, the infant-industry argument, and the use of trade restrictions for strategic purposes. But each of these arguments is frequently abused.

12. **Dumping** will hurt certain domestic producers, but it benefits domestic consumers.

KEY TERMS

Imports   302

Exports   302

Specialization   303

Mutual gains from trade   303

Absolute advantage   305

Comparative advantage   305

"Cheap foreign labor" argument   308

Mercantilism   310

Tariff   311

Quota   311

Export subsidy   311

Trade adjustment assistance   315

Infant-industry argument   316

Strategic trade policy   317

Dumping   318

QUESTIONS FOR REVIEW

1. You have a dozen shirts and your roommate has six pairs of shoes worth roughly the same amount of money. You decide to swap six shirts for three pairs of shoes. In financial terms, neither of you gains anything. Explain why you are nevertheless both likely to be better off.

2. In the 18th century, some writers argued that one person in a trade could be made better off only by gaining at the expense of the other. Explain the fallacy in this argument.

3. Country A has a cold climate with a short growing season, but a highly skilled labor force. What sorts of products do

you think it is likely to produce? What are the characteristics of the countries with which you would expect it to trade?

4. After the removal of a quota on sugar, many U.S. sugar farms go bankrupt. Discuss the pros and cons of removing the quota in the short and long runs.

5. Country A has a mercantilist government that believes it is always best to export more than it imports. As a consequence, it exports more to Country B every year than it imports from Country B. After 100 years of this arrangement,

both countries are destroyed in an earthquake. What were the advantages or disadvantages of the surplus to Country A? To Country B?

6. The following table describes the number of yards of cloth and barrels of wine that can be produced with a week's worth of labor in England and Portugal. Assume that no other inputs are needed.

	In England	In Portugal
Cloth	8 yards	12 yards
Wine	2 barrels	6 barrels

a. If there is no trade, what is the price of wine in terms of cloth in England?

b. If there is no trade, what is the price of wine in terms of cloth in Portugal?

c. Suppose each country has 1 million weeks of labor available per year. Draw the production possibilities frontier for each country.

d. Which country has an absolute advantage in the production of which good(s)? Which country has a comparative advantage in the production of which good(s)?

e. If the countries start trading with each other, which country will specialize and export which good?

f. What can be said about the price at which trade will take place?

7. Suppose that the United States and Mexico are the only two countries in the world and that labor is the only productive input. In the United States, a worker can produce 12 bushels of wheat *or* 2 barrels of oil in a day. In Mexico, a worker can produce 2 bushels of wheat *or* 4 barrels of oil per day.

a. What will be the price ratio between the two commodities (that is, the price of oil in terms of wheat) in each country if there is no trade?

b. If free trade is allowed and there are no transportation costs, which commodity would the United States import? What about Mexico?

c. In what range would the price ratio have to fall under free trade? Why?

d. Picking one possible post-trade price ratio, show clearly how it is possible for both countries to benefit from free trade.

8. The following table presents the demand and supply curves for microcomputers in Japan and the United States.

Price per Computer	Quantity Demanded in U.S.	Quantity Supplied in U.S.	Quantity Demanded in Japan	Quantity Supplied in Japan
1	90	30	50	50
2	80	35	40	55
3	70	40	30	60
4	60	45	20	65
5	50	50	10	70
6	40	55	0	75

Note: Price and quantity are in thousands.

a. Draw the demand and supply curves for the United States on one diagram and those for Japan on another one.

b. If the United States and Japan do not trade, what are the equilibrium price and quantity in the computer market in the United States? In Japan?

c. Now suppose trade is opened up between the two countries. What will be the equilibrium price in the world market for computers? What has happened to the price of computers in the United States? In Japan?

d. Which country will export computers? How many?

e. When trade opens, what happens to the quantity of computers produced, and therefore employment, in the computer industry in the United States? In Japan? Who benefits and who loses *initially* from free trade?

9. Under current trade law, the president of the United States must report periodically to Congress on countries engaging in unfair trade practices that inhibit U.S. exports. How would you define an "unfair" trade practice? Suppose Country X exports much more to the United States than it imports, year after year. Does that constitute evidence that Country X's trade practices are unfair? What would constitute such evidence?

10. Suppose the United States finds Country X guilty of unfair trade practices and penalizes it with import quotas. So U.S. imports from Country X fall. Suppose, further, that Country X does not alter its trade practices in any way. Is the United States better or worse off? What about Country X?

17

The International Monetary System: Order or Disorder?

*Cecily, you will read your Political Economy in my absence.
The chapter on the Fall of the Rupee you may omit.
It is somewhat too sensational.*

MISS PRISM IN OSCAR WILDE'S *THE
IMPORTANCE OF BEING EARNEST*

Miss Prism, the Victorian tutor, may have had a point. In the summer of 1997, the rupiah fell and economic disaster in Indonesia quickly followed. The International Monetary Fund rushed to the rescue with billions of dollars and pages of advice. But its plan failed, and some say it may even have helped precipitate the bloody riots that led to the fall of the Indonesian government.

This chapter does not concentrate on such sensational political upheavals. Rather, it focuses on a seemingly mundane topic: how the market determines rates of exchange among different national currencies. Nevertheless, events in Southeast Asia in 1997–1998, in Brazil and Russia in 1998–1999, and most recently in Argentina in 2001 have amply demonstrated that dramatic exchange rate movements can have severe human as well as financial consequences. This chapter and the next will help us understand why.

CONTENTS

Puzzle: Whatever Happened to Argentina?

The international monetary system seems to lurch from one crisis to another. In 2001, Argentina was at the center of attention.

Only a decade earlier, Argentina was considered a model of success. The Argentine government had overcome its long, unhappy history of inflation by a seemingly simple device: tying the value of the Argentine peso rigidly to the U.S. dollar. Specifically, Argentina created a "currency board," which meant that anyone with an Argentine peso could trade it in for a U.S. dollar—with no limits. By decree, then, the peso, a currency with a checkered inflationary history, became the equivalent of the dollar—the well-trusted currency of a low-inflation country.

The Argentine currency board worked extraordinarily well for a while: Inflation was vanquished and the Argentine economy grew strongly. But troubles came to Argentina following the Mexican crisis of 1994–1995; the country endured a painful recession. Then it all happened again following the Brazilian crisis of 1999. The economy weakened, unemployment rose, and investors began wondering whether the currency board could last. In fact, it did not. Argentina abandoned its currency board amidst political and economic turmoil in January 2002, and the value of the peso tumbled.

What went so badly wrong? What forced Argentina off the currency-board system, leaving the peso to find its own value in the market? We will learn some of the answers in this and the following chapter. But first, we need to understand what determines exchange rates.

WHAT ARE EXCHANGE RATES?

We noted in the previous chapter that international trade is more complicated than domestic trade. There are no national borders to be crossed when, say, California lettuce is shipped to Massachusetts. The consumer in Boston pays with *dollars*, just the currency that the farmer in Modesto wants. If that same farmer ships her lettuce to Japan, however, consumers there will have only Japanese yen with which to pay, rather than the dollars the farmer in California wants. Thus, for international trade to take place, there must be some way to convert one currency into another. The rates at which such conversions are made are called **exchange rates.**

The **exchange rate** states the price, in terms of one currency, at which another currency can be bought.

There is an exchange rate between every pair of currencies. For example, one British pound is currently the equivalent of about $1.80. The exchange rate between the pound and the dollar, then, may be expressed as roughly "$1.80 to the pound" (meaning that it costs $1.80 to buy a pound) or about "55 pence to the dollar" (meaning that it costs 55 British pence to buy a dollar).

Exchange rates vis-à-vis the United States dollar have changed dramatically over time. In a nutshell, the dollar soared in the period from mid-1980 to early 1985, fell relative to most major currencies from early 1985 until early 1988, and then fluctuated—sometimes sharply—with no clear trend until the spring of 1995. From then until 2002 the dollar was mostly—but not always—on the rise. But lately, the dollar has been falling. This chapter seeks to explain such currency movements.

A nation's currency is said to **appreciate** when exchange rates change so that a unit of its currency can buy more units of foreign currency.

Under our present system, currency rates change frequently. When other currencies become more expensive in terms of dollars, we say that they have **appreciated** relative to the dollar. Alternatively, we can look at this same event as the dollar buying less foreign currency, meaning that the dollar has **depreciated** relative to another currency.

A nation's currency is said to **depreciate** when exchange rates change so that a unit of its currency can buy fewer units of foreign currency.

What is a depreciation to one country must be an appreciation to the other.

For example, if the cost of a pound rises from $1.40 to $ 1.80, the cost of a U.S. dollar in terms of pounds simultaneously falls from 71 pence to 55 pence. The United King-

TABLE 17-1   Exchange Rates with the U.S. Dollar

SOURCE: International Financial Statistics and The Wall Street Journal.

Country	Currency	Symbol	Cost in Dollars				
			July 1980	Feb. 1985	June 1995	April 2002	March 2004
Australia	dollar	$	$1.16	$0.74	$0.72	$0.53	$0.75
Canada	dollar	$	0.87	0.74	0.73	0.63	$0.76
France	franc	FF	0.25	0.10	0.20	*	*
Germany	mark	DM	0.57	0.30	0.71	*	*
Italy	lira	L	0.0012	0.00049	0.0061	*	*
Japan	yen	¥	0.0045	0.0038	0.0118	0.0076	0.0090
Mexico	new peso	$	44.0†	5.0†	0.16	0.11	0.09
Sweden	krona	Kr	0.24	0.11	0.14	0.10	0.13
Switzerland	franc	S.Fr.	0.62	0.36	0.86	0.60	0.78
United Kingdom	pound	£	2.37	1.10	1.59	1.44	1.80
—	euro	€	—	—	—	0.88	1.22

NOTE: Exchange rates are in U.S. dollars per unit of foreign currency.

*These exchange rates were locked together at the start of the euro in January 1999.

†On January 1, 1993, the peso was redefined so that 1,000 old pesos were equal to one new peso. Hence, the numbers 44 and 5 listed for July 1980 and February 1985 were actually 0.044 and 0.005 on the old basis.

dom has experienced a currency *appreciation*, whereas the United States has experienced a currency *depreciation*.

Notice also that, when many currencies are changing in value, the dollar may be appreciating with respect to one currency but depreciating with respect to another. Table 17-1 offers a selection of exchange rates prevailing in July 1980, February 1985, June 1995, April 2002, and March 2004, showing how many dollars or cents it cost at each of those times to buy each unit of foreign currency. Between February 1985 and April 2002, the dollar *depreciated* sharply relative to the Japanese yen and most European currencies. For example, the British pound rose from $1.10 to $1.44 During that same period, the dollar *appreciated* dramatically relative to the Mexican peso; it bought about 0.2 pesos in 1985 but more than 9 in 2002.[1]

Although the terms "appreciation" and "depreciation" are used to describe movements of exchange rates in free markets, a different set of terms is employed to describe decreases and increases in currency values that are set by government decree. When an officially set exchange rate is altered so that a unit of a nation's currency can buy fewer units of foreign currency, we say that a **devaluation** of that currency has occurred. When the exchange rate is altered so that the currency can buy more units of foreign currency, we say that a **revaluation** has taken place. We will say more about devaluation and revaluation shortly, but first let's look at how the free market determines exchange rates.

A **devaluation** is a reduction in the official value of a currency.

A **revaluation** is an increase in the official value of a currency.

EXCHANGE RATE DETERMINATION IN A FREE MARKET

At the beginning of 1999, eleven European countries adopted a new common currency, the euro. In early 2002, euro coins and paper money replaced the old currencies in general circulation. But why does a euro now cost about $1.25 and not $0.75 or $1.50? In a world of **floating exchange rates,** with no government interferences, the answer would be straightforward. Exchange rates would be determined by the forces of supply and demand, just like the prices of apples, computers, and haircuts.

Floating exchange rates are rates determined in free markets by the law of supply and demand.

[1] In fact, the dollar bought about 200 pesos in February 1985, but that is because the old peso was replaced by a new peso in January 1993, which moved the decimal point three places.

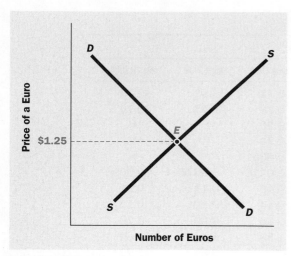

FIGURE 17-1

Determination of Exchange Rates in a Free Market

In a leap of abstraction, imagine that the dollar and the euro are the only currencies on earth, so the market need determine only one exchange rate. Figure 17-1 depicts the determination of this exchange rate at the point (denoted E in the figure) where demand curve DD crosses supply curve SS. At this price ($1.25 per euro), the number of euros demanded is equal to the number of euros supplied.

In a free market, exchange rates are determined by supply and demand. At a rate below the equilibrium level, the number of euros demanded would exceed the number supplied, and the price of a euro would be bid up. At a rate above the equilibrium level, quantity supplied would exceed quantity demanded, and the price of a euro would fall. Only at the equilibrium exchange rate is there no tendency for the exchange rate to change.

As usual, supply and demand determine price. But in this case, we must ask: Where do the supply and demand come from? Why does anyone demand a euro? The answer has three parts:

- *International trade in goods and services.* This factor was the subject of the previous chapter. If, for example, Jane Doe, an American, wants to buy a new BMW, she will first have to buy euros with which to pay the dealer in Munich.[2] Thus Jane's demand for a European car leads to a demand for European currency. In general, *demand for a country's exports leads to demand for its currency.*[3]
- *International trade in financial instruments such as stocks and bonds.* If American investors want to purchase Italian stocks, they will first have to acquire the euros that the sellers will insist on for payment. In this way, demand for European financial assets leads to demand for European currency. Thus, *demand for a country's financial assets leads to demand for its currency.*
- *Purchases of physical assets such as factories and machinery overseas.* If IBM wants to buy out a small French computer manufacturer, the owners will no doubt want to receive euros. So IBM will first have to acquire European currency. In general, *direct foreign investment leads to demand for a country's currency.*

Now, where does the supply come from? To answer this question, just turn all of these transactions around. Europeans who want to buy U.S. goods and services, invest in U.S. financial markets, or make direct investments in the United States will have to offer their euros for sale in the foreign-exchange market (which is mainly run through banks) to acquire the needed dollars. To summarize:

The *demand* for a country's currency is derived from the demands of foreigners for its export goods and services and for its assets—including financial assets, such as stocks and bonds, and real assets, such as factories and machinery. The *supply* of a country's currency arises from its imports, and from foreign investment by its own citizens.

To illustrate the usefulness of even this simple supply and demand analysis, think about how the exchange rate between the dollar and the euro should change if Europeans become attracted by the prospects of large gains on the U.S. stock markets. To purchase U.S. stocks, foreigners will first have to purchase U.S. dollars—which means selling some of their euros. In terms of the supply-demand diagram in Figure 17-2, the increased desire of Europeans to acquire U.S. stocks would shift the supply curve for euros out from S_1S_1 (the black line in the figure) to S_2S_2 (the red line). Equilib-

---

[2] Actually, she will not do so because banks generally handle foreign exchange transactions for consumers. An American bank probably will buy the euros for her. Even so, the effect is exactly the same as if Jane had done it herself.

[3] See Review Question 2 at the end of this chapter.

rium would shift from point *E* to point *A*, and the exchange rate would fall from $1.25 per euro to $1.00 per euro. Thus the increased supply of euros by European citizens would cause the euro to *depreciate* relative to the dollar. (Of course, this is what happened during the U.S. stock market boom of the late 1990s.)

Exercise Test your understanding of the supply and demand analysis of exchange rates by showing why each of the following events would lead to an appreciation of the euro (a depreciation of the dollar) in a free market:

1. American investors are attracted by prospects for profit on the German stock market.
2. A recession in Italy cuts Italian purchases of American goods.
3. Interest rates on government bonds rise in France but are stable in the United States. (*Hint:* Which country's citizens will be attracted to invest by high interest rates in the other country?)

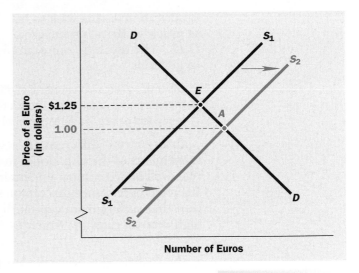

■ FIGURE 17-2
The Effect of a Stock Market Boom on the Exchange Rate

To say that supply and demand determine exchange rates in a free market is at once to say everything and to say nothing. If we are to understand the reasons why some currencies appreciate whereas others depreciate, we must look into the factors that move the supply and demand curves. Economists believe that the principal determinants of exchange rate movements differ significantly in the short, medium, and long runs. So in the next three sections, we turn to the analysis of exchange rate movements over these three "runs," beginning with the short run.

▌ Interest Rates and Exchange Rates: The Short Run

Most experts in international finance agree that interest rates and financial flows are the major determinants of exchange rates—certainly in the short run, and probably (as we shall see next) in the medium run as well. Specifically, one variable that often seems to call the tune in the short run is *interest rate differentials*. A multitrillion-dollar pool of so-called *hot money*—owned by banks, investment funds, multinational corporations, and wealthy individuals of all nations—travels rapidly around the globe in search of the highest interest rates.

As an example, suppose British government bonds pay a 5 percent rate of interest when yields on equally safe American government securities rise to 7 percent. British investors will be attracted by the higher interest rates in the United States and will offer pounds for sale in order to buy dollars, planning to use those dollars to buy American securities. At the same time, American investors will find it more attractive to keep their money at home, so fewer pounds will be demanded by Americans.

When the demand schedule shifts *inward* and the supply curve shifts *outward*, the effect on price is predictable: The pound will depreciate, as Figure 17-3 shows. In the figure, the supply curve of pounds shifts outward from S_1S_1 to S_2S_2 when British investors seek to sell pounds in order to purchase more U.S. securities. At the same time,

■ FIGURE 17-3
The Effect of a Rise in U.S. Interest Rates

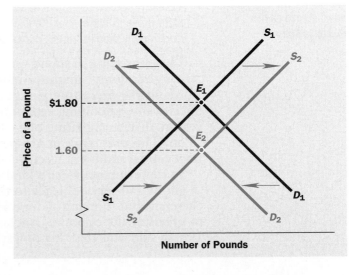

American investors wish to buy fewer pounds because they no longer desire to invest as much in British securities. Thus, the demand curve shifts inward from D_1D_1 to D_2D_2. The result, in our example, is a depreciation of the pound from $1.80 to $1.60. In general:

> **Other things equal, countries that offer investors higher rates of return attract more capital than countries that offer lower rates. Thus, a rise in interest rates often will lead to an appreciation of the currency, and a drop in interest rates will lead to a depreciation.**

Interest rate differentials certainly played a predominant role in the stunning movements of the U.S. dollar in the 1980s. In the early 1980s, American interest rates rose well above comparable interest rates abroad. In consequence, foreign capital was attracted here, American capital stayed at home, and the dollar soared. Similarly, a nation that suffers from capital flight, as did Argentina in 2001, must offer extremely high interest rates to attract foreign capital.

The Medium Run: Economic Activity and Exchange Rates

The medium run is where the theory of exchange rate determination is most unsettled. Economists once reasoned as follows: Because consumer spending increases when income rises and decreases when income falls, the same thing is likely to happen to spending on imported goods. So *a country's imports will rise quickly when its economy booms and rise only slowly when its economy stagnates.*

For the reasons illustrated in Figure 17-4, then, a boom in the United States should shift the *demand* curve for euros *outward* as Americans seek to acquire more euros to buy more European goods. And that, in turn, should lead to an appreciation of the euro (depreciation of the dollar). In the figure, the euro rises in value from $1.25 to $1.35.

However, if Europe was booming at the same time, Europeans would be buying more American exports, which would shift the *supply* curve of euros outward. (Europeans must offer more euros for sale to get the dollars they want.) On balance, the value of the dollar might rise or fall. It appears that what matters is whether exports are growing faster than imports.

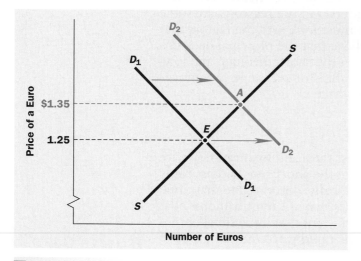

FIGURE 17-4

The Effect of an Economic Boom Abroad on the Exchange Rate

A country whose aggregate demand grows faster than the rest of the world's normally finds its imports growing faster than its exports. Thus, its demand curve for foreign currency shifts outward more rapidly than its supply curve. *Other things equal,* that will make its currency depreciate.

This reasoning is sound—so far as it goes. And it leads to the conclusion that a "strong economy" might produce a "weak currency." But the three most important words in the preceding paragraph are "other things equal." Usually, they are not. Specifically, a booming economy will normally offer more attractive prospects to investors than a stagnating one—higher interest rates, rising stock market values, and so on. This difference in prospective investment returns, as we have seen, should attract capital and boost its currency value.

So there appears to be a kind of "tug of war." As we see, thinking only about trade in goods and services leads to the conclusion that faster growth should weaken the currency. But thinking about trade in financial assets (such as stocks and bonds) leads to precisely the opposite conclusion: Faster growth should strengthen the currency. Which side wins this "tug of war"?

In the modern world, the evidence seems to say that trade in financial assets is the dominant factor. For example, rapid growth in the United States in the second half of the 1990s led to a sharply appreciating dollar even though U.S. imports soared, as investors from all over the world brought funds to America. We conclude that:

Stronger economic performance often leads to currency *appreciation* because it improves prospects for investing in the country.

▌ The Purchasing-Power Parity Theory: The Long Run

We come at last to the long run, where an apparently simple principle ought to govern exchange rates. As long as goods can move freely across national borders, exchange rates should eventually adjust so that the same product costs the same amount of money, whether measured in dollars in the United States, euros in Germany, or yen in Japan—except for differences in transportation costs and the like. This simple statement forms the basis of the major theory of exchange rate determination in the long run:

The *purchasing-power parity theory of exchange rate determination* holds that the exchange rate between any two national currencies adjusts to reflect differences in the price levels in the two countries.

An example will illustrate the basic truth in this theory and also suggest some of its limitations. Suppose German and American steel is identical and that these two nations are the only producers of steel for the world market. Suppose further that steel is the only tradable good that either country produces.

Question: If American steel costs $180 per ton and German steel costs 144 euros per ton, what must be the exchange rate between the dollar and the euro?

Answer: Because 144 euros and $180 each buy a ton of steel, the two sums of money must be of equal value. Hence, each euro must be worth $1.25. Why? Any higher price for a euro, such as $1.50, would mean that steel would cost $216 per ton (144 euros at $1.50 each) in Germany but only $180 per ton in the United States. In that case, all foreign customers would shop for their steel in the United States—which would increase the demand for dollars and decrease the demand for euros. Similarly, any exchange rate below $1.25 per euro would send all the steel business to Germany, driving the value of the euro up toward its purchasing-power parity level.

Exercise   Show why an exchange rate of $1 per euro is too low to lead to an equilibrium in the international steel market.

The purchasing-power parity theory is used to make long-run predictions about the effects of inflation on exchange rates. To continue our example, suppose that steel (and other) prices in the United States rise while prices in Europe remain constant. The purchasing-power parity theory predicts that the euro will appreciate relative to the dollar. It also predicts the amount of the appreciation. After the U.S. inflation, suppose that the price of American steel is $216 per ton, while German steel still costs 144 euros per ton. For these two prices to be equivalent, 144 euros must be worth $216, or one euro must be worth $1.50. The euro, therefore, must have risen from $1.25 to $1.50.

According to the purchasing-power parity theory, differences in domestic inflation rates are a major cause of exchange rate movements. If one country has higher inflation than another, its exchange rate should be depreciating.

For many years, this theory seemed to work tolerably well. Although precise numerical predictions based on purchasing-power parity calculations were never very accurate (see "Purchasing Power Parity and the Big Mac"), nations with higher

Purchasing-Power Parity and the Big Mac

S ince 1986, *The Economist* magazine has been using a well-known international commodity—the Big Mac—to assess the purchasing-power parity theory of exchange rates, or as the magazine once put it, "to make exchange-rate theory more digestible."

Here's how it works. In theory, the local price of a Big Mac, when translated into U.S. dollars by the exchange rate, should be the same everywhere in the world. The following numbers show that the theory does not work terribly well.

For example, although a Big Mac costs an average of $2.80 in the United States, it sold for about 10 yuan in China. Using the official ex-

SOURCE: © 2002 Don Couch Photography

change rate at the time of 8.2 yuan to the dollar, that amounted to just $1.23. Thus, according to the hamburger parity theory, the yuan was grossly undervalued.

By how much? The price in China was just 44 percent of the price in the United States ($1.23/$2.80). So the yuan was 56 percent below its Big Mac parity—and therefore should appreciate. The other numbers in the table have similar interpretations.

True Big Mac aficionados may find these data helpful when planning international travel. But can deviations from Big Mac parity predict exchange rate movements? Surprisingly, they can.

When economist Robert Cumby studied Big Mac prices and exchange rates in 14 countries over a ten-year period, he found that deviations from hamburger parity were transitory. Their "half-life" was just a year, meaning that 50 percent of the deviation tended to disappear within a year. Thus the undervalued currencies in the accompanying table would be predicted to appreciate during 2004, whereas the overvalued currencies would be expected to depreciate.

SOURCE: *The Economist*, December 22, 2001, p. 130, and Robert Cumby, "Forecasting Exchange Rates and Relative Prices with the Hamburger Standard: Is What You Want What You Get with McParity?" Georgetown University, May 1997.

■ Deviations from Big Mac Purchasing Power Parity, January 2004

Country	Big Mac Prices (converted to dollars)	Percent Over (+) or Under (−) Valuation Against Dollar
United States	**$2.80**	—
Sweden	4.15	+48
Great Britain	3.45	+23
Mexico	2.21	−21
South Africa	1.97	−30
Singapore	1.95	−30
Brazil	1.76	−37
China	1.23	−56

inflation did at least experience depreciating currencies. But in the 1980s and 1990s, even this rule broke down. For example, although the U.S. inflation rate was consistently higher than both Germany's and Japan's, the dollar nonetheless rose sharply relative to both the German mark and the Japanese yen from 1980 to 1985. The same thing happened again between 1995 and 2000. Clearly, the theory is missing something. What?

Many things. But perhaps the principal failing of the purchasing-power parity theory is, once again, that it focuses too much on trade in goods and services. Financial assets such as stocks and bonds are also traded actively across national borders—and in vastly greater dollar volumes than goods and services. In fact, the astounding *daily* volume of foreign exchange transactions—more than $1.5 trillion—exceeds an entire *month's* worth of world trade in goods and services. The vast majority of these transactions are financial. If investors decide that, say, U.S. assets are a better bet than Japanese assets, the dollar will rise, even if our inflation rate is well above Japan's. For this and other reasons:

Most economists believe that other factors are much more important than relative price levels for exchange rate determination in the short run. But in the long run, purchasing-power parity plays an important role.

Market Determination of Exchange Rates: Summary

You have probably noticed a theme here: International trade in financial assets certainly dominates short-run exchange rate changes, may dominate medium-run changes, and also influences long-run changes. We can summarize this discussion of exchange rate determination in free markets as follows:

1. We expect to find *appreciating* currencies in countries that offer investors *higher rates of return* because these countries will attract capital from all over the world.

2. To some extent, these are the countries that are *growing faster* than average because strong growth tends to produce attractive investment prospects. However, such fast-growing countries will also be importing relatively more than other countries, which tends to pull their currencies *down.*

3. Currency values generally will appreciate in countries with *lower inflation rates* than the rest of the world's, because buyers in foreign countries will demand their goods and thus drive up their currencies.

Reversing each of these arguments, we expect to find *depreciating* currencies in countries with relatively high inflation rates, low interest rates, and poor growth prospects.

Fixed exchange rates are rates set by government decisions and maintained by government actions.

FIXED EXCHANGE RATES AND THE BALANCE OF PAYMENTS

Some exchange rates today are truly floating, determined by the forces of supply and demand without government interference. Many others are not. Furthermore, some people claim that exchange rate fluctuations are so troublesome that the world would be better off with fixed exchange rates. For these reasons, we turn next to a system of **fixed exchange rates,** or rates that are set by governments.

Naturally, under such a system the exchange rate, being fixed, is not closely watched. Instead, international financial specialists focus on a country's *balance of payments*—a term we must now define—to gauge movements in the supply of and demand for a currency.

To understand what the balance of payments is, look at Figure 17-5, which depicts a situation that might represent, say, Argentina in the winter of 2001–2002—an overvalued currency. Although the supply and demand curves for pesos indicate an equilibrium exchange rate of $0.50 to the peso (point *E*), the Argentine government is holding the rate at $1.00. Notice that, at $1 per peso, more people supply pesos than demand them. In the example, suppliers offer to sell 8 billion pesos per year, but purchasers want to buy only 4 billion.

This gap between the 8 billion pesos that some people wish to sell and the 4 billion pesos that others wish to buy is what we mean by Argentina's **balance of payments deficit**—4 billion pesos (or $4 billion) per year in this hypothetical case. It appears as the horizontal distance between points *A* and *B* in Figure 17-5.

How can governments flout market forces in this way? Because sales and purchases on any market must be equal, as a simple piece of arithmetic, the excess of quantity supplied over quantity demanded—or 4 billion pesos per year in this example—must be bought by the Argentine government.

The **balance of payments deficit** is the amount by which the quantity supplied of a country's currency (per year) exceeds the quantity demanded. Balance of payments deficits arise whenever the exchange rate is pegged at an artificially high level.

■ FIGURE 17-5
A Balance of Payments Deficit

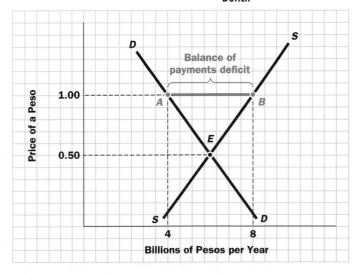

To purchase these pesos, it must give up some of the foreign currency that it holds as reserves. Thus, the Bank of Argentina would be losing about $4 billion in reserves per year as the cost of keeping the peso at $1.

Naturally, this situation cannot persist forever, as the reserves eventually will run out. This is the fatal flaw of a fixed exchange rate system. Once speculators become convinced that the exchange rate can be held for only a short while longer, they will sell the overvalued currency in massive amounts rather than hold on to money whose value they expect to fall.

That is precisely what began to happen to Argentina in 2001. The supply curve of pesos shifted outward, as shown in Figure 17-6, as both domestic and foreign holders sought to "get out of" pesos. This exodus from the peso caused a sharp rise in the balance of payments deficit—from 4 billion to 8 billion pesos in the example. (The numbers are fictitious.) Lacking sufficient reserves, the Argentine government first reacted by blocking withdrawals from banks, but then succumbed to market forces and let the peso float in early 2002. It promptly depreciated.

For an example of the reverse case, a severely undervalued currency, let us go back in history to the case of West Germany in 1973. Figure 17-7 depicts demand and supply curves for marks that intersect at an equilibrium price of 50 cents per mark (point E in the diagram). Yet, in the example, we suppose that the German authorities are holding the rate at 33 cents. At this rate, the quantity of marks demanded (50 billion) greatly exceeds the quantity supplied (40 billion). The difference is Germany's **balance of payments surplus,** shown by the horizontal distance AB.

Germany can keep the rate at 33 cents only by providing the marks that foreigners want to buy—10 billion marks per year in this example. In return, the country receives U.S. dollars, British pounds, French francs, gold, and so on. All of this activity serves to increase Germany's reserves of foreign currencies. But notice one important difference between this case and the overvalued peso:

FIGURE 17-6

A Speculative Run on the Peso

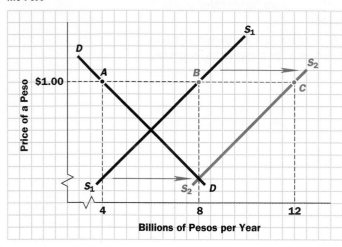

The **balance of payments surplus** is the amount by which the quantity demanded of a country's currency (per year) exceeds the quantity supplied. Balance of payments surpluses arise whenever the exchange rate is pegged at an artificially low level.

The accumulation of reserves rarely will force a central bank to revalue in the way that losses of reserves can force a devaluation.

This asymmetry is a clear weakness in a fixed exchange rate system. In principle, an exchange rate disequilibrium can be cured either by a *devaluation* by the country with a balance of payments deficit or by an upward *revaluation* by the country with a balance of payments surplus. In practice, though, only deficit countries are forced to act.

Why do surplus countries refuse to revalue? One reason is often a stubborn refusal to recognize some basic economic realities. They tend to view the disequilibrium as a problem only for the deficit countries and, therefore, believe that the deficit countries should take the corrective steps. This view, of course, is nonsense in a worldwide system of fixed exchange rates. Some currencies are overvalued *because* some other currencies are undervalued. In fact, the two statements mean exactly the same thing.

FIGURE 17-7

A Balance of Payments Surplus

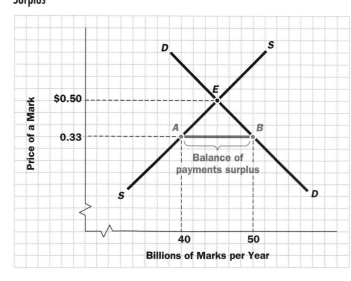

The other reason why surplus countries resist upward revaluations is that such actions would make their exports more expensive to foreigners and thus cut into their sales. And export industries often have the political clout to make their preferences stick.

Defining the Balance of Payments in Practice

The preceding discussion makes it look simple to measure a nation's balance of payments position: Just count up the private demand for and supply of its currency and subtract quantity supplied from quantity demanded. Conceptually, that is all there is to it. But in practice the difficulties are great because we never directly observe the number of dollars demanded and supplied.

Actual market transactions show that the number of, say, U.S. dollars *purchased* always equals the number of U.S. dollars *sold.* Unless someone has made a bookkeeping error, this must be so. How, then, can we recognize a balance of payments surplus or deficit? Easy, you say. Just look at the transactions of the central bank, whose purchases or sales must make up the difference between private demand and private supply. If the Federal Reserve is buying dollars, its purchases measure our balance of payments deficit. If the Fed is selling, its sales represent our balance of payments surplus. Thus, the idea is to measure the balance of payments by *excluding official transactions among governments.* That is, more or less, what is done.

In practice, the balance of payments accounts come in two main parts. The **current account** totes up exports and imports of goods and services, cross-border payments of interest and dividends, and cross-border gifts. The United States has been running large current account *deficits* for years.

> The **current account** balance includes international purchases and sales of goods and services, cross-border interest and dividend payments, and cross-border gifts to and from both private individuals and governments.

But that represents only one part of our balance of payments, for it leaves out all purchases and sales of assets. Purchases of U.S. assets by foreigners bring foreign currency to the United States, and purchases of foreign assets cost us foreign currency. Netting the capital flows in each direction gives us our surplus or deficit on **capital account.** In recent years, this part of our balance of payments accounts has registered persistently large *surpluses* as foreigners have acquired U.S. assets.

> The **capital account** balance includes purchases and sales of financial assets to and from citizens and companies of other countries.

In what sense, then, does the overall balance of payments balance? There are two possibilities. If the exchange rate is *floating*, all private transactions—current account plus capital account—must add up to zero (dollars purchased = dollars sold). But if, instead, the exchange rate is *fixed*, as shown in Figures 17-5 and 17-7, the two accounts need not balance one another. Government purchases or sales of foreign currency make up the surplus or deficit in the overall balance of payments.

A BIT OF HISTORY: THE GOLD STANDARD AND THE BRETTON WOODS SYSTEM

It is difficult to find examples of strictly fixed exchange rates in the historical record. About the only time exchange rates were truly fixed was under the old gold standard, at least when it was practiced in its ideal form.[4]

The Classical Gold Standard

Under the **gold standard,** governments maintained fixed exchange rates by an automatic equilibrating mechanism that went something like this: All currencies were defined in terms of gold; indeed, some were actually made of gold. When a nation ran a balance of payments *deficit*, it had to *sell gold* to finance the deficit. Because the domestic

> The **gold standard** is a way to fix exchange rates by defining each participating currency in terms of gold and allowing holders of each participating currency to convert that currency into gold.

---

[4] As a matter of fact, although the gold standard lasted (on and off) for hundreds of years, it was rarely practiced in its ideal form. Except for a brief period of fixed exchange rates in the late 19th and early 20th centuries, governments periodically adjusted exchange rates even under the gold standard.

money supply was based on gold, losing gold to foreigners meant that the money supply fell *automatically*, which raised interest rates. The higher interest rates attracted foreign capital. At the same time, this restrictive "monetary policy" pulled down output and prices, which discouraged imports and encouraged exports. The balance of payments problem quickly rectified itself.

This automatic adjustment process meant, however, that under the gold standard no nation had control of its domestic monetary policy. The same problem arises in any system of fixed exchange rates, regardless of whether it makes use of gold:

Under fixed exchange rates, monetary policy must be dedicated to pegging the exchange rate. It cannot, therefore, be used to manage aggregate demand.

The gold standard posed one other serious difficulty: The world's commerce was at the mercy of gold discoveries. Major gold finds would mean higher prices and booming economic conditions, through the standard monetary-policy mechanisms that we studied in earlier chapters. When the supply of gold failed to keep pace with growth of the world economy, prices had to fall in the long run and employment had to fall in the short run.

The Bretton Woods System

The gold standard faltered many times and finally collapsed amid the financial chaos of the Great Depression of the 1930s and World War II. Without it, the world struggled through a serious breakdown in international trade.

As the war drew to a close, representatives of the industrial nations met at a hotel in Bretton Woods, New Hampshire, in 1944. They sought to establish a stable monetary environment that would restore world trade. Because the United States held the lion's share of the world's reserves at the time, these officials naturally turned to the dollar as the basis for the new international economic order.

The Bretton Woods agreements reestablished fixed exchange rates based on the free convertibility of the U.S. dollar into gold. The United States agreed to buy or sell gold to maintain the $35 per ounce price that President Franklin Roosevelt had established in 1933. The other signatory nations, which had almost no gold in any case, agreed to buy and sell *dollars* to maintain their exchange rates at agreed-upon levels. Thus, all currencies were indirectly tied to gold. A holder of French francs, for example, could exchange these for dollars at (roughly) 5 francs per dollar and then exchange the dollars for gold at $35 per ounce. In this way, the value of the franc was fixed at 175 francs per ounce of gold (5 francs per dollar times $35 per ounce).

The *International Monetary Fund (IMF)*, which has been much in the news of late, was established in 1944 to police and manage the Bretton Woods system. Using funds contributed by member countries, the IMF was empowered to make loans to countries that were running low on reserves. Letting the exchange rate adjust was viewed as a last resort, for it was believed that fixed exchange rates were essential to world trade.

The Bretton Woods system inherited the flaws of any fixed exchange rate system. A change in exchange rates was to be permitted only in the case of a "fundamental disequilibrium" in a nation's balance of payments—for it was believed that only relatively fixed exchange rates could provide the stable climate needed to restore world trade.

Of course, the Bretton Woods conferees did not define clearly what a "fundamental disequilibrium" was, nor could they have. As the system evolved, it came to mean a chronic *deficit* in the balance of payments of sizable proportions. Such nations would then be allowed to *devalue* their currencies relative to the dollar. So the system was not really one of fixed exchange rates, but rather one where rates were "fixed until further notice." Because the IMF sanctioned devaluations only after a long run of balance of payments deficits had depleted the country's reserves, these devaluations could be clearly foreseen and normally had to be large. Speculators therefore saw glowing opportunities for profit and would "attack" weak currencies with waves of selling.

This problem led many economists to question whether the system of fixed exchange rates really provided the stable climate for world trade that had been intended. Was a system where rates remained constant for long periods and then were altered by large amounts really more conducive to international trade than one in which overvalued currencies would gradually depreciate, as they would under a system of floating rates?

A second problem arose from the asymmetry mentioned in the previous section: Deficit nations could be forced to devalue while surplus nations could resist upward revaluations. Because the value of the U.S. dollar was fixed in terms of gold, the United States was the one nation in the world that had no way to devalue its currency. The only way exchange rates between the dollar and foreign currencies could change was if the surplus nations revalued their currencies upward relative to the dollar. They did not adjust frequently enough, so the United States developed an overvalued currency and chronic balance of payments deficits.

The overvalued dollar finally destroyed the Bretton Woods system. By August 1971, the depletion of America's reserves and the accumulation of foreign debts forced President Richard Nixon to end fixed exchange rates—which he did by announcing that the United States would no longer buy or sell gold at $35 per ounce. After some futile attempts to reestablish fixed rates, the Bretton Woods system died in 1973.

ADJUSTMENT MECHANISMS UNDER FIXED EXCHANGE RATES

Under the Bretton Woods system, devaluation was viewed as a last resort, to be used only after other methods of adjusting to payments imbalances had failed. What were these other methods?

We encountered most of them in our earlier discussion of exchange rate determination in free markets. Any factor that *increases the demand* for, say, Argentine pesos or that *reduces the supply* will push the value of the peso upward—if it is free to adjust. But if the exchange rate is pegged, the balance of payments deficit will do the adjusting instead. Specifically, the Argentine balance of payments deficit will *shrink* if either the demand for pesos increases or the supply decreases.

The two panels of Figure 17-8 illustrate these adjustments. In each case, Argentina has a payments deficit, because the official exchange rate (1 peso = 1 dollar) exceeds

■ FIGURE 17-8
Adjusting to Balance of Payments Deficits

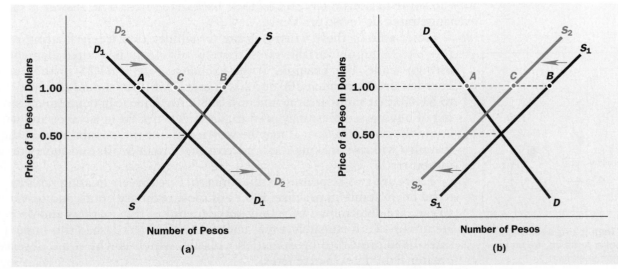

Number of Pesos
(a)

Number of Pesos
(b)

the equilibrium rate (1 peso = 50 cents). The deficit starts at *AB* in each diagram. Then either the demand curve moves outward, as in Panel (a), or the supply curve moves inward, as in Panel (b). With the exchange rate held at 1 peso to the dollar, the balance of payments deficit shrinks—to *CB* in Panel (a) or to *AC* in Panel (b).

Recalling our earlier discussion of the factors that underlie the demand and supply curves, we see that one way a nation can shrink its balance of payments deficit is to *reduce its aggregate demand*, thereby discouraging imports and cutting down its demand for foreign currency. Another is to *lower its rate of inflation*, thereby encouraging exports and discouraging imports. Finally, it can *raise its interest rates* to attract more foreign capital.

In other words, deficit nations are expected to follow restrictive monetary and fiscal policies *voluntarily*, just as they would have done *automatically* under the classical gold standard. However, just as under the gold standard, this medicine is often unpalatable.

A surplus nation could, of course, take the opposite measures: pursuing *expansionary* monetary and fiscal policies to increase economic growth and *lower* interest rates. By increasing the supply of the country's currency and reducing the demand for it, such actions would reduce that nation's balance of payments surplus. But surplus countries often do not relish the inflation that accompanies expansionary policies, and so, once again, they leave the burden of adjustment to the deficit nations. The general point about fixed exchange rates is that:

Under a system of fixed exchange rates, a country's government loses some control over its domestic economy. Sometimes balance of payments considerations may force it to contract its economy so as to cut down its demand for foreign currency, even though domestic needs call for expansion. At other times, the domestic economy may need to be reined in, but balance of payments considerations suggest expansion.

That was certainly the case in Argentina, where interest rates soared to attract foreign capital, and the government pursued contractionary fiscal policies to curb the country's appetite for imports. Both contributed to a long and deep recession. Argentina took the bitter medicine needed to defend its fixed exchange rate for quite a while. But high unemployment eventually led to riots in the streets, toppled the government, and persuaded the Argentine authorities to abandon the fixed exchange rate.

WHY TRY TO FIX EXCHANGE RATES?

In view of these and other problems with fixed exchange rates, why did the international financial community work so hard to maintain them for so many years? And why do some nations today still fix their exchange rates? The answer is that floating exchange rates also pose problems.

Chief among these worries is the possibility that freely floating rates might prove to be highly variable rates, thereby adding an unwanted element of risk to foreign trade. For example, if the exchange rate is $1.25 to the euro, then a Parisian dress priced at 200 euros will cost $250. But should the euro appreciate to $1.40, that same dress would cost $280. An American department store thinking of buying the dress may need to place its order far in advance and will want to know the cost *in dollars*. It may be worried about the possibility that the value of the euro will rise, making the dress cost more than $250. And such worries might inhibit trade.

There are two responses to this concern. First, freely floating rates might prove to be fairly stable in practice. Prices of most ordinary goods and services, for example, are determined by supply and demand in free markets and do not fluctuate unduly. Unfortunately, experience since 1973 has dashed this hope. Exchange rates have proved to be extremely volatile, which is why some observers favor greater fixity in exchange rates.

"Then it's agreed. Until the dollar firms up, we let the clamshell float."

A second possibility is that speculators might relieve business firms of exchange rate risks—for a fee, of course. Consider the department store example. If each euro costs $1.25 today, the department store manager can assure herself of paying exactly $250 for the dress several months from now by arranging for a speculator to deliver 200 euros to her at $1.25 per euro on the day she needs them. If the euro appreciates in the interim, the speculator, not the department store, will take the financial beating. Of course, if the euro depreciates, the speculator will pocket the profits. Thus, speculators play an important role in a system of floating exchange rates.

The widespread fears that speculative activity in free markets will lead to wild gyrations in prices, although occasionally valid, are often unfounded. The reason is simple.

> **To make profits, international currency speculators must *buy* a currency when its value is low (thus helping to support the currency by pushing up its demand curve) and *sell* it when its value is high (thus holding down the price by adding to the supply curve). This means that successful speculators must come into the market as *buyers* when demand is weak (or when supply is strong) and come in as *sellers* when demand is strong (or supply is scant). In doing so, they help limit price fluctuations. Looked at the other way around, speculators can *destabilize* prices only if they are systematically willing to lose money.[5]**

Notice the stark—and ironic—contrast to the system of fixed exchange rates in which speculation often leads to wild "runs" on currencies that are on the verge of devaluation—as happened in Mexico in 1995, several Southeast Asian countries in 1997–1998, Brazil in 1999, and Argentina in 2001. Speculative activity, which may well be *destabilizing* under fixed rates, is more likely to be *stabilizing* under floating rates.[6]

We do not mean to imply that speculation makes floating rates trouble-free. At the very least, speculators will demand a fee for their services—a fee that adds to the costs of trading across national borders. In addition, speculators will not assume *all* exchange rate risks. For example, few contracts on foreign currencies last more than, say, a year or two. Thus, a business cannot easily protect itself from exchange rate changes over periods of many years. Finally, speculative markets can and do get carried away from time to time, moving currency rates in ways that are difficult to understand, that frustrate the intentions of governments, and that devastate some people—as happened in Mexico in 1995 and in Southeast Asia in 1997.

Despite all of these problems, international trade has flourished under floating exchange rates. Perhaps exchange rate risk is not as burdensome as some people think.

THE CURRENT "NONSYSTEM"

The international financial system today is an eclectic blend of fixed and floating exchange rates, with no grand organizing principle. Indeed, it is so diverse that it is often called a "nonsystem."

Some currencies are still pegged in the old Bretton Woods manner. One example is Hong Kong, which maintains a fixed value for its currency by standing ready to buy or sell U.S. dollars as necessary. China also pegs its currency to the dollar, without enunciating that as its official policy. A few small countries, like Panama and Ecuador, have taken this theme even further by actually adopting the U.S. dollar as their domestic currencies. Other nations tie their currencies to a hypothetical "basket" of several currencies, rather than to a single currency.

---

[5] See Review Question 11 at the end of the chapter.

[6] After their respective currency crises in 1995 and 1999, both Mexico and Brazil floated their currencies. Each weathered the subsequent international financial storms rather nicely. But Argentina, with its fixed exchange rate, struggled.

More nations, however, let their exchange rates float, although not always freely. Such floating rates change slightly on a day-to-day basis, and market forces generally determine the basic trends, up or down. But governments do not hesitate to intervene to moderate exchange movements whenever they feel such actions are appropriate. Typically, interventions are aimed at ironing out what are deemed to be transitory fluctuations. But sometimes central banks oppose basic exchange rate trends. For example, the Federal Reserve and other central banks sold dollars aggressively in 1985 to push the dollar *down*, and they bought dollars in 1994 and 1995 to push the dollar *up*. As we will discuss in the next chapter, the Japanese have spent hundreds of billions of dollars trying to prevent the yen from floating up. The terms *dirty float* or *managed float* have been coined to describe this mongrel system.

The Role of the IMF

The role of the International Monetary Fund in the current nonsystem is quite different from what it was under the old Bretton Woods system. No longer the police officer of fixed exchange rates, the IMF has evolved into a general-purpose, international fire-and-rescue squad instead.

The IMF examines the economies of all its member nations on a regular basis. When a country runs into serious financial difficulties, it may turn to the Fund for help. The IMF typically provides loans, but with many strings attached. For example, if the country has a large current account deficit—as is normally the case when countries come to the IMF—the Fund will typically insist on contractionary fiscal and monetary policies to curb the country's appetite for imports. Often, this mandate spells recession.

During the 1990s, the IMF found itself at the epicenter of a series of very visible economic crises: in Mexico in 1995, in Southeast Asia in 1997, in Russia in 1998, and in Brazil in 1999. In 2001, Turkey and Argentina ran into trouble and appealed to the IMF for help. While each case was different, they shared some common elements.

Most of these crises were precipitated by the collapse of a fixed exchange rate pegged to the U.S. dollar. In each case, the currency plummeted, with ruinous consequences. Questions were raised about the country's ability to pay its bills. In each case, the IMF arrived on the scene with both money and lots of advice, determined to stave off default. In the end, each country suffered through a severe recession—or worse.

The IMF's increased visibility has naturally brought it increased criticism. Some critics complain that the Fund sets excessively strict conditions on its client states, requiring them, for example, to cut their government budgets and raise interest rates in a recession—which makes a bad domestic economic situation become even worse.

Other critics worry that the Fund is serving as a bill collector for banks and other financial institutions from the United States and other rich countries. These banks loaned money irresponsibly, these critics argue, and therefore deserve to lose it. By bailing them out of their losses, the IMF simply encourages more reckless behavior in the future.

Suggestions for reform are everywhere (see "Does the International Monetary System Need Reform?"), and some changes have been made in the IMF's procedures. But the debate rages on.

The Volatile Dollar

As mentioned earlier, floating exchange rates have not proved to be stable exchange rates. No currency illustrates this point better than the U.S. dollar. (See Figure 17-9.)

In 1977 and 1978, the international value of the dollar plummeted until a concerted effort by central banks to buy dollars stopped the fall. The dollar then stabilized for almost two years before rising like a rocket for a period of almost five years. As Table 17-1 showed, in July 1980 a U.S. dollar bought less than 2 German marks,

POLICY DEBATE   Does the International Monetary System Need Reform?

Robert Rubin, America's former Treasury secretary, wants to "modernize the architecture of the international financial markets." Eisuke Sakakibara, Japan's top international finance official, is thinking of a "Bretton Woods II." Alan Greenspan, chairman of the Federal Reserve, wants to review the "patchwork of arrangements" governing international finance. After East Asia's crisis, activism is in the air. . . .

It is easy to see why. . . . Policymakers worry that today's financial architecture, designed at Bretton Woods in 1944 for a world of limited capital mobility, may not be capable of dealing with an ever more global capital market. For international finance has been revolutionised. Formerly closed economies have cast off controls and embraced foreign funds. Better technology and financial innovation have made it easy to move money instantaneously.

The benefits are obvious: the expansion of private flows to developing countries. . . . But vast inflows can quickly become huge outflows. And financial crises can spread overnight between apparently unconnected markets. The five worst-affected Asian economies (South Korea, Indonesia, Thailand, Malaysia and the Philippines) received $93 billion of private capital flows in 1996. In 1997 they saw an outflow of $12 billion.

[One] reform to reinforce capital markets is better regulation. . . . Countless banking crises—in rich and poor countries alike—have shown that the combination of free capital flows and badly regulated banks is disastrous. . . . Others go much further, arguing that a global capital market needs global financial regulation, not a hotch-potch of national supervisors of varying quality. . . .

For many conservatives, particularly in America's Congress, the answer is to curb, or even eliminate, the IMF. It is the prospect of bail-outs, they argue, that encourages governments to profligacy and investors to recklessness. . . .

SOURCE: © Serge Attal/Getty Images/Gamma-Liaison

For those who see East Asia's crisis primarily as one of panic, . . . far more urgent is the need to control the capital flows themselves. . . . For those who are uneasy with the speed with which funds flow around the globe, the perennial idea of a tax on currency transactions has surfaced again. . . .

With such an array of possible reforms, it is hardly surprising that international officials are confused and uncertain [whereas] their political masters demand quick action.

SOURCE: "The Perils of Global Capital," *The Economist*, April 11, 1998. © The Economist Newspaper Group, Inc. Reprinted with permission. Further reproduction prohibited. www.economist.com

Authors' note: Politicians may have wanted "quick action" in 1998, but few of the items on this list have actually happened. The debate goes on.

---

about 4 French francs, and about 830 Italian lira. By the time it peaked in February 1985, the mighty dollar could buy more than 3 German marks, about 10 French francs, and more than 2,000 Italian lira. Such major currency changes affect world trade dramatically.

The rising dollar was a blessing to Americans who traveled abroad or who bought foreign goods—because foreign prices, when translated to dollars by the exchange rate, looked cheap to Americans.[7] But the arithmetic worked just the other way around for U.S. firms seeking to sell their goods abroad; foreign buyers

[7] *Exercise:* How much does a 100-euro hotel room in Paris cost in dollars when the euro is worth $1.25? $1? 80 cents?

■ FIGURE 17-9
The Ups and Downs of the Dollar

SOURCE: Federal Reserve System.

NOTE: Exchange rate relative to major currencies, March 1973 = 100.

found everything American very expensive.[8] It was no surprise, therefore, that as the dollar climbed our exports fell, our imports rose, and many of our leading manufacturing industries were decimated by foreign competition. An expensive currency, Americans came to learn, is a mixed blessing.

From early 1985 until early 1988, the value of the dollar fell even faster than it had risen. The cheaper dollar curbed American appetites for imports and alleviated the plight of our export industries, many of which boomed. However, rising prices for imported goods and foreign vacations were a source of consternation to many American consumers.

Since 1988, the overall value of the dollar has not changed much—on average. But quite a few appreciations and depreciations have occurred that were sharp enough to gain the attention of the world's financial markets and central banks. (In recent years, the dollar has been mostly falling.) The international currency markets are anything but boring.

The Birth of the Euro

As noted earlier, floating exchange rates are no panacea. One particular problem confronted the members of the European Union (EU). As part of their long-range goal to create a unified market like that of the United States, they perceived a need to establish a single currency for all member countries—a monetary union.

"His mood is pegged to the dollar"

The process of convergence to a single currency took place in steps, more or less as prescribed by the Treaty of Maastricht, over a period of years. Member nations encountered a number of obstacles along the way. But to the surprise of many skeptics, all such obstacles were overcome, and the euro became a reality in 1999.

Electronic and checking transactions in 11 of the 15 EU nations were denominated in euros rather than in national currencies as of January 1999. The number of participating countries rose to 12 when Greece joined the monetary union,[9] and the new euro coins and paper money were introduced successfully in January 2002. By now French francs, German marks, Italian lira, and nine other national currencies have been withdrawn from circulation—and are relics of the past. Each of these transformations has taken place remarkably smoothly.

The establishment of the euro and the withdrawal of the other national currencies is a great economic experiment that marks a giant step beyond merely fixing exchange rates. A fixed exchange rate regime can be abolished at any time by decision of the relevant governments. And, as we have seen, speculators sometimes break fixed exchange rates even when governments want to maintain them. Europe's monetary union was created by an international treaty, however, and it is more or less invulnerable to speculative attack because it *abolished* exchange rates among the participating nations. Just as there has long been no exchange rate between New York and New Jersey, now there is no exchange rate between Germany and France. Monetary unions may create other problems, but exchange rate instability should not be one of them.

But a monetary union fixes the exchange rate only *within* the union. The common currency (in this case, the euro) continues to fluctuate in value vis-à-vis other currencies. After introduction, the euro fell significantly relative to the U.S. dollar. In January 1999, one euro was worth about $1.17. It subsequently sunk below 85 cents. This

---

[8] *Exercise:* How much does a $55 American camera cost a German consumer when the euro is worth $1.20? $1? 80 cents?

[9] As of this writing, three EU members (Sweden, Denmark, and the United Kingdom) have chosen not to join the monetary union.

large depreciation of the euro has had its usual positive (stimulating exports) and negative (inflationary) effects on Europe's economies. But it also wounded European pride. Lately, the euro has risen to above $1.25, leaving EU nations worried about their ability to export.

 ## Puzzle Resolved: The Fate of the Argentine Currency Board

What we have learned in this chapter helps us understand what went wrong with Argentina's fixed-exchange-rate system in 2001 and 2002. The story actually begins at the time of the Mexican crisis in 1995.

When the Mexican peso fell, international investors began worrying about other Latin American currencies that were pegged to the dollar, including the Argentine peso. They offered pesos for sale and demanded dollars in return, which Argentina was bound to provide under the terms of its currency board. Argentina was determined to maintain parity between the dollar and the peso, which it viewed as the key to its conquest of inflation. So it followed the orthodox prescription for currency defense: It raised interest rates and cut its budget deficit. The medicine worked; the value of the peso was preserved. But this remedy brought a painful cost—a serious recession.

Unfortunately for Argentina, the U.S. dollar then rose in value against most of the world's currencies over the next six years, pulling the Argentine peso with it. As a result, Argentine goods became increasingly expensive. Bad luck struck again in 1999 when Argentina's largest neighbor, Brazil, was forced to abandon its own fixed exchange rate system. The Brazilian real plunged in value, making the Argentine peso (which was tied to the dollar) terribly expensive by comparison.

Argentina soldiered on for several more years, successfully maintaining its currency board at the cost of a multiyear recession. But in the closing months of 2001, as we have seen, chaos erupted in the streets and the currency board was doomed. Argentina now has a floating exchange rate.

SUMMARY

1. **Exchange rates** state the value of one currency in terms of other currencies, and thus translate one country's prices into the currencies of other nations. Exchange rates therefore influence patterns of world trade.

2. If governments do not interfere by buying or selling their currencies, exchange rates will be determined in free markets by the usual laws of supply and demand. Such a system is said to be based on **floating exchange rates.**

3. Demand for a nation's currency is derived from foreigners' desires to purchase that country's goods and services or to invest in its assets. Under floating rates, anything that increases the demand for a nation's currency will cause its exchange rate to **appreciate.**

4. Supply of a nation's currency is derived from the desire of that country's citizens to purchase foreign goods and services or to invest in foreign assets. Under floating rates, anything that increases the supply of a nation's currency will cause its exchange rate to **depreciate.**

5. Purchasing-power parity plays a major role in very-long-run exchange rate movements. The **purchasing-power parity theory** states that relative price levels in any two countries determine the exchange rate between their currencies. Therefore, countries with relatively low inflation rates normally will have appreciating currencies.

6. Over shorter periods, however, purchasing-power parity has little influence over exchange rate movements. The pace of economic activity and the level of interest rates exert greater influence.

7. Capital movements are typically the dominant factor in exchange rate determination in the short and medium runs. A nation that offers international investors higher interest rates, or better prospective returns on investments, will typically see its currency appreciate.

8. An exchange rate can be fixed at a nonequilibrium level if the government is willing and able to mop up any excess of quantity supplied over quantity demanded, or provide any excess of quantity demanded over quantity supplied. In the first case, the country is suffering from a **balance of payments deficit** because of its overvalued currency. In the second case, an undervalued currency has given it a **balance of payments surplus.**

9. The **gold standard** was a system of **fixed exchange rates** in which the value of every nation's currency was fixed in terms of gold. This system created problems because nations could not control their own money supplies and because the world could not control its total supply of gold.

10. After World War II, the gold standard was replaced by the **Bretton Woods system,** in which exchange rates were fixed in terms of U.S. dollars, and the dollar was in turn tied to gold. This system broke up in 1971, when the dollar became chronically overvalued.

11. Since 1971, the world has moved toward a system of relatively free exchange rates, but with plenty of exceptions. We now have a thoroughly mixed system of "dirty" or "managed" floating, which continues to evolve and adapt.

12. Floating rates are not without their problems. For example, importers and exporters justifiably worry about fluctuations in exchange rates.

13. Under floating exchange rates, investors who speculate on international currency values provide a valuable service by assuming the risks of those who do not wish to speculate. Normally, speculators stabilize rather than destabilize exchange rates, because that is how they make profits.

14. The U.S. dollar rose dramatically in value from 1980 to 1985, making our imports cheaper and our exports more expensive. From 1985 to 1988, the dollar tumbled, which had precisely the reverse effects. Since then, the dollar has fluctuated in value with no clear trend, rising substantially from 1995 to 2002 and falling since then.

15. The European Union has recently established a single currency, the euro, for most of its member nations.

KEY TERMS

Exchange rate   324

Appreciation   324

Depreciation   324

Devaluation   325

Revaluation   325

Floating exchange rates   325

Purchasing-power parity theory   329

Fixed exchange rates   331

Balance of payments deficit and surplus   331, 332

Current account   333

Capital account   333

Gold standard   333

Bretton Woods system   334

International Monetary Fund (IMF)   334

"Dirty" or "managed" float   338

Euro   340

QUESTIONS FOR REVIEW

1. What items do you own or routinely consume that are produced abroad? From what countries do these items come? Suppose Americans decided to buy fewer of these things. How would that affect the exchange rates between the dollar and these currencies?

2. If the dollar appreciates relative to the euro, will the German camera you have wanted become more or less expensive? What effect do you imagine this change will have on American demand for German cameras? Does the American demand curve for euros, therefore, slope upward or downward? Explain.

3. During the first half of the 1980s, inflation in (West) Germany was consistently lower than that in the United States. What, then, does the purchasing-power parity theory predict should have happened to the exchange rate between the mark and the dollar between 1980 and 1985? (Look at Table 17-1 to see what actually happened.)

4. Use supply and demand diagrams to analyze the effect of the following actions on the exchange rate between the dollar and the yen:

   a. Japan opens its domestic markets to more foreign competition.

   b. Investors come to believe that values on the Tokyo stock market will rise.

   c. The Federal Reserve raises interest rates in the United States.

   d. The U.S. government, to help settle the problems of the Middle East, gives huge amounts of foreign aid to Israel and her Arab neighbors.

   e. Japan has a recession while the United States booms.

   f. Inflation in the United States exceeds that in Japan.

5. How are the problems of a country faced with a balance of payments deficit similar to those posed by a government regulation that holds the price of milk above the equilibrium level? (*Hint:* Think of each in terms of a supply-demand diagram.)

6. For each of the following transactions, indicate how it would affect the U.S. balance of payments if exchange rates were fixed:

   a. You spent the summer traveling in Europe.

   b. Your uncle in Canada sent you $20 as a birthday present.

   c. You bought a new Honda, made in Japan.

   d. You sold some stock you own on the Tokyo Stock Exchange.

7. Suppose each of the transactions listed in Review Question 6 was done by many Americans. Indicate how each would affect the international value of the dollar if exchange rates were floating.

8. Under the old gold standard, what do you think happened to world prices when a huge gold strike occurred in California in 1849? What do you think happened when the world went without any important new gold strikes for 20 years or so?

9. Explain why the members of the Bretton Woods conference in 1944 wanted to establish a system of fixed exchange rates. What flaw led to the ultimate breakdown of the system in 1971?

10. Suppose you want to reserve a hotel room in London for the coming summer but are worried that the value of the pound may rise between now and then, making the room too expensive for your budget. Explain how a speculator could relieve you of this worry. (Don't actually try it. Speculators deal only in very large sums!)

11. We learned in this chapter that successful speculators buy a currency when demand is weak and sell it when demand is strong. Use supply and demand diagrams for two different periods (one with weak demand, the other with strong demand) to show why this activity will limit price fluctuations.

12. In 2003, market forces raised the international value of the Japanese yen. Why do you think the government of Japan was unhappy about this currency appreciation? (*Hint:* Japan was trying to emerge from a recession at the time.) If they wanted to stop the yen's appreciation, what actions could the Bank of Japan (Japan's central bank) and the Federal Reserve have taken? Why might the central banks have failed in this attempt?

18

Exchange Rates and
the Macroeconomy

No man is an island, entire of itself.

JOHN DONNE

Surveying the problems afflicting a number of the world's economies in the late 1990s, Federal Reserve Chairman Alan Greenspan famously declared that the United States could not long remain an "oasis of prosperity" in a troubled world. The nations of the world are indeed locked together in an uneasy economic union. Fluctuations in foreign growth, inflation, and interest rates profoundly affect the U.S. economy. Economic events that originate in our country reverberate around the globe. Anyone who ignores these international linkages cannot hope to understand how the world economy works.

The macroeconomic model we developed in earlier chapters does not go far enough. In particular, it ignores such crucial influences as exchange rates and international financial movements. The previous chapter showed how major macroeconomic variables such as gross domestic product (GDP), prices, and interest rates affect exchange rates. In this chapter, we complete the circle by studying how changes in the exchange rate affect the domestic economy. Then we bring international capital flows into the picture and learn how monetary and fiscal policy work in an **open economy.**

CONTENTS

An **open economy** is one that trades with other nations in goods and services, and perhaps also trades in financial assets.

 Issue: Should the U.S. Government Try to Stop the Dollar from Falling?

For years, economists predicted that America's huge—and growing—trade deficits would *eventually* drive the international value of the U.S. dollar down. In the early months of 2002, the prophecy finally started to come true, as the greenback began an irregular decline that continues to this day. For example, in the first quarter of 2002, a euro was worth about 88 cents; at this writing (in March 2004), it is worth about $1.23. Looked at the other way around, a dollar could buy about 1.13 euros in early 2002, but only about 0.8 euro two years later. That is a very large change.

As the dollar fell, the U.S. economy recovered from the 2001 recession, and generally grew much faster than either Europe or Japan. By the time 2004 began, both the European and Japanese governments were complaining that their businesses were losing export markets to the Americans, and that was damaging European and Japanese growth. They urged the United States government to stop the dollar's decline. But the United States insisted that currency values should be "flexible," determined in world markets by the forces of supply and demand that we studied in the previous chapter.

Who was right? We will examine this question as the chapter progresses.

INTERNATIONAL TRADE, EXCHANGE RATES, AND AGGREGATE DEMAND

We know from earlier chapters that a country's net exports, $(X - IM)$, are one component of its aggregate demand, $C + I + G + (X - IM)$. It follows that an autonomous increase in exports or decrease in imports has a multiplier effect on the economy, just like an increase in consumption, investment, or government purchases.[1] Figure 18-1 depicts this conclusion on an aggregate demand and supply diagram. A rise in net exports shifts the aggregate demand curve outward to the right, pushing equilibrium from point A to point B. Both GDP and the price level therefore rise.

■ FIGURE 18-1

The Effects of Higher Net Exports

But what increases net exports? One factor mentioned in Chapter 7 was a rise in foreign incomes. If foreign economies boom, their citizens are likely to spend more on a wide variety of products, some of which will be American exports. Thus, Figure 18-1 illustrates the effect on the U.S. economy of more rapid growth in foreign countries. Similarly, a recession abroad would reduce U.S. exports and shift the U.S. aggregate demand curve inward. Thus, as we learned in Chapter 8:

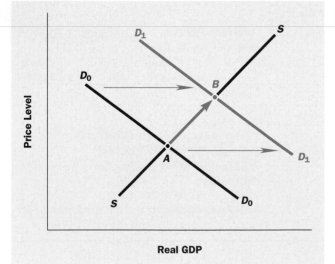

Booms or recessions in one country tend to be transmitted to other countries through international trade in goods and services.

One other important determinant of net exports was mentioned in Chapter 7, but not discussed in depth: the relative prices of foreign and domestic goods. This idea involves a simple application of the law of demand. Namely, if the prices of the goods of Country X rise, people everywhere will tend to buy fewer of them—and more of the goods of Country Y. As we will see next, this simple idea holds the key to understanding how exchange rates affect international trade.

---

[1] An appendix to Chapter 8 showed that international trade lowers the numerical value of the multiplier. Autonomous changes in C, I, G, and $(X - IM)$ all have the same multiplier.

Relative Prices, Exports, and Imports

First assume—just for this short section—that exchange rates are *fixed*. What happens if the prices of American goods fall while, say, Japanese prices are constant? With U.S. products now less expensive *relative to Japanese products*, both Japanese and American consumers will buy more American goods and fewer Japanese goods. As a result, America's exports will rise and its imports will fall, adding to aggregate demand in this country. Conversely, a rise in American prices (relative to Japanese prices) will *decrease* U.S. net exports and aggregate demand. Thus:

A *fall* in the relative prices of a country's exports tends to *increase* that country's net exports and hence to raise its real GDP. Analogously, a *rise* in the relative prices of a country's exports will *decrease* that country's net exports and GDP.

Precisely the same logic applies to changes in Japanese prices. If Japanese prices rise, Americans will export more and import less. So $X - IM$ will rise, boosting GDP in the United States. Figure 18-1 applies to this case without change. By similar reasoning, falling Japanese prices decrease U.S. net exports and depress our economy. Thus:

Price increases abroad raise a country's net exports and hence its GDP. Price decreases abroad have the opposite effects.

The Effects of Changes in Exchange Rates

From here it is a simple matter to figure out how changes in exchange rates affect a country's net exports, for *currency appreciations or depreciations change international relative prices.*

Recall that the basic role of an exchange rate is to convert one country's prices into another country's currency. Table 18-1 uses two examples of U.S.–Japanese trade to remind us of this role. Suppose the dollar depreciates from 120 yen to 100 yen. Then, from the American consumer's viewpoint, a television set that costs ¥30,000 in Japan goes up in price from $250 (that is, 30,000/120) to $300. To Americans, it is just as if Japanese manufacturers had raised TV prices by 20 percent. Naturally, Americans will react by purchasing fewer Japanese products, so American imports will decline.

Now consider the implications for Japanese consumers interested in buying American personal computers that cost $1,000. When the dollar falls from 120 yen to 100 yen, they see the price of these computers falling from ¥120,000 to ¥100,000. To them, it is just as if American producers had offered a 16.7 percent markdown. Under such circumstances, we expect U.S. sales to the Japanese to rise, so U.S. exports should increase. Putting these two findings together, we conclude that:

A currency *depreciation* should *raise* net exports and therefore *increase* aggregate demand. Conversely, a currency *appreciation* should *reduce* net exports and therefore *decrease* aggregate demand.

The aggregate supply and demand diagram in Figure 18-2 illustrates this conclusion. If the currency depreciates, net exports rise and the aggregate demand curve shifts outward from D_0D_0 to D_1D_1. Both prices and out-

■ TABLE 18-1   Exchange Rates and Home Currency Prices

Exchange Rate	¥30,000 Japanese TV Set		$1,000 U.S. Home Computer	
	Price in Japan	Price in the U.S.	Price in the U.S.	Price in Japan
$1 = 120 yen	¥30,000	$250	$1,000	¥120,000
1 = 100 yen	30,000	300	1,000	100,000

■ FIGURE 18-2
The Effects of Exchange Rate Changes on Aggregate Demand

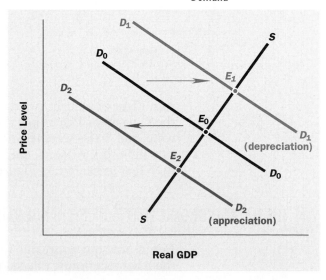

put rise as the economy's equilibrium moves from E_0 to E_1. If the currency appreciates, everything operates in reverse: Net exports fall, the aggregate demand curve shifts inward to D_2D_2, and both prices and output decline.

This simple analysis helps us understand why the U.S. trade deficit grew so enormously in the late 1990s and early 2000s. We learned in the previous chapter that the international value of the dollar began to climb in 1995. According to the reasoning we have just completed, within a few years such an appreciation of the dollar should have boosted U.S. imports and damaged U.S. exports. That is precisely what happened. In constant dollars, American imports soared by roughly 50 percent between 1997 and 2002, while American exports rose by less than 10 percent. The result was that a $105 billion net export deficit in 1997 turned into a monumental $509 billion deficit by 2002.

AGGREGATE SUPPLY IN AN OPEN ECONOMY

So far we have concluded that a currency depreciation increases aggregate demand and that a currency appreciation decreases it. To complete our model of macroeconomics in an open economy, we turn now to the implications of international trade for *aggregate supply.*

Part of the story is already familiar to us. As we know from previous chapters, the United States, like all economies, purchases some of its productive inputs from abroad. Oil is only the most prominent example. We also rely on foreign suppliers for metals such as titanium, raw agricultural products such as coffee beans, and thousands of other items used by American industry. When the dollar depreciates, these imported inputs cost more in U.S. dollars—just as if foreign prices had risen.

The consequence is clear: With imported inputs more expensive, American firms will be forced to charge higher prices at any given level of output. Graphically, this means that *the aggregate supply curve will shift upward* (or inward to the left).

■ FIGURE 18-3

The Effects of Exchange Rate Changes on Aggregate Supply

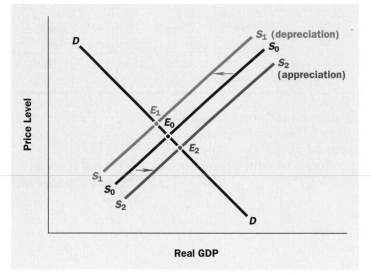

> When the dollar *depreciates,* the prices of imported inputs rise. The U.S. aggregate supply curve therefore shifts *inward,* pushing up the prices of American-made goods and services. By exactly analogous reasoning, an *appreciation* of the dollar makes imported inputs cheaper and shifts the U.S. aggregate supply curve *outward,* thus pushing American prices down. (See Figure 18-3.)

Beyond this, a depreciating dollar has additional inflationary effects that do not show up on an aggregate demand and supply diagram, which depicts *the price of domestic product* on its vertical axis. Most obviously, prices of imported goods are included in U.S. price indexes like the Consumer Price Index (CPI). So when the dollar prices of Japanese cars, French wine, and Swiss watches increase, the CPI goes up *even if no American prices rise.* For this and other reasons, the inflationary impact of a dollar depreciation is even greater than that indicated by Figure 18-3.

THE MACROECONOMIC EFFECTS OF EXCHANGE RATES

Let us now put aggregate demand and aggregate supply together and think through the macroeconomic effects of changes in exchange rates.

First, suppose the international value of the dollar falls. Referring back to the red lines in Figures 18-2 and 18-3, we see that this depreciation will shift the aggregate demand curve *outward* and the aggregate supply curve *inward*. The result, as Figure 18-4 shows, is that the U.S. price level certainly rises. But whether real GDP rises or falls depends on whether the supply or demand shift is the dominant influence. The evidence strongly suggests that aggregate *demand* shifts are usually larger, so we expect GDP to rise. Hence:

A currency depreciation is inflationary and probably also expansionary.

The intuitive explanation for this result is clear. When the dollar falls, foreign goods become more expensive to Americans. That effect is directly inflationary. At the same time, aggregate demand in the United States is stimulated by rising net exports. As long as the expansion of demand outweighs the adverse shift of the aggregate supply curve brought on by currency depreciation, real GDP should rise.

But wait. By this reasoning, the massive depreciations of several Southeast Asian currencies in 1997 and 1998 should have given these economies tremendous boosts. Instead, the so-called Asian Tigers suffered horrific slumps—as did Mexico when the peso tumbled in 1995. Why? The answer is that our simple analysis of aggregate supply and demand omits a detail that, although unimportant for the United States, is critical in many developing nations.

Countries that borrow in foreign currency will see their debts increase whenever their currencies fall in value. For example, an Indonesian business that borrowed $1,000 in July 1997, when $1 was worth 2,500 rupiah, thought it owed 2.5 million rupiah. But when the dollar suddenly became worth 10,000 rupiah, the company's debt skyrocketed to 10 million rupiah. Many businesses found themselves unable to cope with their crushing debt burdens and simply went bankrupt.

Now let's reverse direction, and look at what happens when the currency *appreciates*. In this case, net exports *fall* so the aggregate demand curve shifts *inward*. At the same time, imported inputs become cheaper, so the aggregate supply curve shifts *outward*. Both of these shifts are shown in Figure 18-5. Once again, as the diagram shows, we can be sure of the movement of the price level: It falls. Output also falls if the demand shift is larger than the supply shift, as is likely. Thus:

A currency appreciation is disinflationary and probably also contractionary.

This analysis explains why many economists and financial experts cringed when both the yen and the euro appreciated relative to the dollar in 2002–2004. Japan, in particular, was already experiencing deflation and very slow growth. The last thing it needed, they argued, was a decrease in aggregate demand.

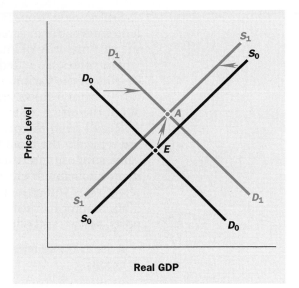

■ FIGURE 18-4
The Effects of a Currency Depreciation

■ FIGURE 18-5
The Effects of a Currency Appreciation

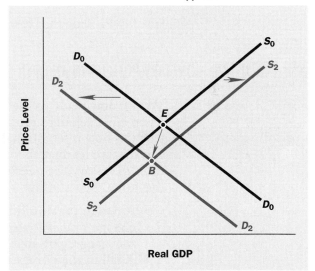

Interest Rates and International Capital Flows

One important piece of our international economic puzzle is still missing. We have analyzed international trade in goods and services in some detail, but we have ignored international movements of *capital*.

For some nations, this omission is inconsequential because they rarely receive or lend international capital. But things are quite different for the United States because the vast majority of international financial flows involve either buying or selling assets whose values are stated in U.S. dollars. In addition, we cannot hope to understand the origins of the various international financial crises since the 1990s without incorporating capital flows into our analysis. Fortunately, given what we have just learned about the effects of exchange rates, this omission is easily rectified.

Recall from the previous chapter that interest rate differentials and capital flows are typically the most important determinants of exchange rate movements. Specifically, suppose interest rates in the United States rise while foreign interest rates remain unchanged. We learned in the previous chapter that this change in relative interest rates will attract capital to the United States and cause the dollar to appreciate. This chapter has just taught us that an appreciating dollar will, in turn, reduce net exports, prices, and output in the United States—as indicated in Figure 18-5. Thus:

> **A rise in interest rates tends to contract the economy by appreciating the currency and reducing net exports.**

International capital flows are purchased and sales of financial assets across national borders.

Notice that this conclusion has a familiar ring. When we studied monetary policy in Chapter 12, we observed that higher interest rates deter investment spending and hence reduce the I component of $C + I + G + (X - IM)$. Now, in studying an open economy with **international capital flows,** we see that higher interest rates also reduce the $X - IM$ component. Thus, *international capital flows strengthen the negative effects of interest rates on aggregate demand.*

If interest rates fall in the United States, or rise abroad, everything we have just said is turned in the opposite direction. The conclusion is:

> **A decline in interest rates tends to expand the economy by depreciating the currency and raising net exports.**

Exercise Provide the reasoning behind this conclusion.

FISCAL AND MONETARY POLICIES IN AN OPEN ECONOMY

We are now ready to use our model to analyze how fiscal and monetary policies work when the exchange rate floats and capital is internationally mobile. Doing so will teach us how international economic relations modify the effects of stabilization policies that we learned about in earlier chapters. Fortunately, no new theoretical apparatus is necessary; we need merely remember what we have learned in the chapter up to this point. Specifically:

- A rise in the domestic interest rate leads to capital *inflows* and makes the exchange rate *appreciate*. A currency appreciation *reduces* aggregate demand and *raises* aggregate supply (see Figure 18-5).
- A fall in the domestic interest rate leads to capital *outflows* and makes the exchange rate *depreciate*. A currency depreciation *raises* aggregate demand and *reduces* aggregate supply (see Figure 18-4).

Fiscal Policy Revisited

A **closed economy** is one that does not trade with other nations in either goods or assets.

With these points in mind, suppose the government cuts taxes or raises spending. Aggregate demand increases, which pushes up both real GDP and the price level in the usual manner. This effect is shown as the shift from D_0D_0 to the red line D_1D_1 in Figure 18-6. In a **closed economy,** that single shift is the end of the story. But in an *open economy* with international capital flows, we must add in the macroeconomic effects that work through the exchange rate. We do this by answering two questions.

First, what will happen to the exchange rate? We know from earlier chapters that a fiscal expansion pushes up interest rates. At higher interest rates, American securities become more attractive to foreign investors, who go to the foreign exchange markets to buy dollars with which to purchase them. This buying pressure drives up the value of the dollar. Thus:

A fiscal expansion normally makes the exchange rate appreciate.

Second, what are the effects of a higher dollar? We know that when the dollar rises in value, American goods become more expensive abroad and foreign goods become cheaper here. So exports fall and imports rise, driving down the $X - IM$ component of aggregate demand. The fiscal expansion thus winds up increasing both America's *capital account surplus* (by attracting foreign capital) and its *current account deficit* (by reducing net exports). In fact, the two must rise by equal amounts because, under floating exchange rates, it is always true that:[2]

Current account surplus + Capital account surplus = 0

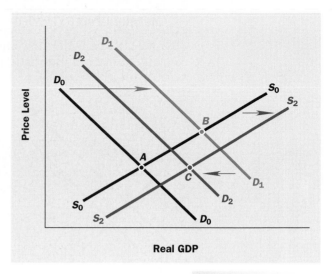

■ FIGURE 18-6
A Fiscal Expansion in an Open Economy

Because a fiscal expansion leads in this way to a trade deficit, many economists believe that the large U.S. trade deficits of the 1980s were a side effect of the large tax cuts made early in the decade—and that the tax cuts of 2001–2003 once again pushed the trade deficit up. We will return to that issue shortly.

For now, note that the induced rise in the dollar will shift the aggregate supply curve *outward* and the aggregate demand curve *inward*, as we saw in Figure 18-5. Figure 18-6 adds these two shifts (in blue) to the effect of the original fiscal expansion (in red). The final equilibrium in an open economy is point C, whereas in a closed economy it would be point B. By comparing points B and C, we can see how international linkages change the picture of fiscal policy that we painted earlier in the book.

Two main differences arise. First, a higher exchange rate makes imports cheaper and thereby offsets part of the inflationary effect of a fiscal expansion. Second, a higher exchange rate reduces the expansionary effect on real GDP by reducing $X - IM$. Here we have a new kind of "crowding out," different from the one we studied in Chapter 14. There we learned that an increase in G will crowd out some *private investment* spending by raising interest rates. Here an increase in G, by raising both interest rates and the exchange rate, crowds out *net exports*. But the effect is the same: The fiscal multiplier is reduced. Thus, we conclude that:

International capital flows reduce the power of fiscal policy.

Table 18-2, which shows actual U.S. data, suggests that this new international variety of crowding out was much more important than the traditional type of crowding out in the 1980s. Between 1981 and 1986, the share of investment in GDP barely changed despite the rise in the shares of both consumer spending and government purchases. Only the share of net exports, $X - IM$, fell—from +0.2 percent to −2.8 percent.

American economists learned this important lesson in the 1980s. In 1981, many economists worried that large government budget deficits would crowd out private investment. By the end of the decade, most were more concerned that deficits were crowding out net exports and producing a massive trade deficit.

■ TABLE 18-2   Percentage Shares of Real GDP in the United States, 1981 and 1986

Year	C	I	G	X − IM
1981	64.5%	14.3%	20.5%	0.2%
1986	67.3	14.5	21.2	−2.8
Change	+2.8	+0.2	+0.7	−3.0

NOTE: Totals do not add up because of rounding and deflation.

---

[2] If you need review, turn back to Chapter 17, page 333.

Monetary Policy Revisited

Now let us consider how *monetary policy* works in an open economy with floating exchange rates and international capital mobility. To remain consistent with the history of the 1980s, we consider a *tightening*, rather than a loosening, of monetary policy.

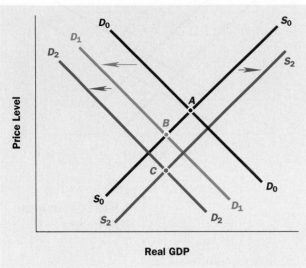

As we know from earlier chapters, contractionary monetary policy *reduces* aggregate demand, which lowers both real GDP and prices. This situation is shown in Figure 18-7 by the shift from D_0D_0 to the red line D_1D_1, and it looks like the exact opposite of a fiscal expansion. Without international capital flows, that would be the end of the story.

But in the presence of internationally mobile capital, we must also think through the consequences for interest rates and exchange rates. As we know from previous chapters, a monetary contraction *raises* interest rates—just like a fiscal expansion. Hence, tighter money attracts foreign capital into the United States in search of higher rates of return. The exchange rate therefore *rises*. The appreciating dollar encourages imports and discourages exports; so $X - IM$ falls. America therefore winds up with an inflow of capital and an increase in its trade deficit.

FIGURE 18-7

A Monetary Contraction in an Open Economy

In Figure 18-7, the two effects of the exchange rate appreciation appear in blue: aggregate supply shifts *outward* and aggregate demand shifts *inward*. This time, as you can see in the figure:

International capital flows increase the power of monetary policy.

In a closed economy, higher interest rates *reduce investment* spending, I. In an open economy, these same higher interest rates also appreciate the currency and reduce *net exports*, $X - IM$. Thus the effect of monetary policy is enhanced.

It may seem puzzling that capital flows *strengthen* monetary policy but *weaken* fiscal policy. The explanation of these contrasting results lies in their effects on interest rates. The main international repercussion of either a fiscal *expansion* or a monetary *contraction* is to raise interest rates and the exchange rate, thereby crowding out net exports. But that means that the initial effects of a fiscal expansion on aggregate demand are *weakened*, whereas the initial effects of a monetary contraction are *strengthened*.

INTERNATIONAL ASPECTS OF DEFICIT REDUCTION

We have now completed our theoretical analysis of the macroeconomics of open economies. Now let us put the theory to work by applying it to the events of the 1990s, when fiscal policy was tightened and monetary policy was eased. Should reducing the budget deficit (or raising the surplus) strengthen or weaken the dollar?

As discussed in Chapter 14, the U.S. government transformed its mammoth budget deficit into a notable surplus during the 1990s by raising taxes and cutting expenditures. Column (1) of Table 18-3 reviews the predicted effects of a fiscal contraction: It should lower real interest rates, make the dollar depreciate, reduce real GDP, and be less disinflationary than normal because of the falling dollar. This information is recorded by entering + signs for increases and − signs for decreases.

TABLE 18-3   Expected Effects of Policy

Variable	(1) Fiscal Contraction	(2) Monetary Expansion	(3) Combination
Real interest rate	−	−	−
Exchange rate	−	−	−
Net exports	+	+	+
Real GDP	−	+	?
Inflation	−	+	?

Eliminating the budget deficit reduced aggregate demand. But the Federal Reserve restored the missing demand by lowering interest rates so that the economy would not suffer a slump. According to the analysis in this chapter, such a monetary expansion should lower real interest rates, make the dollar depreciate, raise real GDP, and be a bit more inflationary than usual because of the falling dollar. These effects are recorded in Column (2) of Table 18-3.

Column (3) puts the two pieces together. We conclude that a policy mix of fiscal *contraction* and monetary *expansion* should reduce interest rates strongly, push down the value of the dollar, and strongly stimulate our foreign trade. The net effects on output and inflation are uncertain, however: The balance depends on whether the fiscal contraction overwhelms the monetary expansion, or vice versa.

What actually happened? First, interest rates did fall, just as predicted. The rate on ten-year U.S. government bonds dropped from almost 7 percent in late 1992 to just over 4.5 percent in December 1998, and by 1998 American households were enjoying the lowest home mortgage rates since the 1960s. Second, the U.S. economy expanded rapidly between 1992 and 1998; apparently, the monetary stimulus overwhelmed the fiscal contraction. Third, inflation fell despite such rapid growth. As we explained in Chapter 9, one major reason was a series of favorable supply shocks that pushed inflation down.

But what about the exchange rate and international trade? Here the theory did less well. The dollar generally declined from 1993 to 1995, as the theory predicts. But then it turned around and rose sharply from 1995 to 1998, just when the budget deficit was turning into a surplus. America's trade performance was even more puzzling. According to the theory, a lower budget deficit should have led to a lower exchange rate, and therefore to a smaller **trade deficit.** But, in fact, America's real net exports sagged from just $-\$16$ billion in 1992 to $-\$204$ billion in 1998. What went wrong?

> A country's **trade deficit** is the excess of its imports over its exports. If, instead, exports exceed imports, the country has a **trade surplus.**

◼ The Loose Link between the Budget Deficit and the Trade Deficit

To answer this question, let's explore the connection between the budget deficit and the trade deficit in more detail. To do so, we need one simple piece of arithmetic.

Begin with the familiar equilibrium condition for GDP in an open economy:

$$Y = C + I + G + (X - IM)$$

Because GDP can either be spent, saved, or taxed away,[3]

$$Y = C + S + T$$

Equating these two expressions for Y gives

$$C + I + G + (X - IM) = C + S + T$$

Finally, subtracting C from both sides and bringing the I and G terms over to the right-hand side leads to an accounting relationship between the trade deficit and the budget deficit:

$$X - IM = (S - I) - (G - T)$$

Notice that this equation is a matter of *accounting*, not economics. It must hold in *all* countries at *all* times, and it has nothing to do with any particular economic theory. In words, it says that a trade deficit—a *negative* value of $(X - IM)$—can arise from one of two sources: a government budget deficit (G larger than T) or an excess of investment over saving (I larger than S).

Now let's apply this accounting relationship to actual U.S. events in the 1990s. As we know, the government deficit, $G - T$, fell precipitously. Other things equal, that

---

[3] If you do not see why, recall that GDP equals disposable income (*DI*) plus taxes (*T*), $Y = DI + T$, and that disposable income can either be consumed or saved, $DI = C + S$. These two definitions together imply that $Y = C + S + T$.

should have *reduced* the trade deficit. But other things were not equal. The equation reminds us that the balance between saving and investment matters, too. As shares of GDP, business investment boomed while household saving declined from 1992 to 1998. So $S - I$ moved sharply in the negative direction. And that change, as our equation shows, should *raise* the trade deficit (reduce net exports).

In brief, taken by itself, deficit reduction would have increased net exports. But in reality, sharp changes in private economic behavior—specifically, less saving and more investment—overwhelmed the government's actions and made net exports fall instead. The link from the budget deficit to the trade deficit can be a loose one!

IS THE TRADE DEFICIT A PROBLEM?

The preceding explanation suggests that the United States' large trade deficits over the past decade are a symptom of a deeper trouble: The nation as a whole—including both the government and the private sector—has been consuming more than it has been producing for years. The United States has therefore been forced to borrow the difference from foreigners. The trade deficit is just the mirror image of the required capital inflows.

Those who worry about trade deficits point out that these capital inflows create debts on which interest and principal payments must be made in the future. In this view, Americans have been mortgaging their futures to finance higher consumer spending.

But another, quite different, interpretation of the trade deficit is possible. Suppose foreign investors come to see the United States as an especially attractive place to invest their funds. Then capital should flow here, not because Americans need to *borrow* it, but because foreigners are eager to *lend* it. The desire of foreigners to acquire American assets should push the value of the dollar up, which should in turn push America's net exports down. In that case, the trade deficit would still be the mirror image of the capital inflows. But it would signify America's economic *strength*, not its weakness.

Each view holds elements of truth, but the second raises a critical question: How long can it go on? As long as the United States continues to run large trade deficits, foreign investors will continue to accumulate large amounts of U.S. assets. At some point, economists and financial experts fear, these investors may conclude that they have acquired about all the American assets they want. Indeed, that day may now have arrived. If so, the U.S. trade deficit must now be sharply reduced. The only question is how.

ON CURING THE TRADE DEFICIT

How can we cure our foreign trade problem and end our addiction to foreign borrowing? There are four basic ways.

▌ Change the Mix of Fiscal and Monetary Policy

The fundamental equation

$$X - IM = (S - I) - (G - T)$$

suggests an *increase in the budget surplus* (turning $G - T$ sharply *negative*) as one good way to reduce the trade deficit. According to the analysis in this chapter, a reduction in G or an increase in T would lead to lower real interest rates in the United States, a depreciating dollar, and, eventually, a shrinking trade deficit.

When the government curtails its spending or raises taxes, aggregate demand falls. If we do not want a larger budget surplus to slow economic growth, we must therefore compensate for it by providing monetary stimulus. Like contractionary fiscal policy, expansionary monetary policy lowers interest rates, depreciates the dollar, and should therefore help reduce the trade deficit. So the policy recommendation actually amounts to tightening *fiscal* policy and loosening *monetary* policy.

As we have noted, the U.S. government—after years of vacillation—changed the policy mix decisively in this direction in the 1990s. But our trade deficit rose anyway because private investment spending soared while private saving stagnated. Then, starting in 2001, the U.S. fiscal surplus turned rapidly into a large fiscal deficit, which pushed the trade deficit up further. What else might work?

More Rapid Economic Growth Abroad

One factor behind the growing U.S. trade deficit in the 1990s was that the economies of many foreign nations—the customers for our exports—grew slowly while the U.S. economy boomed. If foreign economies would grow faster, the U.S. government argued, they would buy more American goods, thereby raising U.S. exports and reducing our trade deficit. So we urged our major trading partners to stimulate their economies and to open their markets more to American goods—with only modest success. When the U.S. economy slowed down in 2000–2001, our trade deficit did recede a bit—but no one thinks that is a very good remedy.

Raise Domestic Saving or Reduce Domestic Investment

Our fundamental equation calls attention to two other routes to a smaller trade deficit: more saving or less investment.

The U.S. personal saving rate (saving as a share of disposable income) has hit postwar lows in recent years. The 2 percent saving rate recorded since 1999 is the lowest since the Great Depression of the 1930s! If Americans would simply save more, we would need to borrow less from abroad. This solution, too, would lead to a cheaper dollar and a smaller trade deficit.

The trouble is that no one has yet found a reliable way to induce Americans to save more. The government has implemented a variety of tax incentives for saving, and more are suggested every year. But little evidence suggests that any of them has worked. Instead, large increases in stock market wealth in the second half of the 1990s convinced Americans that it was prudent to save even *less* than they normally do.

If the other cures for our trade deficit fail to work, the deficit may cure itself in a particularly unpleasant way: by reducing U.S. domestic investment. The 2001 recession accomplished this to some extent, reducing the share of investment in real GDP from 17.8 percent in 2000 to 15.7 percent in 2003. (It also curbed our appetite for imports.) That effect is only temporary, however, and there is a potential longer-run problem.

As our trade deficits and foreign borrowing persist, foreigners wind up holding more and more U.S. dollar assets. At some point, their willingness to acquire yet more dollar assets will begin to wear thin, and they will start demanding higher interest rates. At best, higher interest rates will lead to lower investment in the United States. At worst, foreigners will cease lending to the United States, interest rates will skyrocket, and we will experience a severe recession.

Protectionism

We have saved the worst remedy for last. One seemingly obvious way to cure our trade deficit is to limit imports by imposing stiff tariffs, quotas, and other protectionist devices. We discussed protectionism, and the reasons why almost all economists oppose it, in Chapter 16. Despite the economic arguments against it, protectionism has an undeniable political allure. It seems, superficially, to "save American jobs," and it conveniently shifts the blame for our trade problems onto foreigners.

In addition to depriving us and other countries of the benefits of comparative advantage, protectionism might not even succeed in reducing our trade deficit. One reason is that other nations may retaliate. If we erect trade barriers to reduce our imports, *IM* will fall. But if foreign countries erect corresponding barriers to our exports, *X* will fall, too. On balance, our *net* exports, *X* − *IM*, may or may not improve. But world trade will surely suffer. This game may have no winners, only losers.

Even if other nations do not retaliate, tariffs and quotas may not improve the U.S. trade deficit much. Why? If they succeed in reducing American spending on imports, tariffs and quotas will thereby reduce the supply of dollars on the world market—which will push the value of the dollar up. A rising dollar, of course, would hurt U.S. exports and encourage more imports. The fundamental equation

$$X - IM = (S - I) - (G - T)$$

reminds us that protectionism can raise $X - IM$ only if it raises the budget surplus, raises saving, or reduces investment.[4]

CONCLUSION: NO NATION IS AN ISLAND

The poet John Donne wrote that "no man is an island." Similarly, no nation is isolated from economic developments elsewhere on the globe. Instead, we live in a world economy in which the fates of nations are intertwined. The major trading countries are linked by exports and imports, by capital flows, and by exchange rates. What happens to national income, prices, and interest rates in one country affects other nations. No events make this point clearer than the international financial crises that erupt from time to time—most recently in Argentina (see the previous chapter).

As we noted in Chapter 17, one root cause of almost all of these crises was the countries' decisions to fix their exchange rates to the U.S. dollar. Unfortunately for such nations as Thailand, Indonesia, and South Korea, the dollar rose spectacularly from 1995 to 1997. With their exchange rates tied to the dollar, the Thai baht, the Indonesian rupiah, and the Korean won automatically appreciated relative to most other currencies—making their exports more costly. Soon these one-time export powerhouses found themselves in an unaccustomed position: running large trade deficits.

"But we're not just talking about buying a car—we're talking about confronting this country's trade deficit with Japan."

Then the crisis hit, and all four of these countries watched their currencies tumble in value. The sharp depreciations restored their international competitiveness, but it also impoverished many of their citizens. Naturally, the shrinking Asian economies curbed their appetites for American goods, so our exports to the region fell—which contributed to further deterioration in the U.S. trade deficit.

---

[4] Here tariffs, which raise revenue for the government, have a clear advantage over quotas, which do not.

Thus a primarily American development (the rise of the dollar) harmed the Asian economies, and then a primarily Asian development (deep recessions in the Asian tigers) hurt the U.S. economy.

 ## Issue Revisited: Should the Dollar Be Allowed to Fall?

Recall the question with which we began this chapter: Should the U.S. let the dollar fall or try to stop it? Remember that a falling dollar boosts exports and growth in the United States but *reduces* exports and growth in, say, Europe and Japan. With economic growth in both Japan and Europe already slow, it was easy to understand why foreign leaders wanted the U.S. government to stop, or at least slow down, the dollar's rapid descent.

But it is also easy to understand why the United States was not eager to do so. 2004 was an election year, and a falling dollar could reasonably be expected to help the U.S. grow faster—even if that meant that Europe and Japan would grow slower.

There was no way to avoid this conflict of interests. For better or for worse, we all live in one world.

SUMMARY

1. The nations of the world are linked together economically because national income, prices, and interest rates in one country affect those in other countries. They are thus **open economies.**

2. Because one country's imports are another country's exports, rapid (or sluggish) economic growth in one country contributes to rapid (or sluggish) growth in other countries.

3. A country's net exports depend on whether its prices are high or low relative to those of other countries. Because exchange rates translate one country's prices into the currencies of other countries, the exchange rate is a key determinant of net exports.

4. If the currency depreciates, net exports rise and aggregate demand increases, thereby raising both real GDP and the price level. A depreciating currency also reduces aggregate supply by making imported inputs more costly.

5. If the currency appreciates, net exports fall and aggregate demand, real GDP, and the price level all decrease. An appreciating currency also increases aggregate supply by making imported inputs cheaper.

6. **International capital flows** respond strongly to rates of return on investments in different countries. For example, higher domestic interest rates lead to currency appreciations, and lower interest rates lead to depreciations.

7. Contractionary monetary policies raise interest rates and therefore make the currency appreciate. Both the higher in-terest rates and the stronger currency reduce aggregate demand. Hence, international capital flows make monetary policy more powerful than it would be in a closed economy.

8. Expansionary fiscal policies also raise interest rates and make the currency appreciate. But in this case, the international repercussions cancel out part of the demand-expanding effects of the policies. Hence, international capital flows make fiscal policy less powerful than it would be in a closed economy.

9. Because eliminating the budget deficit in the 1990s combined tighter fiscal policy with looser monetary policy, it lowered interest rates. That should have pushed the dollar down and led to a smaller **trade deficit** in the United States. However, changes in private economic behavior—specifically, lower saving and higher investment—offset the presumed international effects of deficit reduction.

10. Budget deficits and trade deficits are linked by the fundamental equation $X - IM = (S - I) - (G - T)$.

11. It follows from this equation that the U.S. trade deficit must be cured by some combination of lower budget deficits, higher savings, and lower investment.

12. Protectionist policies might not cure the U.S. trade deficit because (a) they will make the dollar appreciate and (b) they may provoke foreign retaliation.

KEY TERMS

Net exports 346

Open economy 346

Exchange rate 347

Appreciation 347

Depreciation 347

Closed economy 350

International capital flows 350

Trade deficit 353

Budget deficits and trade deficits 353

$X - IM = (S - I) - (G - T)$ 353

QUESTIONS FOR REVIEW

1. For years, the U.S. government has been trying to get Japan to expand its economy faster. Explain how more rapid growth in Japan would affect the U.S. economy.

2. If inflation is lower in Germany than in Spain (as it is), and the exchange rate between the two countries is fixed (as it is, because of the monetary union), what is likely to happen to the balance of trade between the two countries?

3. Explain why a currency depreciation leads to an improvement in a country's trade balance.

4. Explain why American fiscal policy is less powerful and American monetary policy is more powerful than indicated in the closed-economy model described earlier in this book.

5. Use an aggregate supply-demand diagram to analyze the effects of a currency appreciation.

6. Explain why $X - IM = (S - I) - (G - T)$. Now multiply both sides of this equation by -1 to get

$$IM - X = (I - S) + (G - T)$$

and remember that the trade deficit, $IM - X$, is the amount we have to borrow from foreigners to get

$$\text{Borrowing from foreigners} = (I - S) + (G - T)$$

Explain the common sense behind this version of the equation.

7. Given what you now know, do you think it was a good idea for the United States to adopt a policy mix of tight money and large government budget deficits in the early 1980s? Why or why not? What were the benefits and costs of reversing that policy mix in the 1990s?

8. In 2001, Congress passed the large tax cut that President Bush had requested. What effect is this policy likely to have on the U.S. trade deficit? Why?

9. In 2001, the international value of the yen declined somewhat. This development was viewed as good news by many economists. Why?

10. **(More difficult)** Suppose consumption and investment are described by the following:

$$C = 150 + 0.75DI$$

$$I = 300 + 0.2Y - 50r$$

Here DI is disposable income, Y is GDP, and r, the interest rate, is measured in percentage points. (For example, a 5 percent interest rate is $r = 5$.) Exports and imports are as follows:

$$X = 300$$

$$IM = 250 + 0.2Y$$

Government purchases are $G = 800$, and taxes are 20 percent of income. The price level is fixed and the central bank uses its monetary policy to peg the interest rate at $r = 8$.

a. Find equilibrium GDP, the budget deficit or surplus, and the trade deficit or surplus.

b. Suppose the currency appreciates and, as a result, exports and imports change to

$$X = 250$$

$$IM = 0.2Y$$

Now find equilibrium GDP, the budget deficit or surplus, and the trade deficit or surplus.

GLOSSARY

Absolute advantage One country is said to have an absolute advantage over another in the production of a particular good if it can produce that good using smaller quantities of resources than can the other country. (p. 305)

Aggregate demand Aggregate demand is the total amount that all consumers, business firms, and government agencies are willing to spend on final goods and services. (p. 122)

Aggregate demand curve The aggregate demand curve shows the quantity of domestic product that is demanded at each possible value of the price level. (p. 62)

Aggregate supply curve The aggregate supply curve shows the quantity of domestic product that is supplied at each possible value of the price level. (p. 62)

Aggregation Aggregation means combining many individual markets into one overall market. (p. 60)

Allocation of resources Allocation of resources refers to the society's decisions on how to divide up its scarce input resources among the different outputs produced in the economy and among the different firms or other organizations that produce those outputs. (p. 27)

Appreciate A nation's currency is said to appreciate when exchange rates change so that a unit of its own currency can buy more units of foreign currency. (p. 324)

Asset An asset of an individual or business firm is an item of value that the individual or firm owns. (p. 213)

Automatic stabilizer An automatic stabilizer is a feature of the economy that reduces its sensitivity to shocks, such as sharp increases or decreases in spending. (p. 190)

Autonomous increase in consumption An autonomous increase in consumption is an increase in consumer spending without any increase in incomes. It is represented on a graph as a shift of the entire consumption function. (p. 157)

Balance of payments deficit The balance of payments deficit is the amount by which the quantity supplied of a country's currency (per year) exceeds the quantity demanded. Balance of payments deficits arise whenever the exchange rate is pegged at an artificially high level. (p. 331)

Balance of payments surplus The balance of payments surplus is the amount by which the quantity demanded of a country's currency (per year) exceeds the quantity supplied. Balance of payments surpluses arise whenever the exchange rate is pegged at an artificially low level. (p. 332)

Balance sheet A balance sheet is an accounting statement listing the values of all the assets on the left side and the values of all the liabilities and net worth on the right side. (p. 213)

Barter Barter is a system of exchange in which people directly trade one good for another, without using money as an intermediate step. (p. 204)

Bond A bond is simply an IOU by a corporation that promises to pay the holder of the bond a fixed sum of money at the specified *maturity* date and some other fixed amount of money (the *coupon* or *interest payment*) every year up to the date of maturity. (p. 229)

Budget deficit The budget deficit is the amount by which the government's expenditures exceed its receipts during a specified period of time, usually a year. (p. 265)

Budget surplus The budget surplus is the amount by which the government's receipts exceed expenditures during a specified period of time, usually a year. (p. 265)

Capital Capital refers to an inventory (*stock*) of plant, equipment, and other (generally durable) productive resources held by a business firm, an individual, or some other organization. (p. 110)

Capital account The capital account balance includes purchases and sales of financial assets to and from citizens and companies of other countries. (p. 333)

Capital formation Capital formation is synonymous with investment. It refers to the process of building up the capital stock. (p. 110)

Capital gain A capital gain is the difference between the price at which an asset is sold and the price at which it was bought. (p. 95)

Central bank A central bank is a bank for banks. America's central bank is the *Federal Reserve System*. (p. 225)

Central bank independence Central bank independence refers to the central bank's ability to make decisions without political interference. (p. 226)

Closed economy A closed economy is one that does not trade with other nations in either goods or assets. (p. 350)

Commodity money A commodity money is an object in use as a medium of exchange, but which also has a substantial value in alternative (nonmonetary) uses. (p. 207)

Comparative advantage One country is said to have a comparative advantage over another in the production of a particular good *relative to other goods* if it produces that good less inefficiently than it produces other goods, as compared with the other country. (pp. 28, 305)

Consumer expenditure Consumer expenditure, symbolized by *C*, is the total amount spent by consumers on newly produced goods and services (excluding purchases of new homes, which are considered investment goods). (p. 122)

Consumer Price Index (CPI) The Consumer Price Index is measured by pricing the items on a list representative of a typical urban household budget. (p. 100)

Consumption function The consumption function shows the relationship between total consumer expenditures and total disposable income in the economy, holding all other determinants of consumer spending constant. (p. 128)

Convergence hypothesis The convergence hypothesis holds that nations with low levels of productivity tend to have high productivity growth rates, so that international productivity differences shrink over time. (p. 109)

Coordination failure A coordination failure occurs when party A would like to change his behavior if party B would change hers, and vice versa, and yet the two changes do not take place because the decisions of A and B are not coordinated. (p. 152)

Correlated Two variables are said to be correlated if they tend to go up or down together. Correlation need not imply causation. (p. 11)

Cost disease of the personal services The cost disease of the personal services is the tendency of the costs and prices of these services to rise persistently faster than those of the average output in the economy. (p. 118)

Crowding in Crowding in occurs when government spending, by raising real GDP, induces increases in private investment spending. (p. 274)

Crowding out Crowding out occurs when deficit spending by the government forces private investment spending to contract. (p. 273)

Current account The current account balance includes international purchases and sales of goods and services, cross-border interest and dividend payments, and cross-border gifts to and from both private individuals and governments. (p. 333)

Cyclical unemployment Cyclical unemployment is the portion of unemployment that is attributable to a decline in the economy's total production. Cycli-

cal unemployment rises during recessions and falls as prosperity is restored. (p. 88)

Deflation Deflation refers to a sustained decrease in the general price level. (p. 101)

Demand curve A demand curve is a graphical depiction of a demand schedule. It shows how the quantity demanded of some product will change as the price of that product changes during a specified period of time, holding all other determinants of quantity demanded constant. (p. 36)

Demand schedule A demand schedule is a table showing how the quantity demanded of some product during a specified period of time changes as the price of that product changes, holding all other determinants of quantity demanded constant. (p. 36)

Demand-side inflation Demand-side inflation is a rise in the price level caused by rapid growth of aggregate demand. (p. 280)

Deposit creation Deposit creation refers to the process by which a fractional reserve banking system turns $1 of bank reserves into several dollars of bank deposits. (p. 214)

Deposit insurance Deposit insurance is a system that guarantees that depositors will not lose money even if their bank goes bankrupt. (p. 212)

Depreciate A nation's currency is said to depreciate when exchange rates change so that a unit of its currency can buy fewer units of foreign currency. (p. 324)

Devaluation A devaluation is a reduction in the official value of a currency. (p. 325)

Discount rate The discount rate is the interest rate the Fed charges on loans that it makes to banks. (p. 230)

Division of labor Division of labor means breaking up a task into a number of smaller, more *specialized* tasks so that each worker can become more adept at a particular job. (p. 27)

Dumping Dumping means selling goods in a foreign market at lower prices than those charged in the home market. (p. 318)

Economic model An economic model is a simplified, small-scale version of some aspect of the economy. Economic models

are often expressed in equations, by graphs, or in words. (p. 11)

Efficiency A set of outputs is said to be produced efficiently if, given the current technological knowledge, there is no way one can produce larger amounts of any output without using larger input amounts or giving up some quantity of another output. (p. 26)

Equation of exchange The equation of exchange states that the money value of GDP transactions must be equal to the product of the average stock of money times velocity. That is,

$$M \times V = P \times Y \text{ (p. 242)}$$

Equilibrium Equilibrium is a situation in which there are no inherent forces that produce change. Changes away from an equilibrium position will occur only as a result of "outside events" that disturb the status quo. (pp. 42, 144)

Excess reserves Excess reserves are any reserves held in excess of the legal minimum. (p. 214)

Exchange rate The exchange rate states the price, in terms of one currency, at which another currency can be bought. (p. 324)

Expenditure schedule An expenditure schedule shows the relationship between national income (GDP) and total spending. (p. 146)

Export subsidy An export subsidy is a payment by the government to exporters to permit them to reduce the selling prices of their goods so they can compete more effectively in foreign markets. (p. 311)

Externality An activity is said to generate a beneficial or detrimental externality if that activity causes incidental benefits or damages to others not directly involved in the activity, and no corresponding compensation is provided to or paid by those who generate the externality. (p.6)

45° lines Rays through the origin with a slope of 1 are called 45° lines because they form an angle of 45° with the horizontal axis. A 45° line marks off points where the variables measured on each axis have equal values. (p. 17)

Fiat money Fiat money is money that is decreed as such by the government. It is of little value as a commodity, but it maintains its value as a medium of exchange because people have faith that the issuer will stand behind the pieces of printed paper and limit their production. (p. 208)

Final goods and services Final goods and services are those that are purchased by their ultimate users. (p. 65)

Fiscal policy The government's fiscal policy is its plan for spending and taxation. It is designed to steer aggregate demand in some desired direction. (p. 186)

Fixed exchange rates Fixed exchange rates are rates set by government decisions and maintained by government actions. (p. 331)

Fixed taxes Fixed taxes are taxes that do not vary with the level of GDP. (p. 186)

Floating exchange rates Floating exchange rates are rates determined in free markets by the law of supply and demand. (p. 325)

Fractional reserve banking Fractional reserve banking is a system under which bankers keep as reserves only a fraction of the funds they hold on deposit. (p. 211)

Frictional unemployment Frictional unemployment is unemployment that is due to normal turnover in the labor market. It includes people who are temporarily between jobs because they are moving or changing occupations, or are unemployed for similar reasons. (p. 87)

Full employment Full employment is a situation in which everyone who is willing and able to work can find a job. At full employment, the measured unemployment rate is still positive. (p. 89)

GDP deflator The price index used to deflate nominal GDP is called the GDP deflator. It is a broad measure of economy-wide inflation; it includes the prices of all goods and services in the economy. (p. 102)

Globalization Globalization refers to the increasing share of sales and purchases in any country coming from other countries, with more and more countries playing a role in the markets of any country. (p. 302)

Gold standard The gold standard is a way to fix exchange rates by defining each participating currency in terms of gold and al-

lowing holders of each participating currency to convert that currency into gold. (p. 333)

Government purchases Government purchases, symbolized by G, refer to the goods (such as airplanes and paper clips) and services (such as school teaching and police protection) purchased by all levels of government. (p. 123)

Gross domestic product (GDP) Gross domestic product is the sum of the money values of all final goods and services produced in the domestic economy and sold on organized markets during a specified period of time, usually a year. (p. 64)

Gross private domestic investment Gross private domestic investment includes business investment in plant, equipment, and software; residential construction; and inventory investment. (p. 137)

Human capital Human capital is the amount of skill embodied in the workforce. It is most commonly measured by the amount of education and training. (p. 107)

Income-expenditure diagram An income-expenditure diagram, or 45° line diagram, plots total real expenditure (on the vertical axis) against real income (on the horizontal axis). The 45° line marks off points where income and expenditure are equal. (p. 148)

Index number An index number expresses the cost of a market basket of goods *relative to its cost in some "base" period, which is simply the year used as a basis of comparison.* (p. 100)

Index number problem The index number problem is the fact that there is no perfect cost-of-living index because no two families buy precisely the same bundle of goods and services, and hence no two families suffer precisely the same increase in prices. (p. 100)

Indexing Indexing refers to provisions in a law or a contract whereby monetary payments are automatically adjusted whenever a specified price index changes. Wage rates, pensions, interest payments on bonds, income taxes, and many other things can be indexed in this way, and have

been. Sometimes such contractual provisions are called *escalator clauses*. (p. 296)

Induced increase in consumption An induced increase in consumption is an increase in consumer spending that stems from an increase in consumer incomes. It is represented on a graph as a movement along a fixed consumption function. (p. 157)

Induced investment Induced investment is the part of investment spending that rises when GDP rises and falls when GDP falls. (p. 146)

Industrial Revolution The Industrial Revolution is the stream of new technology and the resulting growth of output that began in England toward the end of the 18th century. (p. 27)

Inflation Inflation occurs when prices in an economy rise rapidly. The rate of inflation is calculated by averaging the percentage growth rate of the prices of a selected sample of commodities. (p. 62)

Inflationary gap The inflationary gap is the amount by which equilibrium real GDP exceeds the full-employment level of GDP. (p. 151)

Innovation Innovation is the process by which new products or new methods of production are introduced, including all the steps from the inventor's idea to bringing the new item to market. (p. 114)

Inputs The inputs used by a firm or an economy are the labor, raw materials, electricity and other resources it uses to produce its outputs. (pp. 22, 78)

Intermediate good An intermediate good is a good purchased for resale or for use in producing another good. (p. 65)

International capital flows International capital flows are purchases and sales of financial assets across national borders. (p. 350)

Invention Invention is the act of generating an idea for a new product or a new method for making an old product. (p. 114)

Investment Investment is the *flow* of resources into the production of new capital. It is the labor, steel, and other inputs devoted to the *construction* of factories, warehouses, railroads, and other pieces of capital during some period of time. (p. 110)

Invisible hand The invisible hand is a phrase used by Adam Smith to describe how, by pursuing their own self-interests, people in a market system are "led by an invisible hand" to promote the well-being of the community. (p. 34)

Labor force The labor force is the number of people holding or seeking jobs. (p. 80)

Labor productivity Labor productivity is the amount of output a worker turns out in an hour (or a week, or a year) of labor. If output is measured by GDP, it is GDP per hour of work. (p. 79)

Law of supply and demand The law of supply and demand states that in a free market the forces of supply and demand generally push the price toward the level at which quantity supplied and quantity demanded are equal. (p. 43)

Liquidity An asset's liquidity refers to the ease with which it can be converted into cash. (p. 209)

Long run The long run is a period of time long enough for all of the firm's current commitments to come to an end. (p. 329)

M1 The narrowly defined money supply, usually abbreviated M1, is the sum of all coins and paper money in circulation, plus certain checkable deposit balances at banks and savings institutions. (p. 209)

M2 The broadly defined money supply, usually abbreviated M2, is the sum of all coins and paper money in circulation, plus all types of checking account balances, plus most forms of savings account balances, plus shares in money market mutual funds. (p. 209)

Marginal analysis Marginal analysis is a method for calculating optimal choices- the choices that best promote the pertinent objective. It works by testing whether, and by how much, a small change in a decision will move things toward or away from the goal. (p. 6)

Marginal propensity to consume (MPC) The marginal propensity to consume is the ratio of changes in consumption relative to changes in disposable income that produce the change in consumption. On a graph, it appears as the slope of the consumption function. (p. 128)

Market system A market system is a form of economic organization in which resource allocation decisions are left to individual producers and consumers acting in their own best interests without central direction. (p. 29)

Medium of exchange The medium of exchange is the object or objects used to buy and sell other items such as goods and services. (p. 206)

Mercantilism Mercantilism is a doctrine that holds that exports are good for a country, whereas imports are harmful. (p. 310)

Monetarism Monetarism is a mode of analysis that uses the equation of exchange to organize and analyze macroeconomic data. (p. 245)

Monetary policy Monetary policy refers to actions that the Federal Reserve System takes to change the equilibrium of the money market—that is, to alter the money supply, move interest rates, or both. (p. 234)

Monetize the deficit The central bank is said to monetize the deficit when it purchases bonds issued by the government. (p. 272)

Money Money is the standard object used in exchanging goods and services. In short, money is the medium of exchange. (p. 206)

Money-fixed asset A money-fixed asset is an asset whose value is a fixed number of dollars. (p. 130)

Money multiplier The money multiplier is the ratio of newly created bank deposits to new reserves. (p. 217)

Multiplier The multiplier is the ratio of the change in equilibrium GDP (Y) divided by the original change in spending that causes the change in GDP. (p. 152)

National debt The national debt is the federal government's total indebtedness at a moment in time. It is the result of previous deficits. (p. 265)

National income National income is the sum of the incomes that all individuals in the economy earned in the forms of wages, interest, rents, and profits. It excludes government transfer payments and is calculated before any deductions are taken for income taxes. (pp. 123, 138)

National income accounting The system of measurement devised for collecting and expressing macroeconomic data is called national income accounting. (p. 136)

Natural rate of unemployment The economy's self-correcting mechanism always tends to push the unemployment rate back toward a specific rate of unemployment that we call the natural rate of unemployment. (p. 288)

Near moneys Near moneys are liquid assets that are close substitutes for money. (p. 209)

Net domestic product (NDP) Net domestic product is calculated by subtracting payments derived from production in other countries form net national product and adding back factor payments made by American businesses to citizens of other countries. (p. 138)

Net exports Net exports, symbolized by $(X - IM)$, is the difference between U.S. exports and U.S. imports. It indicates the difference between what we sell to foreigners and what we buy from them. (p. 123)

Net national product (NPP) Net national product is national income plus indirect business taxes, such as sales taxes, excise taxes, and the like. (p. 138)

Net worth Net worth is the value of all assets minus the value of all liabilities. (p. 213)

Nominal GDP Nominal GDP is calculated by valuing all outputs at current prices. (p. 64)

Nominal rate of interest The nominal rate of interest is the percentage by which the money the borrower pays back exceeds the money that he borrowed, making no adjustment for any fall in the purchasing power of this money that results from inflation. (p. 94)

On-the-job training On-the-job training refers to skills that workers acquire while at work, rather than in school or in formal vocational training programs. (p. 113)

Open economy An open economy is one that trades with other nations in goods and services, and perhaps also trades in financial assets. (p. 346)

Open-market operations Open-market operations refer to the Fed's purchase or sale of government securities through transactions in the open market. (p. 227)

Opportunity cost The opportunity cost of some decision is the value of the next best alternative that must be given up because of that decision (for example, working instead of going to school). (pp. 4, 21)

Origin The "0" point in the lower-left corner of a graph where the axes meet is called the origin. Both variables are equal to zero at the origin. (p. 14)

Outputs Outputs are the goods and services that consumers want to acquire. (pp. 22, 78)

Phillips curve A Phillips curve is a graph depicting the rate of unemployment on the horizontal axis and either the rate of inflation or the rate of change of money wages on the vertical axis. Phillips curves are normally downward sloping, indicating that higher inflation rates are associated with lower unemployment rates. (p. 283)

Potential GDP Potential GDP is the real GDP that the economy would produce if its labor and other resources were fully employed. (p. 80)

Price ceiling A price ceiling is a maximum that the price charged for a commodity cannot legally exceed. (p. 47)

Price floor A price floor is a legal minimum below which the price charged for a commodity is not permitted to fall. (p. 50)

Principle of increasing costs The principle of increasing costs states that as the production of a good expands, the opportunity cost of producing another unit generally increases. (p. 23)

Production function The economy's production function shows the volume of output that can be produced from given inputs (such as labor and capital), given the available technology. (p. 80)

Production indifference map A production indifference map is a graph whose axes show the quantities of two inputs that are used to produce some output. A curve in the graph corresponds to some given quantity of that output, and the different points on that curve show the different quantities of the two inputs that are enough to produce the given output. (p. 18)

Production possibilities frontier A production possibilities frontier shows the different combinations of various goods that a producer can turn out, given the available resources and existing technology. (p. 22)

Productivity Productivity is the amount of output produced by a unit of input. (p. 170)

Property rights Property rights are laws and/or conventions that assign owners the rights to use their property as they see fit (within the law)—for example, to sell the property and to reap the benefits (such as rents or dividends) while they own it. (p. 111)

Purchasing power The purchasing power of a given sum of money is the volume of goods and services that it will buy. (p. 90)

Quantity demanded The quantity demanded is the number of units of a good that consumers are willing and can afford to buy over a specified period of time. (p. 35)

Quantity supplied The quantity supplied is the number of units that sellers want to sell over a specified period of time. (p. 39)

Quantity theory of money The quantity theory of money assumes that velocity is (approximately) constant. In that case, nominal GDP is proportional to the money stock. (p. 243)

Quota A quota specifies the maximum amount of a good that is permitted into the country from abroad per unit of time. (p. 311)

Rational decision A rational decision is one that best serves the objectives of the decision maker, whatever those objectives may be. Such objectives may include a firm's desire to maximize its profits, a government's desire to maximize the welfare of its citizens, or another government's desire to maximize its military might. The term *rational* connotes neither approval nor disapproval of the objective itself. (p. 21)

Rational expectations Rational expectations are forecasts that, while not necessarily correct, are the best that can be made given the available data. Rational expectations, therefore, cannot err systematically. If expectations are rational, forecasting errors are pure random numbers. (p. 292)

Ray through the origin (or Ray) Lines whose Y-intercept is zero have so many special uses in economics and other disciplines that they have been given a special name: a ray through the origin, or a ray. (p. 16)

Real GDP Real GDP is calculated by valuing outputs of different years at common prices. Therefore, real GDP is a far better measure than nominal GDP of changes in total production. (p. 64)

Real GDP per capita Real GDP per capita is the ratio of real GDP to the population. (p. 82)

Real rate of interest The real rate of interest is the percentage increase in purchasing power that the borrower pays to the lender for the privilege of borrowing. It indicates the increased ability to purchase goods and services that the lender earns. (p. 94)

Real wage rate The real wage rate is the wage rate adjusted for inflation. It indicates the volume of goods and services that money wages will buy. (p. 90)

Recession A recession is a period of time during which the total output of the economy declines. (p. 62)

Recessionary gap The recessionary gap is the amount by which the equilibrium level of real GDP falls short of potential GDP. (p. 150)

Relative price An item's relative price is its price in terms of some other item rather than in terms of dollars. (p. 92)

Required reserves Required reserves are the minimum amount of reserves (in cash or the equivalent) required by law. Normally, required reserves are proportional to the volume of deposits. (p. 213)

Research and development (R&D) Research and development is the activity of firms, universities, and government agencies that seeks to invent new products and processes and to improve those inventions so that they are ready for the market or other users. (p. 114)

Resources Resources are the instruments provided by nature or by people that are used to create goods and services. Natural resources include minerals, soil, water, and air. Labor is a scarce resource, partly because of time limitations (the day has only 24 hours) and partly because the number of skilled workers is limited. Factories and machines are resources made by people. These three types of resources are often referred to as *land, labor,* and *capital.* They are also called *inputs* or *factors of production.* (p. 20)

Revaluation A revaluation is an increase in the official value of a currency. (p. 325)

Run on a bank A run on a bank occurs when many depositors withdraw cash from their accounts all at once. (p. 204)

Scatter diagram A scatter diagram is a graph showing the relationship between two variables (such as consumer spending and disposable income). Each year is represented by a point in the diagram. The coordinates of each year's point show the values of the two variables in that year. (p. 126)

Self-correcting mechanism The economy's self-correcting mechanism refers to the way money wages react to either a recessionary gap or an inflationary gap. Wage changes shift the aggregate supply curve and therefore change the equilibrium GDP and the equilibrium price level (p. 175)

Shift in a demand curve A shift in a demand curve occurs when any variable other than price changes. If consumers want to buy *more* at any given price than they wanted previously, the demand curve shifts to the right (or outward). If they desire *less* at any given price, the demand curve shifts to the left (or inward). (p. 37)

Shortage A shortage is an excess of quantity demanded over quantity supplied. When there is a shortage, buyers cannot purchase the quantities they desire at the current price. (p. 42)

Slope of a straight line The slope of a straight line is the ratio of the vertical

change to the corresponding horizontal change as we move to the right along the line or, as it is often said, the ratio of the "rise" over the "run." (p. 14)

Specialization Specialization means that a country devotes its energies and resources to only a small proportion of the world's productive activities. (p. 303)

Stabilization policy Stabilization policy is the name given to government programs designed to prevent or shorten recessions and to counteract inflation (that is, to *stabilize* prices). (p. 74)

Stagflation Stagflation is inflation that occurs while the economy is growing slowly ("stagnating") or in a recession. (p. 72)

Store of value A store of value is an item used to store wealth from one point in time to another. (p. 206)

Structural budget deficit (or surplus) The structural budget deficit (surplus) is the hypothetical deficit we *would have* under current fiscal policies if the economy were operating near full employment. (p. 268)

Structural unemployment Structural unemployment refers to workers who have lost their jobs because they have been displaced by automation, because their skills are no longer in demand, or because of similar reasons. (p. 88)

Supply curve A supply curve is a graphical depiction of a supply schedule. It shows how the quantity supplied of some product will change as the price of that product changes during a specified period of time, holding all other determinants of quantity supplied constant. (p. 40)

Supply-demand diagram A supply-demand diagram graphs the supply and demand curves together. It also determines the equilibrium price and quantity. (p. 42)

Supply schedule A supply schedule is a table showing how the quantity supplied of some product changes as the price of that product changes during a specified period of time, holding all other determinants of quantity supplied constant. (p. 40)

Supply-side inflation Supply-side inflation is a rise in the price level caused by

slow growth (or decline) of aggregate supply. (p. 280)

Surplus A surplus is an excess of quantity supplied over quantity demanded. When there is a surplus, sellers cannot sell the quantities they desire to supply at the current price. (p. 42)

Tangent The tangent to a curve at some point, Z, on that curve is a straight line that touches point Z but does not cross the curve at that point. (p. 16)

Tariff A tariff is a tax on imports. (p. 311)

Theory A theory is a deliberate simplification of relationships used to explain how those relationships work. (p. 10)

Trade adjustment assistance Trade adjustment assistance provides special unemployment benefits, loans, retraining programs, and other aid to workers and firms that are harmed by foreign competition. (p. 315)

Trade deficit A country's trade deficit is the excess of its imports over its exports. (p. 353)

Trade surplus A country's trade surplus is the excess of its exports over its imports. (p. 353)

Transfer payments Transfer payments are sum of money that the government gives certain individuals as outright grants rather than as payments for services rendered to employers. Some common examples are Social Security and unemployment benefits. (p. 125)

Unemployment insurance Unemployment insurance si a government program that replaces some of the wages lost by eligible workers who lose their jobs. (p. 89)

Unemployment rate The unemployment rate is the number of unemployed people, expressed as a percentage of the labor force. (p. 84)

Unit of account The unit of account is the standard unit for quoting prices. (p. 206)

Value added The value added by a firm is its revenue from selling a product minus the amount paid for goods and services purchased from other firms. (p. 139)

Variable A variable is something measured by a number; it is used to analyze what happens to other things when the size of that number changes (varies). (p. 14)

Variable taxes Variable taxes are taxes that vary with the level of GDP. (p. 186)

Velocity Velocity indicates the number of times per year that an "average dollar" is spent on goods and services. It is the ratio of nominal gross domestic product (GDP) to the number of dollars in the money stock. That is:

$$\text{Velocity} = \frac{\text{Nominal GDP}}{\text{Money stock}} \text{ (p. 242)}$$

Vertical (long-run) Phillips curve The vertical (long-run) Phillips curve shows the menu of inflation/unemployment choices available to society in the long run. It is a vertical straight line at the natural rate of unemployment. (p. 288)

Y-intercept The Y-intercept of a line or a curve is the point at which it touches the vertical axis (the Y-axis). The X-intercept is defined similarly. (p. 16)

INDEX